Dark Journey

Dark Journey

Black Mississippians in the Age of Jim Crow

Neil R. McMillen

University of Illinois Press
Urbana and Chicago

Publication of this book was supported in part by a grant from the University of Southern Mississippi. Farm Security Administration and Work Projects Administration photos courtesy of Mississippi Department of Archives and History.

Illini Books edition, 1990

This book is printed on acid-free paper.

Library of Congress Cataloging-in-Publication Data

McMillen, Neil R., 1939–
    Dark journey: black Mississippians in the age of Jim Crow / Neil R. McMillen.
      p. cm.
    Bibliography: p.
    Includes index.
    ISBN 0-252-01568-1 (cloth : alk. paper). ISBN 0-252-06156-X
    (paper : alk. paper).
    1. Afro-Americans—Mississippi—History.   2. Afro-Americans
—Mississippi—Segregation—History.   3. Mississippi—Race relations.
I. Title.
E185.93.M6M33 1989
976.2′00496073—dc19   88–17123
                                               CIP

For
Mac and Pinky

It seems to me I've lived
pretty close to slavery.

—St. Elmo Bland
  (b. Coffeeville, Miss., 1895)

Contents

CHAPTER 9
The Gathering Challenge

Tables

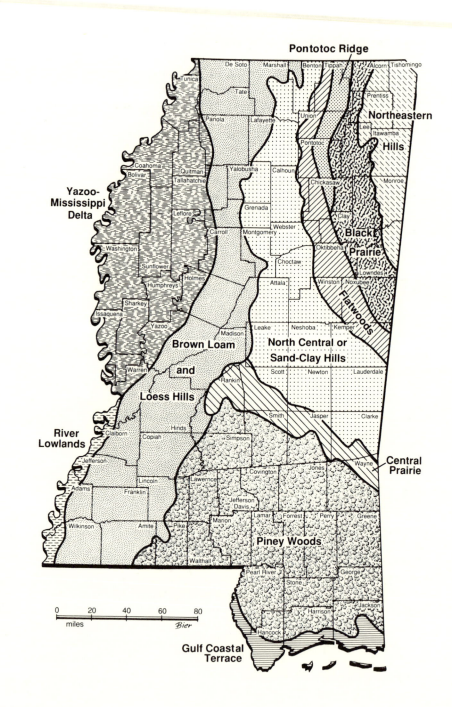

Pontotoc Ridge

Northeastern

Hills

Black
Prairie

Flatwoods

North Central or
Sand-Clay Hills

Central
Prairie

Yazoo-
Mississippi
Delta

Brown Loam

and

Loess Hills

River
Lowlands

Piney Woods

Gulf Coastal
Terrace

De Soto | Marshall | Benton | Tippah | Alcorn | Tishomingo
Tunica | Tate | Prentiss
Panola | Lafayette | Union | Lee | Itawamba
Coahoma | Quitman | Yalobusha | Calhoun | Pontotoc | Monroe
Bolivar | Tallahatchie | Chickasaw
Leflore | Grenada | Clay
Carroll | Montgomery | Webster | Oktibbeha | Lowndes
Washington | Holmes | Choctaw | Attala | Winston | Noxubee
Sunflower | Humphreys | Madison | Leake | Neshoba | Kemper
Sharkey | Yazoo | Scott | Newton | Lauderdale
Issaquena | Warren | Rankin | Smith | Jasper | Clarke
Claiborn | Hinds | Simpson | Jones | Wayne
Copiah | Lawrence | Covington
Jefferson | Lincoln | Jefferson Davis | Lamar | Forrest | Perry | Greene
Adams | Franklin | Marion | Pearl River | Stone | George
Wilkinson | Amite | Pike | Walthall | Hancock | Harrison | Jackson

0   20   40   60   80
miles   Bier

Preface

This is a history of Mississippi's black people, its majority people, and their struggles to achieve autonomy and full citizenship during the critical period of disfranchisement, segregation, and exclusion following 1890. As such, it is both more and less than the book I set out to write some years ago. My original intention, shaped by the new historiography of slavery, was to write black history, to focus rather narrowly on the culture and community of the Afro-Mississippians themselves, to describe the world they made in the aftermath of emancipation and reconstruction. In the now well-worn terms of the historical profession, my purpose at the outset was to make the black Mississippians the subjects rather than the objects of their own story.

In the years between its inception and completion, the book's larger design changed substantially—but the purpose remained the same. From the early phases of my research it became increasingly difficult to ignore the obvious fact that Afro-Mississippians, perhaps more than any other people in United States history, were indeed both objects and subjects; that while they were always actors in their own right, the range of their actions was nevertheless often profoundly influenced by white supremacy. Thus, it seemed to me, until historians adequately explored the exterior forces that operated on the black community there could be no truly adequate histories of the interior life of the people within that community. At the same time, however, my reading of the evidence convinced me more than ever that the Jim Crow system in this most race-haunted of all American states could never be fully understood until it was seen as black Mississippians saw it and until it was described, whenever useful and possible, in their own words.

Accordingly, I have attempted to position this book at the intersection of two increasingly divergent fields of inquiry. Neither precisely black history nor race relations history, this volume is something of a hybrid of the two: an effort to study black-white relations and the black circumstance from the bottom up. I cannot pretend that I, a northern-born white resident of the post–Second Reconstruction South, possess what has come to be called black soul and black consciousness. I have, however, tried to see things as late nineteenth and early twentieth-century black Mississippians saw them, to understand the dilemmas of a color-caste system in a nominal democracy as they understood them, to analyze the conflict between white constraints and black aspirations from their vantage point. Believing as I do that the oppressed cannot be studied in isolation from the oppressor, I have examined in some detail the structure and nature of white supremacy. Yet it has been my persistent wish to keep the Afro-Mississippians at the center of this work. While I have permitted the white supremacists to intrude on the black story even as they intruded on black lives, I have focused primarily on blacks themselves and particularly on their responses to the coercive and often bloody dominion of Jim Crow. Above all, I have tried to be mindful that Afro-American resistance to white dominance in that time and place necessarily often assumed forms other than the merely material, that defiance can be as much a state of mind as a physical act.

The book is organized topically, rather than chronologically. Of course, all organizational decisions entail unattractive trade-offs, and the topical approach, in particular, compounds the risk of undue repetition and the difficulty of establishing a sense of historical development over time. While some may quarrel with my decision to arrange the book in this fashion, many will agree, I think, that by subordinating time to theme—or, more precisely, by subsuming chronology under subject—I have been able to explore more systematically and coherently the several problems to which this book is addressed.

Chapter 1, an overview of the origin, development, and enforcement of the color-caste system from Reconstruction to World War II, provides an introduction to the black "place" as whites defined it. Chapters 2 and 3 examine the separate and unequal black political and educational experiences, while Chapters 4 and 5 analyze the patterns of black economic endeavor, and particularly black efforts to realize the American dream of material security and independence. Chapters 6 and 7 turn to matters of criminal justice and community-sanctioned violence, to the mutually reinforcing roles of Jim Crow and Judge Lynch in the defense of white supremacy. To my mind, these chapters on popular and formal justice are the most disturbing in the book, and they reinforce my conviction that historians must fully understand how blacks have been acted upon before they can fully appreciate how resourcefully and effectively they have acted in their own cause. Chapter 8 depicts black population movement in the half century following 1890, with emphasis on the race-conscious diaspora known as the Great Migration. In this chapter, the "great northern drive" is analyzed as an instrument both of protest for a politically impotent and economically dependent people and of social leverage for those blacks who remained behind. The ninth and last chapter, an examination of the feasible limits of protest in a closed social order, draws together the several strands of black resistance developed in early chapters and delineates three comparatively distinct periods in the black Mississippians' challenge to white rule.

The book's title relates directly to this periodization. By Dark Journey I allude not simply to the obvious—to pigmentation and subjugation, to the burdens of color in a benighted age—but to a journey toward freedom, a journey of three stages beginning with the collapse of Reconstruction and ending in the civil rights struggles of our own time. I do not mean to suggest, of course, that even now the journey is complete, merely that the third leg of this journey, the one beginning with the American intervention in World War I, found its logical conclusion in the more militant confrontations of the Second Reconstruction following World War II. In this third stage, a stage prompted by a gradual reconfiguration of the race problem nationwide, black expectations and black consciousness in Mississippi quickly outran the black capacity to influence social change. Yet, if World War I was a turning point that scarcely turned, if a second reconstruction necessarily awaited the more favoring national and international milieu that followed World War II, black Mississippians in the interwar years nevertheless began to reimagine their place in a democratic society. During this third stage, the forces of change slowly gathered in Mississippi and black agitation for political and social rights became the impending civil rights revolution.

Far better even than at the outset of this project, I understand at its conclusion that the black Mississippians' experience under white supremacy cannot be captured in a single volume. In population terms alone the task is more than daunting, for throughout much of its history the state has been as regards both soil and people one of the blackest realms of the great southern black belt. In 1890, when nearly 60 percent (743,000) of Mississippi's 1,300,000 people were black, the state was home to nearly one in ten of all Afro-Americans. By World War II, under the pressure of massive black outmigration to northern industrial cities, the state's racial balance, for the first time in more than a century, had tipped in the white favor. Yet well over a million blacks still lived in Mississippi, proportionally more (49.2 percent in 1940) than in any other state.

In writing *Dark Journey* I do not claim to have written a complete history of all of these people through all of these years. Indeed, at best this book represents a voyage of discovery, an exploration of selected regions of the Afro-Mississippians' past that have been heretofore neglected or incompletely understood. For the most part I have selected traditional topics and studied them in more or less traditional ways. Focusing on the black response to Jim Crow, I have necessarily included little here that might be called the "new" social history. This is not, then, a community and culture study, and I have not examined such interesting and vital "interior" subjects as black leisure, health, family life, and musical or religious expressions.

Finally, a word on the period of time here under review. For the most part, I have begun my analysis with disfranchisement in 1890 and terminated it with the onset of the Great Depression in 1930. I have not, however, been the slave of chronology and I freely plead guilty to some temporal untidiness at both ends of my period of greatest concentration. For reasons of comparison and whenever it suited my analytical and descriptive purposes, I have ventured into the years both before and (more frequently) after these four decades. In fact, in some respects I regard World War II as a more logical terminus for this study than the advent of the New Deal and have therefore found it necessary to carry aspects of the black Mississippians' story to and beyond 1940. But in these pages I have addressed neither the economic crisis of the 1930s nor FDR's programs. My decision not to include the depression years in more than passing fashion was dictated by my concern that the welter of New Deal programs and the dominating presence of Franklin Roosevelt in the black imagination might unduly encumber an already substantial undertaking—and by my wish to treat the black Mississippian's depression story in a separate volume now in progress. The Roosevelt years in depression and war are among the most pivotal in the black experience and they merit full and separate analysis.

My obligations are manifold, and can be only partially acknowledged here. I am particularly grateful to those friends and colleagues who read all or parts of several drafts and who shared with me their learning and wisdom—not least of all the discipline of their editorial pencils. In addition to John Dittmer and Jack Temple Kirby, who read the manuscript and prepared insightful critiques for the University of Illinois Press, my deepest debts are to John Marszalek, Noel Polk, Arvarh

Strickland, Lester Lamon, Samuel Shannon, Terry Alford, Kenneth McCarty, David Bodenhamer, James Cobb, August Meier, Gary Stringer, Hunter Wahli Watson, Allison Steiner, and Susan Gibbs. Although not a few of these generous contributors to my work may wish that I had more fully heeded their many useful suggestions, all should know that I have benefited richly from their insights. Nor should I forget the many students in my classes, and particularly those in History 340, who perhaps without ever suspecting as much inspired me to write this book in the first place.

I must also acknowledge the assistance of far too many librarians and archivists to list here. Special thanks, however, are due two dedicated professionals: Henry L. Simmons and Karolyn S. Thompson, friends and associates at the University of Southern Mississippi who aided my research more often than even I can now remember. I am grateful, too, to Cleveland Payne, Kat Bergeron, and Terry Alford, who shared with me their personal collections.

Colleagues and administrators in my department and college helped provide me with valuable increments of time released from teaching. The University of Southern Mississippi, the University of Missouri at Columbia, and the National Endowment for the Humanities underwrote some of the costs incurred during my years of research. Vice President Karen Yarbrough of USM also helped in a most material way.

Although I typed every page of the manuscript with my own fingers, Ms. B., my wife of nearly thirty years, read, criticized, and encouraged every phase of my writing. I value her judgment and I appreciate her patient indulgence of a sometimes irascible scholar. The same should be said for my children, Caroline Leslie, Hunter Neil, and the most recent addition to our family circle, Randall Craig; only now do I fully sense how much I have missed during my many absences from their loving company. Finally a grateful accolade is due Larry Malley, as good a friend in a dark hour as this historian will ever know!

PART **I**

The Black Place

Mississippi . . . to my mind was the darkest section of the South for a colored man.
                                        —William Henry Holtzclaw, 1915

You have got to be a black man in Mississippi at least 24 hours to understand what it means to be a Negro.
                                        —Dr. Theodore Roosevelt Mason Howard, 1951

Mississippi was everybody's choice as the state that was the South at its worst.
                                        —Arvarh E. Strickland, on the Jim Crow years

CHAPTER **1**

Jim Crow and the Limits of Freedom, 1890-1940

Don't monkey with white supremacy: it is loaded with determination, gun-powder, and dynamite.
—Vicksburg *Commercial Herald,* May 1889[1]

The first necessity is for the absolute social separation and isolation of the negro. He will never be accepted as an equal no matter how great his future advancement. He may gain the culture of the schools and acquire something of the polish of polite society, but he can never beat down the barriers between white and black.
—Dunbar Rowland, 1903[2]

No Foolish Consistency Here

In Mississippi the color line was drawn in the attitudes and habits of its people, black and white, well before it was sanctioned by law. By 1885, three years before the state enacted its first Jim Crow statute, the practice of racial discrimination was so firmly fixed that the Jackson *New Mississippian* dismissed the integrationist arguments of Louisiana novelist George Washington Cable as "obnoxious sentiment" agreeable only to Yankee "negrophilists." Although conceding the freedman "every right he is entitled to," the capital city weekly was confident that "sensible, refined" Mississippians would never permit the races to be "mixed together promiscuously." "They will set their faces like flint against the sentimentalism of our Mr. Cable, and . . . see to it that the separation of the two races in our theaters, council halls, public schools, churches and so forth, shall be enforced in the interest of both whites and blacks."[3]

Elsewhere in the region, and particularly in such older states of the seaboard South as North Carolina and perhaps Virginia, the patterns of racial segregation and exclusion may not have been rigidly defined until the turn of the century, when an era of relatively fluid race relations was supplanted by one of extreme racism, disfranchisement, and separation.[4] But in the lower South, and most certainly in Mississippi, white sentiment crystallized early. Although not systematically mandated by law even after 1890, a bifurcated social order emerged in these more conservative states before Reconstruction ended.[5] Mississippi could claim, as its Ohio-born Republican Governor Ridgley C. Powers boasted in 1873, to be the first state in the Union to guarantee by statute "full civil as well as political rights to all her citizens, without distinction." But uncompromising white sentiment effectively nullified state laws designed by the Reconstruction legislature to ensure blacks equal access to public carriers and public places.[6] It was probably true, as one historian has written, that "the Negro [in Mississippi] could do things during the first twenty-five years of his freedom that he could not do during the second quarter of a century."[7] Yet black possibilities were already severely limited.

With but rare exception, and then only in the case of the most prominent individuals, black railroad passengers during Reconstruction rode in second-class compartments popularly designated even then as "nigger cars." Steamboat captains likewise defied the law, generally assigning even blacks with first-class tickets to what some called "staterooms for the colored" but what were in fact merely Jim Crow stalls.[8]

Much the same was true of opera houses, hotels, saloons, cafes, and other places of public amusement. In the first blush of freedom, blacks and whites sometimes ate and drank in the same establishments, albeit at separate tables. But during Reconstruction interracial contact of this sort apparently became increasingly rare; in 1874 Congressman John Roy Lynch was ejected from a Holly Springs restaurant.[9] Immediately following the enactment of the comprehensive civil rights law of 1873, hotels, eating houses, and varied centers of resort became "private" institutions, serving guests by invitation only. The new law proved so ineffectual, however, that within a year white proprietors abandoned this artifice, and again opened to the public, serving their exclusively white clientele in flagrant contravention of the law. "Only rarely," William C. Harris has written of Mississippi's Republican period (1867-1875), "did a black man 'create a scene' to secure his rights in public, and except for a few instances on the railroads he was unsuccessful in his efforts."[10]

Yet, though white supremacists in the first decade of freedom fashioned a new, if informal, code of exclusion and discrimination to replace the old code of slavery, separation was incomplete and the color line remained curiously irregular down through the turn of the century. On the state's few streetcars, its most integrated public facilities, blacks and whites sat indiscriminately until segregated by law in 1904.[11] In 1903 the young bandleader W. C. Handy was astonished to find a black assistant cashier in a white Clarksdale bank, "something I had never seen before in all my travels."[12] That same year a federal postal inspector, assigned to investigate violent white opposition to a black postmistress in Indianola, noted the presence of black justices of the peace and constables in several Delta counties. "Verily," he reported to his superiors, "these good people are not hampered with that foolish consistency which, we are told, is the hobgoblin of little minds."[13] Until the late 1880s Jackson, Greenville, and doubtless other communities still had black policemen, though their authority was apparently exercised only over other blacks.[14] In several localities black letter carriers continued to serve both races until early in the next century.[15] Throughout the state, common cemeteries, carefully sectioned off by race, were apparently the rule. And, though state legislators authorized the removal of the remains of black Secretary of State James D. Lynch from a white Jackson cemetery in 1900, a very few favored black retainers were reportedly laid to rest in "white folks ground" in at least Cleveland, Holly Springs, Jackson, and Natchez as late as World War I.[16] Most remarkable of all, an Indianola soda fountain accommodated both races—from separate sets of glassware but at one counter—well into the 1930s.[17]

Too much can be read into such social anomalies. Now well known to historians, they nevertheless often startle, for they demonstrate that race mixing of a kind was possible, if only briefly, even in the most repressive state. Viewed individually, these disappearing exceptions seem to represent areas of unexpected interracial contact, yet they add up to very little. If the color line was not always uniform, if the physical separation of the races was somehow less inclusive in the first decades of freedom than subsequently, white Mississippians had nevertheless carefully defined the black place in what they invariably called a "white man's country." Reviled as inherently dull, servile, and vicious, set apart by habits of mind and social convention that made skin color the mark of human worth, black Mississippians were Jim Crowed early, well before a rising tide of extreme racism swept across the state after 1890.

The Logical Extreme

Fresh from his doctoral studies at Columbia University, the young Mississippi-born scholar James Wilford Garner surveyed the lowering racial scene in his native state in 1903 and recoiled in horror. Judging the negrophobia of the recent gubernatorial campaign to be without precedent "for low-down vulgarity and indecency," he concluded that "the race question which is now uppermost in this state . . . has reached a more serious aspect than at any time since the days of Reconstruction." "There can be no doubt that the hostility of the white to the black is increasing."[18] The Reverend Charles B. Galloway, bishop of the Methodist Church South in Mississippi, examined the other side of the same issue and discovered in 1904 "a measure of despair" among blacks in "Mississippi—the most intensely Southern of all Southern States . . . where because of their immense numbers the so-called 'problem' of the negroes is most acute." "There is great unrest and growing discontent among the negroes," the progressive white churchman believed. "They are beginning to feel friendless and hopeless."[19]

Less sympathetic observers also occasionally rued what one state legislator called "this constant crusade against the inferior race." The Jackson *Weekly Clarion-Ledger* denied the "base slander" that race relations at the turn of the century were less harmonious than at any time since emancipation, but it conceded that "existing conditions" were the source of much "uneasiness and dissatisfaction" within the black community. Even John Sharp Williams, whose own campaign rhetoric had grown increasingly negrophobic, used the occasion of his victory over Governor James K. Vardaman in the Senate race of 1907 to deplore the "ceaseless agitation," the "indiscriminate cursing of the whole negro race."[20]

The surest sign of the times, many observers believed, was a loosening of the bonds of affection that once linked white and black. "The older persons of both races, with their peculiar and pathetic attachments, are fast passing away," Bishop Galloway remarked in 1904. "Between the younger generation there are no such ties of sympathy, but rather, I fear, a growing estrangement."[21] The record abounds in such testimony: the aging Confederate brigadier who, though disenchanted with the freedman, remembered the wartime gallantry of a favorite manservant; the elderly planter who lamented the faithlessness of his own hands, but recalled the childlike loyalty of his father's slaves; the fragile dowager who deprecated her "thieving" household staff but never forgot the protective warmth of a long-departed slave nurse. A white Mississippian, born during the Civil War to a plantation family and raised by a black servant, recognized the abasement of the aristocratic ideal in three generations of his own family. "In a way I'm fond of the Negro . . ." he observed in 1918, "but the bond between us is not as close as it was between my father and his slaves. On the other hand, my children have grown up without black playmates and without a 'black mammy.' The attitude of my children is less sympathetic toward the Negroes than my own."[22]

Such sentiment bespoke much nostalgic foolishness, but also some truth. Strained by emancipation and Reconstruction, the old paternalism persisted feebly into the twentieth century. No doubt it occasionally still softened the harder edges of white supremacy, particularly in plantation counties. As a social ideal, however, it was no match for the more savage impulses of racism; after 1890 it was honored more often in the breach than in practice.

The South's "capitulation to racism" in the quarter century after 1890 has been examined by others, most elegantly by C. Vann Woodward, and needs little further analysis here.[23] Born in part of the frustrations of agricultural depression in the eighties and nineties and the fear that Populism threatened both white cohesion and a renewed black political influence, the increasingly virulent social distemper of Mississippi and her sister states was sustained by a cluster of related national currents ranging from the vogue of Social Darwinian "survival of the fittest" and Anglo-Saxon scientific racism to the immigration restriction movement and the American assumption of the "white man's burden" in Hawaii and the Philippines. Not least of all, the excesses of the period were encouraged by a growing Yankee readiness to accept a "southern solution" to the race problem.

Perhaps the most telling evidence of what the white press in Mississippi took to be a "wholesome change"[24] in northern attitudes came from the Supreme Court. In *Plessy* v. *Ferguson,* the separate-but-equal ruling of 1896, but also in a series of decisions from the *Slaughter House Cases* (1873) to *Williams* v. *Mississippi* (1898), the high court effectively denied blacks the protection of federal civil rights law.[25] A generally reliable if sometimes laggardly barometer of national opinion, the court did not always speak plainly. But its rulings could hardly be misunderstood. "Does not the South perceive that all the fire has gone out of the Northern philanthropic fight for the rights of man?" wrote the racially moderate Professor Thomas Pearce Bailey of the University of Mississippi. "*The North has surrendered!*" With federal constitutional and statutory restraints all but nullified, Bailey believed, southern whites were now free "to treat the negroes as aliens," to "enact discriminatory suffrage laws, Jim Crow laws, and the like."[26]

In this favoring climate, white supremacy in Mississippi reached its logical extreme, sometimes through the force of statute, more often by dint of custom. Beginning in 1888 with a separate coach law, "an act to promote the comfort of passengers on railroad trains," the state mandated "equal but separate accommodations" in sleeping cars (1888), railroad waiting rooms (1888), and trolleys (1904).[27] After 1906 cities of more than 3,000 were directed to maintain three rest rooms in train depots, one each for white men and women and one for "colored." Taxi drivers were forbidden in 1922 to carry both races at one time. A separate bus bill failed during World War II, largely for economic reasons. But state lawmakers kept up with changing mass-transit patterns by requiring black passengers in 1940 to sit behind white passengers on motor buses. On all conveyances black nurses in the company of their mistresses or white children were usually seated in white compartments.[28] The object of these laws, whites insisted, was to prevent "friction, disorder, and general unhappiness." Without them, one white editor asserted in 1910, Mississippi would be the scene of "more race clashes and dead niggers than have been heard of since reconstruction."[29]

Blacks and whites apparently never attended the same schools in Mississippi. In 1878, biracial education was proscribed by statute and in 1890 it was made unconstitutional.[30] In the latter year, polling places, already effectively closed to blacks by force and fraud, were formally reserved for whites by ostensibly legal means. It was, of course, unlawful for the two races to intermarry or otherwise cohabit; state law also required the specification of race on all bills for divorce.[31] Black and white patients were kept apart by law in hospitals, public or private, and were prevented even from using the same entrances to state health care facilities. Black and white nurses could tend only the sick of their own race; black nurses employed by public institutions were required to work under white supervision. An annex to the state asylum was reserved for black lunatics. Blacks and whites could not be lawfully incarcerated in the same jail cells, and they could not be confined or worked together in the penitentiary system.[32]

In 1940, the state senate narrowly rejected a Jim Crow textbook measure that would have required the exclusion of all reference to voting, elections, and democracy in civics books used by black public school children.[33] Two decades earlier, however, the legislature had outlawed the advocacy of social equality. Under a law of 1920, anyone found "guilty of printing, publishing or circulating printed, typewritten or written matter urging or presenting for public acceptation or general information, arguments or suggestions in favor of social equality or of intermarriage" was subject to a fine of not more than $500, imprisonment of not more than six months, or both.[34]

Beyond these formal provisions for the recognition of caste, however, racial segregation in Mississippi was largely a matter of custom. Service establishments—including barber shops and beauty parlors, and such places of public amusement and public accommodation as hotels, lodging houses, restaurants, theaters, saloons, and billiard halls—did not fall under the purview of state law until 1956, when proprietors during Mississippi's period of "massive resistance" to federal civil rights law were authorized to "choose or select" their patrons.[35] Nor did municipal ordinances fill this gap in the legal code. During the civil rights era after World War II, some communities attempted to curtail direct-action campaigns for voter registration and desegregation by formally requiring segregated waiting rooms and toilet facilities or by proscribing such activities as parading, demonstrating, picketing, praying, singing, or orating on public streets and sidewalks.[36] Prior to the 1950s, however, municipal law largely ignored the color line. Some towns and cities before World War I indirectly legislated against blacks through curfew and vagrancy laws that, though officially color-blind, were applied primarily to blacks.[37] But throughout the Jim Crow years municipal laws regulating interracial contact were limited almost exclusively to cemeteries and jails. Excepting these measures and the occasional provision for the construction of a white library or for the repair of a racially separate school building, the pre–civil rights era ordinances of Mississippi's towns and cities did not address racial issues.[38]

Thus, while the state's canon of racial exclusion or separation could hardly have been more complete, it was in substantial part informal. In Mississippi, as elsewhere in the region, there was a pronounced movement after 1890 from a system of de facto to one of de jure segregation. Perhaps more than any other state, Mississippi, as Joel Williamson has written, was "thoroughly and deeply Radicalized" by turn-of-the-century Negrophobia: "To be a Mississippian . . . was ipso facto to be a Radical [Negrophobe] or else to be alone in one's racial views."[39] Yet this radical distemper was never fully institutionalized and the process of formally transcribing custom into law was fitfully pursued and never finished. Indeed, Mississippi seems to have had *fewer* Jim Crow laws during the entire segregation period than most southern states.

The explanation for this apparent paradox—the relative exiguity of legal apparatus in the most racially restrictive state—can be found in the confidence of the dominant race. Having defined the limits of freedom early, almost at the moment of emancipation, white Mississippians capitalized on increasing northern indifference late in the nineteenth century by closing some remaining loopholes in their social code with laws requiring segregation in public transportation, health care facilities, and state institutions. But little additional legislation was required, for there was no need legally to enjoin the unthinkable. Where deeply ingrained social habit prohibited interracial dining and drinking, law was superfluous. Where popular convention and white sensibilities governed virtually every phase of interracial contact, there was little cause legally to separate black from white. Quite simply, in places of public accommodation, at funerals or weddings, in courtrooms, tent shows, theaters, and other places of public assembly—indeed wherever the two races came together—the forces of social habit and white opinion were in themselves usually sufficient to ensure that the races knew their places and occupied them with neither a statute nor a white or "colored" sign to direct the way. "White supremacy," as one black Natchezian has written, "was based on oral or traditional discrimination without legal sanction. Negroes accepted these traditions as a way of life and as a method of survival."[40] Indeed, so powerful was the force of custom that even the legal pretense of equality in separation was unnecessary.

Let there be no confusion, however. Because blacks normally lived within the letter of the racial canon, it does not follow that they were comfortable in subordination or that they accepted white dominance as either natural or just. As subsequent chapters of this book will document (Chapter 9 most systematically), the black Mississippians' response to the tightening noose of white racism was anything but docile. When it was feasible—and sometimes when it was not—they resisted white injustices and asserted their civil and political rights. To a degree even they sometimes underestimated, they managed to modify in small but psychologically meaningful ways the terms of their subordination. In the end, however, their possibilities were severely circumscribed. Fettered by a social system based on black disfranchisement and economic dependence and, ultimately, on the force of white arms, they could condition their circumstance but not fundamentally alter it. A few chose virtual suicide through open defiance; a great many left the state in search of personal dignity and material betterment. Those who remained accepted white-imposed limits on black freedom because they had no practical alternative.

More often than not Jim Crow custom required exclusion, not merely separation. Most recreational facilities, public and private, denied admission to blacks. Roller rinks, bowling alleys, swimming pools, and tennis courts opened only to whites. Dr. Theodore Roosevelt Mason Howard of Mound Bayou built the state's first swimming pool for blacks during World War II; until then, he believed, Delta field hands had no public places to go after sundown except black churches, schools, and "jook joints."[41] Cinemas normally maintained Jim Crow ticket windows and entrances, and seated blacks only in "buzzard roosts" or "nigger galleries."[42] Municipal libraries with but few exceptions were for whites only. Except for those facilities kept by educational institutions, the Carnegie Negro Library in Meridian was the state's only black library until after World War I. In Clarksdale, where black patrons had once been segregated in a small basement room of Carnegie Public Library, a "colored branch" was opened in 1930, in large part through black fund-raising efforts. After World War II, Jackson, Oxford, and other communities followed suit with black branch libraries of their own.[43]

Black motorists apparently bought gasoline wherever it was sold, but few service stations maintained "colored" rest rooms, and none seem to have kept them clean. Inconvenience, humiliation, and uncertainty nearly always accompanied the black traveler. Overnight lodgers throughout the Jim Crow period depended largely on the hospitality of their race or the chance discovery of a Negro rooming house. According to the U.S. Department of Commerce, only Columbus, Laurel, Mc-Comb, Meridian, and Yazoo City had black-operated hotels by 1938.[44] Early in the automobile age white opinion and the local constabulary in some communities arbitrarily denied black motorists access to the public streets. Many towns informally restricted parking to whites on principal thoroughfares; for a time following World War I, Jackson's Capitol Street, portions of Greenwood, the entire city of Laurel, and doubtless all or parts of many other communities were known to be open only to white motor traffic. In the Delta, custom forbade black drivers to overtake vehicles driven by whites on unpaved roads. "Its against the law for a Negro to pass a white man," a black Holmes Countian reported in 1940, "because the black man might stir up dust that would get on the white folks."

Precisely because so much was left to custom, particularity seemed to be the only universal rule. Much as they agreed that the black place was a separate and subordinate place, whites even in Mississippi, the heartland of American apartheid, were not precisely of one mind on how to address the "negro question." Racial practices and the attitudes they reflected varied somewhat from social class to social class, from locality to locality, and over the sweep of time. White gentlefolk in such older river cities as Natchez, Port Gibson, or Greenville often thought of themselves as not only more refined but more indulgent of blacks than their plainer counterparts in such recently developed Piney Woods communities as Brookhaven or Picayune. Although the pale flame of noblesse oblige that once presumably distinguished "white quality" from "white trash" flickered ever lower in the postbellum period, it seemed to burn somewhat brighter and longer in the older, large-scale cotton districts of the Delta than in the hardscrabble regions of the North-Central and Northeastern Hills. The Gulf Coast, with its faintly Latin character and its numerous Catholic churches—its many descendants of French and Spanish settlers and its admixtures of eastern Europeans —was more ethnically and culturally pluralistic, and perhaps a bit more racially tolerant, than the homogeneous Protestant and Anglo-Saxon hinterland. To an outsider, these individual and regional variations might seem too small to matter much. Black Mississippians, however, understood the importance of social nuance. To avoid trouble with the dominant race they had to know that what one community or one individual permitted, others might proscribe. Because Jim Crow could be a stickler for minutia, even the young learned to attend carefully to the variety of local and personal white customs. "Every town had its own mores, its own unwritten restrictions," a black educator remembered of the period before World War II. "The trick was to find out from local [black] people what the 'rules' were."[45]

The "niggertown" slums that dotted the landscapes of most Mississippi cities and towns were also the consequence of white social pressure and black poverty, not of law. No Mississippi locality had a residential segregation ordinance,[46] but housing configurations in the state invariably served the needs of caste. Briefly and far too simply put, close study of representative urban places reveals that there were many lesser variations but essentially only two basic residential patterns.[47] In the first of these, in such antebellum communities as Natchez, Vicksburg, Columbus, and Greenville—older river communities formed under a cotton and slave economy—black housing well into the twentieth century was widely scattered, marked by what social scientists call a "backyard pattern" of settlement. To be sure, there were in cities of this type racially identifiable neighborhoods. Yet blacks in these older towns and cities typically lived in most residential areas, including the "better districts"—sometimes in the same blocks with whites; sometimes in quarters on or near the property of their white employers; sometimes in a servant room within a white home. The resulting residential mix must not be misunderstood, however, for even in spatially close circumstances a sense of distinction prevailed. Typically, in these racially mixed areas, either a vacant lot separated black and white residences or the two races occupied opposing sides of the same street. Invariably, there was a mutual recognition of the separate spheres.

In the second pattern—in more recently settled towns and cities without antebellum traditions of house slaves and free blacks living near their white masters—physically separate neighborhoods were the rule from the outset. Typically, in such postbellum railroad and lumber centers as Hattiesburg, Laurel, and Meridian, black housing was concentrated in one or more racially exclusive areas well removed from respectable white neighborhoods. Ultimately, this second and more conventionally segregated configuration prevailed.

After 1900, as racial sentiment hardened and white demands for black exclusion mounted, the tendency everywhere in the state was toward physically discrete neighborhoods. For a time, class and social standing sometimes overrode racial concerns in some communities and wealthy blacks occasionally continued to live beside or near whites of similar standing. Prosperous blacks, including the attorney M. M. McLeod and fair-skinned Republican leader James Hill, for example, both lived after Reconstruction on Jackson's fashionable West Capitol Street, not far from the home of prominent white Democratic leader James Z. George. James D. Lynch, the light-complexioned "founder of the Mississippi Republican Party," made his home in an otherwise white section of Capitol Street.[48] As late as 1903, the wealthy landowner and future insurance pioneer Wayne W. Cox lived in "one of the best resident houses in Indianola," a white traveler reported, "in a part of the town where other colored men seem to be not desired."[49] By that date, however, whites virtually everywhere in the state were less tolerant of such breaches of caste. The antebellum "backyard pattern" still obtained in the older cities, and a scattering of black cabins could be found along the bayous or back alleys of the better white districts of many towns. But exclusion became increasingly common.

In 1904, a black physician elected not to buy one of "the handsomest and finest residences" in Jackson after white property owners threatened to use violence to keep their neighborhood lily-white.[50] A few years later, Thomas Pearce Bailey reported an extreme form of residential exclusion in a small community near Clinton, where "all negroes have been driven out."[51] After World War I in Natchez—where the most elegant antebellum mansions were sometimes flanked by tumbledown servant shacks and whites were thought to be "too lenient" in racial matters—a wealthy black was forced out of his newly purchased home in a middle-class white neighborhood.[52] In subsequent years the areas of black settlement in Natchez and the other river cities shrank as whites displaced blacks in many mixed neighborhoods and the checkerboard effect gradually gave way to racially identifiable residential clusters. By World War II the housing pattern of the old cities approximated that of the new.[53]

Whatever their location, black housing districts, the "nigger sections" and "Darktown" slums, were instantly recognizable. Hortense Powdermaker's description of Indianola in 1939 could be applied to nearly any town or city in the state: "The most striking physical feature of the community is the segregation of Negro and white dwellings, and the contrast between the two sections." Black homes were nearly always found in the least desirable sections, across or along the tracks in any community served by a railroad, in low-lying areas, along flood-prone rivers and drainage ditches, abutting cemeteries and jails, adjacent to or within the local version of a tenderloin or industrial district. Public services were minimal, reflective of the Negro's inability to vote. Street paving and lighting, sidewalks, sewage and water systems, and other such amenities as a pre–World War II Mississippi community might afford were reserved with few exceptions for white residential areas.[54]

"Blood Will Tell"

Of all interracial proscriptions, none was more fiercely held by whites and none more frequently transgressed through white initiative than the taboo on interracial sex. Whatever its origin and character, whether the product of violence and exploitation or of mutual consent and affection, sex between the races was Jim Crow's most vexatious problem. Whites "instinctively" understood that "sex is at the core of life," the Mississippi writer David Cohn believed, and in their "conscious or unconscious minds" they knew that the "negro question" was "at bottom a blood or sexual question."[55]

This fearful conjunction of race and sex haunted the white imagination. The subject was too delicate for polite conversation, but whites alluded to it frequently in such turn-of-the-century expressions as "race purity" or "blood will tell," and later in the presumably unanswerable query: "Would you want your daughter to marry a Negro?" The unthinkable horrors of "race degeneracy" justified the most barbarous forms of interracial violence and made the injunction against "amalgamation" the first law of white supremacy. But the appetites of the flesh were not easily governed by the logic of Jim Crow and the color line was rarely so permeable as when it passed through the bedroom.

During Reconstruction, the state had no law against intermarriage.

The constitution of 1869 recognized common-law unions, and thus legitimated long-standing informal biracial relationships. The following year, lawmakers repealed the ban on intermarriage, and despite the ridicule and bitter disapproval of the white population, an undetermined but apparently small number of mixed marriages did occur. With the return of Democratic rule in 1876 interracial unions were again prohibited and in 1890 the prohibition was written into the new constitution, where it remained for some three-quarters of a century.[56]

Marriage is one thing, however, and sex quite another. Although white opposition to formal interracial unions was virtually unanimous, the white community — or at least the community of white men — was more tolerant of out-of-wedlock intimacy between white men and black women. Sexual congress between black men and white women, of course, was all but unthinkable. As the savage tradition of unpunished lynchings suggests, it was the presumption of both white public and white law that intercourse between white women and black men could result only from rape. As one editor asserted, there had never been a southern white woman so depraved as to "bestow her favors on a black man."[57] White men, Theodore Bilbo admitted, had "poured a broad stream of white blood into black veins." Whites remained "absolutely pure," nonetheless, because "white women have preserved the integrity of their race." The lapses of white men notwithstanding, the virtue of the southern lady, Bilbo insisted, assured the "preservation of the blood of the white race."[58]

Black Mississippians knew only too well that women of the opposite race were more accessible to white men than to black men. Yet they discounted the chivalric myth of the Fair Maiden, the angelic, passive, and inaccessible white "ice goddess" of the double standard and the pedestal who found sex with her own white husband distasteful and with black men beyond the realm even of imagination.[59] "According to Negro accounts," an interracial team of anthropologists reported of Natchez in the 1930s, "it is quite common for white women to 'have' Negro men; 'plenty of 'em, and those white women [are] crazy about 'em.' "[60] Indeed, blacks generally believed that the mystique of white feminine "purity" was an excuse for lynching but not a description of social reality. Early in her career as an antilynching crusader, Mississippi native Ida B. Wells investigated the problem and concluded that the ritual of the rope and the faggot was used by white men to exorcise the interracial love affairs of their women more often than to punish black sexual violence. "Nobody in this section of the country," she wrote in 1892, "believes the old thread-bare lie that Negro men rape white women."[61] More than half a century later, Charles Evers qualified the argument but made the same claim: "In most cases, but not all, she has bothered him."[62]

No doubt, even in Mississippi, some white women did deliberately fall from racial grace and take black lovers. But such transgressions could never have been numerous, for the risks were simply too high for both parties. Always inflammatory, race mixing of this variety was never more dangerous than during the half century after 1890. Obsessive white fear of black rape and extreme black caution marked nearly every encounter between black men and white women. Often characterized as ravenous primitives—insatiable black satyrs lusting for white females—black men moved among white women with inordinate care. As one authority noted in the mid-1930s of the Delta, "Negro men are careful not to look or act offensively in the presence of a white woman, and in general attempt to minimize contacts with them in order to avoid the too-ready suspicion of the white men."[63] "You couldn't smile at a white woman," a Jones County black man said. "If you did you'd be hung from a limb."[64] There were dangers even in early childhood. Although close same-sex interracial friendships often survived into adolescence, the more heedful parents of both races usually terminated the play of black boys and white girls early, sometimes by the age of four or five.[65]

As a practical matter, then, in this environment it mattered little whether a black male was guilty of sexual assault or merely sexual indiscretion. Either way, whites viewed the act as "the unspeakable crime," the "sum of all villainies." Even when the circumstances were clearly consensual—even when the woman was a prostitute—interracial couples known to have violated the region's sex taboo nearly always received the worst: death or at least castration and banishment for the black man; ostracism for his white partner.[66]

When white men took black sexual partners, however, the dominant race often asked only for discretion. "A white man has nothing to lose even if he sees fit to live in concubinage with a colored woman," wrote John Roy Lynch, himself a product of a biracial union. "Society draws the line only at the marriage altar."[67] Although white sensibilities dictated that such relationships receive little public notice, they did not escape attention. Until World War I they were apparently common, perhaps even fashionable—at least among the wealthier plantation county whites.[68] Noting that his northern-born father was something of a social misfit in late nineteenth-century Greenville, Judge Percy Bell explained that this abstemious gentleman indulged neither in drink, gambling, nor black women. According to the younger Bell, "The keeping of negro mistresses was a widespread evil but he was strictly a family man."[69] Another resident of the black belt believed that "if some daring woman, not afraid of being dubbed a Carrie Nation, were to canvass the delta counties of Mississippi taking the census [in 1910], she would find so many cases of miscegenation, and their resultant mongrel families, that she would bow her head in shame for the 'flower of Southern chivalry'— gone to seed."[70] In 1907 the white citizens of Vicksburg became so exercised by the problem that they formed an Anti-Miscegenation League; about the same time, irate Greenvillians, noting that interracial love "has wrecked more young lives [than] all other vices," drove an offending couple from their town. In pre–World War I Meridian the district attorney warned citizens that "the accursed shadow of miscegenation hangs over the South to-day like a pall of hell." An Adams County grand jury reported in 1921 that Natchez was so "honeycombed with white gentlemen who have their Negro concubines" that this "disgraceful vice . . . threatens our commonwealth with a mongrel race."[71]

More often than not these relations were casual and commercial in character. Until World War I many towns in the state had "restricted districts" where vice openly flourished in "assignation houses" and white men could find black women for a price. When W. C. Handy arrived in Clarksdale in 1903, he discovered in that community's New World district "latticed houses of prostitution" within which whites enjoyed exclusive access to "richly scented yellow girls"—"lush octoroons and quadroons from Louisiana, soft cream-colored fancy gals from Mississippi towns."[72] Indignant white Jacksonians reported in 1908 that the capital alone had a hundred such "abodes of infamy and shame," a great many of them in the city's black business district. Greenville's largest bordello early in the century was "The Mansion," which featured "nice clean colored girls . . . for white gentlemen." As in all such establishments, black men normally entered only as servants. "You know," one black Greenvillian said, "you don't tamper with these white gentlemen's girls!"[73]

In a great many cases interracial sex was simply exploitative and the black objects of white attention were neither paid nor willing. In a society characterized by white dominance and black dependence, even the most virtuous black woman could be victimized with impunity. Among the most bitterly resented legacies of slavery was the white conviction, reiterated ad nauseam, that no female black above the age of puberty was chaste. Blacks also claimed that many white men thought every day to be open season on black women, that the law effectively provided even black children no protection from white rape, and that police and white rowdies sometimes molested black women and girls on the city streets.[74] When a progressive lawmaker in 1904 sought to raise the age of consent from ten to fourteen years of age, conservatives in the state senate blocked the measure because, as one historian noted, it would "enable Negro girls to sue white men." A decade later the statutory age was raised to eighteen, but the problem of white sexual abuse did not go away.[75] As we shall see (Chapter 5), it was severe enough in Indianola to figure in Mississippi Life Insurance Company's decision to leave the state in 1919.

Some interracial entanglements became lasting relationships that in exceptional cases approximated marriage. Usually cohabitation meant simply that a white man took a concubine, more or less temporarily, setting her up in a house in the black district where he paid court as his schedule permitted. Sometimes what began as casual pleasure became abiding commitment; sometimes an interracial couple formed a stable, presumably loving union and lived together as discreetly or furtively as circumstances required. The mulatto children of these unusual relationships were from time to time frankly acknowledged by the father, who might provide for their education and remember them in his will.[76] Relatively open arrangements of this kind, however, were never common in Mississippi and after World War I they grew increasingly rare; by World War II they were all but unheard of.

In fact, interracial cohabitation of every variety became less common (or at least less apparent) in the twentieth century than it had been in the nineteenth. Of course, old habits persisted. For example, during a Yazoo City childhood in the period of World War II, twelve-year-old Willie Morris was shocked to discover that white men had sexual intercourse with white women for reasons other than procreation. "I had thought that only Negro women engaged in the act of love with white men just for fun." To this future writer, as for many whites of his time and place, "Negro girls and women were a source of constant excitement and sexual feeling"; they filled his adolescent "day-dreams with delight and wonder."[77] Similarly, the black civil rights activist and writer Anne Moody who came of age in Wilkinson County in the 1950s, remembered, in angry overstatement, that "just about every young white man in Centreville had a Negro lover." While affairs between black men and white women were said to be virtually unknown in her community, white men still had ready access to black women. "Everybody knows it too," one of Moody's classmates said. "Look how many white babies we got walking around in our neighborhoods."[78]

Yet, though these and other examples suggest the continuity of Deep South sexual mores, miscegenation—used in both senses, as "interbreeding" and the race mixture resulting from "interbreeding"—

apparently declined steadily after World War I. In small part, this development can be attributed to the increased use of contraceptives by mixed couples. But more important reasons are to be found in the changing social attitudes of both races. Heightened white opposition to this form of interracialism, mounting white fear of venereal disease among blacks, the increased availability of white women to white men as white sexual standards were relaxed—these and other factors played a part in the decline of miscegenation.

Not least of all, as black pride and caste solidarity grew apace in the 1920s and 1930s, blacks became less tolerant of "kept women." Always deeply frustrated by the double standard of interracial congress, black Mississippians closed ranks against miscegenation. The high social status once enjoyed by the concubines of influential whites declined markedly by World War II.[79] "To have white folks [i.e., white kinfolks] was good a quarter of a century ago," black historian Saunders Redding reported in 1942, following a trip through Mississippi. "Now it is contemptible. Now attaches to it all the distrust, suspicion, and fear that attaches to a 'white folks' nigger.' "[80]

There are no reliable estimates of the size of the mulatto population in Mississippi or anywhere else. Whites often said, sometimes in the same breath, that (a) there was not a "full-blooded nigger" in the state, and that (b) there were more "genuine Africans" in Mississippi than anywhere else in the South.[81] Census statistics are scarcely more revealing. Federal enumerators counted 8.5 percent (or 37,200) of the state's black population as mulatto in 1860; in 1890 the figure was listed at 11.5 percent (or 85,166). In 1890 enumerators were instructed not only to count Negroes of "pure" or "mixed" blood, but to distinguish between blacks, mulattoes, quadroons, and octoroons. The patent absurdity of this effort and the general difficulty of distinguishing the mixed from the unmixed, a problem brilliantly illuminated by the racially ambiguous figure of William Faulkner's Joe Christmas (*Light in August*) led to the abandonment of the mulatto category altogether. After 1920 persons with visible admixtures of "black blood" were counted, along with those with no visible admixtures of "white blood," simply as Negroes.[82]

Blacks of mixed blood predominated within the black elite in Mississippi, not merely during Reconstruction but during the first decades of the twentieth century and later, though to a diminishing extent. Precise measurement again is clearly impossible, yet members of the state's small and interlocking black leadership class, its more notable political, business, professional, religious, and fraternal figures, were more often than not men of comparatively light complexion. To be sure, the correlation between social status in the Afro-American community and skin color was anything but complete. Mound Bayou's Charles Banks, the state's foremost black businessman, was thought to have "no mixture of blood"; and Isaiah T. Montgomery, first citizen and founder of the same Bolivar County town, was once described by Jefferson Davis as "black as the ten of spades." The same was surely true of other influential black Mississippians, including John M. Strauther, a Greenville banker and investor who was one of the state's wealthiest Afro-Americans.[83]

Many others were clearly mulattoes. Perry Wilbon Howard and Willis E. Mollison, the leading lawyers of the period before World War I, were both extremely fair, and Howard at least was blue-eyed. Howard's law partner and political associate, W. L. Mhoon, was described as "just say, a white man," "so nearly white that thousands of white men have greeted him as 'Mr. Mhoon.'"[84] Similarly, Eugene Parker Booze, Montgomery's son-in-law and himself a prominent businessman and planter, was so light-complected that some thought it nearly "impossible to distinguish him from one of the white race."[85] Even a highly abbreviated list of Mississippi race leaders would necessarily include such men of mixed ancestry as Sidney D. Redmond, lawyer and physician; the fraternal leaders Edward P. Jones, Thomas W. Stringer, and Louis Kossuth Atwood; insurance pioneers Wayne W. Cox, Merah Steven Stuart, Dr. W. A. Attaway, and George W. Lee; clergymen Bishop Elias Cottrell and Bishop E. W. Lampton; and bankers C. W. Gilliam and J. W. Francis.[86] The lives of these personalities intersected at a number of points and their names appeared continually in the same social, business, professional and political circles. Although evidence is scanty, their influence apparently owed more to wealth, education, and personal ability than to skin color. Mississippi's Negro upper crust was lighter than the generality of its black population—and fair skin was an important advantage—yet positions of race leadership in the state were not closed to talented men of dark skin.

The Afro-American community, however, was not untouched by the Caucasian notion that whiter was better. Not a few believed that to "marry right" one must "marry light." Fair-skinned Negroes, in the once nearly universal fashion of Afro-America, generally sought mates of similar hue. Successful, upwardly mobile dark-skinned men, Montgomery and Banks among them, tended to take wives of lighter coloring.[87] Color also figured in admission to some ladies' clubs and campus organizations. The light-skinned young women of Tougaloo College near Jackson preferred, as one study concluded, to "sit together in church, pointedly excluding their darker sisters."[88] Nor were such practices limited to the Jim Crow years. In the early 1960s, when Anne Moody prepared to transfer from Natchez College to the liberal arts institution near Jackson, she was advised by a friend that "Tougaloo was not for people my color": " 'Baby, you're too black. You gotta be high yellow with a rich-ass daddy.' "[89] Well into the civil rights period, some Tougaloo students believed that "bright" skin favorably influenced the grading practices of some black teachers.[90]

At Piney Woods Country Life School, Mexican children were thought to enjoy preferment over local blacks and, as Alferdteen Harrison has written, "very light girls with long curly hair" enjoyed advantages not accorded darker-skinned coeds. "The whiter you were," one graduate remembered, "the better off that you were in Piney Woods." Tension and derision between some Piney Woods mulattoes and dark-skinned blacks—between those called "Old Yellow Thing" and those called "Black and Nappy Headed"—moved schoolmaster Laurence Jones to remind the student body that "the real attributes that are worthwhile in a human being . . . are found in black, brown, yellow or lily-white people of the race regardless of what kind of hair they have."[91]

Even in the all-black town of Mound Bayou, the question of color was not entirely absent. Prior to World War I, an Episcopal mission was erected, as one scholar has noted, "for residents with lighter-than-average complexions." An object of suspicion in a community thought to consist largely of "pure blacks," the church was not well attended and its principal organizer, blue-eyed Eugene P. Booze, was dismissed as a "half-white niggah." It soon failed, yet it left its mark. In Saunders Redding's judgment, "Color became a factor in the town's life."[92]

These irritants notwithstanding, color preference seriously challenged black unity only in Natchez, where miscegenation was probably more pervasive than in any other Mississippi community. Elsewhere in the state, mulatto exclusiveness retreated steadily as the black community came to question the value it had once vested in white skin. By World War II, it was a diminishing factor. Very likely, though most black Mississippians looked upon "passing" as "treason to the race,"[93] some light-skinned Negroes, weary of the struggle, continued to exercise the "mulatto escape hatch" and pass into white society.[94] Their number of course is unknowable, but they were probably fewer after 1925 than ever before. Far better known are the cases in which mulattoes who were white enough to go undetected among whites chose, like both the principal of Tougaloo High School and insurance executive Merah S. Stuart, to identify with their darker kinsmen. Taken for a white person by an indignant conductor, the Tougaloo educator kept her seat in a

Jim Crow car with a curt: "I know where I belong." Similarly, Stuart, who had scarcely "an atom of Negro blood" and who might have been "classed as white," identified with his fellow black Mississippians and spent his life, as one of them reported, in "vociferous . . . denunciation of the evils of racial prejudice." Not unlike one-sixteenth black Charles Etienne de Saint Valery Bon in Faulkner's *Absalom, Absalom!,* these Mississippians found the door to a more comfortable and secure world ajar and refused to pass through it.[95]

Significant exceptions to the progressive decline of color consciousness among black Mississippians included the exclusive "blue-vein" society of Natchez and the remnants of smaller, scattered enclaves of Catholic, French-speaking "colored Creoles" on the Gulf Coast. Although the coastal mulattoes have never been studied, some evidence suggests that their sense of exclusivity—though waning—survived well into the interwar period. Their claims to a tenuous racial middle ground were apparently discounted by both whites and blacks. Yet in Hancock and Harrison counties racially mixed "Cajun" families readily acknowledged their Indian but not their black Afro-American forebears; and some "free-born colored" of Bay St. Louis and Pass Christian saw themselves as late as the 1930s as neither whites nor, as one of them expressed it, "real negroes."[96]

Much more is known about their Natchez counterparts. Numbering some thirty families of planters, shopkeepers, and artisans in 1900, the Adams County "blue-veins" occupied an intermediate status not unlike that of the half-castes in some Latin societies or the mixed-blood aristocrats of Charleston, Nashville, New Orleans, or Savannah. As a group they enjoyed high social and economic status and positions of leadership in the black community. Resentful blacks called them "color struck," not remarkably, and accused them of "sellin' out to white folks." The social scientists who studied them in 1934 noted that though their ranks were somewhat depleted by outmigration, they remained a cultural and genetic enclave governed by endogamy and "organized chiefly around 'white' physical appearance"—"olive, light yellow or white skin color, with white hair-forms." Occasionally, dark-skinned children born to this group were quietly sent to live with darker relatives in other communities.[97]

Elsewhere in the state whites operated under the "one drop rule," agreeing with the Mississippi sheriff in Edna Ferber's *Showboat* (1924) that "one drop of nigger blood makes you a nigger in these parts." But relatively permissive Natchez whites until after World War I apparently recognized the "blues-veins" as a "different race" and, in small but psychologically meaningful ways, treated them accordingly. As late as the mid-thirties, these "white Negroes" denied kinship with the larger black community and excluded even the wealthiest brown skins from their inner circle.[98]

Yet even in this old river city "bright" skin and "good" hair mattered less in 1940 than in 1890. Once virtually the sole nonwhite claimants to high status in Natchez, they were outnumbered at the end of the period by a brown-skinned, phenotypically negroid middle class. In this latter group, color was not incidental, but it counted less than education, occupation, and polished manners. The process had only begun, but the leadership class was nevertheless gradually darkening in Natchez much as it had elsewhere in the state. Indeed, as the period ended, Mississippi's mulatto elite was rapidly merging into a black elite. As the decades passed—and as black-white miscegenation declined and black-mulatto intermarriage increased—the state's mixed-blood population became at once larger and darker. In line with tendencies elsewhere in Afro-America, the black part became somewhat less black; the mulatto part became somewhat less white; and the whole became somewhat browner.[99]

The Etiquette of Race

The black Mississippians' "place," as whites defined it, was always more behavioral than spatial in nature. The dominant race understood that it was often neither possible nor desirable to separate physically two people living and working in close proximity. Valuing hierarchy more than they feared propinquity, whites casually rubbed elbows with blacks in contexts that sometimes startled northerners. Yet the requirements of caste, most particularly of social distance, were zealously enforced. Unlike his Yankee counterparts, the conservative and paternalistic planter-scholar Alfred Holt Stone believed, the white Mississippian "does not object to personal association with the negro—provided it be upon terms which contain no suggestion of equality of personal status."[100]

The point of caste was made most characteristically in the everyday courtesies whites routinely withheld from blacks. In Mississippi, as elsewhere in the South, good manners were emphasized from birth and even close friends often addressed each other formally. Black Mississippians, on the other hand, were generally called—even by much younger whites—only by their first names, nicknames, or simply "boy" and "girl." A favored person, particularly when old, might be called "auntie" or "uncle," "sister" or "elder"; a well-regarded lawyer "esquire," a physician "doctor," a half-educated one-room school teacher "professor." For a decade or two following Reconstruction, the leading men of the race, particularly such political figures as John Roy Lynch or James Hill, were actually addressed in some newspapers as "Mr."[101] After 1890, however, conventional terms of respect were rarely extended. Until the practice was stopped by federal authorities, postal officials in at least one Delta town effaced "Mr." and "Mrs." on envelopes thought to be addressed to blacks.[102] In 1909, African Methodist Episcopal Bishop Edward Wilkinson Lampton and his family were forced to flee Greenville for the North after the clergyman's daughter imprudently insisted that a local telephone operator address her as "Miss."[103] Similarly, much of the hostility initially directed toward Sherwood Eddy's short-lived Delta Cooperative Farm in Bolivar County near Hillhouse, a biracial but otherwise deliberately segregated depression-era communal experiment, could be traced not only to black participation in community decisions but to the practice of using courtesy titles for all members. Sensitive to what its deeply religious founders called "external pressures"[104]—attentive to the racial code lest they, in Jonathan Daniels's words, "complicate the cooperative experiment unduly by unnecessarily alarming Mississippi"—the farm's business, religious, and social meetings were segregated and its two dozen families lived in separate-but-equal cabins. These concessions notwithstanding, white opinion was not assuaged, and farm leaders ultimately suggested that all but the most elderly residents be addressed by their Christian names. "Its crazy," a planter told Daniels. "Crazy mistering niggers in Mississippi."[105]

White men, however chivalrous toward white women, neither tipped nor removed their hats for black women, and of course shook black hands only in exceptional circumstances. Blacks on the other hand were expected to show deference at every turn: to wait in nearly any line until all whites were served; to approach a white home only by the back door; to yield the right of way to whites when walking or driving;[106] to show respect even to the poor whites they privately mocked as "peckerwoods." As blacks sometimes joked among themselves, white sensitivities were so easily roiled in the timber districts of the Piney Woods that heedful black customers ordered "Mr. Prince Albert" tobacco.[107]

The racial code also prohibited all forms of interracial activity that might imply equality: eating or drinking, card playing, a social chat in a white family's parlor or front porch. In rural areas, prudent blacks did not smoke cigars in white company, wear dress clothes on weekdays, drive large or expensive cars, or otherwise carry an air of prosperity.

Indeed, any deviation from the Sambo style could result in trouble. "There was a day when the average Negro householder was afraid to paint his house and fix up his premises because of the attitude of some white man," conservative Piney Woods schoolmaster Laurence Jones observed. Not every sign of black ambition was perceived as "being uppity," Jones added, "but the fact remains that a Negro did not always feel as safe in a neat cottage with attractive surroundings as he did in a tumbling-down shack." As late as the 1930s, affluent black Natchezians commonly took the precaution of concealing their wealth by depositing savings in several banks and, occasionally, even in northern institutions.[108] Virtually everywhere in the state, the most educated and articulate blacks knew when they could afford to be themselves and when they could not.

Nor was it enough merely to observe the letter of the social ritual. Lest they appear "sassy" or "sullen," the black anthropologist Allison Davis has written, blacks had to show ready acquiescence by inflection and gesture, to appear by every outward sign to be "willingly and cheerfully" humble.[109] "Whites are not satisfied if Negroes are cool, reserved, and self-possessed though polite," John Dollard discovered in Sunflower County; "they must be actively obliging and submissive." Few blacks risked seeming "biggity," a black Lawrence Countian remembered of the early post–World War II years. "At that time in Mississippi it was tough enough being black; to be known as a smart nigger would have been unbearable." "The white man is the boss," another black Mississippian observed. "You got to talk to him like he is the boss."[110]

Above all, black Mississippians were expected to avoid controversy with the dominant race. It was a breach of caste to contradict any white; an angry exchange, even when provoked, was a foolhardy act; a flash of black rage could be as dangerous as physical assault. Some subjects, in fact were simply too sensitive for interracial discourse. Richard Wright's catalog of forbidden topics is incomplete but suggestive: "American white women; the Ku Klux Klan; France; and how Negro soldiers fared while there; French women; Jack Johnson; the entire northern part of the United States; the Civil War; Abraham Lincoln; U. S. Grant; General Sherman; Catholics; the Pope; Jews; the Republican party; slavery; social equality; Communism; Socialism; the 13th, 14th, and 15th Amendments to the Constitution; or any topic calling for positive knowledge or manly self-assertion on the part of the Negro."[111]

By his own account, Wright never cultivated what black Mississippians called a "white folks' manner." While a Jackson teenager, he remembered in his autobiography, a classmate instructed him in the mid-1920s on the ways of survival: "Dick, look, you're black, black, *black*, see? . . . White people make it their business to watch niggers. . . . And they pass the word around. . . . When you're in front of white people, *think* before you act, *think* before you speak. Your way of doing things is all right among *our* people, but not for *white* people. They won't stand for it." Try as he did, the future novelist found it "utterly impossible . . . to calculate, to scheme, to act, to plot all the time." Although he marveled at how skillfully the young people of his generation "acted out" their assigned roles, he could not play the part himself. "I would remember to dissemble for short periods, then I would forget and act straight and human again, not with the desire to harm anybody, but merely forgetting the artificial status of race and class."[112]

Wright's path carried him out of Mississippi, first to Memphis in 1925 and then, in 1927, to Chicago. Those who stayed behind necessarily learned more accommodative behavior, usually at a very young age. No doubt black children quite unconsciously discovered the social utility of deference by observing their elders. Yet a substantial body of social science literature—and the testimony of the people themselves—demonstrates that the black community left little to chance, that the black child was usually given "specific training . . . within his own family to enable him to adjust to . . . white demands."[113] By most accounts, black children in Mississippi were fully "adjusted" by as early as five or six years of age and no later than ten or twelve. "Being black is part of the air you breath," observed Charles Evers (who in 1969 became the first black mayor of Fayette): "Our mothers began telling us about being black from the day we were born. The white folks weren't any better than we were, Momma said, but they sure thought they were. . . . We got it hammered into us to watch our step, to stay in our place, or to get off the street when a white woman passed."[114] The form and content of their training, of course, were as varied as the families that provided them. Some children, like some adults, no doubt internalized their subservient roles and accepted caste degradations and the master-servant relationship as somehow natural. Yet a great many more rejected the white worldview. Evers, once again, remembered with admiration the disingenuousness of his Uncle Mark Thomas who "used a lot of psychology on white people." He "yes *sirred* and no *sirred*"; "he played them for fools, and he got almost anything he wanted. He wasn't a *Tom*, but he played it real cool." James Farmer, on the other hand, looked back in anger, remembering the humiliation of deference. Of a childhood spent, in part, in Holly Springs, Farmer vividly recalled "the complexity and absurdity of southern caste" and his own anguish at "my father's accommodation to a system that made him less than a man." Though he recognized even then that the elder Farmer was a "highly complex man" who projected several "distinct faces," the ten-year-old son nevertheless resented his father's "compromising if not subservient" behavior and he vowed "I'll never do that when I grow up. They'll have to kill me." "Scared or not," he thought, "I'd never kowtow to meanness."[115]

The "white folks' manner"—whether of the Sambo type so common to rural blacks or the more refined forms of deference adopted by the educated black middle class—was not to be taken at face value. Although he personally found "the 'Massa' style of politeness in negroes," distasteful, Thomas Pearce Bailey recognized it for what it was. "Most negroes are naturally astute in dealing with the white man. . . . I doubt whether the negro that always has the word 'Boss' on his lips is either especially polite or especially humble; rather he is habituated to servile words, or else cunning enough to know they serve as a convenient mask."[116]

Black Mississippians rarely spoke so plainly to whites, but among themselves or to trusted outsiders they could be brutally candid. "I know just how to get along with them," a Cleveland day laborer told a black sociologist on the eve of World War II. "I can make them think they own the world. It is nothing but a lot of jive that I hand them." But for his poverty, he said, he'd find a more hospitable place to live and "all the white folks could kiss where the sun don't shine." "Mississippi is awful," a Bolivar County woman told the same researcher. "All the important things Negroes can't do."[117] Such resentment could, of course, explode into violence. As we shall see, unduly imperious whites sometimes learned that the obliging comment and the passive demeanor of the field hand and the domestic servant could melt away in a moment of passion.

The best strategy, most blacks agreed, was to minimize contacts with whites wherever possible and to appear obedient when necessary. "I stayed out [of] the way," reported Phil Larkin, a Laurel sawmill hand. "When you were told to get off the streets, you would get off the streets." For themselves, pretended servility was widely regarded as a loathsome but necessary act; for their children, many parents found it increasingly unacceptable after World War I. After sending her son to a northern school, a Greenville mother explained her reluctance to see him return: "For him to accept the same abuses to which we, his parents, are accustomed, would make him much less than the man we would have him to be." In the same ambivalent spirit, other blacks looked to the visits of their northern relatives with a mixture of anticipation and dread, longing to see them but fearing they could not make the required behavioral adjustments.[118]

All told, this was a social code of forbidding complexity. Largely unwritten and subject to widely varying individual and local interpretations, it was nevertheless enforced in uncounted and often trivial ways. Yet it was anything but irrational, and its purpose must not be underestimated. If violence was the "instrument in reserve"—the ultimate deterrent normally used only against the most recalcitrant—social ritual regulated day-to-day race relations. Within the context of a biracial social order based on white dominance, it served much the same function as "good manners" in any society. For the most part, the code assured white control without the need for more extreme forms of coercion.

Finally, it seems useful to remember that the black journey through Jim Crow Mississippi was not one of unrelieved darkness and that even within the cramped boundaries of the social code there was often room for the civility that seemed second nature to the southern region. Whatever they may have lacked in theoretical idealism for the black race in general, not a few whites, irrespective of wealth or breeding, were capable of practical acts of great decency to its individual members. "Personal relationships, the solving touch of human nature," as journalist Ray Stannard Baker discovered at the turn of the century, "play havoc with political theories and generalities. Mankind develops not by rules but by exceptions to rules."[119] Indeed, race relations in Mississippi, as elsewhere in the South, were too fraught with paradox and contradiction to be easily described. Individually, whites and blacks sometimes defied the rules of caste, forming deep attachments and lifelong friendships that served both races well. Linked by a web of feeling and mutual dependency spun by generations of intimate association, whites and blacks often managed to behave as individuals with a warmth and deeply felt concern that went beyond mere paternalism and seemed curiously out of place in a society dominated by race. Although whites generally read more into these acts of interracial humanity than did blacks, the personal affections and the frequent courtesies were nonetheless genuine and they form a small but important part of a very complex story.

The Instrument in Reserve

If the tenor of everyday race relations was generally even, the threat of physical aggression was nevertheless ever present. When violence shattered the racial calm, some whites deplored it and many attributed its "excesses" to ungovernable redneck passions. But white Mississippians of every class seemed to regard coercive acts against erring black individuals as object lessons of universal benefit to the subordinate race. A judicious flogging here—and, in extreme circumstances, an isolated lynching there—allayed white anxieties by reaffirming the color line and striking fear into black hearts.

Considerations of the utility of black fear seemed to recur in white conversation. In moments of agitation, white exchanges, as Dollard learned in the 1930s, turned easily, almost naturally, to stories of "the 'what I did with that uppity nigger' type."[120] Some of this was loose talk, a kind of racial one-upmanship that should not be taken at face value. Yet the confidence and frequency with which white Mississippians described retributive racial violence, even to outsiders, suggest not only its pervasiveness but its general acceptability as an instrument of white control.

White violence and the racial fears that engendered it were telling refutations of the standard myths of white supremacy. For if the Afro-American had been by nature the "servile and contented darky" who, as whites endlessly assured themselves, cared little for citizenship and nothing at all for suffrage and social equality, force would not have been a requirement of white dominance and, indeed, the color line would have borne less watching. As it was, however, whites were forever monitoring the behavior of both races, watching for the telltale transgressions that betrayed the "nigger lover" and the "uppity nigger." Representative examples abound, but three should suffice.

In 1891 an "impudent" sleeping-car porter was dragged from a train near the town of Lake and flogged for having "sassed" a white telegrapher. The Vicksburg *Evening Post* reported that white vigilantes "did not want to shoot him," so he was merely "badly disfigured."[121] In 1906, a northern white missionary was assaulted and run out of Columbus when he was caught walking "arm-in-arm in close conversation" with a local black, an offense "not often witnessed" in Mississippi. The Columbus *Commercial* thought the transgressor's primary assailant did "JUST WHAT ANY OTHER GOOD CITIZEN SHOULD HAVE DONE."[122] In 1934, a white mob near Pelahatchee beat to death seventy-year-old Henry Bedford, a black tenant farmer. He was said to have "talked disrespectfully" to his landlord.[123]

Because the black sphere, as whites defined and enforced it, was not merely separate from but subordinate to that of the dominant race, caste discipline was administered almost as readily for what a black individual represented as for specific infractions. Although evidence of black success was in itself sometimes offensive, an accommodating demeanor might neutralize white resentment of a well-situated Afro-American's wealth, education, or occupation. Yet blacks who deviated too markedly from the Sambo model, who however unwittingly defied white notions of the black place, were nevertheless vulnerable; the chronicles of small-town Mississippi afford numerous illustrations, often centering on persons of the professional or business class. Thus, in 1925, a black physician and his fiancee were beaten and seriously wounded by gunfire when whites forced them off a road near Meridian. The National Association for the Advancement of Colored People investigated, and attributed the assault to "jealousy among local whites of the doctor's new car and new home."[124]

Recurring throughout the postbellum period, violence of this kind, designed as it was to affirm white dominance by punishing black dignity or achievement, was particularly widespread during and immediately following the unsettled years of World War I. In the autumn of 1917, soon after the bloody rioting between black army regulars and whites in Houston, Texas, white soldiers and civilians in Vicksburg, acting out ancient white-supremacist fears of black men-at-arms, ordered black enlisted men off the streets and on at least two occasions threatened to tear the uniforms from black officers.[125]

The most notorious of these incidents involved George Washington Lee, who later won wealth and celebrity as a Beale Street businessman and "Black and Tan" Republican party leader. Enroute from Memphis to a speaking engagement at Alcorn College, his alma mater, the native Mississippian stopped in Vicksburg to renew old friendships. The very antithesis of Sambo, he proudly appeared on Washington Street in a crisp new uniform with second-lieutenant bars, swagger stick, jaunty barracks cap and chin strap—and was jeered by Mississippi National Guardsmen. Later, following rumors that he had forced a white enlisted man to salute, a white mob drove him from the "buzzards' roost" of a movie house into hiding in the black community. Early the next morning he left town in civilian dress, convinced that white Mississippians could tolerate blacks only as menials and certain that he had narrowly escaped a lynching. A committee of prominent local black business and professional leaders complained of this and other outrages to the commander of the 155th Infantry at nearby Camp Hayes. They received assurances that future offenses by white service personnel would be dealt with by military police. City officials, on the other hand, merely instructed the delegation to keep uniformed black soldiers out of Vicksburg.[126]

Similarly, in July 1918 in the same city, surely one of the most racially tense communities in the wartime lower South, a white "vigilance committee"—composed of "leading citizens" and a police officer and clearly encouraged by city officials and the local War Savings Committee—tarred and feathered a distinguished black physician, Dr. J. A. Miller, who had practiced in Vicksburg for eighteen years. Charged with "sedition," Dr. Miller was then paraded through town, displayed near City Hall, put in jail, and finally banished under threat of death. That same day three other black "disloyalists," a dentist, a pharmacist, and an attorney, were also scheduled by the committee for tar and feathers but were luckily out of town. Only the attorney, allegedly a "safe negro" with influential white friends, was permitted to return to Vicksburg. The dentist, Dr. William P. Harrison, was reclassified by the local selective service board and later inducted. Like Miller, both Harrison and the pharamacist, D. D. Foote, were forced to sell their property in absentia at great loss.[127]

Beyond the absurd charge of sedition, the vigilantes offered no explanation. The three victims had discreetly organized Mississippi's first NAACP branch; they had also complained to municipal officials of the harassment of black soldiers. Their primary offense, however, may have been, as national officers of the NAACP believed, that they were prosperous, well-educated professional men in a community eager to be rid of blacks of that class.[128]

Acts such as these, whether directed at black accomplishment or at particular black departures from the ritual of submission, were not quite routine, but they were anything but uncommon. The Jim Crow years, and particularly the thirty years from 1889 through 1919, are among the most repressive in Mississippi history. By nearly any measure—the frequency and sadism of lynching and other forms of white vigilantism; the extension and formal codification of black disfranchisement, segregation, and exclusion; the prejudicial character of the criminal justice system and the size of the black prison population; the prevalence of peonage and the adoption and selective application of stringent vagrancy and contract labor laws—the current of white fear and repression ran wide and deep during these years. Although quantitative comparisons are impossible, the use of violence as an instrument of social control and race subordination was perhaps as flagrant during this extended racial "hot time" as it was during the last decades of the embattled slave regime and the turbulent last years of Reconstruction.

Following World War I, the more virulent forms of racial tension subsided somewhat and the color line grew marginally less troubled. Not until the advent of a second and more disruptive world war and the civil rights revolution that followed would the racial waters of the state again be so easily roiled. Yet, though the social temper seemed to moderate slightly during the 1920s and 1930s, direct physical compulsion continued to condition race relations in the state and fear of white violence remained one of the constants in the black Mississippian's life. As the chapters that follow demonstrate, the dominant race throughout the long Jim Crow era, even as in slavery, looked to physical intimidation as an essential tool in the "management" of Negroes.

PART II

Separate and Unequal

The Negro has . . . despaired of obtaining his rights as a citizen in this section. . . . The Negro, generally finds himself wholly excluded . . . from all participation whatsoever, in the State and National Government under which he lives.

This he holds responsible for all of his many inequalities and injustices under the law, and feels that . . . such a state and condition must ever remain, just so long as he is denied the ballot, since history affords no example of mutual cooperation, contentment, and mutual welfare, where one groupe [*sic*] assumes guardianship of another, and attempts to govern them without the consent of the governed.

—Black Mississippians' Convention Resolution, 1923

CHAPTER 2

The Politics of the Disfranchised

A people who cannot vote in a republic are at the mercy of those who can.
—William Henry Holtzclaw, 1930[1]

The Negro's status in Southern politics is dark as Hell and smells like cheese. There is an unwritten law in the state of Mississippi that not enough Negroes shall be allowed to register to jeopardize white supremacy. . . . On one occasion, a Negro applicant went up to register. Said the registrar: "Get the hell out of here, nigger, before I take something and knock you in the head. You niggers are looking for trouble. What you want to vote in a white man's election for? You think you are equal to a white man, don't you."
—Sidney D. Redmond, 1930s[2]

How could I fail to love my party, the party which took the shackles off my mother and father.
—Perry Wilbon Howard, 1954[3]

Legitimate Interlude

Politics, political scientists like to say, determines who gets what, when, and how. Black and white Mississippians never doubted that. Outnumbered by blacks throughout most of the state's history, the white minority insured its dominance by denying or limiting black suffrage. Under territorial law (1808) and the earliest state consitutions (1817 and 1832), the ballot was restricted to "free white males." The color bar was dropped from the Reconstruction constitution of 1868, yet the period of "black rule" in Mississippi was brief and never characterized by black political supremacy. From the initial registration of freedmen under military authority in 1867 until the implementation of "legal" disfranchisement under the constitution of 1890, black registrants outnumbered white registrants by substantial margins (see Table 2.1). Throughout most of these years, however, white force and fraud effectively deterred black political participation. Reconstruction ended in 1875, when well-armed Democratic "white liners" drove from power an uneasy Republican coalition of blacks, Whiggish native whites, and transplanted northerners. Thereafter, year by year until even the pretense of equal suffrage was dropped, whites narrowed the sphere of permissible black political activity. By 1890, when white rule was formalized under a new consitution, the Fifteenth Amendment scarcely figured in the state's political life.[4]

In retrospect, the failures of the Reconstruction era seem unremarkable. If, as Du Bois observed, the American nation "was not ready for Negro suffrage" in 1865, white Mississippians found the idea all but unthinkable. Provisional Governor William L. Sharky declared in 1865 that even if limited to the most educated and propertied blacks, enfranchisement would be impossible in the state. General William T. Sherman doubted that it could be imposed by force.[5] Sharky's successor, Governor Benjamin G. Humphreys, conceded that "the Negro is free, whether we like it or not." But lest too much be read into emancipation, he thought to remind the first postwar legislature in November 1865 that the freedmen were not citizens and could never be permitted to vote.[6] That same year, whites expressed shock when an assembly of

TABLE 2.1. Mississippi Voting-Age Population (VAP) and Voter Registration, by Race, 1868-1964.

	Black		White	
	Registered[1] voters	Percentage VAP[2] registered	Registered voters	Percentage VAP registered
1868	86,973	96.7	68,587	80.9
1892	8,922	5.9	69,641	57.7
1896	16,234	8.2	108,998	72.4
1899	18,170	9.1	122,724	81.5
1940	2,000	0.4	—	—
1947	5,000	1.0	—	—
1955	21,502	4.3	423,456	59.6
1964	28,500	6.7	525,000	70.2

[1] Figures for 1868, 1892, 1896, 1955 are official; others are estimates.

[2] Voting-age population: men 21 years and older, 1868-1899; men and women 21 years and older, 1940-1964.

Sources: Harris, *Day of the Carpetbagger,* 76n; Stone, "Note on Voter Registration," 295-296; *Voting in Mississippi,* 8; *V.E.P. News,* April, 1968, 3.

Vicksburg blacks petitioned Congress for the franchise. One influential Democratic editor predicted that enfranchisement could only be followed by white exodus or race war: "The whites must either abandon the territory, or there would be another civil war in the South—a war of the races . . . a war of extermination."[7]

Against the grain of such sentiment, black Mississippians entered the body politic. Registered to vote under the Reconstruction Act of 1867, they helped to draft and ratify a new state constitution. Largely through their efforts a new legislature was elected that endorsed the Fourteenth and Fifteenth Amendments and brought Mississippi back into the Union in 1870. Yet, despite their commanding numbers (54 percent of the population in 1870), blacks controlled neither the state Republican party nor state government. Hiram Rhodes Revels (1870-1871) and Blanche Kelso Bruce (1875-1880), it is true, served in the United States Senate. John Roy Lynch was speaker of the state house of representatives (1872-1873) and a three-term congressman (1872-1876, 1880-1882). Both James D. Lynch (1870-1872) and James J. Hill (1874-1878) were secretaries of state, and A. K. Davis was lieutenant governor (1874-1875). With such notable exceptions, however, most black officials served in minor capacities. Whites dominated the government of every town and city except Natchez; by most estimates, whites held more than 95 percent of all county offices. There were a few black county supervisors, perhaps eight black sheriffs, and a small number of black chancery and circuit clerks; but no freedman held a judicial post above the level of justice of the peace. Though represented in substantial numbers, blacks never controlled either chamber of the state legislature.[8]

However incomplete and transitory, this experiment in biracial democracy figures importantly in the black Mississippians' story. White mythology notwithstanding, Reconstruction did not set the bottom rail on top. Yet, while it lasted, the state's freedmen registered in impressive numbers and developed sufficient leadership and group solidarity to translate their votes into generally favorable public policies, a reasonable share of community services, more police protection and judicial equity, and more freedom of movement, of expression, and of association than they would know for a hundred years. Long after white conservatives returned to complete control, blacks would remember this "Radical" interlude as a golden age of harmony and progress.[9]

In his *The Facts of Reconstruction,* written in 1913 to correct white misinterpretations of Reconstruction, John R. Lynch characterized the period in Mississippi as one without "fraud, violence and intimidation at election," when "criminal assaults and lynching were seldom heard of," and "race proscription and social ostracism had been completely abandoned." It was a time when "cordial, friendly and amicable relations between all classes, all parties, and both races prevailed everywhere." When it passed, the former congressman believed, "the legitimate State Government—the one that represented the honestly expressed will of a majority of the voters in the State"—passed with it.[10]

Unquestionably, this bright and nostalgic view of Reconstruction is overdrawn. But it is not unrepresentative of the collective memory of a people who voted freely during only about five of their first hundred years of citizenship. Compared to the ensuing dark years of Jim Crow, Reconstruction was the black Mississippians' heroic age. Next to emancipation itself, it was the headiest moment in their history.

"We Came Here to Exclude the Negro"

Without the ready acquiescence of northern white sentiment, the national Republican party, and the three branches of the federal government, blacks could not have been driven from politics in any state. Beginning with the prohibitions of the Fourteenth and Fifteenth Amendments against voter discrimination, the obstacles to disfranchisement were formidable. When Mississippi reentered the Union in March 1870 it did so under a state constitution that enfranchised "all male inhabitants" and a federal statute that proscribed any state effort to limit further the right of suffrage.[11] In an 1873 ruling upholding an equal accommodations law, the state supreme court affirmed its belief that the United States Constitution "guarantees to all [male] citizens forever the elective franchise."[12]

Additional protection to black voters seemed to rest in the administration of federal law. The enforcement measures passed by Congress in 1870 and 1871, however ineffective, were apparent symbols of a federal commitment to political equality. Even after President Ulysses S. Grant refused to send troops to Mississippi to suppress antiblack political violence in 1875, and the United States Supreme Court eviscerated federal voting-rights enforcement procedures in 1876, the possibility remained that wholesale disfranchisement might reawaken federal interest in black rights.[13] For the moment, prudent white Mississippians contented themselves with the substance of white control and eyed northern sentiment warily. Not a few agreed with Senator L. Q. C. Lamar when he said in 1879 that disfranchisement was a "political impossibility."[14]

Actually, as Lamar understood, the process was already well advanced. Faced with a forbidding array of constitutional and statutory restraints, whites evolved a two-stage approach to voter discrimination. The first of these, the so-called First Mississippi Plan, was the work of the "re-deemers" of 1875. Its provisions included both a complicated election law, which assigned voter registration to local (and presumably white) registrars, and the racially gerrymandered Sixth or "Shoe String" District, which meandered through the predominantly black river counties leaving the other five congressional districts predominantly white.[15]

The redeemers' most effective deterrents to black political partici-pation, however, were intimidation and sham. By all accounts the elec-toral process became a farce. "Our present pretended State Govern-ment," former Congressman Lynch advised a correspondent in 1885, "was brought into existence, and is maintained, through usurpation, violence and fraud." In the privacy of his correspondence, accommo-dative Isaiah Montgomery, black planter and founder of Mound Bayou, later remembered the era as one "of unblushing fraud and false swearing to nullify the coloured vote, or substitute their ballots."[16] Even some conservative whites feared that the First Mississippi Plan threatened to "pollute the very sources of representative government." Judge J. J. Chrisman, a member of the Constitutional Convention of 1890, thought it "no secret that there has not been a full vote and a fair count in Mississippi since 1875—that we have been preserving the ascendency of the white people by revolutionary methods."[17]

But if some found the redeemers' methods unsavory, none could deny their practical results. Following Reconstruction, black voter turnout dropped off more sharply in Mississippi than in any southern state. In the face of mounting white violence, fully 66 percent of the state's black registrants did not vote in the presidential canvass of 1880. Among those who did, nearly half prudently voted Democratic, leaving Re-publican candidate James A. Garfield with only 18 percent of the po-tential black vote. Much the same happened in the gubernatorial race of 1881. Although roughly three in four whites voted (73 percent), scarcely one in three blacks (38 percent) did—and once again a sizable black percentage (13 percent) cast Democratic ballots.[18] Similarly, in Jackson, the one municipality in which Republican control (white in this case) survived the counterrevolution of 1875, white terror effectively eliminated the black vote two years before legal disfranchisement. Dur-ing the municipal election of 1888 that restored Democratic control in the capital city, race tension was so acute that by all accounts only one of the city's 270 black voters cast a ballot.[19] In subsequent presidential and gubernatorial contests black voting continued to dwindle statewide until 1890, when it virtually ceased.

The final stage, the Second Mississippi Plan, came with the new constitution of 1890. No doubt a general disenchantment with the malodorous character of redeemer politics strengthened demands for a new constitution. There was also an ill-defined but widespread white uneasiness with government under the "Black and Tan Constitution" of 1868, a document that bore the taint—as conservative Democrats would have it—of the "aliens, strangers, carpetbaggers, and ignoramuses," the "wild and imported animals," the "negroes, mulattoes and brazen adventurers of the white race" who had drafted it.[20] "Strangely enough," the president of the 1890 convention acknowledged, the instrument "was not, as [a] whole, a bad constitution." What galled, what "aroused intense indignation and scorn," was the "effrontery of such a collection of irresponsible men undertaking to frame organic law."[21]

Yet there were other pressures for change that were not—or at least were not directly—racial in character. In fact, the call for a new constitution originated in the predominantly white counties, where discontented small farmers and other reformers chafed under conservative black-belt planter dominance and pushed for legislative and school-fund reapportionment, prohibition, penal reform, and railroad regulation. At first, then, there was no irresistible ground swell of opinion favoring suffrage restriction by constitutional means. The white press and white public teetered between indifference and opposition to a new constituent assembly. A bill calling for a constitutional convention, first introduced in 1877, met defeat in the House in 1886; Governor Robert Lowry vetoed a similar measure in 1888. To be sure, there was little white support for black suffrage—and virtually none at all from the white underclass that attributed black-belt planter preeminence to the "stolen negro vote." At the same time, many whites recognized that an instrument which could circumvent the Fifteenth Amendment and yet disfranchise blacks could also be used by the entrenched ruling class to disqualify large numbers of poor whites. Moreover, Delta conservatives, satisfied that "our present condition is tolerable" and that the "negro problem" was under control, initially feared that a new constitution risked not only federal intrusion but unwanted socioeconomic reform. Much of the preconvention debate, then, turned not on disfranchisement but on the conflicting interests of whites from the Delta and whites from the hills.[22]

In the end, the suffrage issue was paramount. "The convention is called," the Raymond *Gazette* reported in June, 1890, "for the purpose of divising means by which the negro can be constitutionally eliminated from politics."[23] This triumph for disfranchisement could be traced, in substantial part, to Senator James Zachariah George, one of the principals in the counterrevolution of 1875 and chief architect of the Second Mississippi Plan. Although such powerful Democratic leaders as L. Q.

C. Lamar, Edward C. Walthall, and Anselm J. McLaurin opposed a constitutional convention, George used his estimable eloquence and energies to overcome all resistance. Fearing inundation by a rapidly expanding black population,[24] he saw suffrage restriction as the central issue: "Our chief duty when we meet in Convention," he told a statewide assembly of whites, "is to devise such measures . . . as will enable us to maintain a home government, under the control of the white people of the State." "The plan," the senator often said, "is to invest permanently the powers of government in the hands of the people who ought to have them—the white people."[25]

State and national political developments also provided the disfranchisers with timely support. In 1888, for the first time since 1872, the Republican party won control of the presidency and both houses of Congress. The following year, President Benjamin Harrison asked for new measures to protect the black franchise. In 1889, for the first time since redemption, the largely black Mississippi Republican party nominated a complete (but virtually all-white) state ticket. Then, only a month before the convention, Henry Cabot Lodge introduced a bill to permit federal oversight of congressional elections. Those who sought popular support for the formalization of white rule in Mississippi could not have asked for more. In each case, the threat to white control proved to be more imagined than real. The national Republican party evinced little sustained interest in black rights. The state Republican ticket was immediately withdrawn under threat of violence and after calls for the revival of armed "white men's clubs" prepared to march, as in 1875, to "the music of unadulterated Democracy." The "Lodge Force Bill" passed the House but died in the Senate. Yet the dread specter of "black domination" had been aroused. Only formal disfranchisement, white Mississippians now generally believed, would put it to rest.[26]

With the way thus cleared, the Mississippi disfranchisers turned in August 1890 to the challenge of circumventing the federal Constitution. Some favored a forthright approach. One proposed to deny public office to citizens with "as much as one-eighth negro blood"; another demanded nothing less than repeal of all federal suffrage laws.[27] Throughout the convention, discussions were frankly racial in character. "Let us tell the truth if it bursts the bottom of the Universe," declared President S. S. Calhoon. "We came here to exclude the negro. Nothing short of this will answer." Indeed, so single-minded were the framers that Judge Chrisman was said to cry "My God! My God! Is there to be no higher ambition for the young white men of the south than that of keeping the Negro down?"[28] Yet the finished product was, if not subtle, at least not explicitly discriminatory. The suffrage provisions set forth in Article

12 did not mention race. An adult male who would vote after January 1, 1892, was required: to be "duly registered" by state officials at least four months prior to an election; to be a resident of the state for two years and his election district for one year; to have paid all taxes including a $2.00 annual poll tax; to have committed none of a specified number of crimes; and, most transparently, to read any section of the state constitution or "be able to understand the same when read to him, or give a reasonable interpretation thereof." Lest these measures be struck down by the courts, the framers added two other safeguards: legislative reapportionment to increase white-county representation and an electoral college scheme to insure white control of the governor's office.[29]

The "understanding clause" was easily the most objectionable. Its advocates assured the convention that it was a white supremacy loophole, designed not to disfranchise blacks but to permit the registration of illiterate whites. It was included, all understood, as a grudging black-belt compromise to appease white-county sentiment. In plantation districts, where the interests of the redneck had few champions, whites generally opposed the provision. Conservative newspapers that favored the enfranchisement of only the "better class" of even the white race called it the "odious section," "a shameless fraud," and a "mongrel hotch-potch suffrage scheme." In the face of widespread and influential opposition to this and other provisions of the constitution, the convention, by majority vote, found popular ratification of the controversial charter both "unnecessary and inexpedient" and voted not to submit it to a popular referendum. Although this decision too aroused indignation, most discord ended in the general recognition that black voting could at last be "legally" denied.[30]

Legality, like beauty, is largely in the eye of the beholder. Most certainly Mississippi could not have reentered the Union under such a constitution in 1870. Nor could the document, as drafted in 1890, have withstood the scrutiny of the federal judiciary in the 1960s. But when the new suffrage provisions were tested in state and federal courts in 1892 and 1898 respectively, they were found constitutional. A unanimous United States Supreme Court concluded that the laws of Mississippi did not contravene federal safeguards because "they reach weak vicious white men as well as weak vicious black men" and "they do not on their face discriminate between the races."[31]

Blacks, of course, could read between the lines and so could nearly everyone else. Under the 1890 constitution, one black community leader has written, "the Emancipation Proclamation, the 13th, 14th and 15th Amendments were 'annulled' in the State of Mississippi." Nor did whites necessarily disagree. Rarely circumspect, James K. Vardaman saw no reason to deny the framers' intent: "There is no use to equivocate or lie about the matter. . . . Mississippi's consitutional convention of 1890 was held for no other purpose than to eliminate the nigger from politics; not the 'ignorant and vicious,' as some of those apologists would have you believe, but the nigger. . . . Let the world know it just as it is." The point was also underscored in the white press. Black educational progress notwithstanding, the *Clarion-Ledger* predicted, whites would never again permit black enfranchisement. "They do not object to negroes voting on account of ignorance, but on account of color."[32]

Despite these admissions, most officials chose to read their constitution as literally as they read their Bible. The candor so evident preceding and during the convention surfaced less frequently thereafter. In their public pronouncements, state and local officers disingenuously emphasized the equitable language of the law, attributing its discriminatory effects not to the document itself but to black moral and mental deficiencies. Federal suffrage guarantees had not been violated, asserted Judge R. H. Thompson, one of the framers—they were "only circumvented by Anglo-Saxon ingenuity": "There is not a word in the constitution of 1890 which discriminates against the colored people; race characteristics alone can be said to have been made causes of disfranchisement."[33] Vardaman did not disagree, but he spoke more plainly: "In Mississippi we have in our constitution legislated against the racial peculiarities of the Negro. . . . When that device fails, we will resort to something else."[34]

Whether delivered with a sly wink or a sledgehammer, the message was unmistakable. Uneradicable differences set the races apart, and those differences now assured white rule. Residency requirements, for example, applied to all citizens, but whites thought that an inherently "rootless" and "migratory race" was more likely to be disqualified. The cumulative poll tax was burdensome to all poor people; but because it had to be paid well in advance and two years in succession, the levy, whites believed, rested most heavily on the naturally "shiftless" Negro. Even the list of disqualifying offenses—which included arson, bigamy, fraud, and petty theft, but not murder, rape, or grand larceny—was tailored, in the opinion of the state supreme court, to bar blacks, a "patient, docile people . . . given rather to furtive offenses than to the robust crimes of the whites."[35]

The literacy requirement, more than any other, seemed to promise whites sure and immediate relief. By even the most conservative estimates, 53 percent of the state's blacks—but only 8 percent of the whites—had no formal schooling in 1900.[36] Of course, the education gap could be narrowed, but grossly discriminatory allocations of school funds practically guaranteed little immediate change. Whites also found assurance in the nearly universal belief that literacy was in itself a poor guide to electoral fitness, that as Senator George had said, even the educated black lacked the unlettered white's "aptitude of free government." "If every negro in Mississippi was a graduate of Harvard, and had been elected class orator, . . . " the *Clarion-Ledger* affirmed, "he would not be as well fitted to exercise the rights of suffrage as the Anglo-Saxon farm laborer."[37]

Yet too much can be made of such legal obstacles. For the ultimate white safeguard was not law but the administration of law by white supremacists. In the last analysis white rule owed less to the letter of the new constitution than to the spirit in which it was drafted, less to formal proscription than to informal sanctions. The creature, not the mother, of white political control, suffrage law — indeed any law — was secondary to the higher law of white supremacy. As a generation of unpunished political violence had demonstrated, the dominant race would remain dominant, legally if possible but illegally if necessary.

Blacks understood this, and because they did, the great mass of them apparently chose not to challenge the new arrangement. Whites often attributed black disfranchisement to apathy rather than to discrimination. While that argument was both self-serving and false, there is little reason to question contemporary white assertions that relatively few blacks actually attempted to register. Whites invariably insisted that voting was "white folks' business" and blacks had every reason to believe that "uppity negroes," those who insisted overmuch on their rights of citizenship, risked white hostility and worse. Because the high cost of voting might not be limited to the poll tax, not a few blacks apparently concluded that the franchise was a civil amenity they could ill afford.

The available record is often silent when we want it to speak. It tells us how many blacks actually registered during the early years of disfranchisement but not how many were turned away. Surely more tried than succeeded. Yet there is some evidence of an unexpected measure of impartiality in the initial administration of the suffrage laws. Of the 2,142 voters registered under the understanding clause in 1892, nearly half (49 percent) were black. In fact, in twenty-five of the seventy-five counties for which there are figures — fourteen white counties and eleven black counties — more blacks than whites entered through the loophole designed expressly for white illiterates.[38] Regrettably, there are no comparable figures for any other year. But in 1898 Mayre Dabney, a member of the constitutional convention, investigated voter registration practices in the Delta (Third Congressional District), and found that though the poll tax was a formidable obstacle to both races, black-belt registrars did not often deny either blacks or whites by reason of illiteracy. The "educational clause," he concluded, was "of little effect or value . . . in precluding the negro from voting."[39]

By 1904, I. T. Montgomery reported, Delta officials usually followed the practice—"well laid down" by the constitutional framers—of registering only white illiterates without restriction. Unlettered blacks routinely encountered difficulties, he believed, but "reasonably intelligent" Negroes who could "read and write fairly well" were "generally accepted," though their names might be struck if their votes proved "troublesome later on." Along the Gulf Coast, Jacob L. Reddix, the black Jackson County native who would become president of Jackson State College, could remember "no opposition" to black voting prior to 1910. Elsewhere, by that date, the registration process was less open. B. Baldwin Dansby, then dean of faculty (and later the fourth president) at Jackson College, registered in Hinds County in 1913 without a literacy test; he understood that democracy in Mississippi was a "ticklish business," however, because other literate blacks in the same area were required to interpret the state constitution after reading it backwards. Others reported that Hinds County blacks were denied voter registration when they failed correctly to answer such questions as "How old was Christ when he was born?"[40]

Because so much of the exclusionary process was necessarily left to the discriminatory application of otherwise racially neutral law, voter registration practices were never uniform. Generally, however, only a favored few blacks—usually men of high community standing and relative economic independence, or "good negroes" who enjoyed the patronage of influential whites—remained on the rolls. Ike Pringle of Lincoln County, for example, apparently first registered in 1867 and continued to exercise his political rights for more than fifty years. According to a white admirer, he was "totally unreconstructed, a true negro of the Old South" who "always sided with his white folks and, so highly regarded is he that, although not legally entitled to do so for many years, he is still permitted to cast his ballot unchallenged." As "Uncle Ike" put it, "I always voted for our side de house."[41] Similarly, in the 1930s eighty-four-year-old Jerry Cook of Gulfport informed a WPA slave-narrative project interviewer that "I ain' seen de dey when any white man tried to keep me from votin'." Although too old and crippled to accept the local registrar's personal invitation to "vote any way I want to," he was nevertheless confident that "any cullud man aroun' here, who knows de Constitution of de law, has paid his taxes, an' ain' no law violator, ain been barred from votin' ifn he wants to in de general 'lections."[42]

Of course anecdotal evidence that particular blacks registered easily, even under the understanding clause, must be weighed against registration figures for the race as a whole. When the new rolls were released in 1892, the Jackson *Daily Clarion* exulted that the black vote had been reduced to "a harmless minority." "The political map of Mississippi no longer contains a black belt." A decade later, a Piney Woods editor thought that "the negroes are as far from participating in governmental affairs in this state as though they were [in] a colony in Africa."[43] These judgments were not excessive. As Table 2.1 demonstrates, black voters were qualified after 1890 only in numbers too small to alarm whites. Even at peak strength in 1899, the electorate never included as many as one in ten of the black voting-age population. Thereafter, as official apprehension of renewed federal intervention proved groundless and white paternalism increasingly gave way to the virulent racism blacks called the "Vardaman influence," the black share of the electorate diminished further. Following World War I, Sidney D. Redmond, then state chairman of the Mississippi Republican party, attempted unsuccessfully to compile statewide black voter registration data. Although his letters to county clerks went unanswered, some responded to his telephone inquiries and their answers were more than revealing: "Don't allow niggers to register in Sharkey County." "Seventy-five niggers registered in Madison County." "About twenty-five niggers registered in Copiah County." "Only four of 'em here [in Forrest County]." "Only three niggers vote here [in Yazoo County], thank God." "None. You know we don't allow niggers to register in Humphreys County."[44]

Table 2.2 supplements Table 2.1, suggesting the early effects of the 1890 constitution. Because there are neither official statistics nor trustworthy estimates of Mississippi voter registration for the predisfranchisement period,[45] the impact of the 1890 constitution cannot be satisfactorily gauged. A comparison of the adult male population in 1890 with official data for 1892 and 1896, however, suggests that the devastation was fairly uniform and very nearly complete. Black majority counties were particularly hard hit, notably such Delta counties as Washington, Warren, and Yazoo and such rich prairie counties as Noxubee and Lowndes. Of the state's thirty-nine black counties, only Quitman retained a black electoral majority in 1892 and white liners corrected that oversight in 1896. In Hinds, the county with the second-largest black voting-age population, scarcely a hundred were qualified in 1892. In some districts and especially in such Piney Woods counties

TABLE 2.2. Impact of Suffrage Restrictions on Voter Registration in Selected Mississippi Counties, 1892 and 1896.

	Black			White		
	1890 VAP[1]	1892 voters	1896 voters	1890 VAP	1892 voters	1896 voters
White Counties:						
Benton	877	188	174	1,230	637	938
Calhoun	619	62	103	2,229	1,235	1,523
Covington	487	70	359	1,053	513	1,152
Hancock	577	50	64	1,296	399	679
Harrison	735	64	199	2,030	575	1,382
Jasper	1,256	45	72	1,487	974	1,304
Jones	289	7	108	1,346	682	1,530
Marion	542	109	420	1,314	639	1,520
Black Counties:						
Adams	4,009	342	342	1,620	682	839
Claiborne	2,155	125	122	836	728	850
Hinds	5,566	101	169	2,700	1,764	3,324
Holmes	4,750	220	421	1,712	1,023	1,593
Lowndes	4,412	19	98	1,437	878	1,270
Noxubee	4,312	4	39	1,075	641	988
Tunica	2,797	103	167	437	190	312
Warren	5,552	149	293	2,471	1,061	1,537
Washington	9,103	132	332	1,700	853	1,317
Wilkinson	2,412	153	117	928	550	912

[1] Voting-age population: adult men, 21 years and older.

Sources: Stone, "Note on Voter Registration," 295-296; *Biennial Report of the Secretary of State to the Legislature of Mississippi, 1896-1897* (Jackson, 1897), 66-67.

as Covington and Marion, black voter registration increased markedly between 1892 and 1896. These gains were more than offset by increased white registration, however, and they reflected rapid population growth rather than lessening white opposition. The decimation reached even into the relatively cosmopolitan coastal counties of Hancock and Harrison, where white sentiment was thought to be more moderate than elsewhere in the state.

The new voter registration figures, it should be reemphasized, brought satisfaction to white supremacists but little else, for the state's political revolution came in 1875, not in 1890. Whatever the larger regional pattern, in Mississippi formal disfranchisement affected voter registration more dramatically than voter turnout. The new constitution dealt a crushing blow to black morale, but its suffrage measures had little practical impact on a people already largely hounded from politics. In fact, the constitutional convention itself offers perhaps the most obvious and telling proof that the Negro was effectively barred from politics before he was "legally" disfranchised. As we shall see, black political leaders, with but one notable exception, openly opposed the convention, but were powerless to prevent it or even to influence its course. Only one black, "safe" and conservative Isaiah T. Montgomery, was elected as a delegate, and though his seat was challenged by a white rival, he enjoyed the support of the dominant faction. "Under the then existing conditions," one convention member later remembered, "it would have been a technical error to have excluded the only negro claiming to be a delegate to the convention."[46] Montgomery's election and his assignment to the convention's most important committee, that on elective franchise, appointment, and elections, may have been a personal triumph for the Mound Bayouan and a sop to northern sentiment, but it was not a reflection of black electoral strength on the eve of disfranchisement. Nor did his decision to vote for disfranchisement reflect the will of his people.

"My People Cannot Vote Down Here"

Black men, whites often told themselves, did not seek the ballot, had little interest in public affairs, and turned to politics only under the goad of self-seeking outsiders. Once free of Radical Republican oversight, the great mass of Negroes cheerfully lapsed into civic apathy, disfranchising themselves through ignorance and neglect or, paradoxically, through a recognition that the races could coexist harmoniously only under white rule. As the new era of political exclusion unfolded, Governor John M. Stone found it to be one of interracial good feelings in which all Mississippians joined in the general rejoicing that "conflicts between the races have happily ceased to occur." "In State or local matters," Secretary of State J. L. Power added, blacks "manifest little or no concern, and so long as white folks pay the taxes, and they [blacks] enjoy the schools and churches, and get plenty of work, they are more than willing to let the white folks do the voting and hold the offices." "Disfranchisement was accepted by the masses of the sons of Ham without show of sorrow and resentment," another constitutional convention delegate affirmed: "Suffrage had come to them unsolicited, it departed from them unregretted."[47]

These were comfortable delusions, self-serving but not insincere. White supremacists were not necessarily hypocritical: they simply heard what they wanted to and discounted everything else; they convinced themselves that southern whites alone understood the Negro, and their black retainers prudently declined to set them straight. Coachmen and cooks listened respectfully to their "white folks' " views and kept their own counsel. Like their slave forebears, these black dissemblers feigned contentment when the occasion required it; they knew that when whites sought black opinion, they really wanted only their own.

If whites found the testimony of their servants and field hands credible, they found that of Isaiah Montgomery positively conclusive. A prosperous businessman and planter, the founder and first citizen of the all-black colony of Mound Bayou, Montgomery was an examplar of the more conservative, self-segregating tendencies of post-Reconstruction black thought. Later, after Booker T. Washington was thrust into national prominence, Mississippi whites sometimes compared Montgomery's long and eloquent defense of the franchise committee's report to the Tuskegean's speech at the Atlanta Exposition. They meant this as a compliment and Montgomery apparently took it that way.

The Mound Bayou patriarch was not apolitical. Although his father, Benjamin, had thought suffrage to be "of doubtful and remote utility" to the freedmen,[48] Isaiah was active in the factional struggles of the state Republican party and he served briefly (1902-1903) and somewhat ingloriously as receiver of public monies in the federal land office in Jackson.[49] As Saunders Redding has written, he was skilled at the "ceremonial submissiveness" required of blacks who would "stay right" with southern whites. He took no part in the Reconstruction government and declared himself to be "mighty dissatisfied" with some blacks who did. Bruce and Revels, Montgomery said, were "outsiders." He falsely criticized Lynch as a "Douglass man," and absurdly put Bruce in the same militant category. After a brief flirtation with the dream of mass black outmigration from the South, he opposed the exodus of 1879 to what he called a "fools' paradise" in Kansas.[50] He withdrew from the Colored Farmers' Alliance when he thought it had become "too political" and too closely aligned with the white Southern Farmers' Alliance. "This is a white man's country," he concluded. "Let them run it."[51] Accepting the black place as whites defined it, he asked little more than that his people be given the protection of the law, that they might be allowed to pursue their own independent economic destiny, and, by no means last, that his beloved Mound Bayou might enjoy freedom from white intervention.

Whites found him to be "safe" and "sensible," a black leader who emphasized duties more often than rights, who favored a conciliatory black response to racial exclusion. Upon his death in 1924, white planters bought the aged town builder's tombstone and conservative Democratic leaders praised him as "the outstanding man of his race," "one of the profoundist thinkers, most logical reasoners, and greatest leaders" of his people. "He was," his white eulogist affirmed, "the first to draw the color line in Mississippi."[52] In sum, Montgomery was cast in the Washington mold of black self-help, separate economic development, and accommodation with the "better class" of white southerners. In a modest way, his speech on the convention floor, and the rush of acclaim and censure that followed, anticipated Washington's Atlanta Compromise address of 1895.

The most striking feature of Montgomery's address was its tone of racial sacrifice and resignation. He supported the convention's endeavors to "purify the ballot," to "restrict the franchise to a stable, thoughtful and prudent element of our citizens," never doubting its impact on "the swarthy sons of Ham." By his own calculations, the new suffrage provisions would "secure unquestioned white supremacy" by disfranchising roughly two-thirds of the black voters, leaving an electorate of 66,000 blacks and a white majority of more than 40,000. This was "a fearful sacrifice laid upon the burning altar of liberty," "an olive branch of peace," offered "to bridge a chasm that has been widening and deepening for a generation" and to avert a mutually destructive and otherwise "irrepressible conflict" between blacks and whites. Having laid "the suffrage of 123,000 of my fellow-men at the feet of this convention," he asked in return only that the laws be fairly applied, that whites join in the search for peace through "Truth, Justice and Equality," that "the race problem" be resolved, and that future public issues be addressed "on some basis other than the color line." Closing dramatically, he "press[ed] the fated question home to your conscience and to your hearts—'What answer?'" "Is our sacrifice accepted? Shall the great question be settled?"[53]

The speech was all that whites could have hoped for. The delegates, it was reported, received it with "a deep sense of relief and surprised wonder." "The Convention was with him." The members were said to have been "carried away," and further debate was limited to "matters of detail." The state's Democratic press was enthusiastic, and former President Grover Cleveland expressed approval. A reporter for the New York *World,* perhaps the only journal to reprint the full text, thought it to be "a generous offer of peace" that could "settle the race question once and forever."[54] Some Republicans in Congress vigorously opposed the new suffrage restrictions, but northern whites, in their eagerness to put to rest the "southern problem," generally accepted Montgomery's "sublime sacrifice" as the will of his people. Vernon Wharton thought that "it probably did more than anything else to allay suspicion and opposition in the North."[55]

The overall black response was more ambivalent. Mississippi's conservative race leaders then and later applauded Montgomery's "act of statesmanship."[56] But there were many cries of shock and dismay reviling Montgomery as a "traitor" and "turncoat," and these judgments did not quickly fade. Fifty years after the sole black framer voted for "the infamous Constitution of 1890," Sidney D. Redmond, one of the state's most prominent black politicians, thought he would be ever remembered as "the Judas of his people."[57] Another observer believed that the Mound Bayouan was "thoroughly hated" by a younger generation of black Mississippians who remembered "Old Man I. T." as the "dictator . . . who had sold them out." Even the official historian of Mound Bayou conceded that "his address was received with varying emotions throughout the country, many of his own people dissenting from the compromising tenor assumed by him."[58] Montgomery was not alone among conservative southern black leaders in advocating literacy qualifications. But because he insisted less on equal rights—and because he was among the first black advocates of suffrage restrictions—his rationalization of disfranchisement aroused more indignation.[59]

Historians have generally been puzzled by Montgomery's role at the convention. It was "strange," "unfathomable," an "inexplicable mystery," a "jangle of contrarieties."[60] John R. Lynch speculated obliquely that Montgomery promised his support to the disfranchisers in exchange for the empty favor of a convention seat. Saunders Redding concluded that he traded his vote and his eloquence for an "exemption from [white] interference" in the affairs of Mound Bayou.[61] Yet given Montgomery's own conservative instincts and the hostile political and social milieu in which he functioned, his behavior seems neither puzzling nor inconsistent. Nor is there compelling reason to suspect that he betrayed his race for personal advantage. He gave away little but his consent: with or without his vote, disfranchisement was an accomplished fact. Through his act of race abnegation, he clearly hoped, blacks might find an opportunity for the educational and economic progress that would ultimately assure the restoration of their political rights. He was wrong, of course, but it does not follow that he was insincere, recreant, or self-seeking.

In time Montgomery changed his mind and expressed his second thoughts in the privacy of his correspondence. In 1904, after he was forced out of his job in the federal land office, he confessed to Washington a growing sense of betrayal, and suggested that only federal intervention could bring democracy to Mississippi. White talk of restoring "pure government" by purging ignorance, he admitted to a sympathetic white northerner, was insincere. "It should be fully understood that the contention now is against the black as an effective voter, irrespective of qualifications." Having effectively denied black citizenship, he believed, the dominant race now sought the formal repeal of the Thirteenth, Fourteenth, and Fifteenth Amendments, "nothing less than a retrogression of the Negro back towards serfdom and slavery."[62]

These private disillusionments notwithstanding, the Mound Bayouan apparently never publicly looked back with regret at what he and other conservative black Mississippians called the "peace bush" of 1890. On the twentieth anniversary of his controversial speech, he offered a "calm and dispassionate" defense of a "fundamentally just" state constitution that "brought order . . . out of chaotic uncertainty, and gave peace to a confused people." Obscuring his personal resentments and misgivings in the equivocal language of accommodationism, he attributed racial inequities to the administration of law rather than to the law itself. Under a charter that "providentially divorced [race] from politics for all time," he said, Mississippi had enjoyed two decades of "marvelous progress."[63] Neither here nor in any public forum did he repeat his private call for armed federal intervention.

Whites raised Montgomery's example as proof that black Mississippians acquiesced in their own disfranchisement. And the orator himself insisted that his views were known to the black Bolivar Countains who helped to elect him as their convention delegate.[64] Perhaps. But Montgomery did not speak for the state's first generation of black political leaders, those old-line Republican figures who as John R. Lynch put it, "bravely refused to surrender their honest convictions." These dissenters—among them Lynch, Blanche K. Bruce, James J. Hill, and other leaders prominent during what we shall call the first stage of the black Mississippian's journey toward full civil equality—resisted white encroachments on black civil and political rights by every practical means. Preferring confrontation on this issue to conciliation, Lynch delicately described Montgomery's acquiescence as "a great disappointment to his friends."[65] Well before suffrage restrictions were enacted, this former congressman demanded federal intervention in Mississippi where "an election . . . is a travesty indeed" and where the majority could not vote because "they fear murder." Then fourth auditor of the United States Treasury, Lynch publicly advocated, even as Montgomery prepared to offer his "fearful sacrifice," both federal supervision of Mississippi elections and a reduction of the state's congressional representation in proportion to the number of its disfranchised black cit-izens.[66]

Led by Bruce, Hill, and Lynch, race leaders from forty counties met in Jackson in June, 1889, to denounce the "violent and criminal suppression of the black vote." Noting that flagrant white electoral irregularities and terror had made "a mockery and a sham" of de-mocracy in Mississippi, the conferees, in what some whites thought to be "the largest colored convention" in state history, demanded federal intervention "to break up lawlessness and ballot-box stuffing" and "bring about a respect for the rights of citizens."[67] When the state legislature called for the election of delegates to the constitutional convention, race lawmakers—their numbers reduced from twenty-one in 1876 to but six members of the lower chamber in 1890—were outspoken in op-position. Speaking for the unified black minority, Representative George F. Bowles of Natchez declared that "the right to suffrage once granted should stand for all time." To abrogate that right only twenty-five years after emancipation, he believed, invited the "odium of the world" and threatened to reverse "the grand results of the late war" and reduce the former slaves to "a position more intolerable than the old-time slavery."

Outvoted in the legislature by white convention supporters, black leaders, in a second major conclave, met again in the capital to urge the people of their race to organize politically in every county, demand "a free ballot and a fair count," and fight this "unjust scheme," this "policy of crushing out the manhood of the negro citizen," by electing delegates of their own. "Every man who is not blinded by prejudice," these spokesmen declared in a circular issued to blacks throughout the state, "will admit that the negro citizen is entitled of right to represen-tation in the constitutional convention." Soon thereafter, F. M. B. Cook, a black Republican who was actively campaigning for election as a delegate in Jasper County, was assassinated.[68]

Unable to pack the convention with opponents of disfranchisement, blacks in some communities prepared to minimize their political losses by subverting the new system from within its own rules. Even before the framers had completed their work, the *Clarion-Ledger* reported, dissident blacks were plotting ways around the proposed educational restrictions: "Night schools for negro men have already been established in the Delta," the paper noted. "All that these men have to learn is the alphabet. Perfect familiarity with that will enable them to vote." Alarm-ism such as this underestimated the ingenuity of local white voter registrars, but it accurately represented the refusal of even many un-lettered blacks to accept disfranchisement. Black obduracy on this point was forcefully expressed by the Meridian *Fair Play.* Every black prayer meeting, editor L. W. W. Mannaway exclaimed, must become a night school; every educator and preacher must teach the illiterate to read: "Do away with the midnight dance and the cheap excursion; stop taking Saturday evening vacations and let every negro who can stammer over the alphabet consider himself appointed by the Lord to teach one another of his race so much as he knows." By such means, this journalist believed, the race might limit white political control.[69]

The Jackson *Colored Journal* denounced Montgomery's "peace bush"; the editor of the Natchez *Brotherhood* protested the suffrage restriction in language that no white community in Mississippi would have tolerated a decade later: "Disfranchise the negro! Keep him from holding office! In the name of God, where now are the last two amendments to the federal constitution? Will an American congress permit a state to set up an oligarchy by reversing the intents and purposes of the organic law of the land?"[70] Even the white press, which often understated such things, took note occasionally of "colored Republicans" and the organization of scattered Loyal Leagues or Negro Taxpayers' Leagues, as blacks assembled to discuss their political frustrations and aspirations and sometimes to petition for longer school terms so that they might meet literacy requirements. Often, as the times would increasingly require, such meetings emphasized black opportunities more than white discrimination. But white Democratic editors correctly interpreted them as expressions of protest—and warned blacks not to "fight a cyclone" or commit acts "worse than folly."[71]

Black Mississippians also opposed the new suffrage law in both state and federal court. When these legal challenges failed, Cornelius J. Jones, a doughty Greenville attorney who was among the last blacks to serve in the state legislature, sought unsuccessfully in 1896 and 1899 to unseat white congressmen on the ground that they were elected under an unconstitutional election code. Because Mississippi's election procedures were based on disfranchisement, Jones boldly contended, no congressman from a black majority district was entitled to a place in the House of Representatives.[72]

Clearly, then, in 1890 Montgomery was out of step with the state's recognized black leadership. Although the views of plainer folk cannot be measured, available evidence suggests that a great many rank-and-file black Mississippians also deplored the new voter restrictions. Try as they might to conclude otherwise, even some conservative whites, to quote prominent redeemer Democrat and one-time state Attorney General Frank Johnston, found no "disposition on the part of the negroes to acquiesce in the suppression of their votes or to retire from politics."[73] Regrettably, contemporary black sources do not speak directly to the issue; and the slave narratives of the 1930s (largely, one suspects, because whites did most of the interviewing) are inconclusive. James Lucas, for example, a former slave from Adams County, said that he "nevah keered 'bout votin'"; and Henry Lewis of Pike County claimed that "I never wanted to vote; I always tried to stay in my place." Squire Irvin, an ex-slave from Coahoma County, on the other hand, coyly insisted that he "never heared there is any objection to the colored folks voting." But other WPA interviewees were more forthright: "I quit votin' kase dey 'franchised us from votin'. I thought dem was good times in de country 'fore de [dis]franchised us." "Dar wus so much fuss gwine on at dat time I stayed way in didn't go to vote." "I use to vote years ago . . . but quit as some folks didn't lak it." "Dis nigger kno'd bettern den to try to vote; dem white folks wud git yo'."[74]

Unremarkably, the most straightforward repudiations of Montgomery-style accommodationism are to be found in the private letters black Mississippians addressed to the National Association for the Advancement of Colored People after World War I. "We want only one thing, primarily," C. E. Johnson, a black agriculture demonstration agent from Prentiss, reported in 1920. "That is the ballot. Ballot everywhere. My people cannot vote down here. . . . We want the damnable curse of disfranchisement in primary elections [re]moved in every form of state government."[75] These letters, so eloquently at odds with white mythology, capture some of the frustration of the disfranchised and much of the dangers of citizenship. Consider Mack Holliman, whose experience was exceptional perhaps only because he hoped to win full citizenship through legal action. In August, 1927, after learning that the United States Supreme Court, in *Nixon* v. *Herndon,* had voided a Texas white primary election law, Holliman tried to participate in a Democratic primary in Jones County, where he had been registered to vote for fourteen years. Refused by reason of color, he decided to seek redress in court and, after much difficulty, secured a white attorney. Before his case could be heard, however, Holliman withdrew the suit and fled the state, leaving his 130-acre farm and livestock: "My life has ben threten and I will hafter move off and leave my home if they Dont Kill me before. . . . I dont think they aim for me to me[et] cort." From the relative safety of Mobile, he wrote the NAACP's New York office several more times: "I am in much troble over the suit. . . . The threts was made at night." The association refused the exiled Negro's requests for NAACP legal assistance when he would not risk returning to Jones County even to appear in court. Although acknowledging its interest in additional cases to test southern white primary laws, the association's legal division nevertheless concluded that in Mississippi "the stakes may be too high" for black litigants.[76] Similarly, in 1928 when a Tunica County black sought the NAACP's help in his effort to register, the association again refused because "it has been not only futile but dangerous for individuals to enforce their right to vote in some southern communities."[77]

The evidence presented here does not prove that Mississippi blacks were either typically conciliatory or typically litigious. It does suggest that voting could be a discouraging and hazardous undertaking for blacks—and that the distance between an Isaiah Montgomery and a Mack Holliman, between one who would compromise and one who would not, was less great than it would first appear. Clearly these two black men responded very differently to white policies of exclusion, yet neither could be called apathetic. And if Montgomery surrendered, he did so not because he wanted less for his people, but because to him, in that dark moment of rising negrophobia, accommodation seemed to promise blacks a greater return. Above all, the Mound Bayouan was a realist who recognized and worked within the permissible limits of black political activity in a white world. In 1890 he accepted as unavoidable a severely restricted black electorate. Yet until he died in 1924 he remained an active force in his party and an important, if ambiguous, example of black refusal to abandon entirely the game of politics to the white oppressors.

Finally, it should be said of Montgomery that he became a symbol for his age, a representative advocate of the strategy of conciliation embraced by many southern blacks in the second generation of freedom. If not precisely the architect of race compromise, he was among the earliest, most articulate and visible spokesmen for the new black accommodationism so characteristic of the period after 1890. His unctuous humility in the presence of whites and his too-ready cooperation with the disfranchisers were anathema to the generation of Bruce, Lynch, and Hill, to the state's relatively militant first-stage black political activists. Following World War I, during what might be called a third stage in the dark journey through the Jim Crow years, his views again became unrepresentative of black thought; by World War II, no black Mississippian could endorse his frankly accommodating stand on the suffrage question and yet aspire to leadership. As we shall see in subsequent chapters, the Mound Bayou patriarch's emphasis on self-help, group solidarity, and race pride would never fully go out of fashion; but to younger, less patient black Mississippians in the interwar years, his willingness to soft-pedal black grievances and to purchase racial peace and white good will with the dearly won coin of civil and political rights became increasingly less acceptable. During the quarter century after

1890, however, during the period of the second stage, his ideas were widely shared by conservative race spokesmen in Mississippi and throughout the South. During the heyday of the "group economy"—those oddly sanguine years of separate economic development and deteriorating black status preceding the Great Migration and World War I (see Chapter 5)—Isaiah Montgomery was very much in the Deep South black mainstream of caution, compromise, and Black and Tan politics.

Blacks and Tans

Mississippi's black Republicans, like their counterparts elsewhere in the South, were often characterized as "patronage farmers," "palace politicians," and "rotten borough" or "post office Republicans." Used by white Democrats who opposed "nigger politics" in all forms, these maledictions flowed from racial and partisan animus. But scholars have also found them to be useful descriptions and, in truth, once stripped of sectarian content, these labels seem neither misrepresentative nor unfair. In the period after disfranchisement the Republican organization in the state was no organization at all—or, at best, it was a paper organization, a formless and ever-shifting tangle of factions that performed few of the functions normally associated with political parties. The oft-repeated charges that it sought neither electoral victory nor party strength—that it made no real effort to turn out the vote, had no programs, and did not even offer slates of candidates in local, county, and state elections—were true, but immaterial. In a political order inflexibly governed by the principles of white supremacy, black disfranchisement, and one-party Democratic rule, a nearly all-black Republican organization could find no meaningful role in the conduct of public affairs. As party stalwart Charles Banks of Mound Bayou put it, Republican candidates had "no possible chance of election" and would align "the negroes against the whites, which in itself is fraught with dangers and altogether unwise." The organization's raison d'être, then, was to distribute political spoils. "There is," as Banks conceded, "hardly any Republican Party in the South when there are no offices to give."[78]

Black Mississippians found their principal avenue of political expression in party factionalism. They maneuvered for party favors for their race and for themselves. They jockeyed for the perquisites of party office. They fought for the prestige of being party functionaries, convention delegates, and patronage dispensers. As political realists in a solidly Democratic state where the only election that mattered was the all-white primary, their principal concern was control of the party and its patronage and not voter preference. They kept Republican machinery intact and usually under black leadership from one presidential election to the next. But they never managed to build a party worthy of the name. "During the presidential campaign our committee performs its only cause for being," explained the chairman of the Warren County Republican Committee in 1940. "We proselytize these few score Negroes to vote . . . and, after pocketing the handouts from the party slush fund . . . we put our committee back in moth balls to await another presidential election." As for other functions: "Hell, naw! We got no local program. We are doctors and preachers and barbers. We make enough money to buy enough liquor to wash the inconveniences of being a nigger out of our brains."[79]

Although impotent in the state and local context, Mississippi's 'Blacks and Tans,' like Republican party functionaries elsewhere in the rotten boroughs of the South, took an important part in the nomination of presidential candidates. Both victims and beneficiaries of an anomalous candidate-selection process that permitted delegates from the over-whelmingly Democratic South to exercise disproportionate influence at Republican national conventions, they performed their duties in a system that invited corruption. "Every four years," as W. E. B. Du Bois reported, "the disgrace of buying up certain delegates for the Republican convention is repeated." Characterized as "expense funds," campaign dollars flowed from candidate slush funds into the pockets of southern party leaders who, as the *Crisis* editor believed, "are for sale to the highest bidder."[80]

These were harsh judgments, but not gratuitous. Although the practice was not unique to the South or to the GOP, nearly every major Republican leader piously denounced it. Yet even Theodore Roosevelt, William Howard Taft, and Herbert Hoover, the presidents who professed to be most offended by rotten-borough venality, found the system too useful to abandon.[81] Southern Republicans generally denied that their delegates were for sale, or that the payments involved more than routine campaign expenses.[82] But whatever its nature, the practice Du Bois deplored was apparently widespread.

So too was intraparty strife, the most characteristic form of Republican political behavior in Mississippi. An uneasy alliance of "Negroes and Northern men with lily-white tendencies,"[83] the party was vexed from its inception in 1867 by racial tensions. Whites controlled it during Reconstruction, but during the last decades of the nineteenth century its recognized leaders were Bruce, Lynch, and Hill, who though often at odds were united in their determination to maintain black control. Indeed, black Republicans generally agreed that while whites were welcome to participate in party affairs, the leadership of an overwhelmingly black political organization should not be white. "No white man can ever become a successful leader of the Republican party in this State," the Greenville *Republican* insisted, "—and we do not favor elevating them, to the exclusion of worthy colored race [men], to offices of trust and honor."[84]

Black racial solidarity was strengthened by the persistence of lily-whitism among such "carpetbag Republicans" as former Union General George C. McKee, the postmaster at Jackson who led a small but influential rival faction of native whites and transplanted northerners.[85] The McKee Republicans, joined by James R. Chalmer, a formidable Independent Democrat and former Confederate general, challenged the virtual black monopoly on party machinery and patronage in the early 1880s. In language that was already the staple of the lily-whites, these "reformers" dissociated themselves from "negro Republicanism" and promised a new and "respectable" party, one with which white southerners of "ability and integrity" might proudly identify. With a little help from leading white Democrats, who understandably wished to keep the political opposition "disreputable," the black Republicans gave ground only slightly, briefly sharing some of the spoils with the lily-whites but keeping key positions of party leadership.[86]

By 1892 the principal rivalry was among the blacks themselves, and by 1896 a destructive feud between Lynch and Hill resulted in two black Republican state conventions, two slates of black delegates to the Republican national convention, and two separate black Republican electoral tickets. Early in the next century when Bruce and Hill died and Lynch left the state, party leadership passed for a time to a succession of white national committeemen: H. C. Turley (1900-1904); L. B. Moseley (1904-1917); and Michael J. Mulvihill (1919-1924).[87]

In one sense the change was merely administrative. Black voters in Mississippi remained loyal to the Republican party, and the party remained virtually all black. Although these white committeemen could be both autocratic and patronizing in their association with blacks, none sought to limit party participation to whites.[88] As Sidney D. Redmond later said of the most durable among them, "Mosley [*sic*] was not anti-Negro. He was more liberal than the present lily whites and accepted collaboration with Negroes. He had a considerable Negro following." Yet a substantial portion of the party's "colored wing," and especially leaders of the stature of Redmond, Banks, Jackson attorney Perry Wilbon Howard, and Vicksburg attorney Willis E. Mollison, frequently and vigorously opposed Moseley's leadership. The white committeeman, as Banks confided to Emmett Scott, "will not suit at all." Party control by "his kind, is not calculated to inspire or appeal to the man-hood and patriotism of the class I am trying to lead. . . . Nothing which we desire can be accomplished by working under the leadership of [Moseley]."[89] So bitter was the rivalry that at state conventions in 1908 and 1912, delegates arrived with side arms, and on at least one occasion the two sides exchanged gunfire.[90]

If Moseley was not a negrophobe, he was also not an advocate of black rights and political ambitions. Unlike the independent white Republicans of the 1930s—Redmond's "present lily whites" who refused all association with the regular or Black and Tan party—he did not try to build an all-white organization to rival the Democrats. But he was as capable as any lily-white of lamenting the "discordant and venal element in our party, notably some of those formerly allied with the late James Hill."[91] And he was more than cooperative with those who sought to limit federal preferment exclusively to whites.

As Redmond suggested, Moseley was more symptom than cause. The exclusion of blacks from public office could be traced not to white party leadership but to a pervasive and mounting white racism that afflicted American politics at every level. That Moseley's tenure and this development coincided was perhaps not fortuitous, but neither did one cause the other. Yet their concurrence made blacks all the more resentful of white party control.

The process of excluding black Mississippians from office began in 1875. But through a peculiar arrangement known as "fusion"—under which white Democrats and black Republicans in a half dozen black-majority counties cooperated informally in the post-Reconstruction period to elect biracial and bipartisan slates of candidates—blacks continued to hold elective positions until the turn of the century. At best this black-Bourbon entente was an alliance of unequals in which whites held the veto over "unacceptable" black candidates. The fusion system, as a white Deltan explained it, permitted "the Negroes to have some of the offices, and the whites, of course, the best ones."[92] Yet the arrangement had a measure of reciprocity, of mutual if not equitable privileges and obligations. Through it blacks found a way to offset the racial advantages of their white Republican factional rivals in minor county offices and even to acquire a token few seats in the state legislature.[93] After 1890, however, fusion was sharply curtailed. Three black state representatives were elected in 1892, and one as late as 1898. Thereafter, until Congress enacted the revolutionary Voting Rights Act of 1965, only whites held elective office in Mississippi, and blacks were denied state appointments even as notaries public.[94]

Federal appointments remained open only slightly longer. Despite local white objections, blacks shared the patronage of the Harrison and McKinley administrations. James Hill, for example, was named by Harrison as postmaster of Vicksburg, the state's most desirable and remunerative postal appointment. Although whites held an "indignation meeting" and local black leaders feared violence, Harrison did not back down and Hill occupied the position without incident.[95] Under McKinley, Hill and Lynch were given minor federal jobs and Bruce, the "dean of Negro federal officeholders," was named registrar of the U. S. Treasury, a position Lynch thought to be "the most lucrative, important, and dignified" ever offered to an Afro-American.[96] Under Theodore Roosevelt and William Howard Taft, however, blacks were often denied even the lesser plums of office. Although Theodore Roosevelt named several Afro-Americans to federal posts — including the collector of the port of Vicksburg and the postmaster of Dry Grove (Hinds County)[97] — mounting white opposition and the president's own efforts to improve Republican standing among white southern voters combined to eliminate black officeholding in Mississippi. In the most notorious example, white Indianolans challenged the chief executive and won.

At the center of the Indianola controversy was Minnie M. Cox, the dignified, efficient, and Fisk-educated wife of businessman Wayne W. Cox. One of only five blacks to hold third-class postal appointments in Mississippi, Cox had been the postmistress of this Delta county seat under both Harrison and McKinley. But in 1902, whites who coveted her job raised the cry of "nigger domination." Vardaman, then campaigning for governor, joined the crusade and chided the community for "tolerating a negro wench as postmaster." Almost immediately some white Indianolans concluded that her occupation of the position was a "menace to white civilization," even a "constant incitement" to black rape of white women. Following several angry public meetings and much talk of violence, the postmistress resigned and left the state.[98]

Briefly, local whites thought they had an ally in Roosevelt. They had not forgiven his White House dinner with Booker T. Washington in 1901, but the president had at least criticized the "utterly rotten" Mississippi Republican organization. He had also refused an appointment to Hill, the state's most prominent black Republican, and he had named Edgar S. Wilson, a Democrat and one of the framers of the 1890 constitution, as his patronage referee. But those who believed the time ripe for the elimination of all black officeholders had not reckoned with Roosevelt's sense of fairness. Following a less celebrated precedent set by William McKinley at Pickens in 1898, Roosevelt refused to accept Cox's resignation and suspended postal service to the community. Whites then had their mail shipped to nearby Heathman—and employed a black to transport it to Indianola. Their point was clear enough: blacks could serve whites in Mississippi, but only as menials. In the end the extremists prevailed. After the expiration of Cox's commission in 1904, the post office was reduced to a fourth-class facility, but it was reopened under a white postmaster. Indianola had served notice, as Governor Vardaman put it, that white Mississippians *are not going to let niggers hold office.*[99]

Very likely Roosevelt's action temporarily cut short other attacks on black postal appointees in the state, and Isaiah Montgomery, at least, thought his administration had "frustrated a movement to drive from positions all [black] Federal officer-holders of importance." In 1903, an effort to force out a black postmaster in Goza in Copiah County (population 22) failed for want of community support, and in a few relatively tolerant cities along the Gulf Coast black postmasters served without appreciable opposition until at least World War I.[100]

But antiblack sentiment was increasing. Many communities still accepted black mail carriers, perhaps because the work was hard and poorly compensated, and perhaps because, as Hattiesburg authorities reported, "they are polite and accommodating, know their place and stay there." Black postal clerks, however, were rapidly losing favor and black postmasters had become virtually intolerable. In 1908, when the white postmaster of Meridian resigned unexpectedly, the *Evening Star* advised the incoming Republican administration that his replacement must be "acceptable" to the white community.[101]

Taft was more than accommodating. As a presidential candidate he had wooed southern black delegates and even assured Booker T. Washington that he was "opposed to lily-whitism." But during the campaign of 1908 he also characterized southern suffrage restrictions as a "turn for the better," and after the election he tried his hand at building "a decent white man's party" in the South.[102] In the interest of party "reform" he refused appointment to blacks and in some cases encouraged the removal of those still in office. For example, despite some early opposition, the attorney Thomas Richardson had been postmaster in Port Gibson for some two decades. Taft thought him to be "an excellent postmaster" and seemed disposed to permit him to serve out his appointment. But local white complaints, the urgings of Senators John Sharp Williams and LeRoy Percy, and "the presence of a number of female schools" in the area, moved the president to act. Working through Moseley, his patronage referee, Taft secured Richardson's resignation and gave him a lesser and more anonymous federal post. Richardson said nothing publicly, but Moseley assured the president that the black man "deeply appreciated your kindly interest in him and his race."[103]

Taft's handling of the postmastership in Ocean Springs was more typical. When Thomas I. Keys's commission expired after twelve years of service under three Republican presidents, black leaders petitioned the White House for his reappointment. As they often did, they also reached out to Tuskegee and to influential northerners for assistance. Keys had no local opposition, but Taft replaced him with a white Democrat.[104]

Elsewhere the story was much the same. Charles Banks, the state's foremost black business leader, noted a federal reluctance even to employ black census supervisors in all-black districts. " 'Sambo' is left out," the Mound Bayouan complained. "The Negroes have lost heart, they feel they have less friends about the White House than in 50 years"; "we are now worse off in Mississippi than ever since emancipation." Lynch knew of but one black Taft appointment in Mississippi, and that to a "small and unimportant" job in the federal land office. "In fact," Lynch concluded, "the colored American had been practically outlawed."[105]

Although Taft justified his action in the name of reform and vital party interests, black Republicans were embittered. Much of their criticism was directed at Moseley, who as one leader put it, "is opposed to and fights bitterly any man of color in Mississippi who shows any manliness and independence in politics."[106] But Moseley was merely Taft's agent, and blacks generally understood that the real problem lay not with the national committeeman but with a rising tide of white racism.

The administration's undisguised hostility tested the party loyalty of even the more conservative black Republicans in Mississippi. Their Tuskegee ally quietly urged fidelity to the incumbent president, and older blacks, including Isaiah Montgomery and Jackson business and fraternal leader Louis Kossuth Atwood, stood by Taft in 1912. But Howard, Redmond, Banks, Mollison, Dr. W. A. Attaway (Indianola physician and businessman), and Samuel A. Beadle (Jackson attorney) did not.[107] In deference to Washington, his political and business mentor, Banks did not immediately join the Roosevelt exodus, but Howard left the Republican convention and with Redmond, Mollison, Beadle, and other dissaffected blacks supported a third-party movement. Their efforts were discouraged by Roosevelt's managers, who welcomed the formation of a "white man's party" led by Mississippi national committeeman Benjamin F. Fridge of Ellisville. But Howard expressed confidence that when the two delegations arrived in Chicago the Roosevelt Progressives would not seat the lily-whites. If the black delegates from Mississippi were turned away, he insisted, they would "put the matter up to their brethren" elsewhere in the nation. Whatever Colonel Roosevelt's personal preferences, "he is too good a politician to risk the African vote of the North."[108]

The colonel's support, however, went to the lily-whites, and the black delegates from Alabama, Florida, and Mississippi were excluded. Yet, as Howard recognized, there was nowhere else to turn. Although Woodrow Wilson promised the race "absolute fair dealing"—and though Du Bois gave the Democrat an unenthusiastic endorsement and an embittered Redmond campaigned for his election among the state's black voters—there was no discernible black shift in Mississippi to the candidate for the white man's party. However unattractive, Roosevelt was less objectionable than Taft. In November, the normal Republican vote of 3,000 to 5,000 (at least 90 percent of it presumably black) declined to 1,565. The Bull Moose ticket polled 3,646. Even Montgomery's home precinct, Mound Bayou, deserted the GOP. Indeed, Roosevelt led Taft in every Mississippi county except Claiborne, where he trailed the president by a single vote.[109]

Black indignation also found expression in the renewed struggle for party leadership. Although anti-Moseley blacks failed to win control of party machinery in 1912 and 1916, their efforts were redoubled upon Moseley's death in 1917. Led by Perry Howard, a largely black faction sought recognition at the Republican National Committee meeting in St. Louis in 1919 and at the national convention in Chicago in 1920. Both times it lost to a largely white faction led by Michael Mulvihill. But soon after the new white committeeman refused to name blacks to key party positions, Mulvihill's leadership was doomed by the defection of his principal black allies, Montgomery and his son-in-law, Eugene P. Booze.[110] In 1924, with virtually unanimous black support, Howard challenged Mulvihill again at the national convention in Cleveland. This time he and Mary Booze, Montgomery's daughter, were elected to become the first blacks seated on the RNC in this century, and Redmond was made state Republican chairman.[111]

The resumption of black party control temporarily brought increased black influence over patronage distribution, but little else. With the notable exception of Perry Howard's appointment as assistant United States attorney general, federal jobs went entirely to whites and nearly always to Democrats. Howard and his associates frequently managed to win offices for "sympathetic whites" and occasionally even blocked the confirmation of those whom blacks found most objectionable.[112] But the slightest mention of appointments for blacks themselves invariably brought indignant white protest followed by earnest assurances that the Howard organization would never "offend" white sensibilities by forwarding the name of any Afro-American nominee.[113] The depth of white hostility was expressed in 1929 by a Hinds County chancery court judge who presided over the disbarment of a black attorney on questionable charges stemming largely from the black man's political activities: "The question of Niggers participating in politics has been settled and set at rest. Niggers in politics, handling Federal patronage, what do you think of that Gentlemen? What are we coming to? This must be stopped."[114]

More thoughtful white supremacists, however, recognized the utility of an opposition party dominated by a despised race. As long as Republicanism could be equated with what some called "niggerism," as long as the organization functioned primarily as the instrument of the state's minuscule black electorate, the party threatened neither the Democracy nor the status quo. An all-white party, on the other hand, might prove more formidable. Native whites, as nearly all agreed, would never identify with the party of the old-line Black and Tan regulars, the party of "black domination" and "carpetbag rule." But a lily-white organization led by conservative representatives of the state's business community might cast off the burdens of Reconstruction. It might compete with the Democracy in state and local contests. Worst of all, it might divide the white vote, giving blacks the balance of power.[115] Such fears had contributed to the vitality of fusion politics in the 1880s and 1890s and such fears now brought Democratic support for Howard's Black and Tans in their factional struggles with a new generation of lily-whites.

The object of white Democratic concern was an independent Republican organization led by northern-born Picayune lumberman Lamont Rowlands and former Nebraska Governor George L. Sheldon. A whiggish coalition of local business people and transplanted northerners, the Sheldon-Rowlands faction was formed prior to the election of 1928 as a "responsible," "respectable," and "representative" all-white alternative to the Black and Tans. It quickly won the endorsement and the patronage of President Herbert Hoover.[116] In the time-honored fashion of Republican presidential aspirants, Hoover's southern managers had stalked the South's rotten boroughs, cash in hand, in search of delegate support. "They needed the Mississippi fellows, . . ." one observer wrote, "and they were, therefore, courting and loving Perry Howard . . . as though he were a prince from the celestial world."[117] But once nominated, Hoover spoke of a southern "house-cleaning" and promised to build a "sound" party in the South, one led by Republicans of the "highest type." In private conversations with a former president he was more candid. Following one such discussion, William Howard Taft confided to a correspondent that Hoover was "intensely interested in his purpose to break up the solid south and to drive the negroes out of Republican politics."[118]

The president's motives were very likely mixed.[119] However conventionally conservative his own social values, he was a man of high principles who was genuinely offended by the seamier aspects of post office Republicanism and devoted to both honest government and party reform. Yet he was also committed to his party's political welfare, and like nearly every Republican president since Rutherford B. Hayes, he dreamed of forging an anti-Democratic alliance with business-minded southern whites. With the solid South already disintegrating under the forces of economic and demographic change—and his own impressive electoral sweep in five southern states—he apparently believed that the sole surviving obstacles to the growth of a two-party system in the region were white memories of Reconstruction and black control of Republican organizations.

In Mississippi Hoover's southern policy seemed likely to benefit from a patronage scandal that threatened to discredit Howard and the entire Black and Tan organization.[120] The charges were nothing new. For decades, southern Republicans were thought to traffic in federal jobs. Evidence gathered by the Post Office Department and the Federal Bureau of Investigation against black Mississippians suggested that lesser postal positions were peddled for up to $1,500 and that more lucrative posts, including those of revenue collector and United States marshal, sometimes commanded as much as $2,500. In his varied capacities as assistant attorney general, national committeeman, and state patronage referee, Howard was the one Mississippian who could most influence Republican appointments. It was widely assumed, although never proved in court, that he received the lion's share of the graft.[121]

Howard and his principal lieutenants were tried and acquitted twice on these charges in federal proceedings that revealed much not only about the character of the regular Republican organization and the nature of the federal patronage system but also about the conflicting demands of white supremacy and the quality of justice in a Jim Crow state. Often a figure of controversy in the black community, Howard was a prudent accommodationist who quarreled frequently with "hot heads" and "wild-eyed radicals" and was not well respected by race spokesmen as diverse as Du Bois and Kelly Miller of Howard University, socialist labor leader and editor A. Philip Randolph, and NAACP leader Walter White.[122] But following the indictments in 1928, Howard emerged as a race martyr, the victim of Republican political strategy. Blacks closed ranks behind the national committeeman and his codefendants.

Whatever they had done, black leaders plausibly concluded, they were no guiltier than the next spoilsmen. Having been used to win Hoover's nomination they were now being cast aside in order to build a lily-white southern party.[123]

Whatever its legal relevance, this argument could not be gainsaid. Although the national rumor mill had, for decades, churned out similar allegations against Republican organizations in nearly every southern state, the specific charges against Howard could be traced to his political factional rivals, the Sheldon-Rowlands faction favored by Hoover. Moreover the timing of the trials and Hoover's obvious personal interest in their outcome suggest that politics was not a secondary consideration. Nor did Mississippi Democrats, themselves not unduly fastidious in matters of political morality, fail to link Howard's fate with the future partisan alignment of the state. On the eve of the first trial, Major Fred Sullens, editor of the Jackson *Daily News,* used the pages of his influential journal to remind Mississippians that "a Republican party in Mississippi under the leadership of Negroes offers no peril to white supremacy. A Republican party led by white men . . . would constitute a decided menace." A guilty verdict, the fiery Democrat predicted, would bring a "return of an era of carpetbaggers," the "return of the negro as a menacing factor in political affairs."[124]

Certainly the defendants were given every consideration by prominent Mississippi whites. Governor Bilbo expressed his preference for the Black and Tan leadership. The chief justice and an associate justice of the state supreme court, bankers, merchants, lawyers, and law enforcement leaders offered sworn testimonials to the good character of Howard. Senators Byron Patton ("Pat") Harrison and Hubert Durrett Stephens—and even the grand dragon of the state Klan—were said to favor acquittal. Attorneys for the defense reminded native white Mississippi Democratic jurors that 93 percent of the Black and Tan patronage went to Democrats, that these were "white men's negroes and they have been good to the Democratic party." When the jury returned an innocent verdict after the first trial, Sullens explained that the "real psychology of the trial" lay not in issues of law but with a "firmly established conviction that if a Republican party is to exist in Mississippi it is better to have it under the leadership of negroes than white men."[125]

Sullens also predicted acquittal in the second trial before the case was heard. The guilt or innocence of the defendants, as he said, would be secondary to the question of "whether a jury will be willing to encourage the establishment of a white Republican party in Mississippi."[126] The expected verdict came on the first ballot. A jubilant Howard—who had earlier expressed readiness "to submit any action of mine to the calm judgment of the white men of my native state"—declared the white southerner to be the black southerner's "best friend." Whites found in the verdict proof of the impartiality of Mississippi justice.[127]

The irony here is too obvious to require much comment. As Ralph Bunche has said, Howard had a knack for " 'staying in' with the white folks." Yet in a state not notably solicitous of black welfare, Howard was an unlikely creature of white concern. Indeed, the nattily dressed, articulate, well-educated, fair-skinned, and blue-eyed attorney—the man who was widely thought to be not only a favorite of influential Yankee Republicans but the "smartest negro in politics" and the "highest paid" black in government service—was the very model of everything a southern darkey must never be.[128] Threatened by "reformers" who would purge blacks in order to build a viable southern party, he and his associates found sanctuary in the house of the political opposition. The government's evidence, though never impartially weighed on the scales of justice, suggested that his organization had honored the ancient practice of levying toll on its beneficiaries. But whatever the merits of the case against them, the black Republicans salvaged their political careers because they were valuable to whites who benefited from the patronage they distributed, who feared the political and social consequences of a two-party system, who honored Jim Crow more than the rule of law.[129]

The trials effectively ended old-line regular control of patronage but not of the state party. Although forced to resign his position in the Department of Justice, Howard—with the assistance of such influential black Republicans as party boss Robert Church of Memphis and Congressman Oscar DePriest of Chicago—continued as titular head of the "official" Republican party in Mississippi. For the remainder of Hoover's term, Rowlands was the president's "personal representative."[130] But the practical effects of even this presidential slight were minimal, for Rowlands had reason to believe that the skillful Howard still pulled the patronage strings. Frequently unable to move his important nominations through the Senate Judiciary Committee, the new Republican referee attributed the delays to the obstructionism of Mississippi Senators Harrison and Stephens, Howard's allies in opposition to the establishment of a viable white Republican party in Mississippi.[131] Upon Hoover's defeat in 1932, the struggle for patronage control lost all meaning.

Deprived of a presidential ally, the independent Republican movement quickly withered, leaving the regulars without effective competition until the return of the Republicans under Dwight D. Eisenhower.

With his co-workers Mary Booze (committeewoman 1924-1948) and Edna E. Redmond (committeewoman 1948-1960), Howard kept his seat on an otherwise all-white national committee and in fact became its ranking member. Elsewhere in the region, urban white business leaders replaced old-line Black and Tans. But in Mississippi, the regulars beat down all contenders until 1956, when they were forced to share Mississippi's national convention seats with an all-white slate of independents. In 1960, the year before Howard died at the age of eighty-four, the regulars lost national party recognition altogether.[132]

Until the end, the party operated as it had operated throughout the century, as a closed, almost private, club less concerned with winning voter support than in managing conventions and delivering delegates. By any measure it was an anachronism, one of what Kelly Miller called the "residuary legatees" of Reconstruction.[133] The patronage trials of the Hoover years demonstrated that the organization functioned at the sufferance of white Democrats. The plaything of the small, conservative black bourgeoisie, it was free to dabble in national politics. But within the state there were sharp and unmistakable limitations on the range of permissible actions. The Black and Tans rarely forgot those limits and for that reason they became the objects of black criticism years before their demise. Although Mississippi's sociopolitical order permitted little race militance, Howard was sometimes dismissed even at home as "outdated," "a good white man's negro," and not a "true Race leader."[134]

Much of this criticism could be credited to the chronic absenteeism of a national committeeman who spent half of a long lifetime in Washington as bureaucrat and lawyer, and who after 1920 never again lived or voted in Mississippi. Part of it, too, could be attributed to a black leadership that often campaigned for Republican candidates among northern blacks, but who could neither organize nor expand the black electorate at home. Most of all, the Black and Tans fell from favor because time passed them by. Blacks mistrusted them for the very reason they were valued by white national party leaders who permitted them seats at national conclaves. Trotted out quadrennially for what Bunche called a "robust, all-out, Lincoln-freed-the-slaves, the-Democrats-be-damned brand of Republican soap-boxing,"[135] they were used as symbols to northern blacks that the party of emancipation still cared for racial justice long after that party ceased to care at all.

Given the opportunity to vote, there is no reason to assume that black Mississippians after 1936 would have been any more loyal to the GOP than were their counterparts elsewhere in the nation. In all likelihood, most would have agreed with George Washington Albright, an ex-slave and two-term member of the Reconstruction legislature who changed parties after fifty years as a Republican. Pressed by a reporter for his reasons, the ninety-one-year-old Mississippi emigré replied with a question of his own: "Do you suppose that at my age I can't tell the difference between a Lincoln Republican and a Landon Republican?" Indeed, even the conservative Mound Bayouan Eugene Booze confessed that in other circumstances—were he younger and less closely tied by family and sentiment to the Republican party—he would "head or join a movement to organize a Democratic League among the Negroes of Mississippi."[136] It seems more than suggestive, then, that when Mississippi's black veterans attempted to register after World War II, they generally did so not under the banner of the GOP but under those of newly organized black Progressive Voters' Leagues and the Mississippi Negro Democrats' Association.[137]

But the anachronistic character of the later old regulars—or even the unseemly dimensions of post-office Republicanism—cannot diminish the place of the resouceful Black and Tans in the history of Jim Crow Mississippi. Except in the most negative sense in which the black presence in itself aroused white fears of "negro domination," the black Mississippians' role in public policy formation declined sharply after Reconstruction and by 1900 had all but disappeared. Yet they maintained their own political institutions, nurtured a tradition of political activism, and kept alive a black interest in public affairs that brought heightened purpose and dignity to black lives. They accommodated themselves to a system they could not materially change, but they never conceded that politics was "white folks' business." Their small and vulnerable place in the scheme of national Republican politics served their party better than their people. Still, it provided opportunities that would otherwise have been closed. It gave them places of leadership and status among their own people, channels of communication with the larger Afro-American community, and useful ties with prominent white leaders and public officials.

Not least of all, "patronage farming," for all of its less savory dimensions, gave Mississippi's black politicos a measure of control over the spoils of office, including such potentially crucial positions as federal marshals, judges, and attorneys. Under Republican administrations, patronage politics, as one scholar has observed, provided southern blacks "one of their few effective ways of securing some degree of protection and prestige in an otherwise hostile society."[138] Token seats at national conventions and token places on the national committee could not carry black Mississippians into the mainstream of either party or nation, but these modest advantages served to limit the oppressive isolation of caste. Altogether, it was not much. but it was the most the system permitted and it was considerably better than nothing.

Expecting Little, Getting Less

Finally we turn again to the ballot as the coin of what Gunnar Myrdal called "legal justice"—of community services, impartiality in the courts, and social equity, of who gets what, when, and how. Suffrage, it is now generally recognized, is in itself not enough. Without parallel educational and economic progress, an expanded electorate alone cannot topple deeply entrenched racial barriers to full citizenship or even to full political participation. But if the right to vote is not a panacea, it is nonetheless one of the keys to meaningful social change. "Political power," as Du Bois wrote, "is the beginning of all permanent reform and the only hope for maintaining gains. . . . No permanent improvement in the economic or social condition of Negroes is going to be made, so long as they are deprived of political power to support and defend it."[139]

The first imperative of white supremacy, then, was disfranchisement. Without the ballot, emancipation lost much of its meaning, and the herrenvolk democracy of the slave South emerged from the crucible of war and postwar Reconstruction substantially intact. Once effectively stripped of their Fifteenth Amendment rights, blacks were driven from public office, refused equality under the law, excluded from places of accommodation and amusement, and denied the public services for which they were taxed. Because all institutions are political in one degree or another—because the conduct of hospitals, orphanages, charitable agencies, and agricultural demonstration agents, scarcely less than that of police courts, penal institutions, city halls, county governing agencies, and state legislatures, reflect the distribution of political power—the white minority's control of the ballot assured the subordination of Mississippi's black majority. As the pages that follow document, black Mississippians expected little from their government and, sadly, often got less.

CHAPTER 3

Education: The "Mere Faint Gesture"

In educating the negro we implant in him all manner of aspirations and ambitions which we then refuse to allow him to gratify. It would be impossible for a negro in Mississippi to be elected as much as a justice of the peace. . . . Yet people talk about elevating the race by education! It is not only folly, but it comes pretty nearly being criminal folly. The negro isn't permitted to advance and their education only spoils a good field hand and makes a shyster lawyer or a fourth-rate teacher. It is money thrown away.

—James K. Vardaman, 1899[1]

We cannot understand by what process of reasoning that you can conclude that [it] is humane, just or reasonable to take the common funds of all and use it to the glory of your children and leave ours in ignorance, squalor and shame. The negro has been silent, gentlemen, but not asleep to these gross neglects, for these facts are too patent, even to the most obtuse.

—Black Appeal to the State Legislature, February, 1918[2]

Of Burdens White and Black

Black education in Jim Crow Mississippi was separate but never equal. Paying little but lip service to a dual system of public education, the state invested most of its meager school dollars throughout the half century after 1890 in the education of its white minority. "It will be readily admitted by every white man in Mississippi," state Superintendent of Education A. A. Kincannon wrote in 1899, "that our public school system is designed primarily for the welfare of the white children of the state, and incidentally for the negro children."[3] After World War II, as the state launched a belated "equalization" campaign designed to preclude federally mandated school desegregation, the Jackson *Daily*

News conceded: "In the past we actually have not maintained a dual system of schools, financially. We have maintained a white system and left the negro schools to go with meager attention." As the newspaper repeatedly informed its readers, Mississippi's neglect of its black children was "shameful," a "public scandal," and a "flagrant violation" of both the letter and the spirit of federal law.[4]

In fact, no state spent less on black education. The great regionwide educational awakening of the Progressive Era (1900-1920) brought modest advances for the state's white children, but left its black children further behind. As was true of the public school movement throughout the South, such educational progress as white Mississippians enjoyed after 1890 came directly and quite deliberately at black expense. The poorest of the poor, Mississippi lacked the per capita wealth to support a satisfactory public education system for its entire population.[5] Accordingly, financially starved black schools served white interests in several ways. By limiting the quality and the extent of black education, the white minority could hope to cramp black political aspirations, inhibit black ability to compete economically, and assure an adequate supply of low-wage menial black labor. It could also allocate the larger portion of its meager educational funds to white schools. At the turn of the century, blacks comprised 60 percent of the state's school-age children but received only 19 percent of the state's school funds. By World War II, the gap had widened: the black 57 percent of the school population received only 13 percent of the total annual state school appropriation.[6] Table 3.1, a comparison of expenditures for white and black pupils, reveals the magnitude and persistence of the problem. Table 3.2 demonstrates that the disparities were greatest in counties where the great majority of the state's black population was concentrated.[7] The picture of relative black deprivation becomes darker still

TABLE 3.1. Mississippi School Expenditures, per Pupil and by Race, 1913-1914 to 1949-1950.

Year	White	Black	Black percentage of white
1913-1914	$ 8.20	$ 1.53	19
1929-1930	31.33	5.94	19
1940-1941	38.96	4.97	13
1949-1950	122.93	32.55	26

Sources: Monroe Work, ed., *Negro Year Book, 1913-1914,* 221; Joint Committee, *Progress of the Education of Negroes, 1870-1950,* Part 2 (n.p., 1954), 25; Harry Ashmore, *The Negro and the Schools* (Chapel Hill, 1954), 153.

TABLE 3.2. Mississippi School Expenditures, per Pupil and by Race, in Selected White and Black Counties, 1908-1909 and 1929-1930.

	Blacks in school pop.		Black share of enrollment		Expeditures per pupil			
	1908-1909	1929-1930	1908-1909	1929-1930	1908-1909		1929-1930	
					White	Black	White	Black
Black counties								
Noxubee	90%	82%	86%	83%	$14.08	$1.69	$47.86	$3.08
Washington	88	71	92	69	12.29	2.50	42.41	6.01
Yazoo	80	71	69	69	8.40	1.83	37.59	3.78
White counties								
Greene	25	23	21	27	9.22	4.59	30.42	5.23
Itawamba	7	6	10	7	3.76	1.70	14.56	5.91

Sources: Report of the State Superintendent, 1907-1908 and 1908-1909, 97-103; 1929-1930 and 1930-1931, 93-99.

TABLE 3.3. School Expenditures in Mississippi Cities of 10,000 or More, 1908-1909 and 1920-1921.

	Blacks in total pop. (1910)	Per capita expenditures (1908-1909)		Blacks in total pop. (1920)	Per capita expenditures (1920-1921)	
		White	Black		White	Black
Greenville	63%	$30.06	$2.98	60%	$51.22	$10.57
Hattiesburg	37	17.71	2.41	37	—	—
Jackson	50	18.48	6.32	44	34.31	8.00
Meridian	40	14.28	4.16	36	—	—
Natchez	57	17.10	5.05	54	29.00	7.65
Vicksburg	58	20.33	4.73	50	33.30	12.41

Sources: Report of the State Superintendent, 1908-1909 and 1909-1910, 144-147; 1919-1920 and 1920-1921, 226-230.

when examined against a regional backdrop. In 1930, when Mississippi's per pupil expenditure differential was $5.94 for blacks to $31.33 for whites, the average comparable figures for thirteen southern and border states were $12.57 to $44.31.[8]

Compared to their rural cousins, urban blacks throughout the South were often relatively advantaged; as Table 3.3 suggests, Mississippi was no exception.[9] In 1920-1921, for example, the average black child in the separate districts of the state's six largest cities received in excess of three to four times more in state aid than the average black child in either white or black counties. They suffered greatly by comparison to their white counterparts, however. In that school year, Mississippi's largest cities distributed an average of $36.96 for the education of every white child, but only $9.66 (26 percent as much) for every black one.

These figures say something about the quality of black education, of course, but they say a great deal more about white racial attitudes. Throughout the period, whites appeared to believe that blacks were poorly suited for book learning, that even such formal schooling as they received was an undue burden on white taxpayers. Those who favored a fairer shake for black children were minority voices in a chorus of white opposition to equal education for blacks. When reformers raised the question of equitability in school-fund distribution, they were generally concerned not with black children but with the sons and daughters of white hill county farmers.

Most of the lingering opposition to "free schools" centered on white objections to black public education. The state's segregated public school system was established by the Republican regime in 1870. Following the restoration of white rule there was some sentiment, as Wharton has written, for its abolition as "a Yankee importation and a monstrous evil."[10] Saner judgments prevailed, however, and though state appropriations were drastically reduced, conservative Democrats accepted public education as a necessary departure. If the schools did not flourish under the Bourbons, then, they nevertheless gradually gained in public favor. By 1890, one state education official believed, opponents were "rapidly diminishing, and the mass of the people are beginning in earnest to back the public school."[11] Dissent was generally racial in character; most whites agreed that black education was "an expensive luxury."[12] The superintendent of Yalobusha County found sentiment "largely" supportive of public education; "the greatest objection . . . is the education of the negro." On "that ground and that ground alone," he reported, many whites still resisted the system. In 1893, local officials from a dozen counties reported "want of confidence in the education of the negro" and "skepticism concerning the utility" of schools for blacks. The superintendent of Grenada County thought that "public sentiment . . . [was] decidedly inimical to free schools under the existing state of things."[13]

White criticism often accompanied demands that blacks pay for their own education. "If it is within the constitution of the United States to have separate cars, separate depots, and separate schools, . . ." inquired a Jefferson County education official, "why cannot Mississippi allow her white citizens to run their own schools at their own expense and the negroes to do the same."[14] Similar proposals to provide blacks just such schools as their taxes could support were adopted in the District of Columbia, Delaware, Kentucky, and Maryland immediately after the Civil War. In the states of the lower South the idea was violently agitated well into the new century, and in Mississippi, Governors James Kimble Vardaman (1904-1908) and Edmond Favor Noel (1908-1912) were elected on platforms promising a division of school taxes along racial lines.[15] For reasons related less to fair play than to white self-interest, the legislature let the proposition die. Some Delta conservatives feared that this kind of Vardamanism could drive needed black labor into adjoining states. Others may have recognized, as we shall see, that tax segregation would very likely have resulted in significant *increases* in public spending for black education.

Under existing state law, common school funds went to county and separate school districts "in proportion to the number of educable children in each."[16] In an equitable social and political order this arrangement should not have been objectionable. However, in Mississippi, where blacks were disfranchised and where the doctrine of white supremacy was beyond public debate, local officials were free to misappropriate state funds technically designated for the black population by simply diverting the greater share of public moneys to white schools. In such a system, plantation county whites benefited handsomely from the Afro-Americans' very presence, managing not only to keep their labor force ignorant, and therefore presumably more docile and dependent, but to educate their own children at black expense.[17] However much they may have shared hill county doubts about the benefits of black education, black county whites clearly preferred not to tamper with measures that worked to their advantage. Table 3.2 reveals that white per capita education expenditures were greatest in counties of greatest black population density. Table 3.4, which offers a percentage comparison of appropriations based on black population to funds actually expended on black education, suggests the extent to which black school funds were diverted to white education. Some white counties, notably the three coastal counties of Jackson, Harrison, and Hancock, actually appropriated (by adding local supplements) more for black education than the state provided; but no predominantly black county— except for Warren, the second most urban county, and the old and relatively genteel plantation county of Claiborne—distributed school funds equitably to black schools.

Of course, there were "idealists" who favored schools for blacks on moral and religious grounds, but even they generally couched their arguments in practical terms and emphasized the need for the "right

TABLE 3.4. Ratio of Per Capita Black School Appropriations to Black School
Expenditures in Representative Black Counties, 1932-1933.

County	Percentage expended	County	Percentage expended
Desoto	28	Issaquena	53
Bolivar	34	Wilkinson	56
Tunica	36	Noxubee	57
Tallahatchie	38	Leflore	59
Marshall	43	Claiborne	134
Quitman	45	Warren	147
Madison	52	State average	74

Source: Mississippi Department of Education, "Mississippi's Negro Schools," Division
of Negro Affairs, Records of the National Youth Administration, Record Group 119,
NA.

kind" of education. Thus when Governor Vardaman protested the expenditure of white taxes on black schools, he was answered by Alfred
Holt Stone, the aristocratic and paternalistic Delta planter-scholar, not
simply in the name of justice but from "the standpoint of enlightened
selfishness." To abandon black education to the black's own small devices, Stone argued, was to invite the growth of independent and private
institutions organized by meddling Yankees, by "strangers, alien and
antagonistic to our ideas." The cost, as he said, was "meager enough,
in all conscience, and why not, in the name of reason and prudence,
let us retain its control where it is—absolutely within our hands."[18]
With conscience thus wedded to prudence—and with demands for
racially segregated school taxes confined largely to the representatives
of poor whites—inertia triumphed. The tax receipts of both races continued to flow into a common fund which, though technically appor-
tioned on a per capita basis, was actually expended primarily on whites.

The argument over how much of the white man's burden should
include black education was gratuitous at best. On the lowest plane of
civic duty it denied the theory of the public school, which posited
community responsibility for the education of all children.[19] Moreover,
white demand for a distribution of black and white school moneys
according to black and white tax receipts was based on a false assumption, which, if implemented, would have produced results white
supremacists neither intended nor desired. It incorrectly assumed—
because roughly two-thirds of all school revenues were derived from
property taxes[20] and because blacks were largely landless—that whites
paid most of the taxes. It did not, therefore, distinguish between what
economists call "legal tax burden" and "ultimate tax incidence"; it

failed to recognize the nature and extent of "tax shifting," the process whereby those who bear initial legal responsibility for tax payment ultimately manage to shift part or all of that burden to others.[21]

The white tax burden argument, then, did not recognize that taxes can be levied indirectly as well as directly, that planters "shared" their property taxes with tenants, just as producers and retailers "shared" theirs with consumers. This argument failed to take into account black payment of a range of nonproperty taxes, including excise taxes, poll taxes, and (after 1932) sales taxes; it did not recognize that blacks were entitled to a per capita share of corporation taxes and sixteenth-section land revenues, that they paid civil and criminal fines, and that black convicts were a major source of state revenues in a notoriously exploitative twentieth-century penal farm system that regularly produced enormous annual profits;[22] not least of all, it ignored the fact that in freedom no less than in slavery, such wealth as the state possessed was based on black labor. Although whites owned most of the land, blacks raised most of the cotton upon which the state's economy was almost entirely dependent. White conventional wisdom notwithstanding, then, if in fact there was a white burden, it rested lightly and only in the first decades of the public school experience.

Indeed, many prominent black Mississippians believed that public school expenditures for blacks would actually have increased had black tax moneys not been diverted to white schools. "If school taxes were divided on the basis of collections from the races seperately [*sic*]," Isaiah Montgomery advised a northern correspondent, "and the colored people were allowed their proratta [*sic*] of corporation taxes, they would receive a considerably larger fund than under the present regime." Recognition of that fact, Montgomery thought, ultimately led white opponents of black education to abandon the scheme for dividing tax money along race lines.[23] Similarly, a school-finance study sponsored by a northern foundation reported that the public debate over tax segregation in Mississippi ended once it was generally understood that blacks would benefit. Instead of dividing the school tax along racial lines and thus increasing black school appropriations, whites, as black leaders often said, "just decided to take it all."[24]

Although scholars have been more interested in the distribution of tax benefits than in the distribution of tax loads, the evidence suggests that blacks did pay a disproportionate share of public education costs. In his pioneering study of the relative racial burdens and benefits of education in the South, W. E. B. Du Bois found in 1901 that "the negro school systems of the former Slave States have not cost the white taxpayers a cent." In Mississippi and three other lower South states, Du

Bois noted, blacks met not only their own educational bills but part of the whites' as well. By his estimate, even as Mississippi lawmakers debated a measure to relieve allegedly aggrieved white taxpayers of the burden of black education, black Mississippians paid 113 percent of the costs of their own schools.[25] A recent statistical analysis confirms these conclusions: in the period from 1880 to 1910, one economic historian has argued, "black taxpayers were subsidizing white school systems in every southern state." In Mississippi the gap between lagging expenditures for black education and increasing receipts from black taxpayers gradually widened after 1870, pushing annual net transfers of black tax dollars to white schools to well over $1 million by 1910. Measured another way, for every black child enrolled in school, whites exacted a subsidy for white education of $3.30. Had that tax money remained in the black community where it was collected, this scholar estimates, state expenditures for black education would have been 150 percent larger in 1910.[26]

In the end, discriminatory funding procedures meant not only that black taxes were diverted for white purposes but that black schools were largely dependent on private donations and what blacks called "second taxes." Some public funds, to be sure, were used in the construction of improved rural schools built through Rosenwald Fund grants, and some individual white Mississippians gave generously to black school campaigns. But because public tax-fund contributions for rural schools were comparatively small, much of the matching local money required by this northern foundation was raised through a second tax by private subscription in the black community.[27] However grateful they were for Rosenwald Fund generosity, black community leaders nevertheless resented the terms under which these schools were built. Such education facilities as rural black school children enjoyed, a black taxpayers' convention reported in 1924, were products not of governmental concern but of "distant charity and the Negroes' double tax." As such, they were, these conventioneers believed, both a "disgrace to the state and nation which allows a private citizen to do the state's work" and "a liability on the Negro . . . since having already paid general tax to help build the white school, he must now take his own private funds . . . and build his own."[28]

The urban school-building process was much the same. Believing as they did that education was the key to race "uplift," and deeply influenced by the ideals of racial solidarity and self-help, black Mississippians in community after community compensated for official white neglect by second-taxing themselves to help their children succeed in a hostile white world. In Tupelo, black schoolmaster A. M. Strange mobilized the black community in the 1920s to build a twelve-grade black school, initially without public funding of any kind. In a Delta town near Indianola, authorities met black requests for educational opportunities following World War I with "a shell of a building" and the promise of some support for teacher salaries. "The rest of the work was done by Negroes," John Dollard has written, "and an unexpected lot it was." Volunteer black craftsmen finished the interior and black community organizers collected funds for blackboards, desks, and fuel. Noting "a great reluctance to spend money for Negro education," Dollard concluded that "it is really the fervor of Negro belief in education as a means of advancement that has been responsible for much of the development."[29] In Laurel, where per capita spending for white children exceeded that for blacks by more than three to one, Sandy Gavin Colored Primary School (Southside No. 2) was constructed in the early 1920s substantially through second taxes on black citizens. Built at a cost of $30,000, the school was financed by equal grants from a local mill owner, the city, and private subscription. Whatever their complaints with a system that used public tax dollars largely for white schools, local black leaders nevertheless conducted an imaginative year-long fund-raising drive that tapped both the black community's enthusiasm for education and its meager financial resources. Mill hands (including some whites) contributed a day's wages; parents were asked to donate twenty-five cents a week and students a dime; teachers canvassed door to door; and school-boosters sponsored molasses pulls, minstrel shows, "penny socials," and concerts. The black middle class called upon its white friends for contributions and black children chanted:

> We want a brick school,
> We want a brick school,
> We want a brick school,
> Just—like—yours!

As one black Laurelite remembered, "This was . . . the first worthwhile project done in Laurel by the Negroes that involved the total Negro community. Man, it was beautiful."[30]

These examples of black institution building demonstrate both the practical application of Bookerite doctrines of self-help and racial solidarity and the political impotence of black taxpayers. As in all questions of public resource allocation, disfranchisement was the root of the second-tax evil. Practically speaking, J. C. Flowers, state director of the National Youth Administration, explained in 1938, Mississippi had "no taxing authority whatever for the support of Negro schools." "A large proportion of the buildings being used for Negro schools are not even publicly owned." Because public officials were beholden only to white voters, this white man observed, black school committees were "seldom, if ever," able to secure public funds for improved facilities and were therefore driven to the expedient of informally "taxing" themselves through private contributions. "Usually they are able by volunteer 'pass the hat' procedure to collect from the Negro citizenship sums of money... to build facilities."[31]

Black Mississippians repeatedly made the same argument, though seldom more systematically or forcefully than in 1923 at a convention in Jackson. "The Negro ... is equally taxed with the white man," these race spokesmen noted, but "he gets only about one-twentieth of his share." "Though all schools for whites are built out of the common fund, raised by the taxation of both white and black, the Negro is called upon by the State ... to solicit charity, to build his own little, meagre school house of his own personal funds, supplemented by philanthropy." In their catalog of neglect, convention leaders reported that Mississippi operated more than a thousand high schools, but only one for blacks. It maintained some fifty agricultural high schools, perhaps 800 consolidated rural schools, a public school transportation system, and institutions for the care and education of the blind, the delinquent, the tubercular, and the feeble-minded—all exclusively for white use.[32]

These resentments were the more acute because black efforts to resist special taxes for exclusive white educational purposes had so often failed. Black taxpayers in Brookhaven, for example, had objected in 1890 to a $15,000 school-bond levy because most of the issue was intended for white classroom construction. Denied in the Lincoln County chancery court, they appealed, alleging in the state supreme court the unconstitutionality of a state law authorizing Brookhaven to establish a separate school district and to issue bonds because under that law "equal advantages are not secured to the colored children of the city." Recognizing that segregation was no longer a judicable issue, they did not precisely attack the legality of separate-but-equal public education; they argued rather that under the state constitution of 1868 and the Fourteenth Amendment the city could build "a common free school-building" but not one for whites only. Unremarkably, the appeals court disagreed; the law was upheld, the white school was constructed, and the special tax was collected from both races.[33]

In 1922 Covington County authorities—a decade after establishing a consolidated school district for whites—responded to black petitions for improved educational opportunity by creating Hopewell Colored Separate School District. Whites viewed the proposed black school as a good-will gesture. But blacks cried foul in 1924 when a ten-mill tax was levied on each district, arguing that they were "doubly taxed" because the lines of the two districts were so drawn that the larger white district wholly encompassed the black district and the black district encompassed only the property of blacks. The new black school, therefore, was dependent exclusively on black taxes, but Hopewell's black property owners were also taxed a second time to support the white district. When authorities denied either an equitable division of the school funds or black exemption from white-district taxes, black property owners sued under the equal protection clause, only to lose once again.[34] In an earlier ruling, upon the petition of William J. McFarland, a black Jasper County taxpayer, the state supreme court in 1909 had struck down a state law permitting counties to construct agricultural high schools for whites only. No court, it declared, could stay within the constitution and uphold laws that permitted the taxation of "the property of the two races for the benefit of the one."[35] But in subsequent cases the judges saw no evil when discrimination was rooted in the application of the law and not in the law itself, when officials were permitted by law to build schools for both races but chose to do so only for whites. By such logic—and by arguing that the tax rates in the two Covington County districts were identical and that the mere happenstance of residence placed all blacks but no whites in both districts—the appeals court could in the Hopewell matter affirm both that "the law does not permit discrimination" and that this form of double taxation was unobjectionable. Although district lines permitted black property owners no escape from both taxes, the court found equity in the fact that should whites buy property in the Hopewell district they too would bear a double burden. If there was discrimination here, it was "accidental" and temporary, subject to change "at any moment."[36]

Angered by such practices, and with an inspired sense of irony, blacks appropriated the whites' own argument. In 1924, as the Hopewell case worked its way through court, an ad hoc black leadership conference led by Sidney D. Redmond, the most forceful critic of educational discrimination in Mississippi during the interwar years, petitioned the legislature to segregate taxes by race: "In view of the very great discrimination in the application of the public school funds contrary to law . . . we would most respectfully ask . . . [for] a division on racial lines, of the taxes levied for school purposes, giving to the whites all taxes paid by individual whites . . . and let the Negroes receive all taxes paid by them."[37] In the same mordant spirit, the Mississippi Association of Teachers in Colored Schools (MATCS) gently scolded lawmakers in 1937 for the gross inequities in black and white teacher salaries: "No red blooded white man wants [tax] money paid by Negroes to go for the education of his children."[38]

Professor Hopkins's Schools

Bricks and mortar, as James A. Garfield believed, are not the better part of a formal learning environment: "Give me a log hut with only a simple bench, Mark Hopkins on one end and I on the other."[39] By this austere standard, Mississippi's black common school children had everything but Professor Hopkins. But in more conventional terms—measured by such tangibles as facilities and equipment, length of school calendar, curriculum, teacher salaries and training, student-teacher ratios, average daily attendance, and pupil "survival rates"—the state's black children had few of the advantages generally associated with quality in education. By virtually every objective measure, they were the nation's most educationally deprived people.

Their schoolhouses were the rudest anywhere. Describing a typical rural school at the turn of the century, a black schoolmaster noted that it was "little better than teaching out of doors. When it rained the water not only came through the top, but through the sides as well." Although he usually kept himself dry with overcoat and galoshes, his pupils were rarely so well prepared. "The little fellows would be standing in the water below like little ducks. . . . Many of them were not protected with overshoes or any shoes, but they came to school each day much as if they had been properly clad."[40]

The passing decades—and the assistance of northern foundations and the New Deal—brought only modest improvement, as Table 3.5 suggests. Although total public expenditures for the state's education plant increased markedly during the period, all but a diminishing frac-

TABLE 3.5. Total Investment in Mississippi School Property, per Pupil and by Race, 1913-1914 to 1941-1942.

	1913-1914	1921-1922	1935-1936	1941-1942
White	$8.00	$18.00	$147.00	$175.00
Black	1.00	4.00	11.00	11.00

Source: Work, ed., *Negro Year Book, 1913-1914,* 221; *Negro Year Book, 1921-1922,* 240; Wilson, *Education for Negroes in Mississippi,* 56; Wilkerson, *Special Problems of Negro Education,* 30-31.

tion went to white schools. Federal funds channeled through such Roosevelt programs as the Civil Works Administration, the Public Works Administration, and the Work Projects Administration were used almost exclusively to upgrade white facilities: $8 million for whites to $400,000 for blacks.[41] Nearly all public moneys spent on rural black school buildings during the half century after 1890 were appropriated as matching grants for the construction of the state's so-called Rosenwald schools. In fact, by 1932, when its regionwide black school building program was terminated, the schools constructed through Rosenwald Fund grants represented 89 percent of the value of all black school property in Mississippi. (Elsewhere in the region the figure ranged from a low of 24 percent in Georgia to a high of 74 percent in Arkansas.) All told, the fund aided the construction in Mississippi of 633 black school buildings valued at $2,850,000—more than for any southern state except North and South Carolina. Rosenwald gifts helped to neutralize the opposition of white taxpayers and transformed individual black rural schoolhouses in nearly every Mississippi county. Because the fund required official cooperation and local assistance, it stimulated public support for black education, prying desperately needed tax funds from state and county government and contributions from sympathetic private citizens, white as well as black. Yet, though it sometimes countered the prejudice and apathy that hobbled black education and brought schools to many of the state's schoolless black children, even Rosenwald generosity could not reverse a trend toward ever more discriminatory school appropriations. By the mid-1930s, despite some two decades of Rosenwald schoolhouse construction, the average valuation of black schools in the southern states was $36 per pupil, compared to $183 for whites. In Mississippi, the black-white disparity was greater by far than in any other southern state: $11 to $147.[42] Expressed in other terms, for every $1.00 invested in Mississippi's white physical plant, blacks received only $.07. To make matters worse, the white official charged with supervising black education in Mississippi was found guilty in 1932 of embezzling more than one of every ten dollars given to the state by the northern foundation.[43]

By 1940, roughly half of all black common schools in the state still met in tenant cabins, lodges, churches, and stores—privately owned structures that under Mississippi law could not be improved with public funds.[44] A survey commissioned by the Sunflower County Board of Education reported in 1950 that the county had no four-year black high schools, no publicly owned black school buildings, and that "the colored schools . . . as they now exist, are in deplorable condition."[45] In another county during World War II, a local official admitted, 75 percent of all black school buildings were still unfit even for cotton storage. Elsewhere in the state, hundreds were said to be "hardly better than cattle sheds."[46] A great many, according to the state superintendent of education, were "just four blank, unpainted walls, a few old rickety benches, an old stove propped up on brickbats, and two or three boards nailed together and painted black for a black board." More than two-thirds had no water supply and well over 90 percent had no outhouses. Where there were erasers, maps, pictures, chalk, or even fuel, they were supplied privately.[47] A task force designated by the state Department of Education found conditions in the Negro elementary schools so deplorable in 1935 that "it is hard to imagine how any work at all could be done." Only 5 percent of the black schools had any library or supplementary books at all, and these were "not related to the children's needs."[48]

City schools were generally thought to be better. But in 1940, health department officials inspected Yazoo City's only black school—where "classes were being held . . . recently, with temperatures in the rooms below freezing"—and found it to be "unsatisfactory" and a "fire-trap." The Jackson *Daily News* thought conditions in that community to be "quite common in the state."[49]

Until after 1950, when the state began its massive school construction program for blacks, 60 percent of all black public schools were rural, elementary, one-teacher institutions.[50] There were few high schools for blacks, and students who wished to pursue education beyond the eighth grade frequently could do so only by leaving home to attend privately operated boarding schools. In 1916, there were nearly a thousand black secondary students in the state, but not a single four-year public high school.[51] Ten years later, the state had forty-nine agricultural high schools, only one of which (Coahoma County's) was for blacks—and it alone among schools of its class had no library. During the 1920s, amid rising white fears that the Great Migration to northern industrial centers was stripping the state of black labor, a number of cities—including Clarksdale, Hattiesburg, Jackson, Meridian, Natchez, and Vicksburg—supported modest bond issues for the construction or improvement of black high schools.[52] Yet by 1940, twenty-five of the state's eighty-two counties still had no black secondary schools of any kind.[53] All told, there were some ninety black high schools, most of them either privately operated or built through grants from northern foundations. Nearly all were woefully underfunded and only three, one public and two private, were accredited by the Southern Association of Colleges and Secondary Schools.[54]

The teachers, the black Mark Hopkinses at the far end of Mississippi's school bench, were as neglected as the physical plant. It does them no injustice to say, as contemporaries frequently did, that in many instances they were "the blind leading the blind." Although commended by local white school officials for their "professional zeal" and lauded by a state superintendent for "the persistency with which they seek to better their qualifications," they were often little better educated than their charges.[55] It was generally assumed, one critic noted, that "if a man could write, count to a hundred and spell Constantinople, he was competent enough to teach a Negro school in the rural districts of Mississippi." "You won't believe this," another black Mississippian confided to a visiting sociologist in the 1930s, "but it's the honest-to-God's truth. We had one teacher who didn't know her multiplication tables."[56] Doubtless this was an exceptional case, for a great many black teachers, and particularly those in urban schools, were well educated and highly competent, and not a few were important and worthy role models for black youth. Teaching, after all, was one of but a very few challenging outlets for black talent in a society that otherwise limited blacks largely to menial occupations. Poorly compensated though they were, black teachers, compared to others of their race, occupied relatively high-status, high-wage jobs. Yet early in the century Laurence Jones doubted that teachers in Piney Woods counties could "measure up" to fifth graders in his home state of Iowa. In Du Bois's estimate of 1920, the "average preparation" statewide was the seventh grade. As late as World War II not one in ten of all Mississippi black elementary and secondary teachers had a college degree; more than half did not have a high-school diploma.[57] In most cases, the one- and two-teacher rural schools, where the majority of Mississippi's black young people still received all of their formal education, were still staffed largely by teachers who had little if any training beyond the eighth grade. Excepting perhaps only Georgia, Mississippi's black teachers were the South's most poorly trained educators.[58]

Whatever their deficiencies, the teachers themselves could not be blamed. From their inception, the Mississippi Association of Teachers in Colored Schools (founded 1906) and the Mississippi Congress of Colored Parents and Teachers (founded 1926) lobbied vigorously for equal educational opportunities and equal pay for black teachers.[59] Almost annually, supervisors of Negro education identified better-trained black educators as the state's "greatest need." But from 1904, when Vardaman closed the State Normal School at Holly Springs, to 1940, when private Jackson College was reopened as a publicly funded two-year teacher training center, there was no normal college for blacks in Mississippi. Teacher education was available only at isolated Alcorn Agricultural and Mechanical College, the state's only black public institution of higher learning; at such private institutions as Tougaloo College, Piney Woods Country Life School, and the Mary Holmes Seminary; and at six-week "summer normals" and a number of un-accredited "county training schools," most of which did not offer four years of secondary training.[60] Within the state, blacks could not obtain training beyond the baccalaureate level. Indeed, the qualities white officials most highly prized in black teachers had little to do with ed-ucation. The northern-born and northern-educated, those thought most likely to entertain "vicious thoughts" and "pernicious doctrines," were generally suspected by whites, who preferred "safe" and "suitable" blacks, particularly native Mississippians who understood and accepted "our way of life."[61]

Salaries for Mississippi teachers of both races were the nation's lowest. During the early years of public education there seems to have been no color distinction in teacher pay, and as late as the 1890s the most highly qualified blacks in some counties were paid more than any whites. By the turn of the century, however, the salary gap (see Table 3.6) was well established, only to widen appreciably as the years passed. During the twentieth century white salaries improved steadily, but by 1940 black salaries in at least fourteen counties were actually lower than in 1890.[62] In that year the average black teacher taught nineteen more pupils (forty-nine compared to thirty) than his or her white counterpart and was paid only 32 percent as much; in no other state was the color disparity so great. In some cases, the black monthly wage was as low as $18.00 (less than the wages drawn by many cooks and handimen) and the teaching load as high as seventy-five to 150 students. These conditions, as Sidney Redmond observed, could only drive from the classroom "most of those . . . who are qualified to teach." Indeed, the annual black teacher turnover was astronomical—25 per-cent in the early 1920s—and the supply nearly always chronically short.[63]

TABLE 3.6. Average Annual Teacher Salaries in Mississippi, by Race, 1885-1886 to 1945-1946.

	1885-1886	1890-1891	1912-1913	1939-1940	1945-1946
White	$125	$130	$323	$750	$1,211
Black	110	90	173	237	426

Sources: Report of the State Superintendent, 1889-1890 and 1890-1891, 7; 1941-1942 and 1942-1943, 11; 1947-1948 and 1948-1949, 11; U.S., Bureau of Education, Negro Education, 1:34; Wilson, Education for Negroes in Mississippi, 585.

Tables 3.7, 3.8, and 3.9 reveal similar disparities in literacy and enrollment. In each area blacks made progress but still lagged well behind whites. In 1930, by even the most optimistic standard of literacy, "the slightest amount of schooling," one in four blacks was illiterate (Table 3.7).[64] Table 3.8 demonstrates that the state's compulsory school attendance law of 1918 was never effectively enforced.[65] In 1940, the peak year, scarcely half of the black children were in average daily attendance, and those in school attended under calendars that were the nation's shortest. Fixed at four months in 1890 and increased to six months by 1940, the average black school term was three months shorter than the average white term.[66]

Most discouraging of all, as Tables 3.8 and 3.9 show, black pupils suffered a vastly higher attrition rate than whites. The great bulk of the

TABLE 3.7. Black and White Illiteracy Rates in Mississippi, 1900-1930.

	1900	1910	1920	1930
White	8.2%	5.2%	3.6%	2.7%
Black	49.1	35.6	29.3	23.2

Sources: Oliver H. Campbell, *Progress of the Negro in the United States and Mississippi* (Washington, D.C., 1936); U.S., Bureau of the Census, *Negro Population, 1790-1915* (Washington, D.C., 1918), 415.

TABLE 3.8. Average Daily Attendance (ADA) in Mississippi Schools, 1930-1950.

	1930-1931		1940-1941		1950-1951	
	White	Black	White	Black	White	Black
School-age population	379,678	493,987	382,705	481,777	393,804	492,349
ADA grades 1-12	232,420	205,617	257,201	241,173	247,306	229,554
Grade 1	43,469	72,991	36,991	83,797	29,944	64,788
2	24,316	31,222	24,314	29,965	25,951	27,962
8	15,696	7,164	19,642	9,550	19,734	12,321
1-8	189,842	201,726	199,175	230,575	190,644	209,983
9	14,405	1,945	17,982	4,160	17,646	7,870
12	7,615	304	12,260	1,523	10,450	2,626
9-12	42,578	3,891	58,026	10,598	56,662	19,571

Sources: Report of the State Superintendent, 1929-1930 and 1930-1931, 106ff.; *1939-1940 and 1940-1941,* 61; *1949-1950 and 1950-1951,* 116.

TABLE 3.9. Secondary School Enrollment in Mississippi, by Race, 1930-1950.

	1930-1931		1940-1941		1950-1951	
	White	Black	White	Black	White	Black
Population aged 15-19 years enrolled in grades 9-12						
Population	107,509	114,893	115,232	114,415	101,499	93,889
Enrollment	49,698	5,029	64,388	12,495	62,666	22,985
Percentage enrolled	46	4	56	11	62	25
Total secondary enrollment by grades						
Grade 9	35%	51%	31%	40%	31%	41%
10	27	29	27	26	28	28
11	21	13	22	19	23	19
12	18	7	20	16	18	13

Sources: Report of the State Superintendent, 1929-1930 and 1930-1931, 103, 111; 1939-1940 and 1940-1941, 61; and 1949-1950 and 1950-1951, 116.

school population of both races was concentrated in the early grades (Table 3.8). But in 1940 nearly half (47 percent) of all black children enrolled in school were enrolled in grades one and two. By 1950, black first graders (many of whom were overage) were still more than twice as numerous as black second graders and more than five times more numerous than black eighth graders.

At the high-school level the figures are much worse: worse, again, by far than in any other state. Table 3.9 reveals that black secondary enrollment rose sharply between 1930 and 1950. Yet by the latter date, 75 percent of the black high-school age population were not enrolled in high school—and of those enrolled, only 13 percent were in the twelfth grade.[67] Much of the attendance gap could be attributed to the state's lily-white school bus policy. Except for North Carolina, no southern state spent more tax dollars on the transportation of white rural students; but Mississippi was the only southern state that did not appropriate public funds for black school transportation.[68]

"Educate a Nigguh"

Statistics tell only part of the story. They help to define the relative place of black children in the march of education, but they tell us little either of the black community's endeavors to push its children forward or of the white community's endeavors to keep them back. To understand these things, we must look beyond the tables to more subjective evidence.

Throughout the Jim Crow era, the single greatest impediment to better Afro-American schools was white fear of the revolutionary social and economic implications of educating a subservient workforce. The oft-repeated allegation that the generality of blacks was incapable of formal learning might rationalize official neglect of black schooling, but it was not to be taken seriously. In fact, although few whites thought to question the comfortable doctrine of innate black inferiority, white concerns centered on a well-founded suspicion that blacks would learn too much in school, not too little. Broader educational opportunity for blacks, many whites recognized, could profoundly unsettle the patterns of southern life. It could breed black discontent; it could technically qualify blacks for suffrage. Educated blacks were thought to be less dependent and deferential than their ignorant cousins, less comfortable with caste sanctions, more likely to challenge the acceptable limits of white supremacy. Not least, they were less likely to work for whites on white terms. Vardaman understood the problem as well as anyone: "Literary education—the knowledge of books—does not seem to produce any good substantial results with the negro, but serves rather to sharpen his cunning, breeds hopes that cannot be gratified, creates an inclination to avoid honest labor."[69]

Even an inferior education might have a subversive effect. Asked why the dominant race was so "unsettled" by "a few... grotesquely inefficient negro schools," Thomas Pearce Bailey, a University of Mississippi professor, answered: "Because the white people want to 'keep the negro in his place' and educated people have a way of making their own places and their own terms." Whites feared even "a crude smattering of literary education," Bailey believed, because they feared "liberated minds," because they understood that "education is a mockery in the case of people who are fundamentally unfree, who are held in the position of a permanently inferior caste, who are deprived of the normal accompaniments of citizenship." In 1940, even as President Franklin Roosevelt asked the nation to serve as "the great arsenal of democracy" in a Second World War, the state legislature nearly adopted a separate textbook bill that would have sanitized civics books used by black children of all reference to democratic political procedures. "There was opposition," state Supervisor of Black Education P. H. Easom privately lamented, "on the point of teaching Negroes about voting and other matters pertaining to running the government."[70]

Nor was the tension between education and subordination overlooked by black Mississippians. In the abstract, they unquestionably shared the American faith in education as the way to a better life.[71] But little in their daily experiences suggested that the avenues of progress were open

even to the most qualified Afro-Americans. Although the accommodationists among them might contend, with Booker T. Washington, that
the race had only to prove its worthiness to win white acceptance, black
circumstances argued that black opportunities were limited almost exclusively to common labor. In the words of a Bolivar County father
who wanted no more for his sons than that they "take a trade": "What's
the use of learnin' how to be a bookkeeper if you ain't never gonna
have no books to keep? That ain't for no niggers."[72] Or, as a frustrated
black Natchez teacher put it: "You educate your children—then whatcha
gonna do? You got any jobs for 'em? You got any business for 'em to
go into?" In much the same vein, another black Natchezian, a businessman, spoke to an anthropologist about the perils of educating the
Afro-American beyond his place: "As long as you keep him ignorant,
he's satisfied to work for some white man on the plantation; but as
soon as he learns to want other things, he comes to the city to try to
get them. When he gets here, he finds the white man has everything,
and he can't get the kind of work or job he wants, and he is dissatisfied.
And then you have a dangerous situation."[73]

To avoid such dangers, the sovereign race seemed content to starve
the black schools. Extremists often opposed any education, even manual
training. During the 1907 senatorial campaign, Vardaman forced his
Democratic rival, John Sharp Williams, to deny that he had ever advocated vocational schooling for blacks. It would be, Williams said, the
"worst thing that could be given them" for it would threaten the racial
equilibrium and white good will by bringing them "into competition
with white mechanics and artisans."[74] The state's educational establishment, on the other hand, took a somewhat longer view and denied that
black education and white supremacy were necessarily incompatible.
"If he is educated in the right way," state Superintendent of Education
Willard F. Bond said of the black child, "he will become a valuable
asset. He no longer pays any attention to false prophets of his own race
who try to interest him in social equality, the franchise and other rot,
but has turned to other leaders whose ideas coincide with those of the
southern white people."[75]

Although vigorous in the advocacy of schooling for blacks, the education that white reformers like Bond advocated was "negro education," a special curriculum designed to meet the "peculiar" aptitudes
and needs of a race of manual laborers. To be sure, these otherwise
humane-spirited school men were subject to enormous public and political pressure. Agricultural and industrial education for blacks, moreover, was widely stressed, not merely by southern white supremacists
but by northern philanthropies and church mission boards that looked

toward "practical education" as an instrument of race uplift and interregional reconciliation. A more enlightened approach based on equalitarian assumptions would have been self-defeating. If blacks were to be educated at public expense, white school reformers all but universally recognized, black education must be not only separate but subordinate.[76] But however much their good intentions may have been circumscribed by tactical considerations, the reformers' public argument with the demagogues was in the end a small one, quite literally of degree, not kind. Blacks needed schools, they said, but not the same kind of schools that whites did. Foreign language, formal science, technical grammar, and advanced arithmetic—"cultural, disciplinary, linguistic, and symbolic types of training"—had little place in the black curriculum. The three R's should be emphasized only in the lower grades and the study of history limited to an explanation of the "status and relationship" of the two races. Above all, as a consultant to moderate Governor Henry L. Whitfield counseled in the mid-1920s, the daily regimen of black schools "should not be idealistic beyond the sphere of negro life." Its object should be to produce a class of "efficient," "disciplined," "punctilious" workers well drilled in the habits of personal hygiene, honesty, and loyalty.[77] Using Vardaman's distinction, this was education for the Negro's "hand and heart," not for his head. On this the White Chief and the state's educational establishment were one.

Even so, it was mostly talk. In Mississippi, black industrial education—what one historian has called "schooling for the new slavery"[78]—was confined largely to such private institutions as the "little Tuskegees": Piney Woods Country Life School, Prentiss Normal and Industrial Institute, and Utica Normal and Industrial Institute. State and federal appropriations for the development of vocational education went almost entirely to white schools.[79] White Mississippians may have wanted a more "efficient" workforce, but they would not pay for it. Except for the relatively modest sums provided by such philanthropic agencies as the General Education Board, the Jeanes Fund, and the Slater Fund,[80] grants largely outside the state's control, black public schools were scarcely touched by the industrial education movement. In fact, from the white supremacists' point of view, "practical" education for blacks was scarcely more desirable than "theoretical" education. In a system designed to limit black opportunity to unskilled, low-wage occupations, there was little need to teach them scientific, mechanized farming, much less the technical and vocational skills required of artisans in a modern industrial economy.

In cotton counties, white doubts about the utility of formal education for blacks often turned on the planters' chronic need for labor, their fear that even casual encounters with books made the workforce more migratory, and their suspicion that blacks who could read and figure might prove troublesome at settlement time. Some landlords, to be sure, seemed to recognize the value of rudimentary schooling even for field hands; some bowed to growing demands and tolerated the organization of plantation schools in order to retain their workers.[81] But others were opposed: "Damned niggers don't need any education," a Delta planter told the writer David Cohn following World War II. "Education ruins 'em, makes 'em unhappy." Blacks, too, understood that an educated field hand might prove troublesome. Explaining why "these white people are against educating these negroes," a river county black addressed the problem from the planter's perspective: "They say: 'Educate a nigguh an' you ruin him for the farm!' And they're absolutely right, too. As soon as they get a little education, they're simply not going to stay on these farms. The white man knows that, and that's why he won't give these Negroes good schools."[82]

The experiences of black school-builders early in the period provide useful illustrations of white opposition. Tuskegee graduate William Henry Holtzclaw organized Utica Institute in Hinds County in 1903 after searching in vain for a hospitable place in the Delta. "The majority of the planters I interviewed in the Delta seemed to be afraid of the results of Negro education." Even "high-grade men" advised Holtzclaw not to settle in plantation counties. A typical planter near Minter City (Leflore County) told him: "What I want here is Negroes who can make cotton, and they don't need education to help them make cotton. I could not use educated Negroes on my place."[83] Although Hinds Countians proved more receptive, Holtzclaw was advised by a leading white man that he could stay if he would "teach the 'nigger' to be useful; . . . but if you have come to educate him to dress up and quit work, my advice would be to . . . pass on."[84] Laurence Clifton Jones, founder of Piney Woods Country Life School, encountered the same hostility in the Delta and fared no better in the timber districts until he convinced whites in Rankin and Simpson counties that practical schooling would "make better workers out of the niggers." "He says he ain't gwine to teach 'em so much book larnin'," commented one relieved sawmill operator, "but he wants to learn 'em to do more and better work, so when we wants good work done we can git it. That nigger seems like a good nigger. I like him." Years later, another white observed: "a book larnin' school for the negroes would have gotten no support whatever, and Jones would have aroused prejudices that would have been fatal."[85]

Without white good will, no black schoolmaster could expect to succeed. "Public relations" and "useful friendships in the white community," the son of pioneer black educators Jonas and Bertha Johnson recalled, were necessarily among the school-builders' first concerns.[86] An educator of lesser skills, one less adroit in the manipulation of white sensibilities or more insistent on the Afro-American's right to a literary education, might encounter overwhelming local opposition. Such was the fate of Wallace A. Battle, the Talladega College graduate who founded Okolona Industrial School in 1902. Despite its name, the struggling institution in Chickasaw County aspired to more than elementary and industrial training. Battle was himself educated in the liberal tradition, and his school, true to the Talladega model of liberal education,[87] emphasized academic rather than vocational education. "The white people in and around [the town of] Okolona resented his efforts from the beginning," a younger contemporary remembered. "He was harrassed and his life was threatened many times." Never able to win acceptance and apparently convinced that his presence jeopardized the institution's future, the schoolmaster left the state in 1927, soon after independent Okolona became affiliated with the American Church Institute for Negroes (Protestant Episcopal Church). Having learned from Battle's "mistakes," subsequent administrators increasingly emphasized the school's vocational mission.[88]

Okolona's problems were exceptional. Tougaloo College near Jackson, for example, also emphasized liberal rather than industrial education, and it coexisted in comparative harmony with the surrounding white community. Yet, as we shall see, Tougaloo, and indeed all black educational institutions in Mississippi, carefully honored the rules of social distinction. As a matter of course, black educators nurtured white friendships as buffers for their institutions. Even the most conservative among them lived in fear that a careless act or a misunderstanding might provoke conflict with the dominant race.

With whites so often opposed to black education, some black parents risked much in their children's interest. During the 1930s the little school on the Delta Cooperative Farm (Bolivar County) was flooded by black children from the surrounding plantations where white sentiment, as the farm's director noted, was "bitter against us."[89] With no other school in the area, these families weighed the dangers of an angry landlord against the future of their children and pushed fear aside. William Holtzclaw remembered that his mother was prepared to make the same sacrifice late in the nineteenth century. "When the landlord came to the quarters early in the morning to stir up the cotton pickers, she used to out-general him by hiding me behind the skillets, ovens, and pots, throwing some old rags over me until he was gone." Then after slipping him off to school "through the woods and underbrush" she joined the other pickers in the field, working at double-time to "make up to the landlord for the work of us both." When the future educator became a full hand at the age of nine, his mother contrived to continue his education on alternate days, sending his brother to school on one day and him the next. "What he learned on his school day he taught me at night," Holtzclaw reported, "and I did the same for him."[90]

In other cases poverty and distance were as much obstacles as white hostility. In his unfinished autobiography, Sidney D. Redmond, the lawyer-physician-entrepreneur, remembered that the ramshackle one-room schoolhouse he sporadically attended in Holmes County was seven miles from his parents' cabin, "across fields . . . through briar patches, cane brakes, and swamps." Although he was bookish by inclination, the intervening miles and the demands of the cotton patch conspired against Redmond's formal education and he was thirteen before he could write his name. Driven by his own astonishing talent and his unlettered mother's determination, he eventually made his way first to Rust College, then to the Meharry and Illinois Medical Colleges, to the Illinois College of Law, and finally, for postgraduate studies, to Harvard Medical College and the University of Michigan School of Law.[91]

Though perhaps not unique, Redmond's example was not easily followed. To a tenant family subsisting from crop to crop on plantation commissary credit and heavily dependent on the labor of young and old alike, education was an unaffordable luxury. A child in school was not only a lost hand but a drain on family resources for books and presentable clothing. Landlords usually insisted, moreover, that work came first. In these circumstances even the most concerned parents often kept their children in the fields until after harvest. "I didn't get no higher than fourth grade," an elderly black county woman reminisced in 1971. "I had to work all the time." "When you lived on white people's place," Mary Barr, another former tenant, remembered of the pre–World War II era, "you couldn't go [to school] like you wanted to, . . . [you] had to work." Once the crop was in, black rural schools, so empty during the picking season, often filled to overflowing. "If you went to school," one black Washington County teacher explained, "you went after Christmas . . . because the cotton had been harvested and you had money to buy clothes." In lean years, many children didn't go at all because, without shoes, they could not walk the long distance in cold weather. As Mary Barr recalled, except in seasons of plenty, she and her siblings could not attend school because "we didn't have nothin' fitting to wear."[92]

Because public schools were so often unavailable, much of the burden of black education even at the elementary level was assumed by private institutions.[93] Pupils without money for board and tuition, always the majority, paid in kind or worked their way through as "industrial" students. Patterned in some cases after Hampton and Tuskegee, these "work-your-way" institutions were largely built by the labor of needy students who divided their time between their books and such trades as carpentry, bricklaying, and plastering.[94] Although enrollment was primarily at the elementary level, the students were not necessarily children. Parents and their offspring sometimes worked at the same jobs and attended the same classes. Unembarrassed illiterates of middle age registered as beginners. Among the 200 boarders at Piney Woods Country Life School in 1922 were "Pa" Collins, an illiterate field hand, his wife, their seven children, and his mother and father. Like so many others, they came, wrote school founder Laurence Jones, with nothing but "a desire for an education and a willingness to work for it." Others brought rations—a milk cow, gallon tins of molasses, a wagon-load of corn, a flock of geese—in lieu of part of their fees. Georgie Lee Myers, a penniless orphan and one of Professor Jones's favorite success stories, came with the offerings of nearly everyone she knew: "Aunt Hester Robinson gave a pound of butter and a dime, Grandma Willis a chicken, Aunt Lucy McConnell 'four bits' (fifty cents), Sarah Pernell a chicken, Effie McCoy a cake and five cents, Sam McCoy five cents, . . . Bessie Harvey one of her dresses, Washington Lincoln Johnson two pecks of meal, Mandy Willis a dozen eggs."[95] Jones promised "anybody that wants to come here, [even] if you haven't got a penny, I'll never turn you down."[96]

The oldest of the private institutions were denominational or religious in character. Southern Christian Institute at Edwards, chartered in 1875, was operated by the American Christian Missionary Board. Haven Institute of Meridian, Natchez College, and Campbell College of Vicksburg (later Jackson), all essentially elementary schools, were organized, respectively, by the Methodist Episcopal Church (1878), the Negro Baptist Convention of Mississippi (1885), and the African Methodist Episcopal Church (1890). Mary Holmes Seminary in West Point was established in 1892 by the Presbyterian Church, U.S.A., and the Mississippi Industrial College of Holly Springs was founded in 1906 by the Mississippi Conference of the Colored Methodist Episcopal Church. Mound Bayou Normal and Industrial Institute (1892), Mount Hermon Seminary of Clinton (1875), and Tougaloo College (1869) were all American Missionary Association institutions.[97] Although only marginally funded, these schools at least benefited from more or less regular sources of outside institutional support.

The "little Tuskegees," on the other hand—Utica Normal and Industrial Institute, Piney Woods Country Life School, Prentiss Normal and Industrial Institute—were independent institutions, the work of individual black visionaries who took great pride in their humble beginnings. When Jones, the University of Iowa–trained son of a hotel porter, arrived in Braxton in October 1909 to found Piney Woods he had only $1.65 and an indomitable sense of mission. His first lesson, he often recalled, was taught to three students "under the old cedar tree, in God's out-of-doors." As winter set in, he moved his charges into a sheep shed on a forty-acre tract donated by a former slave.[98] The school, as one early graduate proudly affirmed, was a product of black initiative: "The white people didn't give him [Jones] anything in the very beginning. The beginning of Piney Woods School was by black people."[99] Jonas Edward Johnson and his Tuskegee-educated wife Bertha La Branche claimed to have founded Prentiss Institute in 1907 on "faith alone." Although "penniless," they bought forty acres of land and secured operating capital with a loan of $600 from a white banker on a note signed by black Jefferson Davis County farmers who wanted their children to go to school.[100] In similar fashion, the thirty-two-year-old Holtzclaw rode a borrowed bicycle into Hinds County in November 1902 and founded Utica, the first of Mississippi's "little Tuskegees," "in the forest under an oak tree," as he often said, "without a cent and with no house to shelter the pupils." "I went from house to house, among white and colored people seeking funds until I finally got a start." As the school caught on, children came with their "mothers' mites," and donations arrived without solicitation: "dear fesser Please cept dis 18 cents it is all I has I save it out n my washing dis week god will bless you will send some more next week."[101] Parents sent baskets of eggs, garden produce, and painfully scribed letters that "breathed the fervent prayer . . . that their children might have a chance to go to a good 'school 'ouse.' "[102]

Such tokens were welcome symbols of local black support, but Mississippi's private schools (and many public ones too) always depended heavily upon Yankee dollars. A substantial number cultivated cotton and truck gardens or kept dairy herds and other livestock; at least one maintained a sawmill. But much of their expenses were met through the philanthropies of assiduously cultivated benefactors, most of them northerners, and the contributions garnered by the spiritual-singing groups annually dispatched throughout the nation and even abroad.[103]

At Piney Woods student tuition met only about 10 percent of the school's operating costs. "The Cotton Blossom Singers," as one of Jones's associates reported in 1937, "have come to be one of the schools main sources of income." Similarly, Utica's income for 1914-1915 was $14,170, nearly $12,000 of which came from northern benefactors. By 1922, the cost of operating the school had increased to $80,000. One third of that amount was derived from its farm and industrial operations. Student labor also produced lumber and bricks, and student carpenters erected campus dormitories and other buildings. Yet the great bulk of the school's operating expenses was raised by Principal Holtzclaw, who like Jones and Johnson, devoted roughly half of every year to raising funds in northern cities.[104] During these long absences, the day-to-day management of the "little Tuskegees" often fell to the principals' wives— Bertha LaBranche Johnson, Grace Morris Allen Jones, and Mary Patterson Holtzclaw—whose contributions to the school-building experience have never been fully recognized.[105]

Higher Education in the "Emergency Period"

Until World War II, observed Jacob Reddix, first president of Jackson State College, black higher education in Mississippi remained in an "emergency period" of extreme privation and white hostility: "Hindered not only from a financial point of view, but also by the suspicious attitude of certain elements of the dominant white political leaders," black colleges, he said, "had to struggle for mere existence." Victims of grossly discriminatory public appropriations and northern philanthropic preferences for vocational rather than classical learning, the state's black colleges struggled against seemingly insuperable odds.[106] Most in fact were not colleges at all, but schools of elementary and secondary grade. Where college departments existed, they were the relatively minor appendages of institutions whose major function was precollegiate education. Of course, colleges that were really not colleges were not unique to Mississippi.[107] Despite the early appearance of institutions with ambitious names, higher education for blacks nearly everywhere in the region developed slowly and only as satisfactory systems of public education developed. This southern tendency, however, was most pronounced in Mississippi, a state that seemed to follow all others in nearly every category of education.

For the origins of black higher learning in Mississippi one must look to the foundation in 1866 of Rust College by the Methodist Episcopal Church. But Rust was opened as an elementary school, and though it operated under such names as Shaw University and Rust University, and briefly offered training in both law and medicine, the institution at Holly Springs remained largely a secondary school until well after World War I. Similarly, Tougaloo University was organized near Jackson in 1869 but did not issue its first baccalaureate degree until 1901. Thereafter, for the next three decades, it averaged only two such degrees a year. By 1930 it had granted some 1,000 degrees, but only sixty of them were of college level.[108] State-supported Alcorn Agricultural and Mechanical College near Lorman produced its first bachelor's degrees in 1882. For many years its graduates were few, however, and in 1916, when Thomas Jesse Jones of the federal Bureau of Education published the first systematic survey of black higher education, all of its 448 students were enrolled in programs below college grade, roughly two-thirds of them in the elementary program.[109]

Much the same was true of both Jackson College, which operated for nearly half a century before offering its first college course in 1921, and Mississippi Industrial College, the small denominational school (Colored Methodist Church) that opened its doors in Holly Springs in 1905 but enrolled no college-grade students for many years.[110] Other institutions, including such short-lived and obscure establishments as Stringer University at Friars Point (African Methodist Epsicopal) and the three Negro Baptist colleges, Mound Bayou, Central Mississippi at Kosciusko, and Sardis Industrial, were apparently never more than elementary schools.[111] Campbell College, Natchez College, Mary Holmes Seminary, Southern Christian Institute, and the "little Tuskegees" eventually became junior colleges. Yet prior to 1940 they rarely enrolled students above the secondary level.[112]

Even the strongest of these institutions lacked the resources, facilities, and faculty required of collegiate education. Tougaloo, the first to be recognized by the Southern Association of Colleges and Schools (1931), was far and away Mississippi's best black college. Wharton thought it to be the one institution where black Mississippians by 1890 could obtain "competent training" at the elementary and secondary levels. Others ranked it in later decades as one of the best small black liberal arts colleges in the South. Yet it too was a struggling institution, ill-equipped for its stated purpose. Students at such institutions as Fisk and Talladega called it "poor little Tougaloo," the "country cousin" and "poor relation" of black mission schools.[113] In common with the region's other schools of its type, Fisk and Talladega among them, it suffered from inadequate funding, dependence on northern foundations, and administration by long distance. All policy and often even the most trivial administrative decisions were tightly controlled from New York by the American Missionary Association.[114]

Among other matters, the AMA's white directors, and the conservative northern foundations upon which the school so heavily depended, kept a close watch on the color line. Although Tougaloo was theoretically open to all races, it was throughout most of its history an all-black school with a largely white faculty and administration.[115] In the 1960s its students and faculty played a major role in the origins of the Jackson civil rights movement and during the administration of President Adam Daniel Beittel (1960-1964) Tougaloo emerged as a haven of interracialism and an effective thorn in the side of white supremacy.[116] But in earlier years the school, in the nearly universal fashion of southern black educational institutions, prudently lived within the mores of the state and region. Tougalooans were encouraged to avoid politics or other "offensive" activities and to accept white discrimination without complaint. Although an abused student might expect the support of white administrators in specific instances of off-campus injustice, the school as a matter of policy and necessity pointedly accepted Jim Crow. Campus publications were routinely screened of materials thought to be racially sensitive. The children of white administrators and faculty were sent off campus to attend white schools. On campus, an undercurrent of racial tension between white missionary teachers and their black co-workers and students occasionally surfaced; and the AMA itself resisted local black pressures for more black representation on the staff. At nearby Jackson College, a northern missionary board appointed a black president and an all-black faculty in 1911; the first black president of Rust College was appointed in 1920. But though the AMA began to add black faculty in the late 1920s and black administrative advisors a few years later, Tougaloo did not have its first black president until 1965.[117]

Fortunately, what Clarice T. Campbell and Oscar A. Rogers have called the "unconscious 'benevolent' racism" of some white administrators and white faculty was substantially offset by the influence of the early black faculty, an influence suggested by the appearance in the later 1920s of the Paul Robeson Dramatic Club, the Phillis Wheatley Club, and Scribia, a student organization formed to bring the Harlem Renaissance to Tougaloo. Scribia sponsored campus appearances of Countee Cullen, Langston Hughes, and James Weldon Johnson. Black faculty members also introduced courses in black history and black literature. But the gradual influx of black teachers, some of whom saw themselves as "Young Turks," brought little change in rules against social activism. After World War II, for example, President Harold C. Warren (1947-1955) relaxed the school's policies against Greek letter societies, but denied a charter for a campus branch of the NAACP. Similarly, a crisis precipitated by the interracial marriage of two instructors—an act that was both illegal and death-defying in Mississippi—was resolved only when the couple was forced to resign.[118]

For the most part, it must be emphasized, Tougalooans of both races seemed to regard social acquiescence as a matter of strategy rather than of personal preference, as a necessary compromise without which the institution could not have survived in Mississippi. No doubt, as August Meier discovered during his tenure at the institution following World War II (1945-1949), the campus had its share of "old fashioned 'do-gooders' " intent on "doing things for a degraded people rather than working with individuals on a democratic level."[119] Yet if the missionaries were never the band of Yankee fanatics many white Mississippians feared them to be, the AMA was nevertheless committed to a policy of equal educational opportunity and such Tougaloo presidents as Frank G. Woodworth and A. D. Beittel were worthy embodiments of the association's egalitarian traditions. From the very outset, the school implicitly rejected white notions of black potential. The decision to call the institution a "university" in 1871 may not have reflected immediate reality but it suggests the asssociation's long-range ambitions for black academic achievement. "Educate not the Negro," an early Tougaloo administrator advocated, "but the child, not for his place but that he may find his place." Virtually alone among Mississippi's black schools, then, Tougaloo was unambiguously dedicated from the beginning not to "negro education," as that patronizing term was understood in the Jim Crow era, but to the education of Negroes. By all accounts, its single greatest contribution to a state that until after 1940 had no publicly supported black normal college was the training of qualified black teachers.[120]

Founded in 1869 as Tougaloo Normal and Manual Training School (its name was changed to Tougaloo University in 1871, Tougaloo College in 1916, and Tougaloo Southern Christian College in 1953), the institution was originally designed as a 500-acre plantation school where students could find part-time employment in field and kitchen. In some cases, students with no money for tuition were admitted as full-time workers (ten hours a day) and enrolled in night courses. Until 1931 all students, regardless of their financial condition, were expected to work one hour daily in the school's kitchen, laundry, fields, shops, or woodlot. Indeed, despite the AMA's emphasis on liberal learning, Tougaloo's developmental years were devoted in substantial part to agricultural and mechanical training. The institution inaugurated an ambitious program of industrial education in 1871; and in 1883, following the receipt of the first of a continuing series of grants from the Slater Fund, it expanded its manual training staff and equipment. The school's agricultural and industrial departments taught agronomy, dairying, carpentry, blacksmithing, shoe repairing, and wheelwrighting. Such programs encouraged donations from paternalistic northern philanthropists and good will from southern whites. "It is the industrial education the negroes are receiving there," an AMA publication concluded, "which so thoroughly commends the university to the dominant race."[121] But Tougaloo was no "little Tuskegee," and Tougalooans, like black students elsewhere in the region, clearly preferred classical training. With the inauguration of the college preparatory department in 1893 and the college department in 1897, industrial and agricultural education were eventually overshadowed by liberal higher education. What had been essentially a manual training high school at the turn of the century, became in the period after World War I an accredited college emphasizing teacher training and liberal arts.[122]

The process, however, was slow in development. When the school was evaluated in 1927 by the U.S. Bureau of Education, its college curriculum was found to be "extremely thin in some departments of instruction, and the entire program is limited in scope." In the bureau's judgment, Tougaloo did not meet "modern scholastic standards," was unprepared to grant baccalaureate degrees, and should be reorganized as a two-year junior college emphasizing teacher training. At the time there were ten college students enrolled in the junior and senior classes, all of them in liberal arts.[123] Although Tougaloo's faculty and library were among the best in the state, there was little separation of the institution's collegiate and secondary functions and three of its five full-time instructors divided their time between both divisions. Faculty were poorly paid and in some years library acquisitions, as this study noted, were devoted entirely to a small number of periodicals. Through the mid-1920s, the school's library was a helter-skelter assortment of books housed (often in boxes) in a room open to students only on Sunday afternoons. After 1926, Tougaloo did have a dedicated, full-time librarian and with the help of grants from the Rosenwald Fund, and later from the Carnegie Foundation and the General Education Board, a growing collection was placed in Woodworth Library, a wing of newly constructed Holmes Hall.[124]

Fortunately, Tougaloo's future was brighter than its present. After World War II, it absorbed Southern Christian Institute and was fully accredited by the Southern Association. Although plagued by the financial and enrollment problems generally associated with small, private black colleges, Tougaloo entered its second century of service as a healthy and respected institution, recognized for its leadership in both education and human rights.

The history of Alcorn A & M is more melancholy. Despite auspicious beginnings this public institution became not so much a stepchild of Mississippi higher education as an orphan. As even whites sometimes acknowledged, Alcorn, the state's only black four-year public institution of higher learning until 1940, drew "very little water" and was "simply a sop thrown to the negroes."[125] Created as Alcorn University by a Republican state legislature in 1871, the institution was endowed with 60 percent of the state's land-grant funds and the promise of annual appropriations of $50,000 for ten years. Although black leaders initially preferred the integration of the University of Mississippi to the creation of an all-black institution, they were generally won over by the state's early generosity and the governor's appointment of an all-Negro board of trustees. But if they expected an equitable share of state financial support they were soon disappointed. The decline of Republican strength prompted the transfer of 10 percent of Alcorn's agriculture fund and the reduction of its annual appropriations to $15,000 in 1875 and to $5,500 in 1876, and eventually the appointment of a lily-white board. In 1878, the legislature deleted "University" from its name and added "Agricultural and Mechanical College," words that, as one scholar has noted, assured whites that the school "had no pretensions to higher education."[126]

Yet function did not follow form at Alcorn. Created in the image of "Ole Miss" at Oxford and established on the premises of defunct Oakland College, an antebellum liberal arts school for the sons of planters, Alcorn's academic orientation was fixed in its early years. Its first president, Hiram Revels (1871-1882), whatever his administrative shortcomings, was educated in the classical tradition and he staffed the new institution with black men much like himself, most of them graduates of Fisk University.[127] Its first generation of students wrestled with Latin and Greek as well as with English literature, trigonometry, and chemistry. Its redesignation as an A & M college meant little; the professors and the curriculum remained the same and when Revels retired he was followed by a succession of other liberally trained black educators who did not share white notions about black academic limitations.[128] In deference to white sensibilities, these administrators often spoke the language of vocational training: "The special line of this institution is industrial work, including mechanical and industrial education," President Thomas J. Calloway reported to the legislature in 1895. The many reports of President Levi J. Rowan (1905-1911, 1915-1925) also emphasized "shop and field work" over "instruction in the abstract." The school, he affirmed, was "primarily industrial"; its students were enrolled in a "very practical" curriculum that required all to "pursue some of the industrial courses."[129] It was a harmless charade that fooled few, least of all state lawmakers. Having created two land-grant colleges and funded only one, they could not have expected woefully underfinanced Alcorn to develop the expensive vocational programs available to white students at Mississippi Agricultural and Mechanical College at Starkville.[130]

The gap between Alcorn's stated mission and its actual function was frequently described by white critics and by education consultants commissioned by the state itself. "There are entirely too many courses of the liberal arts type," a prominent school superintendent advised the college board of trustees in 1939. Under the leadership of President William H. Bell, this educator believed, administrators at Alcorn were "obsessed with the idea of turning the institution into a liberal arts college with a high academic rating." A survey in 1945 concluded that "one has to search diligently to find evidence of attention given to the agricultural and mechanical arts." Another consultant reported in 1954 that while the practical trades were taught to secondary students, the school's upper division operated "primarily as a liberal arts college, motivated by a strong classical tradition."[131] It did not offer instructional programs in "superior farming." It maintained no blooded herds and flocks, and engaged in none of the experimental and demonstrational agriculture and horticulture normally associated with land-grant colleges. Its farming operations were practical rather than scientific, designed to provide jobs for needy students and revenue for a chronically needy institution. Only 200 of its 900 acres were suitable for cultivation, and even that portion was not thought to be up to "the requirements of an effective land-grant college."[132]

The liberal arts program, despite a tradition of emphasis in that area, was scarcely better. A federal survey of 1928 was unflattering but not unfair: "It is largely a school of secondary grade, although maintaining extensive and elaborate college curricula on paper." Lacking the facilities and faculty to separate its secondary and collegiate programs, it used the same buildings and teaching staff for instruction at both levels. College and high-school students attended the same recitation and lab groups. The faculty was poorly, often irregularly, paid and afflicted by "serious inbreeding"; faculty preparation was "only fair and not up to the standards set by training in other negro colleges." Laboratories and scientific apparatus were found to be marginally suitable only for the high school, and the library was "below standard," "nearly none at all."

The physical plant, much of it a century old, was also "below the standard" of state institutions. The grounds were tended only by uncompensated student labor. The school annually received more federal than state money, and its largest single source of income—more than one-third of its total operating cost—came from profits produced by students on the school farm. The campus was crowded to overflowing— "at least, one hundred more," the president reported, "than our capacity in the form of dormitory accommodations, class-rooms and teaching force." There were 702 students, but only eighty-eight were enrolled at the collegiate level. Only one of the eleven college seniors was studying agriculture. Finally, the school was situated in a remote corner of the state far from the center of black population, a circumstance that seemed to account for a college enrollment drawn almost entirely from its own preparatory school.[133]

Perhaps the most telling measure of the state's neglect was Alcorn's inability to capitalize fully on handouts from northern foundations. In 1925, the General Education Board offered the institution $100,000 for expansion if the state would provide an additional $200,000. Although two private black Mississippi schools (Tougaloo and Southern Christian Institute) managed to accept similar terms, Alcorn was denied when the state legislature refused to appropriate its matching share. The offer was renewed in 1928, the state cooperated, and Alcorn built several new structures, including a sewing building that doubled as a library.[134] But when the Rosenwald Fund offered a matching grant of $2,500 to buy books, the legislature again refused state support. The college then launched its own campaign and, largely through northern sources, raised the required $5,000 in matching funds. This time the foundation itself decided against the grant when it learned that the school had carried annual deficits for nearly a decade and that its teachers "have had practically no pay for the past year." An institution that could not pay its faculty, Rosenwald officials concluded, had needs more pressing than books.[135]

The last word on Alcorn properly belongs to black Mississippians themselves. In their own informal surveys they could be as critical as any outside expert. They might agree with alumnus Charles Evers (B.S., 1951) that a baccalaureate degree from Alcorn was "the equivalent of a good eighth grade education—maybe."[136] These resentments, however, were often pushed aside by a readiness to celebrate accomplishment in the face of hardship. To its alumni, the institution was affectionately remembered as "Ole Land-Grant," the nation's first black land-grant college, the first publicly supported Mississippi college for blacks, and the first staffed entirely by blacks. However briefly, it alone among the state's public institutions had an all-black board of trustees, and its presidents from the outset were men of the race, most of them natives of Mississippi.[137] For the most part they were, as Alcorn graduates proudly believed, competent and resourceful administrators who managed remarkably well on very little.[138] President Levi J. Rowan, the most able and longest-tenured among them, was himself an alumnus and an inspired educator whose administrative talents were, in the words of Horace Mann Bond, "of such an order that the school could not possibly become as bad as state officials wished it to be."[139] There was, moreover, a distinguished list of graduates, including Dr. Joseph E. Walker (1903) and George Wayne Cox (1914), insurance pioneers; Jonas Edward Johnson (1902), founder of Prentiss Institute; and George Washington Lee (1918), author, businessman, and associate of Memphis Republican boss Robert R. Church. And the school's athletic achievements were already the stuff of sports legend. Beginning with the legendary William ("Big Bill") Foster (class of 1931) of the Chicago American Giants, Alcorn sent a succession of talent to the National Negro Baseball League; with conference victories in 1932 in football and in 1934 in basketball, the purple-and-gold clad Alcorn Braves launched a period of dominance in South Central Athletic Conference competition.[140]

Yet Alcorn's deficiencies by 1940 were too glaring to permit delusion. In a resolution of that year to the governor and state legislature, a statewide convention of race leaders cataloged the "discriminations and injustices practiced against the Negroes in the State." "Education among Negroes," white officials were reminded, "has made practically no advancement in a worthwhile way in the last 40 years." The tax dollars of both races maintained medical, legal, and graduate schools open only to whites. The state's black teacher training facilities were "mere jokes . . . wholly unworthy of even consideration." Of the six state-supported colleges, the one for blacks was, at best, "a mere faint gesture toward higher education." "No state in the Union," the black spokesmen said, "affords a parallel. . . . May we not ask: Is that equal educational opportunity under the law? Is that Justice?"[141]

White Mississippians responded to this petition as they had to others, by ignoring it. Yet modest change in black higher education was already underway. Although Alcorn would languish in near dereliction for many years, whites could no longer ignore the need for a black normal. In 1940, the state assumed control of Jackson College, a foundering, privately operated institution, and reopened it as a public-supported facility for the training of rural elementary teachers. The transfer was made without cost or debt, and with private foundation grants to ease the way.[142] Still there was opposition. "Of course, many objections were raised to the passage of a bill making Jackson [College] . . . a state institution," President Reddix recalled. "Such objections were due mainly to a lack of interest in Negro education among the rank and file of state political leaders." When Governor Paul B. Johnson, Sr., urged the passage of the necessary legislation, one lawmaker snorted: "I consider this the governor's *nigger money*—he can throw it into the Pearl River if he wants to do so."[143]

Nor was this the first time Jackson College found itself unwelcome in Mississippi. Organized in 1877 as the Seminary for Freedmen—a name thought to have a "soothing influence" on whites—the school was originally intended for Canton. But when whites objected, its founders, the American Baptist Home Mission Society of New York, went on "testing out place after place" before finding a home in Natchez. In the interest of a more central location, the school was moved to the northern edge of the capital city in 1882 where it was reopened as Jackson College. But it was soon engulfed by white residential expansion up State Street. Finding it "wise and expedient" to relocate again, the society in 1902 reluctantly sold the desirable property now occupied by Millsaps College. For a year the institution operated out of a borrowed building before resettling at its present site in 1903. Soon thereafter, the northern missionaries appointed a local board of influential white advisors to "serve as buffers to any friction that may occur between Negroes and whites."[144]

For the next quarter century, until it was overtaken by the depression, the little school managed to hold its own and sometimes to inch ahead. About 1930, as foundation support and its own resources declined, the society offered to deed the school to the state. Governor Theodore Bilbo expressed interest in the property, but not in a second state-supported black college. "Bilbo is not in favor," the state superintendent of education confided to a black educator, "unless the school is somewhere way down on the river like Alcorn." A second effort to give the school away also failed in 1936 when a wavering Governor Hugh Lawson White withheld his support in the interest of a further career in politics. Finally, in the spring of 1940, Governor Johnson pushed the enabling legislation through, but not before hard-line negrophobes reduced the school's curriculum to two years and changed its name to the Mississippi Negro Training School, a calculated jeer from lawmakers who had just chartered the Mississippi Training School for Delinquent Colored Youth. Had the black institution been called a college—or even had its chief administrative officer been called president rather than principal—a disappointed P. H. Easom of the state Department of Education believed, "passage [of the adopting legislation] would have been impossible."[145] The legislature also refused to meet a Rosenwald Fund grant designed to ease the transition and upgrade the institution and its physical plant. Although the fund promised to match state moneys up to $105,000 during the first biennium, the legislature appropriated only $20,000, less than 10 percent of its appropriation during the same period for the state's underfunded white teachers' college in Hattiesburg.[146]

Blacks protested both the limited curriculum and the name, and school officials continued to characterize their institution as Jackson College in internal memoranda and in correspondence with outsiders. By 1944, under pressure from Jackson College alumni and their allies in the Department of Education, the legislature relented and the re-named Jackson State College for Negro Teachers began offering a bachelor's degree in teacher education.[147]

In 1946, the state created a third black institution, Mississippi Vocational College (later Mississippi Valley State College) in the Delta community of Itta Bena. Its curriculum was also limited to the "negro's sphere," but in Jim Crow Mississippi this too seemed like progress and one more step out of the emergency period.

PART III

Working and Striving

Negro emancipation was incomplete, for it did not give the freed Negro land. Freedom that has no economic base is a bogus freedom. In a world in which souls are not discarnate there can be no freedom without some degree of power, including economic power.

— Reinhold Niebuhr after visiting Mississippi, 1937

The South will be satisfied with nothing less than a retrogression of the Negro back towards serfdom and slavery.

— Isaiah T. Montgomery, 1904

CHAPTER **4**

Farmers without Land

The story of the Negro in agriculture would have been a rather different one if the Negro farmer had had greater opportunity to establish himself as an independent owner.

—Gunnar Myrdal[1]

De big bee suck de blossom,
De little bee make de honey,
De black man makes de cotton and corn,
And de white man totes de money.

—Black Mississippians' toast[2]

The only thing most niggahs git out of sharecropping is mor'n dey share of trouble.

—"Aunt Mattie," c. 1920[3]

Rungs on the Ladder

When Yankee raiders brought word of the Emancipation Proclamation to slaves on a large plantation near Jackson, their first thought was of land. Although the good news came early in 1863, months before that district fell under Union control, they measured off their master's estate with a plow line and divided it and his tools equally among themselves.[4]

However singular and premature, that act spoke forcefully of the meaning of freedom to a landless people. Like peasants everywhere, the lives of black Mississippians were inseparable from the soil. To possess it, to own the ground they farmed, promised economic security, self-respect, and, not least of all, independence from whites. By war's end the expectation of the imminent apportionment of "Secesh" lands was an article of black faith. Freedmen's Bureau officers in the state found it to be "a fixed and earnest conviction," one held by "nearly all" the former slaves. Whites noted that the newly freed seemed indisposed to accept agricultural employment, as they hoped momentarily "to farm on their own account."[5] Although planters and federal officials alike tried to counter its "baneful" effects, land fever died slowly. The belief in some form of land redistribution persisted even after many former Confederates were pardoned in May, 1865, and permitted to reclaim any confiscated or occupied land. Despite denials and disappointments, the dream was kept alive until almost the end of the decade by periodic waves of rumor that small farms would come to the former slaves as Christmas gifts from their emancipators.[6]

In this world, at least, the meek do not inherit the earth. Despite such promising wartime experiments as that at Davis Bend near Vicksburg, where black refugees were given leases on six plantations, land reform did not accompany abolition. Only a small portion of the state's black agricultural workers managed to acquire farms. All but a few remained farmers without land. In 1880, according to the best estimate available, there were seventeen counties in the state where "not one Negro in a hundred" was a landowner. In other counties the figures were thought to be better: "less than one in fifty" in some; "less than one in twenty" in perhaps twelve more.[7] Unfortunately there are no better statistics until 1890, when the Bureau of the Census began classifying farm operators by race. Thereafter, as Tables 4.1 through 4.3 reveal, the picture, though scarcely less dismal, is more complete.

Throughout the half century before World War II, more than half of all of Mississippi farms and some three-fourths of its tenant farms were operated by blacks (see Table 4.1). Roughly three in every four farm owners, however, were white. Although black landownership was not inconsiderable, approximately 85 percent of all black operators in any given decade did not own the land they farmed (see Table 4.2). Between 1890 and 1900 the number of black-owned farms nearly doubled.[8] But in the next decade farm tenantry among blacks grew faster than farm ownership. In the decades of 1910-1920 and 1920-1930 black landownership actually declined. Much the same was true of total black farm acreage and the total value of black farmland and buildings. In the aggregate, as Table 4.3 reveals, black farmers between 1900 and 1910 managed to increase the size and worth of their holdings. But during the period as a whole, they literally lost ground, owning fewer total acres, operating farms of smaller average size, and possessing a smaller percentage of the value of all farmlands in 1940 than in 1900.

Most black-owned farms were marginal operations, small units on poor land that provided their owners with the satisfactions of propri-

TABLE 4.1. Land Tenure in Mississippi, 1900-1940.

	Operators		Tenants		Owners[1]	
	Total (both races)	Blacks	Total (both races)	Blacks	Total (both races)	Blacks
1900	220,800	58.3%	137,900	78.1%	82,000	25.6%
1910	274,400	60.0	181,500	76.9	92,100	27.2
1920	272,100	59.2	179,800	76.7	91,300	25.4
1930	312,700	58.5	225,600	71.0	86,000	26.3
1940	291,100	54.9	192,800	70.6	97,300	24.1

[1] Includes part owners, operators who owned part and rented from others the remaining part of the land they farmed. Managers, the third and smallest tenure catagory, are not included.

TABLE 4.2. Black Land Tenure in Mississippi, 1900-1940.

	Total Operators	Tenants		Owners[1]	
		Number	Percentage	Number	Percentage
1900	128,700	107,600	83.6	21,000	16.3
1910	164,700	139,600	84.7	25,000	15.2
1920	161,200	137,800	85.5	23,200	14.4
1930	182,900	160,200	87.6	22,700	12.4
1940	159,500	136,100	85.3	23,400	14.7

[1] Includes part owners.

etorship and little more. Generally short of both capital and credit, blacks found their opportunities more often in the hills than the low-lands. "It is often true," as a federal study of land tenure in Mississippi concluded in 1934, "that the negro settles as a farm owner on land that the white people cannot afford to cultivate." Blacks tilled the alluvial bottomlands of the river counties and the rich black loam of the prairies, but nearly always for white landowners. In the ten counties that lie wholly within the Yazoo-Mississippi Delta, for example, 74 percent of the people and 86 percent of all farm tenants were black. Black owners constituted only 2.3 percent of the farm operators and they farmed only 2.4 percent of the cultivated land. In Bolivar, the largest Delta county and the home of the black colony of Mound Bayou, where Isaiah Montgomery encouraged his race to cultivate cotton and economic

TABLE 4.3. Acreage and Value of Mississippi Farms, 1900-1940.

	Acreage			Value of land and buildings		
	Total (in 000s)	Black-owned (in 000s)	Average per black owner	Total (000s)	Black-owned (000s)	Black percentage of total
1900	12,000	1,900	90.2	$152,000	$13,000	8.6
1910	11,500	2,200	89.0	334,000	34,500	10.3
1920	11,500	1,800	78.7	790,000	57,000	7.2
1930	9,500	1,700	76.4	568,000	31,500	5.6
1940	11,000	1,700	74.4	475,000	27,000	5.7

independence, three out of four people were black in 1930 and blacks owned more farmland (14,430 acres) than in any other Delta county. Yet 98.2 percent of all black farm operators were tenants and well over 90 percent of all farmland was owned by whites. The average per-acre value of black-owned land and buildings in the county ($88.72), moreover, was lower than that farmed by either black ($98.06) or white ($94.57) sharecroppers.[9]

Figures 4.1 and 4.2 identify the centers of black landownership in terms of the proportion of owners and of operators and of the absolute number of owners. As Figure 4.1 demonstrates, black landowners constituted a majority of black farm operators primarily only in the infertile pine barrens of the southeast, where the sandy clay soil was generally too poor to support any but the most marginal forms of agriculture. In this region there were four counties in 1940 where more than eight in ten black farmers owned all or part of the land they cultivated.[10] Land values here, however, were the lowest in the state, often not 20 percent of the value of prime Delta land. The data presented in Figure 4.2 are too crude to be easily interpreted, for they do not reflect either soil variations within counties or farm-population densities and they do not derive from a single geographic area. Yet, viewed even through the distorted lense of absolute numbers, the concentration of black farm owners is shown to overlap but yet lie largely outside the heaviest concentration of either black farm operators or large-scale agriculture. Despite the overwhelming presence of blacks in plantation counties, eight of the ten all-Delta counties are not represented in 1910. To be sure, there was an appreciable black ownership class in some black-majority counties, including Bolivar, Hinds, Lauderdale, and Yazoo. But the centers of independent black agriculture, measured in actual

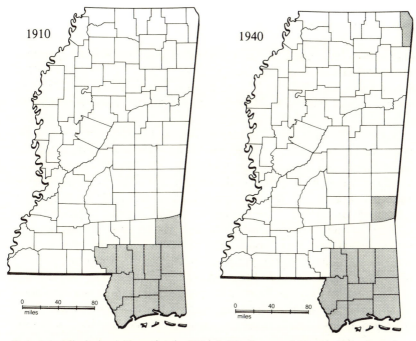

FIG. 4.1. Mississippi Counties in Which Black-owned Farms Constituted at Least Half of All Farms Operated by Blacks, 1910 and 1940.

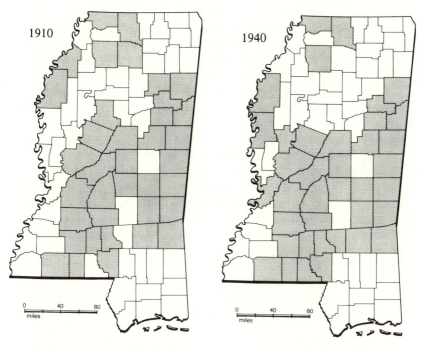

FIG. 4.2. Mississippi Counties with 300 or More Black Farm Owners, 1910 and 1940.

numbers of farm owners or as a proportion of all black farm operators, are found in the central and southern portions of the state, in the Gulf Coastal Terrace, the Piney Woods, and the Sand-Clay Hills, where soils were thin and both farm incomes and black population were notably low.

Some black farms were substantial operations and those owners did considerably better than just get by. In the early postbellum years, the list of major black landowners was led by the former slaves John R. Lynch and Blanche K. Bruce, both of whom owned extensive plantations near Natchez.[11] The most celebrated black landlord was Benjamin Thornton Montgomery, the former bondsman and plantation manager of Jefferson and Joseph Davis, who leased and then bought the vast (4,000 acres) Davis river plantation in Warren County. Montgomery was the third-largest cotton producer in Mississippi. A prominent white admirer thought him to be "the best planter in the county and perhaps in the state."[12] His cotton won all the prizes at the Cincinnati Exposition in 1873. At his death in 1878, the estate went to his son, Isaiah, who managed it for another half decade until forced out by low prices, recurrent natural disasters, and legal difficulties with the Davis heirs. In 1887 the younger Montgomery led a colony of Davis Bend refugees to Bolivar County, where his reputation as a town-builder and his plantation and business interests generally flourished.[13]

Less prominent but no less prosperous twentieth-century black planters included E. W. Green, who but for his black skin could have been the hero of a Horatio Alger novel. Through hard work and good fortune this orphan, who once worked for pennies as an agricultural day laborer, reportedly acquired 1,000 acres and a "magnificent dwelling house" in Jefferson County. In 1912, his land and buildings were valued at nearly $100,000. That year his seventy black field hands and eighty work animals produced 5,000 bushels of corn and some forty bales of cotton. Similarly, Issaquena County planter Johnnie Brown, who began chopping cotton for whites before he was seven, bought his first land (580 acres) in 1934. By 1945 he employed forty-seven black families and owned 7,000 acres, a cotton gin, a general store, and $50,000 in agricultural machinery. Although not yet fifty years old, he was said to be the "third largest individual taxpayer" in the county and "one of the wealthiest and most respected Negroes in the Deep South."[14]

Nearly every plantation county in Mississippi could claim at least one substantial black farmer who through a combination of ownership and rental cultivated several hundred and sometimes even a thousand or more acres, employed numerous sharecroppers, and otherwise operated on a scale normally thought to be limited only to the more successful whites.[15] These "Negro Success Stories," as they were called in the reports of the United States Department of Agriculture, were objects of pride and envy to both races. Officials in the regional offices of the USDA found in them evidence of "the steady progress of Negro farmers throughout the . . . deep south."[16] They were proof, as their more sympathetic white neighbors believed, that the crop-lien system was the "poor man's opportunity," that only the black sharecroppers' profligacy, their penchant for excursions, crap games, and whiskey, kept them down. "The proposition appears too simple to argue," thought Alfred Holt Stone. "The delta negro, by the exercise of common thrift and economy, can become independent as the result of two or three years labor."[17]

Despite mounting evidence that black farmers experienced little upward economic mobility, blacks, too, found these notions appealing. In their search for models of race progress, conservative spokesmen turned to the state's minuscule class of black yeomen for proof, in William Henry Holtzclaw's words, that "here in Mississippi we enjoy privileges along with our disadvantages." Well into the twentieth century, even as black ownership decreased, black rags-to-riches tales were standard fare wherever race leaders gathered. No session of the Mississippi Negro Farmers' Conference or the Mississippi Negro Business League was complete without the testimony of a prosperous few who had scaled the "agriculture ladder" from day laborer to sharecropper to cash renter to owner. Those who would rise above "the mire and filth and dirt of degradation," Holtzclaw often told the landless, need only become independent of whites. Mississippi's black landowner, this Washingtonian asserted, was "the backbone of our beloved commonwealth" and the hope of the race. "You must not get discouraged in your efforts. You must buy land. . . . Every honest effort will bear fruit."[18]

Whatever the psychological benefits of this lively trade in Negro success stories, the practical effects were few, as Holtzclaw's own example suggests. To encourage black landownership, and no doubt to develop a friendly black buffer between his school and the surrounding white community, he organized the Black Belt Improvement Society early in the century to buy land and resell it to enterprising sharecroppers in plots of from ten to twenty acres. The black schoolmaster also designated Utica Institute teachers as "missionaries of rural uplift," and directed them to spend their nonteaching hours encouraging rural blacks to buy land and raise livestock. By 1930 the society had created a colony of small black landowners on several thousand acres in the neighborhood of Utica Institute. One survey reported that "95% of the Negro people near the institution owned their homes and farms." That remarkable achievement, however, was not enough to offset losses elsewhere in Hinds, a county of consistently declining black landownership.[19]

Of the many explanations for black landlessness, some are economic in origin. Like small farmers of every race, the black Mississippians' struggle for survival was frustrated by a generally declining agricultural economy: by erosion and depleting soil fertility, increasing credit costs, and competition with larger and more efficient producers. Not least of all there was the boll weevil, "the world's largest consumer of raw cotton,"[20] which entered the state in 1907, trailing crop destruction and mortgage foreclosures. Indeed the ubiquitous spread of tenantry among the farmers of all races suggests that conditions nearly everywhere in the nation were unfavorable for small landownership.

Yet the most formidable obstacles to black landownership were invariably racial.[21] In the black belt, where the planters' first concern was always for an abundant supply of cheap labor, white landowners had a vested interest in the economic and occupational immobility of their landless workforce, white or black. But even where smaller units of production were the rule, the dominant race was rarely well disposed toward black property ownership. In the immediate aftermath of slavery, Whitelaw Reid discovered in Mississippi an almost universal white hostility to "any ownership of the soil by negroes." "The man who should sell small tracts to them would be in actual personal danger," he believed. "Every effort will be made to prevent negroes from acquiring land."[22] The state's black code of 1865 prohibited black ownership of agricultural land. Although that law never went into effect and white opposition may have softened somewhat during the Reconstruction interlude,[23] the problem persisted into the present century, becoming most critical during the peak years of Negrophobia from 1890 to World War I.

Blacks who managed to buy land (including perhaps even those who homesteaded)[24] were generally those thought by whites to be most acceptable, a quality that might require a reputation for industry and probity but one that demanded, above everything, an accommodative spirit. Social dexterity, perhaps even a measure of servility, was indispensable, a Sunflower County black told Hortense Powdermaker in the 1930s. Although critical of the average sharecropper's penchant for "fast living," this farm owner attributed his own good fortune to more than a willing back: "Hard work, slow saving, and staying in my place, acting humble, that's how I did it."[25]

A special relationship to an influential white man was also a frequent requirement. A white sponsor might be a planter or businessman with no more than a decent concern for an enterprising black neighbor, or the bond might be more intimate. Although the evidence is no more than fragmentary, a high percentage of all black landowners were apparently of mixed blood. In Stone's crude estimate, "the bulk" of blacks owning land in the Delta at the turn of the century were mulattoes, "the larger tracts almost without exception being in their hands." Whether products of long-forgotten master-slave relationships or the issue of more recent interracial liaisons, these blacks often experienced greater white acceptance than did "pure Africans" and some could discreetly claim white kinsmen (often of the same surname). Never eager to acknowledge their mixed-blood offspring, Mississippi whites became much less so in the age of Jim Crow. Yet Allison Davis and his associates discovered that as late as the 1930s, in Adams County at least, a grant of land was still an acceptable form of recognition by a planter of his black children. By Davis's reckoning, one-seventh of the largest black farms in this river county came as gifts from white relatives and many lesser holdings, he believed, were acquired in the same way.[26]

But whatever their relationship to whites, black farmers who would buy property usually had to pay premium prices at exorbitant interest for land that was less desirable to whites. As studies by the U.S. Bureau of Agriculture Economics reveal, blacks often had to pay more per acre than whites, even when black land was less fertile.[27] And because many white-owned banks did not routinely lend money to blacks—and because black-owned banks operated only briefly in the state (see Chapter 5)—many Afro-American land buyers necessarily either paid the higher interest rates demanded by merchants or turned to the doubtful beneficence of landlords. The more unscrupulous of these secondary lenders appear to have made it a practice in good times to "sell" their poorest acres to blacks at inflated prices only to reclaim them, often without benefit of legal proceedings, in bad. The extent of the practice is unknown, but federal investigators found evidence of "a very large number" of such transactions in Mississippi during the 1930s.[28] The Adams County planter who encouraged his black tenants to buy ten-dollar land at $50.00 an acre was doubtless not alone. "In recent years," a black farmer said of him in 1933, "he has sold some little pieces of land to Negroes . . . knowing that they couldn't pay the price. Well, they lose the land as soon as a bad season comes, and he has made about ten times as much as if he had rented it to them." In the same county, according to another black observer, the largest landowners regularly defrauded their land-hungry tenants: "They'll get their money, and yet find ways to keep the title to the land. So Negroes have got wary, and won't try to buy land."[29]

Calculated foreclosures by rapacious mortgagees were, of course, not unique to the southern black belt, and Afro-Americans were not the only victims. But because blacks had few rights that could be protected in Mississippi courts, they were particularly vulnerable. Given the legal double standard—the discriminatory enforcement of property law in interracial cases—and their own prudent indisposition to sue whites, real-estate investments held few attractions for many blacks.

White violence and the fear it engendered was a primary disincentive, particularly in southwestern Piney Woods counties where black land-owners were relatively more numerous and the depredations of the "Cane Hill Billies" were rarely punished. During the early 1890s, years of acute agricultural distress, and then again a decade later during the racially tense years of the Vardaman administration, white dirt farmers in the state's southwestern corner formed secret bands, swore oaths in blood, and set out at night to "gain control of the negro labor, which is by right ours."[30] Called Whitecaps, they sometimes flogged and burned indiscriminately, but their primary targets were independent black rent-ers and farm owners, some of whom were homesteaders. These blacks were singled out, Isaiah Montgomery concluded, because they were "sober, industrious, and reliable," "because they prospered, and their example was likely to be helpful to others."[31] In Amite County in 1902, for example, a clandestine organization thought to be "composed of the leading farmers" declared it to be "bad policy to sell land to negroes." Blacks who sought to "elevate themselves morally" were promised Whitecap protection. Those who sought economic independence were advised to leave the county.[32] Elsewhere signs were posted on black land: "If you have not moved away from here by sundown tomorrow, we will shoot you like rabbits." "All Negroes get out of this county."[33]

The threats were not idle. Night riders destroyed the crops and live-stock of black farmers and torched their barns, churches, and schools. A Marion County editor reported in 1893 that "Negroes are nightly whipped and run off and so common have these occurrences become that the negroes now are afraid to tell when they have been visited."[34] In 1903, a Lincoln County circuit judge feared that violence threatened the "destruction of all legal government and the enthronement of naked brute force as the governing power in the community."[35] All told, in both waves of violence, perhaps a dozen blacks were murdered. But uncounted scores were flogged and driven from their land, and one prominent white churchman predicted that "unless conditions are rad-ically changed" the most industrious blacks would flee the state and "our cotton lands will lie fallow. . . . Already the scarcity of labor is the despair of large landowners."[36]

The black exodus from some counties was great enough by 1903 to affect the economy. Business leaders linked the lawlessness to declining profits; bankers, unable to collect debts from fleeing farmers, threatened to withhold agricultural loans from Whitecap areas; white landlords worried that "our farms will soon be tenantless." With white self-interest so clearly at stake, "anti-Whitecap leagues" were organized in several counties and local and state authorities eventually acted. In 1904, although they were soon pardoned by Governor Vardaman, five Lincoln County whites were sentenced to life in prison for killing a black landowner. Two years later, more than 300 Franklin County Whitecaps received suspended sentences in federal court for intimidating black homesteaders. However tender the mercies of Mississippi justice, these legal proceedings were not without effect. Once out of favor with the law, the night riders quietly disbanded.[37] Isolated acts of Whitecapping continued for nearly another decade, but organized lawlessness against black landownership effectively ended in 1906.[38]

The meaning of the Whitecap phenomenon, however, was not easily forgotten by its principal victims. More than most Americans, black Mississippians had cause to question the work ethic. Whatever the abstract appeal of honest labor, frugality, and accumulation, these traditional virtues entailed for blacks likely risks as well as possible rewards. Assigned the bottom place in the white world, they found little incentive to break out of the vicious circle that bound them to poverty and dependence. "If we own a good farm or horse, or cow, or bird-dog, or yoke of oxen," a black Mississippian said in 1913, "we are harassed until we are bound to sell, give away, or run away, before we can have any peace in our lives."[39]

Although a well-regarded black family with a tradition of landownership was generally secure, the dominant race clearly resented black independence and upward mobility. Tenants who aspired to raise their own cotton on their own land were unwelcome role models for other field hands and their very ambition was evidence that they had ideas beyond their station. Thus, a black Sunflower Countian with the resources to expand his operations explained following World War I that he preferred to farm on a small scale because it was dangerous for a black to "pop his head up too high." One of his neighbors took a bolder if still prudent approach and quietly acquired a substantial plantation, but in scattered parcels in several counties lest his prosperity be "too obvious."[40] Doubtless, the most ambitious put personal success before social peace and pursued the American dream through toil, savings, and eventually landownership. But others succumbed, as Du Bois has written, to "the social environment of excuse, listless despair, careless indulgence and lack of inspiration to work."[41] In such an environment, what some whites thought to be frivolous consumption could also be a strategy for survival. The sharecropper who idled away his slack seasons and squandered his meager earnings on trifles bought neither land nor trouble. In such an environment, the "land mania" of the first generation of Mississippi freemen gave way to a sober realism that restrained aspiration and too readily slaked the thirst for self-improvement.

Finally, the black farmer's aspirations were frustrated by the discriminatory state and local administration of federal programs designed to foster rural prosperity. Although Afro-Americans benefited marginally from the first Morrill Land-Grant College Act and the Smith-Hughes Vocational Education Act of 1917, all but a small fraction of the public funds spent on agricultural education in Mississippi went to white institutions. Similarly, federal appropriations for agricultural experimentation reached blacks only indirectly, if at all. Fearing the unsettling effects of even rudimentary education for blacks, whites carefully channeled tax dollars in their own direction.

The administration of the Cooperative Extension Service provides a useful illustration. Under the terms of the Smith-Lever Act (1914), the conduct of agricultural and home demonstration work was to be non-discriminatory. That provision became meaningless, however, when southern lawmakers led by Senator Vardaman blocked an amendment to the law requiring that federal matching funds to southern states be "equitably divided" between the races.[42] Although the federal share was appropriated on the basis of total rural population, Mississippi whites initially refused to provide local funds for black demonstration work. The program for black farmers, reported the state's first director of extension, was crippled by an "almost general skepticism among the white people" and by "the idea prevalent in some places that the negro must be kept ignorant and destitute in order to manage him safely."[43] Accordingly, while county supervisors granted tax dollars to pay the salaries of white county agents, the first black agents were paid entirely by the USDA and by private subscription ("second taxes") in the local black community.[44] In time, some counties supported extension services for both races, but black farmers never received an equitable share of either state or federal appropriations. In 1915 only five of the state's forty-three county agents were black. Two decades later, there were twenty-nine (roughly one for every 5,800 black farmers) but the white agents had increased to 129 (one for every 1,100 white farmers), and whites still claimed 90 percent of all extension expenditures.[45]

Even these figures probably overstate black participation. Paid only from one-third to one-half as much as whites, black agents were appointed "with the consent and understanding of the white farmers," and they worked with black tenants only "at the request or by the consent of the land-lord." If the annual reports of the state directors are reliable, this screening process produced "suitable" field workers who were not only "capable, energetic, and earnest" but uniformly prudent and conservative, respectful of the "laws of social distinction," eager "to defeat pernicious and hurtful propaganda," as attentive to "clean living" and "moral uplift" as to improved drainage and better herds.[46] Without doubt they performed useful services: organizing boy's corn and pig clubs, encouraging crop diversification, cooperative marketing associations, and the terracing and clearing of land; showing blacks the way to higher crop yields, better land-use planning, and improved diet through subsistence or "live at home" farming. Yet too frequently the black county agents' first duty was not to the farmers of their own race.

Except in rare instances, white agents apparently did not work with blacks; black agents, however, were often assigned to service for whites, including labor recruitment. "The Negro county agent," as an extension service report for 1946 revealed, "was called on by many landlords to assist in finding cooks, drivers, yard boys and other help around the farm home." Or, in the words of one native white critic who believed that "not one Negro farmer in a hundred" had ever seen a county agent, the black extension worker's "principal job" was "to do chores"— to vaccinate livestock, tend orchards, and service machinery—"not for Negro farmers, but for the well-to-do white farmers, who least need assistance but whose opinions carry weight with county politicians."[47]

Such a program could not raise the aspirations of oppressed black tenants or improve the position of marginal black landowners—and that, of course, was precisely as whites intended.

The New Servitude

They might quibble over particulars, but in their attempts to describe the broader contours of life and labor in the cotton belt, black and white Mississippians sometimes found common ground. Blacks had little use for contented-darky fables and were less inclined than whites to romanticize landlord-tenant relations. Yet in the accounts of both races, the plantation emerged as a remarkably resilient institution scarcely touched by either civil war or reconstruction. "The southern planter is lord of all he surveys," the *Weekly Clarion-Ledger* reported some four decades after emancipation, "and still has the cavalier airs and mannerisms of the antebellum days." No section, as Alfred Holt Stone said of his native Delta region, in 1901, was so little touched by "the legacy of [civil] war," and none "emerged with less of violent change as regarded race relations."[48]

The master of Dunleith plantation and one of the most humane landlords in the state, Stone was a thoughtful — if often patronizing — student of Deep South blacks who did not long for the return of slavery. His descriptions of life in the shadows of the postbellum big house, however, often suggested more about contemporary plantation life than he intended: "As in olden time, so now, the word of the planter or his representative is the law of the place, and on the one hand we have implicit obedience, on the other, firmness and moderation. Certainly the relation of master and slave no longer exists, but out of it has been evolved that of patron and retainer."[49]

The view from the retainer's vantage point, not remarkably, was different. But black Mississippians also understood the force of tradition. Whatever their expectations at the moment of emancipation, all but a relative few remained subject to the will of white landlords. Except for the estimable technicality of citizenship, the patterns of their lives were little changed. Pressed by an anthropologist to characterize the plight of the average field hand some seven decades after emancipation, one otherwise articulate Adams County black struggled for words: "Pitiable, pitiable! You can't know what they have to take. . . . You can't imagine." Then, perhaps sensing that his Harvard-trained interviewer had been taken in by the Thirteenth Amendment, he offered a brief exegesis on the continuity of Deep South social and economic institutions. For all practical purposes, he said, "the South won the war." The white planter remained lord and master and the "poor devils" who toiled in his fields "are just the same as his slaves." The major difference between past and present was a diminished sense of white paternalism. The twentieth-century tenant, he believed, was less secure than his slave forebears, for he was not property and white self-interest no longer assured his minimal well-being. "Now, they have him still in economic slavery, and they don't have to feed him, or clothe him or pay a doctor when he's sick!"[50]

From the tenant's perspective, the new order most resembled the old in the area of discipline, in the ways in which blacks still found themselves subject to the arbitrary power of whites. Sharecropper accounts — particularly the oral histories gathered by black interviewers in recent decades — contain little of the nostalgia for "dem olden times" found in some WPA slave narratives dictated to whites in the 1930s. Asked how her life in 1970 compared to what she knew decades earlier as a Clay County field hand, elderly Clara Hampton employed the starkest dichotomy she could imagine: "I would consider we was [now] living in Heaven, considering from that time we was living in Hell." Josephine Beard of Columbus, remembering how blacks feared the riding boss on a northeast Mississippi prairie county plantation, likened tenantry to slavery: "It could have been slavery time . . . the way they act, scared of him. . . . You see our parents wuz scared of white folks." The same thought recurs in interview after interview: "I call it slavery." "Nothing but slavery." "We had to mind them as our children mind us. . . . It was just like slavery time."[51]

The memory of pre–World War II plantation life, to quote Clara Hampton again, still haunted some Mississippi emigres in the 1970s: "At that time, the peoples whupped you here, and they [blacks] are still afraid to come back here[,] still think that's going on now." Eugene Bailey, another former black-belt county tenant, recalled in 1972, "Yeah they whip people on the farm. . . . That's aint been long cut out. That's a few years ago that whipping." Other ex–field hands preferred to recall the floggings that were thwarted by black defiance. Landlords and over- seers, as Robert Allen remembered of plantation management near Houston, were not necessarily foolhardy and not every white was heed- less of black retaliation. "None never did beat me," he proudly affirmed in 1971, "cause I always told um, I say, 'you wont beat me, you might kill me, but won't never beat.'" He remembered, too, the time his father, a redoubtable former slave, faced down a white man: " 'I'll give you some of it,' [the white man threatened]. And he [the elder Allen] said, 'naw, you wont.' He say 'you won't come out like you think you will.' Well, he let him by. . . . That wuz my daddy. My daddy didn't stand for that. He, he wuz full ah African and . . . they didn't fool wid him."[52]

The tenant's choice was not always between the pain and humiliation of the whip or the risk of resistance. The landlord class was not a monolith. Twentieth-century planters, like their antebellum counter- parts, could be stern, even cruel, disciplinarians, but they could also be benevolent employers who enjoyed the respect and indeed the affection of their field hands. Not a few tenants thought of their white folks as generous and fair, and still others remembered that if every planter or riding boss was not virtuous, a great many were fundamentally humane. On model estates—including Trail Lake, the Washington County op- eration inherited by the aristocratic poet William Alexander Percy in 1929 and operated at his direction under the "golden rule"— physical coercion was rarely if ever used.[53] Elsewhere, in times and places of labor shortage, and particularly on the eve of harvest, white self-interest dictated moderation. Violence, as both races recognized, could be counterproductive; whites who employed it too freely risked a sullen and uncooperative work force and even black counterviolence. Because dependency cut both ways, even the hardest riding bosses sometimes foreswore corporal punishment lest their hands leave them with crops still in the field.

But if sharecroppers' experiences varied widely, the fact remains that in Mississippi, as in much of the lower-South black belt, violence or the threat of violence was the most durable legacy of slavery and nearly as central to large-scale cotton production as the mule and the lister plow. In freedom, scarcely less than in slavery, landlords thought of the people who worked their fields as "their niggers," subject to their authority and the ancient work rhythms of the Cotton Kingdom. Confident in the support of the sheriff, the courts, and white public opinion, all too many still believed that economic incentive alone would not drive free blacks to diligent labor. Tenants who were "impudent" or otherwise troublesome, those caught in the act of moving away without permission or while still in debt, might get off with a warning. But when an exasperated landowner concluded that an example was required, he or his manager might assemble all hands and flog an offending black field hand. Sanctioned by the law of tradition and periodic use, applied about as readily to refractory black women and children as to black men, the lash was the symbol of white authority and the all but universally accepted tool of last resort in the management of Negroes. Throughout the period between the two world wars, some landowning families discussed the application of "harness leather"—even in the presence of strangers—as casually as they discussed the weather. "It is the best way," a Wilkinson County white woman matter-of-factly informed an outsider during the mid-1930s: "It frightens them and they are all right after that. If they just whip one, it frightens the others enough."[54]

Under sharecropping and the crop lien, then, the essential socioeconomic patterns of antebellum agriculture survived. Although organized along new lines, the plantation system remained intact well into the twentieth century and the great mass of black agricultural workers remained a dependent, propertyless peasantry, nominally free, but ensnared by poverty, ignorance, and the new servitude of tenantry. On many estates, the hands were still summoned to the fields with bells or bugles—very likely, in some cases, the same bells and bugles that summoned their slave forebears. Even the songs of the new regime evoked antebellum memories:

> Ol' marsh ridin' all time,
> Niggers workin' roun'.

Marsh sleepin' day time,
Niggers diggin' in de groun'.[55]

Many of them came directly from the period of bondage. As late as
World War II, Coahoma County field hands sang a version of the slave
song:

My ole mistress promised me
Before she died she would set me free. . . .
Now she's dead and gone to hell
I hope the devil will burn her well.[56]

Yet the continuities of Mississippi labor practices must not be overstated. Tenants were not slaves and even sharecropping, the most exploitative rung on the land tenure ladder, was not intrinsically an instrument of racial oppression, for it victimized the poor without regard
to color. Moreover, share tenantry in the postbellum South evolved as
something of a compromise. Ideally—because it rested on a reciprocity
of interests, on the tenant's need for land and the landlord's need for
labor—it offered advantages to both parties. In its early development,
the share system could even be considered a concession of sorts to
landless blacks who generally lacked the resources to rent farms of their
own but who were, nevertheless, unwilling to work for wages in tightly
regimented field gangs so reminiscent of slavery. A cropping arrangement seemed to offer former slaves a measure of self-direction, something approximating economic and personal independence: even the
poorest among them could set up for themselves on land marked off
for their exclusive use.[57] Experience quickly demonstrated, however,
that such a compromise, overshadowed as it was by white supremacy
and the habits of slavery, was one of unequal advantage.

Black Mississippians experienced virtually every form of land tenure,
though sharecropping was the most common arrangement. The tenants'
preference, no doubt, was for the greater income and autonomy promised by a fixed-rent contract, or any of several variants thought to be
personally and economically more rewarding than the share system. To
cite only one case, Mattie Lou Bogan and her husband, unable to find
other means of support, reluctantly sharecropped in the state's northeastern black-prairie district during the period between the two world
wars. "We sharecropped a right smart," Mattie Lou remembered years
later; "it didn't leave us wid nothing." Raising melons and hogs on the
side, they eventually acquired a mule and found a landlord willing to
rent them land. "Us thought us was big shots when us went to renting,"
she said. "Us thought us was rich."[58]

Relatively few black tenants were so fortunate. Because they rarely had work stock, tools, or production capital—and because landlords nearly always profited more from croppers than from renters—most black farmers found a share arrangement to be unavoidable. Despite much patronizing white talk about the willful improvidence of field hands who failed to better themselves, planters rarely encouraged tenant movement up the agricultural scale to less dependent positions. Indeed, by the turn of the century, Mississippi planters, like their counterparts elsewhere in the cotton South, increasingly sought to maximize production through tighter day-to-day supervision of labor. Apparently convinced that rental contracts permitted too much tenant control over the cultivation and sale of crops, they preferred croppers and in some cases wage laborers to renters. Although the share system entailed greater risks for landowners, it also afforded higher per-acre yields and, presumably, a more pliant workforce.[59] "The white [man's] control over his sharecroppers is fairly absolute," a federal agricultural survey of Coahoma County reported in 1944. "Supervision of the farming activities of the sharecropper is very close, he has no opportunity to exercise any initiative."[60]

Under a standard share arrangement, tenants worked on "halves." They supplied the labor, and planters supplied the land, seed, tools, and work animals. The two parties shared the cost of the fertilizer and each was entitled to half the harvest. Acreage allotments were small, sometimes only five to fifteen acres and seldom more than twenty-five or thirty.[61] The agricultural year was punctuated by two periods of furious activity: the planting and hoeing season in the spring and early summer; and the picking season in late summer and autumn. Without other assets, the tenants' resources were measured by the size of their "hoe-force," by the number of laborers in their families. Quite simply, because the harvest consumed 60 percent of all cotton production time, a tenant family could plant no more than it could pick. This constraint, of course, served planters better than tenants: small units of production resulted in small volumes of production per unit and small cash earnings per tenant—but also larger yields per plantation. By limiting the size of their croppers' tracts, planters could expect to have their cotton harvested before the onset of winter rains and to squeeze a maximum application of labor from hard-pressed families whose bare subsistence required intensive farming.[62]

Sharecropper families necessarily saw themselves in economic terms, as labor units requiring the work of young and old alike. Remembering her turn-of-the-century childhood in Mississippi, Anna Knight—who eventually abandoned her hoe to study nursing—wrote that "from childhood my lot was hard." "Life was a struggle and there was so much work—work all the time for children as well as for adults." "As soon as I was old enough I took my place beside the older workers in the fields." Very likely, as Edgar T. Thompson has argued, share tenancy exploited child labor more effectively than slavery. The young were often crucial to the household economy, providing the labor that permitted increased acreage and more intensive production methods. Children of five or six, although usually thought too young for field work, tended younger siblings. A youth of nine or ten was already a halfhand; one of thirteen could often do the work of nearly any adult.[63]

Virtually all the women in tenant families toiled alongside the men at peak times in the crop year. In common with working women everywhere, plantation women often worked even harder than their men, attending to the seasonal tasks of agriculture but also to household and motherly chores. "They do double duty," said Martha Robb Montgomery, wife of Isaiah T., "a man's share in the field, and a woman's part at home." Since the dawn of freedom, black families had insisted on the right to allocate their own labor. Some husbands refused to permit their wives to work outside the home and garden. Growing up in Yalobusha County in the 1920s and 1930s, Pearlee Avant, for example, chopped and picked cotton and even cut cordwood for her widowed mother. But "after my husband . . . after I married," she said, "I never did work in the field no more. . . . He didn't believe in women going to the field."[64] Yet, if black tenant families sometimes managed a clear division of labor along gender lines, few could permit their women to withdraw entirely from the field. "Children all went to the field, everyone of 'em worked, wuz raised to work," Christopher Boston of Chickasaw County remembered of his own family in the interwar years. His mother, on the other hand, "kept house. . . . She went to the field some . . . she didn't have to go, but she'd go and help out." Other wives and mothers worked because there was no alternative. Following World War I, Amy Jane Bafford raised ten children and sharecropped with her hard-working husband near Van Vleet (Chickasaw County). Although she remembered "pretty good times back in there," she could not forget the unending toil: "I just had so much to do. I had to . . . prepare breakfast and go to the field and come back out of the field and get over that hot stove and cook and go rat back to the field."[65]

Like Bafford, most women were as agile with a hoe as with a flatiron and though plowing was often thought to be man's work, many a wife could follow a mule as skillfully as her husband. Josephine Beard, a former Lowndes County sharecropper, yielded nothing to any male field hand she could remember. "Field work, child," she told a student interviewer in 1970, "every day I lived in the field chopping cotton, hoeing corn, every day, plowing." If some women knew only the kitchen, Beard remembered breaking the land spring after spring: "[Rise] 'fore daylight, eat your breakfast in the field setting on the plow. That's the truth." Many women could also pick cotton with the best male hand on any plantation. The average worker of either sex picked two hundred pounds from sunup to sundown. Women who could pick three hundred pounds were not uncommon; one, a legendary figure from Issaquena County, was said to have picked 996 pounds in a single day.[66]

Of course not every farm woman had a husband. Those who were widowed, deserted, or otherwise without men often had no choice but to make crops on their own. In fact, in 1940 women operated nearly 10 percent (or a total of 14,000) of all the black farms in Mississippi.[67] Yet the central place of black women in the plantation work force was not entirely a blessing for the dominant race. For while depressed black wages ensured domestic labor to all but the poorest white families, the demands of harvest diverted cooks and laundresses to the fields, making the season, as one Deltan said, "a time of dread" to white households.[68]

The field-workers themselves met the harvest season with mixed emotions. It brought bone-tiring days and nights of distasteful work, but also, at its close, a time of rest and—given a favoring cotton market and an honest landlord—perhaps even a brief period of relative plenty. Too often, however, the end of the picking season brought only loose change and disappointment. Without the resources for either production or subsistence, and without the collateral required by primary sources of credit, sharecroppers and even some fixed-rent tenants (white and black) met their needs during the growing season (March through August) by mortgaging their crops to secure periodic advances of food and supplies from planters or supply merchants. At harvest, when the value of their cotton exceeded the cost of their "furnish," they received a cash settlement.

In years of high cotton prices, a cropper's income might be considerable. In 1919, for example, a banner year when the price soared to a historic high of 85 cents a pound, many black croppers, despite below-average yields, paid out their accounts and still had $500 to $1,000, net earnings that exceeded those of some white industrial workers. At the other end of the spectrum were the crisis years from 1890 to 1902, when yields were uniformly high but prices in a collapsing cotton market ranged from less than five cents to a high of only ten cents, or the drought and depression-ravaged 1930s, when prices sagged to the lowest levels in nearly fifty years. In these periods of crisis, an average family with twenty acres under cultivation might produce a crop valued at

$300. After the landlord took half the lint and seed and the account was settled, the tenants' earnings probably did not exceed $50. Even in relatively flush years when cotton prices fluctuated between ten and thirty cents, most tenants had some cash income but were apparently penniless by Christmas or New Year.[69]

In this time between crops, the "slack" season when according to white lore every darky's day was surrendered to idleness, tenants and their children usually sought other employment, building levee or drainage systems, cutting rail fences, hewing cross ties, clearing woodland, performing domestic services. Without additional income from day wages, winter could be a time of want. With no lien for security, even the most generous landlords were reluctant to advance supplies to workers they thought to be shiftless and migratory. Artley Blanchard's experience was no doubt widely shared. Dependent throughout the growing season on the planter's furnish, this Monroe County tenant's family was thrown back on its own meager resources after the harvest. "When them [commissary] months up, he stop. You got to rute hog or die poor then," he remembered. Every able-bodied family member scrambled for additional earnings and the food supply turned increasingly from the "Three M's" (hog meat, meal, and molasses) to fish and game. "Our whole family, we hunted and fished. Got by like that. . . . Kept us going, you know, what little we wuz getting out the boss man."[70]

All estimates of tenant incomes are crude. Some neoclassical econometricians, persuaded by the logic of competitive-model theory, have recently argued that black sharecroppers enjoyed returns that exceeded their marginal productivity; that relative to slaves, they had comfortable standards of living, "well above the subsistence level."[71] These judgments, however seductive theoretically, must be weighed against a preponderance of empirical evidence which describes the cotton-belt tenant as the poorest of the rural southern poor. Season after season, whatever the fluctuations of the market, croppers with the rarest exceptions remained croppers—living in rude housing often little better than slave cabins; subsisting largely on "pone" and "fatback" (fried corn bread and fat salt pork); ending their agricultural year, when they were lucky, with enough cash to retire their debts, buy shoes for their families, and carry them through until the credit season began with spring plowing.[72] More often than not, as an Anguilla (Sharkey County) sharecropper testified, they settled for little or nothing: "Just work all the year long and at the end of the year, what they say—'You done fine Jim or John, you come out just even. . . . Maybe you do better next year.' "[73]

If next year offered hope, the words to the field hands' songs did not suggest as much:

Niggers plant the cotton,
Niggers pick it out,
White man pockets money,
Niggers does without.

Or:

Done worked all the summer
Done worked all the fall
And here comes Christmas
And I ain't got nothing at all
I'm just a po' cold nigger.

The cotton worker's life, as the blues described it, was one of long days and few rewards:

Ain't it hard? ain't it hard?
Ain't it hard to be a nigger? nigger? nigger?
Ain't it hard? ain't it hard?
For you cain't get yo' money when it's due.[74]

Although the appetite of the boll weevil and the inconstancy of the weather figured importantly in these laments, the problem was attributed principally to white avarice and the planter's accounting practices. From plantation to plantation the couplets varied, but the message remained the same:

Naught's a naught,
Figger's a figger
Figger fer de white man,
Naught fer de nigger[75]

First there was the matter of interest. Although Mississippi's usury law forbade creditors to tax accounts more than 20 percent per annum, tenants generally paid effective rates ranging, as one critic has written, "from 25 percent to grand larceny."[76] Supply merchants, whether at a plantation commissary or country store, usually had both explicit and implicit interest charges, i.e., an annual rate and a credit mark-up. During the growing season, tenants were furnished at "time prices," which though varying from supplier to supplier, were reported at from 10 to 70 percent higher than cash. When accounts were settled, debit entries were subject to an additional charge of from 10 to 25 percent. Although some suppliers scrupulously computed interest from the time of purchase, others simply imposed a flat rate. In the latter case—as apparently nearly always with credit mark-ups—tenants paid effective rates well in excess of the expressed annual charge, for they were assessed as much for a plug of tobacco furnished on the last day of the credit season as for one on the first.[77]

Perhaps one could be too critical of the plantation supply system. As its defenders point out, it gave those without accumulated resources their only chance for credit. No doubt the staggering interest rates owed much to the scarcity of capital in the rural South and to the high risks involved for creditors who were themselves often deeply in debt to primary lending agencies. But the system provided endless, and apparently irresistible, opportunities for landlords and furnish merchants to separate field hands from their money. In seasons of low yield or low prices, the resourceful planter-merchants could be expected to drive hard bargains with their captive black customers. In good years when tenant settlements were likely to be relatively high, some suppliers supplemented their usual stocks of side meat, gingham, and cheap shoes with silk dresses, choice tin goods, second-hand Chevrolets, and even gold teeth and pianos.[78] There was no universal rule on tenant gardens, but some planters discouraged or flatly forbade them, thus forcing their workers into almost total dependence on commissary supplies.[79] At best the system was a necessary evil, one subject to great abuse and deeply hated by its primary victims.

Then there was the matter of cheating, not merely fancy commissary prices or usury, but deliberate miscalculations of a tenant's debts and earnings. The extent of the practice is anybody's guess. Economist Robert Higgs, believing that a competitive labor market tended to keep planters honest, thought it to be relatively uncommon. Hortense Powdermaker, on the other hand, suspected that three out of four planters shortchanged their hands; and Oscar Johnston, president of the Delta and Pine Land Company, the world's largest cotton plantation, admitted privately that "chicanery, larceny (grand and petit), and other forms of dishonesty" were widespread plantation practices — practically "the rule rather than the exception."[80]

The field hands themselves rarely addressed the problem publicly, but they apparently agreed that a fair settlement was a plantation rarity. Traveling through Mississippi during World War I, W. T. B. Williams, a black investigator for the Labor Department, found resentment at every turn. "Many of the Negro tenants," he reported, "feel that it makes little difference what part of the crop is promised them for the white man gets it anyway."[81] Black landlords, on the other hand, though not above the suspicion of their black tenants, were generally thought to be more honest or at least less likely to cheat, for as Powdermaker wrote, black field hands "will not take from a Negro the treatment they are forced to suffer from certain white landlords and overseers." Rather than provoke a confrontation with a white planter, many tenants preferred simply to move on. Although certain that he had been cheated every year for thirty years, a Delta cropper admitted to Laurence Jones that he had never challenged a white planter's balance sheet because "there is no use jumping out of the frying pan into the fire." "If we ask questions we are cussed," he said, "and if we raise up we are shot, and that ends it."[82]

To offset nearly universal black cynicism, the most progressive landlords went to extraordinary lengths. Alfred Stone at the turn of the century, and both William Alexander Percy and Oscar Johnston several decades later, supplied coupon books so that their hands always knew where they stood. After World War II, the managers of the huge King and Anderson plantations near Clarksdale bowed to black wishes and issued statements of account at regular intervals. These procedures, however, were unusual.[83] Most tenants knew little about their own expenses or receipts and few landlords encouraged them to learn. Dr. Dorothy Boulding Ferebee discovered in the 1930s that black rural teachers in Bolivar County were free to instruct their charges in every phase of agriculture except "how to compute their earnings and their share of the produce." Black farm demonstration agents apparently operated under the same strictures. By all accounts tenants with a propensity to figure were objects of deep suspicion on virtually any plantation.[84]

Outdoing Ol' Mostah

Organized black efforts to achieve greater tenant autonomy were even more suspect. The specter of unified black action, particularly that of field hands, aroused the most intense white anxieties, evoking ancient fantasies of Negro "risings," threatening white social and economic control, provoking unreasoning white violence. To landlords, as one northern sojourner in the state observed, even a peaceful demonstration of black solidarity was simply intolerable, for next to the rape of white women, it was the "most heinous crime of all."[85] Though deeply rooted traditions of race dependency greatly minimized collective black action in Jim Crow Mississippi, there were several significant tenant efforts during the period to gain greater bargaining power and independence through collective action. The first of these, the Colored Farmers' Alliance, under the leadership of Oliver Cromwell, was violently suppressed in 1889 by Leflore County whites. When Cromwell, an otherwise obscure alliance leader, began organizing local chapters and persuaded some tenants to trade with a cooperative store in an adjoining county, white merchants and planters ordered him to leave the state. Defiant Colored Alliancemen, audaciously styling themselves "Three Thousand

Armed Men," promised protection for their leader. Three companies of state militia broke their resistance; once the troops withdrew, an orgy of local white violence claimed the lives of perhaps twenty-five blacks. The slaughter was checked, William F. Holmes has written, only by the intervention of the planters, who "probably did not bemoan the killing and driving away of Colored Alliance leaders," but who nevertheless needed substantial numbers of field hands to pick their cotton. Cromwell escaped, but the organization never recovered.[86]

All subsequent efforts by black tenants to improve their lot through organized activity met similar, if less bloody, ends. The Mississippi Negro Farmers' Conference, an early twentieth-century, Tuskegee-inspired companion organization to the Negro Business League, functioned essentially as an annual institute for the inspiration and instruction of black yeomen and, therefore, excited little planter opposition. Sharecroppers' unions were another matter. Fearing a contagion of tenant restlessness, white Mississippians joined in the suppression of the Progressive Farmers and Household Union of America in 1919. Formed in nearby Phillips County, Arkansas, to press landlords for more equitable settlements, the cotton pickers' organization sent waves of alarm through Delta counties on both sides of the river. Amid rumors of a "black insurrection," white Mississippians crossed into Arkansas to take part in a massacre near Elaine.[87] Whites also moved quickly in the early 1930s when Mississippi croppers in perhaps a dozen Delta communities began to join local chapters of the National Federation of Colored Farmers, an obscure black buying and selling cooperative. Authorities arrested a federation organizer; planters warned field hands of "pernicious" influence and "serious trouble"; and the Greenwood *Commonwealth* reminded its readers that "the Delta Negro farmer is a tenant who must buy and sell as his landlord directs." Despite an enthusiastic initial reception from the sharecroppers, the NFCF quietly terminated its efforts in Mississippi.[88]

Other radical depression-era agricultural workers' organizations fared little better. Neither the Share Croppers' Union nor the Farmers' Union (both formed in Alabama in the early 1930s) spilled over into Mississippi. Although Southern Tenant Farmers' Union organizers enjoyed some modest successes in five Mississippi black-belt counties late in the 1930s, this movement came after the STFU's decline elsewhere in the region and it almost immediately collapsed under violent white opposition. Formed in Arkansas in 1934, the STFU quickly expanded into the cotton counties of southeastern Missouri, eastern Oklahoma, western Tennessee, and eastern and south-central Texas.[89] In early 1935, union organizers entered Mississippi and, despite the murder of an

STFU agent near Hernando (DeSoto County) in March, officers claimed three locals by mid-summer. Conditions were such, the union said, that names and places could not be revealed, but a black STFU organizer with a well-deserved reputation for success in "tough places" reported that the "harvest is ripe" for tenant unionism in Mississippi.[90] The following year Mississippi farm workers formed at least two other small locals, both in the Delta: one at the British-owned Delta and Pine Land Company plantation near Scott; and another, surely the only biracial local in the state, at the Delta (Cooperative) Farm near Hillhouse, a short-lived Bolivar County producers' cooperative founded for refugees from the STFU's Arkansas struggles.[91] Little more was attempted in Mississippi until after 1938, however, for as STFU cofounder Harry Leland Mitchell informed a Delta (Cooperative) Farm resident, the union feared that a "premature start" in the most intransigent state could jeopardize tenant organizing elsewhere.[92] The STFU's Mississippi campaign, then, began in earnest only out of desperation, only after the movement's near collapse in Arkansas, Missouri, and Oklahoma forced organizers to seek new grassroots support.

For a tantalizing moment or two, the response from Mississippi share-croppers promised to exceed union expectations. At peak strength by mid-1939, the state had some eighteen locals and three to five hundred members in five counties, all of them in the Delta or Black Prairie.[93] If their numbers were too small to offset membership losses elsewhere in the cotton belt, the Mississippians nevertheless brought new infusions of determination and enthusiasm to a demoralized movement. Virtually denied all participation in New Deal crop-subsidy programs, hoping to obtain decent homes, farms, and increased bargaining power with white planters, these landless peasants turned eagerly to the STFU as a way out of dependency and subordination. Fortunately, for a historical record generally bereft of contemporary sharecropper documents, they also addressed a small avalanche of often painfully scrawled and moving letters to their newfound black and white union brothers at STFU headquarters in Memphis. Noting that "we has Ben Rob and left in Bad condition," one Deltan wrote union officials that the STFU was "the Best Pland that has Ever Ben offer to the negro." "I am proude of this Local," a member of Swift Going No. 14 (Bolivar County) affirmed. "It is jest what we nead amoung . . . the Black race." This surviving trove of documents also speaks to the Mississippi tenants' pride in organization, their well-developed sense of group solidarity, and their conviction that black progress required black unity: "How can we Live unless We Stand together," inquired a day laborer. "We Stand togeather We can Wine togeather; We Stand the Devied We Fall."[94]

Like their Alabama neighbor the remarkable Ned Cobb, these Mississippians believed that collective bargaining could be the counterweight for an imbalanced system. Unionism, as Cobb expressed it, "was a turnabout on the southern man, white and colored; it was somethin unusual." Like Cobb, too, Mississippi blacks found the movement all the more attractive because whites so adamantly opposed it.[95]

In the end, the union's message of hope and solidarity was no match for white terror. Nearly everywhere in the South, tenant organizations met determined and even violent white objection. But nowhere was the climate less favorable than in Mississippi: "When a Mississippi sharecropper stuck his head up," cofounder Mitchell remembered, "he got it shot off."[96] Try as they did to remain undetected by landlords until they found strength in numbers, the black locals were all too quickly discovered and crushed. Many members were threatened; some were driven away and others beaten and arrested; one was castrated. For a time, letters from Mississippi reveal, the movement in some communities survived by moving deeper underground. "This a Bad place Down hear," a local leader wrote from Lowndes County. "I will hafta goe sloe to get By[;] they no me." Though reporting that "our enemies are seeking to find out where we are holding our meetings," a Noxubee Countian affirmed that the members of Local 15 at Mashulaville were still "meeting [and] taking risks of our lives trying to cary the works on."[97] But such unwonted courage could not last. By mid-1940, white pressure had broken the back of the movement in Mississippi and everywhere else. There would be no further attempt to organize tenants until Fannie Lou Hamer formed the Mississippi Freedom Labor Union in 1965.[98]

Powerful as the oppressor was, the oppressed was not impotent. Although often victimized, sharecroppers were not, in Lawrence Levine's apt phrase, "pure victims." Their daily bread, indeed their survival, required accommodation with white rules; but as Levine and others have argued of Afro-Americans generally, they were not wholly powerless to influence the course of their lives.[99] Practically speaking, the planter's will was law. Tenants who were cheated or otherwise abused might take their labor elsewhere, but if they took their grievances to court they could expect only to compound their problems with further personal risk.[100] Some did fight back, legally and physically—and usually paid accordingly. More often the field hands accepted what they could not change even as they searched for methods to resist white control. They never achieved the state of free peasantry they so ardently desired, yet they pushed against the system and refashioned in subtle but meaningful ways the code of plantation life. Like their slave forebears, they knew an infinity of means to frustrate whites and to limit the power they had over their lives.

White jeremiads on black indolence were no doubt useful rationalizations, justifying (at least to the dominant race) the grossly unequal distribution of agricultural income. Yet blacks were not necessarily willing workers, and many field hands in the period after 1890 were about as "lazy" and "shiftless" as many antebellum slaves—and for much the same reason. In one of the more telling examples of continuity between the Old South and the New, planters complained in both periods that blacks were a "troublesome" labor force. In fact, in both periods a subject people countered the day-to-day compulsions of their circumstance by denying white expectations and testing white patience. In both periods, they malingered and dallied, they committed acts of thievery and sabotage, they dissembled, they played dumb and sick. And when they could tolerate no more, they ran away, usually to neighboring swamps during the slave regime, more frequently to the steel mills of Chicago in the twentieth century.

If most whites were apparently content to attribute such behavior to the Afro-American's character, some of the shrewdest among them recognized the natural enmity of the oppressed and the oppressor. Finding no evidence for the popular fiction that "the average Negro in the South adores his 'ol mostah,' " one northern-born Mississippi landlord detected among most black workers an "underhanded antagonism," even a "bitter hatred," toward the planter class: "By no means does the present generation of Negroes believe the white man is their best friend," he wrote in 1924. "Far from it. By every form of cunning and trickery does the average field Negro try to outdo the white man." Ready to concede black victory in this racial tug of war, this transplanted Yankee concluded that the black tenant could be neither coaxed nor driven to conscientious labor for any white: "Leave him for half an hour, and, as surely as the sun shines, he will sit down on you. To send him to the field alone is beyond the most exalted hope of your Southerner."[101]

For a tenant with a stake in the crop, of course, a feigned illness or a slowdown might be a two-edged sword. Self-interest was a powerful incentive and frequently was enough to ensure black diligence. But when there was little hope for an equitable settlement, or where daily wages were the rule, a little indolence held few terrors for the worker. Georgianna Colmer, growing up on a plantation near Louise (Humphreys County) after World War I, watched how black day laborers dealt with a cruel and stingy landowner: "The people don't do nothin' but watch him. They didn't do much work. . . . When he leave, they all lump up in one house an' dance an' drink. An' when . . . they see him comin' back, they get half bent, runnin' to them sacks. They pick hard so when he come back they have somethin' in there." All hands were in place, "fumblin', fumblin' roun' at the cotton," as the white man turned his sorrel down the rows, he "standin' up over 'em on that horse an' the people down there on their knees, peepin' through the cotton." His anger and his inevitable inquiry—"How come you ain't—? What you been doin'?"—brought an unvarying response: "Ah been pickin'." "He was tough," Colmer remembered, "but he couldn't get by them people."[102]

If the planter's word is to be accepted, many tenants were also thieves without compunction, stealing the whites' chickens and hogs, tools, and even cotton at nearly every opportunity. Given the risks involved, it seems improbable that every black hand was somehow in a white pocket. But pilferage was indisputably a problem on some plantations, one greatly compounded by the sharecroppers' distinction between stealing and taking. Croppers, like slaves, were ill-disposed to regard theft always as theft, especially when it meant securing by stealth that which they thought was properly theirs. A ham taken from the plantation smokehouse might not compensate for a dishonest settlement, but it could ease a mind nearly as well as it could fill a stomach.[103]

In the daily routine of plantation life, the field hands' best weapons were often the least confrontational, those that might foil the planters' expectations without provoking their rage: calculated incompetence or stupidity; carelessness and shammed misunderstanding; abuse of machinery, land, or animals; pretended illness, loafing, lying, cheating. But in moments of great anger or indignation an aggrieved tenant might strike out in starkly physical ways. Whites, as Dollard has written, had an "unshakable conviction . . . that danger lurks in the Negro quarter."[104] Although that danger was usually more imagined than real, some tenants did settle their scores violently and no prudent landlord could entirely ignore the possibility that an abused field hand might seek revenge. The fear of arson, for example, seems to have haunted postbellum planters about as much as slave owners, and probably had an equally salutary influence on the management practices of both. Homicide was also widely dreaded. An act of black physical aggression against any white— or even one of self-defense—nearly always resulted in a "nigger hunt" and often in the death of the offender. Yet black rage could not always be suppressed. In a representative case, Sandy Thompson, a Hinds County black, agreed to exchange some portion of his labor for a hog in 1920. A year later, by Thompson's reckoning, the debt was duly paid. The landlord, however, judged the black man's work to be "unsatisfactory" and attempted forcibly to reclaim the animal. Objecting violently, Thompson shot and killed the white man, and was almost immediately lynched.[105]

More often than not the violence was initiated by the planter, as the example of Jim Brady suggests. Thinking that he had been shortchanged in the settlement of his account in 1910, Brady protested and was struck by his employer for his impertinence. Brady struck back, but was promptly seized and flogged by the white man's friends near Mendenhall. Shortly thereafter, as he was chased by a lynch mob, Brady and other black hands exchanged fire with whites. In the end, a white farmer, at least three unidentified blacks, and almost certainly Brady, were dead.[106]

Not every plantation had a Brady or a Thompson willing to risk death for his due. But there is evidence of enough acts of black desperation and defiance to prove that whites who bullied or cheated their field hands did so at some risk.

"Returning Us to Slavery"

"I don' b'lieve in movin' ev'ry yeah, lak a lot o' people," a black Mississippian told a northerner in the 1930s. "But if I tek a mine teh move, I tell you one thing—ain't nobody kin *stop* me!"[107] The thought could not have been more forcefully expressed. If the speaker seemed unduly adamant, it was only because black Mississippians knew that freedom of movement was a right no tenant could take for granted.

In an important sense, the white complaint of black wanderlust was an admission of white failure. For until mechanization supplanted hand labor following World War II, no facet of plantation life commanded more attention than the need for a stable work force. The first post–Civil War legislature refused to ratify the Thirteenth Amendment, choosing instead to defy "sickly modern humanitarians" by enacting laws to require of the former slaves "labor and honest rectitude." To more prudent whites, the Black Code seemed ill-advised, likely in fact to invite further Yankee meddling in state affairs. The freedmen, and even some white editors, thought the code to be a resurrection of the old regime in a new guise. A convention of Vicksburg blacks protested to President Andrew Johnson that the new measures were "returning us to slavery." Most of the code's provisions, those applying exclusively to blacks, were declared void by the state's military commander in 1866; the remainder were swept aside by the Reconstruction legislature in 1870.[108] Though only briefly in place, the laws of 1865 faithfully reflected white determination to perpetuate antebellum work patterns. Stripped of their telltale racial designations, many of them—including the provisions regulating vagrancy, contract labor, emigrant agents, and en-ticement—reappeared in but slightly altered form after Reconstruction, and continued to impede the mobility of black labor well into the twentieth century.

Mississippi's restrictive labor statutes were extensions of white pro-prietary claims on black industry. Twentieth-century landlords, scarcely less than antebellum masters, regarded the field hands in their service as "their niggers." Tenant-stealing was a serious affront, punishable by law and custom. Nothing so excited the planters' passions, a Delta circuit judge believed, as the enticement of their workers; it violated the unwritten code of the cotton belt; it was a "deadly offense" that could result in murder, "as each man regards his labor as his chosen property."[109] Such indignation, it must be said, was not without hy-pocrisy. As hill-county whites had reason to know, labor-hungry Delta landowners frequently recruited in other districts, luring black workers with fantastic stories of riches awaiting them in a cotton paradise. By the same token, the planters of surrounding states often sought hands in Mississippi and just as often complained that shameless Mississip-pians did the same to them.

To protect their own labor supplies, many landlords took extreme measures. A labor agent caught in the act of solicitation could expect little mercy from local vigilance committees. A "Bankers' and Mer-chants' Labor Agency" in Natchez was more indulgent than most when it blocked the attempted departure of "a large group of blacks" by riverboat in 1908 and then merely ordered fifteen suspected recruiters (thirteen of whom were local whites) to leave town. More typically a black agent, apprehended in Noxubee County in 1929 as he tried to transport some two dozen hands to a Delta plantation, was flogged nearly to death. Throughout the period, press reports of lynchings, tar-and-featherings, and other harsh treatment testified to the brutal re-ceptions that awaited competitors for black labor.[110]

Violence of this kind, sanctioned as it nearly always was by white community approval, minimized the need for formal obstacles to labor recruitment. When legal restrictions seemed desirable, however, the state legislature obliged. Under a statute of 1890, anyone who knowingly employed a worker under contract to another was subject to a heavy fine and damages equal to twice the value of any crop the aggrieved first employer may have lost. The damages were later reduced by half, but the enticement law remains in place to the present day.[111] In 1912 the legislature also required emigrant agents to register with local officials and to pay an annual tax of $500 in every county in which they operated. Both measures were reenactments of the laws of 1865 and both were justified in the name of labor stability: "The agricultural labor of the state is overwhelmingly of African descent," the state supreme court noted in upholding the enticement law in 1919. "They are credulous and fickle and are easily persuaded, and thus for the common good this statute was enacted."[112]

Vagrancy and contract labor laws, and an informal criminal surety system, attacked the problem more directly. Under the Black Code, all freedmen over eighteen "with no lawful employment or business, or [those] found unlawfully assembling," could be declared vagrant and subject to fines not exceeding fifty dollars and imprisonment not exceeding ten days. Although that much-abused statute was repealed in 1870, its successors, and particularly the vagrancy law of 1904, were enacted, as one legislative leader said, "to drive negro loafers to the field." As was true of such measures elsewhere in the region, the enforcement of Mississippi's vagrancy law rose and fell with white demand for labor. Typically, "negro round-ups" came at harvest time.[113] During the labor crisis of World War I, municipalities across the state supplemented the law of 1904 with "work or fight" ordinances, which forced black "slackers" into conditions that bordered on peonage.[114]

In a tight labor market, planters might also obtain workers by paying the fines and court costs of blacks convicted of minor offenses, including gaming and public drunkenness. The state had no criminal surety statute. But many communities honored the southern custom of releasing black petty criminals to white landlords, often under circumstances that suggested collusion between police and planter. Although the last vestige of the convict lease system was eradicated in 1908, state prisoners— but apparently only those convicted of crimes against other blacks— were nevertheless sometimes released to planters under contractual obligations that can only be called forced labor. After serving eight years of a life sentence for killing another black, Zodoc Brown, for example, was bound to a white landlord under a "ninety day suspension" in 1928. Believing that he had been pardoned, and apparently grateful to his benefactor, he remained in the white man's employ for six years; when he left without the planter's consent in 1934, he was captured and returned to the state penal farm for having "violated the terms of his suspension." The extent to which commutation became an instrument for private impressment may never be known, but records in the governors' pardon files suggest that influential whites sometimes used the remission of sentences to acquire and hold captive black workers.[115]

The state's contract enforcement statutes were more common means of inhibiting labor mobility. The first of these, "an act to punish a laborer, renter or share cropper who has made one contract in writing and makes a second without giving notice of the first," was enacted in 1900 to make it unlawful for tenants to leave their landlords during the crop year. The second, the so-called false-pretense law of 1906, provided criminal punishments for tenants who entered into contracts with the intent to defraud their landlords. Because the question of intent could be a legal sticking point, the legislature made the violation of a contract by a tenant who had accepted an advance, even if no more than a tin of snuff, "prima facie evidence" of fraudulent intent. The penalties for thus "obtaining property under false pretense" were severe: fines and imprisonment not to exceed $100 or six months. Legislative intent is, of course, no easier to prove than tenant intent. Yet the pattern of arrest and prosecution under this statute suggests that the false-pretense law was itself a false pretense, that the state's purpose was not to punish fraud but to restrain tenant mobility by imposing criminal penalties for civil contract violations and sanctioning, if only indirectly, imprisonment for debt.[116] Together with the state's other restrictive labor statutes, it served as a legal framework for involuntary servitude. Not least of all, it reflected a social ethos that winked at even the less subtle forms of latter-day bondage and that accepted some degree of force as a requirement of black labor.

But for the agility of Mississippi's judiciary, legislative ice as thin as this might easily have given way. For more than a decade the appeals court skated gingerly around the constitutionality question in contract-labor enforcement proceedings, arguing that a ruling on that issue was not necessary for the disposition of the cases at bar. Further avoidance became more difficult, however, after the U.S. Supreme Court, in the celebrated *Bailey* case, overturned an Alabama contract labor law with a false-pretense clause on the ground that it contravened the Thirteenth Amendment.[117] Accordingly, in *Mississippi* v. *Armstead* (1912) the Mississippi high court, in freeing a Panola County black charged with entering into overlapping tenant contracts, struck down the contract labor statute, finding that its effect was "to force citizens into involuntary servitude."[118] Important as that ruling was, it did not fully align Mississippi law with *Bailey* v. *Alabama*. Because the defendant in *Armstead* was charged only with breach of contract, not with intent to defraud—and because the state had a separate statute for each offense—the decision left intact the more onerous false-pretense law, a law directly modeled after the Alabama statute voided by *Bailey*. Although the appeals court spoke eloquently in its *Armstead* decision of an obligation to protect "the weak of our people" from the "unwarranted interference" of the state, Mississippi's false-pretense law survived the Alabama decree by nearly two decades.[119]

The major influence of *Bailey* in Mississippi was greater reliance on the antienticement statute of 1890. This measure, fully as questionable as the contract labor law, was repeatedly challenged over a period of four decades. Skillfully resisting this pressure, the state appeals court gave ground slowly, shielding the law from constitutional attack by construing it in ever narrower terms. In the first major test in 1893, the judges candidly acknowledged that the law was designed not merely to punish tenant-stealing landlords but to "constrain laborers and tenants . . . to performance of their contracts by rendering it difficult for them to secure employment elsewhere." Finding the law to be a legitimate exercise of state police power, the court liberally applied its punitive provisions. In subsequent rulings, however, the appellate body softened its position, frequently ruling for the defense by requiring increasingly strict standards of proof that an accused landlord had "willfully" and "knowingly" induced the tenant of another to break a contract.[120] Following the *Bailey* and *Armstead* decisions, the Mississippi court managed both to reverse itself and protect the statute by ruling that state law could not constitutionally be used to restrict a tenant's freedom of movement. Thus, in *Thompson* v. *Box* (1927), the court left the enticement measure intact but found that the defendant did not unlawfully engage another landlord's workers, for "the darkies in the case at bar" had quit the latter's employ of their own volition after he whipped them and worked them "too rapid."[121]

Interpreted any other way the statute could not stand, the court's majority agreed, for it would mean that tenants must "stay or starve," that they would be "compelled to render service" or find "the hand of every man" against them. A masterpiece of obfuscation and judicial legislation, the *Thompson* ruling seemed to invalidate restrictive labor practices even as it upheld a restrictive labor law. Arguing in effect that it could not be used for its intended purposes, the court wrapped an objectionable measure in the language of the Constitution but left it, nevertheless, on the books where it continued to operate much as it always had. No doubt an occasional curtsy to the Thirteenth Amendment was good exercise for any Mississippi judge. It might even appease a higher court. But for black tenants, there were few practical benefits to be derived from coy declamations against "slavery in any form." After *Thompson,* the enticement statute, Mississippi's legal bulwark of black servitude, was if anything more secure than ever, for it had thus been "freed from constitutional objection."[122]

The practice of black forced labor is harder to track than the laws that fostered it, partly because it so closely resembled farm tenantry, partly because its victims were the poor and inarticulate, and partly because federal and state law enforcement was so indifferent. Yet peonage and even de facto slavery were not uncommon in Mississippi and elsewhere in the lower South.[123] Involuntary servitude flourished from time to time in the southern turpentine, sawmilling, and railroad industries, but most peonage complaints emerged from the cotton belt, a great many of them from the Mississippi Delta. In 1907, Senator John Sharp Williams admitted that strict enforcement of federal antipeonage law would be "to the detriment of southern plantation interests." That same year A. J. Hoyt, an investigator for the Department of Justice, thought that in Alabama, Georgia, and Mississippi, one-third of the larger plantations "are holding their negro employees to a condition of peonage." Three decades later, novelist James Howell Street believed the practice to be still prevalent in his home state: "To this day Mississippi never has voted to free her Negroes and really never has freed them — that is, if peonage is slavery."[124]

Inconclusive though they are, we have no better estimates of the extent of peonage anywhere in the region. As Pete Daniel has noted, forced labor was a hidden crime for which reliable statistics do not exist. The Department of Justice, under heavy diplomatic pressure, suppressed peonage among the South's white immigrant population. Abuse of black agricultural laborers, however, was so pervasive and so widely accepted that it defied the few resources committed by the federal government. Reformers learned to their amazement that slavery, though unconstitutional, was not proscribed by any federal statute. In 1867 Congress had outlawed peonage, but that statute applied only to forced labor for debt and initially only to the exploitation of Indians in New Mexico. Its application when debt was not a factor — and even its constitutionality — remained in question until after 1900. Thereafter, a few peonage test cases were tried and won in federal court. But it was federal strategy, apparently, to try only the tightest cases for demonstration purposes, rather than to attempt a systematic and costly program of eradication.[125]

White Mississippians widely derided allegations of peonage in their state. "Pee-nage," the *Clarion-Ledger* insisted, was a red herring used to excuse absconding black debtors: "When a negro cropper gets considerably behind with his landlord for supplies he tries to sneak off the place. If stopped and made to work out his indebtedness he raises the cry of 'pee-nage' and it interests the federal government in his behalf."[126] State and local authorities, always more responsive to landlord interests than labor rights, apparently agreed. No Mississippi court ever tried a peon master and when peonage cases were brought to the state's federal courts, Mississippi jurors were generally unwilling to convict. Federal proceedings often failed, as a government prosecutor noted, because of the "prejudice of juries" and because "white men contradicted the testimony of the negro witnesses."[127] Even in successful cases the penalties did not reflect the enormity of the crime. In 1921 W. Davis Moore of Pike County was fined $250 after admitting that he had kept Homer Smith in chains while the latter worked out a debt. The court was less indulgent in 1937 when it found J. S. Decker, a Tallahatchie County landlord, guilty of holding in peonage Ethel Lee Davis and her common-law husband, J. W. Wiggins. Capturing the black couple in two attempts to escape, Decker had beaten them, kept them in chains, and forced them at gunpoint to work off a debt of $175. When Wiggins succeeded in a third escape attempt, the black man went to the sheriff, who found Wiggins's wife still chained by the neck to a cabin. Decker was sentenced to three years in federal prison and fined $1,000.[128]

Convictions, or indeed even formal charges, represented only the tip of the forced-labor iceberg in Mississippi. Throughout the half century after 1890, allegations of lawless labor practices were rife.[129] Some of these cases did not come to trial because the victims and other black witnesses to the crime feared to testify against their oppressors. The problem is illuminated by a remarkable exchange of letters from and about Will Davis, a veteran of World War I and a peon on a plantation near Prairie Point in Noxubee County: "Me an my family are chitchen the devel Down here," he wrote his mother, Anne Taylor, in Greensboro, Alabama, in February, 1930; "we Suffers for things we are not uster Don withough." "I wood rather Be in Prison then to Be here." In subsequent letters Davis expressed hope that "we will See one Enether agin," asked his parents for money to help him escape, and urged extreme caution, as "some one haid oping the Last Letter yo rote me." The Taylors sent him cash, and on two occasions the distraught mother naively appealed directly to the planter for Davis's release. Incredibly, the white man responded, telling her that Will and his family "are well and fat," and that, though they "made a very good crop" two years running, they had still "come out behind" and must therefore work off their obligations. The white man assured her that he was "kind & good" and knowledgeable in the management of Negroes: "If they never gives me any trouble I never curse or strike them."

Anne Taylor was apparently not comforted. In April, 1931, she sent the letters from Will and his landlord to the NAACP, which turned them over to the Department of Justice. The resulting investigation brought only terror to Davis. "Mama I am so sorry you did that," he wrote after FBI agents questioned the planter; "you oughter rote and ask me Before yo did that." Noting that the landlord promised to shoot any black who testified against him, Davis poured out his fears: "Mama yo may never see me alive agine[;] the white folks will Kill me if they find out hoo do it."[130] Unfortunately, there appear to be no other surviving Davis letters. Nor is there evidence that he was murdered or that his white captor was prosecuted. Perhaps, as seems likely, the sharecropper and his family were warned of a fate worse than peonage and allowed to slip away quietly. In any event, Davis's experience suggests that black fear of white violence could be a lawless landlord's best defense, surer even than the most sympathetic jury.

Not all involuntary servitude began with indebtedness. Indeed, there is evidence that some Mississippi blacks were held simply as slaves without even the pretext of financial obligation. Often, however, the distinction between peonage and de facto slavery lost all meaning, as in the plantation custom of buying and selling tenant debts. Ray Stannard Baker, using as his example the 1907 "sale" of Dan January in Rankin County, thought the practice amounted to "practically selling the Negro." Baker did not know it, but the hapless January was sold not once but at least four times. That his owners did not recognize his freedom was emphasized by the third one, who caught him in the act of escape, bound him hand and foot and flogged him savagely in the presence of the black debtor's son Jim. Two nights later, when Jim tried to sneak his seriously injured father to freedom, they were again intercepted. This time, the white man threatened to hang them both if they did not either work off Dan's debt or "get somebody to buy him." Happily for January, a landlord more to his liking soon bought the claim against him for more than $1,000—surely a handsome sum to pay for a middle-aged and now-crippled field hand. Jim later managed to take his father's case to federal court, but none of the whites involved were ever punished.[131] Transactions of this kind may have been more common early in the century than later. But the custom of securing workers by buying their debts persisted through the 1930s, despite black efforts to have it prohibited by state law.[132]

The social climate that nourished forced black labor, and the ease with which whites accepted it, is perhaps best illustrated by the flood relief operations of 1927. In one of the great natural disasters of American history, the swollen Mississippi River broke through its levees, pushing thick yellow water over the alluvial plains of Arkansas, Louisiana, and Mississippi and displacing in the state of Mississippi alone nearly 200,000 people, more than three-quarters of them black field hands and their families.[133] Seventy thousand of these Mississippi Delta refugees were placed for up to five months in Red Cross encampments — what black leaders called "concentration camps" and "peonage pens."

Black complaints in Mississippi centered on the role of the National Guard assigned by the governor to "maintain order" in the camps. General Curtis T. Green, the guard commander, first admitted and then denied that his troops forcibly detained refugees. The allegations were also disputed by the director of the Red Cross and by the federal relief coordinator, Herbert Hoover.[134] But Perry Howard, Sidney D. Redmond, and even some native whites reported that the guard kept blacks inside the camps and labor agents out, thus assuring Delta landlords that when the waters receded their workers would return to the plantations. The guardsmen, Delta Red Cross relief administrator William Alexander Percy remembered, "were guilty of acts which profoundly and justly made the negroes fear them."[135]

These charges were borne out in arresting detail in the subsequent field inquiries by a commission of black conservatives led by Robert Russa Moton of Tuskegee (Hoover's so-called Colored Advisory Commission) and by the independent investigations of Walter White and Helen M. Boardman for the NAACP. Among other things, these reports confirmed that before the levees gave way, blacks were conscripted at gunpoint to strengthen the earthen ramparts. At Greenville, it was reported, armed Boy Scouts were assigned guard duty over a contingent of black levee workers until troops arrived. After the levees were breached and relief operations established, soldiers at black camps — but not at camps for whites or Mexicans — controlled all movement in or out. As General Green explained to fair-skinned Walter White, whom he apparently thought to be Causcasian, the state's policy was to hold the refugees until the crisis abated and each planter could claim "his niggers," "no man being allowed . . . any other but *his own niggers*." The Mississippi Delta, he said, was the garden spot of the universe, and "we do not propose to have it stripped of labor" by northern industrialists or landlords from other agricultural districts.[136]

Blacks who attempted to escape or to avoid work details, either in camp or on consignment to local white businesses or plantations, were abused and in some cases beaten with rifle straps. Some were shot. In time, a great many "took to the hills like frightened rabbits" to avoid being sent back to former landlords. In Vicksburg alone, more than 3,000 were reported as "runaways." Others fled after they were forcibly returned to their landlords. "Those who were caught," Moton reported, "were whipped and at times threatened with death if they left the plantations again." Shocking as these revelations were, the investigators may have uncovered only part of the story, for inquiries were often frustrated by black fear of white retaliation. "They tell you frankly," the Moton Commission noted of the detainees, "that they are afraid . . . that they would be killed."[137] Many refugees, however, took the risk. One who did, E. E. Ellsworth of Scott, described "more Cruelty, Savagery and inhuman treatment than you would be willing to believe." "Thousands of us," he informed the NAACP, "will choose death by starvation rather than another Camp. Expose them all you can."[138] Nor did refugee memories of the peonage pens quickly fade. A decade later, as officials prepared for another great inundation, a Washington County planter who led relief operations in 1927 warned that the reintroduction of the militia "would spread terror among the negroes and result in a tremendous evacuation of this immediate territory."[139]

However real the problem of peonage or widespread the practice of forced labor, there were definite limits to white control over black mobility. Through the crop lien and control of the furnish—the rural blacks' primary food source—landlords largely succeeded in stabilizing their labor supplies during the growing season. Whites also managed to restrict black occupational opportunities almost entirely to farm tenantry. Indeed, planters had at their disposal a variety of means, legal and social, to acquire, hold, and otherwise coerce their work force. Through debt servitude and, less frequently, through simple slavery, some maintained nearly absolute control over the movement of their field hands. Mississippi's forced labor system, as one of the state's black lawyers reported, was "as bad as the Serf System under the Czars or the Peonage System in Mexico."[140] Thus, in the language of economics, this was an "imperfect" labor market, one characterized by gross non-market constraints, and one that assured the dominant race an abundant, cheap, and relatively docile labor force. Yet balance requires a recognition that even in darkest Mississippi the old slave regime was not reestablished. Try as whites did to prevent it, there was always considerable black movement: from plantation to plantation, from state to state and, after World War I, from south to north.

How, then, does one explain this apparent paradox of substantial black mobility within a relatively closed system? William Cohen has done so in the context of shifting white labor requirements: unlike slavery, he notes, the postbellum labor system was "a fluid, flexible affair which alternated between free and forced labor in time to the rhythm of the southern labor market." The mechanisms of coercion were always present; but they were generally used only in times and places of labor shortage, leaving blacks free to move about more or less at will in periods of labor abundance.[141] This useful insight, unfortunately, is largely speculative, for no scholar has systematically correlated black interplantation mobility patterns with agricultural labor market fluctuations. Most certainly it exaggerates white ability to manipulate blacks.

The white notion of black wanderlust is at the very bedrock of postbellum plantation lore. By common assent, landlords, from the most exploitative to the most sympathetic, found blacks to be troublesome, innately restless workers, inconstant in their loyalties, and likely to move at the slightest whim. If nothing else, these lamentations about black "migratory instincts" suggest the ultimate failure of white restraints. Annually, during the postsettlement reshuffling process, perhaps as many as one in three tenant families chose, in the plantation idiom, to "hit the grit" or "light a shuck."[142] Some left in search of a better cabin or tenant arrangement, a less miserly furnish, more fertile soil, or decent schools. Some went to avenge an injustice or to leave behind the memory of a disastrous crop. Still others moved after a good year, having learned from bitter experience that a black tenant with an accumulation of corn or livestock could tempt the avarice of all but the most scrupulous plantation bookkeepers. Finally, some simply left when the spirit moved them, for reasons known only to them. But whether they moved for cause or simply to exercise their right to move, they did so often enough to challenge white proprietary presumptions, and, thereby, to fix the limits of white control.

Postscript to the Cotton Patch

Ultimately, of course, it was modernity not wanderlust that swept the great bulk of Mississippi's black field hands off the land. Although the story of the revolution in southern agriculture and the displacement of hand labor in cotton production is itself the subject of entire volumes,[143] its broader outlines can be briefly described.

From Appomattox to the Great Depression cotton culture seemed fixed in time. By the standards of wheat or corn production in the Midwest and Great Plains, cotton had been scarcely touched by the machine age. The one-mule tract was still the standard unit of production. An exploitative and ruinously inefficient labor system, a form of reenslavement developed amid the disruptions of emancipation, remained substantially unchanged. Production methods were ancient and farm machinery primitive. Indeed, the practices of the cotton patch were so rudimentary that one observer thought "Moses and Hammurabi would have been at home with the tools and implements of the tenant farmer."[144]

The glacial pace of southern agricultural change can be explained in part by an abundance of cheap and dependent labor and by a relative shortage of capital that combined to discourage the application of machines to farming. No less important, cotton culture itself seemed to resist modernization. The combustion engine could be harnessed in Mississippi as readily as in Iowa to break land and prepare seedbeds. But until the entire process could be mechanized—until devices could be found to perform the seasonal work of thinning and weeding the cotton plants and picking the lint—there was little practical advantage in tractors, three-bottom plows, and four-row cultivators. Precisely because all producers were dependent on hand labor at peak seasons, hand tools and mule power generally sufficed on even the largest, most innovative, and profit-maximizing plantations.[145]

The region's first tractors appeared soon after World War I. Until well into the thirties, however, they remained a relative novelty. The Dockery Plantation, the largest in Sunflower County, cultivated 8,000 acres entirely with mules through the 1920s.[146] In 1930 the managers of Delta and Pine Land Company still made their daily rounds on horseback. Operating some 38,000 acres in Washington and Bolivar counties, this British-owned company employed 1,200 tenant families and 1,000 mules. Yet it had neither a tractor nor a pickup truck until the implementation of a limited experiment in machine farming in 1931. In fact, by 1940 only 2.7 percent of all Mississippi farm operators owned tractors—compared to 55.3 in Iowa—and no plantation was fully mechanized until after World War II. The mechanical harvester (which could then perform the work of perhaps thirty-five hand pickers) was not used commercially in Mississippi until 1943. Ten years later, 75 percent of all Delta cotton was still handpicked.[147]

Yet if old farming practices endured through the 1930s, there were forces at work that would within a single generation transform southern commercial agriculture. Under the combined pressure of federal farm policy, advancing agricultural science and technology, and increased competition both from foreign and southwestern cotton growers and from synthetic fibers, the cotton South by 1940 was on the brink of social and economic revolution. The change began gradually during the depression with New Deal acreage restrictions and price-support programs that primarily benefited large landowners and reduced their need for tenants, and with the increased utilization of tractors that landowners bought with federal subsidies and credit. It accelerated sharply during the Second World War, which brought higher cotton prices, labor shortages, new opportunities for blacks outside of agriculture, and additional pressures for mechanization. Thus begun in the late 1930s, the transformation was virtually complete by the 1960s.

By the latter decade, cotton production nearly everywhere in the region, and particularly in the Mississippi Delta, was about as capital intensive and labor efficient as the production of any other staple commodity anywhere in the nation. Like the tumbledown tenant shacks that had once defined the southern landscape, the traditional, fragmented plantation system and the institutions it fostered—commissary credit, the crop lien, share tenancy, and landlord paternalism—were all but abandoned. In an era of increasing diversification and consolidation in which fewer but more sophisticated farmers produced higher crop and livestock yields on ever larger farms, the fully mechanized unit—the "neoplantation"[148]—required scarcely one-fifth its former work force. Once subdivided into fifteen- to forty-acre plots, each farmed by a sharecropper family, plantations now operated as single units with resident wage hands. Dispossessed in what has been called the "southern enclosure,"[149] rendered obsolete by flame cultivators, chemical herbicides, and mechanical harvesters, tens of thousands of sharecroppers and other surplus farm workers left the land and often the state in the generally vain search for a better life.

Although this massive reconfiguration of farm life touched Mississippians of both races, blacks outnumbered whites on the lower rungs of the agricultural ladder and, therefore, in the movement off the land. "Our Negroes have moved away," a spokesman for the planters of Greenwood observed in 1944, "and I don't think they will come back unless forced to by necessity."[150] Decades later, recalling the process that in little more than a decade transformed his own "mule and tenant operation . . . into a totally mechanized, scientifically farmed unit," Minor Gray, president of Delta and Pine Land Company, remembered that black field hands left the state "by the train load." "The negra," as he put it, ". . . had to go [North] for economic reasons, he had to leave. It wasn't enough money in the crops for the tenant and the landlord both." Though no other plantation could match its scale, Gray's corporation was something of a microcosm of the cotton South. At the Delta and Pine Land Company, where some 4,000 black tenants had cultivated 16,000 acres of cotton in 1925, no sharecroppers remained by 1969. In their stead, 510 hired hands produced diversified crops on 7,200 acres with 150 tractors, thirty-one mechanical cotton pickers, and nine combines.[151]

In this flight from the fields, the state's farm population declined 94 percent between 1940 and 1980, and the number of its black farmers (owners and tenants) fell from 159,500 to fewer than 9,000.[152] During the same period—for the first time since the massive expansion of slave-based cotton production in the 1830s—the black share of the state's total population dipped below half. Outnumbering whites in every census from 1840 through 1930, blacks were overtaken by whites in 1940 and by 1980 constituted but 35 percent of the state's population.

Unquestionably, this cotton-patch revolution eased the lot of those who stayed behind. Postwar urban and industrial trends, combined with advancing civil rights, gradually eroded the ideology of dependency and brought black Mississippians wider and more remunerative job opportunities. By the 1960s even black farm workers enjoyed somewhat greater bargaining power, higher wages, and improved management-labor relations. Yet, welcome as these changes were, the social cost was fearsome, and most of it was paid by the displaced thousands, the emigres from the cotton patch who, though ill-prepared for city and factory life, found themselves thrust into the nation's urban underclass, where all too often they exchanged one form of dependence for another.

CHAPTER 5

Black Labor / Black Capital

Me and a man was working side by side
This is what it meant,
They was paying him a dollar an hour
And they was paying me fifty cents.

—Big Bill Broonzy, 1945[1]

Despite the political circumstances which render the lives and property of
colored people insecure all over the South, they are gaining a respectable
hold upon the business interests of the country; and just as they adapt
themselves to sound business principles, more and more will come to
them the recognition that is due to every useful and upright citizen.

—Isaiah T. Montgomery, 1901[2]

Following a sojourn in Mississippi of some two years, a white
northerner pronounced the state's black plantation workers in 1922 to
be precisely what their white overlords had made of them: "dull, irresponsible," "without ambition," and "utterly bestial." Town Negroes,
on the other hand, were "markedly different," almost of "another race."
Given the advantages of "training and environment," not least of all
"closer touch with the white race," they were often "immaculate . . . in
appearance and carriage, intelligent, courteous, and able to read." Some,
as she marveled, were useful citizens, "acting successfully" in every
occupation from physician and dentist to dressmaker and bricklayer.[3]

The distinction was, of course, overstated. In a state as rural as
Mississippi, the line between town and country was never sharply drawn.
In the off-season, rural blacks drifted into nearby towns and cities in
search of better jobs or schools. At harvest, ingress became egress, as
village washerwomen and out-of-work mechanics, even many black
schoolteachers and preachers, temporarily entered the fields to supple-

ment meager incomes. Given this seasonal ebb and flow, even the practiced eye of a native could not separate a rudely dressed rural visitor from a large percentage of the black urban underclass. Clearly, as nearly any black non–farm worker knew, the benefits of city life were easily exaggerated.

Yet in nearly every urban place there were "markedly different" blacks, small numbers of semiskilled industrial workers, craftsmen, entrepreneurs, professionals, who in income and life-style approximated white standards. They were the anomalies of a system designed to keep blacks down. From their ranks came the state's minuscule black middle class, its more educated and articulate race spokesmen, and most of such wealth as its black community possessed.

"Nigger Work"

Like peasants throughout the western world, black Mississippians responded to the lure of the city, abandoning farm and countryside as rapidly as urban opportunities permitted. Between 1890 and 1940 the state's black urban population increased five-fold—from 34,200 to 178,000—and its urban places were consistently among the blackest in the South.[4] Yet as Table 5.1 indicates, whites always commanded a disproportionate share of both the urban population and nonagricultural jobs. Despite their continuing rural-to-urban movement, Mississippi blacks remained throughout the Jim Crow years more rural and agricultural than blacks in any other state.

In the cotton counties, where black numbers were greatest, industrial development was limited perhaps not as a matter of public policy but rather of planter indifference bordering in some cases on hostility. As recent scholarship seems to demonstrate, Mississippi's landed elite offered no "sustained, effective opposition to industrialization."[5] But while planters generally did not actively thwart economic development, they

TABLE 5.1. Blacks in Mississippi's Population and Labor Force, 1890-1940.

	Blacks in total population	Blacks in urban population	Urban black population	Black share of work force	Black % of nonagricultural workers
1890	57.6%	48.9%	4.6%	65.7%	55.4
1900	58.5	47.3	6.3	66.0	56.9
1920	52.2	41.5	10.5	59.7	46.8
1940	49.2	41.1	16.6	54.0	40.5

clearly wanted no competition from higher-paying factory employers; and Delta county support for the state's Balance Agriculture with Industry (BAWI) program required repeated official assurances that desirable nonfarm employment would be reserved, particularly in the black belt, for those workers the state's industrial boomers called "native Anglo-Saxons." In fact, such industry as BAWI did attract—principally garment or textile products plants—was located in areas outside cotton districts and employed practically no black workers.[6] Typically, in 1937 when Armstrong Tire and Rubber prepared to open a plant in Natchez, company officials allayed local fears by announcing that the industry would employ "only a few colored for porters and mixing carbon black"—work that was thought to be too unremunerative and distasteful for whites. Well into the 1960s, business leaders in some communities conceded that they sought nonfarm economic development only for whites.[7] Even in Jackson, some blacks believed, whites often opposed industrial growth because they feared that new opportunities for the black underclass would undermine white control. "They figured . . . if a dollar came into the hands of too many. . . Negroes," one black Jacksonian explained, ". . . the Negro would get to be where he was . . . independent."[8]

Black occupations (Table 5.2) were limited almost entirely to domestic and manual labor. There were no legal restrictions on black employment, but employer preference and white public opinion conspired to enforce widespread job segregation. "All the good jobs are for white folks," Jim Evers often told his sons Charles and Medgar, "and the hard ones are for black folks."[9] Town Negroes enjoyed a virtual monopoly on the work of house servants, gardeners, cooks, laundresses, and untrained nurses; hotels and retail establishments retained their services as bellboys, porters, messengers, and janitors. Except when whites de-

TABLE 5.2. Occupational Distribution of the Labor Force in Mississippi, by Race, 1900, 1920, 1940.

	1900 Black	1900 White	1920 Black	1920 White	1940 Black	1940 White
Agriculture	79.4%	60.0%	76.8%	60.5%	67.9%	46.9%
Domestic and personal service	14.9	5.3	9.2	2.0	15.4	3.2
Unskilled non-agricultural labor	5.7	34.7	8.4	4.6	8.4	5.2
Other	5.7	34.7	5.6	32.9	8.3	44.7

manded such service jobs in periods of unemployment, most communities employed blacks as garbage collectors and street cleaners; public officials also preferred them for the construction and maintenance of highways, railroads, and levees. Blacks outnumbered whites as deck and wharf hands, doorkeepers, midwives, and in unskilled, low-wage manufacturing jobs. They invariably performed the most difficult, dirty, and dangerous tasks in gins, compresses, turpentine camps, and sawmills.

As employers usually agreed, black workers held a competitive edge over whites in some jobs because they could be worked harder under the most adverse conditions with fewer complaints. Delta lumbermen nearly always hired black lumberjacks, former Congressman Frank E. Smith remembered, because the work was uncommonly hard and injuries frequent: "Traditionally only black men could work in the swamplands amid the distractions of heat, mosquitoes, bugs and snakes."[10] Although some Piney Woods sawmill operators complained of "no-account and trifling" black labor, others clearly preferred black hands because of "their superior strength and endurance" and because they were "unspoiled by education." A good black hand, one mill boss reported, could do "as much work as two white men." Many other operators apparently agreed: Mississippi lumbermen often called mechanical devices used to turn heavy logs "steam niggers."[11] Blacks also provided virtually all of the physical labor needed to produce naval stores. As the historian Nollie Hickman has written, the black "sapsuckers" and "sorelegs" who chipped (scarified) the trees and gathered or "dipped" the crude gum in the state's vast turpentine forests lived under isolated, "slave-like" conditions and suffered "a ruthless economic exploitation" that whites would not have tolerated. Never abundant, opportunities for better jobs diminished as the decades passed. Late in the nineteenth century, a fortunate few blacks held responsible, good-paying jobs in the timber industry. For example, the legendary former slave John Wesley Fairley (c. 1840-1918)—reputedly a seven-foot-tall "Black Paul Bunyan of Stone County"—was a substantial landowner and "creek runner" (i.e., foreman) who until his retirement at the turn of the century supervised white as well as black rafters and loggers in the Wiggins area.[12] But even then such positions were rarely occupied by blacks, and after 1900 the black worker virtually by definition was an unskilled and low-wage worker.

The question of wage differentials—of whether blacks received less than whites for identical work—is less easily answered than the question of occupational discrimination. Although the census bureau did not systematically compile income statistics by race until 1940, conservative econometricians argue confidently that in competitive labor markets employer interest in efficiency and profit overrides racial considerations and that blacks even in the lower South enjoyed substantial wage parity with whites for unskilled work. What rational cost-minded employer, competitive-market theorists ask, would pay white workers a premium for the color of their skin? The theory of racial discrimination, however, is not (as Gavin Wright concedes) "one of the more firmly grounded branches of economic analysis."[13] Indeed, because "hard" comparative-wage data are lacking and anecdotal testimony is conflicting, even tentative conclusions are hazardous. Yet, for what it may be worth, there is evidence that some Mississippi employers preferred black employees not merely because they could be worked harder but because they could be worked for less. For example, in the sawmills of Laurel, where turn-of-the-century community leaders lured blacks with promises of no "illtreatment or discrimination in business or labor matters," blacks were both excluded from the more desirable and higher-paying "white jobs" and, it appears, paid less for unskilled work. The average black mill worker by 1915 received wages of ten dollars (usually in scrip) for six ten-hour days—well over twice what an agricultural day laborer in the Delta could expect, but roughly 25 percent less than the wage of white Laurel mill hands in comparable jobs.[14] Perhaps the most representative example of the wage problem in Mississippi is to be found in Natchez, where during the labor shortage of World War I a northern-owned lumber planing mill, under a cost-plus defense contract, began paying blacks roughly twice the prevailing community rate for black workers. After white business and plantation interests complained of the destabilizing effect of the higher Negro wage, the mill quickly cut hourly wages by half. Because the jobs in question were all "black jobs" this case does not squarely address the wage-differential issue. It does suggest, however, that in Jim Crow Mississippi the labor market was not necessarily free or competitive, and that racial considerations sometimes outweighed market considerations not only in occupational but in wage decisions.[15]

Blacks could also be handled more roughly than whites. Those thought to be slackers or union agitators were subject to harsh treatment. A Jackson packing plant owner in the 1930s preferred unskilled blacks to whites because, as he said, whenever labor dissatisfaction surfaced, "I take a club and beat the hell out of a couple of Negroes and conditions immediately settle back to normal." An Adams County employer expressed the same preference: "When you just have Negroes, you can make them work by cussing and cuffing them. . . . But with whites you can't do that."[16]

The surest advantage of the unskilled black laborer, however, was the white notion about the proper or natural work of the two races. White definitions of "nigger work" were apparently more rigid early in the period, when memories of slavery were freshest. White notions were also subject to change when unemployment or technical advances rendered particular jobs more attractive. At the turn of the century, a leading white Greenwood attorney noted, poor whites often worked with their hands but the practice was usually frowned upon by their betters, since in plantation districts there was a "social stigma on anyone who did manual labor." "In the rich lands of the Yazoo Delta," Booker T. Washington wrote, "the negro is almost the only man who labors with his hand." Even in the predominantly white counties of the Piney Woods, where not a few white timber and railroad workers necessarily toiled, as the saying went, "like niggers," the hardest labor was the province of blacks. "A white man wouldn't work on a job unless he was a boss," a black Jones County sawmill worker said of the period after World War I. "He wouldn't work like me."[17] In some communities whites who might otherwise have accepted the most arduous manual labor were denied it by public pressure lest they stigmatize the entire race. Some whites even tried to reclassify the "negro jobs" they held by driving off black co-workers. Whitecappers in Lamar, Lincoln, and Forrest counties turned to violence early in this century to rid the area not only of black farmowners but of black loggers and sawmill hands.[18] In one section of Wayne County, turn-of-the-century timber executives agreed to hire only white workers, giving the area a reputation as one "where no negroes were allowed." When shorthanded company officials attempted to import a "train load" of blacks in 1919, armed white bands drove the Negroes out of the district. A "committee" of local whites warned employers that black labor would be tolerated only on railroad beds.[19]

In some instances, black workers were forced out as improved working conditions and white economic needs made their jobs more acceptable to the dominant race. The most notorious example involved black trainmen. The gandy dancers who repaired the roadbeds and aligned the tracks outnumbered all other black Mississippi railroad employees (84 percent in 1910). Although many blacks had been driven from responsible positions in the freight yards early in the century, a substantial number continued to work as switchmen, brakemen, and firemen, positions that until World War I were thought to be too dirty and dangerous for whites. Modernization of equipment and other innovations, however, rendered these jobs more appealing, and the clamor for black exclusion began. When railroad management refused to cooperate, white vigilantes threatened and flogged black trainmen and, in 1921, killed three from ambush on the Illinois Central. Company agents learned that a bounty of $300 had been placed on the head of every Negro who ignored white warnings to resign.[20] During the depression white opposition mounted; snipers killed at least six more on-duty black firemen and brakemen, and wounded more than a dozen others. "Their offense," as the Vicksburg *Evening Post* reported, "was that they sought to earn their bread by the sweat of their brows." Although more than one thousand black Mississippians worked as switchmen, firemen, and brakemen in 1910, there were fewer than one hundred in such positions by 1940. "They used to have Negroes braking and firing on the roads," one Mississippian observed. "The only reason they are not there now is that they will be shot off like dogs."[21]

Similar, if less violent, depression-era pressure forced blacks in some cities from low-status work as municipal garbage collectors, street repairmen, and levee workers. White women in one city tried unsuccessfully to replace black cooks and service workers on a federal relief project for black children. Caught as they were between their own plight and such satisfaction as they found in the comeuppance of whites, black Mississippians viewed shifting perceptions of "negro work" with mixed sentiments. Not a few were willing, as one displaced black laborer said, to "let um know how it feels tuh swing that pick!"[22] Yet, though turnabout was fair play, it put no food on black tables. Occupational mobility in Jim Crow Mississippi was essentially one-directional: whites could move down the employment ladder as their pocketbooks demanded, driving blacks ever deeper into poverty. But black movement upward often entailed great personal risk.

Because their earning capacities were substantially lower, black Mississippians necessarily participated more fully than whites in the labor market, taking jobs at an earlier age and generally remaining in the work force years longer.[23] This disparity was particularly acute among women. In 1910, a time when a white woman's place was thought to be the home, black women swelled the labor force, accounting for more than four-fifths (82 percent) of the state's gainfully employed women and nearly a third (29 percent) of all workers. Thereafter, white female employment levels rose slightly and black female levels declined, but in 1940 black women still outnumbered white women in the state's work force by two to one (66 percent). Table 5.3, which permits comparisons, by race and sex, of both employment levels and occupational distribution, helps to identify the black woman's economic sphere. These data reflect a substantial shift in her place of employment after 1900, but scant change in her occupational alternatives. By 1940, black women

TABLE 5.3. Mississippi Labor Force, by Race and Sex, 1900 and 1940.

	1900[1]				1940[2]			
	Black		White		Black		White	
	Male	Female	Male	Female	Male	Female	Male	Female
Labor force participation: Population employed	87%	47%	82%	13%	84%	33%	79%	19%
Occupational distribution; Employed in: Agriculture	82	74	72	58	76	49	51	15
Domestic service	10	24	4	11	1	38	0	2
Other	8	2	24	31	23	13	49	83

[1] Ten years and older.
[2] Fourteen years and older.

had succeeded far better than black men in finding nonfarm jobs. In that year the total black labor force was more than 70 percent male, but women accounted for nearly half (48.3 percent) of all black urban employment. While black men were increasingly pushed out of the skilled trades into common labor and odd jobs, black women enjoyed job security and often brought in more income than their husbands.[24] These modest advantages notwithstanding, black women workers nevertheless remained locked in the meanest and least remunerative labor.

The contrast with white women was particularly stark. Not only did black women in 1940 enter the labor force in proportions nearly double those of white women, they did so almost exclusively as either farm laborers or domestic and service workers. In that year more than eight in ten (85 percent) of all black women nonfarm workers listed their occupations as either domestic or service workers, primarily cooks, laundresses, servants, and untrained nurses. White women, on the other hand, though themselves the victims of gross sex discrimination, found opportunities as semiprofessional workers, clerical and sales personnel, and semiskilled industrial operatives. In 1940 white women comprised less than 3 percent of the state's female domestic service workers and only 11 percent of its female agricultural day laborers — but 99.5 percent of its female telephone operators, 99 percent of its female stenographers, 97 percent of its female bookkeepers and accountants, 92 percent of its female textile and garment workers, 85 percent of its female commercial proprietors, and 81 percent of its female college professors.

The paternalism that suffused the legend of the antebellum Big House, which tied plantation house servants to their white folks with bonds of mutual affection and obligation, survived into the twentieth century. All but the poorest white families retained blacks for kitchen or yard work and many professed to think of their domestics as "members of the family," "almost one of us." When she died in 1925 at the age of eighty-three Letitia Craig was remembered by the Natchez family she had served for more than half a century as a "faithful, trusted and devoted nurse and friend." After "sharing their joys and sorrows" through two generations, she was "honored and adored," "like a member of the family."[25] Nor was "Aunt Letty" unique. Many a favorite twentieth-century cook or nurse was no doubt petted and otherwise indulged. The lore of Jim Crow, like that of slavery, is too rich in allusions to the semifamilial status of favored retainers to be discounted entirely. Although servant wages were universally low—about the same in 1940 as in 1865—some whites supplied their most faithful black employees not only with the customary offering of food and cast-off clothing but also with health care and, in the most exceptional cases, even a northern education for their children. A highly regarded domestic might also expect some level of continued financial assistance in old age. Upon her death in 1932, Harriet Varnado of Osyka was celebrated in the local press as a "faithful mammy" who had "completed sixty years of continuous and unbroken service" to a single family. In 1872, at the age of nine and apparently orphaned, she had been "given" to her white folks by an ex-slave. She attended to the family's needs through two generations and, in return, was given the family's surname, quarters in the backyard, and such material compensation and love as the paternalistic ideal could supply: "No colored person," some whites said, "has been held in greater respect." When she died, her employers arranged the funeral and, in a spontaneous display of grief and affection, a large attendance of white people paid their last respects.[26]

If some whites repaid black loyalty and industry with gratitude and favors, many more found reason for discontent. Compared to the sainted mammies of old, twentieth-century white Mississippians generally agreed, their own serving people were a sorry lot, faithless, lazy, thieving, hard to come by and harder to keep. A hardworking, reliable domestic was "a jewel beyond price," the Vicksburg *American* observed in 1903. But "such are few and far between" and "at this time . . . almost impossible to secure."[27]

Most employers apparently saw no connection between the quality of their help and the compensation offered. Throughout the period, cooks or cleaning women were rarely paid more than five dollars a week, and sometimes as little as twenty-five cents a day. They worked six and often seven days a week, usually from early morning until at least late afternoon and sometimes until late at night. To make ends meet, as many white mistresses learned to their dismay, they often deserted their domestic chores at harvest season to pick cotton.[28] No doubt these hard-working women of the kitchen and laundry sometimes sincerely loved their white families.[29] Not a few took well-deserved pride in the centrality of their role in white lives. "I have worked for just two families since I was fourteen," eighty-seven-year-old Dinah Hayes of Vicksburg boasted to a WPA interviewer, "and I nursed for both of these and the children called me their black Mammie and I was." She planned and cooked their meals, supervised their play, counseled them and arbitrated their differences, bathed them, told them bedtime stories, and "scolded and whipped them, too, when they needed it": "I loved those children like they be mine."[30]

But if there was often black love and loyalty beyond measure there were also resentments, for service to others brought few rewards and usually required the neglect of one's own children and husband. Having spent a lifetime in white kitchens, nearly blind Nettie Rocket of Tate County recalled her antebellum childhood as a time of relative comfort and security. Her master's "niggers," as she remembered on the eve of World War II, "worked hard as mules," yet "I'd jest as soon be back in slavery as I am now, we have nothing and have to work so hard." White noblesse oblige notwithstanding, domestic workers typically found themselves all but destitute in old age. Harriet Sanders of Starkville, for example, "served many of the best families in the town," yet a Federal Writers' Project field worker noted in the late 1930s that she lived "in the usual condition of most all old negroes. Just existing, at the mercy of her grandchild and kindness of the city."[31]

Nor did the black serving class overlook the contrast in white and black circumstance. In the estimate of Anne Moody, who took her first job as chambermaid at the age of nine, "all white women had colored women working for them" because "they were lazy" and "because white women didn't know how" to care for their own families.[32] The same thought was expressed in a favorite Afro-American tune:

> Missus in de big house
> Mammy in de yard.
> Missus holdin' her white hands,
> Mammy workin' hard.[33]

The Artisans

A small and diminishing segment of the state's black nonfarm workers, nearly all of it male, pursued the skilled trades. Generally thought to be the sons and grandsons of antebellum mechanics, slave and free, these artisans were deeply feared and resented by the white craftsmen who eventually managed to force most of them down into the ever more narrowly defined category of "nigger work." Although Wharton believed them to be already in decline by 1890, black craftsmen still figured importantly in the labor force in 1900, particularly in the building trades. Alfred Holt Stone reported that blacks still dominated skilled labor in the Delta, though by 1908 he sensed an impending "tide of industrial ostracism." Whites, he noted, were increasingly less inclined to patronize black tradesmen, be they barbers or carpenters.[34] In Jackson, Meridian, Vicksburg, Natchez, and nearly every city of any size, enterprising black contractors, some of whom occasionally employed white workers, performed much of the construction work until World War I. But as one observer noted of Jackson early in the century, there was "a growing feeling against negro mechanics in general." "Lately, and particularly since the coming of Governor Vardaman," he wrote, "the thinking Negro has come to realize that conditions are changing somewhat, that the lines are being drawn closer." Only the city's rapid growth, and the resulting demand for skilled labor, seemed to mute the rising protest of white tradesmen against their black co-workers.[35] In 1912, Vicksburg blacks reported that white contractors who but a decade earlier had readily employed Negro skilled labor now generally used only workers of their own race. Black carpenters, masons, and plasterers, it was noted, "are losing because of prejudice."[36]

The fledgling labor union movement, never an important factor in the state until after World War II, moved in much the same direction. Briefly, in the late 1880s, a small but ambitious state assembly of the Knights of Labor recruited the workers of both races. At peak strength the organization could claim some 3,000 Mississippians in at least thirty-three locals, a large but unspecified majority of them rural blacks, principally timber workers. The Knights' public meetings were invariably segregated and the state's grand master workmen were white. But until the union's collapse early in 1890, some locals, including those in Moss Point, Vicksburg, and almost certainly Natchez, were biracial. From the outset, the organization in Mississippi was handicapped by strong antiunion and anti-Negro sentiment and never managed to overcome white reluctance to make common cause with blacks. "In the contest between economic interest and racial prejudice," one labor historian has written, "prejudice won, as usual."[37]

Early in the twentieth century, white bricklayers in at least Jackson and Vicksburg also joined black-dominated and black-led locals. These interracial experiments in organizing the building trades soon ended, however, when whites formed their own organizations and began bargaining for the exclusive favor of white contractors.[38] Following World War I, as whites grew increasingly apprehensive about black out-migration, black workers made modest gains along the relatively moderate Gulf Coast, where some dockworkers joined interracial but white-dominated longshoremen's locals and a relative handful of postal workers (in at least Pascagoula and Ocean Springs) formed independent black unions. Except for trainmen, black nonagricultural workers in the state were apparently otherwise unorganized.[39] Although evidence on the subject is scanty, it appears that they responded to the exclusionary practices of organized white workers, as Booker T. Washington advised, with antiunion sentiment of their own. When a Tougaloo official was asked to characterize the graduates of his institution's industrial departments, he boasted: "They do not join trades unions and find work with but little difficulty."[40] As time passed, the work got more difficult to find; but at least until the rise of the CIO, black Mississippians would take little part in whatever organized labor movement the state possessed.

As elsewhere in the South, black Mississippians at the end of the nineteenth century were distributed unevenly in the skilled trades. They were generally well represented in the older building trades. In 1890 they comprised roughly half of the state's 600-odd brick and stone masons, more than a third of its nearly 4,000 carpenters and joiners, and a fourth of its 600 painters and glaziers. Their position was even stronger in the traditional slave crafts, notably such declining occupations as shoemaking, wheelwrighting, and blacksmithing. Along the Gulf Coast, the race numbered importantly in the naval trades, as master boat and ship builders, caulkers, and steamboat engineers. Beginning with Gilbert Burton, who in 1869 became the first "colored captain" on the Mississippi coast, blacks also commanded schooners and barges on the Pearl River, the gulf sound, and Lake Ponchartrain — sometimes, apparently, with racially mixed crews. By 1900 one black Hancock County native, finding evidence of racial "harmony and progress in the superlative degree," counted nearly 100 Negro captains, "masters from stem to stern," engaged in the coastal carrying trade on some of the area's largest vessels.[41] For the moment blacks also still held a precarious corner on the barber trade. In the new occupations associated with construction they eventually set themselves up in modest numbers as plumbers,[42] but never succeeded in breaching the racially discriminatory apprenticing and licensing procedures required of electricians. They were excluded altogether from telegraphy and rarely found work as machinists, toolmakers, printers, and typesetters.

In the course of the next half century, as Table 5.4 illustrates, black artisans lost ground nearly everywhere. Some of this displacement can be traced to out-migration, which robbed the state of many talented workers, or to the technological innovations and inadequate industrial training that left other blacks marooned in rapidly obsolescing trades. But race lay at the center of the problem. The experience of Richard Wright was representative. Encouraged by a sympathetic northerner, the manager of the American Optical Company in Jackson, the future writer tried to break into the trade of lens grinding in the mid-1920s. His efforts were frustrated by white artisans who accepted him as a janitor but not as a fellow craftsman. When he pressed for the training his employer promised, white workmen taunted his ambition: "What are you trying to do, get smart nigger?" "Nigger, you think you're white, don't you?" "This is a white man's work around here." Relentlessly baited and threatened with death, Wright left the job and eventually the state.[43]

The Professionals

The law, by all accounts, was the most difficult profession for a black to follow. Until the 1960s the law school at the University of Mississippi, though supported by the taxes of both races, was open only to whites. Its graduates, since the first class of 1857, were automatically admitted to the state bar.[44] Black attorneys, and all others who would practice in the state, were admitted through examination. That handicap, however offensive, was initially minor, for well into the present

TABLE 5.4. Black Share of Selected Skilled Trades in Mississippi, 1890-1940.

Trade	1890	1920	1940
Carpenters	38%	31%	26%
Brick and stone masons	49	65	42
Painters and glaziers	25	26	25
Plumbers	—	23	25
Electricians	—	5	6
Printers and typesetters	7	5	2
Blacksmiths	45	32	38
Shoemakers	40	50	38
Barbers	74	37	25

century the aspiring lawyers of both races usually simply "read law" in the offices of established practitioners before undergoing examinations in open court. Although some were well educated in northern, Canadian, and even English universities, other black attorneys in Mississippi, like many of their white counterparts, were essentially self-taught. Before arriving in Mayersville in the 1870s, J. D. Ferrire had studied at Queens College, Oxford University, and practiced in the Inns of Court in London. On the other hand, John F. Harris, who practiced in Greenville during the last quarter of the nineteenth century, learned the law while pursuing his trade as carpenter. One contemporary said that "he carried a saw under one arm and a Mississippi Code under the other, and . . . when he was not doing carpenter work he was reading the Code."[45]

During Reconstruction blacks seem to have entered the profession as easily as whites, but the return of the conservatives was followed quickly by the adoption of more stringent and discriminatory procedures. In 1896, in a notable exception to standard practice, the elegant and widely respected John R. Lynch was admitted (at the age of nearly fifty) to the bar on his second attempt in a proceeding apparently without prejudice. By that date, however, less distinguished blacks were rarely treated so fairly; nor does it seem insignificant that Lynch himself promptly left the state to practice in the nation's capital. More typically, Samuel Alfred Beadle, though he prepared under the direction of one of Jackson's most prestigious white firms, was rebuffed by a judge who would not "examine niggers." Only through the intercession of his patron firm was Beadle later examined. After a meticulous grilling on the intricacies of Blackstone and much heckling by spectators, he was admitted in 1884.[46]

Despite increasingly discriminatory licensing procedures, Mississippi's black attorneys found reason for optimism down through the turn of the century. Numbering more than two dozen in 1890 (perhaps half of them located in Jackson), they formed the nation's first black state association of lawyers, the Colored Bar Association of Mississippi, marking, as one charter member thought, "the advent of the colored citizen into a new field of labor."[47] Some black attorneys reported generally good relations with white colleagues; a few were allowed to join otherwise all-white local bar associations, although the Mississippi State Bar Association was open only to whites. One of the most prominent, George F. Bowles of Natchez, was said to have "a large and lucrative practice, being supported by both races." M. M. McLeod of Jackson and Willis E. Mollison of Mayersville and Vicksburg, who served until 1892 as district attorney, also counted whites among their clients. The suave and articulate Samuel Beadle had an extensive civil practice and was general counsel for one of Hinds County's leading white cotton merchandisers until "hard-liners" during the Vardaman years persuaded the firm that the retainer was "too lucrative for a Negro."[48] That and other setbacks notwithstanding, the gamest of the black attorneys continued to believe into the twentieth century that the members of the black bar "were not merely civil rights lawyers . . . but have learned to handle white juries, and are winning their cases every day."[49]

In reality, however, the situation was anything but hopeful. After 1900 fair magistrates and impartial juries became notable exceptions. For a brief time, in Jackson, Natchez, and Vicksburg, lawyers of the race were still tolerated, but elsewhere a favorable verdict in nearly any case required temporary association with white counsel.[50] Some courts denied black lawyers the right to approach the bench or even to sit with the other attorneys inside the railings. Others permitted blacks to try cases, but only from the galleries. A growing number of judges excluded all Negroes from their courtrooms except as spectators, custodians, or defendants. It was, as one black lawyer was advised, simply "against the rules" for Negroes to appear as counsel in some courts. As one authority on the subject observed, black attorneys were increasingly handicapped by the "Vardaman influence" and those who were "resentful or quick to demand all the rights of a human being found it impossible to practice in the State."[51]

Black attorneys were also harassed by the state's white bar association in a series of apparently frivolous disbarment actions. Sidney D. Redmond was twice disbarred by Hinds County chancellors for "unethical conduct" and twice restored to the profession by the state supreme court. He remained in Mississippi after the second attempt in 1929 when a reported 30,000 blacks petitioned him not to leave. The same year, however, his son, Sidney Revels Redmond, grandson of the first black senator and a graduate of Harvard Law School, moved his law office to St. Louis following his suspension from practice in Mississippi.[52] Disbarment proceedings were pressed against Perry W. Howard, a former president of the National (Negro) Bar Association and one of the most celebrated black attorneys in the nation, after his first acquittal on federal charges of patronage abuse. The case was dismissed by the same Jackson judge who disallowed a similar action against W. L. Mhoon, Howard's political associate, after a committee of local white lawyers determined that his professional conduct had always been "humble and modest."[53]

Scarcely less than their black clients, Mississippi's black attorneys found the judicial system stacked against them. "We have faced unreasoning prejudice," Josiah T. Settle, one of the state's pioneer black lawyers and member of the state House of Representatives (1883-1885), reported about 1900. "We have found, not our clients, but ourselves on trial, and not ourselves alone, but the whole race with us."[54] More of a liability than an asset in court, black lawyers were left, as one said, with "only the crumbs of litigation."[55] They represented cases not involving white interests, often for black clients who could not afford the white attorneys they preferred. They handled the foreclosures and mortgages of a small and shrinking number of black banks; they performed such legal services as black benefit and fraternal organizations required. Few grew wealthy (and never as attorneys) and all suffered from the decline of the black fraternal insurance organizations and the collapse of black-owned banks. "My law practice has never amounted to much," conceded the multitalented Sidney D. Redmond, perhaps the state's richest black. "What I have acquired has been from the practice of medicine and transactions in real estate."[56] Similarly, Louis Kossuth Atwood of Jackson and Willis E. Mollison of Vicksburg made their modest fortunes in business, primarily banking and insurance, while Thomas Richardson of Port Gibson published a newspaper and served as village postmaster.[57] Those who could not otherwise support themselves joined the black exodus out of the state during and after World War I. By 1935 only five black attorneys remained (down from 24 in 1900), and as one of them, James A. Burns of Meridian, reported, "We are almost without clientele because they are saying that we can do them no good before the courts."[58] Beyond the personal hardships of the black attorneys themselves stood a much larger tragedy. For, as the often savage drama of the civil rights era would demonstrate, there could be no justice for blacks in a social order in which only whites could administer the law.[59]

Black physicians, dentists, and pharmacists, functioning as they did almost entirely within a separate black world, generally encountered less white hostility than their counterparts in law. If some white professionals accepted their responsibilities to serve the sick without regard to race or remuneration, others clearly preferred to practice only among their own people and were more than willing to share their impoverished black patients with Negro colleagues.[60] Yet until after 1890 there were few black health professionals in Mississippi; not until 1900 was there an association of black physicians, the Mississippi Medical and Surgical Association.[61] By 1930 there were seventy-one black doctors in the state, more than twice as many as in 1890. Thereafter, however, the number declined to fifty-five (five of them women) by 1940. Census enumerators in 1940 also counted twenty-nine black dentists (compared to five in 1900), and eleven black pharmacists.

Inevitably, perhaps, most of these black health professionals settled in the larger cities, where the bulk of the state's tiny black middle class was concentrated. Jackson, for example, had five black doctors in 1940; Greenville had four and Natchez three.[62] There were also black physicians from time to time in smaller communities, including Brookhaven, Clarksdale, Corinth, Greenwood, Holly Springs, Mound Bayou, Okolona, Starkville, and even in rural Claiborne County. On the eve of World War I, Laurel alone had six doctors (four of them apparently retired), a pharmacist, and two dentists.[63] Yet in a state with but one black doctor for roughly every 20,000 black people—the worst such ratio in the United States—medicine was perceived by both races as a white profession. As the reaction of an elderly Indianola woman suggests, the arrival of a "colored doctor" could be an extraordinary event in the life of nearly any town. "My God, what is dis here town coming to," she inquired in 1906, soon after Theodore Roosevelt's celebrated defense of a black federal office holder left that community in turmoil. "Dese white foks just now getting ober habing 'er nigger Postmaster and now here come 'er nigger Doctor—Did Ros'velt send 'm 'ere too?"[64]

The shortage of black health professionals was, and still remains, a nationwide problem. Yet Mississippi, despite its large black population, had substantially fewer black medical practitioners than its sister states of the lower South.[65] The reasons are multiple and include the absence of medical training facilities and the abject poverty of the nation's least advantaged Afro-Americans. But the evidence also points to what one federal study called a "policy of discouraging educated professional men among the negroes from coming to Mississippi." It was an article of faith in black medical circles that Mississippi examiners regularly failed black dentists and doctors—and particularly nonsoutherners—who were then admitted to practice in other states.[66]

Racial considerations generally also required black doctors to avoid sensitive causes and to maintain good relations with influential whites. Those with roots in the locality of their practice usually encountered little trouble. "Before I settled here no one had heard of a 'colored doctor,'" remembered a turn-of-the-century Macon physician. "The history of my parents who have always lived here helped to establish me." The same was true for the Natchez physicians James C. Mazique and William R. Johnson. Both were members of the city's "blue vein" mulatto aristocracy and Johnson was a descendant of its antebellum free black community.[67] An outsider, particularly one educated in a northern medical school, usually needed local white sponsors. Before locating in Greenville, said the daughter of a black practitioner, Negro doctors "had to get on the good side of a white man. . . . They had to have some white doctors vouch for them and say they were needed."[68] The committee of black businessmen who lured Dr. Douglas L. Conner to Starkville in 1951 first won the support of prominent whites. They "checked out the possibility of my coming with the town's white leadership," the Hattiesburg native recalled more than thirty years later. "I noticed how careful black leaders were to gain prior approval of whites for everything they did."[69] Those who lacked influential white support, scarcely less than those who dabbled in racial controversy, might find themselves banished. Recall, for example, the physician J. A. Miller, a graduate of Williams College and the University of Michigan, who was tarred and feathered and the dentist and pharmacist who fled for their lives from Vicksburg during World War I (see Chapter 1). Although Dr. Miller tried, as he said, never to "meddle in the white man's affairs . . . or complain at the many acts of lawlessness against my race," the northern-educated physician's sense of justice ultimately made him unacceptable to whites. White mobs also drove away black doctors they thought to be "too prosperous" or otherwise objectionable from at least Indianola (1903), Greenwood (1903), Laurel (c. 1915), and Meridian (1925).[70]

Whatever their relations with the dominant race, medicine was rarely a passport to wealth for Mississippi blacks. Those who prospered, as some clearly did, generally managed to do so through business activities unrelated to medicine.[71] Some black patients patronized black doctors out of racial pride as well as confidence in their training. But others doubted the skills of their own people. "The poor colored doctor didn't have a chance," a black Jacksonian remembered, "because we wouldn't feel like we had a doctor unless he was white." Black practitioners often complained that Negroes who could pay for their services usually saw white physicians, leaving them too often with poverty cases. Although Dr. J. A. Miller reported that his practice earned more than $5,000 in 1918, Dr. Conner's experience was apparently more typical. Initially the young Starkville physician's patients were largely from "the lowest socioeconomic class." They were "most appreciative of my services," he thought, but few could afford a three-dollar appointment and "some would bring in corn, potatoes, peas, peanuts, or chickens." Noting that Starkville's black middle class continued to prefer white doctors, Dr. Conner concluded that one of the legacies of "slavery and later discrimination" was the black tendency to assume that "if something is done by a white person it is done better."[72]

The black physician's professional prestige and income also suffered from the white-only policies of most hospitals. Except for black-owned clinics, Dr. G. S. Tanner of Brookhaven complained in 1934, "there are no hospitals in the state of Mississippi . . . in which colored physicians may treat patients." Typically, until he founded the state's first small black-owned hospital (1907), the surgeon Lloyd T. Miller of Yazoo City operated in his office, even on his patients' kitchen tables. In the 1930s, Dr. L. L. Rayford of Holly Springs, on the other hand, protested Mississippi's exclusion of black health-care professionals by sending his patients to Memphis hospitals. By 1940, although black patients were treated in the "colored wings" of some "white" hospitals, the state's fifty-five black doctors could use only the sixty-five beds found in small black-owned infirmaries and in a privately operated black facility at Yazoo City, the Afro-American Sons and Daughters Hospital. A second black hospital, the modern, forty-two-bed Taborian Hospital in Mound Bayou (known as Delta Community Hospital after 1967) was completed in 1942. During World War II whites temporarily blocked the construction in Mound Bayou of a federal hospital for black veterans, though it was later approved by President Harry S Truman in 1947.[73]

The primary victims of Jim Crow medicine, however, were not black doctors but black patients. Numbering among the nation's most medically deprived and unhealthy people,[74] black Mississippians knew little of either doctors or hospitals. In 1937 alone, more than 3,000 of them died without any medical care whatsoever, much less hospitalization. In the Delta, where some 70 percent of the state's large black population has concentrated, even tax-supported hospitals by 1940 still admitted only white surgery cases; no hospital in the state provided orthopedic surgery for blacks. Per 1,000 population, Mississippi blacks by 1940 had only 0.7 hospital beds compared to 2.4 for whites. A disproportionate number of those few black beds were to be found in state-owned hospitals, all of them in the southern half of the state. Blacks who could afford hospitalization often chose institutions in Memphis, New Orleans, or Mobile.[75]

If Mississippi had a golden age of black journalism it was during the half century after 1890. In this period from Reconstruction through World War I, well over 100 general-purpose weeklies and several score religious and fraternal organs were published in the state by and for Afro-Americans. For a brief time Mississippi also had a Negro Press Association, which in 1919 reportedly represented thirty-seven newspapers.[76] Had even a representative sampling of this potential mother lode of black lore survived, the record would be immeasurably richer. Tragically, all but a very few scattered issues are lost, forcing those who would know the history of Mississippi's black newspapers to depend heavily on less immediate sources.

The first black newspaper in Mississippi seems to have been the Vicksburg *Colored Citizen,* established in 1867. That short-lived enterprise was followed by the Canton *Citizen* in 1869, the Jackson *Field Hand* apparently in 1870, and many others, making Mississippi by the end of the nineteenth century one of the centers of Afro-American journalism.[77] Nearly all of these papers were transitory endeavors, lasting from but a single fugitive issue to only a half dozen or so. The Jackson *People's Journal* was among the sturdiest. Formed in 1877 and soon reorganized as the *People's Adviser* and then as the *People's Defender,* this newspaper, in all of its forms, survived perhaps five years, though its publication was not continuous.[78]

After 1890 the mortality rate improved slightly, and although few weeklies survived as long as a year or two, some were remarkably long-lived. The Greenville *Delta Light House,* edited by J. C. Chapple from its founding in 1896 until his death in 1919, may have operated through the 1920s; it seems unlikely, however, that its publication was continuous during this extended period of some three decades.[79] The Natchez *Weekly Reporter,* organized early in the twentieth century and reportedly "one of the outstanding publications of its kind," appeared more or less regularly for a quarter century and may once have had a circulation of 1,500 copies.[80] The Mound Bayou *Demonstrator,* founded in 1900 and published fairly continuously for perhaps fifteen years, boasted a circulation of 4,000 copies in 1912.[81] These achievements were apparently not equaled until the appearance of such relatively large and stable papers as the Greenville *Delta Leader* (established 1929) and the Jackson *Advocate* (established 1938).[82] Until World War I, the turnover was such that as rapidly as one paper failed another seemed to emerge. Thereafter, however, the number of new publications declined sharply. Though it still led all southern states except Texas, Mississippi by 1943 accounted for only six of the nation's 144 active general-purpose black newspapers; by 1945 there were only three.[83]

Many of the casualties could be attributed to undercapitalization and the journalistic and business inexperience of their publishers. The high failure rate, as John Roy Lynch saw it, had two sources: "First, the poverty and illiteracy prevailing among the blacks, and, secondly, the inferiority of the papers published as mediums of news."[84] In the twentieth century, all suffered from the heavy out-migration of subscribers and from the increasing competition of widely circulated northern race papers. Not least, the state's black weeklies succumbed for want of sufficient advertisers, the lifeblood of commercial journalism. Yet nearly every Mississippi community of any size supported at least one newspaper, if only briefly, and while these journals lasted they at least partially filled what can only be called a raging hunger for race news.

Black newspapers, like many of the state's black enterprises, were born of exclusion, of an increasingly rigid racial separatism that forced the Afro-American community inward to develop its own parallel institutions. By 1940 a very few white newspapers carried "Negro pages" or "colored columns" written by blacks and devoted to the local social and religious activities of the race. Hodding Carter's *Delta Democrat-Times* even occasionally printed pictures of accomplished blacks, a breach of racial etiquette that provoked much hostility. But most white newspapers still honored the Jim Crow custom of reporting black news largely only when it involved crime.[85] National or international developments with implications unflattering to blacks were often carefully covered, but these stories were widely discounted by black Mississippians who refused to see their race through white eyes. Not remarkably, then, race papers from Chicago, Indianapolis, New York, Pittsburgh, and Washington, D.C., generally smuggled in by Pullman porters, were passed from hand to hand until they fell apart. Local vendors quickly exhausted their supplies and in Greenville alone one black youth reported that he quietly distributed 500 copies of the Chicago *Defender* every week. "Negroes grab the Chicago *Defender*," one black said, "like a hungry mule grabs fodder." Nearly every literate black was thought to read a black newspaper; by one account, "even the sharecroppers are subscribers."[86]

During his early years in Clarksdale prior to World War I, W. C. Handy supplemented his musical earnings by what he called the "risky business" of selling northern race publications, an enterprise "looked upon with strong disfavor by certain of the local powers."[87] Although Handy's brisk trade in forbidden literature went undetected, other vendors were less fortunate. In 1919, a young woman in Yazoo City had to flee for her life for the same activity, and in Tchula and Indianola after World War I whites "mercilessly flogged" blacks even for possessing the *Defender* and the NAACP's *Crisis*.[88] Alarmed by the free flow of information, and particularly of civil rights literature, the state legislature in 1920 made it a misdemeanor "to print or publish or circulate" materials "favoring social equality."[89] That gesture notwithstanding, the race paper "rage," as some called it, continued through World War II. By 1929, one fearful black accommodationist exaggerated, 100,000 copies of "the radical Chicago *Defender*" entered the state every week, "doing inestimable harm" and putting "pernicious ideas" into black heads.[90] Not until well into the 1930s, and then only in the larger cities, could blacks openly possess northern race newspapers.

In the competition with these Yankee publications the local black press was severely handicapped. The New York *Age* or the Indianapolis *Freeman* could speak to racial concerns which no black Mississippi editor could touch. To their credit some of the early Mississippi pioneers, as Irvine Garland Penn wrote nearly a century ago, were "fluent and fearless," "noble reflector[s] of Afro-American sentiment." William E. King, who began publishing the Meridian *Fair Play* in 1889, was said to be dedicated to "equal rights and fair play . . . for every American citizen, without regard to race or color."[91] The editors of some early Mississippi weeklies, including the Jackson *Colored Citizen,* the Meridian *Fair Play,* and the Natchez *Brotherhood,* asserted black political and civil rights and heatedly denounced the constitution of 1890 for its discriminatory suffrage provisions.[92]

In the twentieth century, however, as white racism intensified, black editors increasingly and necessarily became more circumspect. Many of them were apparently captives of whites, either because they published their journals on the presses of white newspapers or because they merely edited "black papers" that were in fact owned and wholly controlled by white businessmen.[93] Even the freest was anything but free: "Juggling torches in a powder magazine," black columnist George S. Schuyler believed, was child's play "compared to editing a newspaper for Negroes in Mississippi." Forced to be all things to all people, the black editor had the difficult task of attracting and holding black readers while avoiding, in Schuyler's words, "nine-tenths of the real news and practically all of the possible topics crying for comment."[94]

In truth, the extant fragments of the black press permit little more than conjecture, but if what remains is representative, the typical black editor was most punctilious: "In racial matters," Aurelius P. Hood said of the Mound Bayou newspaper he edited, the *Demonstrator* "has resolutely declined to cater to the truculent disposition of either side." While this weekly advocated black aspiration, as this editor believed, with "force and dignity," it was never "deluded into the policy of insisting on the practical realization of visionary or impossible conditions." Hood was doubtless more cautious than some, yet his formula for survival has the ring of broad applicability. The publishers of Mississippi's black weeklies substituted conciliation for the combative tone of many northern race papers, frequently reprinting white editorials, sometimes chiding the mistakes of their own people, often praising southern whites for their friendship and cooperation.[95] Some encouraged their patrons to support black enterprise, but even this required tact, for as we shall see, white merchants did not gladly compete with black shopkeepers for the profitable black trade. Like other American country newspapers, their pages were largely devoted to society news, to the doings of church, school, and fraternal groups, to boosterism and community pride.[96]

On balance, then, black journalists after 1890 were conservative realists who understood that white supremacy in Mississippi was a settled issue. Those who expected to survive did not engage in racial controversy. What Greenville writer David Cohn said of one black editor could be said of many others: "There was nothing biggity about him like there is about some educated Nigras, and he got the cooperation of the better element of the white people when they saw he wasn't smart-alecky and started printing the right kind of editorials." Yet, if Mississippi's twentieth-century black editors and publishers exercised a prudent self-censorship, if they were not social crusaders openly agitating for full citizenship for their people, they nevertheless played useful, even vital, roles in their communities. They could not compete in militance with the *Crisis* or the *Defender,* yet their weeklies were organs of racial uplift and black pride. Ready symbols of black literacy and economic achievement to a people who had too little of either, the editors of the state's race papers served as the black town criers: they informed, they encouraged, they advocated, they celebrated their race; they presented black news in a favorable light; they mirrored the concerns of a public that the white press alternately disparaged and ignored. "We are trying to saturate them," one editor said of his readers, "with a realization of the fact that the thrifty, intelligent, well-behaved negro does count."[97]

To try to do more, to advocate racial justice more directly, invited white disfavor and worse. The fate of Eugene N. Bryant, editor of the Brookhaven *People's Relief,* seemed to await other black editors who overstepped themselves on or off the job. Accused of "dabbling in politics" and "stirring up race hatred"—primarily by reprinting editorials from northern race papers—Bryant was ordered out of this Piney Woods community in 1910. Immediately after his flight, a mob led by members of the police force burned his home and press and then, months later, five of his rental houses. Not content with this action, local authorities followed him to Jackson and had him arrested for "criminal libel." His case was ultimately dropped, apparently when a lynching seemed unavoidable.[98]

Bryant's example was not unique, for other black papers were closed when their publishers incurred white indignation.[99] Yet the black press was normally kept in line by means other than violence. An errant editor might be run out of town, but more frequently he was brought to terms by a harsh word from the white community. In Jackson, for instance, Fred Sullens, fire-eating white editor of the *Daily News,* played the role of unofficial censor to the black press, marshaling white indignation and lashing his black counterparts into compliance with not-so-veiled threats of white retribution. In 1931, when the Jackson *Southern Register,* a weekly that had earlier distinguished itself by publishing Richard Wright's first story (1924), seemed too critical of race discrimination, Sullens rebuked the editor, Malcolm D. Rogers, for expressing views "calculated to inspire race violence."[100] During the Second World War, Sullens also threatened Percy Greene, editor and publisher of the Jackson *Advocate,* when the black journalist called for equal educational opportunity and state compliance with federal court rulings banning all-white primaries. Unless Greene mended his editorial ways, Sullens warned, he would be visited by "racial trouble" that "won't contribute to his health or well-being." When black community leaders rallied to Greene's defense, the *Daily News* responded that they too must toe the color line or suffer the consequences of white wrath.[101]

If the work of white censorship was made easier by attrition in the black press, the future for the First Amendment was nevertheless brighter than the past. For the moment, and for some years to come, white control was all but absolute. Yet by 1945 the generation was already born that in early adulthood would witness—through the often shockingly intemperate pages of the *Daily News* if it chose—the unfolding of a new social order in which blacks even in Mississippi could exercise their fundamental American rights of free speech and press.

The Entrepreneurs

To many observers, not least of all to the state's small but exuberant class of black businessmen, Mississippi in the years from 1890 to World War I seemed to lead all states in the development of Afro-American enterprise. In his 1911 celebration of the black entrepreneur, *Beacon Lights of the Race,* the Tennessee writer G. P. Hamilton found Mississippi "unapproachable in the [black] business and financial world." No state, he thought, had "produced a greater percentage of the eminent men of the race," and in no other state had "the race made such marvelous progress along material lines."[102] In 1908, following a six-day trip through Mississippi with Booker T. Washington, another deeply impressed Afro-American reported that contrary to his expectations, he did not find black Mississippians beaten or bowed. He found instead "people with their heads up, determined and in high spirits." "It was a novel thing," he thought, "to see colored people doing their own banking, owning dry good stores and grocery stores and real estate businesses in the way that these Mississippi Negroes do." According to the editor of the New York *Age,* blacks in Connecticut, Massachusetts, New York, and Chicago could not equal the progress of black enterprise in Mississippi.[103]

As these glowing reports often noted, black Mississippians during this period could boast not only of small retail and service establishments—cafes, juke houses, mortuaries, and fly-by-night shops—but of a number of major Afro-American entrepreneurial firsts: the first black-owned legal reserve life insurance company, said at one time to be the "largest negro insurance company in the world"; "the world's only" black-owned cottonseed oil mill; the "only large book store" owned by a black American; and more black-owned banks than any other state in the union.[104]

The apparent vitality of the state's black commercial life was also reflected in its statewide branch of the National Negro Business League (NNBL), the first and, proud black Mississippians justifiably thought, the "most potent" and "most progressive" state Negro Business League in the nation. With a "ladies confederation" and at least thirty more or less active local chapters of the Tuskegee-inspired black chamber of commerce, the state league fostered "a feeling of commercial brotherhood among the negro businessmen in every town and city in the state." By 1910 the organization reportedly represented "bankers, business and professional men whose capital exceeded five millions of dollars," more "Negro capital" than could be assembled anywhere else in the United States.[105] Black Mississippians also occupied many of the most important offices in the NNBL—and in such subsidiary organizations as the National Negro Bankers' Association, the National Negro Bar Association, the National Negro Retail Merchants Association, and the National Association of Negro Insurance Men. Not surprisingly, then, the NNBL at its ninth annual meeting in Louisville in 1909 sponsored "Mississippi Day," an unprecedented tribute to the Deep South capitalists who had shown the race "How to Succeed."[106]

Now all but forgotten, turn-of-the-century black capitalism in Mississippi—although severely handicapped from the outset by black poverty and dependence and never as robust as its boosters believed—represented a promising example of what Du Bois called the "group economy." Denied a place in the mainstream and yet deeply influenced by the values of an expanding commercial and industrial order, enterprising Afro-Americans in growing numbers sought wealth and respectability in an exclusively black economy. To be sure, the wheels of black commerce were not greased by altruism alone, but the group economy found its motive force not merely in the black merchant's desire to monopolize black trade but in a gospel of progress through separate development, in a renewed faith in the doctrines of group solidarity, self-help, and black pride. Briefly, if too simply put, as hope for civil equality dimmed, blacks turned gradually from political to economic arenas where they might, as Booker T. Washington had counseled, "take advantage of the disadvantages" of Jim Crow.[107]

In Mississippi, where black disadvantages were legion, middle-class Afro-Americans embraced the hopeful ideals of racial solidarity and self-help with an enthusiasm remarkable even for the age. By 1889, the black merchants of Natchez had created what they dared hope to be a "southern El Dorado," a model business community distinguished by more black "go-aheadativeness" and "more energetic and enterprising colored men" than could be found anywhere else in the South.[108] In 1899, Vicksburg's black leaders reported more businesses capitalized at above $500 than any other Mississippi town.[109] In Jackson, few black merchants competed for the profits of the Negro market until after 1890. By 1908, however, there were more than 100 race enterprises, including two banks, four pharmacies, two realty companies, a theater, and a bakery that alone grossed $30,000 annually. Farish Street, heart of the black commercial district, the *Clarion-Ledger* reported, was "one of the more progressive, growing business streets in the capital city." By one account, black Jacksonians owned one-third of the city's municipal land area and one-quarter of its real-estate assets. In this wildly optimistic estimate, half of the city's black families owned their homes, and two-thirds of all housing occupied by blacks was black-owned. Caught up in the roseate dreams of separate development, many black Jacksonians accepted an outsider's description of their community as an "oasis in the desert of the South," where the "wonderful progress" of the Afro-American's "splendid business establishments" promised the eventual "dethronement of race discrimination."[110]

Elsewhere—in all-black Mound Bayou and tiny Indianola, along Greenville's flourishing Nelson Street, Clarksdale's Fourth and Issaquena Streets, and Hattiesburg's Mobile Street, indeed in nearly every town of any size—there seemed to be similar evidence, as one black business leader put it, that Mississippi blacks were no longer "backward in coming forward."[111] In fact, the race appeared to have come so far so fast that in 1915 a visiting black Ohioan, apparently all but intoxicated by the spirit of race progress he encountered in the state, predicted that within another quarter century blacks would own 75 percent of the farmland and half of the businesses in Mississippi. "No legislation and no proscription or restriction," he thought, "can stop these Mississippi Afro-Americans."[112]

The most conspicuous and as it developed the most fragile symbols of black enterprise in Mississippi were the thirteen banks organized between 1902 and 1911.[113] Products of the needs of black fraternal and burial societies for depositories and of black businessmen for credit, these institutions operated more often on race pride than on sound business practices. Founded in a period of virtually no state banking regulation, they competed gamely with stronger white institutions and eventually succumbed to inexperience, undercapitalization, overexpansion, and racial antipathy. Like their black counterparts elsewhere in the South, their deposits were numerous but small and their business rarely of the commercial or industrial kind. Because black borrowers usually had little collateral except real estate, they were generally overcommitted to unproductive and illiquid investments. Lacking facilities to clear their own commercial paper, they were routinely dependent on the stronger local white banks they used as correspondents and depositories. In the end they were doomed, like the group economy itself, by the extreme poverty of their clientele.[114]

For a time these deficiencies were obscured by the organization of a Mississippi Negro Bankers' Association (1907) and the apparent success of even the more marginal institutions. For example, the American Trust and Savings Bank, the oldest of two black banks in Jackson, was organized in 1906 with paid-in capital of only $2,700. Yet in its first two years it reported earnings of 23 percent and 29 percent, "the largest dividend," one officer exalted, "earned and paid in . . . Mississippi, where Mr. Vardaman wields the scepter of state and sometimes shapes the destinies of men."[115] Similarly, the Union Savings Bank of Vicksburg opened in 1905 in a hotel basement and served its first customers over a packing crate. Despite almost universal doubts about its viability, and (by 1906) the competition of at least twelve other local banks, it survived the panic of 1907, moved into "commodious" quarters, and in 1908 claimed total resources of nearly $60,000.[116] By that date black banking assets in the state, having nearly doubled five years in succession, approached $750,000, proof, the Mississippi Negro Bankers' Association affirmed, that black banking had passed "the experimental stage."[117] Some white Mississippians, some black contemporaries believed, were so impressed by black financial acumen that they deposited their own funds in black-owned institutions. "Money is almost wholly color blind," Vicksburg banker Willis E. Mollison reported of his Lincoln Savings

Bank. "We have many white depositors, and white borrowers have to be kept off with a club." Such progress seemed all the more promising because it came even as white racial demogoguery escalated. "We are chartered," the president of the Bank of Mound Bayou boasted, "by Governor Vardaman, who, not so much because of kindly feelings towards the members of our race, but mainly because of the indomitable perseverance of the Mississippi Negro, has been forced to sign more charters for negro banks than any other man in the world, living or dead."[118]

But perseverance soon bowed to disaster as nine black institutions perished in a prewar flood of more than 100 Mississippi bank failures. During the severe recession of 1914 the newly organized state banking department closed three other Negro banks, including the Bank of Mound Bayou, leaving the Delta Penny Savings Bank of Indianola— once said to be "the second largest Negro bank in the world"—as the only surviving black facility.[119] For the most part these liquidations, black and white, were attributable to market fluctuations and an over-extended and unsupervised banking industry: quite simply, the weaker ships went down in the economic storms of 1907 and 1914. Black businessmen, however, had reason to complain of the "unwarranted hostility" of elected bank examiners who, under Mississippi's first comprehensive banking act, "did not intend to qualify any . . . colored banks." White Mississippians, as Charles Banks, the state's leading black banker wrote, "think there are some things to which we should not aspire." The banking reform act of 1914, he believed, was "specially framed to eliminate and wipe out any institution the authorities desired." Yet, though required to meet standards higher than those of comparable white institutions, the Mound Bayou bank reopened on October 1915.[120] That same year Delta Penny of Indianola kept its warrant, despite the blatant opposition of state banking officials, by securing the endorsement of two white banks and meeting criteria, as one examiner reportedly conceded, "doubly as rigid as for any other bank in the state." No other black banks were ever chartered and these last two institutions went under in the agricultural crisis of the 1920s.[121]

In symbolic terms, at least, the collapse of black banking was a major blow to the group economy in Mississippi. Widely regarded as evidence of race progress, these institutions seemed to promise eventual independence from white control. In more practical dollars-and-cents terms, however, the very marginality of the black banks surely diminished the impact of their demise. It seems too much to claim, as one scholar has, that the closure of black-owned banks figured importantly in the decline of black landownership.[122] Yet, ill-equipped though these struggling institutions were to meet the capital requirements of black agricultural and business interests, the black bank failures—combined with the color-conscious lending policies of white bankers—further disadvantaged the parallel economy. Although the problem demands further research, the available record suggests that during the segregation years Mississippians of both races took it for granted, once the black banks folded, that anyone could be a bank depositor but only whites could expect bank loans. Of course, the wealthiest blacks, like their white counterparts, had established lines of credit at some banks. And some, including the Farish Street business and professional leader S. D. Redmond, held stocks in several white banks. The average black business, however, rarely if ever borrowed from these lending facilities. "No credit was available to any black business," Jackson undertaker Clarie Collins Harvey recalled in 1981, "and that even continues to a large degree today." In 1941, leading black Jacksonians formed the Hinds County Educational Federal Credit Union (the first such black institution in Mississippi) because, as one of the principal investors reported, "blacks could not get credit at white institutions." In black-belt counties, at least, the very idea of borrowing money from a bank seemed ludicrous to many black farmers. "Couldn't get no money outa no bank," Clinton Anderson of Houston remembered. "Shit, a nigger just can't go in no bank and ask for it. . . . I never did see no Negro in no bank. He just borrow it from the private folks."[123]

The largest single black enterprise in the state was the Mississippi Life Insurance Company, the nation's first black legal reserve company.[124] Like other Afro-American businesses of its type, Mississippi Life could trace its early success to the discriminatory policies of white insurance companies and its institutional roots to black burial and mutual-benefit societies and fraternal orders. In the first years of freedom white companies generally insured both races on equal terms. After 1880, however, ostensibly because of higher black mortality rates, most companies either refused to write black policies or did so at higher premiums. Blacks thereupon turned to their own institutions, first to the often improvident mutual aid or fraternal assessment societies, and then after 1900 to the more businesslike black legal reserve companies.

Among the precommercial mutual assistance organizations, the sums involved were often small. Local "coffin clubs" and church-related aid societies, some of which operated until the end of the period, collected occasional assessments and monthly dues of as little as ten to fifteen cents and paid modest burial and health claims to a few dozen members.[125] The benefit departments of the large multilodge secret orders, however, were often substantial undertakings; between 1870 and 1920, the heyday of the benevolent lodge, some fifty different Mississippi orders distributed a total of $16 million in health and death benefits. The oldest black fraternal order in Mississippi, the Most Worshipful Stringer Grand Lodge of Free and Accepted Masons, formed its endowment department in 1880. By 1905, the 7,000-member Masonic Benefit Association had paid claims totalling more than $500,000, boasted substantial cash assets, and owned 1,000 acres of Delta timberland. "Governor Vardaman and all the other devils this side of Hades," the Grand Master Mason believed, "cannot stay this kind of progress." The state's largest order, the Grand United Order of Odd Fellows, organized its insurance division in 1897 and within a decade claimed 23,000 members. Before its dissolution in the 1920s, some five years after the failure of the Masonic benefit department, the Odd Fellows Benefit Association distributed $8 million in sick and death claims.[126]

Much the same could be said of the "colored" Pythians, Elks, and Woodmen, or the Brothers and Sisters of Love and Charity, the Sacred Order of Perfection, the Fishermen of the Red Cross Relief, the Lone Star Race Pride, and several dozen other orders. All functioned for a time as insurance societies; a few, including the Afro-American Sons and Daughters and the Knights and Daughters of Tabor, continued to write small industrial (weekly premium) policies as late as World War II. Most, however, survived after 1920 as social rather than insurance institutions. Always more than business organizations, black lodges, with their secret rituals, pagentry, and colorful regalia, were among the most important agencies of black social and cultural uplift, providing welcome opportunities for pleasure and leadership and strengthening the black sense of community. But after World War I, when the lodges failed to meet their claims and lost their insurance customers to the more systematized commercial companies, their role as mutual benefit societies declined sharply.[127]

Under the most favorable circumstances, assessment insurance was high-risk enterprise. Operating without actuarial data, unable either to establish rates scientifically or select risks according to age or health, Mississippi's benevolent orders, like assessment societies generally, depended on irregular imposts and lapsed policies to meet their claims. In the competition for new members most offered larger death benefits than monthly collections warranted.[128] Often a disproportionate share of all expenditures, nearly 50 percent in some cases, went for administrative purposes, largely officer salaries. Factional warfare, election irregularities, and financial scandals were widespread. Allison Davis thought that embezzlement was common throughout the state's black lodges, and an investigator for several secret orders found graft to be the "fairly general practice" of Delta fraternal officials. An officer of a large Adams County secret order noted that "the president owns the society; he organized it and has been president of it for 25 years, and he can take all the money he wants and nobody can stop him."[129] That such depredations also occurred in parallel white institutions neither mitigated their ruinous effect nor slowed the drift of black Mississippians to more reliable commercial insurers.

If the decline of the fraternals was a blow to black esteem, it was cushioned by the remarkable success of Mississippi Life. Founded in 1908 by Dr. W. A. Attaway and Wayne Wellington Cox as Mississippi Beneficial Insurance Company, the Indianola firm was originally authorized to write only industrial policies on weekly installments of as little as five cents. In 1910 it was recapitalized (at $100,000) and rechartered as a legal reserve company licensed to write the full range of health and life policies. As Merah Steven Stuart, its first professionally competent general manager has written, the little company's early years were anything but promising. Vexed by "poorly trained" officers, "absconding agents," overdue claims, recurrent "talk of dissolution," and poor risk selection, it somehow survived—Stuart thought to the "amazement and puzzled concern" of the dominant race—until 1916, when it came under the able direction of Stuart and its third president, Dr. Joseph Edison Walker. During World War I it expanded into Alabama, Arkansas, and Tennessee, thereby tripling its annual premium income. By 1919, as the company prepared to relocate in Memphis, Mississippi Life had an annual income of more than $500,000 and a staff of 400.[130] The Sunflower *Tocsin,* a white weekly not otherwise lavish in its praise of black achievement, thought it to be "a decided factor" in the business life of the county and "the largest negro insurance company in the world, and the most reliable." (In fact, though Mississippi Life could be called the "Negro's foremost mid-South firm" in 1919, it was overshadowed regionally by North Carolina Mutual of Durham and perhaps three other black insurance companies.)[131]

White acclaim notwithstanding, much of Mississippi Life's success and indeed its very foundation can be traced to negrophobia. Having fled Indianola for their lives during the Vardaman-Roosevelt post office affray in 1901-1903, the company's principal investors, Wayne Cox and his wife Minnie (the deposed postmistress) returned in 1904, remodeled their home in an otherwise all-white neighborhood, expanded their considerable agricultural holdings, and organized first the Delta Penny Savings Bank and then, four years later, Mississippi Life. Both enterprises, a business associate believed, owed their existence to "Vardamanism" and a black businessman's refusal to be intimidated by the mob spirit; both were viewed by Cox as "monuments of protest" to white injustice. Driven by the "haunting fear" that the insurance company might fall under white control, Cox pointedly reminded Mississippi Life employees, as Stuart remembered, that "they were . . . building . . . an enterprise that might stand through the ages as a credit to the ability of Negroes." Prospective customers were encouraged to patronize an "insurance company of their own."[132]

Company representatives also effectively exploited the everyday discourtesies, the arrogance and "imagined superiority" of competing white agents. Indeed, Mississippi Life's best asset was white ill will. Much of its growth was tied to white malefactions: the harassment of company representatives by police and vigilantes; the open hostility of the state insurance commissioner who repeatedly threatened to withdraw its license; the discovery of a white agent's collection book at the scene of a lynching. During World War I, authorities in Corinth, Meridian, Wiggins, and no doubt other communities warned company agents that they would be in violation of local "work-or-fight" ordinances if they sold insurance.[133] As every black insurance man knew, such acts heightened the group consciousness and strengthened the racial solidarity upon which the business thrived.

Yet if white animus had its short-term uses it also had long-term dangers. In Stuart's discreet explanation, Mississippi Life simply towered "too spectacularly" over the business life of a tiny Deep South agricultural community for "comfort and security." T. J. Johnson, the friend and biographer of president J. E. Walker, attributed the company's decision to leave the state to "the evils of racial prejudice plus the ambitious dream of expansion." Accustomed to illiterate field hands and compliant domestics, white Indianolans, as Johnson noted, "misunderstood" and "mistreated" the educated, well-dressed, self-assured black clerical workers who made up the growing office staff. "As rapidly as they came, just as rapidly did the racial tension in the little village increase." The company's female employees complained of white sexual harassment on city streets.[134]

In 1920 the firm left Mississippi for presumably more hospitable Beale Street only to lose its identity soon thereafter in a confounding series of mergers. Forced out in a dispute with other officers, Dr. Walker left the company in 1923 and organized Universal Life Insurance Company of Memphis. Cox's widow thereupon sold controlling interest in Mississippi Life to the black-owned Standard Life Insurance Company of Atlanta, which was almost immediately absorbed by the white-owned Southern Life Insurance Company of Nashville. To the immense relief of uncounted race-proud Mississippians, however, Southern Life promptly folded and the policies and assets of Mississippi Life were assigned by the Tennessee insurance commission to Walker's new firm. The transfer, an exuberant former Mississippi Life official believed, was "the largest and most important . . . in the history of that race." In effect, the Cox insurance empire lived on under the direction of the late Indianola banker's most talented associate, Joseph E. Walker, who within a decade made his Memphis-based firm one of the nation's largest black insurance companies.[135]

The Mound Bayou Proposition

Promising though their early business ventures often were, the black Mississippians' most striking enterprise was not a bank or an insurance company but the town of Mound Bayou. Founded in 1887 by Isaiah T. Montgomery and Benjamin T. Green, his cousin and fellow freedman, the Bolivar County community was at once a black refuge in a hostile white world and a laboratory of the group economy. Its remote origins, as Janet Hermann has demonstrated, could be traced to the communitarian doctrines of the Scottish visionary Robert Owen and to the idealism of Joseph Emory Davis, the older brother of Jefferson Davis and benevolent slave master who dreamed with his favored man-servant, Benjamin Thornton Montgomery, of founding a slave "community of cooperation" that would be both profitable and just. More directly, Mound Bayou represented the rebirth of General Ulysses S. Grant's "Negro paradise," the doomed wartime experiment in land reform at Davis Bend, and of its successor, the postwar black agricultural colony operated until 1886 at the former Davis plantations on the Mississippi River by Montgomery and Sons, the firm owned by Benjamin T. and his two sons, William Thornton and Isaiah.

Yet Mound Bayou can best be described as a self-conscious experiment in race building, an attempt by Isaiah, the most idealistic of the nation's black town founders, to realize the promise of racial uplift through industry, thrift, self-help, and economic solidarity.[136] From its foundation, the village prided itself on its exclusivity: "Not a single white person resides or owns property within its limits," Montgomery boasted. "Everything here was Negro," Benjamin A. Green, the first native-born Mound Bayouan, remembered of his childhood, "from the symbols of law and authority and the man who ran the bank down to the fellow who drove the road scraper. That gave us kids a sense of security and power and pride that colored kids don't get anywhere else." Town leaders called it the "Jewel of the Delta," "the negro capital of

Mississippi," the "most famous negro town in America." To its founders and to successive generations of citizens Mound Bayou was not merely a town but a showcase of black achievement, "a star of promise in the horizon of a race struggling upward."[137]

Nor did that judgment seem extravagant to others. In 1907 President Theodore Roosevelt called Mound Bayou "an object lesson full of hope for the colored people." Two decades later, despite mounting evidence to the contrary, Mary McLeod Bethune still believed it to be a "demonstration station" of black progress.[138] Booker T. Washington, who repeatedly described the town as a "school" and an "inspiration," took a special interest in the community, procuring funds for its development from such northern philanthropists as Andrew Carnegie, Collis P. Huntington, and Julius Rosenwald. The Tuskegean was allied both personally and through the National Negro Business League with Montgomery and the town's other leading citizen, Charles Banks.[139]

In retrospect, as August Meier has noted, the community's reputation probably rested less on the vigor of its economy than on the celebrity of its first citizens and the close ties they kept with Tuskegee and northern money.[140] Yet until World War I, Mound Bayou was something of a boomtown. Sustained and surrounded by a larger agricultural colony of some 4,000 people and perhaps 30,000 acres, the village by 1890 was a thriving cotton center of some 600 inhabitants with a town hall and depot, plank sidewalks, well-graded and lighted streets, a half dozen churches, public and parochial schools, a telephone exchange and utilities company, a newspaper, and more than forty businesses encompassing "nearly every necessity of the retail and supply trade." Montgomery believed that some day the village would have "industrial plants sufficient to employ a considerable town population . . . and sufficient attractions to hold the younger people."[141]

The community's economic center was the two-story plate glass and brick Bank of Mound Bayou, which in 1910 had deposits of $40,000 and total resources estimated in excess of $100,000. The town's great pride was the $100,000 Mound Bayou Oil Mill and Manufacturing Company, scheduled for completion in 1912 and reputed to be not only "one of the best in the state" but a "monument to the architectural and constructive genius of the negro race."[142] The principal organizer of both enterprises was Charles Banks, Mound Bayou's own "wizard of finance," whose very touch seemed to ensure success.

Banks was the embodiment of bourgeois virtue, an unabashed black Babbitt who, as one admirer believed, found the music of the cash register "as pleasing . . . as the rhapsody of a Beethoven sonata." A self-made man of coal-black skin and "pure African" descent, he rose above the extreme poverty of his Clarksdale youth to become a highly successful speculator in land and cotton with financial interests in nearly every major race enterprise in the state. Booker T. Washington thought him to be "the most influential Negro business man in the United States" and "the leading Negro banker in Mississippi." Like Montgomery he combined opportunism with altruism and benefited handsomely from his Mound Bayou investments. By all accounts he lived in "splendid circumstances." His stylish home, built in 1908 at a cost of $10,000, was big enough, some said, "to house a small-sized army" and worthy of the "rich barons of olden times."[143]

As befit the founder and chief spokesman of the Mississippi Negro Business League, Banks was, like Montgomery again, a sincere evangel of the gospel of uplift. From his arrival in the all-black town in 1903 until his death in 1923, he devoted his enormous energies to fulfilling the promise of the "Mound Bayou Proposition," a separatist utopia built, governed, and occupied exclusively by blacks. In the spirit of the proposition he led in the organization of the bank and oil mill—institutions designed, a close associate affirmed, not merely for profit but as proof of the "Negro's . . . capacity to successfully administer the business of a municipality."[144] To block white encroachment and protect "our whole scheme here," he tried first to organize a trust fund of northern money for the purchase and eventual resale to black farmers of "all the contiguous territory available." Failing there, and yet determined to ensure the future "integrity" of the colony, he joined William Thornton Montgomery, brother of Isaiah, in founding the Mound Bayou Loan and Investment Company in 1906. Capitalized at $50,000, this concern would complement the work of the bank, providing credit to new black settlers and refinancing existing mortgages held by "foreign [white] creditors." As Isaiah advised Dr. Washington, the long-range objective, through "well directed and concentrated efforts for general betterment," was to develop from "the central point of Mound Bayou" black financial, industrial, and agricultural interests that embraced not only central Bolivar County but a "vast territory" encompassing much of the upper Delta, including Tunica, Coahoma, Quitman, Tallahatchie, and Washington counties.[145]

If Mound Bayou was a worthy symbol of the black Mississippians' entrepreneurial aspirations, it also symbolized the ultimate failure of the group economy. Affected by every fluctuation of the cotton market, the town stumbled during the business contractions of 1907 and 1914 and never recovered from the closure of its first bank and the failure of its undercapitalized oil mill. In 1915 the financial institution was reorganized as the Mound Bayou State Bank. Although it survived for nearly a decade, this second bank was hardly stronger than the first and never able to meet the community's chronic need for credit.[146]

The widely heralded oil mill was also a costly disappointment. Following its dedication by Booker T. Washington, the heavily encumbered enterprise stood idle for a year, and then opened in October 1913 only under the direction of a white lessee and with operating capital advanced (at Washington's request) by a white philanthropist. Early in 1914 Charles Banks sent written assurances to Tuskegee that the mill "has its affairs all straightened out and is running full speed night and day and is really making good." In fact, after months of part-time operation, it would permanently close in January 1915, when the white lessee defaulted.[147] Banks refused an offer for a new lease arrangement with the Buckeye Cotton Oil Company, a subsidiary of Procter and Gamble, lest it "mean the loss of our identity as a race with the Oil Mill." His vigorous efforts to reopen the business "absolutely in Negro hands" failed, however, and the idle mill eventually became a dance hall—"a tragic reminder," one Mound Bayouan believed, "of a more prosperous past."[148]

Other misfortunes followed. After a brief interlude of wartime prosperity the state's small cotton farmers entered a period of hard times from which only World War II brought temporary relief. Land values in the colony dropped by nearly half during the recession of 1920-1922; cotton prices fell from a dollar in 1920 to less than twenty cents a pound in 1921. The community's population remained fairly stable at about 800. But "a financial blight," one observer reported, "settled over the town." Having overextended themselves in palmier times, many of the community's land and home owners were wiped out. Once-independent farmers were forced back into tenantry; housewives in growing numbers turned to domestic service. The town's largest retail establishment, the Farmers' Cooperative Mercantile Company, failed in 1922. In 1923 Charles Banks died, his estimable resources depleted by repeated losses. Montgomery died the following year at the age of seventy-seven, leaving a large but heavily encumbered estate.[149] Even the elements and the stock market seemed to conspire against the luckless community. In 1926, and again more disastrously in 1941, fire ravaged the business district. In 1929, scarcely days before the disastrous Wall Street crash, civic leaders launched an ill-fated drive to raise $1 million for the Mound Bayou Foundation, a nonprofit development corporation designed to rehabilitate and perpetuate the Mound Bayou Proposition.[150]

Thus, Mound Bayou, once said to number among the most prosperous communities in the state, entered the Great Depression already profoundly depressed. When Saunders Redding visited it about 1940 he found it to be "more dead than alive," a place of "naked ugliness," virtually without trees or children, with "more buildings . . . empty than in use." By that date, its residents bought their supplies largely from white merchants in surrounding communities. Mayor Benjamin A. Green, son of a founder and a lawyer trained at Harvard, admitted to the black writer that "pride and power and a sense of security no longer apply to the situation here."[151]

Mound Bayou's story, of course, is in one sense that of small-town America, of numberless but once-flourishing agricultural service centers throughout the United States that fell prey to a variety of pressures, direct and indirect: a nationalizing economy and what has been called the "onslaught of modernization";[152] a plague of rural village problems ranging from the demise of the family farm to the appeal of mail-order catalogs and chain stores, rural-to-urban migration, and increased consumer mobility. Yet much as it shared with other farm communities with no special handicaps of race or prejudice, Mound Bayou was not simply one of them. Its problems were less the problems of economic scale than of economic separation; its failures, in the last analysis, were the failures of the group economy itself.

Epitaph for the Group Economy

If nothing else, the experience of Mississippi's stunted black merchant class argues that the doctrines of self-help and racial solidarity were not in themselves the building blocks of a diversified parallel economy. With rare exceptions, the businesses of the race were shoe-string operations, small retail or personal service concerns that teetered precariously between failure and extreme marginality. Even its great successes compared poorly with those of the white competition.

In 1899 Du Bois could find no black enterprise in the state with a capital investment of $10,000 or more. Census enumerators in 1900 identified 505 black Mississippians as "merchants and dealers," but Du Bois's estimates suggest that only seventy-eight of their commercial establishments represented investments of as much as $500. Between 1910 and 1920, a decade of heavy black out-migration, the state's black retail dealers declined from 1,005 to 857.[153] Unfortunately, we cannot determine black sales volume or even the number of black-owned stores prior to the retail census of 1929, the first year in which black business data were classified separately. In that year, though blacks numbered half of the state's population, their businesses accounted for 1,406 (or 12.3 percent) of Mississippi's 17,256 retail establishments, and less than 1 percent of its net retail sales. As Table 5.5 reveals, moreover, the great bulk of all black concerns were either groceries or purveyors of prepared

TABLE 5.5. Black-Operated Stores in Mississippi, 1929.

Groceries and/or meat markets	697
Cafes and refreshment stands	472
General merchandise and apparel	95
Other retail	142

Source: U.S., Bureau of Census, *Fifteenth Census, Retail Distribution* (Washington, D.C., 1930), vol. 1, pt. 2, p. 1395.

TABLE 5.6. Black Retail Trade in Mississippi, 1929, 1935, and 1939.

	Black-owned stores	Net sales	Average per store
1929	1,406	$3,809,000	$2,709
1935	843	841,000	998
1939	1,336	1,803,000	1,350

Sources: U.S., Bureau of Census, *Fifteenth Census, Retail Distribution* (Washington, D.C., 1930), vol. 1, pt. 2, p. 1395; U.S., Department of Commerce, *Retail Trade, Retail Negro Proprietorships, the United States* (Washington, D.C., 1941), 6.

food and drink, businesses that required comparatively little cash outlay. Although government economists estimated that in 1929 a sales volume of $12,000 was the minimum necessary for marginal profitability, Mississippi's black retailers in that year averaged less than one-fourth of that amount. During the depression, as Table 5.6 demonstrates, the picture grew markedly bleaker.

The very size of the average black business dictated a competitive disadvantage and a high probability of failure. The black community had little investment capital of its own and white lenders, influenced by both racial and market considerations, generally staked black ventures only at usurious rates. Hard-pressed black merchants might offer their customers important intangibles, including dignified sales environments free from the traditional observances of caste, but they could rarely compete with larger, more experienced, and better financed white establishments in terms of price, service, and quantity or quality of merchandise. Following the introduction of high-volume chain and mail-order operations many black tradesmen found that they could not buy at wholesale as cheaply as some whites could sell at retail. Nor could they extend the credit upon which seasonally employed black consumers depended heavily.[154]

We cannot trace the distribution of black consumer dollars, but the black merchant's share was never great and it probably declined sharply after World War I. Although race loyalty no doubt influenced the buying habits of many, the fact remains that impoverished field hands could not afford to pay a premium for the satisfaction of trading with their own kind. Indeed, the logic of the marketplace pervaded even Mound Bayou, seemingly the very model of a closed commercial order. Montgomery continually exhorted residents of the all-black town to shop at home, yet in 1914, perhaps the heyday of the community, one of its leading merchants estimated that Mound Bayouans spent nearly three dollars out of every four outside the village, presumably in white establishments.[155]

Nonmarket influences also handicapped black economic development. Black businessmen, like black professionals and skilled trades people, sometimes found their very success to be an affront to white expectations. In a society that defined the black place as one of service to whites, enterprising blacks sometimes found themselves targets of white resentment. Although potentially a problem in any community throughout the Jim Crow period, conditions were especially discouraging at the turn of the century in some northeastern counties and in the Whitecapping counties of the Piney Woods. The Reverend C. S. Buchanan, for example, owner of what Isaiah Montgomery called "the best appointed printing establishment of any colored man in the State," was banished from West Point in 1904 at a "mass meeting" of some 100 whites who objected to his "prospering," to his elegant horse and buggy, his "decent house" and piano. Whites thought that his "mode of living," Montgomery learned, had "a bad effect on the cooks and washerwomen, who aspired to do likewise, and became less disposed to work for the whites." Ordered to sell his business and remove his family under penalty of death, Buchanan fled the Clay County village with scarcely the shirt on his back. Earlier, in the same community, a black grocer had been directed "to sell his Buggy and walk"; a second Negro retailer was ordered to leave town, but permitted to remain "on good behavior"; a third, the owner of two hacks, was "allowed to run only one and was ordered to sell the other."[156]

Nor did white businessmen invariably welcome their black competitors. Although whites generally applauded the self-segregating tendencies of early twentieth-century conservative black thought, white business retailers had no enthusiasm for a parallel black commerce. "Hard work" and "thrift" might be harmless slogans, and even "race pride" was not directly threatening; but the economic implications of "group solidarity" were clearly less acceptable. Whatever their doubts about black worth, white merchants never questioned the value of black money. In the larger cities of the lower South, including Atlanta, New Orleans, and even Memphis, the ideology of black support for black enterprise was a staple of black economic life. In Mississippi, however, and particularly in plantation communities where black consumers predominated, black merchants could not openly urge their own people to "buy black."[157]

As John Dollard has written of one cotton center, there was "definite pressure . . . by the whites to monopolize the business and professional opportunities." Black Indianolans attributed black consumer disloyalty to white coercion. In Clarksdale, and doubtless other cotton towns, white storekeepers regularly trucked the Saturday plantation trade to town; and landlords throughout the state guaranteed their tenants' credit primarily at white businesses.[158] Most telling of all, even some white undertakers coveted black consumer dollars. Although it has long been the conventional wisdom of historians that funeral parlors were among the most segregated enterprises, white Mississippians sometimes (but apparently only in small towns) controlled the business of both races. Here, too, black competition was unwanted. When E. W. Hall and Malachi C. Collins opened the first black funeral home in the Piney Woods town of Hattiesburg shortly before World War I, their white counterpart circulated handbills among blacks: "Don't patronize those niggers, we can give you better service." There were frequent violent threats but apparently no bloodshed and Hall and Collins Funeral Home survived for many years. The atmosphere was intitially so hostile, however, that the partners armed themselves with a shotgun and for a time alternately stood watch over their new firm at night.[159]

To these handicaps one must add the white indisposition to patronize black business. Burdened as they were with "nigger-district" locations and the stigma of color, race merchants rarely sold to whites. Before 1900 some black proprietors, notably barbers, caterers, restaurateurs, and prostitutes, depended exclusively on white customers. Thereafter, however, racial sentiment hardened and whites became increasingly less willing to trade with Negroes. By World War II whites generally entered black firms only on the assumption, usually false, that black retail and service establishments could radically undercut the white competition.[160]

Finally, the development of a viable group economy required a measure of black unity that simply did not exist in Mississippi or anywhere else. All black Mississippians shared a debased citizenship and all but a few knew the common experience of poverty and illiteracy. Yet black society was always less homogeneous than most whites assumed. While the distance between the social and economic extremes in Mississippi was not as great among blacks as whites, it was nonetheless substantial, and not readily overlooked by either the advantaged few or the struggling many.[161] Set apart by the privileges of education, occupation, and sometimes wealth—not least of all by that quality known to those who presumed to have it as "good breeding"—Mississippi's minuscule black business and professional elites exercised influence out of proportion to their numbers and lived in a manner far removed from the black masses. The inevitable tension between the two ends of the black spectrum is suggested by the sidewalk oratory of a black Natchezian in the mid-1930s. Comparing black doctors and merchants to whites, he angrily insisted to thirteen unemployed people of his own race: "de Negro who got somethin' is jus' as bad! Those negroes . . . don't keer uh goddam about *eny* of you! All dey keer about is yo' money. . . . They jus' as bad as them pecks [peckerwoods, i.e., whites]."[162] Perhaps the sentiment was intensified by the hardship of depression. But it demonstrates, nonetheless, that class antagonism sometimes overrode caste solidarity.

A related concern to the black retailer was racial self-doubt. For all their obvious pride in black accomplishments, Mississippi blacks were not unmarked by the psychologically damaging environment of derision and hate in which they lived. The magnitude of the problem can scarcely be surmised. Nevertheless, as Afro-American business leaders seemed to agree, all too many black consumers shared the assumption that "the white man's ice is colder." "Negroes would only go to such [black] businesses as banking and burial associations," one black professional man lamented, "because whites don't offer them these services."[163]

In sum the group economy was doomed from the start. Too poor, too inexperienced, too dependent, too easily victimized to construct a successful economy of their own, black Mississippians could hardly take advantage of the disadvantages when, as Robert Higgs has written of Afro-Americans generally, "the disadvantages were virtually all they had to work with."[164]

Jim Crow's Likeness:
A Photo Essay

Fusing race pride and realism, black Mississippians generally accepted Jim Crow institutions as a fact of life. Segregation was often preferable to exclusion, and separation was not in itself degrading to a race that countered white discrimination with a group identity of its own.

Although whites often assured themselves that blacks were incapable of formal learning, white opposition to equal educational opportunity derived from the well-founded suspicion that blacks would learn too much in school, not too little.

Often victimized by a plantation supply system designed to keep them dependent, Mississippi's sharecroppers moved from landlord to landlord with an annual regularity that defied both the state's restrictive labor statutes and the white planter's claim on black industry.

Sharecropper accounts—particularly oral histories gathered by black interviewers in recent decades—contain little nostalgia for "dem olden times." In narrative after narrative, the image of tenantry as latter-day bondage recurs: "It was just like slavery." "I call it slavery." "Nothing but slavery."

Set apart by the privileges of education, occupation, and wealth, Mississippi's tiny black business and professional elite lived in a manner far removed from the black masses. Above, the home of planter-businessman I. T. Montgomery; below, a "darktown" slum in Tupelo.

Disproportionately concentrated in such traditional slave crafts as blacksmithing, Mississippi's black artisans were gradually squeezed out of the skilled crafts in the twentieth century into unskilled, low-wage "negro jobs" thought to be too dirty or too dangerous for whites.

MARION POST WOLCOTT

In a society in which all but the poorest whites retained black cooks and laundresses, domestic servant wages were universally low—about the same in 1940 as in 1865.

Often unable to compete with better-capitalized white businesses in price or variety of merchandise, black retail establishments such as the Mound Bayou pharmacy (below) offered their customers important intangibles, including race pride and dignified, courteous sales environments.

WPA

While the social costs of the great migration cannot be calculated, the mass black movement to northern cities carried off a disproportionate number of young adults and left an "excess" of children and old people.

ED LISCOMB

Black club women, represented here by middle-class Bolivar Countians gathered in the home of Mary Booze (gesturing, center), quietly challenged white supremacy through strategies of black self-help and prudent social agitation.

PART IV

Under White Law

The fact is that . . . it is somewhat difficult to draw at this time a sharp line marking off distinctly the point where the lynching spirit stops and the spirit of legal procedure commences.

—William Henry Holtzclaw, 1915

To kill a nigger, or a nigger lover, wasn't anything.

—Charles Evers, of the Jim Crow era

CHAPTER 6

Jim Crow's Courts

With every official in Mississippi a white man, and every jury composed of whites; every judge upon the bench white, and all elections conducted by and only participated in by whites, there can be no possible danger of negro rule.

—Yazoo *Herald,* 1907[1]

It is, of course, well known that during and since Reconstruction times, the courts in the South have been used largely as instruments for enforcing caste rather than securing justice.

—W. E. B. Du Bois, 1948[2]

Trial by Ordeal

"Yes sir," Arthur (Yank) Ellington told the prosecutor, "I am scared of all white people." Standing trial for his life in the Circuit Court of Mississippi's Sixth Judicial District, the Kemper County field hand had reason to be afraid. On the evening of March 30, 1934, several hours after the axe slaying of Raymond Stewart, a white farmer, Ellington was delivered by a deputy sheriff for interrogation by some twenty white men at the blood-spattered scene of the crime, a cottonseed storage room attached to the dead man's farmhouse. He was connected to the homicide only by the scantiest of circumstance. He was black; so, most whites assumed, was the killer. He was, as whites put it, "Stewart's nigger." He lived on the white man's place and for two years had worked his fields. Soon after the discovery of the killing Ellington went to Stewart's house, paid his respects, and lingered outside talking quietly with other blacks. On such evidence he was accused of murder. When the young black man denied knowledge of the crime, he was stripped, tied to a tree, and as he later told the court, "they whipped me good." That failing, "they hung me twice; they pulled me up to a limb twice." Unable to force an admission of guilt, the whites permitted the terrified field hand to return to his wife and children.[3]

The following morning the deputy returned to Ellington's cabin, determined this time to make the suspect "belch up the truth." Taking his manacled prisoner across the state line into Alabama, the officer and another white flogged him nearly to death with a metal-tipped strap until he cried: "Tell me what you want me to say and I will say it." With the deputy's coaching, Ellington told a story of guilt. He was then taken to the Lauderdale County jail in Meridian, some thirty miles from DeKalb, seat of Kemper County, and presumably beyond the reach of the mob.

Meanwhile, the deputy had also charged two other blacks, Ed Brown and Henry Shields, with the same crime. Also taken to jail in Meridian, they too professed innocence and they too were stripped and scourged until they confessed. His evidence thus in order, the deputy called in a white minister and the sheriffs of Lauderdale and Kemper counties to attest that the confessions to which the illiterate blacks now put their marks were freely given. In their affidavits, the three whites did not mention that Brown limped severely and could not sit or that Ellington's neck and face bore a rope burn.[4]

The trial was much the same. Fearful that any delay would provoke a multiple lynching in "Bloody Kemper," a county notorious for its racial violence, authorities moved swiftly. Although regular terms of both the grand jury and the circuit court had expired, both institutions were pressed into immediate service. On April 4 the defendants were rushed back from Meridian to DeKalb for arraignment. District Attorney (later U.S. Senator) John C. Stennis conducted the prosecution, and four court-appointed local attorneys were assigned to the defense. The defendants met their lawyers briefly that afternoon and again shortly before trial began the next morning, but only within the hearing of the deputy sheriff who had warned the prisoners to stick to their statements lest he "get meat again."

Three of the defendants' counselors favored prompt conviction. The fourth, state Senator John A. Clark, though ultimately persuaded of their innocence, was initially convinced by peace officers that his clients had voluntarily confessed their guilt. Until he sensed a miscarriage of justice late in the proceeding, Clark by his own testimony had "no doubt of their guilt and was simply going through the form of a trial." His advocacy, he later acknowledged, was compromised by the mob spirit that prevailed in a courtroom guarded by officers heavily armed with machine guns.[5] Warned by an impatient judge not to delay, the defense did not ask for separate trials for the accused, sought neither a change of venue nor a special venire from which to choose jurors, failed to petition the court for a continuance to prepare a case, and did not even question the competence of extorted confessions, the state's only judicable evidence. At a hasty pretrial hearing on the admissibility of the statements, the Kemper County sheriff conceded that he had heard "rumors" that the defendants had been "strapped pretty bad." But the court accepted his assurance that the testimonies had been "freely and voluntarily made," with "no force or intimidation." The evidence went to the jury without objection from the defense.

In due course, the blacks testified in their own defense and the extent of the violence used against them was put into the record without contradiction by the state. Asked about the burn on Ellington's neck and face, the deputy replied: "They didn't hang him. They pulled him up but they didn't hang him." The white officer also acknowledged that the three defendants had been whipped "right smart" before they confessed, but "not too much for a Negro; not as much as I would have done if it was left to me." This testimony and the defendants' repudiation of their confessions notwithstanding, the defense did not move to exclude the confessions and the judge did not direct the jury to declare a mistrial or to find for the defendants. An all-white jury deliberated some thirty minutes before granting District Attorney Stennis's request for first-degree convictions. The judge fixed the execution for May 11 and dismissed the attorneys. Court was adjourned without motion for a new trial.

The entire episode, from the moment of Stewart's death until Yank Ellington and his friends were sentenced to hang, required only seven days. The Meridian *Star,* advocate of a "speedy trial" as an antidote for "mobocracy," noted that "rampant" public discussion of a triple lynching had been cut short by the "quick action" of grand jury and judge. "Group action is unneeded, when courts are 'on the job,' " the editor concluded: "A few more like examples of swift and certain retribution—and 'rabble' illegality will disappear throughout the south."[6]

At this point, only the conscience of defense attorney John Clark prevented the executions. Although released by the court, the courageous country lawyer could not let the matter rest. Shocked by his clients' courtroom testimony and further moved to action by an eleventh-hour interview with the condemned men, he executed a pauper's oath and pressed their cause before the Mississippi Supreme Court.[7] The appeals court, in split decisions that were marvels of evasion, affirmed the convictions twice. The court's majority wished not "to even remotely sanction the methods by which the confessions were obtained," yet it denied the petitions on the ground that the three men could not object on appeal to evidence their attorneys had not challenged during their trial. The confessions, though "apparently coerced," were "properly admitted"; the "alleged whippings" notwithstanding, the majority found that the trial court had honored the "rules of procedure."

Given the trial record and some of the state supreme court's own precedents, these rulings were remarkable. By such logic, scoffed Associate Justice Virgil A. Griffith following the second appeal, the majority could as easily have legitimized a lynching, "because the victims, while being hung by the mob, did not object in the proper form of words at precisely the proper stage of the proceedings." Joined in dissent by Associate Justice William D. Anderson, Griffith pronounced the trial a "solemn farce" beside which "the Scottsboro Cases are models of correct constitutional procedure." For all the "frills and furbelows of a pretended trial," he wrote, it was "never a legitimate proceeding," never anything but a "factitious continuation of the mob."

Judge Griffith's forceful dissent was the turning point in the case. The defense used it to win the secret financial support of the National Association for the Advancement of Colored People, the Commission on Interracial Cooperation, the Association of Southern Women for the Prevention of Lynching—and the assistance of some of Mississippi's most influential legal talent. On appeal to the United States Supreme Court in February, 1936, the convictions were reversed, in a landmark ruling that for the first time overturned state convictions based on coerced testimony. The unanimous decision, written by Chief Justice Charles Evans Hughes—but heavily influenced by the language of Mississippi Justice Virgil Griffith—scolded the state court for tolerating "the rack and torture chamber" in this "trial by ordeal." Where the state appeals court could find no procedural error, the federal judges found "a wrong so fundamental that it made the whole proceeding a mere pretense of a trial." "The duty of maintaining constitutional rights," Justice Hughes affirmed, ". . . rises above the rules of procedure."[8]

Ellington, Brown, and Shields were immediately indicted under "new evidence" brought by District Attorney Stennis and moved to a jail in Jackson amid fears that a second trial would require military protection. In the end, neither the state nor the defense was eager to try the case again. After successive postponements the Kemper County blacks pleaded *nolo contendere* to manslaughter and accepted relatively brief sentences rather than face yet another Mississippi jury. Shields and Brown settled respectively for two and one-half and seven and one-half years in the state penitentiary. Ellington, who had nearly died from internal injuries sustained while in police custody, was given six months. Meanwhile,

John Clark, the object of intense personal abuse in Kemper County, lost his seat in the state senate. His promising political career in shambles, he suffered a physical and mental collapse and retired from the law in 1938 at the age of fifty-four. The district attorney, on the other hand, soon thereafter became Sixth District circuit court judge, and ten years later (1947) a United States senator.[9]

"Negro Law"

Brown v. *Mississippi,* the case of the three Kemper County field hands, is instructive. It ranks, as A. E. Keir Nash has written, with *Powell* v. *Alabama,* the infamous Scottsboro case of the same period, among the Deep South "horribles," one of the worst examples of mob-dominated southern justice. In Richard C. Cortner's words, it is a reminder of "the fragility of the barriers that separate us from human savagery."[10] Yet the quality of justice available to Brown, Ellington, and Shields was not atypical. In cases in which blacks were accused of serious crimes against whites, justice in the courts of Jim Crow Mississippi was often swift and harsh, and rarely color-blind.[11]

Indeed, as a growing body of recent scholarship suggests, black defendants in Mississippi courts in the half century after 1890 may have enjoyed relatively less procedural fairness than did slaves. Accused slaves, of course, were tried under laws that explicitly denied human equality.[12] As both chattel and people they were legally regarded more often as property than persons. And though recognized under the criminal law primarily as persons, they were persons of a particular and carefully circumscribed kind—in the revealing language of the Mississippi Supreme Court, they were "artificial" persons subject not to the common law but to a code "wholly differing in its character" from that created for "natural persons" or citizens. "Experience has proved," the high court affirmed in 1859, ". . . that masters and slaves cannot be governed by the same laws. So different in position, in rights, in duties, they cannot be the subjects of a common system of laws." Whether in the definition of offenses, the assignment of penalties, the designation of special tribunals, the regulation of testimony, or the provision for appeal, in every step of the judicial process, the slave was set apart from "the superior race, the white man."[13]

Such legal anomalies, like the peculiar institution that fostered them, were casualties of the Civil War. In the narrow sense of formal law, black and white defendants of postbellum Mississippi confronted the judicial system on equal terms. "There is no provision in the constitution of this state, no law on the statute book," the state attorney general asserted in 1896, "that *per se* can be said to be directed by way of discriminating against negroes." Although disingenuous, this statement is technically true. So too is the quaint high court dictum of 1906: "Mulattoes, negroes, Malays, whites, millionaires, paupers, princes and kings, in the courts of Mississippi, are on precisely the same exactly equal footing."[14]

As a practical matter, however, the advantages of freedom could be easily overstated. Under the equal protection and due process clauses of the Fourteenth Amendment, blacks had the same claim to justice as whites, yet their circumstances not infrequently precluded the exercise of that claim. Economically dependent and politically impotent, they were at best quasi-citizens without direct influence over public affairs. Effectively denied access to the basic instruments of citizenship by which free peoples safeguard their most elementary civic rights, black demands for police protection and justice in the courts could be safely ignored in a polity exclusively of, by, and for whites.

Indeed, the Fourteenth Amendment notwithstanding, the antebellum slave code had its informal postbellum equivalent in what attorney Sidney Fant Davis called "negro law." De facto distinctions between "artificial" and "natural" persons remained central to day-to-day law enforcement in Mississippi. Davis, a future Sunflower County circuit judge (1920-1928), acknowledged in 1914 that a person reading the state's criminal and civil codes might logically conclude that these laws applied equally to both whites and blacks: "But nothing could be farther from the truth," he noted, for state laws were selectively enforced, and Mississippi judges, lawyers, and jurors knew, as if by instinct, that some applied to both races, some only to whites, and some just to blacks. Negro law, "an important branch of the law here in Mississippi," was unwritten, learned only through experience and observation, and fully understood, Davis believed, only by the native-born. In a society in which race mattered above all else, "negro law" determined who was punished for what. Bigamy, like most other crimes of morality, was a white crime, and one not enforced against a "naturally" promiscuous and faithless race. Saturday night stabbings or thievery between blacks were often not crimes. Petty black theft from a white, on the other hand, was a serious offense in an urban community and often punished by imprisonment. In the rural black belt it was more commonly resolved "out of court," Davis said, in "an ex-parte hearing in the barn," with a "piece of gin belting" or "an old buggy trace."[15]

In freedom as in slavery, then, the planters or, for that matter, the woods-riders or bosses in turpentine and logging camps, were laws unto

themselves who administered the whip for a wide range of lesser infractions. Flogging, many whites believed, was still the most effective
way to deal with most black crime. "Most of the planters when they
catch one of their hands stealing . . . will take them out and give them
a beating and that's the end of it," an Adams County justice of the
peace reported on the eve of World War II. "It never gets into court."
A planter's wife from the same river county noted that officially sanctioned forms of punishing blacks too often worked against the needs
of white landlords: "They can't afford to send them to jail because they
need them on the farms; so they just . . . give them a good beating, and
that teaches them."[16]

Although major black infractions were generally prosecuted formally,
the law was usually applied in the white interest. "When a white man
kills a Negro," Hortense Powdermaker wrote of Indianola and its environs, "it is hardly considered murder. When a Negro kills a white
man, conviction is assured, provided the case is not settled immediately
by lynch law."[17] On the other hand, the murder of a black by a black,
the most common form of homicide in Mississippi during the half
century after 1890, could bring the death penalty if it was exceptionally
brutal or cold-blooded, or if the victim was well thought of by local
whites. In 1911, when one Judge Collins was tried in Sharkey County
for the murder of Rube Boyd, the prosecutor framed his argument for
a "necktie party" with white sensibilities in mind: "This bad nigger
killed a good nigger. The dead nigger was a white man's nigger, and
these bad niggers like to kill that kind." The jury sentenced Collins to
die on the gallows. As Collins's black attorney, Willis E. Mollison,
lamented, "The average white jury would take it for granted that the
killing of a white man's nigger is a more serious offense than the killing
of a plain, every-day black man."[18] Under "negro law" the gravity of
any crime was determined in large part by its impact on white interests.

Thus when black-on-black crimes aroused white racial fears, offenders
were often harshly punished. For example, David Sykes was convicted
for killing George McIntosh in 1906. Both men were black, but the
state's attorney convinced the jury that Sykes's motive was a desire for
McIntosh's wife, a desire that could someday lead to the most heinous
of crimes. "You ought to convict him," the prosecutor argued, "because
he might rape some of the white women of the country." The defendant
was given the death penalty. The honor of white southern womanhood,
as the case of Columbus Story (1923) suggests, could be invoked even
when a black woman was raped by a black man. In his closing argument
for the death sentence, a Holmes county prosecutor reminded the jury

that during Story's attack on a "bright mulatto woman," the black man commanded: "White woman stop your hollerin'." "This shows you," the attorney insisted, "where his passions are leading to."[19]

When white interests were not involved, however, the system was usually less exacting, for the offenses of blacks against other blacks were taken less seriously than were other crimes. "We have very little crime," a white Natchezian boasted in the 1930s: "Of course, Negroes knife each other occasionally, but there is little *real* crime. I mean Negroes against whites or whites against each other."[20] According to the Hattiesburg *Progress,* news of black-on-black homicide was not news at all in Mississippi: "One nigger cuts another's throat about the former's wife and that is the last heard of it." In this editor's judgment, "nigger crap shooters kill each other in different parts of the state nearly every day" with impunity; murder among black railroad construction gangs was too common even to be investigated: "Perhaps not one-third of the murder[er]s are ever arrested. It is like dog chewing on dog and the white people are not interested in the matter. Only another dead nigger—that's all."[21]

When black capital offenders were arrested and tried, the proceedings were often tainted by white notions about "negro characteristics." The criminal justice system reflected the values of the larger white society that regarded blacks as naturally more impulsive and violent than whites and that placed less value on the life and honor of blacks than whites. Brought before the bar of justice for the rape or murder of a person of his own race, the black defendant was far more likely than his white counterpart to confront an indulgent prosecutor willing to exchange a guilty plea for life imprisonment.[22] Such permissiveness, whatever its advantages to the accused, seemed to condone intraracial black lawlessness and offered inadequate protection for black life and property. While it generally served the black community poorly, the paternalistic side of "negro law" had its defenders. As one trial judge explained, it produced verdicts in black cases that were "perfectly satisfactory to all parties concerned"—taxpayers were spared the expense of lengthy trials, defendants eluded the hangman, and the state got additional field hands for the prison farm.[23]

Occasionally, whites interceded with the law on behalf of their black tenants, domestics, or other employees. When "Ike" killed his wife after World War I, he was convicted in Adams County largely on the testimony of "Wash," "a white man's nigger." But Ike's landlord—who thought "I could have gotten him off, but I didn't attend to it in time"—arranged to have him released from prison after only one year so that the black man could return to the fields. "He was a good steady negro,"

the planter noted, "since he came back." In 1922 Elizabeth H. Rowe, a black Vicksburg woman, watched as her husband's black murderer was acquitted upon the request of an influential white. It was common knowledge, she bitterly observed, that many Mississippi whites were loath to lose a good hand to prison, as "the live nigger is worth more than the dead one."[24]

Given the personal nature of law enforcement and the imperatives of the double standard, a relationship with a white, that of patron to protégé, could figure importantly in court. One of the first questions a black-belt magistrate might ask was, "Whose nigger are you?" A defendant linked to a white man of influence could expect to be "let off lightly," as David Cohn explained. One identified with a lesser white could expect to receive harsher treatment: "If he has no white folks at all, his fate is in the lap of the gods."[25]

Most crime in Mississippi was intraracial, but when whites victimized blacks, they often escaped trial, even for serious offenses. In an interracial altercation resulting in the death of a black, nearly any white man of good standing could avoid the indignity of a trial, whatever the circumstances. When a Hinds County landlord killed two unarmed black trespassers in 1911, for example, the Jackson *Daily News* explained, under the headline "FARMER SLAYED TWO BAD BLACKS," that the killings were "justifiable," so the white man "was not put to any trouble by the county authorities."[26] Moreover, black victims of white crime often prudently declined to press charges.[27] White lawyers were reluctant to accept such cases, white police and prosecutors rarely encouraged blacks to press charges, and some local magistrates simply denied black victims the protection of the law. Again, a Hinds County incident illustrates the problem. In 1897, a black woman who complained that she had been beaten with an axe handle was denied her hour in court by a justice of the peace who could find "no law to punish a white man for beating a negro woman." When a Jackson police court also turned her away, the local press dismissed the matter as "a very funny incident."[28]

In apparently open-and-shut cases whites could be convicted, but the punishments assigned often reflected white notions of black worth. In 1930, for example, a Yazoo City white man was charged with raping a seven-year-old black girl in the presence of her five-year-old sister. Because whites generally agreed that no black female above the age of puberty was chaste, the victim's age seems at least as crucial to the proceeding as the quality of the state's evidence. After extended deliberation, the jury voted to convict, but then could not agree on the sentence. By default, the defendant received a life term. If the race of the child and her attacker had been reversed, no sentence less than death would have been imaginable.[29]

In sum, "negro law" was, to quote Judge Davis again, "one of the most complicated branches of the law," one learned only by "experience and observation." To the literal-minded—and particularly to outsiders bewildered by the obvious gap between the letter of the state's formal legal code and its day-to-day applications—the legal system seemed hopelessly capricious, at once both permissive and severe.[30] Yet "negro law" was anything but irrational. Under its many-layered provisions, white interests were a major concern of prosecutors, jurors, and judges; law enforcement, with rare exception, served the needs of caste. Viewed as a logical and coherent response to the demands of the dominant race, one might even say that the criminal justice system in Mississippi performed its appointed task well. Although scrupulous impartiality is the ideal, courts in virtually any society are assigned what might be called a parapolitical role. They serve as "access points" at which popular or institutional pressures can be applied to resist social change or to promote majority values.[31] In open societies this role is often subordinated to the citizens' demand for equity and minority rights are advanced. In Jim Crow Mississippi, however, where justice was bound by caste and where full citizenship was a white prerogative, the tension between social justice and social control was nearly always resolved in the interests of the dominant race.

We know much less about what might be called class law, about the relative weight of class vis-à-vis caste on the scales of justice. No doubt poor whites, too, encountered inequities in the criminal justice system. Economic circumstance, however, is the as-yet-unexamined variable in the legal history of Jim Crow Mississippi. The annals of Deep South social relationships, and the evidence presented in this chapter, suggest that race was paramount. But until legal scholars provide the necessary quantitative analyses, until problems of class and caste are studied comparatively, the question must remain open and conclusions must be tentative.

The Mob in the Courtroom

Tom Carraway, an apparently innocent black youth, was charged in 1931 with the rape of a white woman. He was tried in a Jackson County circuit court under moblike conditions nearly indentical to the *Brown* case and convicted and sentenced to hang on testimony known by both prosecutor and judge to be false. Fearing white retaliation, black material witnesses critical to the defense refused to appear in court and were not formally summoned. Carraway's attorney—ordered by the prosecutor "not to start any monkeying business" and advised that delay might make matters "worse" for the defendant—asked for neither a continuance nor a change of venue. On appeal, two justices of the state supreme court found that the denial of due process in Carraway's case was "stronger than it was in the 'Scottsboro cases.' " His conviction was nevertheless upheld. If this case was notable it was not because the state's evidence was so questionable or the defense so ineffectual—but rather because the suspect was not lynched. According to the Jackson *Clarion-Ledger,* this alleged rapist was "one of the first negroes in Mississippi" not to die "at the hands of indignant white citizens."[32]

Carraway was not mobbed, but he was tried at a moment and in a place of extreme racial excitement, and both the pace and the conduct of his trial were influenced by the threat of white violence. In cases involving black defendants accused of capital crimes against whites—always the most severe test of Mississippi justice—the fear of violence was an all-too-frequent feature of the judicial process. Thus when Isaac Howard, Ernest McGehee, and Johnnie Jones were tried in Hernando in 1934 for the rape of a white teenager, the DeSoto County courthouse was ringed by barbed wire, machine guns, and more than 300 national guardsmen equipped with gas masks and fixed bayonets. At one point in a proceeding that lasted only four hours, a mob of several thousand whites attempted unsuccessfully to breach the county's defenses. In the face of this pressure, the jury deliberated for only six minutes before returning the expected verdict. The judge then condemned the prisoners to be hanged and delivered one of the period's more notable statements on law and order. Asking jurors, relatives of the victims, and other whites in the courtroom to help disperse the crowd, he reminded them that an extralegal hanging could insure the passage of federal antilynching legislation then before Congress, legislation that would "destroy one of the South's cherished possessions—the supremacy of the white race." Whatever his higher motives—his respect for human life, his concern for the integrity of his court and the judicial process—this judge called for peace and dignity in the language of expedience: "In this case a lynching would have been against the interests not only of DeSoto County and Mississippi, but of the whole south."

There was no lynching that day, but the mob's demand for personal vengeance was satisfied when a state senator, a cousin of the young female accuser, promised to sponsor a bill to permit her father to serve as executioner at a public hanging. That proposal won the support of Governor Martin Sennett Conner and quickly cleared the upper house only to be blocked by the chairman of the House Judiciary Committee. When the youths were hanged, however, the father was on the gallows as a guest of the sheriff. When the bodies were taken to a common grave other relatives of the white teenager rode on their coffins as onlookers sang "Bye, Bye, Blackbirds" and "I'm Glad You're Dead, You Rascals You."[33]

There were other instances when whites were less patient or less satisfied with the work of the courts. In 1892, a Hinds County mob broke into a formal inquest and seized and summarily hanged a black man accused of well poisoning. His wife, mother-in-law, and two other male blacks were lynched later the same day, after they were exonerated of the same charge by the coroner's jury.[34] In 1911, although the Jackson *Daily News* thought it "inconceivable" and "an outrage on justice," a Sunflower County court sentenced a black convicted of murdering a white to life in prison rather than to the gallows. Following the trial, the newspaper protested, the public will was again denied when the sheriff outraced a lynch mob and placed his prisoner in a "mob-proof" jail in another county.[35]

Other officers were less resourceful. In Poplarville in 1918 and Laurel in 1942 black defendants were lynched after they were sentenced to life in prison for murdering whites. In 1920, whites in Tylertown, having killed one young black man before he could be tried for rape, smashed through locked courtroom doors to seize and lynch his brother during trial for the same crime. Later that year a convicted black murderer, whose execution was stayed pending appeal, was killed by a mob in Quitman. Another man tried for the murder of a white in 1935 was taken by some hundred whites from the county jail in Oxford and put to death even as a jury deliberated his fate.[36]

The most sensational of all such disruptions of the judicial process occurred in Clarksdale in 1925, where Lindsey Coleman was tried for the murder of a white plantation manager, largely on self-incriminating evidence extorted by force. At the close of a rowdy trial—during which defense counsel Thomas S. Ward, Grand Dragon of Mississippi's Ku Klux Klan, repeatedly warned authorities of possible mob action against his client—the jury shocked and dismayed local whites by acquitting the defendant. As he left a tense courtroom in the company of the Grand Dragon, Coleman was seized and shot to death.[37]

Of course not every courtroom was ringed with barbed wire and not every defendant was mobbed. But well into the 1930s, rumors of mob action frequently plagued judicial proceedings in Mississippi, and many blacks were tried in courtrooms heavily charged with racial tension. During periods of extreme disquietude that nearly always followed the commission of serious black-on-white crime, Mississippi justice often bordered on lynch law. In such moments the bench itself seemed unduly influenced by the spirit of the mob, and the trial served merely to validate pretrial accusations.

The remarkable case of Ely Pigott, charged in Lincoln County in 1908 with assault on a white woman (but not rape), is a useful illustration. The alleged offense, always serious in Mississippi, was particularly inflammatory because it was not then a capital crime and carried a maximum sentence of ten years' imprisonment. Pigott was held in jails in New Orleans and Jackson, while local authorities attempted to assure his safe return for trial by negotiating with the aggrieved party's relatives and friends. The circuit judge, M. H. Wilkinson, hoping to avert private vengeance, apparently convinced the defendant that he could have the dignity of a state execution only by pleading guilty to rape, a capital crime for which he was not initially charged. Pigott did apparently so plead, and the Lincoln County *Times* announced that mob action was unnecessary for the judge had promised that "a legal hanging is sure to follow the holding of court." Following a "mere formality of a trial," the editor reported, the community would have a "legal execution." However, when two companies of state militia escorted Pigott back for trial he was seized and shot to death by a mob of some 500 whites.[38]

Even by the standards of his time and place, the conduct of this magistrate was extraordinary. It was not routine for a Mississippi trial judge to pronounce sentence before a case was heard; nor did magistrates normally force pleas substantially greater than an alleged offense. Yet the episode seems otherwise unexceptional. Ostensibly the symbol of calm reason in an hour of savagery, Judge Wilkinson was the architect of a travesty of justice. Yet he went out of his way to prevent a lynching. In his own deplorable fashion, Pigott's judge tried to uphold what he surely thought to be the majesty of the law in a society that too often viewed mob action as "popular justice." His first concern was with the forms, rather than with the substance of justice. Under the circumstances—and putting his actions in the best possible light—he may have thought that he had done all he could to uphold the law in a lawless moment. Whatever its ethical deficiencies, and however self-serving, such a thought cannot be easily dismissed, for in the aftermath of the violence the state's white press all but ignored official efforts to uphold the rule of law but widely applauded the lynchers.[39]

Most trial judges in the state, perhaps even Judge Wilkinson, viewed themselves as professionals, as local embodiments of justice. Many seem to have been men of dignity and courage to whom impartiality, even in cases involving black capital crimes against whites, was not merely legal cant. Collectively and individually they had a stake in the integrity of the judicial process. But they were also elected officials in a state that generally honored white supremacy above the rule of law. The evidence suggests that their courtroom behavior was influenced as much by societal pressures and personal values as by the content and spirit of the law.[40] Often called upon to function in the eye of a storm of local white passions, not a few of them apparently shared the nearly universal white belief that mob action could be effectively combated only by the swift punishment of black crime.[41] Not remarkably, fairness in such circumstances was less important than efficiency, and the judicial ideals of independence and detachment became subordinate to the desire to maintain at least the forms of justice in periods of virtual anarchy. Try as we might to appreciate the complexities of the problem, the conclusion seems inescapable: all too many justices were unjust.

In moments of extreme popular excitement, the patterns of Mississippi justice were all too predictable. Following arrest, the accused was spirited away for safekeeping—often to the "mob-proof" jail in Jackson—only to be raced back for trial in the very community in which the crime had occurred. The trial itself was, if nothing else, a model of brevity. Conviction was all but assured. Sentencing could follow arrest by a week or less. The execution was carried out as soon as the law allowed.

White offenders, too, could be tried with unseemly dispatch. In an age in which judges frequently prided themselves on the "economy and expedition" with which their dockets were cleared, many courts simply discouraged procedural delays, without respect to race.[42] In matters of interracial capital crime, however, black and white trials differed substantially in both character and pace. Community passions might be stirred by serious white infractions, but in the twentieth century, at least, threats of mob intervention rarely if ever conditioned the very atmosphere in which white defendants were investigated, indicted, tried, and sentenced. Nor did the principals in white legal causes—from prosecutors and grand jurors to judges and jury foremen—feel compelled to protect the integrity of the law through headlong justice.

When the defendant was black and the victim white virtually all parties agreed that only official celerity would deny private vengeance. In the case of Lawson Davis—who in 1911 was nearly lynched and then persuaded to plead guilty of sexual assault after he had allegedly *attempted* to enter the bedroom of a white woman—it took only seven minutes to impanel a jury, present the evidence, and impose a sentence of ninety-nine years in prison.[43] Surely this was among the fastest trials for a capital offense in state history. But even when defendants professed their innocence, some proceedings against blacks took less than one hour and trials of only four to six hours' duration were fairly common.[44] Under pressure from state and federal appeals courts, Mississippi trial courts grew marginally more sensitive to procedural fairness during the 1930s and 1940s. Yet in 1946, only twenty-four hours after fifteen-year-old Charles Trudell was declared indigent, assigned an attorney, and indicted for the murder of his white employer in Wilkinson County, he was sentenced to die in the electric chair.[45]

In this rush to judgment, jury prejudice was often not a major concern of the court. With the local press and white public demanding "swift and certain" justice, procedural delays were unwanted, even dangerous, and few judges encouraged such safeguards as peremptory challenges, challenges for cause, continuance, and change of venue. It was not extraordinary, therefore, when a circuit judge in 1903 refused Thomas Brown's request for a trial in a neutral setting but assigned sixteen well-armed deputies to protect him from a Montgomery County mob that had already mistakenly killed one black and was now threatening to dynamite the jail and take the defendant. The judge could see, as could nearly anyone in the county, that whites shared an "almost universal expression" of guilt, but he was blind to the community's obvious inability to provide Brown an impartial trial.[46]

Yet even when a change in locale was granted, the passions of the aggrieved community were sometimes transferred to the new setting. When William Harris was accused of attempting to murder a white in Amite County in 1909, his trial was moved to adjacent Pike County. As the evidence was heard, however, the judge—overruling five objections from the defense—permitted the prosecutor to pit the "courage" of jurors in the trial county against that of whites in the county where the crime had occurred. The accused, the state's attorney taunted Pike Countians, had been shrewd to seek a different venue: "The time to turn a nigger loose for shooting a white man will never come in Amite County," he asserted. "He never would have gotten a verdict of not guilty in Amite County." Harris was convicted and sentenced to hang.[47]

Trial courts could also be casual about the quality of evidence used in proceedings against blacks. Even by the standards of the day, a Bolivar County prosecutor went to extremes in the trial of a black man in 1935 when he presented to an all-white jury a sack containing what he said were the remains of the murdered white woman. The court's indulgence of this macabre exhibit was surely extraordinary, and no doubt influenced by a mob of several hundred whites that threatened to breach the ring of barbed wire and national guardsmen around the courthouse in Cleveland.[48] A circuit court in Hinds County admitted a more conventional, if still questionable, variety of evidence against Lonnie Hunter and three other black male teenagers in 1924. Although a number of witnesses, some of them white, placed the four youths miles from the scene at the moment of the crime, they were tried and convicted for the hatchet slaying of a white woman. The prosecutor won death sentences on the contradictory and unsubstantiated confession of a severely retarded alleged accomplice with a reputation for wildly implausible accusations; on a garment stained with what may have been rabbit blood; and the "testimony" of a pack of tracking dogs that traced a scent to his door. In ordering a retrial, the state supreme court acknowledged the popular "reverence for bloodhound testimony" but found the evidence in the case at bar "far below the standard required for conviction."[49]

Evidentiary standards varied widely from bench to bench, but questions involving coerced testimony came before the appeals court often enough to suggest that some circuit judges received into evidence tainted admissions of guilt by black criminal defendants. If many magistrates exercised reasonable care even in periods of public unrest, all too many others were less than rigorous. Although the problem awaits more methodical examination, it seems clear that trial judges—even by the comparatively relaxed rules then governing confessions—often took little interest in the methods police used to extract self-incriminating testimony. To be sure, not every Mississippi lawman employed third-degree methods to obtain evidence, yet as black Mississippians universally understood, white supremacy was a major concern of law enforcement in the state and black rights under the Fourteenth Amendment were never more theoretical than when they were accused of murdering or raping whites. Sometimes police acquired confessions merely with promises of protection from mob violence; sometimes, as in the case of Oscar Perkins of DeSoto County, they employed less subtle methods. Convicted in 1930 for the murder of a white who may have died of natural causes, Perkins signed an incriminating statement dictated by arresting officers who struck him with a pistol, hanged him by the neck over an open fire, and measured his body for a coffin.[50] As we shall see, under steady pressure from federal tribunals and from its own increasing standards of professionalism, the state supreme court gradually forced trial judges to become more exacting. Yet until late in the period here under review, black defendants were frequently tried before judges who seemed ill disposed to question the admissibility of the state's evidence.

The problem of coerced evidence was compounded by the widespread use of private white citizens in the apprehension and interrogation of black suspects. Nearly every "negro hunt" featured a large number of armed, but informally deputized, whites who accompanied authorities as they followed the bloodhounds on the offender's trail. On occasion, whites acting in wholly private capacities detained and questioned a suspect before calling in authorities, and were later allowed to present the evidence so gathered in court.

Consider the case of Gerrard White. Arrested in 1921 following the robbery and hatchet murder of the postmaster of Holly Springs, White was questioned and quickly released. Almost immediately, however, an armed and angry planter seized the black man and took him to the murder scene, where the bloody corpse still lay. According to this white man, the suspect then admitted his guilt, though not within the hearing of a dozen other whites also present. When White refused to repeat his confession for all to hear, the planter, "a very heavy man," threw him to the floor and, with one foot on his neck and the other on his chest, administered the "water cure"—a method that entailed, in the words of a supreme court justice, "pouring water from a dipper into the nose . . . so as to strangle him, thus causing pain and horror, for the purpose of forcing a confession." White confessed and tried unsuccessfully to direct his inquisitors to stolen money he apparently knew nothing about. At a pretrial hearing, the circuit judge excluded the second or "water cure" testimony, but admitted the first confession and a third, one the planter claimed the defendant made to him while in jail. Thus, however questionable the state's case against White, his conviction and death sentence technically did not rest on coerced testimony.[51]

In a second and related case, John Fisher was tried in 1925 before a less fastidious magistrate. Arrested at his home in Coahoma County when dogs tracked a scent from the murder scene to his doorstep, Fisher was convicted entirely on "bloodhound testimony" and a confession extracted by "water cure," administered this time in the presence of peace officers. Both White and Fisher appealed and the Mississippi Supreme Court in separate decisions overturned both convictions. In the latter ruling, *Fisher* v. *Mississippi,* the court also noted that Lindsey Coleman, who had been lynched immediately after his acquittal in 1925, was tried on "water cure" testimony. Having identified at least three such cases in a span of four years, the high court directed the attention of the courts below to "the crowning infamy of the Star Chamber, and the Inquisition," and rebuked the practice of "coercing the supposed state's criminals into confession."[52]

Under Mississippi law, even defendants who could not pay for legal services were entitled to "adequate counsel" in capital cases.[53] An enlightened guarantee that dated from the pre–Civil War era, the right to an attorney was fundamental to the quality of justice in a state that trailed all others in literacy and per capita income. But because defendants were required to affirm their penury—and because indigent blacks, whether in fear, pride, or ignorance, often did not petition the court for lawyers—all too many were permitted to face the law alone. Thus, as late as the post–World War II period, Leroy Miller was convicted of burglary and attempted rape in Monroe County without benefit of attorney. Mentally retarded, unable even to sign his own name, Miller completed one year of a twenty-year sentence before he secured a lawyer through the NAACP. His case was then appealed on grounds that he had been bludgeoned into confessing and that "he was unfamiliar with courts, had no attorney to advise him of his rights, and plead[ed] guilty because he knew nothing else to do." His petition to the state supreme court in 1949 was, nevertheless, denied and the United States Supreme Court refused to hear the case.[54]

The presence of a lawyer did not, of course, guarantee an adequate defense. The Mississippi bar was virtually lily-white, and black defendants, in nearly every case, were represented by white counsel. Even when assigned by court, white attorneys could not always defend blacks accused of serious crime without fear of retribution. In the emotional context of a rape or murder trial, the Fifth Circuit Court of Appeals noted, only the most "courageous and unselfish lawyers" raised sensitive points of law. Vigorous white advocates of black causes, the federal court noted, risked "personal sacrifice which may extend to loss of practice and social ostracism."[55] A white Mississippi attorney after World War I admitted that he could not defend blacks accused of sexual crimes against whites. Juries were "openly antagonistic" and verdicts a "foregone conclusion." Although affirming his own "full sympathy" with a black accused of killing his wife's white paramour, the lawyer said, "I have to live here and support my family. . . . I cannot take the case."[56]

In the trial of Brown, Ellington, and Shields, court-appointed lawyers were so reluctant to challenge county law enforcement officers that they flipped coins in a game of "odd-man out" to determine who would cross-examine state witnesses. When John Clark, a floor leader in the state senate and defense attorney in the *Brown* case, decided to appeal the verdict, a Meridian judge who served as his closest political adviser warned him that he was "too valuable and greatly needed in Mississippi public affairs to be permitted to sacrifice his life for three negroes."[57]

Although the problem seems to have been greatest in small rural communities, the defense could encounter what one lawyer called "a legal mob" even in Hinds, the state's most urban county. When four male adolescents were tried jointly for the murder of a white woman in 1924, the Hinds County district attorney persuaded the defense that "grave danger of mob violence" precluded anything but a "speedy trial." The two court-appointed Jackson attorneys later explained that although the youths were "absolutely innocent" and even the prosecution had "strong doubt as to their guilt," the case was argued under the "most trying circumstances" in a courtroom "jammed to its utmost capacity." The "tenseness of the situation" was palpable and affected the proceedings, although this fact "cannot be reduced to black and white and does not appear in the record." "I dare say," one of them informed a correspondent, "there were hundreds of pistols in the pockets of spectators." There was also loose talk "by irresponsible people" about the dangers awaiting the attorneys. "But for the vigilence of the officers," the lawyer believed, "we would be attacked as well as the prisoners."[58]

Black attorneys were, in every respect, more vulnerable. Hindered by the same racial prejudice as their black clients, race lawyers might by their very presence before the inevitable all-white jury do a black client's cause more harm than good.[59] After 1890, and particularly in interracial litigation, black counselors appeared in court on behalf of black defendants usually only in the company of white colleagues. Even so, there could be physical risk. When S. D. Redmond, Jackson's only practicing black attorney in the 1930s, defended an alleged black rapist in Biloxi, he was associated with Bidwell Adams, prominent white Gulf Coast lawyer and former lieutenant governor. After the conviction of his client, Redmond was threatened by angry whites, but managed to escape his pursuers in a high-speed automobile chase on the road home to Jackson. "The worst charge that could come against me," he wrote Roy Wilkins, "would be [that] I defended Negroes charged with raping white women."[60]

Time was also a factor. Given the speed with which black capital crimes were prosecuted there was frequently no opportunity for adequate preparation, even with the most conscientious of counsel. An attorney frequently had only the briefest conference with the defendant before improvising a case in court. When counsel was indifferent or incompetent, or when close personal and professional ties with the prosecutor seemed to militate against forceful advocacy, the defense was at best perfunctory, making no motion for retrial and attempting no appeal. At Tom Carraway's trial in 1931, Mississippi Supreme Court Justice Griffith concluded that "he had counsel only in form." According to this judge, the attorney in question " 'laid flat down on the job,'... even to the extent of allowing a fictitious confession to be used." The trial judge overruled a motion for a retrial, but agreed that Carraway's lawyer "at every step of the proceeding evidenced an absolute indifference as to the result of the trial and the fate of his client."[61]

No doubt indigent white defendants, particularly those charged with grave or inflammatory offenses, also suffered the neglect and incompetence of some court-appointed defense attorneys. Records in the governors' pardon files suggest, however, that in matters of defense caste considerations loomed larger than those of class, and that assigned attorneys were rarely less diligent than when defending black causes.[62]

Much the same argument emerged from Governor Martin Sennett Conner's "Court of Mercy" hearings in 1935. Fulfilling an inaugural pledge to investigate the plight of Mississippi's "forgotten men," Conner reviewed the cases of 160 convicts, most of them blacks "without means or friends." Professing astonishment that black children were assigned to the penitentiary, he ordered the release of perhaps two dozen prisoners, including an inmate known for fourteen years by his judge to be innocent, and "three little nigger boys," ages eleven and twelve. The inquiry demonstrated, the Governor believed, that the price of cotton and the availability of plantation labor sometimes determined both the solicitude of the bench and the vigor of the defense available to a black defendant. In Conner's judgment, planter interests figured importantly in the judicial process, for when cotton was cheap and the white need for black hand labor easily met, blacks were too often persuaded by court-appointed defense counsel to plead guilty regardless of the merits of their cases. "It is obvious to me," Conner said, "that when labor is plentiful in the delta the accused is permitted to go to the penitentiary."[63]

There were notable exceptions, court-assigned attorneys who risked much and faithfully defended their black clients. A Jones County defense lawyer may have spoken for a substantial segment of the state bar when he argued that "whatever else we may deny the negro, we do give him the same measure of even handed justice we claim for ourselves."[64] Moreover, a recent (and notably sympathetic) historian of the Mississippi Bar Association gives its members generally high marks for fairness. They were, he notes, representatives of "the state's professional, upper class elite." They "tended to regard blacks with benevolent paternalism and apparently felt that, though they might not be in all respects the equals of whites, they were entitled to the equal protection of the law." But if that were true, and it was surely true of some, there were many other attorneys who in the face of white community pressure abandoned both the abstraction of equal justice and their paternalism in favor of an expediency that served the prosecution better than the defense.

Indeed, as the same scholar conceded, well into the 1960s "white Mississippi attorneys who took on 'outside agitators' or 'uppity' blacks as clients were apt to come under intolerable pressure from their friends, neighbors, and other clients."[65]

Perhaps the record holds no more telling judgment on the quality of the legal services available to Mississippi blacks than the one offered inadvertently by United States Senator Hubert D. Stephens. In a patronage letter to President Herbert Hoover, the federal lawmaker from Mississippi searched for words to prove the exceptional impartiality of a candidate for the office of the United States attorney for Mississippi's northern district, and then settled for these: "I have seen him represent negroes against white men. In such cases he was as active, earnest and vigorous as if his client were white."[66]

On Appeal: Between Caste and Law

The black defendant was not entirely at the uncertain mercies of lawyers and circuit judges. The state supreme court could correct trial-court injustices. Because the state had no intermediate appellate body and the high court had no discretionary power to choose or refuse cases, review by the superior court was theoretically available to every defendant. But for the poor, the practical availability of the appeal process was limited. Direct review of trial decisions was not mandatory even in capital cases and could be undertaken only upon formal petition. Poor people of both races apparently found appeal to be costly and difficult—and blacks sometimes found it to be dangerous. Court-appointed attorneys generally lost interest in their indigent clients upon conviction. As legal scholars frequently remind us, then, judicial review was not a realistic possibility for social mudsills, and particularly for Negroes.[67] In a system in which the court of first resort could also be the last, trial-level errors often went undetected.

Nor was appeal necessarily a guarantee of justice. In an earlier era, the Mississippi High Court of Errors and Appeals, like the appellate courts of most of the newer states of the Old South, offered the slave essentially fair treatment in an otherwise oppressive era. The antebellum high court was, of course, a bulwark of the peculiar institution; its rulings invariably recognized human bondage as the "natural condition" of a "degraded" and "inferior" species of humanity. Yet when the interests of slavery as an institution were not in question, the court could be sympathetic, at times even indulgent, to a particular slave. Its decisions in the relatively narrow area of criminal law, as one scholar put it, were "enlightened and well reasoned, compassionate and yet scholarly."[68] Among the fairest courts of the slave South, Mississippi's High Court of Errors apparently offered blacks about as much justice as a society based on caste could tolerate.

Less should be claimed for the state supreme court in the half century after 1890, although it too could apply the law with striking impartiality. Its justices also worked within the circumscriptions of caste. To a man, they seemed to share the racial values of their time and place. After 1914, when their terms were reduced from nine to eight years and their offices were changed from appointive to elective, they were, moreover, directly answerable to a lily-white electorate. They were not, however, merely politicians in robes. Compared to other public officials, they enjoyed long and uncontested tenures. Between 1916 and 1940, only two of nine full-term judges on a six-judge court were denied reelection. Their electioneering was notably free of the racial mudslinging generally characteristic of Mississippi political campaigns.[69]

More insulated and therefore less identified with local influences and less responsive to popular pressures than trial judges, the supreme court justices often managed a sufficient sense of distance to remedy the worst abuses of the courts below. Although precise comparisons must await further research, they also appeared to be generally more professional, more paternalistic, and more committed to the rule of law than trial-court judges. And while they did not eagerly intrude on the prerogatives of lower tribunals, they were capable of responsible supervision of trial-level justice.

Among the black defendants' most common complaints was the prosecutor's resort to race issues in criminal trials. When such cases were unambiguous and sufficiently egregious, the high court usually granted relief. In a characteristic ruling, Associate Justice Sam C. Cook wrote for a unanimous court in 1912: "The race question and all of its vexations should be dropped at the outer door of all courts of justice. When a black man is on trial for his life, he, of course, should be . . . convicted or acquitted according to the evidence and law that would lead a fair and impartial jury to convict or acquit a white man."[70] Prosecutors who failed to heed these noble sentiments were routinely scolded for "the unfair and barbarous practice of trying the accused upon his color"; trial judges who permitted the state to employ racial arguments were reminded of the magistrate's duty, "sua sponte," to interfere "of his own motion" lest his failure be interpreted, "sub silentio," as an endorsement of "race prejudice" and "popular clamor."[71]

When fair-skinned Ezra Hampton appealed a conviction in 1906 for the murder of another Negro he did so on the ground that he had been prejudicially characterized by the state as a representative of a race "worse than negroes," one "accursed by every white man." The high court ruled in his favor. Justice Solomon Saladin Calhoon advised the court below that "only impartial trials can pass the Red Sea of this court without drowning." Such dicta, the black attorney Willis E. Mollison believed, were "the pillar of fire by night and cloud by day to all who seek to administer justice with 'unfevered hand.' "[72]

Even in more sensitive cases—as when the testimony of a white accuser was opposed only by that of the black accused,[73] or when blacks were charged with serious crimes against whites—the appeals court often insisted on the same color-blind standard. William Harris, for example, was convicted in 1909 of assault with intent to kill a white man, but he was granted a retrial when the supreme court determined that the closing remarks of the district attorney "were a direct appeal to race prejudice, and are of such a highly inflammatory character, and so manifestly transcend any legitimate bounds of argument as to necessitate reversal of themselves."[74]

Self-defense, as virtually all black attorneys agreed, was generally no defense in a Mississippi court when the decedent was white.[75] Yet on at least two occasions the high court overturned convictions in such cases because the evidence suggested justifiable homicide rather than murder. In a 1929 case, the judges not only set aside the verdict of the lower court but also discharged the appellate on the ground that "if this had been a case where a white man had killed a white man, or a negro had killed a negro, or a white man had killed a negro, there would never have been a conviction."[76] A 1919 case—though it presented greater difficulties for the court because it involved the death of a white police officer—was also fairly resolved. The black appellant, Anthony Williams, was arrested in Arcola (Washington County) on unspecified charges after he allegedly brandished a pistol at another Negro in a game of dice. When he denied possession of the weapon, the officer took him behind a cotton gin, flogged his bare back, hit him with a pistol, and kicked him in the mouth. Williams then produced the handgun and killed the officer. He was convicted, and on first appeal the six justices divided evenly. Appealed again on suggestion of error, the conviction was reversed and remanded in a four-two decision. The majority found that the officer was killed while on an "unlawful mission" by an appellant who had acted while under "unlawful duress."[77]

At its evenhanded best, then, the high court insisted that blacks be tried within the framework of law. In 1942, when it reversed the conviction of Willie Upton, a black man convicted in Warren County for raping a teenage white girl, the editor of the NAACP's *Crisis* magazine applauded: "The Mississippi supreme court has seen fit to consider the merits of the case, rather than the color of the persons involved." On its face, that reversal appeared routine enough: an appellant with a credible alibi and a "physical incapacity" had been convicted on the contradictory and uncorroborated testimony of a fifteen-year-old accusor. Nevertheless, as the black editor knew, convictions for rape were rarely set aside by the popularly elected judges of a Deep South court. The ruling suggested that even in Mississippi there was "progress toward the goal of justice for all."[78]

But progress followed an erratic path. When the court found that "law knows no color" or when it reversed convictions grounded on "racial prejudice and Southern sentiment";[79] when it remanded black causes based on coerced testimony or overturned black death sentences for rape or murder of whites because the evidence would not sustain the verdict; when it followed the high road to these decisions, it demonstrated that it understood and could enforce the Constitution. But in other cases, some of them fully as irregular as those it overturned, the high court demonstrated that it could not apply it consistently. It would generally tolerate neither wholesale departures from due process nor convictions based on naked appeals to race. It repeatedly affirmed that equality before the law "is a firm and settled proposition in this court,"[80] but it was too easily beguiled by the form of law. When the issues were relatively subtle, when juridic forms were duly observed, or when white dominance itself was in question, the appeals judges presumed that justice had prevailed in the court below.

In its decisions in *Brown* v. *Mississippi,* the court's majority side-stepped the merits of the appellant's case and pursued a technicality. Although conceding that the convictions of the petitioners were based on involuntary confessions, it upheld the death sentences because during the trial the defense had not objected to the state's evidence and because the court below had not blatantly violated established rules of procedure. With much the same logic the supreme court's majority let stand the death sentence of Tom Carraway, who as we have seen was convicted on testimony that during the appeals process was admitted to be false by both the prosecutor and the trial judge. The majority reasoned that because during the original proceeding the flawed nature of the state's evidence had been known to the defendant and thus necessarily, it presumed, to his attorney, and because that issue had not then been raised, it could not on appeal be called "newly discovered" evidence and could not therefore be ground for a retrial.[81]

A third and final example of the high court's penchant for legal formalism is the conviction of Sonnie Dobbs, which it affirmed because

Dobbs's court-appointed attorney had not filed for a retrial within the term of court. In few cases was the denial of justice clearer. A World War II veteran only ninety days out of uniform, Dobbs was attacked in 1946 by seven drunken whites in Attala County. He fought back, killing one of his assailants with a knife. In a proceeding that conformed in virtually every particular to other mob-dominated black criminal trials of the period, court-assigned counsel failed even to raise the issue of self-defense.[82]

In each of these three cases, a black respondent was denied substantive justice by an appeals court that dodged its obligation to protect human life. In rulings that were not so much judgments as casuistries, a procedure-bound high court acquiesced in legal lynchings and discovered in the canon of process the way around its supervisory responsibility. In these decisions it seemed to deny its own precedents. Earlier, in *Fisher* v. *Mississippi* (1926), the rights of a black petitioner had been upheld in language that was broadly applicable: "The duty of maintaining constitutional rights of a person on trial for his life rises above mere rules of procedure."[83] Duty in the three later cases seemed to demand no less, but as Justice Griffith wrote in his dissent in *Carraway,* "technical rules," "mere rules of procedure" were honored above "common and honest justice." "In such a case," Griffith argued, "the court of last resort, far removed from the scene and the influence which often so strongly operates to bring about results such as are here shown should apply a corrective and grant a new trial." Instead it neglected its "judicial duty," submerged the merits of the Negro's cause in sophistic argument, and permitted him to be "ordered to the gallows out of respect to technical rules."[84]

The court's see-no-evil literalism, so apparent in these cases, was never so patent as when the racial composition of juries was at issue. During Reconstruction, Mississippi courts honored the federal prohibition against racial discrimination in the selection of jurors, and even after the white Democratic restoration (1875) blacks appeared (albeit in declining numbers) on jury panels in most counties through the mid-1880s. After disfranchisement, however, black jurors were effectively, although not explicitly, eliminated by a state constitutional provision that restricted jury service to qualified electors of "sound judgment and fine character." By 1900, Mississippi juries virtually by definition were lily-white.[85]

Asked to rule on the issue for the first time in a series of cases in 1895 and 1896, the state appeals court refused to intervene. And so, too, did the United States Supreme Court. Blacks tried by all-white juries had not been denied equal protection, the federal court concluded, because Mississippi laws governing jury selection "do not on their face discriminate between the races." Admitting that these laws granted official discretion that "has been exercised against the colored race," the federal justices ruled nevertheless that appellants had failed to show that "their actual administration was evil, only that evil was possible under them."[86]

When the issue reemerged early in the twentieth century the state court softened its position slightly, ruling this time that a black citizen's right to an impartial jury prohibited the "purposeful" or "willful" exclusion of blacks from jury lists. The absence of black veniremen was not in itself judged to be discriminatory and did not in itself suggest that race was a factor in jury selection. Where black electors were in short supply, the court reasoned, so too must black jurors be.[87] By such logic, the justices could affirm their demand for an abstract fairness without challenging laws that in their effects were blatantly discriminatory.

Such was the standard for jury selection until 1946, when Eddie Patton carried an appeal to the United States Supreme Court. Convicted for murdering a white man in Lauderdale County, he based his petition directly on constitutional grounds: indictment by an all-white grand jury, trial by an all-white petit jury in a county that, though 35 percent black, had not had a black juror for more than thirty years. The state appeals court rejected his argument, but the federal court found in it "very strong evidence of purposeful racial discrimination." Patton's cause was remanded for retrial.[88]

That rebuke required the appeals judges to shift ground, but again only slightly. For nearly twenty years thereafter, they upheld convictions by all-white juries whenever local authorities merely denied discriminatory procedures. In a typical post-*Patton* affirmation, the court found that "no Negro had actually served on either the grand or petit juries in the county [of Lincoln] during a period of more than thirty years," yet it accepted the testimony of county officials that the condemned Negro's jury was all white merely by happenstance—testimony the appellate body thought to be disputed only by the "circumstance that in years past no Negro had been summoned or had served." If that circumstance could nullify this proceeding it could, as the judges recognized, also nullify black convictions in "a large majority, if not all, of the eighty-two counties of this state."[89] That, of course, was the rub. The Negro was denied equal protection because he was denied political power. On this knottiest of judicial problems the court could not serve both the Fourteenth Amendment and Jim Crow; it could not open the jury box to blacks without opening the Pandora's box of black suffrage.

In the last analysis, then, justice for Mississippi's Afro-American population was necessarily qualified because it was dispensed by courts that honored white supremacy above the rule of law. In important respects those courts were more vulnerable to racial pressures than were their predecessors of the antebellum period. So long as blacks were property, so long as their place was permanently fixed by their status as slaves, the justices of the High Court of Errors and Appeals might stretch an otherwise harsh slave code in their favor. It could often do so with white approval, for not the least of the bond servants' courtroom advantages was the capital investment they represented. Because their lives and labor were sources of white wealth it was usually not in the white interest to judge them hastily or to punish them unduly. Although acts of resistance or rebellion routinely met brutal treatment in a society that lived in dread of servile insurrections, the court was free in the more routine areas of slave criminality to display a measure of equity often denied black defendants in the postbellum period.

Without materially changing the black circumstance, emancipation brought presumptive freedom, theoretical equality with whites, statutory and constitutional guarantees to the same rights under the same law. And precisely because it did these things, it blunted the paternalism that often characterized white behavior under slavery and it quickened the repressive tendencies of a society of white supremacists who had every reason to fear the implications of freedom.

More than its antebellum counterpart, then, the high court in Jim Crow Mississippi was an institution in the middle, caught between the conflicting demands of caste and law. Because it could not serve two such disparate masters with equal fidelity, it often spoke eloquently in defense of equity even as it acquiesced in a double standard of justice designed to keep the races separate and unequal.

CHAPTER 7

Judge Lynch's Court

If it is necessary every Negro in the state will be lynched; it will be done to maintain white supremacy.

—James K. Vardaman, 1907[1]

In those days it was "Kill a mule, buy another. Kill a nigger, hire another." They had to have a license to kill anything but a nigger. We was always in season.

—A Black Mississippian remembering the lynching era[2]

I led the mob which lynched Nelse Patton and I am proud of it. I directed every movement of the mob and I did everything I could to see that he was lynched. Cut a white woman's throat? . . . Of course I wanted him lynched. . . . I don't care what investigation is made. . . . I will lead a mob in such a case any time.

—Former U.S. Senator William Van Amberg Sullivan, 1908[3]

White Death

His verse rarely rose above the romantic conventions of love— of country, women, mother, and life. Yet the Jackson attorney and writer Samuel Alfred Beadle was so tormented at the turn of the century by the rising toll of mob violence that he wrote one "unashamedly angry" poem, "Strike for Equal Rights."

> Think of the price of liberty,
> Think of the lash and slavery,
> of lynch rule and its massacre
>   And strike for equal rights.
>
> Say, must we longer trust the law,
> Class-enacted to hide the flaw

of the crimson hand that strikes to awe
And terrorize us into slaves?

Let him who thinks or has fears,
When the cowardly mob appears,
Receive a coward's mud and tears,
Death and a piece of hemp.
. . . .

Come the valiant, and come the brave,
Come all except the abject slave —
Let him fall in a bondman's grave —
And strike for liberty![4]

From the pen of a black Mississippian not otherwise identifiably radical, the unmistakable tit-for-tat fury of these lines fairly startles. Described in an unpublished biography as "a stirring call to latent bravery," an appeal to blacks to "weight the price of liberty against the cost of the lash and slavery,"[5] the poem evokes the militant tradition of black protest thought. Its explicit contrast between slave submissiveness and the defiant courage of free men recalls the antislavery pyrotechnics of David Walker's *Appeal* (1829): "Are we not men! . . . Kill or be killed . . . had you not rather be killed than to be a slave to a tyrant. . . ." And Henry Highland Garnet's "Address to the Slaves" (1843): "Liberty or death. . . . Rather die freemen than live to be the slaves." Or Claude McKay's more recent poetic summons to black arms, "If We Must Die" (1919): "Like men we'll face the murderous, cowardly pack, Pressed to the wall, dying, but fighting back!"[6]

Happily, Beadle died of natural causes, never having to test his own resolve against the mob. All too many other black Mississippians, however, experienced firsthand the terror of trial by torchlight. Some of them found the means to fight back, meeting vigilante violence with counterviolence and nearly always dying in the act of self-defense. Dave Hagen, for one, preferred suicide to the noose: accused in 1916 of assaulting a police officer and tracked by bloodhounds through rural Madison County, he slit his own throat with a razor rather than submit to capture.[7]

At other times, black fugitives from vigilante justice and those to whom they turned for protection in the black community directed their weapons on the pursuer. In 1906, in what one observer thought to be "the most strenuous excitement . . . since the civil war," Wiggins blacks exchanged more than 500 shots with a white mob bent on indiscriminate punishment of blacks for attempting to prevent the lynching of a "bad nigger." After dynamiting the jail to seize "Dollar Bill" Smith, enraged whites entered the Negro section where blacks were rumored to be massing for an armed defense of the incarcerated man. Apparently, no one died in the shoot-out, but the casualties were said to be heavy on both sides.[8]

Similarly, blacks in the Wahalak community of Kemper County had a reputation for armed resistance to white terror; twice in two decades they waged race war against invading vigilantes. In 1888, after an inconclusive fight between a black and a white youth, a white "posse" pursued the offending Negro into the black section of Wahalak, where "organized and armed" black men met fire with fire. At least two whites and "several negroes" died in the exchange.[9] In 1906, Governor Vardaman dispatched state militia to the same community to put down a Christmas Eve riot. Having lynched one black, a band of white men invaded Wahalak and surrounding black districts, in order, as newspapers reported, to punish "impudent and quarrelsome" blacks and "strike terror into the negroes, who had been getting defiant of late." Although the blacks were thought to be well-armed and prepared to "fight if necessary," the timely arrival of state troops and an influx of whites from surrounding communities assured that the casualties would be unequally shared: all told, one white and at least sixteen blacks died in some forty-eight hours of intermittent fighting. Three days after the melee began, the *Weekly Clarion-Ledger* feared that white lives would not be secure until "the last of the obnoxious negroes have been done away with."[10]

These bloody encounters notwithstanding, armed black resistance to mob violence was rarely possible. Typical victims—lone fugitives trailed by bloodhounds or unarmed prisoners taken from a sheriff—could rarely defend themselves, and concerted action by an intended victim's friends or family was scarcely more conceivable. Sidearms were widely carried by men of both races, but whites usually enjoyed a clear preponderance of firepower and could virtually always count on the support of police and militia. Blacks who attempted to conceal, much less openly defend, the object of a "nigger hunt" invited white fury upon themselves. When, as the saying went, white "feelings ran high," even the rumor of a black rising brought swift retribution as armed men from throughout a given district converged to "set the niggers right."

Although whites often spoke of "orderly" lynchings, vigilantes had a well-deserved reputation for indiscriminate violence. "You don't understand how we feel down here," a young white Mississippian explained to the historian Albert Bushnell Hart in 1908: "When there is a row, we feel like killing a nigger whether he has done anything or not."[11] Thus mob actions often resulted not merely in the summary execution of the offending Negro, but in looting, arson, more or less aimless "nigger whippings," accidental shootings, even random murders.[12] "It is generally a bad negro who starts crime and before he is caught or hanged," the editor of the Greenville *Times* noted, "many innocent ones suffer from the temper of the mob."[13]

Given such odds, black Mississippians typically responded to white lawlessness either by retreating to the relative safety of their own community or by out-migration. "Every lynching almost without exception is followed by a departure of numbers of colored people," James Weldon Johnson believed. Robert R. Moton described mob violence as "the chief cause of unrest among Negroes" during World War I and "the cause most often given as a reason for wanting to migrate to the North."[14]

However appealing, immediate flight to safer environs was less practical than self-imposed isolation from whites. In 1919, after a black was burned in Vicksburg, a local newspaper reported "a noticeable absence of negroes on the streets"; local merchants "missed the negro trade."[15] Following another burning that same year near Laurel, one local historian has written, blacks minimized contacts with whites and race leaders "were silenced by their belief that a protest might result in things being made harder for the masses of their race. . . . When racial troubles occurred the colored citizens . . . remained in their homes." A Delta lynching in 1930, as one young black Coahoma Countian recalled, left blacks frozen in fear: "This mob had all the niggers in town scared. . . . None of 'em would come out on the streets. . . . That mob would push you around and beat you up if you acted funny. They went through all the niggers' houses and nobody tried to stop 'em." Nor did black memories of white terror quickly fade. In 1968, more than four decades after a particularly barbarous mob execution in Rocky Ford, an effort to record the tragedy was frustrated by black reticence. Negroes in the area, it was noted, "won't even mention the [victim's] name." "There has been a hush-hush in Union County for forty-three year[s]."[16]

Black fear, of course, did not merely attend a particular event. Writing of "the threatening atmosphere in which Negroes live," Dollard reported in 1937 that though Indianola had not had a lynching in many years, fear of lynching in that community was "one of the major facts in the life of any Negro." Drawing on interviews with black Sunflower Countians, Dollard concluded that "the threat of lynching is likely to be in the mind of the Negro child from the earliest days." The young Richard Wright agreed. The fear of lynching, what he called the "white death," "hung over every male black in the South." When he was scarcely ten years old, Wright later remembered, "a dread of white people . . . came to live permanently in my imagination." "I had already grown to feel that there existed men against whom I was powerless, men who could violate my life at will." Although in his youthful fantasies he was prepared to "kill as many of them as possible before they killed me," Wright also "felt completely helpless in the face of this threat that might come upon me at any time . . . because there did not exist to my knowledge any possible course of action which could have saved me if I had ever been confronted with a white mob."[17]

First on the Roll

Although antebellum Mississippi had a well-established reputation for mob violence, lynching was not a distinctly interracial phenomenon until the Civil War. Before 1860 racial concerns rarely figured in vigilantism and victims of mob violence were far more likely to be white than black.[18] During the Confederate period, however, white terror was increasingly visited on the black community. By war's end, one historian has written, Negro lynchings were "commonplace" in Mississippi; by the end of Reconstruction racially motivated extralegal executions were a state "tradition," a "characteristic of society." Charles Sumner's estimate for the Republican years — "a daily average of two or three black men killed" — may be too high, but well before the return of white rule Mississippi had established its leadership among lynching states.[19]

During the 1870s and 1880s, mob executions of blacks were so common that they excited interest only in the black community. State and local authorities kept no records and never sought the arrest of vigilantes. Most of what was known about mob violence appeared in the highly sectarian pages of the white press, where the subject was typically covered, when it was covered at all, among the "Mississippi Brevities" or "Miscellaneous Items." In fairly typical fashion, an 1885 issue of the Raymond *Gazette* noted in a single line of small type: "Four negroes were lynched in Grenada last week; also one at Oxford."[20] Vernon Lane Wharton, who studied the problem more closely than anyone else, found it "impossible to make any estimate" of the number of lynchings in Mississippi during the first quarter century of freedom.[21]

For the years after 1890, the tally is somewhat more complete, though blacks generally believed that the numbers actually reported were a pale reflection of the violent truth. In 1919, when Holmes County blacks informed a Memphis newspaper of the lynching of a recently discharged black soldier and young black woman near Pickens, the paper ran into a wall of silence. Community leaders indignantly denied rumors of the double lynching, and the acting marshal, although acknowledging that vigilantes had stormed the jail and taken the young veteran, suggested that his prisoner had somehow escaped from the mob: "I guess he got clear away. . . . No, I haven't heard of any lynching."[22]

In 1934, the NAACP officially attributed six lynchings to Mississippi but a Meridian race leader placed the figure "nearer 20." Except in the state's larger cities, he advised the association, "such news is hardly ever published." In 1939 Madison County blacks informed Walter White that local authorities had suppressed news of two unrelated lynchings within ten months: "The newspapers of Canton, Miss., have not written a word and there have been no arrests made and the Negroes have been told not to discuss the incident." Other country editors in the state suppressed news of local mob violence because "such things always result in hard feelings" and "publicity on such matters merely results in a lot of adverse criticism by outside papers."[23]

Clearly, then, lynching data are scarcely more than suggestive. Mississippi communities sometimes, perhaps frequently, managed to bury the evidence of their racial crimes along with their black victims. What astonishes is not that some lynchings were covered up but that so many lynchers felt at liberty to operate so openly in the confidence that their deeds were sanctioned by the community and beyond the reach of law or even serious public censure.

No agency kept systematic records until 1882, when the Chicago *Tribune* began producing annual estimates. The first yearly report of Tuskegee Institute appeared in 1913 and the NAACP did not collect annual data until 1917. But because these keepers of the lynching record depended upon local press reports or letters from local blacks, even such records as they kept must be viewed as crude and probably very conservative estimates.

The figures are, nevertheless, shocking. During the period from 1889 to 1945, the half century Roy Wilkins called the "lynching era," Mississippi accounted for 476, or nearly 13 percent, of the nation's 3,786 recorded lynchings. If the beginning date is pushed back to include the 1880s, the bloody decade immediately preceding disfranchisement, the toll in Mississippi exceeded 600. Twenty-three of the victims (after 1888) were white men and one was a white woman. Fourteen were black women, at least two of whom were well advanced in pregnancy. The remainder were, of course, male blacks, most of them relatively young, a great many of them still minors, some scarcely adolescents.[24]

Although Georgia and Texas were close rivals, Mississippi was the state most embarrassing to congressional opponents of federal anti-lynching legislation. It ranked first in virtually every category—the most total lynchings, the most multiple lynchings, the most per capita, the most female victims, the most victims taken from police custody, the most lynchings without arrest or conviction of mob leaders, the most public support for vigilantism.[25] Standing in the statistical and geographic center of the national lynching belt, Mississippi's record, the Norfolk *Journal and Guide* observed, made the other southern states "look like pikers." The Chicago *Defender* described the state as "the most brutal community in history"; Walter White placed it at the top of his list of "hopeless states." It was, in the opinion of one North Carolina editor, "without peer," "first on the roll," the state with "the blackest mob-murder record in the country."[26]

As Figure 7.1 demonstrates, mob violence was widely distributed in Mississippi. Essentially a rural small-town phenomenon, lynchings also occurred in the state's largest population centers: Columbus, Greenville, Hattiesburg, Jackson, Laurel, Meridian, Natchez, Vicksburg, and Yazoo City. By 1936, however, when Ellwood Higginbotham was taken from jail during a trial for murder and summarily executed in Oxford, population 3,890, vigilante executions in communities that large were unusual.[27] Eight counties had no reported lynchings (1889-1945), but mobs were active in every region of the state, irrespective of demographic, historical, or cultural differences. Vigilantes struck even in the noncotton counties where white majorities were greatest — including Tishomingo and Itawamba of the northeastern hills (the counties with the lowest percentage of black population), Harrison and Jackson of the coastal plain, and Greene and George of the sparsely populated Piney Woods.

As Table 7.1 reveals, however, the great majority of lynchings — 70 percent of the sample — occurred in the state's black belt, in the plantation districts with the greatest density of black population. Of the counties with no record of mob violence, only Tate was a black-majority county. Hinds, the county with the highest total black population at the turn of the century, led all others, followed by the Black Prairie counties of Lowndes and Kemper and the all- or part-Delta counties of Desoto, Bolivar, and Washington.[28] Yet bloody as the record of the black belt was in absolute terms, Mississippi Negroes were relatively less vulnerable to the mob in counties in which their numbers were greatest. Statistically, per 10,000 black population, individual blacks were less at risk in such old plantation counties as Adams, Jefferson, or Claiborne — even in Bolivar and Washington — than in such timber counties as Perry and Jones, or even rugged, "disloyal" Tishomingo, the stronghold of nonslaveholding Unionist hillbillies who voted against secession in 1861.[29] Measured in this way, in proportion to black population density, lynching rates, unlike other forms of race oppression, rise as black population decreases and fall as it increases.[30] As a practical

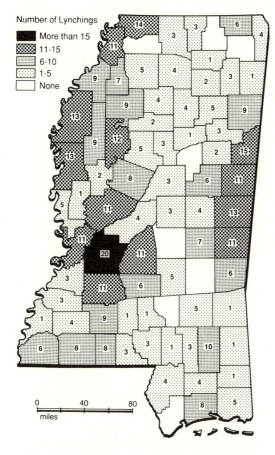

FIG. 7.1. Mississippi Lynchings, 1889-1945.

Table 7.1. Distribution of Mississippi Lynchings, 1889-1939.

Black population of counties[1]	Number of counties	Percentage of all lynchings[2]
Less than ¼ black	12	6
¼ to ½ black	34	24
More than ½ black	36	70
Totals	82	100

[1] Average black population, 1890-1930.
[2] Based on a 20 percent random sample, i.e., 87 of 434 lynchings.
Sources: Adapted from NAACP, *Thirty Years of Lynching,* 74-80; NAACP, *Annual Reports,* 1919-1939.

matter, however, the per capita rate seems less significant than the absolute numbers of mob deaths. Because lynching, as object lesson, touched the entire black community and not merely the victims and their families, the larger total number of mob deaths in the Delta may have produced more fear than the higher statistical probability of lynching in the white counties. To the Washington County blacks who in the course of one lifetime could have witnessed at least thirteen vigilante executions in their county alone, there was cold comfort in the fact that they were somehow statistically safer than their hill county counterparts.[31]

There were two sustained periods of peak mob activity in Jim Crow Mississippi: 1889-1908 and 1918-1922. The first coincides with what has been called the South's "capitulation to racism"; the second with the uneasy years during and immediately following World War I. Although early data, as we have seen, are unreliable, the lynching curve began to rise sharply during Reconstruction as conservative Democrats moved to consolidate white control. The violence reached record levels during the agricultural depression of the 1890s and the era of radical racism that culminated in the triumph of "Vardamanism." Half of the 476 Mississippi lynchings during the fifty years after 1888 occurred before 1904: twenty-five of them in 1889, twenty-four in 1891, twenty-one in 1900. In 1903, the year the "White Chief" captured the redneck vote and the governor's mansion with his earthy brand of racial vitriol, there were eighteen. From 1904 through 1908, the Vardaman years, there were seventy-four more, or an average of one every twenty-five days. Thereafter, the number declined precipitously until the unsettling wartime years brought a second great surge. After 1921 there were never as many as ten authenticated summary executions in a single year and in 1932, 1940, 1941, 1943, and 1945 there were none at all. Race

number lynched per year

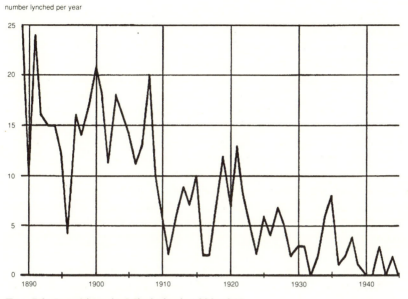

FIG. 7.2. Lynchings in Mississippi, 1889-1945.

murder, as we shall see, assumed new forms in the 1930s and 1940s, but lynching in the classic sense never again reached major proportions in Mississippi. By the early 1950s it had been so fully supplanted by other means of white control that Tuskegee's Department of Records no longer considered it a barometer of race relations in the South.[32]

"Negro Barbeques"

Savage as the statistical record was, postbellum mob violence did not turn truly sadistic until after 1890. Until late in the century, hanging and shooting were the customary forms of lynching; in the twentieth century, however, as the number of victims gradually declined, mobs grew more barbarous. Once comparatively rare, some form of mutilation became commonplace, either preceding or following an execution; lynchers and spectators frequently gathered souvenirs—small bones, ears, toes, and fingers—for use sometimes as watch fobs or for display as curiosities in service stations or general stores. Even the methods of execution changed as the noose increasingly gave way to the faggot and to varied and often highly inventive forms of torture.[33]

Invariably, what Wilbur Cash called the "rape complex" brought out the worst in any mob, but black Mississippians charged with violence against white men also met indescribable cruelties: two were executed by blow torch, one was tortured to death with a hot iron, others were drowned, bludgeoned, and dragged to death behind automobiles. Between 1900 and 1940 at least fifteen blacks died in public burnings,[34] a method described by one newspaper as "NEGRO BARBEQUES"[35] and one generally reserved for male blacks accused of sexual crimes or improprieties against white women. In some instances the agony of the victim was reported in graphic detail by local white journalists apparently eager to satisfy the public appetite for gore, what Jacquelyn Dowd Hall has called "the late-Victorian relish in the details of death."[36] Before Luther Holbert and his wife were burned by whites who charged them in 1904 with murdering a planter, the Vicksburg *Evening Post* noted, they suffered the "most fiendish tortures" at the hands of whites who chopped off their fingers and ears, one by one, gouged their eyes until they "hung by a shred from the socket," and pulled "big pieces of raw, quivering flesh" from their bodies with corkscrews. A crowd estimated at one thousand observed the butchery.[37]

In 1919, following the burning of Lloyd Clay, readers of the same city's newspapers were told how "the flesh on the body began to crinkle and blister," how "the face of the negro became horribly distorted with pain," how "the legs of the corpse curled backward grewsomely [*sic*]."[38] When I. Q. Ivy, an accused rapist, died at the stake at Rocky Ford in 1925 a Mississippi correspondent for the Memphis *News-Scimitar* described the "leaping blaze," the "odor of the baking flesh," the "cry of agony as the flames reached him"—" 'Oh God; Oh God,' he shouted, 'I didn't do it. Have mercy.' "[39]

In early 1929 the Jackson *Daily News* used its front page and its most matter-of-fact style to describe the burning near Shelby (Bolivar County) of mentally retarded Charley Sheppard, noting that for seven hours "the enraged farm and townspeople of the Delta went methodically about their work of torturing"; that before his gasoline-soaked body was ignited his "mouth and nose were partly filled with mud to prevent him from inhaling gas fumes which might cause his instant death"; that "it was 45 minutes before the powerfully built negro finally quit his convulsive twitching and agonized fighting at the ropes and flames"; that "the blackened skull . . . smoked in a ditch beside the road this morning, tossed there by a souvenir hunter."[40]

These barbarities were routinely excused in the name of white womanhood.[41] Although black crimes against white women remained comparatively rare, the post-1890 defenders of lynching increasingly found justification for mob violence in an alleged epidemic of black rape and the parallel myth of black atavism—of the Negro savage now freed from the restraints of slavery and rapidly retrogressing toward his natural, lustful, bestial state. Following a "nigger burning" near Corinth in 1902, Vardaman expressed his preference for legal executions or even extralegal live burials. A public burning, the state's next governor wrote in his Greenwood *Commonwealth,* "is not elevating"; it could be "rather hardening" and perhaps contribute to the "moral deterioration" of white civilization. Yet mob violence in some form, he thought, was often the only "adequate punishment" for a black "two legged monster" who defiled "the exalted virtue, the vestal purity and superlative qualities of southern woman."

Following World War I, Mississippi Congressman John Rankin opposed a federal antilynching proposal as "a bill to encourage rape."[42] Most white Mississippians apparently agreed. Mob violence was generally described, even by some who openly lamented its frequency, as a necessary evil, an unseemly but effective deterrent to black lust. In the estimate of one clergyman, the witness to a lynching near Carrollton in 1901, "the greater part of the educated, conservative, thoughtful, and in ordinary situations, more influential citizens, approve of lynching for the rape of a white woman but deplore the seeming necessity for it." Nearly four decades later, Hortense Powdermaker sampled adult white opinion in Sunflower County and discovered that 64 percent believed "lynching for rape is justifiable."[43]

Mounting white fears of the black "beast-rapist" notwithstanding, sexual congress in any form was a relatively minor "cause" of mob violence in Mississippi or any southern state. As nearly every serious student of vigilantism since Ida B. Wells's pioneering research of the 1880s has recognized, chivalry was more often an excuse than an explanation for lynching. Drawing on records kept by the Chicago *Tribune,* Wells, the Mississippi-born antilynching crusader, concluded that rape was alleged—much less proved—in only one third of the nation's summary executions. The NAACP reduced the figure still more. Based on its data for the period from 1889 to 1935, the association estimated that 19 percent of all blacks lynched in the United States—and 12.7 percent of those lynched in Mississippi—were accused of rape.[44]

Observers closer to the scene sometimes also agreed that black sexual violence against white women was more often imagined than real. In 1902, even as the white obsession with black rape neared pathological proportions, Alfred Holt Stone thought such "violations" to be "an unknown crime" in the state's plantation counties. Another white Deltan conceded in 1908 that in twenty years he had heard of but one case in his district, yet "we never take our eyes off the gun. . . . I never leave my wife and daughter at home without a [white] man in the house after ten o'clock at night—because I am afraid."[45] The offense did occasionally occur, but the record of mob violence in the state suggests that interracial intimacy perhaps figured as importantly as forcible rape, and that some Mississippi blacks who were lynched on accusations of sexual crimes against white women had merely violated the taboo against interracial sex.[46] Moreover, in a society in which black men habitually averted their eyes from white women and otherwise learned to move circumspectly in their presence, an act of minor disrespect or even a careless gesture might result in the charge of attempted assault, a charge often not distinguished from that of rape itself. There is also reason to believe that chivalry was sometimes merely the pretext for punishing uppity Negroes. The Stone County mob that lynched Wilder McGowan in 1938, for example, charged the young black man with criminally assaulting an elderly white woman when in fact he was merely guilty, as one investigator learned, of "manly" pride, of "not knowing his place."[47]

Murder, not rape, was the allegation most often leveled against Mississippi's mob victims. But the record abounds in lynchings for lesser affronts: "insubordination," "talking disrespectfully," striking a white man, slapping a white boy, writing an "insulting letter," a personal debt of fifty cents, an unpaid funeral bill of ten dollars, a $5.50 payroll dispute, organizing sharecroppers, being "too prosperous," "suspected lawlessness," horse killing, conjuring, and, of course, mistaken identity.[48] However trivial these accusations now seem, whites then thought them to be serious because they represented transgressions of caste, the one cause common to nearly all Mississippi lynchings. Regional mythology notwithstanding, mob violence was tolerated by the ruling class because it helped to keep the Negro in line, because many whites—by no means all of them rednecks—viewed a "good lynching" as an instrument of social discipline, an object lesson of general value to the entire black community. Thus, in 1929 when proud, elderly Mose Taylor overstepped the limits of permissible black behavior in an "altercation with whites" and was mobbed in Georgetown, a Simpson County newspaper used the incident to remind other blacks of white expectations: "Negroes must learn—and most of them do know—that they occupy a peculiar place in this land and must keep it."[49]

In 1938, three years after a summary execution in Oxford, a white resident of that community reflected on the symbolic importance of violence. When an individual black was lynched, he informed Arthur Raper, the entire race was put on notice and the color-caste system reaffirmed: "It is about time to have another lynching. . . . When the niggers get so that they are not afraid of being lynched, it is time to put the fear in them." So long as day-to-day controls proved effective and blacks stood in deference and fear, this white man believed, violence itself was unnecessary.[50]

In fact, implicit in the apology for lynching was the admission that blacks did not share the white worldview, that for all the self-serving white rhetoric about "darky contentment" whites kept Negroes in their place, ultimately, through force. For example, Governor Theodore Bilbo, as accurate a barometer of majority white sentiment in Mississippi as any public figure, attributed the sharp increase in mob violence in 1919 to "the attempt of the negro race to seek social and political equality." "This desire on the part of the negro," Bilbo believed, "seems to have been increased since the World War by the social reception and familiarity with the negro soldiers by a certain class of white women in France." Responding to a northern black newspaper's inquiry into the rising incidence of racial violence in the state, the Piney Woods politician proposed a way to end mob activity: "This is strictly a white man's country . . . and any dream on the part of the negro race to share social and political equality will be shattered in the end. If the northern negro lover wants to stop negro lynching in the South, he must first get the right conception of the proper relation that must necessarily exist between the races and teach and train the negro race along these lines and in this way remove the cause of lynching."[51]

This was vintage Bilboese. But it was also sentiment that no white politician could openly oppose. The Jackson *Clarion-Ledger,* a newspaper generally out of sympathy with Bilbo's brand of populism, applauded the governor's advice and offered some of its own: "There is a cure for lynchings in the South and that cure lies within the hands of the negroes themselves—remove the cause and the lynchings will stop of themselves, but so long as busy-bodies . . . preach social equality to the negro, drastic measures will be taken to impress upon him that this is a white man's country to be ruled by white men as white men see fit." Although confident that "few negroes in this part of the country" shared the aspirations of "their sweet scented brothers of the North," this editor warned that those who "demand or seek social equality . . . will get it in the neck."[52]

In the last analysis, then, lynching was deemed necessary because black Mississippians could not otherwise be trained to subordination, because they rejected the ideology of a white man's country. Black aspirations could be checked, in the end, only through violent measures.

Popular Justice

Paradoxically, though lynchers seldom attempted to conceal their identities until well after World War I, their socioeconomic status remains subject to speculation. Some mobs, as in the case of a "perfectly orderly" crowd in Union County in 1925, posed with both the sheriff and the victim while news reporters took before and after photographs of a burning.[53] Condoned, if not always openly commended by community leadership, those who took the law into their own hands had little to fear from local authorities. Yet precisely because they could act with such impunity—because arrests were extremely rare and indictments even rarer—the surviving record says little directly about the composition of any given mob. Conventional wisdom argues that lynchers were the less respectable folk, the rednecks and the peckerwoods who translated their touchy Anglo-Saxon pride and their class resentments into race-baiting and physical violence.[54] The victims deserved their fate, the white "quality" generally agreed, but they were denied the dignity of a state hanging by ruder types. James Street, the Mississippi writer who covered his first lynching as a cub reporter of fourteen, expressed the idea perfectly: "Halfway law-abiding" people did sometimes take the law into their own hands, he admitted, but in nine out of ten cases the state's "lynching citizenry" was drawn from "the ignorant, hot-blooded trash, the leavings," the denizens of "the pool rooms and log cabins." Hodding Carter, in his "Ballad of Catfoot Grimes," identified the mob with the same social class, with

> Poolroom fleecers
> and crap-game touts,
> Pimps and brawlers
> And corner louts,
> Scum of the small town's
> Stagnant cess,
> Spawned in boredom
> and ugliness. . . .[55]

Yet both Street and Carter knew that when rednecks played their roles as the heavies in the lynching tragedy they often did so with the tacit consent, sometimes the active participation, and nearly always the close observation of their social betters. The so-called grit thesis notwithstanding, then, violence was not exclusively, or even primarily, the work of the "grits," the lower orders. As Joel Williamson has argued, styles of repression varied from class to class, but whites of every station shared a common body of "essential assumptions and consequent attitudes."[56] No doubt, a public act of community vengeance—whether sponsored by the state or conducted unofficially—brought excitement, perhaps even a sense of caste solidarity to the white underclass that more socially and economically secure whites did not need. No doubt, too, many community leaders feared the rowdy excesses of the mob, preferring to maintain racial hierarchy through what Williamson has called "quiet violence," the less physical instruments of economic or legal coercion. Yet, because they often looked the other way it hardly follows that "responsible" whites were either out of sympathy with vigilante justice or powerless to prevent it.

If Mississippi's rabble was more easily roused than that of any other state, it was precisely because its ruling class was so conveniently permissive. Accordingly, when the Association of Southern Women for the Prevention of Lynching formed a Mississippi council in 1931, the targets of its law-and-order crusade were middle- and upper-class whites, not the unwashed white masses.[57] Similarly, the president of the Mississippi Bar Association, noting that lynching persisted only through the indulgence of the white leadership class, reminded the "decent citizens" of Mississippi in 1925 that to end lawlessness they had only to demand that law enforcement officers enforce the law: "Who," he inquired in a widely circulated tract, "has ever heard of a member of a mob in this state being killed or wounded while acting in the mob enterprise?"[58]

Blacks, too, sometimes discounted class theories of racial violence and saw lynching as a white communal ritual, an expression of caste solidarity. Despite the praise of their more conservative leaders for influential whites and their own special contempt for the point-blank bigotry and the social pretensions of "poor white trash," some black Mississippians understood who manipulated whom within the master race. Recalling the upsurge of lynching following World War I, a black Laurelite, though unwilling to absolve the mean-spirited "peck," traced the disorder to its source, to "the middle class white man [who] would sic him on you." When a merchant or landlord sought to punish caste infractions, this mill worker said, "he wouldn't do it himself, he put that low class white man on you. . . . That's how it was."[59]

Throughout most of the period, whites, whether upper or lower class, did not generally regard lynching as a lawless act. It was understood as law enforcement by informal means, a community-sanctioned extension of the criminal justice system. Editors and public officials sometimes deplored mob excesses, but they frequently described the lynchers themselves not as a mob but a posse, thereby cloaking them in quasi-official authority. "The men who do the lynchings," the Meridian *Star* declared in 1919, ". . . are not men who flout law but men who sincerely believe they have the best interest of their fellow men and women at heart."[60]

Lynching was spontaneous justice, an expression of the peoples' will, not so much the contravention of established legal procedure as a supplement to it; it might be homicide, but when committed in defense of race or tradition it needed no other justification. "No right-minded citizen approves of lynching," Fred Sullens of the Jackson *Daily News* declared in 1935, "but right-minded persons realize that public sentiment is the law."[61]

This tendency to blur distinctions between popular violence and the formal administration of law was not unique to Mississippi, but it was probably more pervasive there than in any other southern state. As one circuit judge explained, turn-of-the-century white Mississippians were "bold and daring folk willing to make and enforce their own laws, or in case of necessity to dispense with them altogether." "An old fashioned state" still influenced by "frontier conditions," Mississippi had developed "a very self-reliant people whose occasional apparent disregard for legal form was not lawlessness but self-reliance and individuality." Impatient with the awkward conventions of state-sponsored justice, the judge observed, the white Mississippian might "constitute himself a governing power," an "absolute monarch," in the perfect confidence that "to the individual must be left the solution of the problems affecting him and that recourse to the Courts is frequently not to be considered."[62]

The point here is not that whites disdained law, but that they shared an expansive view of it, one not limited by the conventional meaning of law, one that embraced such cultural codes as community tradition, family pride, personal vengeance, feminine virtue, male honor, and white supremacy. Where matters of hierarchy were concerned, the difference between the law as an abstraction and the white code of family-honor-race could be conveniently overlooked and lynching could be viewed as a legitimate, at times even gallant, defense of all that whites held sacred. Mob violence was the preferred form of retribution; to white men of pride and honor some crimes were simply too hateful to be left to the ordered redress of the state.[63] Lynching, as United States Senator Bilbo said in 1938, was often the only "immediate and proper and suitable punishment." When effected in defense of a white woman's virtue it was not merely the public will summarily executed, it was the highest form of justice known in this world or the next. Although he could hardly have put it better, it was not Bilbo, vulgar Prince of the Peckerwoods, but Mississippi's classic southern gentleman, John Sharp Williams, who said that "race is greater than law now and then, and protection of women transcends all law, human and divine."[64] It was a law unto itself.

White notions of racial honor were flexible enough to excuse a wide variety of lawless behavior, but wanton savagery was not necessarily acceptable. When a lynching was thought to be "unnecessary" or when a mob was "unduly brutal," some Mississippians, even some newspaper editors, openly deplored the action.[65] James Street described this seemingly widespread white capacity to distinguish between acceptable and unacceptable popular violence: "Lynchings, like liquor and Negroes, are divided into two classes. It's a good lynching or a bad lynching. He's a 'good niggah' or a 'bad niggah.' " Good lynchings were tidy affairs in which a relatively few disciplined whites swiftly executed a "bad niggah" charged with a heinous crime. Bad lynchings featured a surfeit of liquor and firearms and an unruly, indiscriminate mob that threatened the peace and dignity of an entire community. Above all, Street wrote, "a bad lynching means a burning."[66]

Although lynchings often fell somewhere between Street's extremes, Lloyd Clay's execution was definitely bad: anarchic, poorly planned, crudely effected—and widely disapproved by white Mississippians. A twenty-two-year-old day laborer from a well-respected family, Clay was arrested in Vicksburg in 1919 and accused of rape, though even his alleged white victim denied he was her attacker. Taken from the jail by whites who accidentally shot two people of their own race in the excitement, he was burned alive near the center of town in what local newspapers thought to be a "hideous" and "horrible" execution, "one of the worst lynchings in history." The *Daily Herald* reported that Clay was "probably an innocent man, and one wholly out of the classes of the 'bad negro.' " The *Evening Post* typed the lynchers as a "green mob," an "amateur organization," whose "ring leaders had no experience in such affairs and showed lack of skill in carrying out their purposes." Of over a thousand more or less passive spectators, many reportedly believed that the mob itself was inordinately clumsy, that it unintentionally inflicted "needless suffering" on Clay because its leaders could not fashion a proper noose and therefore had to resort to fire. Other whites lamented the impatience of the lynchers, who "picked the first tree which came handy," one that happened to be in a white neighborhood. Six white ladies fainted and there were uncounted others, one reporter thought, whose "sensibilities were shocked."[67]

More orderly lynchings aroused little public censure. In 1935, a year in which Mississippi accounted for two-thirds of all lynchings reported in the United States, the *Clarion-Ledger* thought a double lynching near Columbus "more than regrettable," but found it "to the credit of the Lowndes County citizens forming the mob, that they did not indulge in the barbarism of torture but inflicted the death penalty with as much mercy as the state itself allows."[68] In extralegal executions such as these, the lynchers were few in number and recognized leaders maintained relatively tight discipline, often taking care to establish (to white satisfaction) the victim's guilt. At such times the mob was not necessarily "moblike" and the entire proceeding might become a quasi-juristic act, a grim parody of the criminal justice system, in which deadly earnest vigilantes, operating under the authority of popular assent, meted out such judgments as white supremacy required. Properly administered, then, vigilantism was not mere anarchy, and the "orderly lynching," in nearly every respect, conformed to the patterns of state-sanctioned public hangings. More often than not, one editor believed, a mob "may almost be termed a jury of the whole people." Judge Lynch, as another editor noted, "is a stern justice" presiding over a "rapid-transit tribunal" imposing "speedy punishment" that in "most cases . . . received the hearty endorsement of the people."[69]

In 1903, Samuel Adams was "tried" and condemned in a parajudicial setting in Pass Christian. Accused of raping a white woman, he was placed in a Harrison County jail while community leaders assembled "the men of the town," black and white, at the Woodman Hall. At the appointed hour, a white participant-observer has written, the victim identified the accused and a "jury of the whole" heard the case: "The matter was explained, the witnesses examined, and it was decided that the only thing to do was to put the criminal to death." Following sentencing, the citizens took Adams to a grove, permitted him to make a final statement, and then hanged him: "Not a shot was fired, not a loud word was spoken; everything was quiet and orderly." Two physicians and the coroner certified his death. A hastily impaneled grand jury reported that Adams "came to his death at the hands of the male citizens of Pass Christian, both white and colored, who met, tried and condemned [him] . . . for the crime that should and will, meet with speedy death wherever perpetrated." Nothing in the history of this coastal community had done more "to quiet the feeling between the races," this white man believed, than this singular act of popular justice.[70]

Although death was the usual penalty assigned by such tribunals, there were exceptions. Accused of winking at a white woman, a black Sunflower Countian with an apparent facial tic was tried by a "crude court" at an "informal trial" sometime after World War I. Perhaps because the offense was mitigated by the nervous disorder, the accused man was upon conviction permitted to choose his sentence: hanging, one hundred and fifty lashes, or surrender to the state for long imprisonment. When he logically chose the whip, it was applied by the aggrieved party's husband—but under the supervision of a "friend at court," a sympathetic white assigned to see that the punishment did not exceed the sentence.[71]

Incredible as it was, the scene was not without precedent. At least two other black Mississippians actually convinced popular "tribunals" of their innocence and survived to tell about their day in Judge Lynch's court. Both were men of prominence and both generally well regarded by whites as "safe" black leaders. Piney Woods schoolmaster Laurence Jones and leading Montgomery County religious figure Valley L. Lester where charged in separate incidents during World War I with promoting a black "rising" against white rule. Lester was seized at a black church in D'Lo and taken by a "mob thirsty for a Negro's blood" to a lynching tree. While onlookers wrangled over his watch and ring—and even over who would claim his fingers and toes—he used his soon-to-be legendary powers of elocution and the timely intervention of an influential white friend to save his life. Professor Jones, apprehended following a speaking appearance at a black revival, had a noose around his neck and was trussed to a "brush pyre" when he found the words that saved his life: "I spoke as I have never spoken before about the life in our Southland. . . . I told stories that made the crowd laugh . . . I referred to different white men in the South with whom I had had helpful dealing." So persuaded, a mob leader cried "This must be a good darky" and Jones was freed. His would-be executioners then collected fifty dollars for the education of Rankin County black children.[72]

It matters little whether, as both Jones and Valley apparently believed, these were spontaneous acquittals, unwonted and artless expressions of mob clemency in cases involving white misunderstanding, or whether they were calculated acts in a theater of white terror designed to feature black leaders as object lessons for the race in general. Either way, these remarkable incidents help to demonstrate the deliberate, purposeful quality of some mob action. If few blacks had a "friend at court" and few vigilantes were subject to black persuasion, lynchings were not necessarily unchecked carnivals of white fury. When "good order" prevailed, mob savagery might be restrained until the moment of execution and the victim was sometimes accorded what, under the circumstances, seems even now to be a measure of solicitude. The lynchers of Pony Poe, a field hand taken from Walthall County authorities in 1888 following his arrest for assaulting a white woman, honored his request that he not be hanged until after black spectators finished praying for his immortal soul. In 1902, patient Corinth vigilantes accommodated a Negro's last wish by burning him alive twenty-four hours behind schedule, so that his next of kin could attend the execution.[73] In 1925, the whites who overpowered a Union County sheriff to seize L. Q. Ivy, an alleged rapist, showed "no sign of mistreatment," and even stopped at a country store to buy the captive a last meal of cheese, crackers, and milk before torching his gasoline-soaked body. In 1930, a leader of a mob that lynched "Pig" Lockett and Holly Hite at Scooba (Kemper County), a man reportedly "active in the local church," bought coffins for the Negroes to insure them a decent burial.[74]

Not least of all, well-conducted acts of popular justice were viewed by the white community as a measured response to the most serious black caste depredations. If the bad lynching was characterized by a trigger-happy swarm indiscriminately wreaking terror on the entire black community, the good lynching was notably free of unfocused "nigger whippings" or random acts of arson and looting against black homes, churches, and lodges.[75] Indeed, because the vigilantes were directly in control and the outcome predetermined, Judge Lynch's court might perform its task more deliberately than a mob-dominated, state-sanctioned trial in circuit court. The burning of John Hartfield in 1919 near Ellisville, for example, was described by elderly white citizens as one of the state's "most orderly" executions.[76] So inclusive were white notions of justice and so deeply entrenched were the canons of popular vengeance that the lynching, as described in the state's papers, seemed more a murder trial followed by a legally sanctioned public hanging than an act of social mayhem. Although five innocent parties were wounded in the confusion surrounding the event, local authorities nevertheless affirmed that the mob's work was not marred by frenzied shouting, indiscriminate use of firearms, unscheduled turmoil, or accidental deaths.

Hartfield's lynching was said to have been carefully planned days in advance by a "citizens committee," and the mob's rank and file reportedly "pledged itself to act in conformity with the arrangements." Pursued by posse and bloodhounds for ten days through three counties, the accused rapist was treated upon capture for gunshot wounds by a physician who determined that he would live long enough to be hanged. While some mob leaders permitted the curious, two by two, to see the condemned man, others quietly established the place and means of execution. Cautioned by a local minister to "use discretion," the committee had the black man "positively identified" by his alleged victim and pursuaded an apparently reluctant sheriff to surrender Hartfield without resistance. Meanwhile, the word was carried throughout the area. Sawmills released their employees, farmers brought their families and dogs, and whites jammed interurban trains as several thousand spectators—some with picnics of fried chicken and layer cake—arrived to see a spectacle that Governor Bilbo declared he was "powerless to prevent." The afternoon editions of newspapers in Jackson and New Orleans announced the impending event—"3,000 WILL BURN NEGRO," "JOHN HARTFIELD WILL BE LYNCHED BY ELLIS-VILLE MOB AT 5 O'CLOCK THIS AFTERNOON," "NEGRO JERKY AND SULLEN AS BURNING HOUR NEARS."[77] At the appointed hour, the black man was kicked unconscious, hanged from an ancient sycamore tree, and riddled with bullets before his body was engulfed by flames.

"Unknown Causes"

The most important single fact in the story of lynching in Mississippi is that for most of the Jim Crow period the mob had little articulate opposition. Whites who lynched Negroes, the Jackson *Clarion-Ledger* reported in 1889, were, "like the offspring of royalty," not subject to public censure or legal control. "Mobs feel licensed to do as they please, conscious that they will not be held accountable for their conduct."

During the next half century little seemed to change. Although gratified to note the declining frequency of lynchings, Arthur Raper concluded in 1936 that "in most of Mississippi and in considerable areas in other deep South states, the community leadership still considers lynching necessary." Citing the examples of recent executions in Wiggins, Calhoun City, Slayden, and Oxford, Raper asserted that Mississippi mobs were still "commonly made up of the leading people of the community."[78]

Perhaps the most visible component of what might be called Mississippi's prolynching consensus was the white press. Surveying the southern response to the acetylene torch murders at Duck Hill (Montgomery County) in 1937, the NAACP attributed to Mississippi "the worst editorials in the whole country in favor of lynching." Reflecting the values of the communities in which they did business, the state's newspapers generally either justified lynching by reference to the South's "peculiar situation" or offered sympathetic excuses for the "inevitable" acts of "well-intentioned citizens" enraged by black depradations or frustrated by a dilatory judicial system.[79] Some individual editors objected to the more barbarous rituals of mob violence, and some, by the late 1930s, declared their opposition to summary justice. But no influential Mississippi journalist played a public role in the antilynching crusade. When news of a lynching appeared in the local press, it was reported, as one NAACP investigator said, in "routine pro-lyncher fashion—the lynching had occurred, the mob victim deserved his fate, the lynchers had expressed the will of the people."[80]

Little more can be said for the state's religious institutions. Although noted clergymen sometimes committed their personal moral authority to the cause of law and order, Mississippi's Protestant churches, like their counterparts elsewhere in the fundamentalist Bible belt, preached the gospel of personal experience and piety, but rarely addressed social issues. With few exceptions, Episcopal Bishop William Mercer Green noted in 1942, "the white churches, as such, show generally little interest in the Negroes."[81] Much as they might deplore lawlessness elsewhere in the region, most pastors fell silent when lynchings occurred in their own communities. "The only way to keep the pro-lynching element in the church," one white Mississippian concluded, "is to say nothing which would tend to make them uncomfortable as church members." Accordingly in 1930, after two blacks suspected of robbery were hanged by a mob near Scooba, the local clergy ignored the violence lest they cause "dissension in church organization."[82] When state leaders of the Association of Southern Women for the Prevention of Lynching, themselves active in Methodist missionary societies, sought the support of fellow churchwomen in the 1930s they were attacked in the press, often opposed by the men of their denomination, and sometimes criticized by their own husbands and by other women who thought them afflicted by a "Negro Complex." Although they won ready support from the state federation of women's clubs, they found statewide denominational bodies "very evasive."[83] In 1933, in the face of opposition from the conference floor, the ASWPL failed to collect a single antilynching pledge at the Mississippi Baptist Convention, official body of the state's largest denomination and the one white moderates thought to be "the farthest behind" on matters of social justice.[84] The Mississippi Conference of the Southern Methodist Church did not adopt its first explicitly antilynching resolution until 1936, after five years of lobbying by the ASWPL.[85] "Perhaps lynchings would not have been so common in Mississippi during this period," one historian has written, "if more clergymen and congregations had taken strong stands against it."[86]

State and local authorities were, if anything, less helpful. Given its widespread acceptance, few elected officials could be expected to oppose popular justice; those who did risked public disfavor. In his gubernatorial campaign of 1899, Andrew H. Longino said nothing about white outrages against blacks. At his inauguration, however, he proposed legislation to compensate families of lynch victims and to dismiss peace officers who failed to protect their prisoners. The legislature failed to act and Longino did not push the measure—nor did he condemn the mobs that killed fifty-seven blacks during his administration. His anti-lynching bill, however, returned to haunt him twenty years later when he sought a second term as governor in 1919. Longino "Freely Admits Mistake," the *Clarion-Ledger* noted, and the former governor declared that he was "big enough, honest enough, and brave enough" to concede his error. He ran third in the Democratic primary. Also defeated in campaigns for United States senator and Supreme Court justice, Longino concluded that his "very unpopular" proposal sounded his "political knell."[87]

Even Governor Vardaman, whose credentials as a white supremacist were above suspicion, challenged the mob spirit warily. When he used the militia to prevent a double lynching in 1904, he was opposed, the Natchez *Democrat* estimated, by "almost every white man in the state."[88] And after Governor Dennis Murphee, then serving an unexpired term and seeking a full term in his own right, lost to Theodore Bilbo in 1927, he attributed the defeat to his use of the Mississippi National Guard to prevent a lynching.[89]

With these and other examples before them, law enforcement officials rarely offered protection for blacks. In the most blatantly open circumstances, coroners' juries routinely found that mob victims met "death at the hands of unknown parties." Grand juries even when in session often took no official notice of a popular execution.[90] The police were frequently and conveniently absent during a lynching. "Officers do not resist the mob," a president of the State Bar Association said, "and the mob knows the officers will not resist."[91] The district attorney of Jones County, who was later elected to Congress, watched the Hartfield burning and even used the occasion for a little electioneering. He brought no charges against mob leaders. A Marshall County justice of the peace who watched the execution of Ab Young in 1935 admitted to news reporters: "I'm an officer. But my friends mean more to me than being an officer."[92] One of the whites who burned L. Q. Ivy scoffed at Governor Henry Whitfield's order for an investigation in 1925: "Not an officer in Union County or any of the neighboring counties will point out any member of the crowd. . . . Sure the officers know who were there. Everybody down there knows everybody else. We're all neighbors and neighbors' neighbors."[93]

The whites who executed Roosevelt Townes and "Bootjack" Mc-Daniels by blowtorch near Duck Hill in 1937 seized the two Negroes in broad daylight in downtown Winona immediately following their arraignment for murder. A former mayor of Winona thought that "there are a thousand people in Montgomery County who can name the lynchers." But neither the sheriff (who apparently arranged to yield his prisoners without resistance), nor the district attorney and secretary of state (both of whom reportedly watched as twelve unmasked whites seized the Negroes), nor anyone else in this town of several hundred people, would identify even one member of the mob.[94]

Congressmen from other southern states, fearing that the Duck Hill atrocity could undercut their efforts to defeat a federal antilynching bill, urged "speedy and adequate punishment." A circuit judge and the state's governor ordered investigations.[95] But authorities arrested no one. The editor of the Sunflower *Tocsin,* who thought "the two brutes at Duck Hill richly deserved what they got," accurately predicted that "nothing will ever come of any investigation." Editor Fred Sullens of the Jackson *Daily News* dismissed an international storm of outrage, some of it coming from within Mississippi itself, as "a lot of tommy-rot."[96] The NAACP's undercover agent, a white southerner, reported to the New York office: "The citizens of Duck Hill seemed rather well pleased with themselves. The only feature of the incident displeasing to them was the pictures taken of Townes and McDaniel and widely circulated through the press." Local blacks believed the two Negroes were lynched because whites feared that the state had insufficient evidence to convict them.[97]

Sheriffs and other police officials did from time to time heroically resist mob action, and mobs sometimes took prisoners only after battering through the masonry and steel of reputedly impregnable jails.[98] Although Governor Bilbo used the National Guard in 1919 to hunt down a black fugitive but not to stop his lynching, every other governor from Henry L. Whitfield (1924-1927) to Paul B. Johnson (1940-1943) used state troops to protect a black suspect from a mob.[99] Toward the end of the period there were usually more "prevented lynchings"— recorded cases in which police by one means or another denied the mob—than there were lynchings.[100] But at least through World War II, law enforcement was frequently either actively or passively an accomplice of the crime and all too many members of the state National Guard, as one reformer lamented, were "imbued with much the same spirit as the mob itself."[101]

The black Mississippian stood virtually alone against the mob. As Vernon Wharton has written, there was "some opposition" to lynching in the state as early as 1890. But those who opposed it generally did so discreetly and only after the fact, only after "immediate passions had had time to cool."[102] Although race leaders repeatedly linked black discontent to white lawlessness, whites in significant numbers did not openly condemn mob violence until after World War I.[103] Then, for a variety of reasons—the out-migration of black labor, organized pressure from outside the South and the introduction of federal antilynching bills, moral outrage quickened by wartime idealism, the postwar effort to diversify the economy by attracting industry—a growing body of white professional, business, religious, and civic leaders began to place their influence on the side of law and order.

All but inaudible at first, these voices of moderation—the Pittsburgh *Courier* called them Mississippi's "civilized minority"—were joined in the 1930s by the all-white Mississippi Council of the Association of Southern Women for the Prevention of Lynching. As Jacquelyn Dowd Hall has written, this organization was the ASWPL's "model" state council and the "most active" in the South. Led by Bessie C. Alford of McComb and Ethel Featherstun Stevens of Jackson, it sponsored community forums and antilynching institutes, spoke to service clubs and ladies' church, bridge, and literary societies, pressed the law-and-order cause on law enforcement personnel and elected officials, quietly investigated lynchings and focused the glare of unfavorable publicity on lawlessness. On several occasions, it even confronted mobs of prospective lynchers.[104] Accompanied as these efforts were by the larger, modernizing postwar patterns of improving transportation and communication, of diminishing rural isolation and cultural change, such efforts at public education ultimately helped to undermine white public support for the mob.

At no point in the entire period, however, did vigilantes have cause to expect punishment. The problem was regionwide, but Mississippi seemed to be the southern state most tolerant of lawlessness.[105] White solidarity and black fear usually hindered official inquiries, however well intended. Even the most prudent investigations by antilynching reformers generally met a wall of silence. Although state authorities seemed amenable, the NAACP's efforts to prosecute leaders of a Madison County mob failed in 1939 when neither local officials nor prospective witnesses would cooperate. "People were loath to talk to me," Howard Kester advised Walter White. "There seemed to be genuine fear that there would be reprisals against the Negroes of Canton if there was any talk." Kester's attempts to gather evidence from professors at a nearby black college were blocked by the institution's president, who thought it "extremely dangerous" even to meet with him and who feared that "his buildings might be burned any moment."[106]

These problems notwithstanding, the mob's immunity from justice always owed less to the quality of the evidence than to the solicitude of the veniremen. For if Mississippi grand juries were loath to indict, Mississippi petit juries simply refused to convict. In one of the first actions of its kind in the state's history,[107] a special grand jury did return true bills in 1925 against a sheriff and four members of the Coahoma

County mob that killed Lindsey Coleman only minutes after he was acquitted of murdering a white planter. The sheriff was found guilty of misprison and was fined $500 but was permitted to keep his office; three others were tried and acquitted.[108]

During the next two decades, a period in which at least fifty-three black Mississippians were lynched, the leaders of three other mobs were indicted (twenty-seven whites in all). None was found guilty. During World War II, as the case against the killers of Howard Wash suggests, Mississippi was no more ready to punish its lynchers than it had been a half century before. In October, 1942, after pleading self-defense to the charge of murdering his white employer, Wash was convicted by a Jones County jury, sentenced to life in prison—and promptly seized and executed by a mob of fifty to 100 men. Only five days before, Quitman whites had hanged two black fourteen-year-olds, allegedly for attempted rape. A fourth lynching within a week was prevented only when troops and highway patrolmen restored order in Hazelhurst.[109]

These developments brought a wave of indignation from a wartime nation. A. Philip Randolph's March-on-Washington Movement held a public prayer in the streets of New York; NAACP officials wired President Roosevelt that "the Mississippi mobs gave important aid to Tokyo." United States Attorney General Francis Biddle sent in the FBI and promised "relentless prosecution." In Jackson, blacks led by Sidney D. Redmond demanded immediate state action; and a "deeply outraged" Governor Paul Johnson ordered the state guard to arrest mob leaders and promised "to do everything that I possibly can."[110] The Laurel *Leader-Call* joined "responsible persons" in this Piney Woods city of 20,000—including the sheriff, a judge, and a clergyman—in denouncing the Jones County outrage. But when the report of a special session of the grand jury failed even to mention the lynching and local authorities refused to file charges, the only recourse was to federal statutes protecting Wash's civil rights. The deputy sheriff, who had delivered the black man to the mob, and four whites described by federal authorities as "ring leaders" were indicted by a federal grand jury.[111]

At the trial in federal court, both sides argued race rather than the merits of the case. The lynching, the prosecution said, was not only a "dark and damnable" crime but an affront to white supremacy. Because Wash was tried in "a white man's country, [where] white men rule the proceedings, a white judge presided, a white jury tried the negro and a white Sheriff had him in charge," an attack on him was an attack on white authority itself. This approach was creative, but that of the defense was surer. "One of the brightest spots in the South," counsel for the accused whites argued, "was what southern people did at night, when the South protected itself in one of its darkest moments." Evoking memories of Reconstruction—when the "South lay bleeding," when "the Thirteenth, Fourteenth and Fifteenth Amendments were imposed on us"—the defense suggested that the issue at trial was not the guilt or innocence of the defendants but federal meddling in Mississippi's affairs. The defendants faced maximum sentences of ten years; an all-white jury found them not guilty.[112]

Such experiences convinced blacks that only direct federal intervention would end lawlessness. The Jackson *Advocate,* one of but three surviving black Mississippi weeklies, noted that the acquittal had been a blow to black "faith and hope." Enlightened Mississippians of both races, the paper reported, "had been looking forward to the trial to furnish the restraints that appear . . . to be so urgently needed at this time." The NAACP, which had heavily invested its limited resources in the investigation and exposure of unpunished white violence in the state, concluded that the trial of lynchers by Mississippi jurors was futile. "The situation in Mississippi is so bad," Walter White informed another officer of the association in 1939, "that beyond publicity . . . there is nothing we can do in the Mississippi courts. Our only hope is through continued efforts for passage of the federal anti-lynching law."[113]

Going Underground

White refusal to punish vigilante crimes against blacks undercut otherwise encouraging post–World War I developments. Following the war, the racial climate moderated somewhat and the number of authenticated lynchings steadily declined; during five of the years between 1930 and 1945 no lynching was officially reported in the state. Despite the social disruption and the heightened anxieties of wartime, the bloody record of the First World War was not reenacted during the Second. From 1939 through 1945 the NAACP counted twenty-seven lynchings in the nation, and attributed six of those to Mississippi. In such statistics not a few observers, and especially congressmen searching for reasons to oppose a federal antilynching statute, found cause for optimism. An increasingly enlightened South, it was often argued, had its vigilantes on the run. Even in darkest Mississippi, many believed, trial by torchlight was out of popular favor. In Hodding Carter's phrase, lynching was the state's "almost vanished" crime.[114]

Other observers were less hopeful. Black Mississippians had reason to know that lynching was but part of a larger pattern of extralegal physical coercion and that while the character of white racial violence was changing, its frequency had scarcely diminished. The NAACP, the Commission on Interracial Cooperation, and its affiliate, the Association of Southern Women for the Prevention of Lynching, noted that the old-fashioned "nigger hunt" and lynching bee were being supplanted by more subtle varieties of race murder.[115] Lynching was now rarely defended publicly; communities in which mobs once operated openly now tried to suppress news of race violence. Following the infamy at Duck Hill, the number of blacks "killed while resisting arrest" by informal posses of private white citizens was thought to have increased markedly.[116] Rumors of "covert lynchings" surfaced thoughout the plantation counties. The president of Lane College in Tennessee revealed information given him by Coahoma County blacks of "ten or twelve lynchings" near Clarksdale in 1939, about which "not one word had appeared in any newspaper."[117] That same year Howard "Buck" Kester, the Southern Tenant Farmers' Union official who frequently investigated mob violence in Mississippi, uncovered four "underground lynchings" in the vicinity of Cleveland and two more near Canton—all of which had been kept out of the news by local authorities. In his dispatches to the New York office, Kester reported that since the Duck Hill atrocities lynching in Mississippi had entered a "new phase." Many blacks were killed annually, he believed, "but their disappearance is shrouded in mystery, for they are dispatched quickly and without general knowledge. In some lonely swamp a small body of men do the job formerly done by a vast, howling, blood-thirsty mob."[118]

And so the period ended much as it began. Black life was still cheap. White violence against Afro-Americans, although assuming new forms, was still rife. The keepers of the lynching record still found it all but impossible to estimate the numbers murdered. If the mob rode less brazenly, its specter continued to haunt the color line for years to come. After World War II, in the long dark night of Mississippi's massive resistance to the Second Reconstruction, a resurgent tradition of unpunished white vigilantism brought new infamy to the state, reaffirming its reputation as "the land of the tree and the home of the grave." In 1955 the self-confessed killers of Emmett Till were tried and acquitted at Sumner; in 1959 two grand juries refused to indict the band of whites who dragged Mack Charles Parker from a Poplarville jail and lynched him; in 1967, after state and federal prosecutors agreed that Klansmen would not be convicted for murder by a Mississippi jury, the Freedom Summer lynchers of James Chaney, Michael Schwerner, and Andrew Goodman were tried in federal court for depriving the victims of their civil rights. Although the firebomb snipers who murdered NAACP activist Vernon Dahmer served brief sentences, the assassins of such black voting-rights activists as Lamar Smith, George Lee, and Medgar Evers escaped punishment altogether.[119]

PART **V**

A Resistant Spirit

How do Negroes feel about the way they have to live? How do they
discuss it when alone among themselves? I think this question can be
answered in a single sentence. A friend of mine who ran an elevator once
told me: "Lawd, man! Ef it wuzn't fer them polices 'n them ol lynch mobs,
there wouldn't be nothin' but uproar down here!"
—Richard Wright, "The Ethics of Living Jim Crow"

CHAPTER 8

"Northboun'": Mississippi's Black Diaspora

Huh! de wurl' ain't flat
An' de wurl' ain't roun'
Jes' one long strip
Hangin' up an' down.
Since Norf is up,
an' Souf is down,
an' Hebben is up,
I'm upward boun'.

—Lucy Ariel Williams, "Northboun'" (1926)[1]

When a man's home is sacred; when he can protect the virtue of his wife
and daughter against the brutal lust of his alleged superiors; when he can
sleep at night without the fear of being visited by the Ku Klux Klan
because of refusal to take off his hat while passing an overseer, then I will
be willing to return to Mississippi.

—Anonymous Mississippi emigre, 1919[2]

Prewar Patterns

In the 1910 revision of his *American Commonwealth,* James
Bryce examined the patterns of black movement in the United States
and concluded that the future would bring the "African" of North
America ever closer to the regions most resembling "his ancient seats
in the old world," to "the low warm regions that lie near the Gulf Stream
and the Gulf of Mexico and especially to the . . . banks of the lower
Mississippi." There, south of latitude 33°N and east of longitude 94°W,
"he finds conditions which are at once most favorable to his development and most unfavorable to that of the whites." "It is certainly in

those southernly regions," the viscount believed, "that his chief future increase may be expected."[3]

As events soon demonstrated, Lord Bryce perceived the past more clearly than the future. Yet, while he did not foresee the mass exodus of blacks to northern cities during and after World War I, his was a reasonable projection of earlier demographic trends. Although the population of the United States had grown whiter as the black minority declined from 19.3 percent of the total in the first census of 1790 to 10.7 percent in 1910, the "lower and hotter regions" of Mississippi and the newer states of the cotton South had grown progressively blacker. In the period from 1800 to 1910, the black proportion of Mississippi's population increased from 42 percent to 58 percent. By 1910, 10.3 percent of all American blacks were Mississippians. Blacks outnumbered whites in thirty-eight of the state's seventy-nine counties, and in Issaquena (94.1 percent black) and Tunica (90.6 percent black)—the first- and third-blackest counties in the United States—the black majority was more than nine to one.[4]

Despite persistent white dissatisfaction with the "indolent" Negro and a vigorous postbellum search for a "safer," more "stable" work force, the state's economy was by 1910 more dependent than ever on black labor. Successive efforts to supplant black agricultural workers with immigrants—first with northern Europeans and Chinese and finally with Italians—came to little. Planters as influential as Senator LeRoy Percy and Alfred Holt Stone frequently predicted the arrival of massive numbers of docile, tractable, and nonblack workers. But while foreign-born workers in apparently endless streams flooded the labor markets of the East and Midwest, immigrants found conditions in the plantation states of the lower South singularly unfavorable. By 1910 the foreign-born population in Mississippi was smaller than in 1870.[5]

Bryce's projection also seemed consistent with trends in the native white population. In a development generally overlooked, the traditional influx of whites from the Carolinas, Georgia, and Alabama slowed markedly after the Civil War and native white Mississippians deserted the state in substantial numbers. Unfortunately, census data for the period are too flawed to permit any but the crudest analysis. But as Table 8.1 suggests, the dramatic surge of black out-migration after 1917 tends to obscure a very sizeable white out-migration.

For more than a century one of Mississippi's principal exports had been people, and prior to the Great Migration its biggest losses through migration occurred in the white population. In both 1900-1910 and 1910-1920—and in every decade thereafter—black emigration was greater than white emigration. But if the temporal unit is expanded to

TABLE 8.1. Net Intercensal Migration of Mississippi Blacks and Whites, 1870-1950.

	1870-1880	1880-1890	1890-1900	1900-1910	1910-1920	1920-1930	1930-1940	1940-1950
Black	+22,200	−17,100	−13,900	−35,500	−148,500	−83,000	−68,100	−314,200
White	−30,300	−34,500	−27,100	−34,300	−111,900	−80,300	−35,200	−202,600

+ = Net population increase through migration.
− = Net population loss through migration.
Source: Kuznets et al., *Population Redistribution,* 1: 74-90.

the half century from 1870 to 1920, the state's net loss through migration was significantly greater for whites than for blacks (238,100 to 192,800).[6] Measured another way, in terms of native Mississippians living in states other than Mississippi, the magnitude of the white exodus is even more clearly demonstrated. As Table 8.2 reveals, the percentage of Mississippi-born whites not in residence was greater than the same percentage for blacks in every decade from 1870 through 1940.

These tables also clarify tendencies in the state's black population that have been often misunderstood—and that were missed by Bryce. Blacks did not leave in droves until World War I; yet a consistent pattern of black out-migration had been established well before the decade of 1910-1920. During the antebellum period and for a decade after the Civil War, the influx of black labor from the worn-out agricultural districts of the upper Southeast accounted for much of the black increase in Mississippi. By 1870, 28 percent, or 124,400 of the state's 444,300 nonwhites, were born elsewhere—three-quarters of them in Virginia, North and South Carolina, Georgia, and Alabama.[7] Although the non-native black percentage fell to 22 percent in 1880 (142,000 of 652,000), heavy black in-migration continued until white Democratic rule was reestablished in 1875.

In the early 1870s labor agents representing the rapidly expanding railroad and cotton interests of the river counties vigorously recruited in the states to the east, luring away blacks with what one disillusioned migrant of the seventies remembered to be "fantastic stories about the richness of the Mississippi Delta," where cotton grew so tall it could be picked only from horseback and where "money could be gathered from the trees." In 1869 and 1870, blacks left the eastern seaboard by the trainload, and during the winter of 1873-1874, flood tide of the black migration into Mississippi, a fleet of covered wagons and the cars of the Vicksburg and Meridian Railroad shuttled between Alabama and the Delta carrying black agricultural workers and their families out of

TABLE 8.2. Nonresident, Mississippi-born Whites and Nonwhites, 1870-1950.

	1870	1880	1890	1900	1910	1920	1930	1940	1950
Black									
Total natives	377,400	583,700	705,300	901,600	1,035,100	1,073,500	1,230,300	1,331,000	1,441,600
Natives nonresident	57,500	73,800	82,300	108,800	134,100	211,100	289,700	313,100	504,700
Percentage nonresident	15.2	12.6	11.7	12.1	13.0	19.7	23.5	23.5	35.0
White									
Total natives	325,300	473,300	583,000	720,500	880,100	1,014,100	1,172,100	1,287,200	1,433,300
Natives nonresident	81,100	120,000	142,300	187,400	217,200	281,400	321,100	328,100	442,500
Percentage nonresident	24.9	25.4	24.4	26.0	24.7	27.7	27.4	25.5	30.9

Source: Kuznets et al., *Population Redistribution,* 1: 271, 321.

a region of successive crop failures into the "Promised Land." Returning from Alabama with thirty hands in January, 1874, a Hinds County planter reported that blacks by "the hundreds of thousands" were leaving the state for Mississippi.[8] That same month a newspaper correspondent noted that "ten thousand have passed Meridian up to this time, and thousands are waiting for transportation." By mid-decade, so many had come that planters in the neighboring state wrung their hands over the "wholesale exodus" and some Mississippi whites—usually the spokesmen for the hill counties least dependent on black labor—lamented the almost daily "inundations" of "ragged, penniless, worthless-looking negroes from Alabama."[9]

The considerable riches of the Delta, however, were to be gathered largely by whites. That fact, plus the ascendancy of "white liners" after 1875, slowed and then reversed the black movement into the state. By decade's end—in the brief but frenzied 1879 mass exodus to Kansas and the less dramatic departures of individuals and single families to Tennessee, Arkansas, and Missouri—black Mississippians by the hundreds and perhaps thousands were seeking better opportunities elsewhere.[10] Although in 1870-1880 the state's net gain through the migration of blacks was nearly equal to its net loss of whites (see Table 8.1), the era of heavy black migration into Mississippi ended when Reconstruction collapsed.[11] In succeeding decades some black in-migration continued and, no doubt, many of the disillusioned emigres of the seventies returned. Yet in the exchange with other states, in the balance between immigration and emigration, Mississippi became a consistent net loser of blacks as well as whites.

For a time relatively high rates of natural increase kept the populations of both races growing, and the lower volume of black emigration assured the continued, slow expansion of the black majority (from 53.7 percent in 1870 to 58.7 percent in 1900). But in 1900-1910, when for the first time more blacks than whites departed, the population balance began to shift. Each decade thereafter, the proportion of blacks to whites decreased; by 1940, for the first time since 1840, blacks were a numerical minority in Mississippi.

In a state that permitted blacks few other avenues of protest, this comparatively small pre–World War I out-migration must not be overlooked. The headlong flight toward a better life did not begin until 1915. But in the two generations after Reconstruction, black Mississippians by the thousands exercised the ultimate freedom—the freedom to move, to search elsewhere for the political and economic opportunities, the human dignity, and the personal security they could not find at home.

"Many Thousand Go"

Although white newspaper editors seemed determined not to alarm their readers by overstating the movement, a breathless quality characterized much of the early reportage of the Great Migration. During its wartime phase alone (1915-1920), the exodus carried roughly half a million blacks out of the South, 100,000 of them out of Mississippi.[12] To the reader who followed early local press accounts of this mass movement, it surely seemed that an entire people were abandoning the state for the packinghouses and steel mills of Chicago, Detroit, and St. Louis as fast as the railroads could carry them.

In October, 1916, the Memphis *Commercial-Appeal,* the paper most widely read by Delta whites, reported that the state's "Blackbelt is being stripped of farm laborers."[13] Dispatches came from Lowndes County that 60 percent of the Negroes had left the farms and "a large proportion of the best land in the county promises to remain uncultivated." "It has proved impossible to check the exodus," the Meridian *Star* concluded; "the blacks are leaving in large numbers daily." The movement was so rapidly draining the labor supply that the *Star* urged officials to impress convicts for the cotton harvest. During the spring and summer of 1917 Jackson newspapers announced that "there is not a night but negroes leave [the capital] for the North" aboard the Illinois Central. "Practically all of the young negroes have left this section." If the black "wanderlust" could not be curbed, the *Daily Clarion-Ledger* predicted, "the railroads soon will have hauled all of the negroes out of Jackson."[14] Dispatches from the sawmill districts of the Piney Woods, the turpentine camps of the coast, and the textile mill towns of the northeast were no less startling. The economy of Hattiesburg was reported to be "seriously hurt," its black sections for a time "almost depopulated"; the freightyards of Tupelo and Gulfport reportedly often lacked the workers to unload railroad cars.[15]

Much of this coverage was overwrought. But the wartime labor shortages were very real and the volume of the black diaspora from Mississippi and the other states of the lower South was unprecedented. In the decade after 1910 the state's net loss through black migration was nearly 150,000. The proportion of blacks to whites declined in seventy-two of (the then existing) eighty-one counties, and so too, for the first time ever, did the total black population. In subsequent decades the movement out continued (see Table 8.1), stripping Mississippi during the half century from 1910 to 1960 of nearly a million blacks (938,000)—a figure larger than the state's entire black population in 1900 (908,000).[16] Inevitably, the heaviest emigration came during the two world wars, periods of peak industrial expansion; yet even during the depression losses were heavy. All told, this was a folk movement of inestimable moment, destined to transform not only the face of the South and the texture of Afro-American life but the very character of American institutions and values.

Its immediate causes were economic and are too well known to require much explanation here. Blacks migrated from the South, scholars agree, largely for the same reasons that whites did. Indeed, as the British pioneer demographer E. G. Ravenstein concluded, virtually any mass migration could be described as a "safety valve for relative population pressure," "a rough adjustment to the distribution of economic opportunities."[17]

In their own considerations of the relative merits of staying or leaving, Mississippi blacks rarely resorted to the colorless language of demography, of "cotton price demoralizations" or "adjustment mechanisms." Yet they understood the meaning of the hard times that followed the boll weevil and the floods of 1915 and 1916; they knew firsthand the ravages of pellagra, the disease of malnutrition that accompanied cheap cotton and successive short crops. The sharecropper who received no share at settlement time, the agricultural day laborer who struggled for sixty cents, the cook or the laundress who sometimes earned two dollars or less a week, the poorly paid laborers in the oil mills, cotton compresses, and railroad shops — all felt the impact of sharply rising wartime inflation and all responded eargerly to news of shorter hours and higher pay in northern cities.[18]

Their letters to contacts in the North, far better than austere scholarly analyses, reveal the "hunger push" behind the decision to abandon familiar ground for the uncertainties of urban life. "Wages here are so low [we] can scarcely live," wrote an Ellisvillian: "We can only buy enough to Keep us alive." A "willen workin woman" from Biloxi, who hoped to find jobs for herself and her family asked a Chicago editor for "healp," "as we are in a land of starvation."[19] As he prepared to board a northbound train, a Hinds County man answered a white query: "Cap'n, I've been working here for a dollar and four bits a day and that's good wages for a nigger in Jackson. Flour is costing me nearly two dollars a sack, meat is so high I can't eat it. I am leaving because I can't buy food . . . on what I can make. If you white folks wants de niggers to stay in the South you will have to . . . pay us more money."[20]

But if blacks often cited hard times as their reason for leaving, they also frequently alluded to social causes, to caste discriminations, dilapidated housing and inferior schools, legal injustices, and mob violence. Indeed, the decision to migrate was usually an intensely personal one, each emigrant having private notions of why he or she would abandon the familiar haunts and friendship of a lifetime to risk a new start in a strange place. As often as not, as an unknown versifier explained, there was a complexity of causes:

> Boll-weevil in de cotton,
> Cutwurm in de cawn,
> Debil in de white man,
> Wah's goin' on.[21]

In many instances, however, black explanations were less ambiguous:

> I'm tired of this Jim Crow, gonna leave this Jim Crow town,
> Doggone my black soul, I'm sweet Chicago bound,
> Yes, I'm leavin here, from this old Jim Crow town.[22]

Drawn as well as driven, southern blacks answered the beckoning of wartime opportunity. With normal sources of cheap, white immigrant labor disrupted and the nation's labor needs sharply accelerated by the draft and industrial expansion, Afro-Americans who were once welcome in the urban North only in personal service occupations now found themselves in demand as unskilled and semiskilled industrial workers. Notices of job opportunities published in northern race papers invariably brought an avalanche of mail from Mississippi, asking for "infermation of labor situations in your city" and usually promising "I will come at once."[23]

The economic dimensions of the migration, then, were major; certainly they determined the timing and the direction of flight. Without wartime labor shortages the impoverished refugees would have had little reason to crowd into blighted northern slums. Yet it is important to remember that the emigres saw themselves not simply as job-seekers but as expatriates. Although rarely candid in the presence of whites, they often expressed themselves freely to one of their own; thus, when the Department of Labor dispatched a black field investigator to the centers of heaviest out-migration, he went to Mississippi and found the frustrations and humiliations of Jim Crow foremost on the black mind. The "matter of treatment," he noted, was the "all-absorbing, burning question." Whites seemed oblivious to the issue, but blacks never met "without finally drifting into some discussion of their treatment at the hands of white people." Similarly, in his inquiries for the Department of Agriculture at northern points of debarkation, a black agent found the new arrivals interested not only in "better opportunity" but "better privileges." While they cared little for interracial contact, they felt strongly about the need for personal safety: "I just want to be somewhere where I won't be scared all the time"; "I just want to feel safe."[24]

Letters written by black Mississippians to the Chicago *Defender* and the Detroit Urban League underscore the same theme: "I want to bring my family out of this cursed southland[.] down here a negro man is not as good as a white man's dog"; "i am sick of the south"; "we are anxs to get of[f] southern soil"; "I want to live in a state among gentle men who have fealing for a colored man"; "I am so tired of such conditions that I sometimes think that life for me is not worthwhile." Often these letters included a plea for anonymity: "done use my name in print, for it might get back down here."[25]

Given the intensity of these sentiments, the trek North, not remarkably, sometimes assumed the character of an escape from slavery. In one example, a scene that recalled the most dramatic moments of the Underground Railroad, a band of 147 Hattiesburg emigres stopped their watches as their train crossed the Ohio River, knelt to pray, and with tears of joy sang the still-remembered songs of deliverance:

> I done come out de land of Egypt
> aint that good news.
>
> O Canaan, sweet Canaan
> I am bound for the land of Canaan.

Well-versed in the Israelites' flight from bondage, these deeply religious and expressive pilgrims assumed the role of "de Hebrew Children" as easily as their slave forebears—and with no more compunction to separate rigidly the sacred from the secular.[26] This scene must have been repeated many times, for the figurative language of black migration was by tradition highly charged with biblical imagery. Just as Canaan symbolized more than heaven to the fugitive slave—"We meant to reach the *North*," Frederick Douglass remembered, "and the North was our Canaan"[27]—a new generation of Mississippi Israelites surely crossed their own River Jordan singing:

> We'll soon be free
> . . . .
> It won't be long
> 'Fore de Lord will call us home.
>
> Slavery chain done broke at last
> . . . .
> 'Cause my Jesus set me free.

Perhaps, too, they sang *Many Thousand Go:*

> No more peck o' corn for me
> . . . .
> No more hundred lash for me
> . . . .
> No more mistress' call for me.[28]

In the early stages of the movement, whole communities and churches appear to have transplanted themselves substantially intact to northern cities. In his wartime field research in Mississippi, the sociologist Charles S. Johnson found evidence of something akin to crowd hysteria that led blacks to abandon homes and jobs in a race-conscious gesture of escape from oppression. When the "northern fever" struck, he noted, "there was no subject of discussion but the migration." It dominated every conversation. "The packing houses in Chicago for a while seemed to be everything," one respondent told Johnson. "You could not rest in your bed at night for Chicago." Movement itself created pressures for further movement. Those left behind were haunted by darkened windows and vacant places at lodge or church. A property owner in one small southern Mississippi city unburdened herself to Johnson: "If I stay here any longer, I'll go wild. Every time I go home I have to pass house after house of all my friends who are in the North and prospering." Although she stayed behind for business reasons, she worried about the future: "There ain't enough people here I now know to give me a decent burial."[29]

The fever was also fed by daily conversations at the local depot with sleeping-car porters, ready symbols of the freedom to move. There were also weekly infusions from the militant Chicago *Defender,* which promoted the "great northern drive" on nearly every page. Copies of the *Defender,* the most widely read race paper in Mississippi, were usually snapped up the day of arrival and passed from hand to hand. Whites in Hattiesburg credited the sheet with "ruining" the city.[30]

Letters from recently immigrated friends and relatives were equally persuasive. By Emmett Scott's estimate, at least half of all Mississippi emigres left upon "the solicitation of friends through correspondence."[31] Whether written by the merely lonely or by the truly proud, a glowing letter home was sure to be studied carefully and widely shared. One particularly vivid example, sent by a newly elevated "first assistant to the head carpenter," was read in the correspondent's home church: "What's the news generally around Hattiesburg? I should have been here 20 years ago. I just begin to feel like a man. It's a great deal of pleasure in knowing that you got some privileges. My children are going to the same school with the whites and I don't have to umble to no one. I have registered — will vote the next election and there ain't any 'yes sir' — it's all yes and no and Sam and Bill."[32] Powerful enticements in themselves, such letters might be particularly effective if they came in moments of acute race tension — or if they carried money, easily the most persuasive evidence of the good northern life. Routinely, Scott discovered, husbands who preceded wives and adult children who preceded their parents made the sacrifices required to send traveling money to loved ones.[33]

The Distant Magnet

Since the dawn of the industrial age the direction of human movement in the United States, as throughout the western world, has been from farm to factory. Until after 1914, however, the tide of agricultural workers flowing into the industrial labor pool of the nation's cities was white, either native-born or European. Blacks were not immobile, but the direction of their movement was generally south and west, from one point in the rural South to another. During the 1880s, a decade of unprecedented American urban growth, the comparatively small number of Mississippi black emigrants went to adjacent states, primarily to the plantation counties of Arkansas.[34] In 1910, more Mississippi-born blacks lived in each of the three states of Arkansas (39,500), Louisiana (26,600), and Tennessee (26,100) than in all the Middle Western, Middle Atlantic, and New England states combined (12,700).[35]

The pattern changed abruptly, as we have seen, during World War I. What had once been a trickle into the agricultural districts of adjoining states became a torrent that flowed out of the rural areas into nearby towns and cities and then northward through Memphis and across Tennessee toward St. Louis, Chicago, and Detroit. Between 1910 and 1920, the number of Mississippi-born blacks more than doubled in the urban centers of Ohio and Missouri and more than quadrupled in urban Illinois and Michigan. For the decade as a whole, rural Arkansas was still the primary destination; but after 1915 northern cities drew black Mississippians in growing numbers.[36] By 1930 Chicago claimed 38,400 native black Mississippians, more than any non-Mississippi city—nearly as many, in fact, as Jackson, Meridian, and Greenville combined.

But if the North was, in Lord Acton's phrase, the black Mississippians' "distant magnet," not all of the movement went out of state. As Table 8.3 reveals, rural-to-urban migration carried a growing number of rural black Mississippians to the state's towns and cities. Throughout the period the proportion of the total black population living in areas officially classified as urban increased, in relatively small and even increments from 1890 to 1920 and more sharply thereafter, particularly in the period of the Great Depression and World War II. Between 1890 and 1910, the state's urban black population nearly tripled; between 1920 and 1940 it nearly doubled again. But industrial underdevelopment insured low rates of urbanization for both races, and a consistent

TABLE 8.3. Black Urban[1] Population in Mississippi, 1890-1970.

	1890	1910	1920	1930	1940	1970
Total urban	70,000	207,300	240,100	338,800	432,900	986,600
Black urban	34,200	95,400	98,600	134,000	178,000	331,900
Percentage black	48.9	46.0	41.1	39.6	41.1	33.6

[1] Cities and towns of 2,500 and more.

Source: Kuznets et al., *Population Redistribution,* 1: 356.

pattern of employment discrimination insured a lower rate for blacks than whites.

In the South at large, blacks were generally, if only slightly, more urban than native whites.[37] In Mississippi where the practice of restricting blacks to "nigger jobs" was more systematically applied than in the region as a whole, native whites were consistently more urban than blacks, and urban areas were whiter than the total population. Except in the depression decade, when the movement to northern cities slowed everywhere in the South, the black Mississippian's share of the total urban population declined in every decade after 1870. This development was consistent with a long-term southern regional pattern of increasingly white urban populations.[38] But there was one major difference. Following World War II, the great cities of the South (though not the general southern urban population) became progressively blacker as rural Negroes moved into decaying urban cores and whites fled to outlying areas. Mississippi had no Memphis or New Orleans, much less an Atlanta or Birmingham. But even in its largest urban centers— Jackson, Meridian, Greenville—the black presence (see Table 8.4) was proportionally, and substantially, smaller in 1970 than in 1890. There was, then, a striking uniformity to the black exodus from Mississippi, where cities no less than the countryside gave up their black people to the opportunities of the North.

For a time, the movement also brought blacks to the labor-starved plantation counties. During World War I, many Delta communities served as staging areas for northbound migrants. But the losses were more than offset by a long-term black influx into the Delta counties (both intra- and interstate) that continued through the war and at least through the next decade. In fact, during the period from 1910 to 1940, much of the black flight out of the poorer agricultural districts of the

TABLE 8.4. Black Population in Mississippi Cities of 10,000 or More,[1] 1890-1970.

	1890[2]	1910	1920	1940	1970
All cities					
Total blacks	27,327	56,499	56,714	93,554	154,404
Percentage black	53.3	48.7	45.3	43.8	37.8
Jackson					
Total blacks	3,127	10,544	9,936	25,256	66,493
Percentage black	52.8	49.6	43.5	39.1	35.0
Meridian					
Total black	5,178	9,321	8,343	12,853	15,106
Percentage black	48.7	40.0	35.7	36.2	33.5
Greenville					
Total black	4,217	6,010	6,939	12,347	20,619
Percentage black	63.3	62.5	60.0	59.1	52.0

[1] Eight cities that had 10,000 population or more in 1920.
[2] Excluding Hattiesburg and Laurel, for which 1890 figures are incomplete.

hills terminated in Delta plantations.[39] During World War II and after — and particularly after the advent of the civil rights movement and the introduction of such labor-displacing devices as mechanical harvesters, flame cultivators, and chemical herbicides — the Delta became a net loser through black migration, and the black population there fell faster than in the state at large. In the thirty years from 1940 to 1970, a period of modest white population growth in both the Delta and the state, the greatest black losses came in the counties where cotton production and black population were heaviest. Indeed, in those years the ten counties and seven partial counties that make up the Delta accounted for more than half (54.6 percent) of the state's total black population decline.[40]

A quality of unwarranted confidence creeps into any analysis of population movement. The approximate volume, the direction, and even the ultimate destination of the migrants can be charted with a fair degree of accuracy. Yet the metaphors so often used to describe human mobility — flow, stream, tide — suggest a continuity of movement that is probably less representative of individuals than of the aggregate. Very likely many field hands did put down their hoes and boarded northbound trains with the dust of the cotton patch still in their throats.

More often the migration seems to have developed in several stages, carrying a worker from a plantation in Coahoma County, say, or a turpentine camp in Hancock County, first to a cottonseed oil mill in Clarksdale or a lumberyard in Gulfport, and then, perhaps, to a job as hotel porter in Memphis or New Orleans, before finally terminating in a St. Louis foundry or a Gary steel mill.

It seems likely, moreover, that the individual who left rural Coahoma or Hancock County was not necessarily the same individual who arrived in St. Louis or Gary. Although large numbers of rural blacks moved to nearby towns, a great many of these individuals may merely have displaced emigrating town Negroes without becoming out-migrants themselves. Available data are simply too crude to tell us how much of the migration went directly from southern farm to northern factory, how much of it came in delayed stages, how much of it was a function of displacement, or, for that matter, how much of it went north but returned within a given census period and thus escaped enumeration altogether.[41]

Nor is it possible to put a price tag on the losses, though the costs to both the state and its people were surely enormous. Although it cannot be measured, out-migration had a devitalizing effect on the remaining black community. The exodus, it was often assumed, drained the state of its best black stock, its most capable and intelligent black role models and community leaders. Some whites, though paradoxically describing the emigres as "shiftless" and "no-account," were comforted by the notion that the most "ambitious" and "aggressive" were the first to leave.[42] These value judgments are at best unprovable and at worst defamatory of nonmigrants. Yet the exodus was in some respects measurably selective.

In Mississippi, as elsewhere in the region, out-migration was positively correlated with years of school completed. Differences at the upper educational levels (high school and college) appear to be negligible, but the loss rate among the least educated was lower than among those relatively more advantaged.[43] Like most migrations, this movement was also age-selective, carrying off a disproportionate number of adults in their most productive years and leaving an "excess" of children and old people. The remaining young adult population, therefore, was left to carry, at an increased per capita rate, the costs of family and community institutions and the responsibilities of leadership. As Table 8.5 shows, the 25-44 age cohort was the most mobile in every decade, accounting for roughly five to six in every ten emigrants.[44]

The table also demonstrates that except in 1910-1920 significantly more women than men emigrated. This sex differential mirrors but

TABLE 8.5. Net Interstate Migration of Mississippi Blacks by Age and Sex, 1910-1950.

Age	1910-1920 Male	1910-1920 Female	1920-1930 Male	1920-1930 Female	1930-1940 Male	1930-1940 Female	1940-1950 Male	1940-1950 Female
10-14	−5,300	−6,500		−700	−1,300	−2,100	−12,800	−13,300
15-24	−23,800	−21,700	−12,800	−13,800	−9,900	−9,400	−30,600	−34,400
25-44	−33,000	−27,900	−19,000	−22,800	−15,200	−17,500	−67,000	−67,700
45-64	−5,900	−4,300	+2,300	−1,600	+1,200	−3,500	−13,800	−15,800
65-	−200	−1,000	−100	−500	−600	+100	−900	−1,900
Total	−68,200	−61,400	−29,600	−39,400	−25,800	−32,400	−125,100	−133,100

+ = Net gain.
− = Net loss.

Source: Kuznets et al., *Population Redistribution,* Table P-1.

does not equal the population distribution in most Mississippi cities, where black women outnumbered black men by some 25 percent. In both cases, the predominance of women can probably be explained by the greater white acceptance of blacks in domestic and personal service occupations than in other forms of employment. The plurality of women emigrants also challenges the myth of black male desertion, a staple in the folklore of out-migration. As bluesman Peetie Wheatstraw saw it:

> When a woman gets the blues
> she hangs her head and cries;
> But when a man gets the blues,
> he flags a train and rides.[45]

Indeed, a field hand in trouble with planter or police might catch the first freight north, leaving a cabin full of children and a wife who did not always respect a mate who could neither provide well nor stand up to whites. Yet statistics do not indicate that the problem was a serious one to black families in Mississippi.

Beyond these few facts, little more can be confidently said about the selective character of the Great Migration. Seeking jobs, human dignity, and personal freedom, hundreds of thousands emigrated from the state, leaving behind disproportionate numbers of the young, the old, the poorly educated—the very population groups least prepared to rock the racial boat. It does not follow, however, that those who stayed were somehow more complacent or less ambitious than those who went.[46] For, if as some whites clearly hoped, the exodus acted as something of a racial safety valve, siphoning off the most malcontented and aspiring blacks, it did so imperfectly. The decision to vote with one's feet, to leave in search of fuller participation in American life, was perhaps the clearest and most frequently exercised expression of black discontent. But it was a relatively costly and wrenching option beyond the reach of many and one that even some of the most alienated black Mississippians might not choose to exercise. Many of the most visible and articulate critics of white supremacy did carry their struggles elsewhere. Others, perhaps not less militant, stayed home, where in spirit if not always in public expression they were closer to W. E. B. Du Bois than to Booker T. Washington on the protest-accommodation continuum of black thought.

A Curse and a Blessing

In his pioneering study of southern race relations, Ray Stannard Baker was struck by the ambiguity of white attitudes toward the Negro. "White people were torn between their feeling of race prejudice and their downright economic needs. Hating and fearing the Negro as a race, . . . they can't get along without him." In one moment, as Baker noted, whites lynched or banished blacks for real or imagined infractions; in the next they resorted to "remarkable measures" to keep them at work.[47]

These observations aptly characterize the white response to the black exodus from Mississippi. On the other hand, there was, as the Hattiesburg *News* put it, a general recognition that "it would be quite as inconvenient for Mississippi to do without negro labor as it would [be] to do without mules." Yet there were many who could still agree with the nineteenth-century editor who thought that "every negro that comes into the State of Mississippi is a curse, every one that leaves a blessing."[48]

Initially, considerable sentiment favored "getting rid of the negro majority." In August, 1916, the Vicksburg *Herald* saw real advantages in a "northern drift" that would ease "negro congestion" in the state, promote greater agricultural diversity, and perhaps even teach smug Yankees something about the "negro problem."[49] Businessmen and planters generally took a longer view, and as the tempo of exodus quickened, so too did white concern. More than any event since emancipation, the migration called the white community's attention to its dependence on black labor.

Once persuaded that their self-interest was involved, whites in some localities tried to restrain the movement of blacks. In many counties, informal "committees" were organized to deal forcibly with the emergency by intercepting northern labor agents and persuading field hands to remain on the plantations. In December, 1917, when agents of northern industries were thought to be "stealthily at work" recruiting "otherwise contented" field hands in the Cleveland area, an organization of bankers, merchants, and planters pledged to take such action "as may be necessary" to protect the local labor supply.[50] Many communities adopted antienticement ordinances, and labor agents generally received rough treatment from the law. In Greenville, police entered northbound trains, dragging off departing workers and ordering other blacks not to board. In Hattiesburg and Jackson departing blacks were arrested. Ticket agents in Natchez refused official requests to deny passage to blacks, but in Meridian and Brookhaven railroad employees sidetracked cars loaded with blacks.[51] Such methods usually succeeded only in strengthening the black resolve to leave. "Our pepel are tole that they can not get anything to do up there and they are being snatched off the trains, . . ." one black Greenvillian reported; "but in spite of all this, they are leaving every day and every night."[52]

More conciliatory tactics, ranging from propaganda to "colored picnics," were also unavailing. Whites were especially fond of citing black authority on the advantages of staying put. Yet, while many prominent race spokesmen argued the whites' case, black Mississippians generally distrusted those who did. Opposing the migration "is the most unpopular thing any professional or business Negro can do," a Labor Department investigator learned. Ministers who preached against the trek north risked losing their collections and perhaps even their congregations.[53] No doubt some leaders—William H. Holtzclaw, Laurence C. Jones, and I. T. Montgomery among them—genuinely believed that the race was better off in the South, its "natural home," but the suspicion persisted that black critics of the exodus were either serving themselves or the whites, or both.[54] Nor did it escape black attention that some of the black speakers most highly favored by whites on the antiexodus circuit were, like former Vicksburg attorney W. E. Mollison, themselves recent emigrants to northern cities.[55]

Whites also tried to exploit northern racial unrest. Following the savage eruptions in East St. Louis in 1917 and Chicago in 1919, headlines in the state's white press proclaimed: "MANY KILLED IN RECENT RIOTS," "NEGROES LEARNING VALUABLE LESSON," "EVERY TRAIN BRINGS NEGROES FROM NORTH."[56] Testimony reportedly taken from terror-stricken returnees (said to be "arriving daily") recounted the horrors of Yankee race hatred: "The negroes were shot down in the streets like dogs"; "negroes were killed simply because they were negroes."[57] Other accounts reported that black migrants starved and froze to death in "bleak and blizzardy" northern streets.[58] Sadder-but-wiser black emigres, having found the North to be "a cold and unsociable place," were said to be "begging to be brought back" and returning "by the thousands," sometimes on foot.[59]

The effect of this propaganda cannot be determined, but it was not great. Black Mississippians evinced little confidence in the objectivity of white journalism, preferring to get their news from northern race papers. In fact, as one white observer discovered, some blacks believed either that the East St. Louis rioting was a white fabrication or that it had been incited by southern whites to stop the exodus. Of course, there was reason for black disappointment in the promised land north of the Ohio. But as black Mississippi often noted, the North, however inhospitable, had unmistakable advantages. "[I'd] rather take a chance of getting shot in East St. Louis den starving in Mississippi," a Jacksonian said as he boarded a northbound train immediately after the riots of 1917.[60] Similarly, a new arrival from the Gulf Coast told a Chicago reporter why he and his party of thirty had left their homes in the dead of winter: "They say that we are fools to leave the warm country, and how people are dying in the east. Well, I, for one, am glad that they had the privilege of dying a natural death there. That is much better than the rope and torch. I will take my chances with the northern winter."[61]

That even northern riots could not drive the Negroes back is illustrated by the ill-fated endeavors of the Mississippi Welfare League. The instrument of prominent planters and businessmen, the league sent its secretary, Jack C. Wilson, to Chicago in July, 1919, immediately after the bloody "Red Summer" race disorders in that city. His mission, Wilson explained, was to prepare the way for the expected return of the lost Mississippians. Perhaps misled by the sympathy and enthusiasm of the white northern press and white Chicagoans, Wilson promptly announced that 20,000 blacks would remigrate in time for the cotton harvest.[62] That claim, however, was denied by the Chicago Urban League, which despite heavy pressure from white civic leaders, vigorously opposed this and all other southern repatriation efforts.

To offset rumors of wholesale black flight, the Urban League monitored Chicago train depots during the week following the rioting and released a survey showing that more blacks arrived than departed. Virtually all who left, the black organization noted, did so for business, vacation, or reasons otherwise unrelated to the rioting. According to T. Arnold Hill, a founder and officer of the local Urban League, Chicago's southern black emigres shared "a pronounced indisposition to return to those conditions in revolt against which they left."[63]

Wilson soon left the city disappointed, but he escorted back to Mississippi a "commission" of three Chicago blacks to "study" race relations in Mississippi. Following a carefully guided tour such as a visitor to Mao's China might have experienced, the commission reported that it knew of no other place on earth where blacks enjoyed the "happiness, contentment and prosperity which prevail among the colored race in Mississippi." Unable to find "any police oppression" or "friction of any kind between the races," the Chicagoans commended the state to northern blacks who would seek their fortunes in a warm and plenteous land where enterprising sharecroppers could become planters and where landlord and tenant shared "the strongest possible ties."[64] The report was well received by white Mississippians.[65]

No Threat Intended

Migration created new possibilities for those who stayed as well as for those who left. With labor in short supply and whites acutely sensitive to their dependence on black workers, Mississippi blacks found increased opportunities to press their demands for better conditions. Although some race spokesmen urged their people to stay at home, others discreetly encouraged (or at least quietly applauded) the migration, recognizing in the growing need for black labor a chance to exact white concessions.

In his wartime investigations in the state for the Department of Labor, R. H. Leavell, a progressive native white Mississippian, discovered that black leaders expected to manipulate white self-interest to black advantage, though they found it imprudent to say so publicly. "At heart they rejoice over it," the white man learned of the migration. "They are silently hoping that the migration may continue in such increasing proportions as to bring about a successful bloodless revolution, assuring equal treatment in business, in the schools, on the trains, and under the law."[66] Indeed, so pregnant was the movement with possibilities that blacks from every station eagerly conspired to advance the "great northern drive." They did so in varied ways, by sharing newspapers and other communications from the North, by protecting those who found it necessary or useful to slip away unannounced, by concealing the movements of the hated labor agents, and by entering into the subterfuge of the chastened "returnees" who were, by one count, "nine times out of ten" busily recruiting workers for northern industries even as they told local whites of the horrors of Yankee life.[67]

Even blacks who opposed the exodus sometimes seized the moment to emphasize the planters' obligation to treat their hands fairly. In December, 1916, Dr. Joseph E. Walker, one of the state's most prominent black physicians and businessmen, used Sunflower County's leading white newspaper to encourage blacks to remain in Mississippi lest they find themselves in "a strange land among strangers . . . [with] the demons of hunger and cold, constantly prowling about their door." But he linked the exodus to black dissatisfactions by identifying "many conditions in the South . . . that ought to be remedied." First among these, he thought, was the landlord's tendency to cheat the "ignorant negro." The paper's few black readers surely understood, if whites did not, that when the physician referred to black interests "identical with those of the white people," he meant to remind the master class of the mutual dependencies that bound those who owned the land to those who tilled it.[68]

Toward the same end, Valley Lester of Montgomery County assumed the role of Sambo to instruct the white race on its Christian duties: "My race works your streets, my race enjoys being your servants, they loved to bring in the bales of cotton for you in the fall of the year. [A man of] my race loves for you to be kind to him . . . and he wants you to prove that you are his friend by the kindly and friendly way which you have treated him." Lester also heaped praise on white benevolence, extolled the "great southland" as "the finest of all" regions, and urged the black field hand to "stay where you are, . . . work on halves or for wages." But his peroration included a delicately circumspect warning that whites must mend their ways or pick their own cotton: "The southern negro only wants a fair and honest treatment and we are willing to forever stay at home and let the north be the north."[69]

If black candor was normally constrained by fear of white retaliation, resourceful black Mississippians nevertheless found ways to identify out-migration with Jim Crow, and particularly with judicial inequities, lynching, and Klan intimidation. In June, 1917, when the Delta Farmers and Businessmen's Club investigated the causes of the "current unrest," Mound Bayou businessman Charles Banks commended the white organization for its "constructive" approach. But he advised his white neighbors not to overlook the "ethnical" dimensions of the migration, and even suggested that the movement owed less to northern opportunities than to southern lawlessness. Blacks, he said, had no sympathy for "brutish" criminals in their own communities. Still they found it "disquieting" when public authority winked at mob violence; nor could they "pretend easiness and satisfaction when charred remains are brought and displayed on the principal street of negro businesses."[70] Similarly, when former Senator LeRoy Percy publicly opposed the organization of the Klan in Greenville in 1922 as a matter of conscience and because he believed that its presence would result in "idle cotton fields" and abandoned lumber mills, Delta blacks hastened to advise white friends that bedsheet violence would indeed accelerate out-migration. "I heard quite a number say they will not remain in this section after this year," a black school principal informed Percy. If responsible whites would prevent organized lawlessness, a petition signed by the "colored citizens of Greenville" affirmed, blacks "will feel safer and much more willing to live here."[71]

Above all, blacks understood that pressure from their community could be counterproductive. Race spokesmen who used the migration crisis to bargain for improved conditions generally found it more fruitful to appeal to white pocketbooks than to white consciences. When the Warren County Colored Ministers' Association petitioned local authorities in 1918 for better black rural schools, it emphasized the relationship between agricultural prosperity and a "contented working class." Existing black education facilities "are not such as might breed contentment," the ministers stated. "We have noticed that the people among whom we work are not settled. Many are leaving. Some are planning to leave."[72]

Perhaps the most dramatic endeavors to convert crisis into opportunity came from a series of conventions that met in the state during the war and early postwar period. In 1918, for example, a delegation of some fifty blacks "from all parts of the state" appeared before the education committee of the state House of Representatives to request that black elementary, secondary, and college students be given the same educational opportunities as whites. "If these matters are given substantial consideration," group spokesman Perry Howard assured the lawmakers, ". . . the exodus which has struck at the very foundation of the labor system of Mississippi will be largely checked."[73]

The statement of a black mass convention organized by S. D. Redmond in 1923 was bolder and more comprehensive. Identifying "a few of the many reasons which cause the Negro to be so easily induced to leave the State," this conference of leaders drafted a twenty-one-point bill of grievances that ranged from mob violence and injustice in the courts, to exploitative labor practices and educational inequalities, to neglected public services and disfranchisement. Affirming their own deep interest "in the future welfare of the commonwealth," the conferees concluded with a "humble judgment": "there is no hope whatever of bringing back the Negroes who have already left the State . . . the only hope now lies in taking the proper steps to retain as many as possible of those who are here."[74]

In 1924, in a petition read before both houses of the state legislature, a group of black leaders again cataloged the inequities and discriminations that kept blacks "in the very highest imaginable state of dissatisfaction." "This is not, of course, intended by any means as a threat," the petitioners avowed, "yet . . . under present conditions, we see nothing short of our beloved state giving up in time, most of its population unless some marked relief is afforded. . . . If one finds that he can do better . . . on one side of a stream than the other, it but stands to reason that he will cross over."[75]

The same spirit of carefully modulated protest animated the Committee of One Hundred, a now little-remembered statewide black leadership conference organized in 1923 "to represent the colored people of Mississippi in inter-racial relation[s]; to petition those in authority for the things we need; . . . and to work for the general improvement of the Negro race in Mississippi." Led by Prentiss Institute schoolmaster Jonas Edward Johnson, the committee characterized itself as a "conservative and patriotic organization" supported by "practically every leading Negro in the state."[76] Operating quietly behind the scenes, committee spokesmen met with white business, civic, and religious groups to "negotiate progress" and express black dissatisfactions. As a friendly lawmaker informed other members of the state House of Representatives in 1923, committee leaders sought only such improvements as would "prevent the great exodus of their people to the Northern states and get them to remain here in the state where their opportunities are good and where they are so much needed." Prompted by committee spokesmen, this Jefferson Davis County legislator supported increased funding for black vocational education to "show the Negroes of the State that we are interested in them and want them to stay here in Mississippi."[77]

Other whites responded to similar pressures. Noting the inadequacy of black schools, the poverty and indebtedness of virtually all tenants, the record of unpunished white lawlessness, and a general white disposition to "keep the nigger down," an enlightened Vicksburg white thought it only natural that blacks should search for greener pastures. "That the South could expect these same benighted people to remain with her and uncomplainingly endure all this when a twenty-dollar bill will carry a man away from it passes my understanding."[78] In 1920 the Mississippi Department of the American Legion urged members of its local posts to "put forth their best effort for the promotion of harmony between the races"; and in 1923, perhaps the peak interwar year of black out-migration, the state Chamber of Commerce called upon white business and civic leaders in every community to sponsor biracial discussion groups designed to address black grievances and thus slow the movement out.[79] Segments of the state's white press also presented the case for adjustments in race relations. Both the Meridian *Star* and the Vicksburg *Daily Herald* identified wage and job discriminations, inferior living standards, and prejudicial legal proceedings as the "causes of [black] migration." "The white people of Mississippi are not giving the Negro a square deal," the Jackson *Daily News* acknowledged. "Until we do there is no reason to hope for a better settlement of our industrial conditions."[80]

The issue was perhaps most squarely addressed in the 1924 inaugural address of Governor Henry L. Whitfield. "The negroes still make up slightly more than one-half of Mississippi's population," the new chief executive noted. "There is a definite relation between their happiness and prosperity and that of the State as a whole. . . . If we would hold these laborers in the South, we must compete with the Northern employer on his own terms." "Our own self interest," he said, required a "new era" for "the less favored black man," on the plantations, in the courts, and in the schools. "Every [white] man and woman in the State must see to it that the laws protecting the negroes in their lives and property are rigorously enforced."[81]

These remarkable examples of self-reproof, unfortunately, were not widely emulated, and the racial soul-searching triggered by the black mass exodus rarely reached more deeply into the white community than the pages of a few dailies. Some optimistic observers detected a "more enlightened" strain of white thought; at least one national periodical predicted that "Vardamanism . . . is on its last legs." A few native whites even professed to see the advent of "a new era of altruism" in which "men of broad vision" were newly awakening to "their duties to their fellow man."[82] But the spirit of white accommodation, meager as it was, scarcely survived the critical labor shortages of the war and its early aftermath.

By 1918, labor market adjustments had pushed up black agricultural and industrial wages across the state 10 to 30 percent, and in some cases more. Sawmill hands, steamboat workers, and Piney Woods lumberjacks were promised "good labor conditions," progressive management and safety practices, and better housing. During the war and into the early 1920s, planters offered tenants improved living quarters, somewhat greater autonomy, and more varied and healthful diets. Representatives of both races agreed that sharecropper settlements were, for the moment, often fairer and that the lash was applied more sparingly. Some landlords closed their commissaries entirely; others continued to operate these often blameworthy institutions but permitted their field hands a welcome measure of consumer discretion through small, periodic cash advances. City officials in Greenwood, Jackson, and Laurel instructed police to deal less harshly with black offenders, and in some areas blacks may have received more evenhanded justice in the courts. Nearly everywhere in the state whites seemed momentarily more attentive to black educational demands. Most promising of all, whites in a number of rural communities talked openly of the need for better treatment of black workers and sometimes even met with "responsible" black leaders to discuss questions of "mutual welfare."[83]

The early impetus for many of these developments came from the Department of Labor's Division of Negro Economics, which worked closely with business and agricultural interests in Mississippi and several other southern states to solve problems "causing [black] restlessness and dissatisfaction." More interested in wartime productivity than social justice, the division's energies were often misspent on public relations endeavors to increase black "morale and efficiency." But it also fostered better employer-employee relations through the creation of a biracial Mississippi Negro Workers' Advisory Committee and the sponsorship of a series of meetings at which representatives of plantation and lumbering concerns were urged to increase wages and improve generally the conditions under which blacks worked.[84]

In some cases, these conferences devoted to black labor problems produced little more than paternalistic rhetoric and probably wounded more black feelings than they salved. All too typically, a "better race relations" meeting sponsored by the earnest white ladies of the Vicksburg Federation of Christian Women began with "a brief address on our duties as superiors toward our inferiors of the colored race" and progressed to adjurations for more sympathetic treatment of cooks, laundresses, and field hands "so that they will be perfectly content to stay in the south, the section best suited to their advancement."[85]

Other endeavors, however, including the widely celebrated but short-lived Bolivar County "Community Congress," resulted if only briefly in what some thought to be "better [race] feelings." Composed of twenty whites and five blacks, this planter-dominated congress met only a few times during the war and was hardly democratic in design. Yet it provided a formal vehicle for interracial contact and can probably be credited with the postwar construction of the state's first black agricultural high school.[86]

In yet another example, this one from the early postwar period, the all-white board of trustees of Alcorn A & M College agreed to restore Latin to the school's curriculum after meeting with representatives of the Committee of One Hundred and learning that black students who would study a foreign language had to do so outside of Mississippi, sometimes at integrated northern universities where they encountered "ideas that don't fit." Skillfully exploiting white fears, black leaders in this instance succeeded, as committee president J. E. Johnson later put it, in "turning race prejudice back on itself." Describing the triumph to his sons—all of whom attended college in other states—the wily black educator explained that in dealings with whites, "there is a very thin line between diplomacy and duplicity."[87]

The fruits of interracial conclaves were rarely so tangible. Blacks usually viewed such concessions as the grudging expedients that they were, and accepted the new-found attentions of whites with a mixture of appreciation and amusement. "The dominant race is just a bit less dominant at present," one black commented to Charles S. Johnson after a meeting with whites. Another marveled that "instead of the old proverbial accusations—shiftless and unreliable—negro labor is being heralded as 'the only dependable labor extant, etc.' "[88] Yet if they found their working conditions momentarily more tolerable, black Mississippians were too seasoned in the ways of white supremacy to expect major adjustments in a system designed to keep them down. Nor were they surprised in the postwar period when white interest in conciliation waned as quickly as labor shortages eased. In the years to come, many continued the struggle to lighten the burdens of black life under Jim Crow; but many others followed increasingly well-worn paths to opportunities elsewhere.

CHAPTER **9**

The Gathering Challenge

The white South said that it knew 'niggers.' . . . Well, the white South had never known me—never known what I thought, what I felt. The white South said that I had a 'place' in life. Well, . . . my deepest instincts had always made me reject the 'place' to which the white South had assigned me. It had never occurred to me that I was in any way an inferior being. And no word that I have ever heard fall from the lips of southern white men ever made me really doubt the worth of my own humanity.

—Richard Wright, *Black Boy* (1937)[1]

Got one mind for white folks to see,
'nother for what I know is me;
He don't know, he don't know my mind.

—Mississippi blues lyrics[2]

Behind the Mask

One of the white Mississippians' "genial delusions," Greenville writer David Cohn observed in 1948, was the assumption that "because they live among masses of Negroes, employ Negro cooks, maids, nurses, washerwomen, they intimately understand Negro life." In truth, Cohn recognized, whites had but the "faintest comprehension" of the "secret and alien" black "inner life."[3]

This delusion, like so many others fostered by white supremacy, was remarkably tenacious. Well into the 1960s, even as the cook and washerwoman entered the civil rights movement in search of full citizenship, white conventional wisdom attributed the "new" black disquietude to outside agitation. But for the revolutionaries in their midst, anxious whites preferred to think, the great majority of Mississippi's blacks would be as content as ever with "our way of life."

Virtually all blacks knew better, and even some perceptive whites suspected that the most ingratiating Sambos were not necessarily what they seemed. Following a period as schoolteacher and graduate student in Mississippi, the young Howard Odum reported in 1910 that nearly every black had two personae: "two distinct social selves, the one he reveals to his own people, the other he assumes among the whites." Dollard amplified the same thought some two decades later when he described the typical field hand as "Dr. Jekyll and Mr. Hyde": "[He] has a kind of dual personality, two roles, one that he is forced to play with white people and one the 'real Negro' as he appears in his dealings with his own people."[4] Now a truism, this insight was lost on most whites. In their eagerness to read the outward signs of black submissiveness as evidence of black recognition of white superiority, most members of the dominant race wished simply to accept Sambo at face value. Elsewhere, and particularly in the North, Mississippi whites believed, all too many Afro-Americans had been corrupted by the false prophets of egalitarianism. Even in the lower South not all blacks were "good negroes," not all were unconditionally submissive. The state had its sullen, sassy, and assertive "bad negroes," and also an occasional "black fiend," the brutish despoiler of white womanhood. Except for these few malefic thorns in Jim Crow's side, however, black Mississippians were thought, as one Delta planter wrote in 1907, to accept white dominance "as a matter of course, as part of their lives—as something neither to be questioned, wondered at, or worried over."[5] Though universally irresponsible and given to lying, thieving, and sloth, they were not malcontented; like their slave forebears, they were born into subordination and therefore accepted it as their natural condition.

If few whites understood the complexity of black social behavior, fewer still suspected the depths of black alienation. At their most candid, black Mississippians normally expressed their grievances to whites in euphemisms, in vague references to "race relations" and "getting along with the white folks." Among themselves, they more commonly spoke of oppression, injustice, and race prejudice. As a black Sunflower Countian informed a northern visitor, black conversation often centered on "the bad treatment received by the Negroes."[6] This point is made most forcefully, again, in Richard Wright's evocation of a Mississippi childhood. Among black teenage schoolboys in Jackson following World War I, Wright remembered, one sought peer acceptance by "subscribing to certain racial sentiments. The touchstone of fraternity was my feeling toward white people, how much hostility I held toward them." Typically, Wright noted, racial bitterness animated youthful street-corner discussions: "The first white sonofabitch that bothers me is gonna get a hole knocked in his head!" "Man, what makes white folks so mean?" "Whenever I see one I spit." "Man, ain't they ugly?"[7]

Resentment ran particularly high against the pretensions of "peckerwoods" and "clay eaters," the poor whites who "ain't got a thing but a lot of tobacco in their jaws." "They think they are better than the Negroes around here," a contemptuous Mississippian told Charles S. Johnson's associate during World War II. "That's the thing that makes me sick."[8]

By the same token, although deference was universally recognized as the price of racial peace, it could be overdone. Blacks who cultivated an excessively obeisant style invited the disfavor of others of their race. For example, Piney Woods Schoolmaster Laurence Jones, as one black contemporary remembered, aroused suspicion in some quarters of the black community "because of his manner," because he was too eager to "suit the white people."[9] To offset black opprobrium for his white-pleasing ways, Richard Wright's friend Griggs denied that his unctuous behavior betrayed a disloyal heart: "You may think I'm an Uncle Tom," he told the future writer, "but I'm not. I hate these white people, I hate 'em with all my heart. But I can't show it; if I did, they'd kill me."[10]

Doubtless the race had its bona fide Sambos, its "handkerchief heads" and Uncle Toms who internalized the white image of themselves as innately servile and inferior. It does not follow, however, that Afro-Mississippians were typically apathetic and acquiescent. Rather, the evidence suggests that an accommodative demeanor often masked a resentful spirit, that black Mississippians generally chafed under white insult and ridicule, that Jim Crow rested easily on only the most dispirited of black shoulders.

Indeed, what seems remarkable is not that some were victimized by self-hatred, but that so many were relatively unscarred by the dehumanizing pressures of white supremacy. Consider the words of elderly Joanna Thompson Isom, a former slave from Oxford, who had seen enough of both races by 1936 to know that "Niggers aint de onliest fools in de worl." Though apparently illiterate and reduced in old age to begging, she neither doubted her own worth nor found logic in racial hierarchy: "Dere aint no diffrunce twixt niggers an' white folks, 'cept dey color; white folks stays out of de sun, but ef you cuts dey finger, dey both bleeds alike; nationality wont let dem be de same; ef hit wuzn't fer station de worl' w'ud be better off; dats what makes dem have to stay on dey own side of de street."[11] And consider, too, the testimony of Lillie Jones of Neshoba County who in 1981, at the age of nearly ninety, described a life-long practice of meeting white racial slurs with affirmations of personal pride: "Whenever they would come any way towards saying something out of the way to me, I'd tell them . . . 'I may not have nothing . . . may not have a dime,' but I said 'I thinks and feels like I am good as anybody on topside earth, I don care who he is.' Thats the way that I feel about myself."[12]

Feasible Limits

If black Mississippians did not eagerly kiss the whip that lashed them, they also did not develop a tradition of sustained, organized challenge to white dominance. Indeed, black resistance in the nadir period of Afro-American history lacked the high drama, perhaps even the sense of heroic purpose, of the later civil rights revolution. With the notable exception of the 1904 streetcar boycotts described below, the half century after 1890 witnessed no direct-action campaigns. Black spokesmen frequently remonstrated for better jobs, better schools, and full citizenship rights. But neither massive street demonstrations against economic and educational discrimination nor voter registration campaigns designed to arouse the disfranchised black underclass were within the realm of possibilities.

To be sure, Jim Crow Mississippi had its uncompromising, race-proud black rebels, most of them historically obscure, a few of them legendary. Robert Charles, for example, a black nationalist and, as one scholar would have it, very likely "the first fully self-conscious black militant in the United States," was born to Copiah County sharecroppers in 1865 or 1866 and remained in the state until 1894. Ida B. Wells, fiery publicist and antilynching crusader, was born in Holly Springs during the Civil War (1862) and spent her formative years in Marshall County. And Sidney Revels Redmond, grandson of the first black United States senator, civil rights activist, and two-term president of the National Bar Association, was born in Jackson in 1903 and practiced law in the state capital during the late 1920s.[13]

Significantly, however, these notable figures won their places in the annals of militant black protest as emigres, outside the borders of Mississippi: Charles as the defiant martyr to black rage in the bloody New Orleans riot of 1900, one of the first serious racial disturbances since Reconstruction; Wells, first in her capacity as co-publisher of the Memphis *Free Speech,* and then (until her death in 1931) as radical activist in New York and Chicago; Redmond as a St. Louis attorney, education reformer, and member of the NAACP legal team in *Gaines* v. *Canada* (1938), the case in which the Supreme Court, for the first time, reexamined the "separate-but-equal" fiction in public education.

Admittedly ahistorical though such "counterfactual" speculation may be, it seems probable, had these exemplars of black assertiveness never left Mississippi, that the patterns of their resistance would have taken different, less overt forms. Because he was a lone rebel and not a public reformer, Robert Charles, the very model of the "bad nigger," is a possible exception. Had he remained a Copiah County day laborer, it is at least conceivable that he could have worn a discreetly proud and defiant black spirit even as he wore a jaunty brown derby and .38 Colt. He might also have been radicalized by mounting white racism, and become a separatist and disciple of Bishop Henry M. Turner's back-to-Africa movement. It seems all but certain, however, that he could not have survived at home without compromise. Whatever anger he carried in his heart of hearts, he simply could not have lived openly in Mississippi as a militant black activist. The same must be said of Ida Wells, whose crusading journalism had no precedent in her home state. Had she continued to teach in a one-room rural school in Mississippi, her militant struggle—her radical advocacy of black suffrage, her campaign against mob violence, her promotion of the NAACP and Garveyism—would have been driven underground, were it waged at all. Redmond's life as public official, member of the NAACP's National Legal Committee, and activist in the campaign to desegregate graduate and professional schools seems equally improbable in a Mississippi setting. In St. Louis this Harvard-educated son and former partner of Jackson lawyer S. D. Redmond could serve as an assistant city attorney, two-term city alderman, and, most telling, local counsel in the NAACP's landmark assault on the exclusion of blacks from the University of Missouri School of Law. In Mississippi, where all public officials were white and black attorneys often found it too risky to defend blacks accused of serious crimes, a judicial challenge to white supremacy would have been, quite simply, suicidal.

This is not to suggest that all militant black Mississippians became emigres—merely that those who did not or could not follow Ida Wells to the comparative freedom of the North also could not follow her example of militant activism. In another era, during the Second Reconstruction, an indigenous black protest movement would emerge in Mississippi and the state would serve, in the judgment of historian Steven F. Lawson, as the "laboratory in which the civil rights movement displayed its most creative energies."[14] But the post–World War II freedom struggles had no precise counterparts in the half century after 1890. Entoiled in a system of racial segregation, degradation, and repression designed to stifle their initiative, insure their poverty and illiteracy, isolate them from national democratic values, and render them politically powerless, black Mississippians in the Age of Jim Crow were poorly situated to articulate candidly and forcefully their own grievances, much less to agitate effectively for full citizenship. Without the favorable interplay of a series of national and international developments during and after World War II, an effective, broad-based social justice movement of, by, and for blacks could not have developed in any American state, least of all in Mississippi.

The continuing struggle to complete the act of emancipation rests on a foundation of black discontent and black agitation dating from the slavery era. But the civil rights movement of the 1950s and 1960s was not one from the social depths; it came not in the darkest hour of racial oppression but in a period of relative social flux and rising black expectations. It was a reflection of long-developing demographic currents that had brought large numbers of southern blacks to northern cities where, despite white Yankee hostility, they found better jobs, better schools, growing cohesiveness and political clout. Animated by black impatience, suffused with black pride and the new "black consciousness," the movement drew not only on the legacies of Frederick Douglass, Marcus Garvey, and W. E. B. Du Bois, but also on the democratic idealism of the war against Hitler, on the anticolonialist strivings of black Africans, and on the moral imperatives of the Cold War. Finally, its way was eased by gradually diminishing white racial animus nationwide, by declining white southern influence on the national Democratic party, by the addition of racial justice to the liberal-reform agenda—not least of all, by increasingly sympathetic federal political and judicial decisions that pulled the remaining legal props from under white supremacy.

By implication, the travail of the post–World War II freedom movement suggests the impediments to civil rights activism in an earlier, less sympathetic age. It takes nothing away from such doughty figures as Fannie Lou Hamer and Aaron Henry of Mississippi's Second Reconstruction to note that circumstance was on their side. In a less favoring milieu their crusades, much less their triumphs, are scarcely imaginable. The argument here is not that the civil rights victories of the 1960s were inevitable or that they came easily, but rather that social movements have contexts and that the character of social agitation, like the pace of social change itself, is conditioned by the environment in which it operates. The study of black protest in the period before World War II, therefore, necessarily begins with an appreciation of its feasible limits. Moreover, those who would understand the black Mississippian's strivings in the age of Jim Crow might also ponder the analogy of slavery historiography. Finding few examples of armed slave revolt, historians once grossly underestimated slave resistance. Encountering few Nat Turners, they postulated too many Sambos, and thereby overlooked the creative capacities of a people who, though trapped in a physically and psychologically coercive system, were neither childlike nor docile; who, though bought and sold like oxen, nevertheless devised safe, often ingenious ways to resist white dominance and influence the rhythms and patterns of their own lives. Similar interpretive pitfalls await historians of the segregation experience, who by looking for too much may see too little.

Dark Journey: Stage One

During the last decades of the nineteenth century, during what might be called the first stage of their dark journey through the Jim Crow years, black Mississippians resisted the erosion of their citizenship by every practical means. Individually, as the record of black counterviolence demonstrates, they sometimes denied their oppressors in starkly physical ways. Moses Weston, an obscure Washington County black, was more assertive than most, but his defiant act suggests not only that the color line rankled but that some blacks would not segregate themselves. Ordered roughly out of a white Greenville saloon in 1889, he claimed the right of a free man to trade where he wished. When a white man tried forcibly to remove him, Weston killed his tormentor with a pistol and was, in turn, shot dead by the proprietor.[15]

Weston's example was not widely emulated. More routinely, the race expressed its disaffections nonviolently: through public and private affirmations of personal dignity and self-worth; through daily, individual acts of passive resistance to white will; or, whenever possible, through the normal channels of protest open to a free people. In the end, there seemed to be no alternative to subordination. Although blacks saw nothing in white supremacy that was either natural or just, they were not, for the most part, foolhardy. Having struggled for equal rights in the face of impossible odds, a great many — perhaps the great majority — ultimately agreed with Booker T. Washington that accommodation was an acceptable alternative to an unrestrained racial conflict they would surely lose.

Here again, those who made the adjustments can tell their own story. The oral histories of elderly blacks, particularly those gathered in the aftermath of the civil rights revolution of the 1960s, often address the resistance-accommodation issue. As this evidence reveals, blacks responded to white dominance in varied ways as their individual personalities and their circumstances required. Some compromised more readily than others. Thus, from the safe distance of 1970, Machen Box of Chickasaw County thought that white supremacy "wasn't so bad" if one understood that it was not negotiable: "When a person know a thing he should not worry over it, 'cause worry will kill you[;] . . . in them times white[s] have things going they way." Similarly, seventy-year-old Maxine Davis of Hattiesburg remembered that fatalism was the best psychological defense against Jim Crow: "It was just something you had to take." Others met white demands for separation with a proud separatism of their own. But most resented their second-class citizenship. Mixing metaphors grandly, seventy-three-year-old Lizzie V. Garner of Jackson seemed to speak for the generality of her race in 1976 when she recalled the bitter cup of white supremacy forced upon those who sat at the back of Mississippi's bus: "I remember vividly, I thought it was the worst thing. I didn't have no other alternative but to sit there and drank it down."[16]

More than a decade before suffrage restrictions were enacted, Afro-Mississippians were effectively denied their political rights through violence and electoral fraud. As the sharp decline in black voter participation during the 1880s suggests, many black Mississippians abandoned a losing struggle before they were "legally" disfranchised. Finding the obstacles overwhelming, no longer willing to pay the price that suffrage required, they simply lost the will to vote. With Isaiah Montgomery, the lone black delegate to the constituent assembly, many perhaps believed that racial peace could be bought only on white terms.

As Chapter 2 emphasized, a great many others resisted the new order by every lawful means: at the ballot box and through voter education, before Congress and the bar of public opinion, and by such legal channels as remained open to them. In the end, their resistance was futile and they were denied the protection of the Fifteenth Amendment as surely as if it had been repealed. From the early 1890s until the mid-1960s, only a diminishing fraction of the former black electorate, and then usually only members of the middle class, managed to overcome the obstacles of official discrimination and white popular hostility to become qualified voters. Restrained by fear and a whites-only primary law of 1902, Mississippi's black electors rarely attempted to vote in local or state canvasses; they nevertheless maintained their own political organizations, participated in federal elections, took an active part in the patronage decisions and the national conventions of the Republican party, and otherwise nurtured a fragile black political tradition. As a practical matter, they exercised no influence over the political decisions that most immediately touched their lives. To their critics, and perhaps sometimes even to themselves, they were merely "post office Republicans" who dabbled harmlessly at the game of politics. Yet, by their very presence in the political arena—by their continued interest in public affairs and the forms of democratic governance—they gave the lie to the myth that whites ruled because blacks wanted it that way.

The black response to mounting white demands for racial separation was more ambivalent, but no more acquiescent. As Charles S. Johnson said of the Jim Crow era, "practically all Southern Negroes *accept* racial segregation."[17] Black Mississippians did so, in part as a matter of pride and preference, and in part as a matter of necessity. Segregation was nearly always more welcome than exclusion, and separation was not, in itself, always degrading to a race that had countered white discrimination with a group identity of its own. The black yearning for assimilation into the American mainstream presupposed equality of opportunity but not necessarily racial integration in every sphere. Nor did all blacks desire white company. Indeed, in some areas of life, separate development was as acceptable, even as desirable, to blacks as it was mandatory to whites. Having hastened to form their own social and religious oranizations in the first years of freedom, black Mississippians continued to evince a strong preference for autonomy, for separate churches, lodges, and other places of assembly and diversion where they might be free from white pretensions and control. Even separate-but-equal drinking fountains, perhaps Jim Crow's most ubiquitous symbols, did not wound every black heart. Expressing her own mixed feelings about interracialism, septuagenarian Betty Gray of Hinds County recalled in 1976 that she resented injustice but not necessarily separation: "They didn't want to drink behind me and I didn't want to drink behind them."[18]

Mississippi public school children never attended biracial classes, and black complaints during the Jim Crow years nearly always centered on inequality within a dual system of education rather than on segregation itself. In a period when most black common schools met in privately owned cabins, churches, and stores—when all but a diminishing fraction of public expenditures went to white students—blacks objected to a system of taxation without benefit. Their own educational facilities were improved, they frequently noted, largely through private subscription in the black community or northern philanthropy, while their taxes were used for the extended school terms, consolidated school districts, agricultural high schools, and transportation of whites. Until after 1954, the redress they sought in court and through public pressure was simple equity, a decent education for their children, not biracial classrooms.

The same was true of higher education. Briefly, during the first years of Reconstruction, some race leaders demanded black admission to the University of Mississippi and some black lawmakers opposed a plan for an all-black university, fearing that it might strengthen "a precedent which we were working hard to break down—that of separate institutions for the races." Black support for Alcorn University solidified, however, after whites refused to "mongrelize" the campus at Oxford and the legislature agreed to an all-black board of trustees and generous state funding for the new institution. Disappointed by the American Missionary Association's decision to use an all-white faculty and administration at Tougaloo University, many black Mississippians looked to Alcorn as a college "of their own."[19] With the return of the Democrats, Alcorn lost most of its appropriation, its status as a university, and eventually even its black governing board. Yet when they addressed, as they repeatedly did, the state's gross neglect of black higher education, race spokesmen invariably appealed for separate-but-equal opportunities, not admission to white institutions. If they recognized that there could never be equality within separation, they also understood that in Jim Crow Mississippi whites would have segregated colleges or none at all.

In relatively fluid areas, where the color line seemed less rigid and white sentiment less volatile, blacks during the post-Reconstruction period asserted their rights to the unimpeded use of public accommodations. Transportation provides a useful example. When the state enacted a separate coach bill in 1888, the effect was to strengthen an existing practice, not to introduce new social policy. Yet, though it effectively changed little, the measure was Mississippi's first Jim Crow law. Leading blacks called it "odious and oppressive," a calculated affront designed to "humiliate and degrade respectable and intelligent colored passengers." Perhaps encouraged by the laggardly compliance of cost-minded carriers reluctant to finance additional passenger facilities exclusively for blacks, the state's prominent race leaders met in June, 1889, to register their opposition. The *Clarion-Ledger* thought that the convention delegates had assembled in Jackson to "whereas and resolve against the white people of Mississippi"; the New Orleans *Picayune* concluded that Mississippi blacks wanted "nothing less than that the social barriers between the superior and inferior races shall be wholly broken down."[20]

In fact, while John R. Lynch, Blanche K. Bruce, James Hill, and the other organizers of the protest promised "to wage a persistent and unceasing war" against "unjust, unfair, and unreasonable discrimination," their stated objective was the derailment of the Jim Crow car, not the toppling of white supremacy. Conceding the railroads' right to enforce "reasonable discrimination in the accommodation of passengers," they argued that it should be accomplished along lines of class rather than race. Convinced that the equal-accommodation clause would "neither be respected nor enforced," they ojected to legislation that for reasons of "mere race or color, regardless of other considerations or conditions," denied to "intelligent and well-dressed and well-behaved colored ladies and gentlemen" the first-class accommodations that were enjoyed by "ignorant, indecent and offensive white persons." The convention resolution instructed delegate leaders to seek legislative repeal of the statute and, failing that, relief in the courts.[21]

Neither approach succeeded. The legislature, having already required separate-but-equal sleeping cars and railroad waiting rooms, would in time extend the logic of the separate coach law to all forms of public transportation. The state supreme court, in the month preceding the 1889 Jackson convention, gingerly skirted the complicating distinctions between intra- and interstate transportation and found the restrictive train law to be a legitimate exercise of state police powers. In 1912, with the concurrence of the United States Supreme Court, the Mississippi tribunal ruled that the state segregation law governed all rail traffic within or through the state, whatever its origination or termination. In these and subsequent rulings, the state court missed few opportunities to lecture operators of public conveyances on their obligations to "prevent race conflict" through "perfect separation" of white from black. Noncompliant carriers—even those that mistakenly assigned fair-skinned Negroes to white compartments—were subject not only to prosecution but to the damage suits of whites who suffered "distress of mind and body" by traveling in proximity to blacks.[22]

Black travelers who expressed public dissatisfaction with Jim Crow arrangements or who asserted their rights as interstate passengers to use sleeping berths or dining cars risked a violent response from police or vigilantes. In 1919, Drummond Leonard, a prosperous barber, traveled from his home in Yazoo City to Jackson to secure drawing-room accommodations for his Atlanta-bound daughters. Indignantly insisting that state law could not deny him interstate privileges, he intimidated a reluctant ticket agent. Returning home, he was dragged from his own train by a white mob at Annie, flogged, and apparently forced to leave the state. Some fifteen years later, Professor Hugh Morris Gloster of Morehouse College objected when black women stood in the crowded black compartment of his Mississippi train while white men sat in half-empty cars. He was ejected near Tupelo, beaten, and thrown in jail by police who thought him lucky, because "many a nigger has been killed here for less."[23]

Although not isolated, such incidents were probably not common after 1900. During the last decades of the nineteenth century, during the first stage of their march toward substantive freedom, black Mississippians directly challenged Jim Crow accommodations and lost. In the twentieth century, with but one major exception—that of the streetcar boycott of 1904—they generally and quite prudently agitated for equal rather than integrated services. Avoiding direct confrontations they could not hope to win, black leaders in the period from the turn of the century through the interwar years—the period of the second and third stages of this dark journey—occasionally sought redress in court and more typically petitioned public carriers and the state legislature for more equitable transportation facilities.[24]

Whatever their strategies, blacks failed to win meaningful concessions. Although some railroads promised "full consideration" of their many complaints, black travel accounts from the period leave little doubt that the Jim Crow car deserved its reputation as a "universally filthy and uncomfortable" facility and a symbol of "indignity, disgrace, and shame."[25] Following a trek from Helena, Arkansas, to Mound Bayou aboard the Yazoo and Mississippi Valley Railroad, perhaps the least discriminatory line in the state, one black passenger observed that the Negro compartment was a noisome, all-purpose "crime against decency," part passenger car, part cattle car, part madhouse: "A well-fitted Jim Crow car in the South carries all the Race people, the porter, the flagman, the conductor, the butcher boy and his boxes, the lanterns and signals[,] . . . the deputy sheriff with five or six race prisoners, all in handcuffs enroute for the state convict farm, and all the chickens, baskets, bags and acting suitcases that weary travelers may claim." "No grander lie was ever enacted into law, than that that declares for 'separate but equal accommodations,' " he concluded. "There will never be equal accommodations for the races. Separation presupposes and invites inequalities."[26]

Widespread black appreciation of that fact, no doubt, inspired the streetcar boycott. In this remarkable example of organized resistance, very likely the last such action in the state until the Second Reconstruction,[27] black Mississippians protested a change in public policy, not merely the enactment of insulting legislation. Until 1904, despite scattered white complaints that white ladies sometimes found it "impossible" to ride with the "unwashed contingent," urban transit systems were perhaps the most integrated public facilities in the state.[28] In

January of that year, however, following the inauguration of Governor Vardaman, the legislature bowed to mounting white public pressure and required street railways to provide either separate trolleys or separate compartments within trolleys. Traction companies resisted the move, finding "no special necessity for such a law," but the editors of several white newspapers thought the statute alone could prevent race war.[29]

In June, 1904, when the law took effect, blacks in at least five of the seven Mississippi cities with street railways boycotted the lines, choosing to walk or go by carriage rather than to be Jim Crowed. In so doing, they participated in an early regionwide direct-action campaign in which blacks in more than twenty-five cities in every state of the former Confederacy protested segregated urban public transit.[30]

Regrettably, the available record tells us nothing of the black mass meetings or petitions to the legislature that surely preceded the enactment of Mississippi's streetcar law. Neither can we know the degree to which the black users' strike was coordinated within and between cities, who the leaders were, nor even precisely how long it lasted. Such news accounts as local black newspaper editors may have published have all vanished. The state's white press, as it did so often in matters of black initiative, deliberately played down the story. Characteristically, white accounts of the action were sometimes accompanied by reports that increased white usage more than offset the loss of black passengers and by letters from conservative Negroes who favored separation as "the only thing possible."[31]

Yet, though the boycott ultimately failed, it was a forceful demonstration of black discontent and perhaps the only practical means to resist changing public policy. Because they constituted some 40 to 50 percent of all trolley-users in the state and because alternative means of transportation were readily available, black Mississippians could exert more pressure on local traction companies than on larger railroad systems. Moreover, as August Meier and Elliott Rudwick have noted, the boycott was a relatively safe and "conservative protest," one that sought to preserve the status quo and did not require direct black confrontation with white law.[32]

For a time, apparently for most of the summer of 1904 in some cities, the boycott was all but complete. During the first week, Vicksburg papers noted that black church and lodge leaders in that city were behind a "mutual and preconserted" action that had produced "an almost absolute boycott." Press dispatches from the Gulf Coast area in mid-June indicated that black Pascagoulans were still striking, though whites were confident that this "mad fit" would soon pass. The Jackson *Clarion-Ledger,* the most vocal advocate of Jim Crow streetcars, ignored the strike; but the Aberdeen *Weekly,* some ten days after the action began, reported that black Jacksonians were "striving for the unattainable" and that only an "occasional lone negro" rode the capital city's trolleys. In late August, the Natchez *Daily Democrat* observed that "the continuous discussion of co-operation among the negroes" was still "knocking flinders out of the Mississippi streetcar business."[33]

But whatever its short-run impact on corporate profits, the urban transit strikes in Mississippi, like those throughout the southern region, were doomed to failure from the outset. In a more auspicious time, as in the Port Gibson buyers' strike of the 1960s, black economic leverage would force social change. In the Age of Jim Crow, however, the power of the black purse was limited. Unable to protest through normal political channels, confronted by a seemingly indomitable white will, and hobbled by a judicial system that sanctioned separate-but-equal law, blacks exercised their only realistic option. But they could not reverse public policy: inevitably, in the face of such odds, their unity collapsed. In Natchez, where for three months local trolley strike coordinators had apparently enjoyed widespread black community support, the movement was undermined late in August by an influx of some 4,000 delegates to the Negro Christian and Education Congress. Led by conservative African Methodist clergy opposed to the boycott, the outsiders freely boarded the street cars enroute to their meetings.[34]

In other Mississippi cities, the most discouraged and foot-weary appear to have already trickled into Negro compartments at the rear of the cars. No doubt there were persistent holdouts, and some may never have patronized segregated trolleys. The strike was clearly futile, however, and black Mississippians would attempt no further organized direct-action campaigns until after World War II.

In a sense, the boycott of 1904 marked a turning point in the black Mississippians' story, the conclusion of the first stage of their journey toward full citizenship. From the end of Reconstruction through the 1890s, blacks responded to the rising tide of racism and proscription with a judicious combination of resignation and resistance, conceding to the dominant race what they could not avoid, opposing caste restrictions as their deteriorating condition permitted. In part because the color line was drawn in the first years of freedom, and in part because restaurant fare, theater tickets, first-class accommodations on public carriers, and (after 1875) even the ballot box, were beyond the practical reach of most of them anyway, black Mississippians made an early though often profoundly uneasy peace with Jim Crow. The currents of their dissatisfactions ran deep, however, and if the public expressions of their recognized spokesmen are representative, they were anything but indifferent to their citizenship.

When whites, toward the end of the century, began further to circumscribe black rights of access and suffrage, to strengthen the devices of control by fixing the habits and practices of exclusion and discrimination into the very law, the most prominent and articulate Afro-Mississippians were virtually united in open opposition. At this point, late in the 1880s, the conciliatory Isaiah Montgomery was rather more the exception than the rule. Anticipating a new generation of more accommodating spokesmen, he acceded to what he knew to be an accomplished fact. Yet among leading black Mississippians his was still a relatively lonely voice, audible above a chorus of black protest only because it was carried on a wave of white acclaim.

In this initial phase of the black struggle, the civil and political aspirations of the race were most faithfully expressed in the words and deeds of such Republican notables as Blanche K. Bruce, James J. Hill, and John Roy Lynch, and also the less well known attorney Cornelius J. Jones of Issaquena County, who argued the unconstitutionality of the state's suffrage restrictions before the Congress and both the state and federal supreme courts.[35] In such political figures, the race found its first generation of leaders and through them it waged a losing counteroffensive against the closing forces of disfranchisement, proscription, and isolation.

Perhaps not militant by the standards of a later era, these black representatives were also not accommodationists. More often than not ex-slaves born in the late antebellum period, they had come of political age during Reconstruction, held public office and influenced public policy, and otherwise participated with dignity and purpose in what later, amid the gloom of the 1890s, seemed to them a golden age of interracial harmony and equal opportunity. When their moment passed, when the conservative Democrats returned to power, they had no illusions about white intentions. The redeemers' triumph, Bruce and Hill predicted in October, 1875, "will . . . sound the death knell of all the hopes that the colored man has indulged of educating, elevating and improving his race in this State. Once under the iron heel of Democracy, the colored man will at once sink back to the status he held in 1865 — free in name, but not in fact — poor, ignorant and helpless, hedged in by unfriendly laws, which he will have no power to circumvent."[36]

By the turn of the century, their worst fears realized and their battles all but lost, most of these first-generation leaders had passed from the scene, either like Bruce (d. 1898) and Hill (d. 1901) in death or like Lynch and Jones through out-migration. Montgomery survived as the very archetype of black conservatism in a new Age of Accommodation. He was a contemporary of Lynch and Hill, and he too came to maturity during the sanguine years of Republican rule. Yet the Mound Bayouan always stood apart from the old-line black Reconstruction figures. He did not want for courage, but he would not fight a whirlwind and, unlike his seemingly more resolute cohorts, he advised his people to steer a safer course into more protected waters rather than to sail futilely (as he would have it) into the eye of a storm. Some thought him disloyal, a black Judas, revenant of the self-abasing darky of antebellum lore. But he was more nearly a harbinger than a throwback, the first and most prominent of the second-generation black Mississippians who emerged in the racial maelstrom of the late nineteenth century and helped to fix the tone of black thought and action until, and indeed well after, World War I.

New Realities: Stage Two

In the period after 1890, during the second stage, Mississippi's "natural" black leaders, the members of its small, interlocking, and migration-ravaged middle class, were conspicuously conservative even by the standards of the lower South. The old Reconstruction figures, many of whom came to prominence as politicians and public officials, drew on the American tradition of egalitarianism and demanded full-fledged citizenship and immediate and complete assimilation into the cultural mainstream. The new spokesmen were not apolitical and many, if not most, were active in Republican party affairs. Their standing in the black community derived from their leadership in such fields as business or the law, religion or education. And though their ends were the same as the Bruce-Lynch generation, their means had to reflect new realities. While their predecessors had challenged the growing political and social reduction of the race through political agitation and public protest, the second-stage leaders emphasized gradualism and concilia-tion, discreetly opposing black subordination but not racial separation itself.

Because white supremacy was, after 1890, not merely a settled issue in Mississippi but a closed subject, one no longer open to public dis-cussion, the new leadership necessarily sought economic rather than political approaches to race advancement. But the differences in black agendas and leadership styles during the two periods were largely tactical, and the changeover from the politics and protest of Bruce and Lynch to the separate development and accommodationism of their successors was a matter of emphasis. In every stage of their journey from slavery to full citizenship, black Mississippians recognized the value of economic development and exercised such political options as they then possessed. Throughout the entire period from the First Reconstruction to the Second the wish for civil rights coexisted with the ideal of group solidarity.

Not remarkably, the most conciliatory of the new breed, notably Montgomery and fellow Mound Bayou businessman Charles Banks, and schoolmasters William Henry Holtzclaw of Utica Institute and Jonas Edward Johnson of Prentiss, were, in their close identification with Booker T. Washington, faithful reflectors both of his optimistic social philosophy of self-help and separate development and of his stategy of compromise and caution. But even those figures with no ties to Tuskegee—the Yazoo City physician Lloyd T. Miller, for example, or attorneys Willis E. Mollison of Vicksburg and Perry W. Howard of Jackson, or Indianola businessmen Wayne Cox and Dr. Joseph E. Walker—were social realists who generally conducted their public lives in scrupulous conformity to the racial code.

In the Bookerite fashion, the new leadership emphasized economic opportunity over social equality and preached the gospel of black uplift through industrial training, right living, thrift, and material accumulation. When they addressed the "Negro problem"—when they took public notice of lynching, peonage, educational inequalities, or discriminatory law enforcement—these second-generation figures typically did so in the language of expedience, obscuring their private aspirations for the race in cautious rhetoric. If they sometimes suggested as even compliant William Holtzclaw did, that "a people who cannot vote in a republic are at the mercy of those who can," they were quick to add that suffrage, whatever its future benefits, was secondary to the black Mississippian's immediate, practical need "to take care of his own progress" through hard work and economy, "to lay hold upon the opportunities that are all around him and to make the best of them."[37] In their hearts and in the company of intimates, they could, as the Jackson attorney Samuel Alfred Beadle did in his life as an obscure poet and man of letters, cry out against the "tyrannous public opinion" that made black Mississippians "alien enemies in the land of their nativity."[38] Their public pronouncements, however, were rarely so forthright. They were not oblivious to the evil that swirled about them. But whatever their private anguish, the leaders of the second stage saw no benefit in open controversy with the dominant white minority.

Thus, when Montgomery sought to quell turn-of-the-century mob violence through public exposure of "the depths to which Mississippi has descended," he did so quietly behind the scenes. Alarmed by an outbreak of Whitecapping against successful Negroes in the state, he carefully monitored the depredations and reported the details to Tuskegee in the hope that "judicious ways" might be found to bring the problem to national attention. When a northern editor asked him to supply particulars, however, he refused, saying that "for reasons which you will understand, I cannot afford any special notoriety in connection with these matters."[39]

In sum, leading black Mississippians after 1890 were characteristically men of public caution who soft-peddled black grievances, advocated alliance with the "better class" of southerners, and counseled patient black acceptance of what they thought to be the best white terms then available. If this was a "white man's country," as the distribution of wealth and influence (and the testimony of virtually every white) proclaimed, then compromise seemed to them wiser than confrontation and the expectation of gradual progress more realistic than the hope of immediate equality. In such a country, there was more to be gained from maneuvering powerful whites into acting out their self-assigned paternalistic roles within the aristocratic tradition than in the open agitation for full social and political rights.[40]

Those who advocated protest, who demanded more for the race sooner, were dismissed as hot heads and pie-in-the-sky idealists who did not understand southern conditions. Although admitting the criticism of "radicals . . . a thousand miles from the scene," Charles Banks would make no apology for the "policy of preaching harmony and . . . holding aloof from politics." "We know that a policy that makes for peace and good-will between the races is best for all concerned, . . . that the Negro has all to gain and nothing to lose by making friends with his white neighbors right here at his very door." The wisdom of that approach, he informed a gathering of black business leaders in Okolona in 1909, would be evident when "the poverty of our race has been decreased in proportion to our illiteracy. . . . Until then, my friends and co-workers, let us be contented to labor and wait."[41]

But how long? The question was never explicitly answered, but implicit in the one-sided "bargain" of black accommodationism, or so most conservative race spokesmen believed, was the promise that in exchange for provisional black acceptance of white supremacy, the Afro-American would gain more than the immediate objectives of an interracial truce and what Washington called "a man's chance" for economic security. At some future point—after the foundation for citizenship was laid, after the freedmen had demonstrated their loyalty to their native Southland, after the former slaves had pulled themselves up by their own bootstraps, become law-abiding, acquired education, wealth, and property—the "negro question" could be reopened and the race could perhaps press the bargain more in its own favor. At such time conservative whites of good conscience, the men who owned and controlled the state, would in simple fairness see that the black Mississippians received their due. Under the new dispensation, the mark of human worth would be personal merit, not race. "While prejudice may predominate today," Edward Wilkinson Lampton of Greenville, Grand Master of the Most Worshipful Stringer Grand Lodge, assured his fellow Masons in 1903, "it must eventually give way to right and justice." Although less patient with present inequities than some, he nevertheless shared a general optimism that black fortitude would ultimately be rewarded and that "the time will yet come when in this country and other countries a man will be measured by the true merits and not the color of the skin."[42]

This conservative formulation of present and future race relations always contained more hope than expectation. It was based, among other things, insofar as it had an objective basis, on flawed assumptions: that the prejudice of the ignorant redneck was the primary obstacle to black progress; that the racial mores of the educated and refined white classes were materially more sympathetic than those of the unwashed masses; that whites of power and wealth were, in fact, the Negroes' "best friend"; and that by emulating white virtues blacks could win white acceptance and ultimately their constitutional rights. The accommodationist argument glossed over the fact that after 1890, even as black rights diminished, white racial depredations mounted. Nor did it recognize that virtually all whites without respect to class or education looked to subordination as the ultimate solution, as an end in itself, not the means to black advancement.

Yet if the black conciliators in the period after 1890 clutched at straws, there was little else to clutch. If they were, as northern black intellectuals often said of race conservatives in general, appeasers and opportunists who appeared to act more readily out of prudence than on principle, the fact remains that they conceded nothing to whites that had not already been taken by force. In truth, the "generation" of Montgomery demanded less for the race than that of Lynch. It did so, however, not because early twentieth-century black Mississippians wanted less, but because their assessments of the power realities of their time and place led them to conclude that conciliation was a more promising path to black progress than confrontation. Whatever the long-range liabilities of accommodationism—and there were many—there were no practical alternatives during the age of Jim Crow.

Of course, accommodation is not necessarily surrender. Even in the ebbtide of black rights there was, as we have noted throughout this volume, black struggle. Black Mississippians were often victimized, but they were never merely victims. Locked out of the mainstream, they sought advantage in disadvantage, strength in group solidarity, hope in an all-black variant of the American Dream. Denied a place in democracy, second-stage race leaders turned to capitalism. As other Afro-Americans have done in times of discouragement and unfulfilled expectation, they deemphasized assimilation and sought advancement through self-help and a heightened group identity. Ultimately, their business enterprises foundered in the backwaters of a white-dominated economic order. Yet during the dark years of exclusion and discrimination the group economy provided outlets for black energy and creativity and sources of black optimism and pride. Moreover, through economic solidarity and cooperation blacks found yet another way to resist white efforts to keep them down.

Amid the lowering shadows of proscription, an exclusive black commerce offered a ray of hope, perhaps a way out of Jim Crow's depths. In Jackson, Natchez, Vicksburg, and other cities confident turn-of-the-century black entrepreneurs pursued private gain *and* human rights through separate development. Mound Bayouans thought of their village as more than a black refuge in a hostile white world. It was a place, as Montgomery boasted, "where Negroes would not have to get off the sidewalks for anybody"; unlike the residents of other Mississippi towns, one of its mayors reported, blacks in this community enjoyed "complete self-respect. In other words . . . a normal life."[43] The town was above all a self-conscious experiment in race building, a showcase of black material achievement, a monument to the black genius for self-government. To Charles Banks, Mississippi's own "black wizard of finance," the Mound Bayou Proposition was an expression of racial "integrity," but not merely the mirror image of white exclusivity. It was an opportunity to demonstrate that left to their own devices and freed from white restraints, Afro-Americans could occupy an independent position of dignity and respect in a nation that valued economic success over nearly all else.

In much the same resistant and race-conscious spirit, enterprising blacks in nearly every community in the state endeavored to build financial, retail, and service establishments that would counter white stereotypes and provide models of black achievement. In their eagerness to read black acceptance of Jim Crow into such endeavors, whites rarely saw black economic and social welfare institutions in all their complexity. Black entrepreneurs, however, understood that black capitalism was animated by pride as well as profit and that the struggle against white dominance could assume economic as well as political forms.

The Resistant Spirit: Stage Three

The third stage in this dark journey began, one might say, on time, during the First World War. Its point of departure can be found in the social ebb and flow of the homefront and war effort and in the resurgent spirit of what is known in Afro-American history as the "New Negro" of the "Militant Twenties." Its earliest and clearest milestones were the great northward exodus and the appearance early in the postwar period of such organizations as a resuscitated state Federation of Colored Womens' Clubs, the now all but forgotten Committee of One Hundred, and the state's first NAACP branches. The way was often obscure and strewn with obstacles, the march not always forward, and progress during the 1920s and 1930s all but imperceptible. Yet on this last passage of the journey through the Jim Crow years, the efforts of black Mississippians gained momentum during the Second World War and reached their summit and terminus in the postwar civil rights revolution.

The differences between the second and third stages, though clear enough in retrospect, were but dimly perceived by contemporaries. The years here in question, the three decades after 1917, were not marked by striking changes in black status or circumstance. But the spirit of social change fostered by the First World War touched the Mississippi homefront in ways that could not be reversed. Although they were less celebrated than their counterparts in Harlem and elsewhere in the urban North, Mississippi, too, had its assertive, race-proud "New Negroes," its vanguard of the civil rights revolution.

Black Mississippians were deeply moved by wartime idealism and were increasingly sensitive to their anomalous position in a democratic nation. The call to serve in the armed forces, if often only in segregated labor battalions, quickened black pride and eroded the oppressive isolation of rural life. As the bonds of a relatively static and agrarian society were loosed, blacks left the state in growing numbers, either to war industries in the North or on military assignment in camps elsewhere in the nation and in France. "Up to the time of the World War," a prominent black educator believed, "the Mississippi Negro seemed fully resigned to his condition." The war with its unsettling impact on southern life — its "shifting about of the people to . . . other States, and across the seas" — however, "put him to thinking — thinking on life and its meaning; thinking on possibilities."[44] Decades later, amid the social ferment of the Second Reconstruction following World War II, B. Baldwin Dansby, retired president of Jackson College, traced the remote origins of the civil rights movement to the black doughboy and the assumption that his service earned for the race a stake in democracy: "It got started with his return. . . . He got the idea in World War I that he was a citizen, fighting for the country just as anyone else. . . . I think the return of the soldier after World War I was really the . . . beginning."[45]

During the war blacks entered eagerly into the patriotic work of the homefront and contributed disproportionately to the state's conscript quotas—supplying 52 percent of Mississippi's draft registrants and 56 percent of its inductees. For the most part, the state's black majority seemed to agree with Du Bois when he argued that during the emergency the higher aspirations of the race should be temporarily submerged in a singleness of national purpose. Yet black Mississippians clearly hoped that democracy's triumph would be felt beyond the trenches of the Western Front. Like Du Bois, they expected that after the armistice their wartime sacrifices would be rewarded with new opportunities for advancement. For the moment, as Perry Howard, chairman of Jackson's black Liberty Bond Committee said in October, 1917, the race should "lay aside all differences of feeling" and "do our whole duty." There would be time enough, he suggested, to carry black complaints, "in a manly and honorable way, . . . to the proper source after the crisis is passed." Toward the end of the war, in an unsigned essay apparently designed to conceal his identity, Howard spoke more forthrightly through the pages of a northern missionary journal: "If the Negro is called upon and furnishes his quota of fighters, man for man, he expects the ballot."[46] Even conservative Laurence Jones linked the war to advancing civil rights when he assured the black citizens of Crenshaw (Panola County) in 1918 that by doing "their very best in answering the call of the government," they might look "to the future prospects of citizenship and democracy which would soon knock at every man's door." Having served the nation in war, Jones believed, black Mississippians "could demand our rights and privileges which have been in store for us a long time."[47]

Even before the Kaiser's defeat, a white backlash against the egalitarian implications of the war effort crushed these hopes. Sharing the general southern ambivalence toward the conflict, white Mississippians responded to American intervention with a volatile mixture of patriotic fervor and heightened racial anxiety. They welcomed the prosperity brought by growing demand for cotton, but feared the disruptive influence of war and wartime democratic ideology on Jim Crow customs.

Inevitably, these fears centered on the black soldier and what the editor of the Vicksburg *Herald* called "the logic of black arms bearing."[48] Recognizing that patriotic sacrifice might strengthen the black claim to full civil and political rights, many whites initially opposed military training for the subordinate race; Senator Vardaman could think of "no greater menace to the South."[49] In the end, as black enlistment became unavoidable, whites assured themselves that "darky conscripts" would be mere uniformed laborers under white leadership.[50] Besides, as the Laurel *Leader* put it, an all-white army would leave "black bucks" at home drawing big wages while young white men died on the firing line.[51]

As the war progressed, race tension mounted. Apprehending a "Frenchified," disciplined, and proud black soldiery—perhaps even an armed black "rising"—whites tightened the reins, making the years from 1917 to 1919 among the most violent and restrictive since the last years of Reconstruction. As the example of J. A. Miller of Vicksburg suggests, blacks who attempted too directly to exploit wartime idealism for racial gain were subject to attack by whites eager to demonstrate that the war had changed nothing. A charter member of the state's first NAACP branch, Dr. Miller resisted the apparently extortionate demands of state and local War Savings Stamp Committees and the Red Cross because, as he said, "my patriotism began at home" and because he shared the founding fathers' aversion to "taxation without representation." Noting the inadequacy of black public education in Vicksburg and Warren County and the fact that black taxpayers could neither vote in the all-important Democratic primary nor use the public library, Miller informed white officials that he would pay only half of the expected assessment because "I had only half my rights." As he later said: "It was not the proper thing to make me share all the burdens and enjoy none of the blessings of democracy."[52]

In the first of several related cases of vigilantism in wartime Vicksburg, the black physician was soon thereafter accused of "sedition," tarred and feathered, and with two other black professional men of that city forced to leave the state. The attack on Miller, conducted as it was by "leading citizens" under tacit official sanction, seemed to open the floodgate of white wartime animus in Vicksburg. That same day an elderly white man with a common-law black wife was also tarred and feathered and banished; his mulatto son was immediately inducted by the local draft board. Early the next morning a band of white rowdies in the same city dragged two black housewives from their beds, stripped them and doused them with creosote and feathers. Both were the wives of black soldiers away on duty and one was in an advanced stage of pregnancy. Although these women were known to take in white people's laundry, their attackers charged them with "idleness."[53]

Already angered by unpunished white assaults on local black soldiers, black Vicksburg met these outrages with restrained fury. Rumors of a wholesale black exodus swept through the community. Feeling ran particularly high among black club women, a federal war worker reported, but "even the most ignorant" Negroes now seemed less supportive of the war. The "colored brass band" that once led black draftees to the railroad station, no longer found "cause for making music." Black Mississippians generally, this observer believed, did "a lot of bitter thinking."[54] From his new home in Detroit, Miller spoke for many of his race when he asked Walter White, "If a country can fight for democracy 3000 miles across the sea, why [can] not simple justice be done at home?"[55] The moment passed without further disorder, but the uneasy racial calm was broken the next year when a young, well-regarded black man—by all accounts the victim of mistaken identity—was burned alive in a white neighborhood for raping a white woman. Fearing a violent black response, the city banned the sale of firearms, converted the jail into an arsenal, and doubled the police force.[56]

Although Vicksburg was perhaps the most troubled city in the state, white wartime repression left a legacy of black resentment in virtually every Mississippi community. Partly to counter rising black expectations and partly to insure a stable black labor supply and drive "negro idlers" into low-wage service jobs, whites in many towns and cities enacted discriminatory "work-or-fight" ordinances,[57] attempted forcibly to impede out-migration, and harassed black servicemen. Local Red Cross units refused to permit black women to become canteen workers at railroad stations, explaining that in Jim Crow Mississippi the women of both races could not wear a common uniform. Some white civilian defense administrators discouraged black participation in federally co-ordinated food conservation efforts because, a representative of the Council on National Defense reported, it seemed "too much like social equality."[58] Throughout the war the white press alternately praised black patriotism and impugned black loyalty. Unsubstantiated reports from every section of the state alleged that "Kaiser-talking negroes" and black "disloyalists" were stockpiling weapons, conducting espionage, and conspiring with enemy agents to resist the draft and overthrow white authority.[59]

Following the armistice, and particularly during the Red Summer of 1919, fearful whites prepared for the worst. State and local officials issued blunt reminders that the old rules still applied. Governor Bilbo warned those blacks "contaminated with Northern social and political dreams of equality" not to return: "we have all the room in the world for what we know as N-i-g-g-e-r-s, but none whatsoever for 'colored ladies and gentlemen.' "[60] Authorities in some communities met with returning black soldiers to explain "what is expected of them"; future Congressman John E. Rankin, then an aspiring Lee County politician, advised black leaders in Tupelo against "action which might prompt racial consciousness"; and *Vardaman's Weekly* called upon Mississippi's "bravest and best" to prepare for armed suppression of "French-woman-ruined" black veterans.[61] Reports of black floggings were numerous[62] and at least three of the state's twelve lynch victims in 1919 were black veterans.[63] As one black Natchez veteran bitterly discovered, even as the truce was signed white Mississippians hastened to "blot out all the memory of the war": "You see they are afraid that if the Negro kept up his idea of his being a soldier and fighting, and wearing guns, etc., that these Negroes wouldn't stand for all the insults which they have to take from white people."[64]

Once peace was restored and rumors of an impending race war in the Delta proved groundless, white fear and repression began to moderate. Physical coercion remained an instrument of social control down through World War II and the threat of violence a fact of everyday black life. But the harsh regimen of the war gave way to a more restrained white dominion. In the early 1920s, responding to black pressure and to their own concerns about the continuing black exodus, responsible white business and civic leaders encouraged improved interracial communication and more equity within separation. Prodded by higher courts, the judicial system grew marginally more sensitive to procedural due process in cases involving blacks. Perhaps because, as an NAACP observer believed, some black Mississippians after 1919 were armed and prepared "to fight fire with fire, to fight back"[65] — and perhaps because of congressional consideration of federal antilynching legislation — vigilantes operated less flagrantly during the 1920s and 1930s. Black life was still cheap in Mississippi, however, and justice was still largely a white prerogative. Until the 1960s the color line scarcely wavered and the right of political expression and active protest demonstration remained tightly circumscribed.

In fact, black economic opportunity and material well-being declined between the two world wars, a development only partially attributable to the depression. In the learned professions, black representation was greatly reduced by out-migration and white hostility. After World War I black lawyers found it all but impossible to practice in the state; the number of black physicians and newspaper editors declined; and despite some modest gains in the quality of black education, the gap between average white and black teacher salaries grew ever wider. The 1920s witnessed the collapse of Mississippi's last black-owned banks, the most visible symbols of black economic aspiration, and a marked reduction in the confidence of the state's black entrepreneurial class. Between 1890 and 1940 the black place in the skilled trades eroded sharply and both the size and value of black-owned agricultural holdings declined substantially. Thus by World War II, more than at any time since emancipation, to be a black Mississippian was to be a menial—a field hand, a domestic servant, or a manual laborer.

Yet if old patterns survived and perhaps intensified, there were nevertheless new if scarcely discernible straws in the wind. Since the first moments of freedom, apprehensive whites, fearing that emancipated blacks might slough off the habits and dependencies of bondage, had mourned the passing of the "old-time darkies," the obliging field hands and loyal retainers who learned their places as slaves and who troubled themselves but little over the meaning of citizenship. As the memories of antebellum ways receded, many whites believed, so too did complacent black acceptance of white supremacy. In 1907 it was still possible for Alfred Holt Stone to imagine that black Mississippians, "just one generation out of slavery," were "still largely controlled by its influences" and, therefore, still "content with their situation."[66] By World War I perceptive white observers sensed a growing black impatience.

Although black leaders continued to advocate gradualism and equality through separation, a mounting black insistence on fair play filled many whites with foreboding. Following the Great War, David Cohn believed, both white paternalism and black accommodationism inched toward extinction. The older generation of Negroes and the older whites, perhaps 'the last exemplars of the tradition of *noblesse oblige*," all too rapidly passed from the scene, and so too did what this Deltan white thought to be their "workable—if perhaps far from ideal—relationship." In this unsettled postwar environment, race relations deteriorated, black discontent and white apprehension grew apace, and mutual "bitter hatreds" emerged. By World War II, Cohn noted, some blacks were talking of "fighting it out," and "a tragic clash between these tragic peoples" seemed increasingly likely.[67]

Blacks too believed that wartime dislocation intensified their own dissatisfactions and hastened generational change, developments that might bring pain as well as progress. With an ambivalence shared by many parents who recognized that their children found life in Mississippi increasingly intolerable, an elderly physician spoke to Emmett Scott early in the Great Migration: "I can't expect my son to accept the treatment under which I have been brought up. My length of residence here and the number of friends whom I know of the older and more aristocratic type of whites will protect me, but as for him, there is no friendship."[68]

Whatever their personal concerns, many blacks sensed that the erosion of old habits they witnessed within their own families presaged change in Mississippi. "My father was born and brought up as a slave," a black minister informed a black outsider during World War I. "He was taught his place and was content to keep it. But when he brought me up he let some of the old customs slip by. But I know there are certain things that I must do and I do them, and it doesn't worry me." In raising his own son, the minister let "more of the old customs slip," so many in fact that life in Mississippi became unbearable to the son. "He says," the father reported, " 'When a young white man talks rough to me, I can't talk rough to him. You can stand that; I can't. I have some education and inside I has the feelings of a white man.' "[69]

Although the preacher's son moved to Chicago, many other perhaps equally restless blacks remained behind. If they normally concealed such feelings from whites, they managed nevertheless to express their dissatisfactions and to press their demands for improved conditions. Indeed, much of the significance of the great migration is to be found in the response of blacks who did not migrate, in the little-known story of those who tried to turn a white problem into black social and economic progress.

Perhaps the most representative institutional expressions of this postwar opportunism were the Mississippi Federation of Colored Women's Clubs and the Committee of One Hundred. Both were race uplift organizations that fused black self-help and prudent social agitation, and both found new ways to manipulate white self-interest to black advantage. The oldest of these, the federation, a product of the reform-conscious Progressive Era, was organized in 1903 by the wives of the state's business, professional, and religious leaders at a meeting of Jackson's Phillis Wheatley Club. The organization flourished for a time, published its own newspaper, the *Woman's Herald* (1907-1913), and then foundered during the early stages of the Great Migration. Reorganized in 1920 by women from twenty-one local clubs, the federation thereafter played a useful role in the life of the black community. By 1921 there were fifty-six affiliates; when the organization convened for an annual meeting at Piney Woods School in 1923, delegates from seventy-three clubs attended.[70]

As suggested by the names of member organizations—the Ladies

Literary Club of Okolona, the Mothers' Club of Ocean Springs, the Woman's Christian Union of Vicksburg, the Willing Workers' Sewing Club of Itta Bena—the movement at the local level often focused on the traditional concerns of middle-class women's organizations: health, home, school, and church.[71] Federation activity at the state level, however, was often bolder and more race-conscious, centering on what an official history called the "cause of right and justice," particularly black demands for an equitable distribution of social services. Under the direction of such resourceful leaders as Grace Morris Allen Jones, wife of the Piney Woods School master; Mary Booze, Republican national committeewoman and daughter of Isaiah Montgomery; and Bertha LaBranche Johnson, cofounder of Prentiss Institute, the federation operated retirement homes for elderly and destitute blacks at Vicksburg and Natchez and lobbied state education officials for the inclusion of libraries in black schools and of Afro-American history in black grammar-school curricula. Beginning in the early postwar period it also waged long-term campaigns to win state support for the care of black tuberculosis patients, the education of handicapped black children, and the construction of a training school for "incorrigible and delinquent colored boys and girls."

Although progress was slow and whites unresponsive, these quiet reformers, so typical of third-stage protest leaders, ultimately prevailed. Under steady pressure from black club women during the 1920s, a "colored wing" was built at the state tuberculosis sanitorium and short-term public funds were appropriated for the establishment of a school for the black visually impaired.[72] Failing to win state legislative support for an institution for black delinquents, the club women opened their own youth facility in 1929. When this facility burned and lawmakers again refused assistance, the federation escalated its crusade for public support and found allies in the Mississippi Federation of [White] Women's Clubs, the Committee of One Hundred, and the Mississippi Council on Interracial Cooperation. Under this combined interracial pressure, the legislature relented and the Mississippi Training School for Delinquent Colored Youth was opened at Okley in 1943.[73]

The Committee of One Hundred, formed amid a postwar surge of out-migration in 1923, took its name from its ambition to be a statewide conference of 100 leading race men and women: one from each of the eighty-two counties and eighteen from the state at large.[74] The committee enjoyed the active support of prominent blacks from every district, including many of the most influential club women. Its early direction and much of its sustaining energy, however, came from educators Jonas and Bertha Johnson of Jefferson Davis County and its strongest representation was always in the nonplantation areas south of Jackson. A campaign in the 1930s to form parallel committees of 100 members in every county broadened the organization's base, but its strength, like its principal leadership, remained in Piney Woods and Gulf Coast counties.[75] Neither a federation nor a dues-paying organization, the committee's informal structure defies efforts to estimate its membership in any given year. Yet its yearly conclaves were usually well attended and its officers could legitimately claim the backing of "practically every leading Negro in the state."[76]

During and after World War II, a less patient generation of black Mississippians minimized the committee's accomplishments and sometimes dismissed its leaders as "ultra conservative, even reactionary." Committee members countered that the organization's patient, behind-the-scenes pressure on the white establishment in the 1920s and 1930s helped prepare the way for the more spectacular breakthroughs of a subsequent age. If committee leaders, as executive secretary Anselm Joseph Finch put it, sometimes "spoke a language, not always understood"[77]—if their public expressions were notably prudent—it was because black protest then required "a delicate touch." More aggressive tactics would have been not only dangerous but counterproductive: "Had blacks pushed in the 1920s like they did in the 1960s," the founder's son recently asserted, "they would have been slaughtered."[78]

For his part, principal founder and perennial president J. E. Johnson always thought of the committee as both "conservative and militant." The organization's leaders, he said, fought for black rights, "not with fire in our eyes, but . . . with grace" and perseverance.[79] During an active life span of some twenty-five years, the Committee of One Hundred advocated a discreet mix of black self-help, interracial cooperation, and fair play. Its charter members and most visible early leaders included not only the always circumspect Johnson, but such conservatives as Holtzclaw, Montgomery, and Eugene P. Booze. Assuring apprehensive whites that theirs was "absolutely not a political or social movement," this self-styled "body of sane and constructive leaders" publicly encouraged black obedience to the law, good citizenship, and race progress through separate economic development.[80]

But if this public side of the committee's work often paralleled prewar accommodationism, there was another more assertive side that developed new channels for interracial communication, contributed importantly to the evolution of a bolder black agenda, and pressed black demands for social justice as no stage-two Mississippi organization could have. Unable to work through normal political channels or to mobilize massive direct-action campaigns, the committee's most effective instruments were always moral persuasion and negotiation with white business, civic, and religious leaders. "It petitioned the powers that be to live up to their duties," one black remembered.[81]

Although it apparently never explicitly demanded desegregation per se, the committee invariably tied black out-migration to discrimination and exclusion. Initially, in the 1920s, its objectives were relatively modest: protection from white lawlessness, higher living standards, and equal-though-separate opportunities. In subsequent years it asked for progressively more. By 1935, the committee was pushing whites not only for better schools, higher teachers' salaries, and public rest rooms, but for suffrage "upon the terms and qualifications as prescribed by the laws of the state of Mississippi." A decade later, its demands included employment of black police in black neighborhoods, the abolition of the poll tax, and equal rights to vote and to hold public office. Directly linking black patriotism and sacrifice in a Second World War to black demands for freedom and democracy at home, the organization insisted following the Allied victory that black Mississippians must now "expect all rights and privileges" of American citizenship.[82]

Perhaps there was more improvisation than long-range planning in this march toward increased militance. Certainly there is no documentary evidence of a conscious strategy for the eventual elimination of Jim Crow through gradually escalating pressures for race equality. Yet by responding to changing circumstances and to the growing discontents of the black rank and file, the organization served as a bridge between pre–World War I Washington-style accommodationism and post–World War II civil rights activism. In this sense, the committee, as one historian has written, was "the forerunner of modern politics among Negroes in Mississippi."[83]

Late in the 1940s the committee quietly dissolved itself in favor of the NAACP. Despite their strikingly different images in the white mind— and the committee's quite deliberate effort to present to whites a conciliatory front—the two organizations were closely aligned. The committee had, from time to time, contributed modest sums to the national organization; representatives of the two organizations often cooperated in lynching investigations and matters of criminal justice. To a degree few if any whites suspected, they shared not only common goals but a common membership. Although the committee apparently did not officially urge its members to join the NAACP until 1944, the two organizations had always overlapped. From the outset, even such conservative committee leaders as Montgomery and Booze were also charter members of their local NAACP branches. During the depression, the

Reverend Roy L. Young of Meridian, perhaps the most able NAACP organizer in Mississippi, was among the most active committee leaders. In Jackson, black community leaders who were active in both organizations included newspaper editor Percy Greene and the lawyers Carsie Hall and Sidney D. Redmond.[84]

The committee's dissolution reflected the growing presence of the national protest organization in the state and the recognition that the time for exclusive dependence on negotiation and persuasion had passed, that the black freedom struggle now often required a more confrontational strategy. In effect, battle-weary committee stalwarts passed the torch to a new generation of black activists—one they described as "further removed from slavery," "not so easily frightened as 20 years ago"[85]—one prepared to make common cause through the NAACP with the larger Afro-American community.

Scattered evidence also suggests that a surprising number of black Mississippians early in the period of the third stage joined chapters of the separatist Universal Negro Improvement Association. Although the history of the UNIA in the South has not been written, it seems clear that the charismatic Marcus Garvey's appeal was not limited to northern inner cities as historians once believed. In Bolivar County alone, there were perhaps eleven different Garvey cells and researchers have recently documented the existence of UNIA chapters in at least thirteen other Mississippi counties. Membership figures are crude estimates at best, but at one time or another during the 1920s and early 1930s Mississippi may have been home to some 500 dues-paying Garveyites.[86] While local records apparently do not survive, it may reasonably be assumed that Garvey's Mississippi followers shared with their northern counterparts a reflexive race chauvinism, a pride in blackness, and perhaps even a longing for a new beginning in a liberated black Africa. Perhaps, too, they numbered among the several thousand black Mississippians who reportedly signed petitions circulated in 1938 by the Ethiopian Peace Movement in support of Senator Bilbo's African "repatriation" bill.[87]

The UNIA virtually escaped white attention in Mississippi, in part because its followers were apparently few and in part because its doctrine did not threaten the status quo. Although planters would not welcome Garveyite talk of a back-to-Africa exodus, the organization was otherwise unobjectionable. Garvey preached race pride but also race purity and separatism and his crusade was widely supported by white supremacists who shared his contempt for intermarriage and his assumption that Anglo-Saxon America would never grant blacks full citizenship. For somewhat similar reasons, neither the Committee of One Hundred nor the Federation of Colored Women's Clubs encountered violent white opposition. Both emphasized self-help and moral uplift, and both employed nonagitational strategies that did not directly confront white dominance. The committee advocated fairness under the state's own suffrage laws and, eventually, equal rights. But it did so gradually, and even after World War II it did not actively or directly challenge either disfranchisement or segregation.

Organizations that were explicitly interracial, or that directly defied the color-caste system, were necessarily more furtive, and their experiences further illuminate both black impatience with white injustice and the practical limits of social protest in a closed society. The NAACP met nearly universal white disapproval and was virtually forced to operate underground. But even the conciliatory Mississippi Council on Interracial Cooperation found it necessary to keep a low profile and to work through other groups, primarily women's religious organizations.

Organized in Atlanta by Will W. Alexander and other white moderates in 1919, the white-dominated, paternalistic Commission on Interracial Cooperation (CIC) cautiously skirted the segregation issue and sought racial harmony and fair play within a separate-but-equal society. Its Mississippi chapter initially maintained a distinctly subordinate and separate "colored division."[88] Although this segregated structure was soon abandoned at the state level, some local "interracial councils" remained lily-white as late as 1943, and the Mississippi organization remained one of the more equivocal and ambivalent examples of the South's interracial movement. In a statewide membership that may never have exceeded 100, blacks outnumbered whites by as much as three to one. Yet the CIC in Mississippi was always led and controlled by whites. In 1941, all but one of its five officers and three of its twelve executive committee members were white.[89]

The immediate objectives of the Mississippi CIC were to ease post–World War I racial tensions, prevent lynchings, and increase white support for black education. Through some two decades of intermittent activity, it distributed quantities of literature, sponsored occasional radio broadcasts on "Race Relations Sunday," organized interracial institutes and community conferences, and otherwise sought to promote "interracial understanding and sympathy" through regular contacts between "the best people of the two races." From first to last, the organization's mission was bounded by its tactical refusal to challenge Jim Crow. Its object was not to erase the color line but to moderate the social climate, to update paternalism and breathe new life into noblesse oblige, "to educate the [white] public to an awareness of conditions which result in injustice."[90]

Perhaps it could be said that the CIC, by its very presence, demonstrated that even in Mississippi the turn-of-the-century tide of racial fear and alienation was at last slowly receding. Perhaps, too, the organization contributed to a gradual leavening of caste oppression in the interwar period. But it never overcame widespread white ill will and, of course, it failed to organize an active network of local interracial committees. Whites who participated in the CIC's work often did so over the protest of their friends and neighbors, and at least one Mississippi officer, a professor at Mississippi Southern College, was forced to resign.[91] Resistance was greatest in the Delta, where regional CIC directors found black concerns to be too sensitive for public discussion and many planters were reportedly determined to destroy "every agency which would put ideas in the Negroes' heads and [to] muzzle every person who would criticize what they are doing."[92] Clearly uncomfortable in close association with such southern liberals as Will Alexander and antilynching activist Jessie Daniel Ames, some white state leaders seemed prepared by 1943 to sever all ties with the Atlanta office.[93] Perhaps only the absorption of the CIC by the newly organized Southern Regional Council prevented this Mississippi secession. At best, the Mississippi CIC—like its 1960s counterpart, the Mississippi Council on Human Relations—was a premature expression of interracialism in a state that viewed such activity with profound suspicion.

However ineffective, the well-intentioned paternalism of the CIC initially seemed to represent a more promising vehicle for racial advancement than the NAACP, the only organizational expression of open black protest in Mississippi during the interwar years. The state's first NAACP branches appeared in Vicksburg in July, 1918,[94] and in Mound Bayou the following year.[95] Both branches folded almost immediately, only to reorganize and fold again repeatedly in the years before World War II. Others were organized during the 1920s in Jackson, Meridian, and Natchez, with the same result. Indeed, though black Mississippians from nearly every sizeable town or city, and not a few rural trading centers, expressed interest in the NAACP during the years between the two world wars, their organizing efforts nearly always failed. By 1929, the association's national officers counted but one branch in the state, in Jackson, and only 100 paid-up members. That branch subsequently collapsed and was reorganized twice in the 1930s (1930 and 1934).[96] By 1940, following the reorganization of other groups in Meridian, Natchez, New Albany, and Vicksburg, Mississippi had five branches and 377 members, fewer than any other southern state. Within a year the total membership had fallen once again to about 100.[97]

The difficulty in these pre–World War II years can be traced in part to the out-migration that deprived many communities of some of their most assertive and advantaged blacks, the very people to whom the NAACP looked for support in a southern state.[98] Poverty was also an important factor. As local organizers and branch officers repeatedly informed national headquarters, the one-dollar annual membership fee and the minimum charter requirement of fifty members per branch were major obstacles in Mississippi. Always difficult, the problem was most severe during the 1930s. "We have the people but we haven't the money," a disappointed Panola Countian advised the New York office in 1932.[99] A Crenshaw resident thought the NAACP to be "the finest thing that the colored race has ever had," but he despaired of organizing a branch in his village: "We all is so poor until We can not do What We Wish to do for our socity[.] some of us has not got Bread and ramon for our Backs and yo just no how we is for Money."[100]

The greatest deterrents, however, were black economic vulnerability and white coercion. The association's branch records reveal that its members in Mississippi were generally representatives of the middle class: ministers, health professionals, lawyers, merchants, self-employed skilled workers, landowning farmers—some of them college educated, many not directly subject to white economic control.[101] But this relatively advantaged segment of the black population was small and it too was subject to white reprisal. In Vicksburg, the state's first branch died in 1918 soon after it was founded when principal officers and organizers were forced to flee the state.[102] Scott County blacks, although "stirred up as never before" by disfranchisement and white sexual abuse of black women, attributed to Klan terror their inability to form a branch in the 1920s. "The K.K.K. is very powerful in here," a resident of Lake community reported, "they term N.A.A.C.P. High Class Meddlers."[103]

In some rural communities it was dangerous to distribute or possess NAACP publications.[104] In 1920, apparently in response to the NAACP's organizing efforts, the state legislature made it unlawful to possess or distribute literature tending "to disturb relations between the races." Even in larger cities the NAACP operated until well after World War II in an atmosphere of fear and secrecy. Members commonly communicated with national headquarters in New York under assumed names, and NAACP materials destined for Mississippi addresses arrived in unmarked envelopes. "I takes chances when ever I rite," a Vicksburg Negro informed the association's national headquarters in 1939: "They will open my mail going or coming."[105]

In Jackson the organization's visibility was so low that its on-again, off-again branch activity escaped the attention of the local press until 1946.[106] The association sent materials to its members in Meridian only through the branch president, because as this officer explained, "they do not feel that it is safe for the white people to know."[107] Within the black community itself, there was reason for caution lest faithless Sambos seek white favor as informants. "All meeting[s] are secret," a Clarksdale organizer informed Ella Baker in 1943. "The whites are bitterly against it—*Bitterly.* I have been asked by some [Negroes] what the organization is . . . and I think 3 times before speaking 1 time." The same activist feared for the future of the Natchez branch when he learned, in 1944, that "some one has undoubtedly told some of the *white people.*"[108]

In this oppressive climate, many blacks weighed the risks of membership against the possibilities for tangible results and decided not to join. Even some national officers came to think of Mississippi, "the savage state," as the association's "lost cause."[109] Although the *Crisis* called for "a few Negroes with backbones" and the leadership in New York often complained that black Mississippians "seem afraid . . . to fight for themselves," the national association also recognized that the NAACP could expect little grassroots support in communities where it could neither carry out its programs nor even reveal itself publicly.[110]

The NAACP encountered intense hostility elsewhere in the region, particularly in the rural black-belt districts of Deep South states. But in no other state was white opposition as violent or as pervasive. In the South's major urban centers, NAACP branches openly agitated for black rights—organizing voter registration drives and "Don't-Buy-Where-You-Can't-Work" campaigns; protesting police brutality and judicial improprieties; challenging inequitable distribution of social services and discriminatory election, housing, and residential laws. In Mississippi, where they could work only behind the scenes, members managed little more than to keep their skeletal organizations, as one local officer put it, "somewhat alive" and to supply national headquarters with such information on lynchings and criminal proceedings as their clandestine investigations uncovered. In hostile Mississippi, some national civil rights leaders believed, blacks "made history" simply by organizing.[111]

Clearly, then, despite some marginal black gains, the essential contours of Mississippi's social order had changed little in the half century after 1890. World War I had been a turning point that turned only slightly. It raised black expectations; it contributed importantly to the gradual reconfiguration of the race problem nationwide; it hastened the developmental processes and the generational changes that modified black circumstances, diminished white control, and ultimately made possible a fundamental transformation of American race relations. For the moment, however, a virtually monolithic white power structure held back the impending revolution. Indeed for more than a generation, the edifice of segregation and discrimination seemed secure; black malcontentment and protest, though mounting steadily, necessarily either remained muted and underground or, when it surfaced, flowed in relatively safe and nonconfrontational channels. The forces of change were slowly gathering, but the objective conditions essential for a Second Reconstruction had not yet fully emerged. During the Great War and the interwar period, black impatience and black consciousness in Mississippi outran the black capacity to influence change. Further racial progress would come only as national socioeconomic developments permitted.

In sum, if the history of the Jim Crow years suggests anything, it is that racial injustice would survive in Mississippi as long as the world's oldest republic would tolerate it; that effective, direct black challenge to white control could not develop without salutary changes in the larger intellectual and political milieu in which American racial attitudes, social policies, and interracial behaviors were shaped; that sustained black agitation could not precede major improvements in the basic conditions of Afro-American life.

The Impending Revolution

The Second World War sent additional tremors of white anxiety and black aspiration along the color line, further eroding the barriers to social change and bringing new vigor and new urgency to the civil rights struggle. Although the story of that war and its impact on Mississippi lies beyond the scope of this volume, it is clear that this second great international crusade for freedom and democracy further dramatized the disparity between the dream and the reality of America and further heightened race consciousness and black unrest. For Mississippi, not less than for the rest of the nation, the war against Hitler's master race ideology marked the beginning of Jim Crow's end, the moment when the gathering challenge of black unrest began the sharp, rapid ascent that would make it a black revolution.

In these fluid years of social change and rising expectations, the limits of black protest were gradually redefined and Afro-Mississippians began to reimagine their place in a democratic society. Recognizing that time and circumstance were at last on their side, convinced of the possibility and necessity for new strategies of opposition to white discrimination and exclusion, growing numbers of blacks, by war's end, were prepared in heart and mind for the impending assault on Jim Crow. As one of them informed a northern journalist, their own emergent tradition of unrest and social agitation propelled them ineluctably toward the increasingly militant protest movement of the 1950s and 1960s: "Lord, child, we colored people ain't nothing but a bundle of resentments and sufferings going somewhere to explode."[112]

Notes

Abbreviations Used in the Notes

AMA   American Missionary Association Archives (microfilm), Amistad Research Center, New Orleans, La.

BAE   Records of the Bureau of Agricultural Economics, Record Group 83, NA

BHP   Benjamin Harrison Papers (microfilm), LC

BMF   Benjamin Montgomery Family Papers, LC

BTW   Booker T. Washington Papers, LC

CGW   Carter G. Woodson Collection, LC

CIC   Commission on Interracial Cooperation Collection, Atlanta University Center, Woodruff Library, Atlanta, Ga.

CPC   Cleveland Payne private collection, Laurel, Miss.

DL   General Records of the Department of Labor, Record Group 174, NA

DPL   Delta and Pine Land Company Records, Mitchell Memorial Library, Mississippi State University

FES   Records of the Federal Extension Service (microfilm), Record Group 33, NA

FHA   Records of the Farmers' Home Administration, Record Group 96, NA

GMP   George Myers Papers (microfilm), Ohio Historical Society, Columbus, Ohio

GPF   Governors' Pardon Files, Record Group 27, MDAH

HPL   Herbert Hoover Presidential Library, West Branch, Iowa

JEJ   Jonas Edward Johnson Papers, in the possession of Alcee L. Johnson, Prentiss, Miss.

JRF   Julius Rosenwald Fund Papers, Fisk University, Nashville, Tenn.

JSU   Piney Woods Oral History Collection, Jackson State University, Jackson, Miss.

LC   Library of Congress, Washington, D.C.

MDAH Mississippi Department of Archives and History, Jackson, Miss.

MHC   Sharecropper Oral History Collection, Mary Holmes College, West Point, Miss.

NA   National Archives, Washington, D.C.

NAACP Papers of the National Association for the Advancement of Colored People, LC

NYA   Records of the National Youth Administration, Record Group 119, NA

PFP   Percy Family Papers, MDAH

SAg   Records of the Secretary of Agriculture, Record Group 16, NA

STFU   Southern Tenant Farmers' Union Papers (microfilm), Southern Historical Collection, University of North Carolina, Chapel Hill

TRP   Theodore Roosevelt Papers (microfilm), LC

WGH   Warren Gamaliel Harding Papers (microfilm), Ohio Historical Society, Columbus, Ohio

WHT   William Howard Taft Papers (microfilm), LC

WPA   Works Progress Administration, Mississippi, source materials for Mississippi History (county histories)

Chapter 1. Jim Crow and the Limits of Freedom, 1890-1940

1. Vicksburg *Commercial-Herald,* quoted in Jackson *Clarion-Ledger,* May 30, 1889.

2. Dunbar Rowland, *A Mississippi View of Race Relations in the South* (Jackson, 1903), 16.

3. Jackson *New Mississippian,* January 13, 1885.

4. The classic argument for the relatively late genesis of proscription, segregation, and disfranchisement is C. Vann Woodward, *Strange Career of Jim Crow* (New York, 1955; subsequent citations are to 2d rev. ed. [New York, 1966]). Race relations in the Old North State are described in Frenise A. Logan, *The Negro in North Carolina, 1876-1894* (Chapel Hill, 1964). On parallel developments in Virginia, cf. Woodward, *American Counterpoint: Slavery and Racism in the North-South Dialogue* (Boston, 1971), 186-187, 212; and Charles E. Wynes, *Race Relations in Virginia, 1870-1902* (Charlottesville, 1961).

5. Among the studies that emphasize the early imposition of a comparatively rigid de facto system of segregation and exclusion, see: Joel Williamson, *After Slavery: The Negro in South Carolina during Reconstruction, 1861-1877* (Chapel Hill, 1965); Vernon Lane Wharton, *The Negro in Mississippi, 1865-1890,* James Sprunt Studies in History and Political Science, vol. 28 (Chapel Hill, 1947); and Wynes, *Race Relations in Virginia.*

6. William C. Harris, *The Day of the Carpetbagger: Republican Reconstruction in Mississippi* (Baton Rouge, 1979), 446 (quotation), 449-452; Wharton, *Negro in Mississippi,* 230-231.

7. William Charles Sallis, "The Color Line in Mississippi Politics, 1865-1915" (Ph.D. diss., University of Kentucky, 1967), 437.

8. Wharton, *Negro in Mississippi,* 230-232; Harris, *Day of the Carpetbagger,* 439-441.

9. Wharton, *Negro in Mississippi,* 230-232.

10. Harris, *Day of the Carpetbagger,* 451-452.

11. See Chapter 9, below.

12. W. C. Handy, *Father of the Blues: An Autobiography* (New York, 1951), 73.

13. Quoted in Willard B. Gatewood, Jr., *Theodore Roosevelt and the Art of Controversy: Episodes of the White House Years* (Baton Rouge, 1970), 76.

14. Jackson *Clarion-Ledger,* May 9, 1889; Jackson *New Mississippian,* November 13, 1889.

15. Lorenzo Greene and Carter G. Woodson, *The Negro Wage Earner* (Washington, D.C., 1930), 121.

16. On Lynch's disinterment, see *Laws of the State of Mississippi, ... January 2, 1900–March 12, 1900,* 171 (hereinafter cited as Mississippi *Laws*); and William C. Harris, "James Lynch: Black Leader in Southern Reconstruction," *Historian,* 34 (November, 1971), 61. On the integration of cemeteries see Etienne William Maxson, *The Progress of the Races* (Wash-

ington, D.C., 1930), 40-41; Celia Herman, oral history, June 14, 1976, Piney Woods Collection, Jackson State University (Jackson, Miss.; hereinafter cited as JSU); Jackson *Daily News,* March 19, 1929; Mt. Olive (Miss.) *Tribune,* May 3, 1946; Allison Davis, "The Negro Church and Associations in the Lower South," Carnegie Myrdal Study of the Negro in America, June, 1940 (microfilm edition), 21; Charles S. Johnson, *Patterns of Negro Segregation* (New York, 1943), 77; Olga Reed Pruitt, *It Happened in Holly Springs* (Holly Springs, Miss., 1950), 112-113.

17. John Dollard, *Caste and Class in a Southern Town* (Garden City, N.Y., 1949), 353.

18. James W. Garner, "A Mississippian on Vardaman," *Outlook,* 75 (September 12, 1903), 139. See also idem, *Studies in Government and International Law by James Wilford Garner,* ed. John A. Fairlie (1943; reprint ed., Urbana, 1972), 76-91.

19. Charles B. Galloway, *The South and the Negro: An Address Delivered at the Seventh Annual Conference for Education in the South, Birmingham, Alabama, April 26th, 1904* (New York, 1904), 5-6.

20. Jackson *Weekly Clarion-Ledger,* May 29, 1902; June 2, 1904; Jackson *Clarion-Ledger,* January 19, 1910 ("constant crusade" quotation); Woodward, *Strange Career of Jim Crow,* 89.

21. Jackson *Weekly Clarion-Ledger,* May 26, 1904 (quotation); Galloway, *The South and the Negro,* 7.

22. Quoted in R. H. Leavell, "Negro Migration from Mississippi," in U.S., Department of Labor, *Negro Migration in 1916-1917: Reports* (Washington, D.C., 1919), 33. On the persistence of the aristocratic ideal of paternalism see also: Allison Davis et al., *Deep South: A Social Anthropological Study of Caste and Class* (Chicago, 1941), 405-406; Thomas Pearce Bailey, *Race Orthodoxy in the South, and Other Aspects of the Negro Question* (New York, 1914), 13; Dollard, *Caste and Class in a Southern Town,* 83, 124; John Roy Lynch, *Reminiscences of an Active Life: The Autobiography of John Roy Lynch,* ed. John Hope Franklin (Chicago, 1970), 52; Beulah Amidon Ratliff, "Mississippi: Heart of Dixie," *Nation,* 114 (May 17, 1922), 588; Jonathan Daniels, *A Southerner Discovers the South* (New York, 1938), 173-176.

23. C. Vann Woodward, *Origins of the New South, 1877-1913* (Baton Rouge, 1951), 321-368; idem, *Strange Career of Jim Crow,* passim.

24. Jackson *Clarion-Ledger,* September 12, 1889 (quotation); Brooklyn (Miss.) *Citizen,* quoted in ibid.; editorial, Greenville *Times,* February 24, 1906.

25. Other such cases include: *Louisville, New Orleans, and Texas Railroad* v. *Mississippi* (1890); *Civil Rights Cases* (1883); *United States* v. *Reese* (1876); and *United States* v. *Cruikshank* (1876).

26. Bailey, *Race Orthodoxy in the South,* 29.

27. Mississippi *Laws,* 1888, chap. 27; Wharton, *Negro in Mississippi,* 230. The state's first Jim Crow law was a statute of 1865 restricting to whites first-class rail transportation. The measure was effectively repealed in 1870 (*Laws,* 1865, chap. 79; *Laws,* 1870, chap. 10).

28. Mississippi *Laws,* 1904, chap. 99; *Laws,* 1922, chap. 217; *Mississippi*

Code of 1906 of the Public Statute Laws of the State of Mississippi (hereinafter cited as *Code*), chap. 4855; *Laws*, 1940, chap. 169; Carey McWilliamson, "Spectrum of Segregation," *Survey Graphic*, 36 (January, 1947), 107; *City Bus v. Thomas, Mississippi Supreme Court Reports*, 172 Miss. 424 (1935).

29. *Bond v. Fung, et al.* (1927), 148 Miss. 462 ("general unhappiness" quotation at 471); Brookhaven *Semi-Weekly Leader*, September 21, 1910 ("dead niggers" quotation). See also: Alfred Holt Stone, *Studies in the American Race Problem* (New York, 1908), 65-66.

30. *Constitution of the State of Mississippi, Adopted November 1, 1890* (Jackson, 1891), art. 8, sec. 207; Harris, *Day of the Carpetbagger*, 148-152; Wharton, *Negro in Mississippi*, 243ff.

31. Mississippi *Code*, 1880, chap. 42, secs. 1145-1147; *Code*, 1906, chap. 37, sec. 1671.

32. Mississippi *Code*, 1892, chap. 87, secs. 2808, 2809; *Laws*, 1910, chap. 115; *Code*, 1930, chap. 108, secs. 4618, 4619; *Code*, 1942, chap. 14, sec. 4259; chap. 1, sec. 7913; chap. 2, sec. 7971.

33. "Textbooks in Mississippi," *Opportunity*, 18 (April, 1940), 99; Mississippi *Laws*, 1940, chap. 202.

34. Mississippi *Laws*, 1920, chap. 214. Before 1920, authorities in some localities punished the offense under obscenity laws (Gatewood, *Theodore Roosevelt and the Art of Controversy*, 88).

35. Mississippi *Laws*, 1956, chap. 257. In 1954 it became unlawful to conspire "to overthrow or violate" state segregation laws (*Laws*, 1954, chap. 20, sec. 7).

36. See, e.g., *Laurel City Ordinance Book No. 6* (n.p., 1956), 149-150; *Laurel City Ordinance Book No. 7* (n.p., 1963), 472-473.

37. Linton Weeks, *Clarksdale and Coahoma County: A History* (Clarksdale, 1982), 108; Johnson, *Patterns of Negro Segregation*, 33. In some communities, the curfew against blacks was a matter of custom rather than law. For the example of Wiggins, see Ollie Reeves, oral history, 1985, Piney Woods Historical Society (Wiggins, Miss.).

38. See representative municipal codes: *Charter and Ordinances, Town of Indianola, Mississippi* (Jackson, 1914); *Charter and Ordinances of the City of Columbus, Mississippi* (Columbus, 1884); *The Code of City of Vicksburg, Mississippi* (Vicksburg, 1907); *Charter and Code of Laws of the City of West Point, Mississippi* (West Point, 1907); *Laws, Ordinances, Rules and Regulations of the City of Winona* (n.p., 1913); *City of Laurel Ordinance Book No. 4* (Laurel, 1916); *Ordinances of the City of Biloxi* (Biloxi, 1908); *Code of Ordinances of the City of Natchez* (Natchez, 1905); *Ordinances of the City of Jackson* (Jackson, 1909); *Code of Grenada* (n.p., 1910).

39. Joel Williamson, *The Crucible of Race: Black-White Relations in the American South since Emancipation* (New York, 1984), 178, 182.

40. Edna White, "Segregation in Natchez, 1865-1960" (course paper, University of Southern Mississippi, 1983, 2; except where otherwise indicated, course papers cited are in the author's possession). See the same argument for a Piney Woods community: Clarice Wansley, "Segregation in the City of

Laurel: Custom or Law?" (course paper, University of Southern Mississippi, 1983).

41. Hodding Carter, "He's Doing Something about the Race Problem," *Saturday Evening Post,* 218 (February 23, 1946), 30, 64; Florence Warfield Sillers, comp., *History of Bolivar County* (Jackson, 1948), 338; Minor S. Gray, "A Short History of Delta and Pine Land Company," undated ms., misc. materials, DPL; Ralph J. Bunche, *The Political Status of the Negro in the Age of FDR,* ed. Dewey W. Grantham (Chicago, 1973), 565. In 1923, Bishop Robert E. Jones of the Methodist Episcopal Church opened Gulfside Resort, a "black Chautauqua" in Waveland ("A Southern Seaside Resort," *Crisis,* 37 [July, 1930], 228-229).

42. Johnson, *Patterns of Negro Segregation,* 72-73; Monroe Work, ed., *Negro Year Book: An Encyclopedia of the Negro for 1921-1922,* 307.

43. Mound Bayou's Carnegie Library never opened, for want of books. Margarete Peebles and J. B. Howell, *A History of Mississippi Libraries* (Montgomery, Ala., 1975), 48, 70, 74, 91, 108, 184; U.S., Bureau of Education, *Negro Education: A Survey of the Private and Higher Schools for Colored People in the United States,* Bulletin 1916, no. 38-39, 2 vols. (Washington, D.C., 1917), 1: 174; Louis R. Wilson and Edward A. Wight, *County Library Service in the South: A Study of the Rosenwald County Library Demonstration* (Chicago, 1935), 45-47.

44. U.S., Department of Commerce, *Hotels Operated by Negroes,* Bulletin 17 (Washington, D.C., 1938), 6.

45. James Harkness, "Mississippi Footprint: Lies They Live in Greenwood," *American Spectator* (February, 1986), 24; Tillman Anderson, "Jim Crow in Mississippi" (course paper, University of Southern Mississippi, 1983), 1; Bobby Daily, "Segregation in Mississippi" (course paper, University of Southern Mississippi, 1983), unpaginated; M. Burgess, oral history, [1982], CPC; H. L. Mitchell, *Mean Things Happening in This Land: The Life and Times of H. L. Mitchell* (Montclair, N.J., 1979), 134 (first quotation); Alcee L. Johnson, interview with author, October 16, 1986 (second quotation).

46. However, the state senate petitioned Congress for the acquisition of territory "to make a suitable, proper and final home for the American Negro" (quoted in Theodore Bilbo, *Take Your Choice: Segregation or Mongrelization* [Poplarville, Miss., 1947], 273). On residential segregation law, see Gilbert T. Stephenson, "The Segregation of the White and Negro Races in Cities," *South Atlantic Quarterly,* 13 (January, 1914), 3; Roger L. Rice, "Residential Segregation by Law, 1910-1917," *Journal of Southern History,* 34 (May, 1968), 179-199.

47. Except where otherwise indicated, this analysis is based on Jessie Oscar McKee, "The Residential Patterns of Blacks in Natchez and Hattiesburg and Other Mississippi Cities" (Ph.D. diss., Michigan State University, 1975); and Sue Anne Leister Rodriguez, "Black Residential Patterns in Hattiesburg, Mississippi, 1905, 1921, 1941" (course paper, University of Southern Mississippi, 1983).

48. Wharton, *Negro in Mississippi,* 130.

49. W. E. B. Du Bois, ed., *Economic Co-operation among Negro Americans,* Atlanta University Publications no. 12 (Atlanta, 1907), 146.

50. Vicksburg *Evening Post,* June 2, 1904.

51. Bailey, *Race Orthodoxy,* 79. Efforts of the "Run, African, Run" vigilante society to "run the negroes out" of Ellisville failed in 1922 (Jackson *Daily News,* January 30, 1922).

52. Davis et al., *Deep South,* 22, 466.

53. McKee, "Residential Patterns of Blacks," 73, 78, 112, 134. Recent patterns are examined in John P. Marcum et al., "Residential Segregation by Race in Mississippi, 1980" (paper, Research Conference on the Experiences of Black Mississippians, Oxford, Miss., 1986).

54. Hortense Powdermaker, *After Freedom: A Cultural Study in the Deep South* (New York, 1939), 9-13, 14 (quotation); David L. Cohn, *Where I Was Born and Raised* (Boston, 1948), 239; Dollard, *Caste and Class in a Southern Town,* 2-4; Rodriguez, "Black Residential Patterns in Hattiesburg," 4-5; Vaughn L. Grisham, Jr., "Tupelo, Mississippi, from Settlement to Industrial Community, 1860-1970" (Ph.D. diss., University of North Carolina, 1975), 315-316.

55. David L. Cohn, "How the South Feels," *Atlantic Monthly,* 173 (January, 1944), 49.

56. Wharton, *Negro in Mississippi,* 227-229; Mississippi *Code,* 1880, chap. 42, sec. 1147; Mississippi *Constitution,* 1890, art. 14, sec. 263. The state had no uniform definition of the Negro race. The constitution of 1890 prohibited whites from intermarriage with persons of "one-eighth or more negro blood," but precise measurement proved impossible and enforcement of the law difficult (see the case of Davis Knight: Jackson *Daily News,* April 18, November 15, 1945). The public schools, on the other hand, operated under a more stringent one-drop definition (see *Moreau et al., School Trustees* v. *Grandich* [1917], 114 Miss. 560; *Rice et al.* v. *Gong Lum et al.* [1925], 139 Miss. 760).

57. Jackson *Daily News,* February, 1931, quoted in Jacquelyn Dowd Hall, *Revolt against Chivalry: Jessie Daniel Ames and the Women's Campaign against Lynching* (New York, 1979), 319.

58. Bilbo, *Take Your Choice,* 57-58.

59. The contours of the myth and its relationship to lynching are delineated in Hall, *Revolt against Chivalry,* 129-157, passim.

60. Davis et al., *Deep South,* 277.

61. Quoted in Hall, *Revolt against Chivalry,* 79. See also: Ida B. Wells, *Crusade for Justice: The Autobiography of Ida B. Wells,* ed. Alfreda M. Duster (Chicago, 1970), 64-65; and Ida B. Wells-Barnett, *On Lynching: Southern Horrors; A Red Record; Mob Rule in New Orleans* (1969; reprint ed. of original 3 vols., New York, 1892, 1895, 1900).

62. Charles Evers, *Evers* (New York, 1971), 68-69. See also Nellie Flowers Cox, oral history, September 6, 1978, JSU.

63. Dollard, *Caste and Class in a Southern Town,* 165. Powdermaker noted that in Indianola the "sex taboo" prevented her from interviewing black men (*After Freedom,* xii).

64. Frank Houston, oral history, August 15, 1981, CPC.

65. Mrs. Medgar (Myrlie Beasley) Evers, "Why Should My Child Marry Yours," *Ladies' Home Journal,* clipping, subject file, *Intermarriage, MDAH.*

66. Hall, *Revolt against Chivalry,* 202 ("unspeakable" quotation); H. S. Fulkerson, *The Negro: As He Was; As He Is; As He Will Be* (Vicksburg, 1887), 76 ("villainies" quotation). See also Cohn, *Where I Was Born,* 281; William Alexander Percy, *Lanterns on the Levee: Recollections of a Planter's Son* (Baton Rouge, paperback ed., 1973), 308-309; Richard Wright, "The Ethics of Living Jim Crow," in idem, *Uncle Tom's Children* (New York, 1965), 12; and the materials related to the particularly telling criminal case against Erwin Pruitt, box D-67, NAACP. For exceptions to the rule of violence described here, see Bailey, *Race Orthodoxy,* 282; and George P. Rawick, ed., *The American Slave: A Composite Autobiography,* 19 vols. (Westport, Conn., 1972), *Mississippi Narrative,* vol. 6, pt. 1, p. 192; and vol. 10, pt. 5, pp. 2268-2269 (hereinafter cited as, e.g., *Miss. Narr.* 6(1), 192; 10(5), 2268-2269).

67. Lynch, *Reminiscences,* 6.

68. Jackson *Daily News,* January 16, 1890; Jackson *Clarion-Ledger,* January 16, 1890; Jackson *Daily Clarion-Ledger,* December 23, 25, 1918.

69. Percy Bell, "Child of the Delta" (unpublished ms., n.d., in the possession of Charles G. Bell, Albuquerque, N. Mex.), chap. 2, p. 2. See also Jackson *Clarion-Ledger,* January 16, 1890; Davis et al., *Deep South,* 31ff.; Dollard, *Caste and Class in a Southern Town,* 150; Powdermaker, *After Freedom,* 181ff.

70. New Orleans *Times Democrat,* June 21, 1907, quoted in Maurice S. Evans, *Black and White in the Southern States: A Study of the Race Problem from a South African Point of View* (New York, 1915), 187.

71. Ray Stannard Baker, *Following the Color Line: American Negro Citizenship in the Progressive Era,* Harper Torchbooks ed. (New York, 1964), 168; Evans, *Black and White,* 187 ("accursed shadow" quotation); [LeRoy Percy], "Did Noel Blunder," May 19, 1908, box 3, PFP ("young lives" quotation); R. Fulton Holtzclaw, *William Henry Holtzclaw: Scholar in Ebony* (Cleveland, 1977), 194 (grand jury quotation). See also: Brandon *News,* June 10, 1909.

72. Handy, *Father of the Blues,* 78-79; Weeks, *Clarksdale,* 107; Jackson *Daily Clarion-Ledger,* February 27, 1919.

73. Meridian *Star,* May 7, 1908 ("abodes" quotation); Daisy Miller Greene, oral history, January 31, 1975, 26-27, MDAH ("tamper" quotation).

74. Greene, oral history, MDAH, 12; Powdermaker, *After Freedom,* 24, 183. See also Ratliff, "Mississippi: Heart of Dixie," 589.

75. Charles Granville Hamilton, "Mississippi Politics in the Progressive Era, 1904-1920" (Ph.D. diss., Vanderbilt University, 1958), 157, 276.

76. See the example of Billie Tim Smith, who left his estate to Mamie Lake and her children (Jackson *Daily News,* October 13, 1920).

77. Willie Morris, *North toward Home* (Boston, 1967), 79.

78. Anne Moody, *Coming of Age in Mississippi* (New York, 1968), 104, 111. See also the childhood recollections of Myrlie Beasley Evers, wife of civil rights martyr Medgar Evers (Evers, "Why Should My Child Marry Yours");

and J. Saunders Redding's observation about interracial sex in Claiborne County in 1940 (*No Day of Triumph* [New York, 1942], 327).

79. On the status once accorded the black concubines of influential whites see Herbert G. Gutman, *The Black Family in Slavery and Freedom, 1750-1925* (New York, 1976), 392-394; on black-white sexual relations in Mississippi and the general decline of miscegenation see: Davis et al., *Deep South*, 31-33, 40; Dollard, *Caste and Class in a Southern Town*, 141-143, 150-151; Powdermaker, *After Freedom*, 181-196; Cohn, *Where I Was Born*, 287. For examples in which interracial couples were prosecuted or punished by mobs see *Miller* v. *Lucks et al.*, 36 So. 2d 140 (1948); *Knight* v. *Mississippi* 207 Miss. 564 (1949).

80. Redding, *No Day of Triumph*, 317. Vestiges of black pride in white ancestry still survive, however. See, e.g., Herman, oral history, June 14, 1976, JSU; Dora J. Adams, oral history, February 22, 1970, MHC.

81. See, e.g., Jackson *Weekly Clarion-Ledger,* January 15, 1903 ("genuine African" quotation); and Ratliff, "Mississippi: Heart of Dixie," 589 ("full-blooded nigger" quotation).

82. Joel Williamson, *New People: Miscegenation and Mulattoes in the United States* (New York, 1980), 112, 114.

83. Booker T. Washington, *The Story of the Negro: The Rise of the Race from Slavery,* 2 vols. (New York, 1909), 1:24; idem, *My Larger Education: Being Chapters from My Experience* (New York, 1911), 206; Janet Sharp Hermann, *The Pursuit of a Dream* (New York, 1981), 170.

84. Frank Craigie, New Orleans *Morning Tribune,* reprinted in Chicago *Defender,* December 1, 1928. See also the description of Mhoon and Howard's brother-in-law, S. D. Redmond, in Herman, oral history, June 14, 1976, JSU.

85. Joseph H. Douglass, "A History of E. P. Booze," 24 undated mss., BMF.

86. Edward Byron Reuter, *The Mulatto in the United States: Including a Study of the Role of Mixed-Blood Races throughout the World* (Boston, 1918), 238, 241, 253, 275, 296-297, passim. Although Reuter's work is useful, it is marred by the author's racial assumptions and by error.

87. Hermann, *Pursuit of a Dream,* 170.

88. Clarice T. Campbell and Oscar Allan Rogers, Jr., *Mississippi: The View from Tougaloo* (Jackson, 1979), 168.

89. Moody was relieved to learn that in spite of her apprehensions, other Tougaloo students were dark-skinned (Moody, *Coming of Age,* 213, 215).

90. John Dittmer to author, June 5, 1987.

91. Monroe White, oral history, October 14, 1978, JSU ("whiter" quotation); Alferdteen Harrison, *Piney Woods School: An Oral History* (Jackson, 1982), 116-117 (subsequent quotations). White's oral history contains a particularly revealing exchange with Alferdteen Harrison on the question of color preferment at Piney Woods and Jones's own ambivalence on the subject. But see also Katie Catherine Love Donnel, oral history, October 14, 1978, JSU.

92. Redding, *No Day of Triumph,* 303 ("half-white" and "factor" quotations); Norman L. Crockett, *The Black Towns* (Lawrence, Kans., 1979), 72

("complexions" quotation); Hiram Tong, "The Pioneers of Mound Bayou," *Century Magazine,* 79 (1910), 390-400.

93. Laura Beam, *He Called Them by the Lightning: A Teacher's Odyssey in the Negro South, 1908-1919* (Indianapolis, 1967), 41.

94. Williamson, *New People,* 100-106, 119-120.

95. Clarice T. Campbell, "History of Tougaloo College" (Ph.D. diss., University of Mississippi, 1970), 333-334 ("I belong" quotation); T. J. Johnson, *From the Driftwood of Bayou Pierre* (Louisville, 1949), 39 ("vociferous" quotation). See also Merah S. Stuart, *An Economic Detour: A History of Insurance in the Lives of American Negroes* (New York, 1940), 179; Williamson, *New People,* 105.

96. As used along the Mississippi Gulf Coast, neither *Cajun* nor *Creole* has precise meaning. *Cajun* is a corruption, and technically refers to people of Acadian lineage; *Creole* includes people with Spanish as well as those with French ancestry. But the terms are often used interchangeably in both Mississippi and Louisiana. "Pure white" Creoles and Cajuns, of course, usually object when the terms are applied to the racially mixed. There are no scholarly references for Mississippi, but see the testimony of two such "people of color" in Rawick, ed., *Miss. Narr.,* 6(1), 189-191 and 9(4), 1700-1709; and also Jacob L. Reddix, *A Voice Crying in the Wilderness: The Memoirs of Jacob L. Reddix* (Jackson, 1974), 53; and Henry Fly, oral history, July 27, 1973, MDAH. A smaller and more isolated mixed settlement was to be found at the Piney Woods community of Free Woods, near Crosby (McComb *Enterprise-Journal,* June 3, 1984, July 23, 1986).

97. Davis et al., *Deep South,* 21, 215-217, 230-238, 244-248.

98. Williamson, *New People,* 1 (Ferber quotation).

99. Ibid., 111-139. Vestiges of Afro-American color preferment survived in Mississippi at least through 1966. As one thoughtful dark-skinned Mississippian put it, "Only black power ended it" (Alferdteen Harrison, conversation with author, November 5, 1986).

100. Alfred Holt Stone, "Is Race Friction between Blacks and Whites in the United States Growing and Inevitable?" *American Journal of Sociology,* 13 (1907-1908), 685. See also: Bailey, *Race Orthodoxy,* 41; David L. Cohn, "How the South Feels," *Atlantic Monthly,* 173 (January, 1944), 48; George M. Fredrickson, *White Supremacy: A Comparative Study in American and South African History* (New York, 1981), 254.

101. The standard treatise on the manners of white supremacy is Bertram Wilbur Doyle, *The Etiquette of Race Relations in the South: A Study in Social Control* (Chicago, 1937); but see also Powdermaker, *After Freedom,* 43-49; and Dollard, *Caste and Class in a Southern Town,* 343-363. On the early use of courtesy titles see Wharton, *Negro in Mississippi,* 233; Natchez *Democrat* quoted in Woodville *Republican,* December 24, 1887; Davis et al., *Deep South,* 53-55; Grisham, "Tupelo," 312-314.

102. Johnson, *Patterns of Negro Segregation,* 39. For related acts in the period after 1954, see Frank E. Smith, *Congressman from Mississippi* (New York, 1964), 104.

103. *History of Blacks in Greenville, Mississippi, 1863-1975: National Homecoming, July 1975* (n.p., 1975), unpaginated pamphlet; LeRoy Percy to Lampton, June 17, 1909, box 4, PFP.

104. Charles S. Johnson, "Personal Note for Trustee Meeting, November 1, 1938," box 4, Reinhold Niebuhr Papers, Manuscript Divison, LC. The concern with which the farm's trustees and managers viewed their Mississippi environment is suggested in William R. Amberson to Niebuhr, July 18, 1938, ibid.; Sherwood Eddy to Julius Rosenwald, March 25, 1936, and Eddy to Sam Franklin, April 19, 1936, box 191, JRF.

105. Daniels, *A Southerner Discovers the South,* 150-151. See also John Dillingham, "Cooperative Farm," *Brown American,* 1 (December, 1936), 22; Donald H. Royer, "A Comparative Study of Three Experiments in Rural 'Community' Reconstruction in the Southeast" (M.A. thesis, University of North Carolina, Chapel Hill, 1943), 37-39; Mitchell, *Mean Things Happening in This Land,* 134; "Croppers' Co-op," *Literary Digest,* 123 (February 6, 1938), 8.

106. Likely exceptions to the white-first rule include the first-come tradition honored generally at cotton gins and many gasoline stations (Jack Temple Kirby, "Black and White in the Rural South, 1915-1954," *Agricultural History,* 58 [July, 1984], 421).

107. Lenzie Braddy, oral history, September 15, 1978, JSU.

108. Laurence C. Jones, *The Bottom Rail: Addresses and Papers on the Negro in the Lowlands of Mississippi* (New York, 1935), 35; Davis et al., *Deep South,* 466.

109. Allison Davis, "Caste, Economy, and Violence," *American Journal of Sociology,* 51 (July, 1945), 10; Davis et al., *Deep South,* 23.

110. Dollard, *Caste and Class in a Southern Town,* 185; John Perkins, *Let Justice Roll Down: John Perkins Tells His Own Story* (Ventura, Calif., 1976), 48 (Lawrence Countian's quotation); Johnson, *Patterns in Negro Segregation,* 251 ("boss" quotation).

111. Richard Wright, *Black Boy: A Record of Childhood and Youth,* Perennial paperback ed. (New York, 1966), 253.

112. Ibid., 202-204. Wright's classmate was Dick Jordan (Michel Fabre, *The Unfinished Quest of Richard Wright* [New York, 1973], 56-57).

113. Allison Davis, "The Socialization of the American Negro Child and Adolescent," *Journal of Negro Education,* 8 (July, 1939), 270; Powdermaker, *After Freedom,* 215-216; Davis, "Caste, Economy, and Violence," 11; Robert Coles, "It's the Same, But It's Different," *The Negro American,* ed. Talcott Parsons and Kenneth Clark (New York, 1967), 262-264.

114. Evers, *Evers,* 29-30. But see the example of exceptionally protective parents who managed largely to insulate their daughter even from the knowledge of white discrimination: Clarie Collins Harvey, oral history, April 21, 1981, MDAH.

115. Evers, *Evers,* 168-170; James Farmer, *Lay Bare the Heart: An Autobiography of the Civil Rights Movement* (New York, 1985), 58, 63, 65 (but see generally 33-65). Differing styles of family race education are adumbrated

in the autobiographies and biographies of black Mississippians. See, e.g., Moody, *Coming of Age,* 26-27; Wright, *Black Boy,* 55-56, passim; O. L. Elliot, *The Mississippi Girl* (Toledo, 1947), 77; Jessie O. Thomas, *My Story in Black and White: The Autobiography of Jessie O. Thomas* (New York, 1967), 11-17; George Mitchell, *Blow My Blues Away* (Baton Rouge, 1971), 110-112.

116. Bailey, *Race Orthodoxy,* 296.

117. Johnson, *Patterns of Negro Segregation,* 307 (first quotation); Charles S. Johnson, *Growing Up in the Black Belt: Negro Youth in the Rural South* (Washington, D.C., 1941), 304 (second quotation).

118. Phil Larkin, oral history, September 13, 1981, CPC; Emmett J. Scott, *Negro Migration during the War* (New York, 1920), 24-25 (second quotation).

119. Baker, *Following the Color Line,* 251.

120. Dollard, *Caste and Class in a Southern Town,* 77.

121. Vicksburg *Evening Post,* November 5, 1891, quoted in Wiliam Ivy Hair, *Carnival of Fury: Robert Charles and the New Orleans Race Riot of 1900* (Baton Rouge, 1976), 14. Although such misdeeds were normally corrected privately, local courts also punished caste violations. See a 1908 Brookhaven case involving a nondeferential black woman (Lincoln County *Times,* February 7, 1907).

122. Columbus *Commercial,* October 16, 1906. See also an example from Hattiesburg, described in Jackson *Daily News,* August 4, 1919.

123. NAACP, *Annual Report for 1934* (New York, 1935); Jessie Daniel Ames, *The Changing Character of Lynching: Review of Lynching, 1931-1941* (1942; reprint ed., New York, 1973), 43. For other examples, see Chicago *Defender,* June 21, 1919; Lincoln County *Times,* February 7, December 19, 1907; Clarksdale *Register,* January 10, 1918.

124. "General Synopsis of Legal Cases, 1925," box D-11, NAACP.

125. J. A. Miller to Walter White, September 3, 1918, William P. Harrison to John Shillady, September 25, 1918, box C-361, NAACP; Jackson *Daily Clarion-Ledger,* November 13, 14, 1917.

126. David M. Tucker, *Lieutenant Lee of Beale Street* (Nashville, 1971), 30-34. Lee tells his own story in the more autobiographical passages of his roman à clef: *River George* (New York, 1937), 220-232.

127. Vicksburg *Evening Post,* July 26, 28, 29, 30, 1918; Vicksburg *Daily Herald,* July 24, 25, 27, 1918.

128. William P. Harrison to John R. Shillady, September 25, 29, 1918, box C-361, NAACP. In the same file see also J. A. Miller to Walter White, September 3, 1918; Miller to Shillady, October 15, 16, 29, 1918; White to Department of Justice, August 1, 1918; White to William G. McAdoo, October 10, 1918; Shillady to Justice Department, August 1, 1918.

Chapter 2. The Politics of the Disfranchised

1. William Henry Holtzclaw, "Present Status of the Negro in Mississippi," *Southern Workman,* 59 (August, 1930), 344.

2. Quoted in Bunche, *The Political Status of the Negro,* 435.

3. Quoted in Jackson *Clarion-Ledger,* September 15, 1954.

4. Harris, *Day of the Carpetbagger,* 67ff.; Wharton, *Negro in Mississippi,* 181-215; J. Morgan Kousser, *The Shaping of Southern Politics: Suffrage Restriction and the Establishment of the One-Party South, 1880-1910* (New Haven, 1974), 14, 16, passim.

5. C. Vann Woodward, "The Political Legacy of Reconstruction," in his *The Burden of Southern History,* rev. ed. (Baton Rouge, 1968), 91 (Du Bois quotation); Wharton, *Negro in Mississippi,* 140.

6. James W. Loewen and Charles Sallis, *Mississippi: Conflict and Change* (New York, 1974), 146 (Humphreys quotation); James Wilford Garner, *Reconstruction in Mississippi* (New York, 1901), 111-112; William C. Harris, *Presidential Reconstruction in Mississippi* (Baton Rouge, 1967), 126, 133-134.

7. Natchez *Tri-Weekly Courier,* July 18, 1865, quoted in Wharton, *Negro in Mississippi,* 141.

8. The most exhaustive analysis of this eventful period is Harris, *Day of the Carpetbagger,* 67-290. But see also Wharton, *Negro in Mississippi,* 144-150; Garner, *Reconstruction in Mississippi,* 171-371; John R. Lynch, *The Facts of Reconstruction* (New York, 1913), 44-45, 92-99.

9. Mrs. Charles C. [Jessie] Mosley, *The Negro in Mississippi History,* 2d ed. rev. (Jackson, Miss., 1969), 63; Robert Fulton Holtzclaw, *Black Magnolias: A Brief History of the Afro-Mississippian—1865-1980* (Shaker Heights, Ohio, 1984), 67.

10. Lynch to Carter Woodson, May 7, 1917, con. 6, CGW; Lynch, *Facts of Reconstruction,* 115-116.

11. *Constitution of the State of Mississippi . . . 1868* (Jackson, 1868), art. 7, sec. 2; Harris, *Day of the Carpetbagger,* 115-154, 268.

12. *Donnell v. State,* 48 Miss. 661 (1873).

13. Harris, *Day of the Carpetbagger,* 663-669; *U.S. v. Cruikshank,* 92 U.S. 542 (1876); *U.S. v. Reese,* 92 U.S. 214 (1876).

14. L. Q. C. Lamar, "Ought the Negro to Be Disfranchised," *North American Review,* 128 (1879), 231-232. See also Jackson *Clarion-Ledger,* August 15, October 31, November 14, 1889; May 1, 1890; Jackson *New Mississippian,* December 9, 1884; April 30, 1890; Wesson *Mirror,* September 20, 1890.

15. Accounts of the "Revolution of 1875" and the "First Mississippi Plan" include Harris, *Day of the Carpetbagger,* 623-699; Garner, *Reconstruction in Mississippi,* 372-414; James G. Revels, "Redeemers, Rednecks, and Racial Integrity," in Richard Aubrey McLemore, ed., *A History of Mississippi,* 2 vols. (Hattiesburg, Miss., 1973), 1: 590-594; Wharton, *Negro in Mississippi,* 181-198.

16. Lynch to I. T. Montgomery, October 17, 1885, quoted in Sallis, "Color Line in Mississippi Politics," 267; Montgomery to Robert Reinhold, April 4, 1904, con. 242, BTW.

17. J. S. McNeily, "History of the Measures Submitted to the Committee on Elective Franchise, Appointment, and Elections in the Constitutional Convention of 1890," *Publications of the Mississippi Historical Society,* 6 (1902), 130 ("pollute" quotation); Jackson *Daily Clarion-Ledger,* September 11, 1890

("no secret" quotation). See also McNeily, "War and Reconstruction in Mississippi, 1863-1890," *Publications of the Mississippi Historical Society,* Centenary Series, 2 (1918), 532.

18. The voting estimates in this paragraph are drawn from Kousser's *Shaping of Southern Politics,* 15, 28, 145, 241-242 (Tables 1.2, 1.4, 6.3, 9.2, 9.3). Kousser's study tells us much about the impact of white oppression on black suffrage before and after 1890. Yet, while his use of "proportionate reduction statistics" (see ibid., 241-242, 269-270) convinces me that black voter turnout in Mississippi dropped more sharply between 1888 and 1892 than between 1884 and 1888, I believe that he has overstated the effects of formal (i.e., "legal") suffrage restrictions in Mississippi. Other states may have experienced only "relatively small declines in Negro voting previous to disfranchisement" (246), but in Mississippi the pre-1890 decrease—as Kousser's own data reveal—was massive. His critique of Key's so-called fait accompli thesis—the argument that disfranchisement was all but completed before the formalization of white rule—may apply generally to the South and particularly to the white portions of the electorate. But insofar as these arguments can be narrowly applied to black Mississippians, Key's is the better of the two. See V. O. Key, *Southern Politics in State and Nation* (New York, 1949), 533ff.

19. Wharton, *Negro in Mississippi,* 201-202; Jackson *New Mississippian,* November 13, 1889.

20. Harris, *Day of the Carpetbagger,* 131; James P. Coleman, "The Mississippi Constitution of 1890 and the Final Decade of the Nineteenth Century," in McLemore, ed., *History of Mississippi,* 2: 8; J. L. Power, "The Black and Tan Convention," *Publications of the Mississippi Historical Society,* 3 (1900), 73-83.

21. S. S. Calhoon, "The Causes and Events That Led to the Calling of the Constitutional Convention of 1890," *Publications of the Mississippi Historical Society,* 6 (1902), 107.

22. Sallis, "Color Line in Mississippi Politics," 289-290; Hamilton, "Mississippi Politics in the Progressive Era," 36; Albert Dennis Kirwan, *Revolt of the Rednecks: Mississippi Politics, 1876-1925* (1951; reprint ed., New York, 1965), 58-64; Wharton, *Negro in Mississippi,* 206-207; William A. Mabry, "Disfranchisement of the Negro in Mississippi," *Journal of Southern History,* 4 (1938), 318-333; Jackson *Clarion-Ledger,* August 15, 1889.

23. Raymond *Gazette,* June 28, 1890. See also Newton County *Progress,* quoted in Jackson *Clarion-Ledger,* May 29, 1890; Jackson *Clarion-Ledger,* March 6, June 12, 1890.

24. George believed that blacks would soon outnumber whites in Mississippi by 500,000; others predicted an imminent black majority of up to 100,000 (Greenville *Times,* November 2, 1889; Jackson *Clarion-Ledger,* May 8, 1890; Port Gibson *Southern Reveille,* May 23, 1890). For white opposition to the constitution, see Jackson *Clarion-Ledger,* October 31, November 14, 1889; Hamilton, "Mississippi Politics," 36; Coleman, "Mississippi Constitution of 1890," 9.

25. Coleman, "Mississippi Constitution of 1890," 8 (first quotation); Jackson *New Mississippian,* October 23, 1889 (second quotation).

26. For the white response to the Republican ticket, see Jackson *Clarion-Ledger,* September 19, October 3, 10, 1889; Jackson *New Mississippian,* October 2, 1889. For factors contributing to a white consensus favoring formal disfranchisement, see Kirwan, *Revolt of the Rednecks,* 59; Wharton, *Negro in Mississippi,* 208, 209.

27. *Journal of the Proceedings of the Constitutional Convention of the State of Mississippi, August 12–November 1, 1890* (Jackson, 1890), 203, 485.

28. Sallis, "Color Line in Mississippi Politics," 315; Jackson *Daily Clarion-Ledger,* September 11, 1890 (Calhoon quotation); Montgomery to Robert Reinhold, April 4, 1904, con. 242, BTW (Chrisman quotation).

29. Mississippi *Constitution,* 1890, art. 12, secs. 240-243, 256; Eric C. Clark, "Legislative Apportionment in the 1890 Constitutional Convention," *Journal of Mississippi History,* 42 (November, 1980), 298-315.

30. Opposition to the understanding clause is extensively covered in Jackson *Clarion-Ledger,* October 9, 30, 1890; January 8, 1891; and Wharton, *Negro in Mississippi,* 213-214. Much of the early opposition was generated by the *Clarion-Ledger,* which initially dismissed the new document as a "mass of irreconcilable incongruities that nobody can understand" (Jackson *Clarion-Ledger,* December 16, 1890). In time, of course, whites recognized that the constitution's very inscrutability served well the intent of the understanding clause. In the words of an admiring Theodore Bilbo, "Senator George wrote a Constitution that damn few white men and no niggers at all can explain" (quoted in *Voting in Mississippi: A Report of the United States Commission on Civil Rights, 1965* [Washington, 1966], 5).

31. *Sproule* v. *Fredericks,* 69 Miss. 978 (1892); *Ratliff* v. *Beale,* 74 Miss. 247 (1896); *Hill et al.* v. *Duckworth,* 155 Miss. 484 (1929); *Williams* v. *Mississippi,* 170 U.S. 213 (1898).

32. Mosley, *Negro in Mississippi History,* 62 ("annulled" quotation); Greenwood *Commonwealth,* August 17, 1900 (Vardaman quotation); Jackson *Clarion-Ledger,* October 23, 1890. See also Vardaman's views in the *Issue,* January 9, December 19, 1909.

33. *Proceedings of a Reunion of the Surviving Members of the Constitutional Convention of 1890* (Jackson, 1927), 11 (hereinafter cited as *Reunion of Survivors, 1927*). See also Rowland, *A Mississippi View of Race Relations.*

34. Quoted in NAACP, *Annual Report for 1920,* 29.

35. Some of the most candid descriptions of the "primary intention" behind the franchise provisions are to be found in the ruling of the state supreme court in *Ratliff* v. *Beale,* 74 Miss. 247 (1896), and the legal briefs filed therein by Frank Johnston and S. S. Calhoon. But see also *Hill et al.* v. *Duckworth,* 155 Miss. 484 (1929).

36. See Table 2.1 in Kousser, *Shaping of Southern Politics,* 55.

37. Sallis, "Color Line in Mississippi Politics," 316 (George quotation); Jackson *Clarion-Ledger,* August 14, 1890, quoted in Wharton, *Negro in Mississippi,* 210.

38. James M. Stone, "A Note on Voter Registration under the Mississippi Understanding Clause, 1892," *Journal of Southern History,* 38 (May, 1972), 293-296. For slightly different figures, see Jackson *Daily Clarion-Ledger,* August 11, 1892; *Appleton's Annual Cyclopedia, 1892* (New York, 1893), 472.

39. Quoted in *Proceedings of a Meeting of the Surviving Members of the Constitution of 1890, Held November 1, 1910* (Jackson, n.d.), 13-14 (cited hereinafter as *Proceedings of the Surviving Members, 1910*). See also R. H. Thompson, "Suffrage in Mississippi," *Proceedings of the Mississippi Historical Society,* 1 (1898), 43.

40. Montgomery to Robert Reinhold, April 4, 18, 1904, con. 242, BTW; Reddix, *Voice Crying in the Wilderness,* 57; B. Baldwin Dansby, oral history, January 5, 1971, MDAH; Bunche, *Status of the Negro,* 435 ("Christ" quotation).

41. Rawick, ed., *Miss. Narr.,* 9(4), 1760. Blacks residing in such all-black voting precincts as Mt. Carmel (Jefferson Davis County) and Mound Bayou also apparently registered with comparative ease (James Franklin Barnes, "Negro Voting in Mississippi" [M.A. thesis, University of Mississippi, 1955], 33, 35).

42. Rawick, ed., *Miss. Narr.,* 7(2), 499-500. See also the white interviewer's skeptical footnote to this narrative, as well as the narrative of Louis Joseph Piernas, ibid., 9(4), 1707; and Key, *Southern Politics,* 520-521.

43. Jackson *Daily Clarion,* July 16, August 11, 1892 (first quotation); Laurel *Leader,* May 2, 1903, quoted in Cleveland V. Payne, "Economics, Education, and Religious Forces in the Development of a Black Middle Class in Laurel, Mississippi, from 1882-1928" (spec. thesis, University of Southern Mississippi, 1982) (hereinafter cited as Payne, "Black Middle Class in Laurel"), 21 (second quotation).

44. Quoted in Bunche, *Status of the Negro,* 436.

45. Voter registration estimates for 1880 and 1890 range from the merely flawed to the wildly implausible. Although data released by the secretary of state on black and white "electors" in 1880 (130,607 and 110,113 respectively) have sometimes been interpreted as voter registration figures, they are in fact voting-age population figures (*Biennial Report of the Secretary of State to the Legislature of Mississippi, 1880-1881,* 115). The voting-age population in 1890 numbered 271,080, of which 150,469 were black and 120,611 white. Yet one historian estimates that there were 308,774 "voters," 189,884 of them black and 118,890 white (Buford Satcher, *Blacks in Mississippi Politics, 1865-1900* [Washington, 1978], app. D, 209). Although closer to the mark, Kirwan's figures are scarcely more credible. By his count, the state had "approximately 120,000 qualified white voters." He offers no comparable black statistic but notes that the black voting majority "should have been in the neighborhood of 42,000" (*Revolt of the Rednecks,* 67n, 73). Clearly, the number of registered voters in the decade before disfranchisement is anybody's guess.

46. *Reunion of the Survivors, 1927,* 53-54; see also *Journal of the Proceedings of the Constitutional Convention,* 67-74, 76-77.

47. J. M. Stone, "The Suppression of Lawlessness in the South," *North*

American Review (April, 1894), 503; Sallis, "Color Line in Mississippi Politics," 330 (Power's quotation); McNeily, "History of the Measures Submitted to the Committee on Elective Franchise," 138 ("sons of Ham" quotation).

48. Quoted in James T. Currie, *Enclave: Vicksburg and Her Plantations, 1863-1870* (Jackson, 1980), 123. Wharton, *Negro in Mississippi,* 145, notes that Benjamin Montgomery may have been Mississippi's first black public office holder.

49. Hermann, *Pursuit of a Dream,* 233-235; Louis Harlan, *Booker T. Washington,* vol. 2, *The Wizard of Tuskegee, 1901-1915* (New York, 1983), 12-13. For Montgomery's side of the federal land office scandal, see E. P. Booze to Emmett J. Scott, April 9, 1904, con. 234, BTW.

50. J. Saunders Redding, *The Lonesome Road* (Garden City, 1958), 105, 108-109, 114. According to a white sympathizer with long-standing ties to Mound Bayou, Montgomery returned late in his life to the idea of out-migration, in fact African "repatriation," possibly to the Congo. See the statement of Walter Sillers, Sr., in Florence Sillers, comp., *History of Bolivar County,* 593. On Sillers's association with the Mound Bayouans, see Sillers to Charles Banks, April 19, 1917; Banks to Emmett Scott, April 21, 1917 (microfilm, ser. 1, reel 228), TRP.

51. Quoted in George Alexander Sewell and Margaret L. Dwight, *Mississippi Black History Makers,* rev. ed. (Jackson, 1984), 160.

52. Sillers, comp., *History of Bolivar County,* 592-593 (eulogy quotation); "Professional and Civic Leaders," WPA History: Bolivar County; Mississippi Advertising Commission, *Songs of the South* (n.p., n.d.); *I. T. Montgomery,* subject file, MDAH.

53. Montgomery's speech was reprinted in the New York *World,* September 28, 1890. See also *Souvenir Program of the Fiftieth Anniversary of Mound Bayou, Mississippi, July 11-17, 1937* (n.p., n.d.).

54. Jackson *Clarion-Ledger,* September 18, 1890; Raymond *Gazette,* September 20, 1890; Memphis *Avalanche,* September 16, 1890; New York *World,* September 17, 28, 1890.

55. Providence (R.I.) *Journal,* quoted in Coleman, "Mississippi Constitution of 1890," 18; Stephen B. Weeks, "The History of Negro Suffrage in the South," *Political Science Quarterly,* 9 (1894), 700-701; Wharton, *Negro in Mississippi,* 212.

56. See, e.g., New York *Age,* August 25, 1910; John J. Morant, *Mississippi Minister* (New York, 1958), 44-45; Joseph H. Douglass, "A History of E. P. Booze," undated ms., BMF; Aurelius P. Hood, *The Negro at Mound Bayou: Being an Authentic Story of the Founding, Growth and Development of the "Most Celebrated Town in the South"* (n.p., 1909), 59; Maurice Elizabeth Jackson, "Mound Bayou—A Study in Social Development" (M.A. thesis, University of Alabama, 1937), 40; Anselm Joseph Finch, *Mississippi Negro Ramblings* (Chicago, 1969), 196-197. In some quarters the assumption actually persists that Montgomery manfully opposed disfranchisement. See Mosley, *Negro in Mississippi History,* 62.

57. Quoted in Bunche, *Status of the Negro,* 436. See also August Meier and

Elliott Rudwick, *From Plantation to Ghetto,* 3d ed. (New York, 1976), 212; Kirwan, *Revolt of the Rednecks,* 82n; Wells, *Crusade for Justice,* 38-39; Hermann, *Pursuit of a Dream,* 230-231.

58. Beam, *He Called Them by the Lightning,* 179 ("dictator" quotation); Hood, *The Negro at Mound Bayou,* 59 ("compromising" quotation).

59. Louis R. Harlan, *Booker T. Washington,* vol. 1, *The Making of a Black Leader, 1856-1901* (New York, 1972), 289, argues that Montgomery "went farther than Washington in subordinating politics." On the response of Afro-American leaders generally to disfranchisement, see August Meier, *Negro Thought in America, 1880-1915: Racial Ideologies in the Age of Booker T. Washington* (Ann Arbor, 1963), 38-39.

60. Wharton, *Negro in Mississippi,* 212; Redding, *Lonesome Road,* 105; Loewen and Sallis, *Mississippi: Conflict and Change,* 186-187; Holtzclaw, *Black Magnolias,* 67.

61. Lynch, *Facts of Reconstruction,* 265; Lynch, *Reminiscences,* 343; Redding, *Lonesome Road,* 119.

62. Montgomery to Washington, April 5, 1904; Montgomery to Robert Reinhold, April 4, 13, 1904 (quotation), con. 242, BTW. See also, Weeks, "The History of Negro Suffrage," 700.

63. *Proceedings of the Surviving Members, 1910,* 16-20.

64. New York *World,* September 28, 1890.

65. Quoted in Kousser, *Shaping of Southern Politics,* 14n (first quotation); Hermann, *Pursuit of a Dream,* 231 (second quotation).

66. Lynch to Benjamin Harrison, July 2, 1888 (microfilm, ser. 1, reel 9); Lynch to Harrison, November 9, 1894 (ser. 2, reel 89), BHP; Lynch, *Facts of Reconstruction,* 256-257, 284-285; Jackson *Clarion-Ledger,* October 31, 1889; Woodville *Republican,* December 24, 1887.

67. Quoted in Jackson *Clarion-Ledger,* June 20, July 4, 1889.

68. Mississippi *House Journal,* 1890, 232-235 (Bowles quotation); Winona *Advance,* June 27, 1890 (subsequent quotations); *New Mississippian,* June 25, 1890; Raymond *Gazette,* June 28, 1890; Wharton, *Negro in Mississippi,* 210-211.

69. Jackson *Clarion-Ledger,* October 9, 1890 ("night schools" quotation); October 23, 1890 (Mannaway quotation).

70. Jackson *Colored Journal,* quoted in Port Gibson *Southern Reveille,* October 31, 1890; Natchez *Brotherhood,* quoted in Sallis, "Color Line in Mississippi Politics," 332.

71. Aberdeen *Weekly Examiner,* March 22, 1895; Jackson *Clarion-Ledger,* June 26, 1890; West Point *Leader,* July 24, 1903; Sallis, "Color Line in Mississippi Politics," 290-294, 329; Wharton, *Negro in Mississippi,* 210.

72. Jones also carried *Williams* v. *Mississippi* to the United States Supreme Court. See J. Morgan Kousser, "Disfranchisement," *Encyclopedia of Southern History,* ed. David C. Roller and Robert W. Twyman (Baton Rouge, 1979), 363; Chester H. Rowell, *A History and Legal Digest of All the Contested Elections Cases in the House of Representatives of the United States, 1789-1901* (Washington, D.C., 1901), 540-541.

73. Frank Johnston, quoted in Port Gibson *Southern Reveille,* May 23, 1890.

74. Slave narrative quotations, in order of appearance, are in Rawick, ed., *Miss. Narr.,* 8(3), 1348; 9(4), 1400; 8(3), 1089; 6(2), 133-134; 9(4), 1564, 1529.

75. C. E. Johnson to James Weldon Johnson, April 19, 1920, box C-388, NAACP. For another example see Jessie Myles to NAACP, July 30, 1945, box 380, post-1940, NAACP.

76. Holliman to James Weldon Johnson, September 9, 12, October 21, November 28, December 17, 1927; January 26, 1928; Johnson to William T. Holliman, September 16, 26, 1927; William T. Andrews to Holliman, January 30, 1928, box C-285, NAACP.

77. William H. Harrison to Walter F. White, April 14, 1928; William T. Andrews to Harrison, April 17, 1928; William T. Andrews to William H. Harrison, Walter F. White, April 14, 1928, box C-390, NAACP.

78. Charles Banks, quoted in Jackson *Daily News,* July 28, 1919; Banks to Washington, October 25, 1915, con. 68, BTW.

79. Bunche, *Status of the Negro,* 539-540. See also Vicksburg *Light,* January 18, 1900; Jackson *Daily News,* July 28, 1919.

80. W. E. B. Du Bois, "The Republicans and the Black Voter," *Nation,* 110 (June 5, 1920), 758. For the Black and Tan Republicans' role in the nominating process, see Richard B. Sherman, *The Republican Party and Black America: From McKinley to Hoover, 1896-1933* (Charlottesville, Va., 1973), 19-20, 119-120, 156-158.

81. Alexander Heard, *A Two-Party South?* (Chapel Hill, 1952), 223; Sherman, *Republican Party,* 46; U.S., Senate, Special Committee Investigating Campaign Expenditures, *Hearing on Presidential Campaign Expenditures, 1928,* 70th Cong., 1st sess. (Washington, D.C., 1928), 718-735; Norfolk *Journal and Guide,* June 9, 1928; New York *Times,* May 30, July 18, 1928.

82. Perry W. Howard to Theodore Roosevelt, May 1, 1916; S. D. Redmond to Roosevelt, May 1, 1916 (microfilm, ser. 1, reel 208), TRP.

83. Wharton, *Negro in Mississippi,* 145.

84. For Lynch's own account of the Bruce-Hill-Lynch "triumvirate," see Lynch, *Reminiscences,* 89ff. The Greenville *Republican* is quoted in Jackson *New Mississippian,* August 26, 1884.

85. For McKee's unionist background and early political career, see Harris, *Day of the Carpetbagger,* 122-123. For Lynch's favorable estimate of McKee's faction, see John R. Lynch, "Some Historical Errors of James Ford Rhodes," *Journal of Negro History,* 2 (October, 1917), 350-352.

86. Willie D. Halsell, ed., "Republican Factionalism in Mississippi, 1882-1884," *Journal of Southern History,* 7 (February, 1941), 84-101; idem, "James R. Chalmers and 'Mahoneism' in Mississippi," ibid., 10 (February, 1944), 37-58; Vincent DeSantis, *Republicans Face the Southern Question: The New Departure Years, 1877-1897* (Baltimore, 1959), 183-184; Lillian A. Pereyra, *James Lusk Alcorn: Persistent Whig* (Baton Rouge, 1966), 187-190; Kirwan, *Revolt of the Rednecks,* 11-17; Sallis, "Color Line in Mississippi Politics," 239-260.

87. In 1900, with Lynch's support, a white man replaced Hill on the Republican National Committee. On the Lynch-Hill dispute, see Lynch to George Myers, May 14, 1900 (microfilm, roll 3, frames 942-950); June 29, 1900 (roll 4, frames 60-62), GMP; Lynch to J. M. Rusk, January 16, 1892 (microfilm, ser. 1, reel 34), BHP; Lynch, *Reminiscences,* 351-420, passim.

88. Mulvihill is incorrectly identified as a lily-white in Hanes Walton, Jr., *Black Political Parties: An Historical and Political Analysis* (New York, 1972), 68.

89. Quoted in Bunche, *Status of the Negro,* 537 (Redmond quotation); Banks to Scott, March 7, 1908, con. 38, BTW (subsequent quotations). See also Redmond to Roosevelt, May 1, 1916 (microfilm, ser. 1, reel 208), TRP; Banks to Emmett Scott, April 15, 1909, con. 43, BTW; Charleston (W.Va.) *Advocate,* clipping [June, 1912] (microfilm, reel 1, frame 724), Tuskegee Institute News Clippings File; New York *Age,* March 7, 1912; Paul D. Casdorph, *Republicans, Negroes, and Progressives in the South, 1912-1916* (University, Ala., 1981), 55.

90. Moseley's methods of controlling state conventions is described in "Charles Banks Again on the Mississippi Situation" [1912], 3, con. 56, BTW. See also Redmond to Roosevelt, May 1, 1916 (microfilm, ser. 1, reel 208), TRP; Alexander J. Simpson, Jr., "George L. Sheldon and the Beginnings of the Lily-White Movement in Mississippi, 1909-1932" (M.A. thesis, Mississippi State University, 1962), 45; Chicago *Daily Tribune,* March 29, 1912, 1.

91. Moseley to Roosevelt, July 10, 1903 (microfilm, ser. 1, reel 34), TRP.

92. W. B. Roberts, "After the War Between the States," in Sillers, comp., *History of Bolivar County,* 163.

93. Kousser, *Shaping of Southern Politics,* 290-291, argues that the fusion process is known largely through the testimony of disgruntled lily-whites who had reason to exaggerate the party disloyalty of black Republicans, and that its extent has probably been exaggerated. The phenomenon in Mississippi, however, is widely noted: Kirwan, *Revolt of the Rednecks,* 8, 16-17; 99-199; Wharton, *Negro in Mississippi,* 202-203; Simpson, "George L. Sheldon and the Beginnings of the Lily-White Movement in Mississippi," 18-20; Sallis, "Color Line in Mississippi Politics," 257-262; Halsell, ed., "Republican Factionalism in Mississippi," 86-87; Wharton identified Adams, Bolivar, Coahoma, Hinds, Issaquena, Sharkey, and Washington as the counties where fusion tickets met "the general satisfaction of a majority of both races" (*Negro in Mississippi,* 202-203).

94. In the twentieth century the state GOP rarely offered candidates for election, and when it did (as in 1924 and 1932), they were white (Mary Booze to Calvin Coolidge [microfilm, ser. 3, reel 277], WHT; Atlanta *Daily World,* September 2, 1932). When Governor Henry L. Whitfield appointed a black notary public (T. G. Ewing) in Vicksburg, the press called it a "departure" and a "surprise" and Theodore Bilbo was outraged that a "coal black buck" enjoyed the governor's favor (Jackson *Daily News,* May 6, 1924; Bill R. Baker, *Catch the Vision: The Life of Henry L. Whitfield* [Jackson, 1974], 109).

95. Hill served only briefly, however, as Harrison was defeated before the

Mississippian was confirmed by the Senate (Lynch, *Reminiscences,* 352; "Hon. James Hill," *Colored American,* 15 [February, 1909], 103-108).

96. Lynch, *Reminiscences,* 399-406; Wharton, *Negro in Mississippi,* 161, 163.

97. Harlan, *Booker T. Washington,* 2: 11.

98. Quotations are from Gatewood, *Theodore Roosevelt and the Art of Controversy,* 68, 70, 71, 74. See also U.S., Congress, House, *Resignation of the Postmaster at Indianola, Mississippi,* 57th Cong., 2d sess., House Doc. 422 (February 26, 1903); Jackson *Weekly Clarion-Ledger,* January 15, 1903; Indianola *Enterprise,* January 30, 1903.

99. Vardaman quoted in William F. Holmes, *The White Chief: James Kimble Vardaman* (Baton Rouge, 1970), 100. The incident at Pickens is briefly described in U.S., Works Progress Administration, Mississippi, "Source Material for Mississippi History: Holmes County" (microfilm, n.d.), MDAH, unpaginated (hereinafter cited as WPA History: Holmes County).

100. Montgomery to Edward W. Lampton, April 25, 1904, con. 242, BTW (quotation); Gatewood, *Theodore Roosevelt,* 86n; Indianola *Enterprise,* June 5, 1903; Maxson, *Progress of the Races,* 52-53; Jackson *Clarion-Ledger,* August 8, 1889; Rawick, ed., *Miss. Narr.,* 9(4), 1707.

101. Jackson *Weekly Clarion-Ledger,* December 27, 1906; Meridian *Evening Star,* April 24, 25, 26, 1908. See also Columbus *Weekly Dispatch,* December 20, 1906.

102. Taft to Washington, June 9, 1908, con. 7, BTW (first quotation); Sherman, *Republican Party,* 84 (second quotation), 91 (third quotation).

103. "Confidential," Taft to Moseley, June 28, 1911; Moseley to Taft, July 1, 1911 (microfilm, ser. 6, reel 418), WHT. See also "Races and Nationalities," WPA History: Claiborne County, unpaginated; Jackson *Clarion-Ledger,* April 17, 24, 1890; "Hon. T. Richardson," Indianapolis *Freeman,* April 17, 1897.

104. Keys to Charles Banks, January 31, 1910; Banks to Washington, February 1, 5, 1910; Banks to A. I. Vorys, February 8, 1910; Banks to Taft, March 10, 1910; Banks to Fred R. Moore, May 10, 1910, con. 49; Banks to Scott, March 9, 1911, con. 52, BTW.

105. Charleston (W.Va.) *Advocate,* clipping [June, 1912] (microfilm, reel 1, frame 724), Tuskegee Institute News Clippings File; Banks to Washington, August 6, 1909; Banks to F. W. Carpenter, August 11, 1909; Banks to Scott, August 28, 1909 (quotation), con. 43; "Charles Banks Again on the Mississippi Situation" [1912], 4, con. 56, BTW; Lynch, *Reminiscences,* 505-506.

106. "Charles Banks Again on the Mississippi Situation" [1912], 3, con. 56, BTW.

107. Banks to Washington, January 17, 1890, con. 49; W. A. Attaway to Ormeley McHarg, April 20, 1912; Washington to Banks, May 20, June 7, 1912, con. 56, BTW.

108. Memphis *Commercial-Appeal,* July 24, 1912; Paul D. Casdorph, "The 1912 Republican Presidential Campaign in Mississippi," *Journal of Mississippi History,* 33 (February, 1971), 14; Jackson *Clarion-Ledger,* reprinted in Lincoln County *Times,* August 1, 1912 (Howard quotation); New York *Age,* August

1, 1912; New York *Times,* August 4, 1912; George E. Mowry, "The South and the Progressive Lily White Party of 1912," *Journal of Southern History,* 6 (1940), 243; *Official Report of the Fifteenth Republican National Convention . . . June 18-22, 1912* (New York, 1912), 244, 316.

109. Sherman, *Republican Party,* 110, 113; Dunbar Rowland, ed., *The Official and Statistical Register of the State of Mississippi* (Madison, Wis., 1917), 454; Banks to Roosevelt, December 18, 1915, con. 75, BTW; Casdorph, "The 1912 Republican Presidential Campaign in Mississippi," 19.

110. The reluctance of the Mound Bayou leaders to support Howard is explained by Montgomery's daughter: Mary (Mrs. Eugene P.) Booze to Calvin Coolidge, November 12, 1925 (microfilm, ser. 3, reel 277), WHT. On Howard's rise to party leadership see Banks to [Scott], March 1, 1912, con. 56, BTW; Redmond to Roosevelt, May 1, 1916 (microfilm, ser. 1, reel 208); Howard to Roosevelt, January 22, 1918 (ser. 1, reel 273); Howard to Roosevelt, January 22, 1918 (ser. 1, reel 260); Mulvihill to Roosevelt, April 23, 1918 (ser. 1, reel 273), TRP; Howard to George B. Christian, March 5, 1921 (microfilm, reel 195, frame 1270); Montgomery to Harding, March 25, 1922 (reel 200, frames 959-960); and "Minutes of the Meeting of the Republican Executive Committee, Third Congressional District, Mound Bayou, April 28, 1921" (reel 195, frames 1291-1293), WGH; New York *Age,* March 7, 1912; *Crisis,* 20 (August, 1920), 175; Hanes Walton, Jr., *Black Republicans: The Politics of Black and Tans* (Metuchen, N.J., 1975), 132-135; Bunche, *Status of the Negro,* 537-539.

111. Mary Booze's place on the RNC came initially by default after Howard's election, when a white woman favored for the position refused to serve with a black man (Mary Booze to Coolidge, November 12, 1925 [microfilm, ser. 3, reel 277], WHT). See also Bunche, *Status of the Negro,* 538-539.

112. The most notable example was that of a U.S. marshal-designate who refused to meet with the state's Black and Tan leaders in 1931 because there were no "decent or virtuous Negro women in Mississippi." The object of the slur, Mary Booze, with her husband, Eugene, and Perry Howard, directed a successful national campaign of opposition to the offending nominee. See E. P. Booze to [Lamont] Rowlands, July 4, 1932; Rowlands to Booze, July 6, 1932; Walter Newton to Rowlands, July 11, 1932; Booze to Newton, July 14, 1932, box 969, Presidential papers, HPL; Mary Booze to editor, Memphis *Commercial-Appeal,* July 11, 1932; Atlanta *World,* July 12, 1932.

113. Unidentified newspaper clipping, classified subject file, General Records, Department of Justice, Record Group 60, NA; Norfolk *Journal and Guide,* August 25, 1928. Blacks were appointed to postal positions in such all-black communities as Mound Bayou and Utica Institute.

114. "Along the Color Line," *Crisis,* 36 (April, 1929), 139 (quotation); *Crisis,* 37 (March, 1930), 97; Norfolk *Journal and Guide,* January 25, 1930.

115. For the least ambiguous expression of these concerns, see Jackson *Daily News,* December 15, 22, 1928.

116. Simpson, "George L. Sheldon and the Beginnings of the Lily-White Movement in Mississippi"; and David G. Ginzl, "Lily-Whites versus Black-

and-Tans: Mississippi Republicans during the Hoover Administration," *Journal of Mississippi History,* 42 (August, 1980), 194-211.

117. Elvy E. Calloway, *The Other Side of the South* (Chicago, 1934), 94 (quotation); New York *Times,* May 30, 1928; Norfolk *Journal and Guide,* June 9, 1928.

118. "Duty of Reorganization of Republican Party in South to End Abuse of Patronage," Addresses, Letters, Magazine Articles, Press Statements, etc., 40: 995, HPL ("house-cleaning" quotation); New York *Times,* March 27, 1929, 15; and *Literary Digest,* 101 (April 13, 1929), 5-7; Alpheus T. Mason, *William Howard Taft: Chief Justice* (New York, 1964), 152 (Taft quotation).

119. On Hoover's southern policy, cf. the sympathetic studies by Donald J. Lisio, *Hoover, Blacks, and Lily-Whites: A Study of Southern Strategies* (Chapel Hill, 1985), passim; and David Burner, *Herbert Hoover: A Public Life* (New York, 1979), 216, to the more critical accounts, including David J. Ginzl, "Herbert Hoover and Republican Patronage Politics in the South, 1928-1932" (Ph.D. diss., Syracuse University, 1977); Allan J. Lichtman, *Prejudice and the Old Politics: The Presidential Election of 1928* (Chapel Hill, 1979); and Sherman, *Republican Party,* 230-231, 237-239.

120. This scandal and subsequent trials are detailed in Neil R. McMillen, "Perry W. Howard, Boss of Black-and-Tan Republicanism in Mississippi, 1924-1960," *Journal of Southern History,* 48 (May, 1981), 205-224.

121. U.S., Senate, *Reports,* 71st Cong., 2d sess., no. 272: Subcommittee of the Committee on Post Offices and Post Roads, *Influencing Appointments to Postmasterships and Other Federal Offices* (ser. 9107, Washington, D.C., 1930), 3-11; transcript of Department of Justice interview with Howard, May 26, 1925, General Records, Department of Justice; Donovan to John G. Sargent, July 14, 1925, General Records, Department of Justice; bills of indictment, July 14, 1928; November 9, 1928, *United States* v. *Perry W. Howard et al.,* cases 9578 and 9689, Records of the District Courts of the United States, Record Group 21 (Federal Archives Record Center, East Point, Ga.).

122. Quotations from Chicago *Defender,* July 20, 1929. Howard's controversial support of the Pullman Company is described in William H. Harris, *Keeping the Faith: A. Philip Randolph, Milton P. Webster, and the Brotherhood of Sleeping Car Porters, 1925-1937* (Urbana, 1977), 51-53; "Randolph's Reply to Perry Howard," *Messenger,* 7 (October-November, 1925), 350, 352; "A. Philip Randolph Answers New Questions for Perry Howard," *Messenger,* 7 (December, 1925), 381, 400, 402. For examples of black assessments of Howard as Uncle Tom, see Walter White to Redmond, January 8, 1923; James A. Cobb to White, November 10, 1923, box C-389, NAACP. A more favorable judgment is offered by Norfolk *Journal and Guide,* May 12, 1928.

123. *Crisis,* 25 (September, 1928), 312; Chicago *Defender,* July 21, October 20, 1928; March 30, 1929; Norfolk *Journal and Guide,* July 21, August 25, October 20, December 29, 1928; and undated clippings from the Houston *Observer* and the New York *News,* Colored Question, Presidential Papers, HPL.

124. Jackson *Daily News,* December 15, 16, 1928; March 22, 26, 27, April 17, 1929.

125. McMillen, "Perry W. Howard," 217-219 ("white men's negroes" quotation); Jackson *Daily News,* December 15, 16, 1928 (subsequent quotations).

126. Jackson *Daily News,* March 20, 21, 22, 23, 1929.

127. Ibid., December 15, 1928; Chicago *Defender,* July 13, 20, 1929.

128. Bunche, *Status of the Negro,* 81; New York *Times,* July 18, 1928; Samuel Taylor Moore, "Mississippi Auction Block—New Style," *Independent,* 118 (February 21, 1927), 231; Paul Lewinson, *Race, Class and Party: A History of Negro Suffrage and White Politics in the South* (New York, 1965), 181.

129. Of course the questionable circumstances under which Howard was acquitted do not prove his guilt. See Lisio, *Hoover, Blacks, and Lily-Whites,* 131.

130. Helen Hopkins Levings to Republican National Credentials Committee, June 13, 1932; E. M. Hawkins to Newton, June 20, 1932; Rowlands to Hoover, June 14, 1932, Republican National Committee, Presidential Papers, HPL; Atlanta *Daily World,* June 16, 19, 20, July 7, 1932.

131. The administration's factional preferences are reflected in the correspondence in both the State File and Republican National Committee File; for Rowlands's complaints see Rowlands to Newton, August 12, October 17, 1929; March 21, June 7, 1930, Republican National Committee, Presidential Papers, HPL. So closely was Howard allied with Senator Harrison that the black national committeeman was known as "Pat's Perry" (Pittsburgh *Courier,* February 11, 1961).

132. *Report of the Proceedings of the Twenty-Sixth Republican National Convention* (Washington, D.C., 1956), 117; *Report of the Proceedings of the Twenty-Seventh Republican National Convention* (Washington, D.C., 1960), 127-128. S. D. Redmond, the nation's only black Republican state chairman, held his post from 1924 until his death in 1948.

133. Pittsburgh *Courier,* August 7, 1932.

134. See, e.g., B. W. Jackson to James Weldon Johnson, November 19, 1932, box C-391, NAACP; Chicago *Defender,* September 12, 13, October 3, 1931; Atlanta *Daily World,* May 3, 1932; Bunche, *Status of the Negro,* 81, 434.

135. Bunche, *Status of the Negro,* 81.

136. Rawick, ed., *Miss. Narr.,* 6(1), 9 (Albright quotation); Prentiss *Spirit of Mississippi,* January 26, 1935 (Booze quotation).

137. See, e.g., T. B. Wilson to Walter White, May 27, 1946; Robert L. Carter to Theron L. Candle, August 6, 1946, box 380 (post-1940), NAACP; Sewell and Dwight, *Mississippi Black History Makers,* 272; Barnes, "Negro Voting in Mississippi," 54; Jackson *Clarion-Ledger,* August 5, 1947; Heard, *Two-Party South?,* 191; Mosley, *Negro in Mississippi History,* 73; Earl M. Lewis, "The Negro Voter in Mississippi," *Journal of Mississippi History,* 26 (Summer, 1957), 348.

138. Lisio, *Hoover, Blacks, and Lily-Whites,* xvii, 36-37.

139. Gunnar Myrdal, *An American Dilemma,* vol. 1, *The Negro in a White Nation* (New York, 1944), 497, ccxxxvi (Du Bois quotation).

Chapter 3. Education: The "Mere Faint Gesture"

1. Greenwood *Commonwealth,* June 30, 1899.

2. Jackson *Daily Clarion-Ledger,* February 23, 1918.

3. *Biennial Report of the State Superintendent of Public Education to the Legislature of Mississippi for Scholastic Years 1897-1898 and 1898-1899* (Jacksonville, Fla., 1900), 35 (hereinafter cited as *Report of the State Superintendent*).

4. Jackson *Daily News,* March 10, 1954.

5. In 1939, the State Department of Education reported that Mississippi spent a higher percentage of its public revenue on education than any other state. If the state spent all of its public revenue on schools, the department estimated, its per capita spending on education would still be $9 million less than the national average (P. H. Easom and J. A. Travis, "Status of Negro Schools in Mississippi, 1939" [microfilm, reel 13], STFU). Decade after decade, the state ranked last among all American states in its ability to support education. See Joint Committee of the National Education Association and the American Teachers Association, *Progress of the Education of Negroes, 1870-1950,* pt. 2 (n.p., n.d.), 40.

6. Cf. W. E. B. Du Bois, *The Negro Common School* (Atlanta, 1901), 87; editorial, Jackson *Daily News,* June 4, 1942 (World War II figures); *Report of the State Superintendent, 1939-1941,* 75. For white educational advances during the Progressive Era, see Dewey W. Grantham, *Southern Progressivism: The Reconciliation of Progress and Tradition* (Knoxville, 1983), 246. For the role of northern philanthropy in shaping discriminatory southern educational patterns in the name of "black uplift" and intersectional harmony, see Henry Allen Bullock, *A History of Negro Education in the South from 1619 to the Present* (Cambridge, Mass., 1967); and Louis R. Harlan, *Separate and Unequal: Public School Campaigns and Racism in the Southern Seaboard States, 1901-1915* (Chapel Hill, 1958).

7. The expenditure data in Table 3.2 represent instructional costs only and are based on enrollment rather than school-age population. These data, therefore, probably understate black disadvantage.

8. Edwin R. Embree, *Julius Rosenwald Fund: Review of Two Decades, 1917-1936* (Chicago, 1936), 15. In 1930 only South Carolina had a lower per capita figure.

9. The figures in Table 3.3 are drawn from official reports and should be compared to those compiled by the NAACP. See *Crisis,* 32 (December, 1926), 91.

10. Wharton, *Negro in Mississippi,* 247.

11. *Report of the State Superintendent, 1889-90 and 1890-91,* 13.

12. Jackson *Clarion-Ledger,* July 4, 1889.

13. *Report of the State Superintendent, 1891-92 and 1892-93,* 183, 215, 245,

257, 301; Stuart Grayson Noble, *Forty Years of the Public Schools in Mississippi, with Special Reference to the Education of the Negro* (New York, 1918), 108-109.

14. Quoted in *Report of the State Superintendent, 1891-92 and 1892-93,* 236. See also Corinth *Herald,* quoted in Sunflower *Tocsin,* April 10, 1896; Forest *Register,* quoted in Jackson *Clarion-Ledger,* April 25, 1889.

15. Horace Mann Bond, *The Education of the Negro in the American Social Order* (New York, 1934), 98-99; Hamilton, "Mississippi Politics in the Progressive Era," 182.

16. Mississippi *Constitution,* 1890, sec. 206.

17. Horace Mann Bond, "The Cash Value of a Negro Child," *School and Society,* 37 (May 13, 1933), 629; Hamilton, "Mississippi Politics in the Progressive Era," 342ff.

18. Jackson *Weekly Clarion-Ledger,* December 18, 1902. Stone's views were shared by LeRoy Percy and other anti-Vardaman conservatives. See Percy's correspondence to and from Stone, J. S. McNeily, S. S. Calhoon, Pinckney George, A. C. Wharton, and others, box 2, PFP. The speeches and writings of such progressive Mississippi clergy as Bishop Charles B. Galloway and Theodore D. Bratton offer a more idealistic, though less representative, argument to the same effect. See Galloway, *The South and the Negro,* 9-16; Bratton, "The Christian South and Negro Education," *Sewanee Review,* 16 (July, 1908); idem, *Wanted Leaders! A Study of Negro Development* (New York, 1922), 143-172.

19. Meyer Weinberg, *A Chance to Learn: The History of Race and Education in the United States* (Cambridge, Mass., 1977), 49.

20. Richard Kent Smith, "The Economics of Education and Discrimination in the U.S. South: 1870-1910" (Ph.D. diss., University of Wisconsin, 1973), 73.

21. Ibid., 72-79.

22. Mississippi was the first southern state extensively to use convict labor on state-owned farms. In 1910, profits from this source alone approached $180,000 (Grantham, *Southern Progressivism,* 133).

23. Montgomery to Robert Reinhold, April 18, 1904, con. 242, BTW. Much the same argument was made by state Superintendent of Education Henry L. Whitfield (Jackson *Clarion-Ledger,* January 17, 18, 1902; Jackson *Daily Clarion-Ledger,* April 7, May 14, September 3, 1903; West Point *Leader,* August 20, 1903).

24. "The Negro Common School, Mississippi," *Crisis,* 32 (December, 1926), 94.

25. Du Bois, ed., *The Negro Common School,* 91. Other relevant studies include Charles L. Coon, "Public Education and Negro Schools" in *Twelfth Conference for Education in the South, Proceedings* (Atlanta, 1909), 157-167; George W. Cable, "Does the Negro Pay for His Education," *Forum,* 13 (1892), 640-649; Weinberg, *Chance to Learn,* 49-50; Harlan, *Separate and Unequal,* 19; J. Morgan Kousser, "Progressivism—For Middle-Class Whites Only: North

Carolina Education, 1880-1910," *Journal of Southern History,* 46 (May 1980), 169-194.

26. Smith, "Economics of Education and Discrimination," 92-102, 204, 214, 217, 219, 221.

27. Funding patterns varied with community need, but the following representative examples—broken down by race of fund-raiser or source of funding—suggest the extent of black contributions: St. Paul School (Hinds County), $2,800 total cost—$500 from Rosenwald, $400 from public funds, $1,800 from blacks, $100 from whites; Barbee School (Bolivar County), $5,500 total cost—$1,000 from Rosenwald, $1,000 from public funds, $2,600 from blacks, $900 from whites. Very likely some of the moneys raised by blacks came from white contributions. See 1927-1928, "Receipts and Disbursements," Rural School Program files, box 340, JRF.

28. Jackson *Daily News,* January 29, 1924; "The Negro Common School, Mississippi," 96. Of the total cost of Mississippi's Rosenwald schools $1,119,745, or nearly 40 percent, was raised privately at the community level, primarily through black donations, and the remainder through public funds and the Rosenwald Foundation (see Bura Hilbun's annual reports to the fund, Rural School Program files, box 340, JRF; Embree, *Julius Rosenwald Fund,* 23; George Duke Humphrey, "A History of the Public School Funds in Mississippi" [M.A. thesis, University of Chicago, 1931], 64-68).

29. Grisham, "Tupelo," 325-328; Dollard, *Caste and Class in a Southern Town,* 194.

30. Payne, "Black Middle Class in Laurel," 53-55. On the history of black education in Laurel, see also Cleveland Payne, "The History of Oak Park," manuscript [1987], CPC.

31. Flowers to Aubrey Williams, August 19, 1938, State Directors' Reports, Division of Negro Affairs, NYA. For other examples of the taxation of blacks for white school construction see *Southern Frontier,* June, 1942; R. D. Polk to NAACP, April 28, 1937; and Samuel McCormick to Theodore Paige, October 14, 1937, Administrative File, Mississippi Schools, box C-201, NAACP.

32. Press release, Citizens' Mass Convention of the State of Mississippi, May 2, 1923, box C-373, NAACP. Also see other black complaints to the legislature regarding education: Jackson *Clarion-Ledger,* February 23, 28, 1918; Jackson *Daily News,* January 29, 1924; "The Negro Common School, Mississippi," 90-102; Norfolk *Journal and Guide,* June 2, 1928; Resolutions Adopted by the Committee of One Hundred [1934?], JEJ.

33. *Chrisman et al. v. City of Brookhaven,* 70 Miss. 477 (1892).

34. *F. B. Bryant et al. v. Barnes, Tax Collector,* 144 Miss. 732 (1926) and 106 So. 113-116. Black "second taxes" in the financing of Hopewell are described in "Mississippi Building and Equipment Costs," n.d., box 340, JRF.

35. *McFarland et al. v. Goins,* 96 Miss. 67-76 (1909).

36. *Bryant v. Barnes,* 144 Miss. 732 at 747 (1926). See also *Trustees of Walton School et al. v. Board of Supervisors of Covington County,* 115 Miss. 117 (1917); *Barrett et al. v. Cedar Hill Consolidated School,* 123 Miss. 370 (1920).

37. Jackson *Daily News,* January 24, 1924.

38. Editorial, *Mississippi Educational Journal,* 14 (December, 1937), 42.

39. For one variation of Garfield's most memorable aphorism, see John M. Taylor, *Garfield of Ohio: The Available Man* (New York, 1970), 156.

40. William H. Holtzclaw, *Black Man's Burden* (New York, 1915), 94-95. In this instance, and in that documented in note 90 below, Holtzclaw recounted experiences across the state line in his home state of Alabama.

41. P. H. Easom, "Mississippi's Negro Schools," March, 1937, State Directors' Reports, Division of Negro Affairs, NYA; *Report of the State Superintendent, 1935-36 and 1936-37,* 13.

42. See generally, Rural School Program files, 1920-1939, box 340, JRF; Embree, *Julius Rosenwald Fund,* 15, 23; Edwin R. Embree and Julia Waxman, *Investment in People: The Story of the Julius Rosenwald Fund* (New York, 1949), passim; Alfred Gilbert Belles, "The Julius Rosenwald Fund: Efforts in Race Relations, 1928-1948" (Ph.D. diss., Vanderbilt University, 1972), 31-58; Doxey A. Wilkerson, *Special Problems of Negro Education* (Washington, D.C., 1939), 31-33. Except where otherwise indicated, I have relied on Wilkerson for comparative southern school data.

43. Convicted of embezzling funds designated for nonexistent "ghost schools," Bura Hilbun was sentenced to five years in prison. Chicago *Defender,* December 17, 24, 1932; Pittsburgh *Courier,* December 24, 1932. See also materials on the Hilbun investigation, box 340, JRF.

44. "A Classification of Negro School Buildings, Public and Private, in Mississippi," Statistics, box 87, JRF; *Report of the State Superintendent, 1943-44 and 1944-45,* 21.

45. *Report of a Study of the Education for Negroes in Sunflower County, Mississippi,* Bureau of Educational Research, University of Mississippi, March, 1950, 9. See also "Rural Education Studies: Sunflower County" [1939], box 552, JRF.

46. *Southern Frontier,* March, 1940; December, 1940. See also descriptions of county schools in 1912 and 1948: Bailey, *Race Orthodoxy in the South,* 273-286; and Willie Morris, *Yazoo: Integration in a Deep-South Town* (New York, 1971), 17.

47. *Report of the State Superintendent, 1933-34 and 1934-35,* 41; Easom, "Mississippi's Negro Schools"; and idem, "Some Facts about Negro Schools in Mississippi," State Directors' Reports, Division of Negro Affairs, NYA.

48. "General Description of Elementary Schools for Negroes," *Mississippi Education Journal,* 11 (January, 1935), 67. See also "Summary of Facts of Negro Schools in 52 Counties by Jeanes Teachers" [1941], box 299, JRF.

49. *Southern Frontier,* March, 1940 (all quotations). See also "Schools Today," WPA History: Chickasaw County.

50. *Report of the State Superintendent, 1947-48 and 1948-49,* 17, 43. See also Jennings B. George, *The Influence of Court Decisions in Shaping School Policies in Mississippi* (Nashville, 1933), 253; and Florence D. Alexander, "The Education of Negroes in Mississippi," *Journal of Negro Education,* 16 (Summer, 1947), 375.

51. In 1916, Colored High School in Yazoo City had forty-nine students in three grades. Thomas Jessie Jones believed that "there are probably 8 or 10 other public schools enrolling a few pupils above the elementary grades" in Mississippi. U.S., Bureau of Education, *Negro Education,* 1: 41-42, 408; 2: 336, 338.

52. By 1940 there were five black agricultural high schools. *Report of the State Superintendent, 1925-26 and 1926-27,* 36, 38; *1941-42 and 1942-43,* 37. On urban black school construction in the 1920s, see Bura Hilbun to Francis Shepardson, January 30, 1925, box 299, JRF.

53. *Report of the State Superintendent, 1933-34 and 1934-35,* 43; *1939-40 and 1940-41,* 16; Charles H. Wilson, *Education for Negroes in Mississippi since 1910* (Boston, 1947), 63, 77; and Ambrose Caliver, *Secondary Education for Negroes,* U.S., Office of Education Bulletin 1932, no. 17 (Washington, D.C., 1933), 28-29.

54. The state made no effort to accredit black high schools until 1932. The regionally accredited schools were Alcorn, Southern Christian Institute, and Tougaloo. Southern Association of Colleges and Secondary Schools, "List of Approved Colleges and Secondary Schools for Negro Youth, 1940-1941," box 87, JRF.

55. P. H. Easom, "The Greatest Education Need in Mississippi Today," January, 1940, box 299, JRF; Noble, *Forty Years of the Public Schools,* 83; *Report of the State Superintendent, 1889-90 and 1890-91,* 202, 206, 279; *1929-30 and 1930-31,* 59; Bullock, *History of Negro Education,* 182.

56. Johnson, *From the Driftwood of Bayou Pierre,* 25 (first quotation); Johnson, *Growing Up in the Black Belt,* 107 (second quotation).

57. Harrison, *Piney Woods School,* 22; Ambrose Caliver, *Education of Negro Teachers: A National Survey,* U.S., Bureau of Education Bulletin 1933, no. 10 (6 vols., Washington, D.C., 1933), 4: 14; *Report of the State Superintendent, 1921-22 and 1922-23,* 8, 79, 80; *1939-40 and 1940-41,* 22; *1947-48 and 1948-49,* 35; *New South,* 2 (March, 1947), 15; Joseph E. Gibson et al., *Mississippi Study of Higher Education, 1945* (Jackson, 1945), 324-325.

58. Mississippi State Department of Education, *Statistical Data and School Census, 1954-1955* (n.p., n.d.), 21; William P. McClure, *Financing Public Education in Mississippi,* University of Mississippi Studies in Education, no. 1 (n.p., 1948), 16; Wilkerson, *Special Problems of Negro Education,* 23.

59. See, for example, nearly any issue of *Mississippi Educational Journal,* published monthly by the MATCS since 1924; Cleopatra D. Thompson, *The History of the Mississippi Teachers Association* (Washington, D.C., 1973), 12-15, 40-47, 97-101; and MEA, *Report of the Committee on Improvement of Negro Education, November 28, 1940* (n.p., n.d.), in box 168, CIC.

60. Although Alcorn offered programs in agriculture education, it alone among Mississippi's public colleges had no department of education. See S. L. Smith to W. B. Harrell, March 19, 1929, Projects, folder 8, box 156, JRF; Arthur J. Klein, ed., *Survey of Negro Colleges and Universities* (Washington, D.C., 1929). See also, Noble, *Forty Years of Public Education,* 86; Caliver,

Education of Negro Teachers, 4: 3; *Report of the State Superintendent, 1939-40 and 1940-41,* 16; *1955-56 and 1956-57,* 40.

61. See particularly, H. M. Ivy to J. A. Ellard, June 11, 1939, box 254, JRF; but also Alfred H. Stone to editor, Jackson *Weekly Clarion-Ledger,* December 18, 1902; Biloxi *Daily Herald,* March 4, 1904; Noble, *Forty Years of Public Education,* 7-8; Frank D. Alexander, "Cultural Reconnaissance Survey of Coahoma County, Mississippi," December, 1944, Project Files, entry 33, BAE; *Report of the State Superintendent, 1957-58 and 1958-59,* 20.

62. For teachers' salaries during the period after 1890, see National Education Association War and Peace Fund, "Mississippi Must Face These Facts," box 87, JRF; M. E. Fritz, *Our Public Schools: A Report Showing the Unjust Distribution of the Public School Funds* (Lexington, Miss., 1891), 35-36; Noble, *Forty Years of Public Education,* 79-82; and Wilson, *Education for Negroes in Mississippi,* 243-244, 584-585.

63. Wilson, *Education for Negroes in Mississippi,* 585; Jackson *Daily News,* January 24, 1924; "The Negro Common School, Mississippi," 94; *Report of the State Superintendent, 1905-06 and 1906-07,* 40; *1933-34 and 1934-35,* 41.

64. In functional terms, the census bureau's figures undoubtedly understate the problem for both races. See, e.g., the estimates in Davis et al., *Deep South,* 418, and the World War II armed forces induction-refusal rates in "Statistics, Negro Education," undated, box 87, JRF.

65. The last state to adopt a compulsory education act, Mississippi became the first to repeal following the Supreme Court school desegregation ruling of 1954. The attendance law of 1918 was amended in 1920; the 1920 statute excluded many blacks, for counties could elect not to abide by it and families living more than two and a half miles from a school were exempt (*Laws,* 1920, chaps. 156, 216; Hamilton, "Mississippi Politics in the Progressive Era," 349-353).

66. In 1936-1937, when the average school term for rural blacks in Mississippi was still only 100 days, average rural black terms elsewhere in the South ranged from 120 days in Alabama and Louisiana to 165 days in Florida (Easom, "Mississippi's Negro Schools").

67. Nor did the crash "equalization" program then just beginning greatly expand black educational opportunities. See *Report of the State Superintendent, 1963-64 and 1964-65,* 151.

68. Wilkerson, *Special Problems of Negro Education,* 19.

69. For example, see Harvey Wish, "Negro Education and the Progressive Movement," *Journal of Negro History,* 49 (July, 1964), 188-189 (Vardaman quotation). See also Powdermaker, *After Freedom,* 300-303; Dollard, *Caste and Class in a Southern Town,* 201.

70. Bailey, *Race Orthodoxy in the South,* 278; Easom to G. M. Reynolds, February 26, 1940, box 299, JRF.

71. The place of education in the black Mississippian's imagination is suggested by Powdermaker, *After Freedom,* 299-322; Johnson, *Growing Up in the Black Belt,* 90; Reddix, *Voice Crying in the Wilderness,* 58; and "Preliminary

Study of Negro Youth," November 26, 1941, 10, Project Files 1440-45, Division of Program Surveys, BAE.

72. Quoted in Johnson, *Growing Up in the Black Belt,* 119.

73. Both quotations are from Davis et al., *Deep South,* 420.

74. Quoted in George C. Osborn, "John Sharp Williams Becomes a United States Senator," *Journal of Southern History,* 6 (1940), 225. After cutting an appropriation for Alcorn College, Vardaman said: "I am not anxious even to see the Negro turned into a skilled mechanic" (Baker, *Following the Color Line,* 248).

75. *Report of the State Superintendent, 1915-16 and 1916-17,* 17. For similar expressions see, ibid., *1923-24 and 1924-25,* 19; Lewis E. Long, *The Rural Tax Situation in Choctaw County, Mississippi,* Mississippi Agriculture Experiment Station Bulletin 282 (August, 1930), 41.

76. A fuller analysis of the white educator's role in the shaping of black school policy and programs would necessarily credit the enlightened efforts of such liberal school reformers as P. H. Easom, who became state supervisor for Negro schools in 1932. Easom was a tireless advocate of black education who was deeply frustrated by a system he clearly thought to be both short-sighted and unjust. His personal correspondence to trusted allies, unremarkably, is more revealing than his public expressions (see, e.g., Easom to George M. Reynolds, January 22, February 20, 1940, box 254, JRF). Although probably more traditional in his social values, State Superintendent Willard F. Bond (1916-1939) also sought more for black schoolchildren than white public opinion would allow (see Bond, *I Had a Friend: An Autobiography* [Kansas City, 1958], 123-131).

77. M. V. O'Shea et al., *Public Education in Mississippi: Report of a Study of the Public Education System* (Jackson, [1925]), 325-336, 353-354. See also *Report of the State Superintendent, 1939-40 and 1940-41,* 16; Madison County *Herald,* October 3, 1919, reprinted in WPA History: Madison County; Bond, *Education of the Negro,* 102; State Department of Education, "Some Pertinent Reasons for Better School Facilities for Mississippi's Colored Population," August, 1938, box 299, JRF.

78. Donald Spivey, *Schooling for the New Slavery: Black Industrial Education, 1868-1915* (Westport, Conn., 1978).

79. Of all federal vocational education funds sent to Mississippi, the annual black share for the years from 1928 to 1935 ranged from 2.6 percent in 1931-1932 to 17.4 percent in 1934-1935 (Ambrose Caliver, *Vocational Education and Guidance of Negroes: Report of a Survey Conducted by the Office of Education* [Washington, D.C., 1937], 127). See also Sam Cobbins, "Industrial Education for Black Americans in Mississippi, 1862-1965" (Ph.D. diss., Mississippi State University, 1975); David A. Lane, Jr., "The Development of the Present Relationship of the Federal Government to Negro Education," *Journal of Negro Education,* 7 (July, 1938), 277; Charles Wilbur Florence, "The Federally-Aided Program of Vocational Teacher Training in Negro Schools," ibid., 292-302; Charles H. Thompson, "The Federal Program of Vocational Education in Negro Schools," ibid., 307.

80. Easom, "Mississippi's Negro Schools"; *Report of the State Superintendent, 1921-22 and 1922-23,* 74-75, 79; *1939-40 and 1940-41,* 17.

81. C. O. Brannen, *Relations of Land Tenure to Plantation Organization,* USDA Bulletin no. 1269 (October 18, 1924). Too often county superintendents acceded to landlord demands that plantation schools be taught by poorly educated field hands, thus assuring, as Easom believed, that many plantation blacks remained "totally illiterate" (P. H. Easom and J. A. Travis to J. C. Dixon, May 29, 1939, box 299, JRF). But see also a description of what may have been a model plantation school built in the 1940s: Mrs. Early C. Ewing and Mrs. Fred Stout to Hodding Carter, October 18, 1954, box 26, DPL.

82. Cohn, *Where I Was Born,* 251 (first quotation); Davis et al., *Deep South,* 419 (second quotation).

83. Holtzclaw, *Black Man's Burden,* 75-76.

84. Edith McMillan, "In Darkest Mississippi," *Opportunity,* 1 (October, 1923), 294 (quotation); Robert Fulton Holtzclaw, *William Henry Holtzclaw,* 55-63. The latter study is based largely on notes left by the author's father, William Henry Holtzclaw, in preparation for a sequel to *Black Man's Burden.*

85. Laurence C. Jones, narrative biography, pt. 1 [1973], JSU; Harrison, *Piney Woods School,* 29-30 (first quotation), 35, 109; Beth Day, *The Little Professor of Piney Woods: The Story of Professor Laurence Jones* (New York, 1955), 16-17 (second quotation).

86. Telephone interview with Alcee L. Johnson, October 16, 1986. See also Alcee L. Johnson, oral history, June 13, 1975, JSU.

87. Robert G. Sherer, *Subordination or Liberation? The Development and Conflicting Theories of Black Education in Nineteenth Century Alabama* (University, Ala., 1977), 134-148.

88. The school was operated for a time by Battle's wife. Following World War II it became Okolona College. It closed in 1965. See Holtzclaw, *Black Magnolias,* 117-118; Mosley, *Negro in Mississippi History,* 80-81; WPA History: Chickasaw County; Wilson, *Education for Negroes in Mississippi,* 458-463; Thompson, *History of the Mississippi Teachers Association,* 62; interview with Alcee L. Johnson.

89. Sam H. Franklin, Jr., to Trustees, January 17, 1938; March 8, 1938, Delta Cooperative Farm Materials, box 4, Reinhold Niebuhr Papers, LC. The Delta Farm school offered eight months of education, only four of which were supported by public funds (Daniels, *A Southerner Discovers the South,* 150).

90. Holtzclaw, *Black Man's Burden,* 29-31. As noted above, Holtzclaw's recollection in this instance is of an Alabama boyhood.

91. Charles H. Wilson, *God! Make Me a Man: A Biographical Sketch of Dr. Sidney Dillion* [sic] *Redmond* (Boston, 1950), 15-16, 23, 27-29, 46. This volume is based on Redmond's unfinished autobiography.

92. Mary Barr, oral history, July 1, 1971, MHC (first and last quotations); Mattie Lou Bogan, oral history, July 31, 1971, MHC (second quotation); Daisy M. Green, oral history, MDAH (third quotation). See also Dorothy Boulding Ferebee, *The 1938 Mississippi Health Project,* Alpha Kappa Alpha Fourth Annual Report (December 1, 1938), unpaginated; Johnson, *Growing Up in*

the Black Belt, 109; Dollard, *Caste and Class in a Southern Town,* 195-196; WPA History: Humphreys County; "A Tougaloo Teacher in a Rural School," *American Missionary,* new ser., 15 (April, 1923), 39.

93. In 1916 Thomas Jessie Jones fixed the black private school enrollees at 7,044 with 6,278 of them at the elementary level. U.S., Bureau of Education, *Negro Education,* Bulletin 1916, 2: 335.

94. Initially some students worked all day and attended school only at night. At Piney Woods, all students divided the daylight hours equally between work and class, and studied at night. See Harrison, *Piney Woods School,* 67; Joseph H. Armstrong, oral history, n.d., JSU; William H. Holtzclaw, "The Growth of the Normal and Industrial School," *Colored American,* 11 (August, 1906), 115-118.

95. Quotations are from Jones, *Piney Woods and Its Story* (New York, 1922), 133-135. See also Ruth M. Harris, " 'We Come to Git Educated,' " *Liberty Magazine,* undated reprint; and Clarence O. Baker, *Trading Molasses for Learning,* undated pamphlet, both in box 148, JRF. For similar patterns of in-kind payment at Prentiss Institute, see Wilson, *Education for Negroes in Mississippi,* 470.

96. Quoted in Harrison, *Piney Woods School,* 49. See also Ada Adams, oral history, June, 1973, JSU; Lenzie Braddy, oral history, September 15, 1978, JSU.

97. Helen E. Pfeifer, *Something of a Faith: A Brief History of Mary Holmes College* (West Point, Miss., 1982), 7; Holtzclaw, *Black Magnolias,* 9, 100, 114; Wharton, *Negroes in Mississippi,* 250-251.

98. Jones, narrative biography, pt. 1; Rosie Bell Brooks (member of Jones's first class), oral history, September 6, 1978, JSU; Leola Hughes, oral history, September 5, 1978, JSU; Jones, *Piney Woods and Its Story,* 56, 67; Leslie Harper Purcell, *Miracle in Mississippi: Laurence C. Jones of Piney Woods* (New York, 1956), 30-31.

99. George Hall, oral history, April 22, 1973, JSU. Jones and other black Mississippi schoolmasters did, in time, receive modest local, white assistance, as they gratefully acknowledged (Jones, *The Bottom Rail,* 45-55; H. D. Slatter, "Noble Work in the Black Belt," *Alexander's Magazine,* 1 [May 15, 1905], 19).

100. Holtzclaw, *Black Magnolias,* 118-119.

101. William H. Holtzclaw, *Extract from an Address Delivered at St. Mary's Church* (Jackson, Miss., [1905]); Holtzclaw, *Black Man's Burden,* 102 and passim; Slatter, "Noble Work in the Black Belt," 19; Emma C. Penny, "A Light in the Black Belt," *Alexander's Magazine,* 4 (November 15, 1907), 25.

102. Holtzclaw, *William Henry Holtzclaw,* 85.

103. Klein, ed., *Survey of Negro Colleges and Universities,* 440-447; Holtzclaw to Emmett Scott, April 30, 1906; August 24, 1907, regular correspondence, cons. 33 and 36, BTW; Mayme O. Brown, "Mississippi Mud," *Crisis,* 43 (May, 1936), 142; "Utica Normal and Industrial Institute," *Colored American,* 15 (January, 1909), 653-654. According to the estimate of Jessie Mosley, "a third of the operating expenses" of Prentiss Institute were raised by its Jubilee

Singers (Mosley, *Negro in Mississippi History,* 82). For an assessment of the financial importance of the Cotton Blossom Singers to Piney Woods School, see Laurence C. Jones, *The Spirit of Piney Woods* (New York, 1931), 80-82. See also Henry Enck, "Black Self-Help in the Progressive Era: The 'Northern Campaigns' of Smaller Southern Black Industrial Schools, 1900-1915," *Journal of Negro History,* 61 (January, 1976), 76-87; *Rural Plea* (Prentiss Institute), April, 1929, JEJ.

104. Arnie Copper, " 'We Rise upon the Structure We Ourselves Have Builded': William H. Holtzclaw and Utica Institute, 1903-1915," *Journal of Mississippi History,* 42 (February, 1985), 32; McMillan, "In Darkest Mississippi," 294-297; telephone interview with R. Fulton Holtzclaw, October 16, 1986; Holtzclaw, *William Henry Holtzclaw,* 89-95, 136.

105. Ella Carter Jackson, oral history, March 2, 1974, JSU; Eva Weathersby, oral history, June, 1973, JSU; Johnson, interview with author, October 16, 1986; Holtzclaw, interview with author, October 16, 1986.

106. Reddix, *Voice Crying in the Wilderness,* 142. For the discriminatory effects of northern foundations on black higher learning, see the works by Bullock, Grantham, and Harlan cited in note 6 above; and August Meier and Elliot Rudwick, *Black History and the Historical Profession, 1915-1980* (Urbana, 1987), chap. 1.

107. See, e.g., Joe M. Richardson, *A History of Fisk University, 1865-1946* (University, Ala., 1980).

108. Klein, ed., *Survey of Negro Colleges and Universities,* 418-428; Robert Jenkins, "The Development of Black Higher Education in Mississippi, 1865-1920," *Journal of Mississippi History,* 45 (November, 1983), 274-275; American Missionary Association, *Historical Sketch of Tougaloo University* (n.p., [1909]); "Tougaloo College," WPA History: Hinds County; Campbell and Rogers, *Mississippi: The View from Tougaloo,* app.

109. U.S., Bureau of Education, *Negro Education,* 1: 121. Although valuable, Jones's study must be used cautiously, for this Phelps-Stokes Fund official clearly preferred industrial to academic training for blacks. See Meier and Rudwick, *Black History and the Historical Profession,* 17, 37-43; James M. McPherson, "White Liberals and Black Power in Negro Education, 1865-1915," *American Historical Review,* 75 (June, 1970), 1378n.

110. B. Baldwin Dansby, *History of Jackson College: A Typical Story of the Survival of Education among Negroes in the South* (Jackson, 1953), 63; Wilson, *Education for Negroes,* 514.

111. "Stringer University," WPA History: Coahoma County, box 1; Hood, *The Negro at Mound Bayou;* Slater Fund Trustees, *Reference List of Southern Colored Schools,* Occasional Paper, no. 20 (n.p., 1918).

112. Ina C. Brown et al., *National Survey of Higher Education for Negroes,* 2 vols. (Washington, D.C., 1942-1943), 82; *Report of the State Superintendent, 1943-44 and 1944-45,* 21.

113. Wharton, *Negro in Mississippi,* 255; Southern Association of Colleges and Secondary Schools, *Approved List of Colleges and Universities for Negro Youth* (n.p., [1935]); Charles Alexander, "Down in Mississippi," *Alexander's*

Magazine, 6 (February, 1909), 180; Charles B. Galloway, *An Address Delivered at the Fiftieth Annual Meeting of the American Missionary Association* (n.p., n.d.), copy in MDAH; John E. Brewton, *Higher Education in Mississippi: A Survey Report* (Jackson, 1954), 133; Holtzclaw, *Black Magnolias,* 104; Campbell and Rogers, *Mississippi: The View from Tougaloo,* 131.

114. Early administrative and financial problems can be examined in the correspondence between Tougaloo administrators and teachers and the AMA. See, e.g., L. A. Darling to M. E. Strieby, May 4, 1876 (reel 3), AMA. AMA records pertaining to Tougaloo for the period 1879-1939 apparently have not survived.

115. Luella Miner, a white student and the daughter of the school treasurer, graduated from Tougaloo normal department in 1879 (*Tougaloo News,* January, 1944). The college department graduated the first white student in 1964 (Campbell and Rogers, *Mississippi: The View from Tougaloo,* 14, 70).

116. See especially, John Salter, *Jackson, Mississippi: An American Chronicle of Struggle and Schism* (New York, 1979), passim; but also John Dittmer, oral history, August 21, 1980, MDAH; Campbell and Rogers, *Mississippi: The View from Tougaloo,* 196-217.

117. Early local black agitation for the employment of black faculty is described in N. Chase to Strieby, May 31, 1877 (reel 3), AMA. On the larger black struggle for black faculty and administration in mission schools, see McPherson, "White Liberals and Black Power," 1357-1386.

118. Scribia was for college students; the Phillis Wheatley Club was its grammar-school counterpart (Lillian Voorhees, "Student Activities at Tougaloo College," *American Missionary,* new ser., 17 [May, 1925], 62-64). Except as indicated otherwise, this analysis of interracialism at Tougaloo is indebted to Campbell and Rogers, *Mississippi: The View from Tougaloo,* 14, 104-105, 116-118, 132-135, 164-187, and 235 (quotation).

119. August Meier, "Race Relations at Negro Colleges," *Crisis,* 65 (November, 1958), 535-543 (quotation at 537); August Meier and Chester Slocum, "Tougaloo College Revisited," *Unitarian Christian Register,* 130 (November, 1951), 29-30. On the question of missionary paternalism, compare "First Impressions and Christmas Recess at Tougaloo University," *American Missionary,* 61 (February, 1907), 45-46; and Helen Griffith, "The Rich Years of Retirement," *Mt. Holyoke Alumnae Quarterly,* 39 (Winter, 1956), 142-144.

120. *American Missionary,* June, 1881, quoted in Campbell, "History of Tougaloo," 37 (quotation). On Tougaloo's role as a teacher-training institution, see *American Missionary,* new ser., 6 (May, 1912), 94-96; new ser., 10 (June, 1918), 163-164; new ser., 18 (May, 1926), 70-71.

121. "A Day at Tougaloo," *American Missionary,* 42 (July, 1888), 188-189 (quotation); "What Tougaloo Is," ibid., new ser., 8 (February, 1917), 606-607.

122. On student academic preference, see William T. Holmes, "Tougaloo—The Door Opener," *American Missionary,* new ser., 15 (September 1923), 287-288. On the institution's early industrial emphasis and its emergence as a liberal arts college, see William T. Holmes, "After Twelve Years," *American Missionary,* 79 (January, 1925), 398-399; Cobbins, "Industrial Education," 40-

41; August Meier, "The Beginnings of Industrial Education in Negro Schools," *Midwest Quarterly,* 7 (Spring, 1955), 34-35; Campbell and Rogers, *Mississippi: The View from Tougaloo,* 129, 140, 175-176; Edward Mayes, *History of Education in Mississippi* (Washington, D.C., 1899), 259-260; Meier, *Negro Thought in America,* 88, 91, 96-97.

123. Klein, ed., *Survey of Negro Colleges and Universities,* 447-457. See also a similar assessment by a Tougaloo administrator, Henry W. Cobb, "Some Highlights of My Years at Tougaloo, 1919-1944," *Tougaloo News,* 54 (January, 1944), 10-11.

124. Klein, ed., *Survey of Negro Colleges and Universities,* 447-457; Campbell and Rogers, *Mississippi: The View from Tougaloo,* 130, 135, 179.

125. Editorial, Jackson *Daily Clarion-Ledger,* March 17, 1918. Cf. the description in Dunbar Rowland, *Mississippi: Heart of the South* (Chicago, 1925), 2: 504.

126. Horace Mann Bond, "Evolution and Present Status of Negro Higher Education and Professional Education in the United States," *Journal of Negro Education,* 17 (Summer, 1948), 229 (quotation); Harris, *Day of the Carpetbagger,* 347-350; Roy V. Scott, "Land Grants for Higher Education in Mississippi: A Survey," *Agricultural History,* 43 (July, 1969), 365; Samuel H. Shannon, "The Black Land-Grant Colleges: Problems of Identity on the Margins of Higher Education" (paper presented to NEH Fellows in Residence, April, 1976, University of Michigan, Ann Arbor), 4-8.

127. Tougalooans like to point to Alcorn's seventh President William H. Lanier (1899-1905), who reportedly gained "thorough mastery of Latin, Greek [and] Hebrew" at Tougaloo, and then attended Oberlin, Roger Williams, and Fisk colleges. See *Tougaloo News,* 54 (January, 1944), 34; Richardson, *History of Fisk University,* 44-45; and George Sewell, "Alcorn A & M: Pioneer in Black Pride," *Crisis,* 79 (April, 1972), 121-126.

128. W. Milan Davis, *Pushing Forward: A History of Alcorn A & M College* (Okolona, Miss., 1938), 17-18; Gibson et al., *Mississippi Study of Higher Education,* 318; Board of Trustees, Mississippi Institutions of Higher Learning, *Mississippi Study of Higher Education,* pt. 4; *Negro Education* (Jackson, 1945), 2-8, 35-36, passim.

129. *Report of State Superintendent, 1893-94 and 1894-95,* 436; *Biennial Report of Alcorn Agricultural and Mechanical College, 1912-1913* (Nashville, 1913), 8, 18 (hereinafter cited as *Report of Alcorn A & M College*); ibid., *1916-1917,* 6; *1919-1921,* 9-10, 13; *1921-1923,* 4.

130. In 1950, Mississippi's per capita land-grant expenditures for blacks was $379 compared to $1,699 for whites. (Joint Committee of the National Education Association and the American Teachers Association, *Progress of the Education of Negroes, 1870-1950* [Washington, D.C., 1954], pt. 2: 41). On the relative distribution of federal higher education funds in Mississippi see John W. Davis, "The Participation of Negro Land-Grant Colleges in Permanent Federal Education Funds," *Journal of Negro Education,* 7 (July, 1938), 289-291.

131. H. M. Ivy to J. A. Ellard, June 11, 1939, box 254, JRF (first quotation);

Gibson, *Mississippi Study of Higher Education,* 318 (second quotation); Brewton, *Higher Education in Mississippi,* 136 (third quotation). See also Jay T. Smith, Sr., "Origin and Development of Industrial Education at Alcorn Agricultural and Mechanical College" (Ed.D. diss., University of Missouri—Columbia, 1971).

132. Gibson, *Mississippi Study of Higher Education,* 318-319, 333, 340. See also Davis, "The Participation of Negro Land-Grant Colleges," 283.

133. Klein, ed., *Survey of Negro Colleges and Universities,* 404-418; *Report of Alcorn A & M College, 1926-1927,* 9 (president's quotation); *1905-1907,* 32; *1909-1911,* 7; *1916-1917,* 4.

134. *Report of Alcorn A & M College, 1926-1927,* 6; *1928-1929,* 7, 8; "The Negro Common School, Mississippi," 98; "Along the Color Line," *Crisis,* 37 (March, 1930), 97; Davis, *Pushing Forward,* 47-48.

135. S. L. Smith to Rosenwald Fund, February 6, 1932, box 146, JRF (quotation). The background is developed in the following correspondence in the same file: Bura Hilbun to S. L. Smith, May 2, 1928; Smith to Hilbun, May 9, 1928; P. H. Easom to Smith, July 5, 1929; September 14, 1931; Rowan to Smith, September 21, 1931; Smith to Rowan, February 6, 1932. Although Alcorn's financial condition worsened during the depression, the school knew little but hard times after 1875. See for example an appraisal by the secretary of Alcorn's board of trustees in *Report of Alcorn A & M, 1926-1927,* 3-13.

136. Evers, *Evers,* 153.

137. Melerson Guy Dunham, *The Centennial History of Alcorn Agricultural and Mechanical College* (Hattiesburg, 1971), xiii, 151.

138. E. H. Triplett (1896-1899) was a notable exception. See Davis, *Pushing Forward,* 31-32; Dunham, *Centennial History of Alcorn,* 41-42.

139. Bond, "Evolution and Present Status of Negro Higher Education," 228.

140. Dunham, *Centennial History of Alcorn,* 85-175. "Big Bill," younger brother of Andrew "Rube" Foster (president of the Negro League and onetime manager of the Giants), made the Alcorn Braves team when he was thirteen (sixth grade). From 1925 until his graduation from Alcorn in 1931, he pitched for both the Alcorn Braves and the Chicago American Giants. "We had a whole team [at Alcorn] made up of professional players," he recently noted. Foster coached at Alcorn during the 1960s (Jackson *Clarion-Ledger,* August 14, 1977).

141. "To Governor Paul B. Johnson, Jr., and the Members of the Mississippi Legislature," resolution [1940], administrative file, Mississippi Schools, box C-201, NAACP. For similar appraisals by earlier state black leadership conventions, see: Jackson *Daily Clarion-Ledger,* February 23, 28, 1918; "Committee on Address," press release, May 2, 1923, box C-373, NAACP; Jackson *Daily News,* January 29, 1924; Norfolk *Journal and Guide,* June 2, 1928.

142. *Report of the State Superintendent, 1939-40 and 1940-41,* 16; Dansby, *History of Jackson College,* 142, 155.

143. Quotations are from Reddix, *Voice Crying in the Wilderness,* 137.

144. Dansby, *History of Jackson College,* 256-577; B. Baldwin Dansby, oral

history, January 5, 1971, MDAH; Lelia Gaston Rhodes, *Jackson State University: The First Hundred Years, 1877-1977* (Jackson, 1979), 35-36.

145. Dansby, oral history, January 5, 1971, MDAH (Bilbo quotation); Dansby, *History of Jackson College,* 150-156; Reddix, *Voice Crying in the Wilderness,* 137ff.; Bond, *I Had a Friend,* 126-127; Fred G. Wales, "Jackson College, Mississippi," May 8, 1940, box 254 JRF (Easom quotation).

146. Edwin R. Embree to J. A. Ellard, July 2, 1940, box 255, JRF; Wales, "Jackson College, Mississippi."

147. See generally, Jackson College files, boxes 254, 255 (and particularly Embree to Lessing J. Rosenwald, June 5, 1940; and "Resolution to Board of Trustees," April, 1942, box 255), JRF.

Chapter 4. Farmers without Land

1. Myrdal, *American Dilemma,* 1: 237.

2. Rawick, ed., *Miss. Narr,* 8(3), 1130.

3. Quoted in James Howell Street, *Look Away! A Dixie Notebook* (New York, 1936), 41.

4. These "insurgent Negroes" were later captured by Confederate troops. Claude F. Oubre, *Forty Acres and a Mule: The Freedmen's Bureau and Black Land Ownership* (Baton Rouge, 1978), 182; James S. Allen, *Reconstruction: The Battle for Democracy, 1865-1876* (New York, 1937), 43.

5. Quoted in Leon F. Litwack, *Been in the Storm So Long: The Aftermath of Slavery* (New York, 1979), 399-400.

6. Wharton, *Negro in Mississippi,* 59; Edward Magdol, *A Right to the Land: Essays on the Freedmen's Community* (Westport, Conn., 1977), 141, 144, 216.

7. Wharton, *Negro in Mississippi,* 61.

8. Land tenure figures published in the 1890 agriculture census are not fully comparable to the figures for the decennia thereafter, and are therefore not included in Tables 4.1 and 4.2. In 1890, Bureau of Census enumerators counted farm proprietors; beginning in 1900, enumerators counted farms. The figures for 1890 are as follows: 160,800 total farm proprietors; 87,800 black farm proprietors (54.6 percent of all proprietors); 60,600 total farm owners; 11,500 black farm owners (19 percent of all farm owners); 100,300 total tenants; 76,300 black tenants (76 percent of all tenants). According to these figures, 86.9 percent of all black farm proprietors were tenants and 13.1 percent were owners. Unless otherwise identified, all agriculture statistics are those of the United States Census of Agriculture for the years indicated.

9. "Textual Discussion of Problem Area Map of Mississippi," November 1, 1934, 27-28, Project Files, Land Tenure section, BAE (quotation). The cropland percentage for the all-Delta counties is based on 1929 census data. The percentage of land owned by whites in Bolivar County, probably a conservative estimate, is based on a figure derived by dividing the number of acres farmed by black full and part owners into the total acres of farmland.

10. The four counties were George, Greene, Harrison, and Stone. By con-

trast, the figures for selected plantation counties in 1940 were: Bolivar and Quitman, five in 100; Leflore and Sunflower, less than two in 100.

11. Woodward, *Origins of the New South,* 217; Lynch, *Reminiscences,* xxvii-xxviii, 384; *John R. Lynch,* Subject File, MDAH. See also the example of August Mazique of Adams County: Mosley, *Negro in Mississippi History,* 34-35.

12. Susan Dabney Smedes, *Memorials of a Southern Planter* (Baltimore, 1888), 313-314, quoted in Wharton, *Negro in Mississippi,* 42.

13. Histories of the Montgomerys' tenure at Davis Bend include Currie, *Enclave,* 83-144; and Hermann, *Pursuit of a Dream,* 109-216.

14. Pittsburgh *Courier,* September 20, 1912; "Mississippi Farm Empire," *Ebony* (February, 1951), 31-34; Sewell and Dwight, *Mississippi Black History Makers,* 187.

15. The total number, of course, was never large. In 1950 there were only ninety-nine black owner-operators of 500 or more acres (Lewis Jones, "The Negro Farmer," *Journal of Negro Education,* 22 [Summer, 1953], 329).

16. See the releases of the USDA Production and Marketing Administration, Field Service Branch, Little Rock, Ark., "The Door of Opportunity: Success Stories, Negro Farmers" (1949), "Success Stories of Negro Farmers" (1951, 1952, 1953), "Negroes" file, SAg. For other examples of substantial black landownership see Powdermaker, *After Freedom,* 104, 106; John A. Lomax, *Adventures of a Ballad Hunter* (New York, 1947), 214; Davis et al., *Deep South,* 276; "Along the Color Line," *Crisis,* 36 (March, 1929), 89; WPA Histories: DeSoto and Leflore Counties; "Mississippi's Most Controversial Negro," *Our World,* 10 (June, 1955), 30-37.

17. Alfred Holt Stone, "The Negro in the Yazoo-Mississippi Delta," *Publications of the American Economic Association,* 3 (1902), 237-238, 251-252.

18. Quotations are from Jackson *Evening News,* February 15, 1907. See also Holtzclaw, *Black Man's Burden,* 130-131; Charles Banks to "The Negro Farmer," [1908], con. 38, BTW; *Report of the Fifteenth Annual Convention of the National Negro Business League Held at Muskogee, Oklahoma, August 19-21, 1914* (n.p., n.d.), con. 1094, BTW.

19. Finch, *Mississippi Negro Ramblings,* 221 ("95%" quotation); Holtzclaw, "Present Status of the Negro Farmer in Mississippi," 343; Holtzclaw, *Black Man's Burden,* 130, 136-141; Enck, "Black Self-Help in the Progressive Era," 82; Earl W. Crosby, "The Roots of Black Agricultural Extension Work," *Historian,* 39 (February, 1977), 241 ("missionaries" quotation).

20. Rupert B. Vance, *Human Factors in Cotton Culture: A Study in the Social Geography of the American South* (Chapel Hill, 1929), 89.

21. For opposing interpretations, see Alfred Holt Stone, "The Negro Farmer in the Mississippi Delta," *Southern Workman* (October, 1903), 460; and Robert Higgs, *Competition and Coercion: Blacks in the American Economy, 1865-1914* (London, 1977), 51-53, 69-70. On declining black landownership in the region generally, see Manning Marable, "The Politics of Black Land Tenure, 1877-1915," *Agricultural History,* 53 (January, 1979), 142-152.

22. Whitelaw Reid, *After the War: A Southern Tour. May 1, 1865, to May*

1, 1866 (New York, 1866), 564-565. See also the testimony of Cornelius McBride, quoted in Roger L. Ransom and Richard Sutch, *One Kind of Freedom: The Economic Consequences of Emancipation* (London, 1977), 87; and Wharton, *Negro in Mississippi,* 60-61.

23. In Adams County, for example, Davis and his associates found that half of the substantial black landowners acquired their properties between 1865 and 1885 (Davis et al., *Deep South,* 299). Early postbellum black landownership in this river county is described in Kenneth S. Greenberg, "The Civil War and the Redistribution of Land: Adams County, Mississippi, 1860-1870," *Agricultural History,* 52 (April, 1978), 301-302.

24. The extent of black homesteading in Mississippi is an open question, but it may have been a considerable factor in such counties as Forrest, Jefferson Davis, Lawrence, and Simpson, and even in Delta "new ground" areas. For examples from Lawrence and Simpson counties, see the records of Freeman Woodward (Woodard) in the personal collection of Booker T. Woodard, Rockford, Ill.

25. Quoted in Powdermaker, *After Freedom,* 106. For related arguments see Jay Mandle, *The Roots of Black Poverty: The Southern Plantation Economy after the Civil War* (Durham, N.C., 1978), 29; Arthur F. Raper, *Preface to Peasantry: A Tale of Two Black Belt Counties* (1936; reprint ed., New York, 1968), 121-137; Thomas J. Woofter, *Landlord and Tenant,* WPA Research Monograph no. 5 (Washington, D.C., 1936), 23-24; Myrdal, *American Dilemma,* 1: 240-242.

26. Stone, *Studies in the American Race Problem,* 113; Davis et al., *Deep South,* 407. See also the example of black land acquisition by bequest at Sharpley's Bottom (Monroe County) in John R. Kern et al., "Sharpley's Bottom Historic Sites: Phase II, Historical Investigations, Tombigbee River Multiresource District, Alabama and Mississippi," report to the U.S. Department of the Interior, October, 1982, 57; Herman, oral history, June 14, 1976, JSU; and the Benton County case described in Jackson *Daily News,* October 13, 1920.

27. In the Delta, in low-lying sections rescued from annual flooding by federal engineering projects, the median price of so-called new ground was nineteen dollars per acre for whites and twenty-five dollars per acre for blacks—although blacks bought the poorest land (R. Heberle and Udell Jolley, "Mississippi Backwater Study—Yazoo Segment: Report on Social Factors," November 10, 1940; and "Yazoo Segment, Mississippi Backwater Area Study," January, 1942, Land Tenure Section, BAE). In Adams County, the price disparity sometimes exceeded 500 percent (Davis et al., *Deep South,* 293-295).

28. "Textual Discussion of Problem Area Map of Mississippi," 29, BAE.

29. Quoted in Davis et al., *Deep South,* 293-295. See also the case of Pleas Branigan of Noxubee County in [Branigan] to J. R. Butler, September 13, October 10, 1940; and Butler to Curtis Higgins, September 28, 1940 (microfilm, reel 15), STFU.

30. Lawrence County (Whitecap) Central Club "Declaration of Purposes,"

quoted in William F. Holmes, "Whitecapping in Mississippi: Agrarian Violence in the Populist Era," *Mid-America,* 55 (April, 1973), 137.

31. I. T. Montgomery to E. W. Lampton, April 25, 1904, con. 242; see also Richard Browning to Booker T. Washington, January 28, 1902, con. 233, both in BTW.

32. Quoted in Jackson *Weekly Clarion-Ledger,* November 13, 1902.

33. "White Caps and Bull Dozers," WPA History: Hinds County (first quotation); "Outlaw Days," ibid., Amite County; Jackson *Daily Clarion-Ledger,* February 9, 1911 (second quotation).

34. Pearl River *News,* February 17, 1893, quoted in Holmes, "Whitecapping in Mississippi," 138n. Also see a description of Franklin County Whitecap activities in Jackson *Daily Clarion-Ledger,* May 8, 1906.

35. Quoted in "Two Pleas for Negro Rights in Mississippi," *Outlook,* 75 (May 16, 1903), 153. See an account of a second Lincoln County judge who, in the face of death threats, tried Whitecappers: Jackson *Weekly Clarion-Ledger,* December 25, 1902; and Hair, *Carnival of Fury,* 62-63.

36. Charles B. Galloway, *Great Men and Great Movements: A Volume of Addresses* (Nashville, 1914), 314.

37. The fullest accounts of the rise and decline of dirt-farmer violence in the state are by William F. Holmes: "Whitecapping in Mississippi," 134-148; "Whitecapping: Agrarian Violence in Mississippi, 1902-1906," *Journal of Southern History,* 35 (May, 1969), 165-185. In *White Chief,* 55, 97, 134-145, Holmes details Vardaman's role in both the resurgence and suppression of the Whitecaps. For the pardons, unnoticed by Holmes, see Lincoln County *Times,* September 12, 1907.

38. Jackson *Weekly Clarion-Ledger,* April 4, 1907; Lincoln County *Times,* December 5, 1912; Jackson *Daily News,* February 2, 1912.

39. Quoted in *Progressive Farmer,* July 12, 1913, in Tuskegee Institute News Clippings File (microfilm ed., reel 2, frame 417).

40. Dollard, *Caste and Class in a Southern Town,* 300.

41. Quoted in Higgs, *Competition and Coercion,* 128-129.

42. Dewey W. Grantham, Jr., *Hoke Smith and the Politics of the New South* (Baton Rouge, 1958), 256-264; Holmes, *White Chief,* 285-286.

43. For state extension director R. S. Wilson's own ambivalence toward the education of black farmers, see Wilson to Bradford Knapp, February 12, 1916, and February 19, 1917; Wilson to Office of Extension Work, January 1, 1925, State Administration Reports, FES.

44. Wilson to J. A. Evans, February 22, 1915; Evans to Wilson, February 24, 1915; Wilson to Knapp, February 9, 1918, General Correspondence; Wilson to Knapp, February 12, 1916; Wilson to Office of Extension Work, January 1, 1925, State Administration Reports, FES.

45. Of the 218 extension workers (home demonstration and agricultural) in Mississippi in 1936, sixty were assigned to blacks. For expenditures and numbers of workers assigned to each race see the "Annual Inspection Reports," 1915-1939, FES; and W. B. Mercier, *Extension Work among Negroes, 1920,* USDA Circular 190 (Washington, D.C., 1921); Doxey Wilkerson, "The Par-

ticipation of Negroes in the Federally Aided Program of Agricultural and Home Economics Extension," *Journal of Negro Education,* 7 (July, 1938), 331-344; Davis, "The Participation of Negro Land-Grant Colleges," 282-291. To compare the program in Mississippi with that of other states see Earl W. Crosby, "Building the Country Home: The Black County Agent System, 1906-1940" (Ph.D. diss., Miami University, 1977), 97, 107-108, 115, 117.

46. W. F. Reden to Henry Wallace, July 25, 1933, "Negroes" file, SAg; "Mississippi: Annual Report of Progress," November 1, 1911; Wilson to Knapp, February 12, 1916, and February 18, 1917; Wilson to Office of Extension Work, January 1, 1925, State Administration Reports, FES. The regional screening process is described in Earl W. Crosby, "Limited Success against Long Odds: The Black County Agent," *Agricultural History,* 57 (July, 1983), 277, 280.

47. For a suggestive account of the salutary impact of one black agent, see Hodding Carter, *Where Main Street Meets the River* (New York, 1953), 245-53. On the benefits of black extension work, see James A. Booker to Knapp, August 23, 1911, General Correspondence; and I. T. Montgomery to Knapp, October 27, 1910; H. N. Miller to Booker, October 26, 1910; and John A. Wallace, "Narrative Reports, Humphreys County, 1932-1933," State Administration Reports, FES; Charles Banks, "A Negro Colony: Mound Bayou Mississippi," con. 38, BTW. White appropriation of even the black farmers' minuscule share are described in H. C. Galloway, "Emergency Farm Labor," Farm Labor Supervisors Annual Narrative Report, 1946, FES (first quotation); and J. Lewis Henderson, "In the Cotton Delta," *Survey Graphic,* 36 (January, 1947), 50-51 (subsequent quotations).

48. Jackson *Weekly Clarion-Ledger,* January 15, 1903; Stone, "The Negro in the Yazoo-Mississippi Delta," 242.

49. Stone, "The Negro in the Yazoo-Mississippi Delta," 244; Stone, *American Race Problem,* 123-124. For an estimate of Stone's scholarship, see John David Smith, "Alfred Holt Stone: Mississippi Planter and Archivist/Historian of Slavery," *Journal of Mississippi History,* 45 (November, 1983), 262-270.

50. Quoted in Davis et al., *Deep South,* 355. Planters themselves sometimes privately recognized the decline of noblesse oblige. See, e.g., LeRoy Percy to Dr. Dobson, February 15, 1906, box 1, PFP.

51. Clara Hampton, oral history, April 30, 1970; Josephine Beard, oral history, July 13, 1970; Gus Randle, oral history, September 13, 1971; Robert Rogers, oral history, August 9, 1971; Robert Allen, oral history, August 3, 1971, Sharecropper Oral History Collection, MHC.

52. Hampton, oral history, April 30, 1970; Eugene Bailey, oral history, March 6, 1972; Allen, oral history, August 3, 1971, MHC. But see also Mattie Lou Bogan, oral history, July 31, 1971, MHC, on the dangers of protecting loved ones from the lash.

53. On the question of punishment at Trail Lake, cf. Carter, *Where Main Street Meets the River,* 67-78; and Raymond McClinton, "A Social-Economic Analysis of a Mississippi Delta Plantation" (M.A. thesis, University of North Carolina, 1938), 23-24; Lewis Baker, *The Percys of Mississippi: Politics and*

Literature in the New South (Baton Rouge, 1983), 154ff. For Percy plantation practices before William Alexander's tenure, see J. N. Johnson to Sam J. McPeak, April 27, May 2, 1906; LeRoy Percy to Johnson, May 25, 1906; LeRoy Percy to J. B. Ray, December 26, 28, 1906, box 1, PFP.

54. Davis et al., *Deep South,* 395 (quotation); Dollard, *Caste and Class in a Southern Town,* 315ff.; Sidney Fant Davis, *Mississippi Negro Lore* (Indianola, Miss., 1914), 22-28; Ratliff, "Mississippi: Heart of Dixie," 588; and idem, "Mississippi Replies," *Nation,* 115 (August 2, 1922), 126; Indianola *Enterprise,* May 22, 1903; Brookhaven *Semi-Weekly Leader,* September 27, 1911; Jackson *Clarion-Ledger,* August 1, 1946.

55. Quoted in Howard W. Odum and Guy B. Johnson, *Negro Workaday Songs* (New York, 1926), 116-117.

56. Quoted in Lawrence W. Levine, *Black Culture and Black Consciousness: Afro-American Folk Thought from Slavery to Freedom* (New York, 1977), 193.

57. On the origins of sharecropping, see especially Ronald L. F. Davis, *Good and Faithful Labor: From Slavery to Sharecropping in the Natchez District, 1860-1890* (Westport, Conn., 1982); Charles L. Flynn, Jr., *White Land, Black Labor: Caste and Class in Late Nineteenth Century Georgia* (Baton Rouge, 1983).

58. Bogan, oral history, July 31, 1971, MHC.

59. Robert L. Brandfon, "The End of Immigration to the Cotton Fields," *Mississippi Valley Historical Review,* 50 (March, 1964), 592; E. L. Langsford and B. H. Thebodeaux, *Plantation Organization in Operation in the Yazoo-Mississippi Delta Area,* USDA Bulletin no. 682 (May, 1939), 49; E. A. Boeger and E. A. Goldenweiser, *A Study of Tenant Systems of Farming in the Yazoo-Mississippi Delta,* USDA Bulletin no. 337 (January 13, 1916), 9, 13-18; McClinton, "Mississippi Delta Plantation," 21-22; Kern et al., "Sharpley's Bottom Historic Sites," 72-74.

60. Frank D. Alexander, "Cultural Reconnaissance Survey of Coahoma County," BAE.

61. Langsford and Thebodeaux, *Plantation Organization,* 40; Powdermaker, *After Freedom,* 82; Farm Security Summary, Mileston Farms, Mississippi, October 23, 1941, Mileston Project, FHA; C. O. Henderson, "Land Tenure and Tenancy in Mississippi," May, 1937, Land Tenure Section, BAE; Oscar Johnston to D. S. Lantrip, November 15, 1937, box 42, DPL; and Lawrence John Nelson, "King Cotton's Advocate: The Public and Private Career of Oscar G. Johnston" (Ph.D. diss., University of Missouri—Columbia, 1972), 291.

62. See Gavin Wright, "Comment on Papers by Reid, Ransom and Sutch, and Higgs," *Journal of Economic History,* 33 (March, 1973), 175.

63. Anna Knight, *Mississippi Girl: An Autobiography* (Nashville, 1952), 12-13; Edgar T. Thompson, "The Natural History of Agricultural Labor in the South," in Thompson, ed., *Plantation Societies, Race Relations, and the South: The Regimentation of Populations* (Durham, 1975), 253; "Labor Force on Farms Surveyed," pt. 4, Land Tenure Section, BAE; H. C. Galloway, "Annual Farm Labor Report," Farm Labor Supervisor's Annual Report, 1945, FES.

64. Minnie Miller Brown, "Black Women in American Agriculture," *Agricultural History,* 50 (January, 1976), 206 (Montgomery quotation); Pearlee Avant, oral history, July 24, 1970, MHC.

65. Christopher Boston, oral history, February 26, 1970; Amy Jane Bafford, oral history, August 10, 1971, both MHC.

66. Josephine Beard, oral history, July 13, 1970 (quotation); Daisy Archie, oral history, September 12, 1971, both MHC. See also WPA History: Issaquena County; Powdermaker, *After Freedom,* 93; Cohn *Where I Was Born,* 318.

67. U.S., Bureau of the Census, *Population,* 3, Sixteenth Census of the United States (1940), 809.

68. Stone, *American Race Problem,* 104; WPA History: Humphreys County; Stone, "The Negro in the Yazoo-Mississippi Delta," 255.

69. The difficulties entailed in calculating black agricultural income are suggested by an exchange between two economists: Robert Higgs, "Did Southern Farmers Discriminate?" *Agricultural History,* 46 (April, 1972), 325-328; and Charles A. Roberts and Robert Higgs, "Did Southern Farmers Discriminate? The Evidence Re-Examined," ibid., 49 (April, 1975), 441-447. On sharecropper incomes in Mississippi generally, see Dorothy Dickins, *A Nutrition Investigation of Negro Tenants in the Yazoo-Mississippi Delta,* Mississippi Agriculture Experiment Station Bulletin 254 (August, 1928); "Yazoo Segment, Mississippi Backwater Areas Study," January, 1942, Land Tenure Section, BAE; Boeger and Goldenweiser, *Tenant Systems,* 14-15; Charles S. Johnson, Edwin R. Embree, and W. W. Alexander, *The Collapse of Cotton Tenancy: Summary of Studies and Statistical Surveys, 1933-1935* (Chapel Hill, 1935); Davis et al., *Deep South,* 273n, 343-377, 391; Vance, *Human Factors in Cotton Culture,* 125-128.

70. Artley Blanchard, oral history, June 30, 1971, MHC. On black labor in the slack season see Alexander, "Cultural Reconnaissance Survey of Coahoma County," 15-16, BAE; Howard Snyder, "Plantation Pictures," *Atlantic Monthly,* 127 (February, 1921), 168-169; Ratliff, "Mississippi Replies," 126; Harry Oster, *Living Country Blues* (Detroit, 1969), 7; William C. Holley, Ellen Winston, and Thomas J. Woofter, Jr., *The Plantation South, 1934-1937* (reprinted, New York, 1971), 50.

71. Central to the neoclassical argument is Gary S. Becker's distinction between public discrimination and market discrimination. See Becker, *The Economics of Discrimination,* 2d ed. (Chicago, 1971), but also Higgs, *Competition and Coercion;* Stephen J. DeCanio, *Agriculture in the Postbellum South: The Economics of Production and Supply* (Cambridge, Mass., 1974); Joseph D. Reid, Jr., "Sharecropping as an Understandable Market Response: The Post-Bellum South," *Journal of Economic History,* 33 (March, 1973), 106-130. Econometric works critical of the neoclassical position include Mandle, *Roots of Black Poverty;* Ransom and Sutch, *One Kind of Freedom;* and Harold D. Woodman, "Sequel to Slavery: The New History Views the Postbellum South," *Journal of Southern History,* 43 (November, 1977), 523-554.

72. On tenant housing and diet in Mississippi, see especially Woofter, *Landlord and Tenant,* 96-97, 225-229; Dickins, *Nutrition Investigation.*

73. Quoted in "The Rural Negro and Rural Rehabilitation," March, 1935, New General Subject Series, Federal Emergency Relief Administration, BAE. See also virtually any of the sharecropper oral histories at Mary Holmes College.

74. Quoted in Howard W. Odum and Guy B. Johnson, *The Negro and His Songs* (Chapel Hill, 1925), 115; Samuel C. Adams, Jr., "Changing Negro Life in the Delta" (M.A. thesis, Fisk University, 1947), 58; John A. Lomax and Alan Lomax, *American Ballads and Folk Songs* (New York, 1934), 233.

75. Lomax and Lomax, *American Ballads,* 234. For other versions of this black favorite see Paul Oliver, *Blues Fell This Morning: The Meaning of the Blues* (New York, 1960), 18; and Clarence Deming, *By-Ways of Nature and Life* (New York, 1884), 352.

76. C. H. Poe, quoted in Jacquelin Bull, "The General Merchant in the Economic History of the New South," *Journal of Southern History,* 18 (February, 1952), 47.

77. Ibid., 47-50; Thomas D. Clark, "The Furnishing and Supply System in Southern Agriculture since 1865," *Journal of Southern History,* 12 (February, 1946), 28-33; Holley, Winston, and Woofter, *Plantation South,* 24-27; Woofter, *Landlord and Tenant,* 49-63; Brannen, *Relation of Land Tenure to Plantation Organization,* 63; Higgs, *Competition and Coercion,* 55-59. The conditions described here were not unique to agriculture. See the plight of Mississippi forest workers in Nollie Hickman, *Mississippi Harvest: Lumbering in the Longleaf Pine Belt, 1840-1915* (University, Miss., 1962), 139-143.

78. See Snyder, "Plantation Pictures," 168-171; Robert Cecil Cook, *McGowah Place and Other Memoirs* (Hattiesburg, Miss., 1973), 201-203; Alexander, "Cultural Reconnaissance Survey of Coahoma County," BAE. On the nearly total dependence of many tenants on the plantation commissary, see Mark Ham, oral history, November 4, 1971, MDAH.

79. The most avaricious landlords either denied garden privileges or permitted them on a share system that exacted half of all produce, whether staple commodities or garden vegetables. However, more sympathetic and paternalistic planters did much to encourage improved diets and self-sufficiency through tenant gardening. Cf., on the one hand, "A Mississippi Peonage Case," box C-386, NAACP; Sunflower *Tocsin,* October 12, 1916; Howard Snyder, "Negro Migration and the Cotton Crop," *North American Review,* 219 (January, 1924), 22; and on the other, McClinton, "Mississippi Delta Plantation," 79-80; Carter, *Where Main Street Meets the River,* 67-78. See also such county agent reports as A. B. Morant, "Narrative Report of Negro County Agent of Leflore County, 1932-1933"; and A. M. Snowden, "Narrative Report for Bolivar County, 1928," FES.

80. Higgs, *Competition and Coercion,* 53-54, 74; Powdermaker, *After Freedom,* 86; Johnston to William Alexander Percy, November 10, 1938, box 45, DPL. Johnston was less candid when he spoke for public consumption. See his letter to Norman Thomas, quoted in Nelson, "King Cotton's Advocate," 281. See also, Street, *Look Away,* 41; Percy, *Lanterns on the Levee,* 282-283; Jackson *Daily News,* December 14, 1918; January 29, 1924; Memphis *Com-*

mercial-Appeal, September 9, 1917; Dollard, *Caste and Class in a Southern Town,* 122; Davis et al., *Deep South,* 350-351.

81. W. T. B. Williams, "The Negro Exodus from the South," in U.S. Department of Labor, *Negro Migration in 1916-17,* 103. The depths of black cynicism are also probed in Lee, *River George,* a largely autobiographical novel of sharecropper life in Mississippi.

82. Powdermaker, *After Freedom,* 109; Jones, *The Bottom Rail,* 26. The history of one notably generous black landlord, Dr. T. R. M. Howard of Mound Bayou, and his efforts to help tenants become owners is briefly analyzed in George F. David, "Deep in the Delta," *Journal of Human Relations,* 2 (Spring, 1954), 72-75.

83. Stone, *American Race Problem,* 118-119; McClinton, "Mississippi Delta Plantation," 28; Cohn, *Where I Was Born,* 340-345; Minor S. Gray, "A Short History of Delta and Pine Land Company," DPL.

84. Ferebee was a northern volunteer medical worker active in the Delta during the 1930s. [Dorothy Boulding Ferebee], *The 1937 Mississippi Health Project Report,* Alpha Kappa Alpha Third Annual Report (n.p., n.d.), app.; Charles S. Johnson, *The Economic Status of Negroes* (Nashville, 1933), 32.

85. Ratliff, "Mississippi: Heart of Dixie," 588; but see also the suggestive treatment of this subject in Lee, *River George,* 86-140.

86. William F. Holmes, "The Leflore County Massacre and the Demise of the Colored Farmers' Alliance," *Phylon,* 34 (September, 1973), 267-274 (quotations at 271, 273); idem, "The Demise of the Colored Farmers' Alliance," *Journal of Southern History,* 41 (May, 1975), 187-200.

87. Arthur I. Waskow, *From Race Riot to Sit-In, 1919 and the 1960s: A Study in the Connections between Conflict and Violence* (Garden City, N.Y., 1967), 121-142; O. A. Roberts, Jr., "The Elaine Race Riots of 1919," *Arkansas Historical Quarterly,* 19 (1960), 142-150; George Brown Tindall, *The Emergence of the New South, 1913-1945* (Baton Rouge, 1967), 152-153.

88. Editorial, Greenwood *Commonwealth,* February 18, 1931; Chicago *Defender,* August 30, 1930; February 21, 28, 1931; Atlanta *Daily World,* November 7, 1932.

89. Donald H. Grubbs, *Cry from the Cotton: The Southern Tenant Farmers' Union and the New Deal* (Chapel Hill, 1971); Jack Temple Kirby, *Rural Worlds Lost: The American South, 1920-1960* (Baton Rouge, 1987), 259-271.

90. *Sharecroppers' Voice,* July, 1935 ("ripe" quotation); September, 1935 ("tough" quotation); November, 1935 (microfilm, reel 58); STFU; Howard Kester, *Revolt among the Sharecroppers* (1936; reprint ed., New York, 1969), 83.

91. Oscar Johnston to Fine Cotton Spinners and Doublers Association, April 6, 1936, DPL; membership list, Hillhouse local, October 8, 1936 (microfilm, reel 3); H. L. Mitchell to Irma Matheny, May 13, 1936 (reel 2), STFU; Sam Franklin, "A New Way of Life," *Sharecroppers' Voice,* October-November, 1936.

92. Mitchell to Lee Phillips, August 24, 1937 (microfilm, reel 5), STFU.

93. "Complete List of Locals in Mississippi, 1938-1939" (microfilm, reel 9); "Locals, State of Mississippi" [1939] (reel 13), STFU.

94. In order of appearance, the quotations are from STFU Organizers' Report, July 17, 1939 (microfilm, reel 13); Needom Warren to J. R. Butler, June 11, 1940 (reel 15); Report of Local No. 14 (Shaw) [July, 1940] (reel 15); but see generally reels 13-15, STFU.

95. Theodore Rosengarten, *All God's Dangers: The Life of Nate Shaw* (New York, 1975), 296-297.

96. Mitchell, telephone interview, February 2, 1982.

97. George B. Mayberry to Butler, April 27, 1940 (microfilm, reel 14) (first quotation); Local No. 15 (Mashulaville) to Butler, July 4, 1940 (reel 15) (second quotation), STFU. White violence against Mississippi black tenants is voluminously detailed in STFU letters and documents, reels 13-15.

98. Members of the MFLU struck in 1965, but were starved into submission (Philip S. Foner, *Organized Labor and the Black Worker, 1619-1973* [New York, 1974], 355). The only STFU strike called in Mississippi was cancelled in 1936 after Delta Cooperative Farm leaders persuaded strike organizers that at this producers' cooperative they would be striking against themselves (Roger D. Tate, Jr., "Easing the Burden: The Era of Depression and New Deal in Mississippi" [Ph.D. diss., University of Tennessee, 1978], 102).

99. Levine, *Black Culture and Black Consciousness*, x-xi.

100. For exceptional cases of blacks who sued their landlords and won, see *Jackson* v. *Jefferson,* 171 Miss. 774 (1939); and *Mississippi Cooperative Cotton Association* v. *Walker,* 186 Miss. 870 (1939). On the difficulty and risks, see Chapter 6 below, but also C. O. Henderson, "Land Tenure and Tenancy in Mississippi," May, 1937; and "Yazoo Segment, Mississippi Backwater Areas Study," January, 1942, Land Tenure Section, BAE.

101. Quotations from Snyder, "Negro Migration," 27; idem, "Plantation Pictures," 168-169. For a representative planter lament about black "laziness" see LeRoy Percy to E. P. Skene, July 29, 1905, PFP. For the complaint of a black landlord who thought his croppers to be a sorry lot, see Willie Blanchard, oral history, August 27, 1970, MHC.

102. Quoted in Oster, *Living Country Blues,* 121-122.

103. See for example David Cohn, "Share Cropping in the Delta," *Atlantic,* 159 (May, 1937), 585; Davis et al., *Deep South,* 370, 395-396.

104. Dollard, *Caste and Class in a Southern Town,* 287.

105. Baltimore *Afro-American,* April 15, 1921, quoted in Frederick G. Detweiler, *The Negro Press in the United States* (Chicago, 1922), 84. See also the oral history of J. Willie Prince, a World War I veteran who, he claimed, killed a cheating Noxubee County planter in 1929, escaped a lynch mob by hiding in the woods, and eventually walked to Laurel to begin a new life as a tailor (Prince, oral history, July 2, 1970, MHC).

106. Lincoln County *Times,* June 30, 1910. For other examples see *John Gibson* v. *Mississippi,* 17 So. 892 (1895); Jackson *Daily News,* November 15, 1911; Memphis *Commercial-Appeal,* May 12, 1914; Madison County *Herald,*

February 18, 1916; NAACP, *Twentieth Annual Report, 1929* (New York, 1930), 36.

107. Quoted in Davis et al., *Deep South,* 342.

108. Quoted in Harris, *Presidential Reconstruction in Mississippi,* 144n.

109. Bell, "Child of the Delta," app., unpaginated.

110. William Cohen, "Negro Involuntary Servitude in the South, 1865-1940: A Preliminary Analysis," *Journal of Southern History,* 42 (February, 1976), 40; St. Louis *Argus,* November 22, 1929. See also Jackson *Weekly Clarion-Ledger,* December 25, 1902; January 15, 22, 1903; Indianola *Enterprise,* May 22, 1903; Vicksburg *Evening Post,* February 12, 1904.

111. On the evolution of the statute, see Mississippi *Laws,* 1890, chap. 56; *Laws,* 1900, chap. 102; *Laws,* 1924, chap. 160. The extensive use of antienticement law is suggested by the number of appeals. By 1917, the statute had been before the state court more than twenty times. See *Mississippi* v. *Hurdle,* 113 Miss. 736 (1917).

112. Mississippi *Laws,* 1912, chap. 94; *Evans* v. *Mississippi,* 121 Miss. 252 at 256 (1919).

113. Mississippi *Laws,* 1865, chap. 6; *Laws,* 1904, 144; Hamilton, "Mississippi Politics in the Progressive Era," 129 ("negro loafers" quotation); Grantham, *Southern Progressivism,* 137-138; Cohen, "Negro Involuntary Servitude," 50; Vicksburg *Evening Post,* October 9, 1918; New Orleans *Times-Picayune,* September 23, 1936. Black resentment of the vagrancy law of 1904 and a resulting short-lived exodus of black workers are described in Vicksburg *Evening Post,* May 20, 1904; Jackson *Weekly Clarion-Ledger,* May 26, 1904; June 2, 1904; Brandon *News,* June 9, 1904.

114. Walter F. White, " 'Work or Fight' in the South," *New Republic,* 18 (March 1, 1919), 144-146; Jackson *Daily Clarion-Ledger,* June 20, August 15, September 24, 1918; Sunflower *Tocsin,* November 17, 1918; June 3, 1919; Clarksdale *Register,* January 29, May 24, 27, 1918; Vicksburg *Evening Post,* September 20, 1918.

115. See Zodoc Brown material, vol. 693; but also H. N. Graham to M. S. Conner, May 21, 1934, vol. 690, GPF; Frank Jones to James Weldon Johnson, February 5, 1927, box C-386, NAACP; Indianola *Enterprise,* April 3, 1903; Chicago *Defender,* May 25, 1929; October 25, 1930; Kern et al., "Sharpley's Bottom Historic Sites," 69.

116. Mississippi *Laws,* 1900, chap. 101; *Code,* 1906, sec. 1148. The question of legislative intent is addressed by Cohen, "Negro Involuntary Servitude," 42-47; Daniel A. Novak, *The Wheel of Servitude: Black Forced Labor after Slavery* (Lexington, Ky., 1978), passim; Oscar Zeichner, "The Legal Status of the Agricultural Laborer in the South," *Political Science Quarterly,* 55 (September, 1940), 423n, 425; and Charles E. Magnum, Jr., *The Legal Status of the Negro* (Chapel Hill, 1940), 167. The importance that some planters assigned to the false-pretense statute is suggested by the correspondence of LeRoy Percy: Percy to H. C. Niles, February 17, 1908; Sydney Smith to Percy, February 19, 1908; Percy to Smith, February 21, 1908, box 3, PFP.

117. *Bailey* v. *Alabama,* 219 U.S. 219 (1911), 31 Sup. Ct. 145 (1911). But

see Pete Daniel, "Up from Slavery and Down to Peonage: The Alonzo Bailey Case," *Journal of American History,* 57 (December, 1970), 654-670. Pre-*Bailey* cases heard by the Mississippi court include *Hendricks* v. *Mississippi,* 79 Miss. 368 (1901); *Ex parte Harris,* 85 Miss. 4 (1904).

118. *Mississippi* v. *Armstead,* 103 Miss. 90 at 798 (1912).

119. The false-pretense law (Mississippi *Code,* 1906, sec. 1148) remained in Hemingway's annotated *Code,* 1927, sec. 918, but was deleted from *Code,* 1930, 38.

120. *Armstead* v. *Chatters,* 71 Miss. 509 (1893); *Hoole* v. *Dorroh,* 75 Miss. 257 (1897); *Mahoney* v. *McNeill,* 77 Miss. 406 (1899); *Mississippi* v. *Richardson,* 86 Miss. 439 (1905); *Petty* v. *Legett,* 38 So. 549 (1905); *Alford* v. *Peques,* 92 Miss. 558 (1908); *Goolsby* v. *Mississippi,* 98 Miss. 702 (1910).

121. *Shilling* v. *Mississippi,* 143 Miss. 709 at 721 (1926); *Thompson* v. *Box,* 147 Miss. 1 (1927). See also *Mississippi* v. *Hurdle,* 113 Miss. 736 (1917); and *Evans* v. *Mississippi,* 121 Miss. 252 (1919); *Armstrong* v. *Bishop,* 151 Miss. 353 (1928); *Hill* v. *Duckworth,* 155 Miss. 484 (1929).

122. *Thompson* v. *Box,* 147 Miss. 1 at 15 (1927). See also Novak, *Wheel of Servitude,* 70-71.

123. As comparative histories have demonstrated, forced labor was the common postemancipation experience of virtually all societies that practiced chattel slavery. See Pete Daniel, "The Metamorphosis of Slavery, 1865-1900," *Journal of American History,* 66 (June, 1979), 93-95.

124. Hamilton, "Mississippi Politics in the Progressive Era," 138 (Williams quotation); Pete Daniel, *Shadow of Slavery: Peonage in the South, 1901-1969* (Urbana, 1972), 22 (Hoyt quotation); Street, *Look Away,* 136. See also the estimate of an STFU leader: Blaine Treadway to George Smith, June 1, 1940 (microfilm, reel 15), STFU. Peonage in the forests is described by Hickman (*Mississippi Harvest,* 142-144), who notes that it flourished in Mississippi's turpentine industry but apparently not in the sawmills.

125. Daniel, *Shadow of Slavery,* 39, 108, passim.

126. Jackson *Weekly Clarion-Ledger,* October 3, 1903. But see also Vicksburg *Evening Herald,* March 31, 1904.

127. U.S. Attorney William H. Armbrecht, quoted in Daniel, *Shadow of Slavery,* 33.

128. Jackson *Weekly Clarion-Ledger,* July 24, 1919; "Peonage, Mississippi, 1921," box C-386, NAACP; New York *Tribune,* May 10, 1921; New York *Times,* August 26, 1937; January 28, 1938; "Good News from Mississippi," *New Republic,* 94 (February 16, 1938), 31.

129. See, for example, Edgar Wilson to Theodore Roosevelt, March 4, 1904 (microfilm, ser. 1, reel 42), TRP; Emmett Scott to Frank Cole, September 14, 1910, con. 49, BTW; numerous documents, Administrative Files, boxes C-386, C-388, C-415, NAACP; Indianola *Enterprise,* May 22, 1903; Vicksburg *Evening Post,* March 21, 1904; Jackson *Daily News,* November 5, 1911; Jackson *Clarion-Ledger,* April 3, 1927; Norfolk *Journal and Guide,* August 25, September 22, 1928; Chicago *Defender,* March 23, 1929; editorial, *Crisis,* 45 (March, 1938), 81.

130. Davis to Taylor, February 4, 16, August 25, 1930; June 26, August 24, 1931; C. L. Saunders to Taylor, January 20, November 21, 1930; Taylor to W. E. B. Du Bois, April 15, 1931; Walter White to Taylor, April 17, 1931; Taylor to White, June 23, 1931; Will T. Andrews to William D. Mitchell, May 9, 1931; Mitchell to Andrews, May 21, 1931, box C-388, NAACP. See also the materials related to the Noxubee County case of STFU member Claude B. Cistrunk (1940) (microfilm, reel 14), STFU.

131. Baker, *Following the Color Line,* 97; Jackson *Weekly Clarion-Ledger,* December 20, 1906.

132. The practice can be followed in the plantation correspondence of LeRoy Percy: see especially Percy to W. J. Best, December 6, 1905, box 1; Percy to J. E. Branton, March 6, 1907, box 2; Percy to H. B. Duncan, March 27, 1907, box 2; Percy to Charles Scott, December 29, 1906, box 1, PFP. But see also *Thompson* v. *Box,* 147 Miss. 1 (1927); Ratliff, "Mississippi: Heart of Dixie," 588; Jackson *Daily News,* January 29, 1924.

133. See generally, Pete Daniel, *Deep'n as It Come: The 1927 Mississippi River Flood* (New York, 1977).

134. Green to J. H. Noonan, June 8, 1927; and Harry M. Baker to Noonan, June 2, 1927, file 50-637, Department of Justice, Record Group 60, NA; Hoover to Walter White, June 21, 1927, Flood Relief, Commerce, HPL.

135. Howard to Attorney General, May 4, 1927; and Turner E. Campe to Attorney General, April 29, 1927, file 50-637, Department of Justice, NA; Redmond to Calvin Coolidge, April 30, 1927, quoted in Daniel, *Shadow of Slavery,* 153; Jackson *Daily News,* April 30, 1927; William Alexander Percy to Oscar Johnston, February 11, 1937, box 45, DPL (last quotation). See also, Percy, *Lanterns on the Levee,* 249ff.; Baker, *The Percys,* 131ff.

136. Walter White, "The Negro and the Flood," manuscript, 4, 5-6, 10-11, box C-380, NAACP.

137. [Helen M. Boardman], "Vicksburg: A Victory for the South," manuscript, 4, 7-16 ("rabbits" quotation), passim, box C-380, NAACP; Moton to Hoover [Second Report of the Colored Advisory Commission, December 1927], 3-4 (subsequent quotations), Flood Relief, Commerce, HPL.

138. Ellsworth to NAACP, December 20, 1927, box C-380, NAACP. Forced labor and other abuses of black workers in Mississippi River flood-control projects remained a problem at least through the early depression years when, under pressure from the NAACP, a Senate investigation exposed exploitative conditions in the levee camps of private contractors retained by the Army Corps of Engineers. See NAACP, *Twenty-third Annual Report, 1932* (New York, 1933), 8; idem, *Twenty-fourth Annual Report, 1933* (New York, 1934), 9-10; Walter White, *A Man Called White: The Autobiography of Walter White* (New York, 1948), 81-83; and material on the Mississippi Flood Control Project, boxes C-380, C-381, C-382, NAACP. The NAACP's charges were disputed by white planters, including Oscar Johnston. See Johnston's sworn statement, September 30, 1932, box 41, DPL.

139. William Alexander Percy to Oscar Johnston, February 11, 1937, box 45, DPL.

140. W. F. Reden to Henry Wallace, July 25, 1933, "Negroes" file, SAg.

141. Cohen, "Negro Involuntary Servitude," 33.

142. U.S., Bureau of Census, *The Negro Farmer in the United States: 1930* (Washington, 1933), 20; Thompson, "The Natural History of Agricultural Labor in the South," 249. Although labor stability and fair treatment were closely related, even some of the most enlightened landlords complained of an inability to retain their workers. See especially the testimony of the manager of the Delta Farm in Bolivar County: Sam Franklin to Trustees, January 19, 1938, box 4, Reinhold Niebuhr Papers, LC; but also LeRoy Percy to George Hebron, January 20, 1908, box 3, PFP; Adams, "Changing Negro Life in the Delta," 15, 17; and the contrasting judgments of other planters described in: Alfred Holt Stone, "A Plantation Experiment," *Quarterly Journal of Economics,* 19 (February, 1905), 270-87; Baker, *Following the Color Line,* 102-103; Jones, *The Bottom Rail,* 25; and Julia Winklejohn, "The Delta and Pine Land Company: A History" (manuscript, 1964), box 27, DPL.

143. The most recent include Gilbert C. Fite, *Cotton Fields No More: Southern Agriculture, 1865-1980* (Lexington, Ky., 1984); Pete Daniel, *Breaking the Land: The Transformation of Cotton, Tobacco, and Rice Cultures since 1880* (Urbana, 1985); and Kirby, *Rural Worlds Lost.* For a brief summary of plantation consolidation, see idem, "The Transformation of Southern Plantations, c. 1920-1930," *Agricultural History,* 57 (July, 1983), 257-276.

144. Quoted in Fite, *Cotton Fields No More,* 150.

145. M. G. Vaiden, J. O. Smith, and W. E. Ayres, *Making Cotton Cheaper: Can Present Costs Be Reduced,* Mississippi Agriculture Experiment Station Bulletin 290 (February, 1931), 3-8, 20, 22; "Labor Force on Farms Surveyed," pt. 4 (manuscript, March 26, 1942), Land Tenure Section, BAE.

146. Joe Rice Dockery, oral history, December 13, 1979, 4-5, MDAH.

147. Minor Gray, oral history, May 8, 1974, ser. 16, DPL; Fite, *Cotton Fields No More,* 154, 185; *Mechanical Cotton Picker Operation in the Yazoo-Mississippi Delta,* Mississippi State College Agriculture Experiment Station Bulletin 465 (July, 1949), 3. At least one planter, the romantic aristocrat William Alexander Percy, opposed mechanization, and the displacement that inevitably followed, for moral and, perhaps, aesthetic reasons. See Baker, *The Percys,* 155-156.

148. The term apparently belongs to Merle C. Prunty, Jr., who described postwar agricultural consolidation in "Renaissance of the Southern Plantation," *Geographical Review,* 45 (October, 1955), 459-491.

149. Daniel, *Breaking the Land,* 155ff.

150. Quoted in Gilbert C. Fite, "Mechanization of Cotton Production since World War II," *Agricultural History,* 54 (January, 1980), 198.

151. Gray, oral history, May 8, 1974 (quotation), DPL; Ledger no. 26, 1925 Census of Plantations, ser. 1, DPL; Daniel, *Breaking the Land,* 248.

152. See Fite, *Cotton Fields No More,* 238, Table A6.

Chapter 5. Black Labor/Black Capital

1. Quoted in William Lee Conley Broonzy and Yannick Bruynoghe, *Big Bill Blues: William Broonzy's Story* (London, 1955), 56-57.

2. Isaiah T. Montgomery, "The Negro in Business," *Outlook,* 69 (November 16, 1901), 733.

3. Ratliff, "Mississippi: Heart of Dixie," 588-589.

4. Unless otherwise indicated, all statistics in this chapter are taken from occupational data gathered by the United States Bureau of the Census.

5. James C. Cobb, "Beyond Planters and Industrialists: A New Perspective on the New South" (Paper read at the Southern Historical Association Meeting, November, 1985), 25. See also Carter, *Main Street Meets the River,* 207.

6. Jack Edward Prince, "History and Development of the Mississippi Balance Agriculture with Industry Program, 1936-1958" (Ph.D. diss., Ohio State University, 1961), 75, 174, 284-285; Guy Tillman Gillespie, "Mississippi Political Development: The Effects of Democracy on a State Political System" (Honors thesis, Harvard University, 1978), 31; William A. Stacy, "Returned Migrant Attitude Study" (M.A. thesis, Mississippi State University, 1961), 73.

7. Quoted in James C. Cobb, *The Selling of the South: The Southern Crusade for Industrial Development* (Baton Rouge, 1982), 116.

8. Alexander Barron, oral history, March 11, 1976, JSU.

9. Quoted in Evers, *Evers,* 23.

10. Frank E. Smith, *The Yazoo River* (New York, 1954), 210.

11. Hickman, *Mississippi Harvest,* 243-245.

12. Hickman has called Fairley's status "unique" among black forestry workers and suggests that his good fortune owed much to a close friendship with a local white lumber baron. Ibid., 123-125, 138-140; idem, "Black Labor in Forest Industries of the Piney Woods, 1840-1933," in *Mississippi Piney Woods: A Human Perspective,* ed. Noel Polk (Jackson, Miss., 1986), 81-82. The record of Fairley's life has been enriched by the interest of Charles Sullivan. See his interviews: Nollie Hickman, oral history, May 18, 1984; and Lucille Fairley, oral history, June 25, 1984, University of Southern Mississippi; and Hattiesburg *American,* September 1, 1985.

13. For the argument of the cliometricians, see Gavin Wright, *Old South, New South: Revolutions in the Southern Economy since the Civil War* (New York, 1986), 177-197, 181 (quotation); Robert Higgs, "Race and Economy in the South, 1890-1950," in Robert Haws, ed., *The Age of Segregation: Race Relations in the South, 1890-1945* (Jackson, Miss., 1978), 102-111.

14. Laurel *Chronicle,* magazine ed., 1902, quoted in Payne, "Black Middle-Class in Laurel," 9-14 (quotation at 10); Frank Houston, oral history, August 15, 1981, CPC.

15. Davis et al., *Deep South,* 256, 261, 426-427, 432-437. See also Payne interview with Cleveland Heidelberg, August 17, 1981, CPC; Chicago *Defender,* March 1, 1930; W. E. B. Du Bois, ed., *The Negro Artisan,* Atlanta University Publication no. 7 (Atlanta, 1902), 131, 132; Report, National Box Co., February 12, 1925, Research Division, Records of the Women's Bureau, RG 86 NA

(microfilm, reel 18, frame 898-901, Black Workers in the Era of the Great Migration). During the First World War some sawmills on the Gulf Coast paid black and white mill hands the same daily wage (Biloxi *Herald,* May 4, June 1, 1917).

16. Alfred E. Smith to Walter White, November 12, 1937, box C-386, NAACP (first quotation); Davis et al., *Deep South,* 429 (second quotation). See also "Hazelhurst Box Factory" [1925?], Research Division, Women's Bureau (microfilm, reel 18, frame 894).

17. Bell, "Child of the Delta," chap. 11, p. [1] ("stigma" quotation); Washington, *The Story of the Negro,* 1: 118; M. Burgess, oral history, [1981] (Jones County quotation); and Cleveland Heidelberg, oral history, August 17, 1981, CPC.

18. Lincoln County *Times,* October 3, 1907; June 26, 1909; August 8, 1912; Meridian *Evening Star,* April 3, 1908; Brookhaven *Semi-Weekly Leader,* June 26, 1909; Hickman, *Mississippi Harvest,* 246-247.

19. Jackson *Daily News,* July 23, 1919.

20. Indianola *Enterprise,* March 13, 1903; NAACP, *Annual Report for 1921* (New York, 1922), 60; Vicksburg *Evening Post,* April 29, 1919; Memphis *Press,* May 6, 1921; Phil Brown to Secretary of Labor, May 9, 1921, Chief Clerk's file, DL.

21. Pressed by the railroad, police arrested four whites; two were found guilty of assault and sentenced to the penitentiary. NAACP, *Annual Report for 1932,* 18 (*Evening Post* quotation); William Harris, *The Harder We Run: Black Workers since the Civil War* (New York, 1982), 45-48; Myrdal, *American Dilemma,* 2: 1105-1106; Hilton Butler, "Murder for the Job," *Nation,* 137 (July 12, 1933), 44; Charles S. Johnson, "Negroes in the Railway Industry: Part II," *Phylon,* 3 (Second Quarter, 1942), 204-205; idem, *Patterns of Negro Segregation,* 273 (last quotation).

22. Davis et al., *Deep South,* 425-427, 431, 464 (quotation); Tate, "Easing the Burden," 72.

23. In 1900 blacks accounted for 73 percent of all gainfully employed Mississippi children (ages ten to fifteen) and 90 percent of all Mississippi female children in domestic service. In that year 33.3 percent of all black women aged sixty-five and older were still in the labor force (U.S., Bureau of the Census, *Special Reports: Occupations of the Twelfth Census* [Washington, D.C., 1904], 104; U.S., Bureau of the Census, *Statistics of Women at Work, 1900* [Washington, D.C., 1907], 144).

24. Heberle and Jolley, "Mississippi Backwater Study—Yazoo Segment," chap. 1; Johnson, *Growing Up in the Black Belt,* 59; Moody, *Coming of Age,* 95.

25. Rawick, ed., *Miss. Narr.,* 7(2), 532-533. For other examples, see ibid., 6(1), 68-71; Mr. and Mrs. Early Ewing, Sr., oral history, May 7, 1974; and Francis Getze, oral history, May 26, 1974, ser. 16, DPL; Smith, *Congressman from Mississippi,* 16; William Faulkner, "Mississippi," in Faulkner, *Essays, Speeches, and Public Letters* (New York, 1966), 39-43.

26. *McComb Enterprise,* 1932, quoted in Rawick, ed., *Miss. Narr.,* 10(5),

2144-2145. See also Dollard, *Caste and Class in a Southern Town,* 386-387; Davis et al., *Deep South,* 447-448; Powdermaker, *After Freedom,* 117-120.

27. Vicksburg *American,* quoted in Jackson *Weekly Clarion-Ledger,* January 15, 1903. See also Jackson *Daily News,* July 8, 1919.

28. In 1925, weekly wages of the state's small industrial work force of black women ranged from one dollar to over ten dollars, with a median of $5.75. The median for the same category of white workers was $8.60 (U.S., Department of Labor, *Women in Mississippi Industries: A Study of Hours, Wages, and Working Conditions,* Womens' Bureau Bulletin no. 55 [Washington, D.C., 1926], 18, 19, 72, 77; U.S., Department of Labor, *Negro Women: Industry in Fifteen States,* Womens' Bureau Bulletin no. 70 [Washington, D.C., 1929]). To compare the wages of domestic servants over time, see Wharton, *Negro in Mississippi,* 126; Dollard, *Caste and Class in a Southern Town,* 106-107; Davis et al., *Deep South,* 442-443; and Ferebee, ed., *The 1938 Mississippi Health Project.*

29. See, e.g., four folders of uncommonly touching black servants' letters (1945-1968) to the vacationing white Delta plantation family that employed them: James K. Polk, Jr., Papers, MDAH.

30. Rawick, ed., *Miss. Narr.,* 8(3), 962.

31. Ibid., 9(4), 1873 (Rocket quotation); 10(5), 1908 (Sanders quotation). See also, Josephine B. Tibbs, oral history, December 13, 1972, MDAH; and the oral histories of Dora Adams, March 8, 1970; Katie L. Blanchard, June 30, 1971; Nettie Bell, May 7, 1970, all at MHC.

32. Moody, *Coming of Age,* 29.

33. Odom and Johnson, *Negro Workaday Songs,* 117.

34. Wharton, *Negro in Mississippi,* 130; Stone, *American Race Problem,* 88, 168, 170; Greene and Woodson, *Negro Wage Earner,* 114; Rawick, ed., *Miss. Narr.,* 9(4), 1473, 1706; Tupelo *Journal,* January 4, 1902.

35. Jackson's black skilled tradesmen in 1908 included 150 carpenters, forty bricklayers, twenty-five plasterers, thirty-five painters, twelve blacksmiths, and seven shoemakers. D. W. Woodard, *Negro Progress in a Mississippi Town, Being a Study of Conditions in Jackson, Mississippi* (Cheyney, Pa., [1908]), 7-8.

36. W. E. B. Du Bois and Augustus Dill, eds., *The Negro American Artisan,* Atlanta University Publication no. 17 (Atlanta, 1912), 63; "Races and Nationalities," WPA History: Adams County.

37. McLaurin also notes that black loggers participated in the Knights of Labor strikes in Moss Point and Handsboro and that the Vicksburg local, "composed primarily of blacks," backed a slate of candidates in 1888 and helped to elect members of the union to the offices of mayor, alderman, and justice of the peace. See Melton Alonzo McLaurin, *Knights of Labor in the South* (Westport, Conn., 1978), 41, 61, 98, 148 (quotation), 179; Frederic Meyers, "Knights of Labor in the South," *Southern Economic Journal,* 6 (April, 1940), 483; Frank T. De Vyver, "The Present Status of Labor Unions in the South," *Southern Economic Journal,* 5 (April, 1939), 490-493; Sidney H. Kessler, "The Organization of Negroes in the Knights of Labor," in John H.

Bracey, Jr. et al., eds., *Black Workers and Organized Labor* (Belmont, Calif., 1971), 12ff.

38. Woodard, *Negro Progress in a Mississippi Town,* 7-8; Johnson, *Patterns of Segregation,* 97; Greene and Woodson, *Negro Wage Earners,* 189.

39. White hostility to the organization of black trainmen is suggested by the experience of an organizer for the American Brotherhood of Railway Trackmen: James R. Cates to Walker D. Hines, July 3, 1919, file E38-11, Records of the U.S. Railroad Administration, RG 14, NA (microfilm, reel 7, frames 825-826, Black Workers in the Era of the Great Migration). See also National Urban League, *Negro Membership in American Labor Unions* (1930; New York, Negro Universities reprint ed., 1966), 108-112; Donald Crumpton Mosley, "A History of Labor Unions in Mississippi" (Ph.D. diss., University of Alabama, 1965), 99-101.

40. Quoted in Du Bois, ed., *The Negro Artisan,* 74. Earlier, John Roy Lynch took a different position, advocating "political and industrial assimilation" through black participation in trade unions (quoted in August Meier and Elliott Rudwick, "Attitudes of Negro Leaders toward the American Labor Movement from the Civil War to World War I," in Julius Jacobson, ed., *The Negro and the American Labor Movement* [Garden City, 1968], 33).

41. Maxon, *The Progress of the Races,* 23-31.

42. See the example of Charles L. Dickson, who became a plumber in Vicksburg late in the nineteenth century precisely because whites believed no black could develop the skill "to wipe a joint" (Indianapolis *Freeman,* April 17, 1897).

43. Wright, *Black Boy,* 204-212. See also idem, "The Ethics of Living Jim Crow," in Wright, *Uncle Tom's Children* (Perennial Library ed., New York, 1965), 6-8; and Michel Fabre, *The Unfinished Quest of Richard Wright* (New York, 1973), 52, 536n.

44. Briefly, from 1878 to 1889, all-black Shaw University in Holly Springs (now Rust College) maintained a law department; private all-white Millsaps College also had a school of law from 1896 to 1919.

45. Michael de L. Landon, *The Honor and Dignity of the Profession: A History of the Mississippi State Bar, 1906-1976* (Jackson, Miss., 1979), 62; Irvin C. Mollison, "Negro Lawyers in Mississippi," *Journal of Negro History,* 15 (January, 1930), 45-46 (Harris quotation).

46. Lynch, *Reminiscences of an Active Life,* 368-369; Marjorie W. Jordan, "Samuel Alfred Beadle: Victim of the Tightening Web" (manuscript, 1982, in possession of Marjorie W. Jordan, Jackson, Miss.), 6-7; Mollison, "Negro Lawyers in Mississippi," 44.

47. Josiah T. Settle quoted in J. W. Gibson and W. H. Crogman, *The Colored American from Slavery to Honorable Citizenship* (Atlanta, 1903); Indianapolis *Freeman,* December 12, 1891.

48. Indianapolis *Freeman,* May 18, 25, November 16, 1889; July 11, 1903; "Honorable W. E. Mollison," *Alexander's Magazine,* 6 (June 15, 1908), 108; *The Leading Afro-Americans of Vicksburg, Mississippi* (Vicksburg, 1908), 15;

G. P. Hamilton, *Beacon Lights of the Race* (Memphis, 1911), 433-434; Mollison, "Negro Lawyers in Mississippi," 64-65.

49. Perry W. Howard quoted in Little Rock *Our Review,* August 19, 1911. See also Howard's comment in *Report of the Fifteenth Annual Convention of the National Negro Business League,* 225; and the remarks of Ralph W. Tyler on Jackson's black bar, unidentified newspaper clipping, June 19, 1914, Tuskegee Institute News Clippings File (microfilm, reel 2, frame 664). On Howard's own standing in the profession, see *Tuskegee Student,* July 16, 1910.

50. When the NAACP Legal Defense Fund entered a Mississippi case it often used local white legal talent for tactical reasons. See, e.g., James A. Burns to Roy Wilkins, February 6, 1935, box G-106, NAACP.

51. Mollison, "Negro Lawyers in Mississippi," 52-59, 70. See also the example of Ohio-born Nathan Taylor of Greenville, who was banished to Chicago after he was elected president of the National Equal Rights League in 1920 (*History of Blacks in Greenville,* unpaginated; Mollison, "Negro Lawyers in Mississippi," 48).

52. Madison County *Herald,* August 27, 1915; Chicago *Defender,* February 2, 9, May 25, 1929; Norfolk *Journal and Guide,* January 25, 1930; *Crisis,* 36 (April, 1929), 139; *Crisis,* 36 (March, 1930), 97; St. Louis *Argus,* November 29, 1929.

53. Chicago *Defender,* February 2, 1929; Charles S. Johnson, *The Negro College Graduate* (Chapel Hill, 1938), 334.

54. Quoted in Gibson and Crogman, *The Colored American,* 556-557. The son of a planter and a slave woman, Settle was admitted to the Mississippi bar in 1875; he practiced in Panola County until moving to Memphis in 1885 (William J. Simmons, *Men of Mark: Eminent, Progressive and Rising* [reprint ed., New York, 1968], 538-544).

55. Sidney Revels Redmond quoted in Horace Mann Bond, "The Negro Scholar and Professional in America," in John P. Davis, ed., *American Negro Reference Book* (Englewood Cliffs, 1966), 584-585.

56. Quoted in Jackson *Daily News,* December 12, 1928. Redmond speculated in real estate and oil, founded an early black bank, and owned an apparently profitable pharmacy. At his death, he was called "one of America's ten wealthiest Negroes" (Wilson, *Make Me a Man,* 57). Redmond's estate was initially estimated at more than $600,000 (Memphis *Commercial-Appeal,* February 13, 1948; Jackson *Clarion-Ledger,* August 12, 1948).

57. "Honorable W. E. Mollison," 108; *Crisis,* 36 (May, 1929), 166; Hamilton, *Beacon Lights of the Race,* 433-434; "Hon. T. Richardson," Indianapolis *Freeman,* April 17, 1897.

58. James A. Burns to Roy Wilkins, February 6, 1935, box G-106, NAACP. By that date, when a black Mississippian was admitted to the bar it was major news in the black community. See Prentiss *Spirit of Mississippi,* June 1, 1934, in JEJ.

59. See especially Jack Oppenheim, "The Abdication of the Southern Bar," in Leon Friedman, ed., *Southern Justice* (New York, 1965), 127-135; but also

Pat Watters and Reese Cleghorn, *Climbing Jacob's Ladder: The Arrival of Negroes in Southern Politics* (New York, 1967), 146n, 323.

60. Gibson and Crogman, *Colored American,* 689; Carter Woodson, *The Negro Professional Man and the Community* (New York, 1934), 97-98.

61. "A Short History of the Mississippi Medical and Surgical Association," in Finch, *Mississippi Negro Ramblings,* 228-235. A second association, the Tri-State Medical, Dental, and Pharmaceutical Association, was formed by black medical professionals from Mississippi, Arkansas, and Tennessee after World War I (Work, ed., *Negro Year Book, 1913-1914,* 336; idem, *Negro Year Book, 1921-1922,* 368-369).

62. "Health," WPA History: Hinds County, box 2; Greenville *Leader,* February 26, 1938; "Social Conditions of Negroes of Natchez," WPA History: Adams County, box 1.

63. WPA Histories: Chickasaw County, Claiborne County, Coahoma County (box 1), and Leflore County; *Daily Corinthian,* April 15, June 23, 1976; Hood, *The Negro at Mound Bayou,* 35; Payne, "Black Middle Class in Laurel," 15, 41.

64. Quoted in Johnson, *From the Driftwood of Bayou Pierre,* 30-31. On doctor-population ratios, see "Negro Population and Doctors," and Medical Statistics, Negro Physicians, box 87, JRF.

65. In 1936 South Carolina had seventy black doctors (one for every 12,000 black persons); Alabama had 101; Georgia had 156 (*Southern Frontier,* September, 1940; March, 1945); Negro Health, box 76, JRF.

66. R. H. Leavell, "Negro Migration from Mississippi," 35. On this general subject see also "Races and Nationalities," WPA History: Claiborne County; Jackson *Daily Clarion-Ledger,* June 22, 1917; June 20, 1919; Louis T. Wright, "The Negro Physician," *Crisis,* 36 (September, 1929), 305.

67. W. E. B. Du Bois, ed., *The College-Bred Negro* (Atlanta, 1900), 83. See also Mosley, *The Negro in Mississippi History,* 33-34, 103; Rawick, ed., *Miss. Narr.,* 9(4), 1470. For an example of a northern-educated black attorney who was never accepted by whites in his Mississippi hometown, see Scott, *Negro Migration,* 25.

68. Daisy M. Greene (daughter of James Hagan Miller, M.D.), oral history, January 31, 1975, MDAH. S. D. Redmond nearly left Jackson at the turn of the century because he could not find office space (Wilson, *Make Me a Man,* 32-33).

69. Douglas L. Conner with John F. Marszalek, *A Black Physician's Story: Bringing Hope in Mississippi* (Jackson, 1985), 73-75 (quotations); Sadye H. Wier with John F. Marszalek, *A Black Businessman in White Mississippi, 1886-1974* (Jackson, 1977), 55-56.

70. Miller to Walter White, September 3, 1918, box C-361, NAACP. See also Gatewood, *Theodore Roosevelt and the Art of Controversy,* 71-72; Stuart, *An Economic Detour,* 284; Charlie Horne, oral history, August 21, 1981, CPC; "Synopsis of Legal Cases, 1925," box 11, NAACP.

71. The best example is that of Dr. Joseph Edison Walker of Indianola, who served as president of both the Delta Penny Savings Bank and the

Mississippi Life Insurance Company (see Johnson, *From the Driftwood of Bayou Pierre,* passim).

72. Lizzie V. Garner, oral history, April 1, 1976, JSU ("poor colored doctor" quotation); Maxine Davis, oral history, April 4, 1976, JSU; Conner, *Black Physician's Story,* 78-79. For evidence that some black physicians at the turn of the century occasionally treated white patients, see Holtzclaw, *Black Magnolias,* 161-162; Richardson, *History of Fisk University,* 165.

73. Negro Physician Studies, June, 1934, box 545, JRF (Tanner quotation); "White Hospitals in Which Colored Physicians Work" [1934], box 546, JRF; Hodding Carter, "He's Doing Something about the Race Problem," *Saturday Evening Post* (February 23, 1946), 30, 69; *Southern Frontier,* March, 1940; September, 1940; "Mound Bayou's Crisis," *Time,* 104 (November 25, 1974), 107; Wilson, *Education for Negroes,* 156; Baltimore *Afro-American,* March 29, 1947; Chicago *Defender,* March 29, 1947.

74. Venereal disease was a major health problem. Mississippi State Board of Health doctors discovered in the late 1920s and 1930s that roughly one in four black Deltans had syphilis; one in three had some form of venereal illness (H. C. Ricks to M. M. Davis, September 16, 1929; H. S. Cumming to Davis, July 19, 1929, box 231; H. A. Poindexter, "Report of the Glendora, Mississippi Health Unit," October 20, 1937, box 212, JRF.

75. The Julius Rosenwald Fund Papers are the richest single source on Mississippi's black health care facilities. See especially Mrs. J. F. McDougal to M. O. Bousfield, July 24, 1939, box 299; J. B. Snider to Julius Rosenwald Fund, April 30, 1940, box 233, JRF.

76. The most complete list of black weeklies published in this or any state is the register of newspapers published annually since 1870 by N. W. Ayer and Son, Inc. See also the useful annual tabulations published in Work, ed., *Negro Year Book, 1912, 1913-1914, 1918-1919, 1921-1922, 1925-1926,* and *1941-1946).* For a less complete and less accurate listing, see a misnamed document apparently prepared by the Works Progress Administration, "Report on Foreign-Language Press [in Mississippi]" [1939?], MDAH. On the Negro Press Association, see untitled manuscript [June 28, 1910], Charles Banks folder, con. 49, BTW. Julius E. Thomson, *The Black Press in Mississippi, 1865-1985: A Directory* (West Cornwall, Conn., 1988) appeared after this book went to press.

77. Wharton, *Negro in Mississippi,* 273; Julius Thompson, "Mississippi," in Henry Lewis Suggs, ed., *The Black Press in the South, 1865-1979* (Westport, Conn., 1983), 178.

78. Wharton, *Negro in Mississippi,* 273; Irvine Garland Penn, *The Afro-American Press and Its Editors* (Springfield, Mass., 1891), 113. Although Monroe Work listed a Jackson *Peoples' Defender* in 1912, this publication is apparently linked only by name to its predecessor and not at all to the *Peoples' Journal* (Work, ed., *Negro Year Book, 1912,* 193-194). A few religious organs enjoyed uncommon longevity, including the *Baptist Signal,* which appeared in Greenville in 1880 and survived into the post–World War I era as the

Lexington *Signal* (Detweiler, *The Negro Press,* 60; [WPA], "Report on the Foreign-Language Press," 6; Simmons, *Men of Mark,* 595-596).

79. *Delta Light House,* December 13, 1919; Greenville *Leader,* February 6, 1938; Work, ed., *Negro Year Book, 1912,* 193-194; *1918-1919,* 469-470; [WPA], "Report on the Foreign-Language Press," 6. Chapple's son published the short-lived Greenville *Leader* until its demise in October, 1938.

80. During the 1930s, the paper was apparently published as the Natchez *City Bulletin* ([WPA], "Report on the Foreign-Language Press," 5; Work, ed., *Negro Year Book, 1912,* 193-194; *1918-1919,* 469-470).

81. Hood, *The Negro at Mound Bayou,* 28; Isaiah T. Montgomery, *Introduction to Mound Bayou, Mississippi* (n.p., 1913), unpaginated pamphlet.

82. The Greenville *Delta Leader* is not to be confused with the ephemeral Greenville *Leader* (Thompson, "Mississippi," 182-183).

83. There were actually eight black Mississippi weeklies published in 1943, but one was a religious paper and another devoted totally to advertising ("Negro Newspapers and Periodicals in the United States: 1943," *Negro Statistical Bulletin, No. 1,* August, 1944). See also Work, ed., *Negro Year Book, 1912,* 183, 187, 193-194; *1921-1922,* 422, 424; *1941-1946,* 401; [WPA], "Report on the Foreign-Language Press."

84. Quoted in Penn, *The Afro-American Press,* 439. Although many white editors unfairly mocked their less literate black counterparts, something of the literary character of the more marginal Negro papers is suggested in materials reprinted in the state's white newspapers. See editorial, "Manhood," Jackson *Colored Journal,* reprinted in Port Gibson *Reveille,* October 31, 1890; ibid., February 11, 1891.

85. Carter, *Where Mainstreet Meets the River,* 257. For representative complaints from black Mississippians about the kind of black news covered by the white press, see Indianapolis *Freeman,* April 17, 1897, and Chicago *Defender,* February 26, 1916.

86. Scott, *Negro Migration,* 30 ("fodder" quotation); *Vanguard News* (Campbell College, Jackson, Miss.), quoted in WPA History: Hinds County, box 1; Indianapolis *Freeman,* April 17, 1897; Chicago *Defender,* Janaury 15, 1916; Alexander, "Cultural Reconnaissance Survey of Coahoma County," 9.

87. Handy, *Father of the Blues,* 79-80.

88. Chicago *Defender,* January 15, 1916; NAACP, *Annual Report for 1920,* 22; Detweiler, *The Negro Press,* 156; Brooklyn *Daily Eagle,* April 24, 1920; Dollard, *Caste and Class in a Southern Town,* 339; Thompson, "Mississippi," 204n.

89. The Reverend E. R. Franklin, apparently the first to be convicted under the law, was flogged by vigilantes and sentenced to six months of hard labor (NAACP, *Annual Report for 1920,* 22).

90. J. M. Williamson, quoted in editorial, Chicago *Defender,* March 30, 1929.

91. Penn, *The Afro-American Press,* 200-201 (quotation), 228; Thompson, "Mississippi," 178-179.

92. Editorial, Jackson *Colored Journal,* quoted in Port Gibson *Reveille,*

October 31, 1890; Meridian *Fair Play,* quoted in Jackson *Clarion-Ledger,* October 23, 1890; Natchez *Brotherhood,* quoted in Sallis, "The Color Line in Mississippi Politics," 332.

93. For example, the Meridian *Fair Play* was printed by the Meridian *Daily News* until the black editor offended whites and was then forced to publish on a job press (Penn, *The Afro-American Press,* 200-201). In the opinion of one white Mississippian, the state's "so called Negro papers as a rule are owned and controlled by whites and edited from the white not the Negro point of view" (Henderson, "In the Cotton Delta," 109).

94. George S. Schuyler, "Freedom of the Press in Mississippi," *Crisis,* 43 (October, 1936), 302.

95. Hood, *The Negro at Mound Bayou,* 28 (quotation); Jackson *People's Defender,* quoted in Winston County *Journal,* November 25, 1898; Jackson *Enquirer,* quoted in Memphis *Commercial-Appeal,* July 18, 1895; Brandon *Free State,* January 20, 1900; Greenville *Delta Light House,* December 13, 1919.

96. Among the surviving examples see: Brandon *Free State,* January 20, 1900; Vicksburg *Light,* January 18, 1900; Greenville *Leader,* February 26, 1938; but also Schuyler, "Freedom of the Press in Mississippi," 306; [WPA], "Report on the Foreign-Language Press," passim; Thompson, "Mississippi," 179-180, 182-183. Cf. Howard N. Rabinowitz, *Race Relations in the Urban South, 1865-1890* (New York, 1978), 231-232. As this book went to press, the MDAH accessioned issues of the (Senatobia) *Baptist Herald* (January 2, 1891) and the (Meridian) *Echo* and *Weekly Echo,* both published by the Holbrook Benevolent Association (1920s and 1930s).

97. Cohn, *Where I Was Born,* 289 ("nothing biggity" quotation); Crockett, *Black Towns,* 185 ("saturate" quotation).

98. Lincoln County *Times,* May 19, 1910; Brookhaven *Semi-Weekly Leader,* May 18, 21, 25, 1910; and September 13, 27, October 18, 1911.

99. Natchez *Daily Democrat,* August 27, 29, 1904; WPA History: Leflore County; *History of Blacks in Greenville,* unpaginated.

100. Chicago *Defender,* October 3, 1931; Holtzclaw, *Black Magnolias,* 82-83. Wright's story, "Hell's Half Acre," is described in Fabre, *The Unfinished Quest,* 48-49.

101. Jackson *Daily News,* June 17, July 17, 1945.

102. Hamilton, *Beacon Lights of the Race,* 97, 103, 514.

103. Theodore Hemmingway, "Booker T. Washington in Mississippi, October, 1908," *Journal of Mississippi History,* 46 (February, 1984), 31 (second quotation), 37 (first quotation).

104. G. F. Richings, *Evidence of Progress among Colored People* (Philadelphia, 1903), 533-535; Sunflower *Tocsin,* January 22, 1919; Charles Banks to Warren G. Harding, May 30, 1921 (microfilm, roll 174, frame 848), WGH.

105. New York *Age,* July 8, 1909 ("commerical brotherhood" quotation); Charles Banks to "Dear Sir," May 22, 1908, con. 38, BTW; unidentified manuscript [June 28, 1910], con. 49 ("Negro capital" quotation); Emmett Scott, "Advance Matter," con. 1094, BTW; Little Rock *Our Review,* August

19, 1911; I. T. Montgomery, "The Work and Influence of the National Negro Business League," *Colored American*, 15 (February, 1909), 87-88.

106. On Mississippi's leadership in the NNBL's institutional offshoots see: Work, ed., *Negro Year Book, 1912*, 133-134; *1913-1914*, 363; *Report of the Fifteenth Annual Convention of the National Negro Business League*, 15-16; Little Rock *Our Review*, August 19, 1911. On "Mississippi Day" see: *Program, Mississippi Negro Business League, Okolona, June 30 to July 1, 1909*, con. 1094; and Banks to Washington, November 5, 1908, con. 38, BTW; New York *Age*, July 8, 1909; August 25, 1910.

107. Meier, *Negro Thought in America*, 121-157.

108. Indianapolis *Freeman*, May 18, 1889.

109. W. E. B. Du Bois, ed., *The Negro in Business*, Atlanta University Publications no. 4 (Atlanta, 1899), 25-26; J. Cyril O'Neill, *Early Twentieth-Century Vicksburg, 1900-1910* (Vicksburg, 1976), app.

110. Woodard, *Negro Progress*, 3-4; Washington, *The Story of the Negro*, 204; Booker T. Washington, "The Negro's Part in Southern Development," *Annals of the American Association of Political and Social Sciences*, 35 (January, 1910), 129; Work, ed., *Negro Year Book, 1921-1922*, 21; Jackson *Clarion-Ledger*, [1915], quoted in *Clarion-Ledger*, September 26, 1979 (first quotation); Ralph W. Tyler's report in Chicago *Defender* [March, 1914], clipping in Tuskegee Institute News Clipping File (reel 2, frame 663) ("oasis" quotation).

111. Quoted in *Tuskegee Student*, September 11, 1909. For descriptions of Greenville and Indianola, see Baltimore *Afro-American*, February 25, 1921, quoted in Detweiler, *The Negro Press*, 208; and Tucker, *Lieutenant Lee of Beale Street*, 3-4. The "golden period" of black enterprise in Laurel is described in Payne, "Black Middle Class in Laurel," 7-18, 38-48.

112. Ralph W. Tyler in Chicago *Defender* [March, 1914], clipping in Tuskegee Institute News Clipping File (reel 2, frame 663). See also Booker T. Washington, "A Cheerful Journey through Mississippi," *World's Work*, February, 1909, 11282.

113. Mississippi's first black bank was the Lincoln Savings Bank, founded in Vicksburg by W. E. Mollison in 1902. Columbus, Greenville, Indianola, Mound Bayou, Natchez, Shaw, and Yazoo City each had one black bank; there were two each in Hattiesburg, Jackson, and Vicksburg. Total resources in the state's black banks peaked in 1911 at $707,500, compared to a high of $2,555,000 in Georgia (1923), $4,173,300 in Virginia (1926), and $1,466,100 in North Carolina (1925). See: O'Neill, *Early Twentieth-Century Vicksburg*, 31; *Leading Afro-Americans of Vicksburg*, 15; Charles Banks, "Negro Banks of Mississippi," in Woodard, *Negro Progress*, 9-11; Abram L. Harris, *The Negro as Capitalist: A Study of Banking and Business among American Negroes* (Philadelphia, 1936), 191, 193.

114. Ben B. McNew, "Banking, 1890-1970," in McLemore, ed., *History of Mississippi*, 2: 315-317; Harris, *Negro as Capitalist*, passim; and Armand J. Thieblot, Jr., *The Negro in the Banking Industry* (Philadelphia, 1960), 175-191. On the specific problems of representative banks see also, Banks to A. J. Howard, January 1, 1912, con. 56; Banks to Washington, April 15, March

11, 1915, con. 75, BTW; Chicago *Defender,* November 14, 1914; Du Bois, ed., *Economic Co-operation,* 147.

115. Woodard, *Negro Progress,* 5-6; Du Bois, ed., *Economic Co-operation,* 146.

116. *The Union Savings Bank, Vicksburg, Mississippi* (n.p., [1910]), con. 1094, BTW; *Leading Afro-Americans of Vicksburg,* 52.

117. Banks, "Negro Banks of Mississippi," 9-11.

118. W. E. Mollison, "What Banks Managed by Colored Men Are Doing for Their Communities," *Colored American,* 12 (August, 1907), 191-192 ("color blind" quotation); Du Bois, ed., *Economic Co-operation,* 142 ("club" quotation). See also Washington, *My Larger Education,* extracts in Louis Harlan, ed., *The Booker T. Washington Papers* (Urbana, 1972), 1: 436; Du Bois, ed., *Economic Cooperation,* 143 (last quotation).

119. Hamilton, *Beacon Lights of the Race,* 219 (quotation). On the liquidations see Lincoln County *Times,* March 28, 1907; Jackson *Daily News,* February 18, 1912; Indianapolis *Freeman,* September 26, 1914; Chicago *Defender,* November 14, 1914; "Races and Nationalities," WPA History: Adams County; Work, ed., *Negro Yearbook, 1913-1914,* 309-310; *1918-1919,* 368; McNew, "Banking, 1890-1970," 316.

120. Banks to Fred R. Moore, July 14, 1915, con. 75, BTW ("unwarranted" quotation); Stuart, *Economic Detour,* 287 ("intend to qualify" quotation); Banks to Emmett Scott, January 27, 1914, con. 52 ("aspire" quotation); Banks to Washington, October 21, 1914, con. 68, BTW ("wipe out" quotation); see also Banks to Washington, October 22, 1915, con. 75, BTW; and New York *Age,* September 17, 1914.

121. Stuart, *Economic Detour,* 287 (quotation); Sunflower *Tocsin,* May 25, 27, October 28, 1915; January 17, November 21, December 4, 1918. The Mound Bayou State Bank failed in 1922; the Delta Penny Savings Bank folded in 1926. No other black-owned banks were ever chartered in Mississippi (Harris, *Negro as Capitalist,* 191).

122. Marable, "The Politics of Black Land Tenure, 1877-1915," 142-152.

123. Harvey, oral history, April 21, 1981, MDAH ("no credit" quotation); Tommy Lee Johnson, "The Development of Black Banking in Mississippi" (M.A. thesis, Jackson State University, 1977), 26 ("white institutions" quotation); Clinton Anderson, oral history, August 24, 1970, MHC ("shit" quotation).

124. North Carolina Mutual may have been the first black insurance company to operate with legal-reserve status, but Mississippi Life was apparently the first to be so chartered (Walter B. Weare, *Black Business in the New South: A Social History of the North Carolina Mutual Life Insurance Company* [Urbana, 1973], 93n). There were at least four other indigenous black firms, all of them specializing in industrial policies based on small, weekly premiums: Industrial Mutual Relief Association of America and Union Guarantee and Insurance Company of Mississippi, both of Jackson and both operated briefly during and after World War I; Magnolia Mutual Life of Tupelo and Security Life of Jackson were both organized on the eve of World War II (Work, ed.,

Negro Year Book 1918-1919, 360; *Mississippi Education Journal,* 15 [October, 1938], 18; U.S., Department of Commerce, *First Annual Report of Insurance Companies Owned and Operated by Negroes, March 9, 1947* [Washington, D.C., 1947], 6-10).

125. See the examples of two small church-related aid societies in rural Jefferson County (WPA History: Jefferson County), and a much larger yet still local organization in Jackson (Woodard, *Negro Progress,* 7). On the persistence of the local aid society, see the statement of Louis J. Piernas: Rawick, ed., *Miss. Narr.,* 9(4), 1703-1704.

126. Stuart, *Economic Detour,* 20, 25-28, 32; *Biennial Report of the Insurance Department of Mississippi for 1903-1905,* 16, 28, 32; *1909-1911,* 68; *1917-1919,* 96; Du Bois, ed., *Economic Co-operation,* 109-111 (quotation), 121; Mound Bayou *New Light,* June 1, 1913; New York *Age,* September 7, 1911; September 19, 1914; Banks to "Dear Brother," undated form letter, con. 52; Banks to "Dear Brother," November 13, 1913, con. 64; Banks to Washington, January 7, 1914, con. 68, BTW.

127. Powdermaker, *After Freedom,* 121; U.S., Department of Commerce, *First Annual Report of Insurance Companies Owned and Operated by Negroes,* 22. By 1919 only eleven black fraternal orders—compared to forty-seven in 1909—were licensed to sell insurance in Mississippi (*Biennial Report of the Insurance Department of Mississippi for 1917-1919,* 96).

128. Mollison, "Negro Lawyers," 66-67; Du Bois, *Economic Co-operation,* 109-127; New York *Age,* September 9, 1914; Charles Banks to Fraternal Orders of Mississippi, undated form letter [1912], con. 56, BTW; M. S. Stuart, "Life Insurance for and by Negroes of the United States," *Crisis,* 49 (June, 1942), 185.

129. Allison Davis, "The Negro Church and Associations in the Lower South," Carnegie-Myrdal Study of the Negro in America (June, 1940), microfilm ed., 198, 200 (Adams County quotation); Stuart, *Economic Detour,* 18-19 ("fairly general" quotation), 28; Jackson *Daily News,* December 16, 18, 1911; February 21, 1912.

130. Stuart, *Economic Detour,* 284-289. See also George Washington Lee, *Beale Street: Where the Blues Began* (New York, 1934), 184-185; *Report of the Insurance Department of Mississippi for 1920* (n.p., n.d.), 1; *The Negro Race in Sunflower County, Mississippi* (Grenada, Miss., n.d.), 7.

131. Sunflower *Tocsin,* January 22, 1919. On Mississippi Life's relative place in the black insurance field, see Tucker, *Lieutenant Lee of Beale Street,* 48; and Weare, *Black Business in the New South,* 103-104.

132. Gatewood, *Theodore Roosevelt and the Art of Controversy,* 89; Stuart, *Economic Detour,* 277, 286, 302 (quotations).

133. Stuart, *Economic Detour,* 36-37, 178, 286; Jackson *Daily News,* December 7, 8, 1911; Brookhaven *Semi-Weekly Leader,* December 6, 1911; [Walter White], "Report of Conditions Found in Investigation of 'Work or Fight' Laws in Southern States," box C-418, NAACP.

134. Stuart, *Economic Detour,* 168-169, 288-289, 302; Johnson, *From the Driftwood of Bayou Pierre,* 38-39, 51, 57-63, 82. Cf. the company's cautious

public explanation for the decision to relocate: Sunflower *Tocsin,* August 12, 1920.

135. Stuart, *Economic Detour,* 168-169 (quotation); Carter Woodson, "Insurance Business among Negroes," *Journal of Negro History,* 14 (April, 1929), 225; Tucker, *Lieutenant Lee of Beale Street,* 50; Lester C. Lamon, *Black Tennesseans, 1900-1930* (Knoxville, 1977), 202-203. The Cox legacy also includes the Indianolan's nephew, George Wayne Cox, who left Mississippi Life in 1919 to launch a highly successful career with North Carolina Mutual (Weare, *Black Business in the New South,* 112-113, and passim).

136. The most complete scholarly analyses of the rise and decline of Mound Bayou are Hermann, *Pursuit of a Dream;* and Crockett, *Black Towns.* On the Davis Bend experiment see also Currie, *Enclave,* 83-144; and idem, "Freedmen at Davis Bend, April 1964," *Journal of Mississippi History,* 46 (May, 1984), 120-129.

137. Montgomery to A. C. Charleston, July 1, 1904, con. 242, BTW (first Montgomery quotation); Redding, *No Day of Triumph,* 300 (Green quotation); Cleveland *Enterprise,* July 30, 1914 (second Montgomery quotation). On the town's enduring self-image, see: advertisement in Work, ed., *Negro Year Book, 1912,* 10; Hood, *Negro at Mound Bayou,* passim; *"Jewel of the Delta," Mound Bayou, Mississippi, 75th Anniversary, July 12-15, 1962* (n.p., n.d.). Other smaller and less significant all-Negro towns in Mississippi included the sawmill communities of Chambers and Renova, both in Bolivar County.

138. *Address of President Roosevelt at the Laying of the Corner Stone of the Colored Men's Christian Association Building, Washington, D.C., November 26, 1908* (Washington, D.C., 1908), 22; Chicago *Defender,* July 13, 1929 (Bethune quotation). See also: William P. Pickett, *The Negro Problem* (New York, 1909), 485; Day Allen Willey, "Mound Bayou—A Negro Municipality," *Alexander's Magazine,* 4 (July 15, 1907), 159.

139. For Washington's description of the town, see Washington, *My Larger Education,* 209; Booker T. Washington, "Law and Order and the Negro," *Outlook,* 93 (November 6, 1909), 552-554. The close ties between Tuskegee and Mound Bayou are copiously documented by the personal correspondence of Banks to both Washington and Emmett J. Scott in BTW.

140. August Meier, "Booker T. Washington and the Town of Mound Bayou," in August Meier and Elliott Rudwick, eds., *Along the Color Line: Explorations in the Black Experience* (Urbana, 1976), 217. The early years of the town are described in Jackson, "Mound Bayou—A Study in Social Development," 28-45; Hood, *The Negro at Mound Bayou,* 57-61; [anonymous], "The Founding of Mound Bayou, Mississippi," undated manuscript, BMF.

141. Du Bois, *Economic Co-operation,* 171-172 (quotation); Tong, "The Pioneers of Mound Bayou," 393-394; B. F. Ousley, "A Town of Colored People in Mississippi," *American Missionary Association Bulletin, 1904;* Hood, *The Negro at Mound Bayou,* 16-24; Montgomery to Washington, May 19, 1904, con. 242, BTW (last quotation).

142. Banks, "Negro Banks of Mississippi," 9-11; Banks to Theodore Roo-

sevelt, April 23, 1912 (microfilm, ser. 1, reel 172), TRP; Hood, *The Negro at Mound Bayou,* 37-41; Hamilton, *Beacon Lights of the Race,* 208.

143. Hamilton, *Beacon Lights of the Race,* 205, 213-214 ("rhapsody" and "splendid circumstances" quotations); Washington, *My Larger Education,* 207-208 ("pure African" and "most influential" quotations). See also: Gibson Willets, "After Forty Years of Freedom," *Alexander's Magazine,* 1 (November 15, 1905), 12.

144. Charles Banks, *Negro Town and Colony, Mound Bayou, Bolivar County, Mississippi: Opportunities Open to Negro Farmers and Settlers* (Mound Bayou, [1906]); Banks, "A Negro Colony"; Hood, *The Negro at Mound Bayou,* 10 ("capacity" quotation).

145. Banks to Scott, January 10, 1910, con. 49; Banks to Scott, January 13, 1911, con. 52; and Montgomery to Washington, May 19, 1904, con. 242, BTW; Banks, "A Negro Colony"; New York *Age,* April 25, 1912.

146. Among the first bank's most pressing problems was overextension of credit to the oil mill (Banks to Washington, February 20, 1914, con. 68, BTW; New York *Age,* September 17, 1914).

147. Banks to Washington, May 29, 1913, con. 64; Banks to Robert E. Park, September 22, 1911, con. 52; Banks to Scott, April 3, March 22, 1913, con. 64; Frank J. Parsons to Washington, February 28, 1913, con. 64; Washington to Parsons, February 24, 1913, con. 64; unidentified attorney to William C. Greaves, October 4, 1915, con. 75; Banks to Washington, January 7, 1914, con. 68, BTW (quotation); Montgomery, *Introduction to Mound Bayou.*

148. Banks to Washington, February 15, 1915, con. 75, BTW; *Semi-Centennial Celebration—Mound Bayou Mississippi* (n.p., n.d.), 6 ("tragic reminder" quotation).

149. Redding, *No Day of Triumph,* 303 (quotation); Crockett, *Black Towns,* 177-178; Jackson, "Mound Bayou," 36; Douglass, "A History of E. P. Booze," 4; Mary Booze to Calvin Coolidge, November 12, 1925 (microfilm, ser. 3, reel 277), WHT.

150. Chicago *Defender,* June 15, 1929; "Charter and By-Laws of Mound Bayou Foundation," and "Minutes of the First Meeting," Mound Bayou Foundation, subject file, MDAH; Jackson, "Mound Bayou," 76; Webb Waldron, "All Black: A Unique Negro Community," *Survey Graphic,* 27 (January, 1938), 36; Mound Bayou Foundation, *Come to Mound Bayou* (n.p., [1929]), 3.

151. Redding, *No Day of Triumph,* 290-297, 301 (Green quotation). The devastating impact of the Great Depression on the economy of Mound Bayou and its surrounding agricultural "colony" is suggested in the letter of a black county agent, M. M. Hubert, to J. A. Evans, January 23, 1931, President's Personal File 30, Negro Matters, Presidential Papers, HPL.

152. Crockett, *Black Towns,* xiv (quotation), 164-166, 176, 186.

153. Du Bois, ed., *The Negro in Business,* 6, 19, 25-26; U.S., Bureau of Census, *Fifteenth Census, Retail Distribution,* vol. 1, pt. 2 (Washington, D.C., 1930), 1395.

154. Johnson, *Patterns of Negro Segregation,* 64; Davis et al., *Deep South,*

467n; John Henry Harmon, "The Negro as a Local Business Man," *Journal of Negro History,* 14 (April, 1929), 131.

155. Beam, *He Called Them by the Lightning,* 178; Redding, *Lonesome Road,* 110; *Report of the Fifteenth Annual Convention of the National Negro Business League,* 66.

156. Montgomery to Washington, September 6, 1904, in Harlan, ed., *Washington Papers,* 8: 62-63. See also the examples of Memphis Merchant, a tailor, and Dan Gooden, an insurance agent, in Lincoln County (Brookhaven *Semi-Weekly Leader,* December 6, 1911).

157. Davis, "The Negro Church and Associations," 63.

158. Dollard, *Caste and Class in a Southern Town,* 126 (quotation); Adams, "Changing Negro Life in the Delta," 18. The plantation of the Delta and Pine Land Company at Scott (Bolivar County) was a notable exception to the white rule of steering black trade to white merchants. See Johnston, "The Colored Farmers of the Missippi Delta," [1929], reprinted in Mound Bayou Foundation, *Come to Mound Bayou,* 17, 19.

159. Even in the 1980s, Clarie Collins Harvey, Collins's daughter and the heir to his Jackson mortuary, has noted, white undertakers in many small Mississippi towns serve the black community, although not on an equal basis: "They don't bathe the bodies, they don't do their hair." In some cases, services are provided directly by white establishments; in others white funeral homes own black mortuaries and employ black morticians to "front" as owners or managers (Harvey, oral history, April 21, 1981, MDAH).

160. August Meier, "Negro Class Structure and Ideology in the Age of Booker T. Washington," *Phylon,* 23 (Third Quarter, 1962), 259; Judson Byrd, oral history, [1981], CPC.

161. See, e.g., Powdermaker, *After Freedom,* 56-71.

162. Quoted in Davis et al., *Deep South,* 472.

163. Isaiah S. Sanders (interviewed April, 1977) quoted in Johnson, "Development of Black Banking in Mississippi," 21. See also Weare, *Black Business in the New South,* 64-65; and Alean Adams, oral history, May 18, 1970, MHC.

164. Higgs, *Competition and Coercion,* 93. See also Harris, *Negro as Capitalist,* chap. 9; Stuart, *Economic Detour,* xvii-xviii, xix, passim.

Chapter 6. Jim Crow's Courts

1. Quoted in Lincoln County *Times,* May 30, 1907.

2. W. E. B. Du Bois, "Race Relations in the United States, 1917-1947," *Phylon,* 9 (1948), 237.

3. Critical portions of the trial record are reproduced in Robert W. Horton, " 'Not Too Much for a Negro,' " *Nation,* 141 (December 11, 1935), 674-676. The trial and the events leading to it are described in *Brown et al.* v. *Mississippi,* 173 Miss. 572, and Ralph T. Seward, "Another Scottsboro Case?" *New Republic,* 85 (November 13, 1935), 19. The only full analysis of the trial and its larger implications for American constitutional law is Richard C. Cortner, *A "Scottsboro" Case in Mississippi: The Supreme Court and Brown v. Mississippi*

(Jackson, Miss., 1986); but see also Loren Miller, *The Petitioners: The Story of the Supreme Court of the United States and the Negro* (New York, 1966), 277-280.

4. Horton, " 'Not Too Much,' " 676; Cortner, *"Scottsboro" Case in Mississippi,* 3-13. For a description of Ellington's condition and the reluctance of white authorities to permit him medical attention following the beating, see Mrs. J. Morgan Stevens to Mrs. B. L. Johnson, May 7, 1935, JEJ.

5. Cortner, *"Scottsboro" Case in Mississippi,* 24, 44.

6. Meridian *Star,* April 8, 1934.

7. See Clark's affidavit quoted in Horton, " 'Not Too Much,' " 676.

8. *Brown et al.* v. *Mississippi,* 173 Miss. 542 at 559, 572, 574, 579 (1935); *Brown et al.* v. *Mississippi,* 297 U.S. 278 at 285-286 (1936). The NAACP's role is described in its *Annual Report for 1935,* 11; *Annual Report for 1936,* 15-16; and in virtually every issue of the *Crisis,* from (March, 1935), 79; to (May, 1936), 138.

9. "Along the NAACP Battlefront," *Crisis* 46 (January, 1937), 22-23; Cortner, *"Scottsboro" Case in Mississippi,* 156, 158.

10. A. E. Keir Nash, "The Texas Supreme Court and Trial Rights of Blacks, 1845-1860," *Journal of American History,* 58 (December, 1971), 623; Cortner, *"Scottsboro" Case in Mississippi,* xiii.

11. Two caveats are necessary: (1) this essay is based primarily on the appeals record, rather than the trial record of Mississippi's criminal justice system; and (2) its focus is on capital crimes against persons, rather than on crimes against property or morality. The first is a matter of practicality, for the appeals record is the only accessible record. Trial records, for the most part untranscribed documents still in court stenographers' shorthand and housed (in theory, at least) in the eighty-two courthouses of Mississippi, have never been systematically examined. In fact, as attorneys often note, these records in a great many instances no longer survive. Nor are there satisfactory microanalyses of criminal justice in single Mississippi counties for the period after 1890. The second is a matter of choice and interpretation. It is my assumption that a study of how serious crimes against persons—particularly interracial crimes—were handled in the state's circuit and appellate courts reveals more about the quality of justice available to black Mississippians than would the study of the handling of other types of crime.

12. For example, Kier Nash, "The Texas Supreme Court," 622-42; idem, "Fairness and Formalism in the Trials of Blacks in the State Supreme Courts of the Old South," *Virginia Law Review,* 56 (1970), 64-100; Meredith Lang, *Defender of the Faith: The High Court of Mississippi, 1817-1875* (Jackson, Miss., 1977), 94ff.; Daniel J. Flanigan, "Criminal Procedure in Slave Trials in the Antebellum South," *Journal of Southern History,* 40 (November, 1974), 537-564. For a more critical view, see Michael S. Hindus, "Black Justice under White Law: Criminal Prosecutions of Blacks in Antebellum South Carolina," *Journal of American History,* 63 (December, 1976), 575-599. Although Mississippi is not the focus of his study, Edward L. Ayers's *Vengeance and Justice: Crime and Punishment in the Nineteenth-Century American South* (New York,

1984) illuminates changing black experiences with the criminal justice system during the antebellum and postbellum periods.

13. *Minor* v. *Mississippi,* 36 Miss. 630 at 634-635 (1859); Lang, *Defender of the Faith,* 105ff.

14. *Dixon* v. *Mississippi,* 74 Miss. 271 at 275 (1896); *Hampton* v. *State,* 88 Miss. 257 at 259 (1906).

15. Davis, *Mississippi Negro Lore,* 22-28. Much the same point was made by Chancery Judge Percy Bell of Greenville. Although required to report "anything criminal" to the grand jury, this magistrate learned not to report "negro peccadilloes," which he thought were "wisely ignored" and a "waste of time." Bell, "Child of the Delta," chap. 7, p. 9. Judge Davis's career is sketched in Memphis *Commercial-Appeal,* August 24, 1948.

16. Quoted in Davis et al., *Deep South,* 46 (quotation), 394-395. See also Brookhaven *Semi-Weekly Leader,* September 27, 1911; James Harmon Chadbourn, *Lynching and the Law* (Chapel Hill, 1933), 81; Smith, *The Yazoo River,* 202; Alexander, "Cultural Reconnaissance Survey of Coahoma County"; and Hickman, *Mississippi Harvest,* 144-145.

17. Powdermaker, *After Freedom,* 173. See also Davis, "Caste, Economy, and Violence," 11; Ayers, *Vengeance and Justice,* 230-231.

18. *Collins* v. *Mississippi,* 100 Miss. 435 at 437 (1911). See also *Butler* v. *Mississippi,* 146 Miss. 505 (1927).

19. *Sykes* v. *Mississippi,* 89 Miss. 767 at 767 (1906); *Story* v. *Mississippi,* 133 Miss. 476 at 479 (1923). The persistence of the argument employed by the prosecutor in *Sykes* is suggested by *Reed* v. *State,* 232 Miss. 432 at 434 (1958).

20. Quoted in Davis et al., *Deep South,* 499. See also Cohn, "Share-Cropping in the Delta," 581-582.

21. Hattiesburg *Progress,* quoted in Jackson *Weekly Clarion-Ledger,* January 22, 1903. See also the example of Tom Robinson who, though imprisoned in 1924 for killing his wife, had earlier killed (by his count) twelve other blacks without even being arrested (Vicksburg *Evening Post,* May 11, 1935). For other evidence of the casualness with which whites viewed black-on-black homicide, see Brandon *News,* May 26, 1910; Sunflower *Tocsin,* November 16, 1916; Hickman, *Mississippi Harvest,* 144-145; Percy, *Lanterns on the Levee,* 300.

22. Lester Franklin to Martin Sennett Conner, April 29, 1935, vol. 697, GPF. See also Dollard, *Caste and Class in a Southern Town,* 280-283; Snyder, "Plantation Pictures," 171-172.

23. The state treasury was particularly well served by black imprisonment. In the course of a twenty-year sentence, Davis estimated, an inmate–field hand at Parchman prison farm could produce 200 bales of cotton valued at $15,000 (Davis, *Mississippi Negro Lore,* 28).

24. Davis et al., *Deep South,* 521 (first quotation); Rowe to NAACP, June 30, 1922, Legal Files, box D-39, NAACP (second quotation).

25. David Cohn, *God Shakes Creation* (New York, 1935), 155; but see also Dockery, oral history, December 13, 1979, MDAH; and Dixon Pyle, "Mound Bayou, Bolivar County," 9, in *Mound Bayou History,* subject file, MDAH.

26. Jackson *Daily News,* November 15, 1911. See also Port Gibson *Reveille,* October 17, 1890; Brookhaven *Semi-Weekly Leader,* July 17, 1909; Lincoln County *Times,* supplement, December 19, 1907; Sunflower *Tocsin,* April 1, 15, 1915; Vicksburg *Evening Post,* March 22, 1919. Official indifference to white violence against blacks is also suggested by some courtroom humor, a "Sambo and Jerry" story told by an attorney for the state in 1920 to the justices of the Mississippi Supreme Court during the appeal of a murder conviction. "[Sambo:] 'Did you hear about that nigger commitin' suicide in the delta' 'No, why wuz it' asked Jerry, to which Sambo replied. 'He called a white man a liar' " (*Williams* v. *Mississippi,* 122 Miss. 151 at 161 [1920]).

27. But see an exceptional Grenada County case: Walter E. Pittman, "The Mel Cheatham Affair: Interracial Murder in Mississippi 1889," *Journal of Mississippi History,* 43 (May, 1981), 127-133.

28. Jackson *Evening News,* June 7, 1897.

29. Chicago *Defender,* May 3, 1930.

30. Davis, *Mississippi Negro Lore,* 22-23.

31. Kenneth N. Vines, "Southern State Supreme Courts and Race Relations," *Western Political Quarterly,* 18 (March, 1965), 5.

32. *Carraway* v. *Mississippi,* 163 Miss. 639 (1932), 167 Miss. 390 (1933), 170 Miss. 685 at 698-699 (1934). The district attorney was William M. Colmer, future member of the United States House of Representatives. Carraway was spared the gallows by nine reprieves—a Mississippi record—and his sentence was commuted to life by Governor Martin Sennett Conner. See NAACP press releases and other materials in folder "Cases Supported—Tom Carraway," Legal Files, boxes D-49, D-50, NAACP; Jackson *Clarion-Ledger,* October 19, 1932; January 16, 1933; April 24, 1934; Jackson *Daily News,* December 13, 1932.

33. Willie Overton, "Mississippi Spends $5,000 to Protect White Supremacy," undated Associated Negro Press release in folder Howard-McGehee-Jones Case 1934, Legal Files, con. D-18, NAACP; Baton Rouge *Morning Advocate,* February 7, 1934; Pittsburgh *Courier,* March 24, 1934; "Races," *Time,* March 19, 1934, 14; "Races," *Time,* March 26, 1934, 10; "Mississippi Father's Right to Kill Approved by Senate," *Newsweek,* March 17, 1934, 10; [Arthur Raper], *The Mob Still Rides: A Review of the Lynching Record, 1931-1935* (Atlanta, 1936), 6.

34. Ida B. Wells, *A Red Record . . . Lynching in the United States, 1892, 1893, 1894* (Chicago, [1895]), 48-49.

35. Jackson *Daily News,* November 4, 1911.

36. In the latter case, that of Elwood Higginbotham—who pleaded self-defense after killing a white man who had broken into his house at night with pistol drawn—there were reportedly two jurors holding out for acquittal. See [Raper], *The Mob Still Rides,* 8, 12; NAACP, *Annual Report* for the years 1918, 1920, 1935, and 1942; and Jackson *Daily Clarion-Ledger,* April 19, 1918.

37. NAACP, *Annual Report for 1925,* 19; Memphis *Commercial-Appeal,* December 22, 1925; New York *World,* December 23, 1925. Following the Coleman lynching—described by one observer as "the straw that broke the

camel's back"—the state enacted legislation that (a) required local officials, when lynchings seemed imminent, to remove prisoners to other counties for safekeeping and (b) permitted sheriffs to employ "sufficient guard . . . to protect the jail" (Francis Harmon to W. W. Alexander, December 13, 1925, CIC; Mississippi *Code,* 1930, secs. 1295, 3312.

38. Since 1904, attempted rape had been a capital offense in Mississippi. Lincoln County *Times,* January 16, 23, February 13, 20, 1908.

39. See editorials from Yazoo *Herald,* Newton *Record,* Monticello *Press,* Crystal Springs *Meteor,* and Magnolia *Gazette,* reprinted in Lincoln County *Times,* February 20, 1908.

40. The degree to which judicial behavior is influenced, on the one hand, by legal concepts and the content of laws, or, on the other, by societal pressures and personal values, is a question of much interest to legal scholars. On the question and its possible bearing on the problem of justice for blacks see Lawrence M. Friedman, *The Legal System: A Social Science Perspective* (New York, 1975), 170-179; Glendon A. Schubert, *The Judicial Mind Revisited: Psychometric Analysis of Supreme Court Ideology* (New York, 1974); Joel B. Grossman, "Social Backgrounds and Judicial Decision-Making," *Harvard Law Review,* 79 (May, 1966), 1551-1564; idem, "Role Playing and the Analysis of Judicial Behavior: The Case of Mr. Justice Frankfurter," *Journal of Public Law,* vol. 11, no. 2 (1962), 285-299.

41. For evidence of this pervasive white belief, see for example, Walthall *Warden,* September 5, 1988; Brandon *News,* May 27, June 24, 1909; Sunflower *Tocsin,* July 8, 1897; June 2, September 15, 1921; Jackson *Weekly Clarion-Ledger,* October 9, 1902; Meridian *Star,* April 8, 1934.

42. Claudia L. Hajiazimi, "Treatment of Blacks by the Circuit Court System in Hattiesburg, Mississippi, 1920-1939" (course paper, University of Southern Mississippi, December 8, 1980), 6.

43. Brookhaven *Semi-Weekly Leader,* September 13, 16, 20, 1911.

44. In Jackson in 1908 two black "fiends" were sentenced to life in prison for attempted assault, the maximum sentence, "in less than one hour from the time the case was called" (Meridian *Evening Star,* April 8, 1908). "The shortest criminal trial in the history of Rankin County" was that of Will Mack, who was "indicted, tried, convicted and sentenced . . . all in the space of six hours" (Brandon *News,* July 22, 1909; Brookhaven *Semi-Weekly Leader,* June 23, 24, 1909). According to a white editor, "There has never been a fairer trial" in Sunflower County than the one following the alleged rape of an eight-year-old white girl by a black man, wherein a circuit judge organized a grand jury, received a true bill, convened a special session of circuit court, appointed defense attorneys, impaneled a petit jury, heard testimony, instructed jurors and received their verdict, and imposed the death penalty in a single day (Sunflower *Tocsin,* December 2, 1929). See also the more recent case (1968) of John O'Neal in Stanton Hall, "Experiences of a Trial Judge" (manuscript, McCain Graduate Library, University of Southern Mississippi, [1974]), 73-74.

45. Also sentenced to die in the electric chair for the same crime was

fourteen-year-old James Lewis, Jr., who according to testimony of the state's own witnesses took no physical role in the murder. The two were tried separately, Lewis six days after Trudell. In both cases, the state and federal appeals courts refused to intervene. *Trudell* v. *Mississippi*, 28 So. 2d 124 (1946); *Lewis* v. *Mississippi*, 201 Miss. 48 (1946); *Lewis* v. *State*, 331 U.S. 784 (1947); Legal Files, boxes 42, 146, post-1940, NAACP.

46. The state supreme court, ruling that the court below should have granted a change of venue, remanded the case for a new trial. *Brown* v. *Mississippi*, 83 Miss. 645 (1903).

47. A new trial was ordered by the state supreme court. *Harris* v. *Mississippi*, 96 Miss. 379 at 380 (1909).

48. [Raper], *The Mob Still Rides*, 18.

49. *Hunter et al.* v. *Mississippi*, 137 Miss. 276 (1924). For other examples of "tracking dog evidence," see Brookhaven *Semi-Weekly Leader*, December 4, 1909; Vicksburg *Evening Post*, April 23, 1919; *Fisher* v. *Mississippi*, 145 Miss. 116 (1926).

50. *Perkins* v. *Mississippi*, 160 Miss. 720 (1931), 166 So. 357 (1931). Other examples are detailed in *Matthews* v. *Mississippi*, 102 Miss. 549 (1912); *Whip* v. *Mississippi*, 143 Miss. 757 (1926); *Lee* v. *Mississippi*, 201 Miss. 423, 203 Miss. 264, 332 U.S. 742 (1948).

51. *White* v. *Mississippi*, 129 Miss. 182 (1922). Blacks, it should be noted, sometimes also participated in "negro hunts."

52. *Fisher* v. *Mississippi*, 145 Miss. 116 at 134 (1926).

53. Until *Gideon* v. *Wainwright*, 372 U.S. 335 (1963), there was no federal guarantee of the right to counsel.

54. *Miller* v. *Mississippi*, 207 Miss. 156 at 160 (1949); 94 L. Ed. 57 (1949). The NAACP's role is described in *Leroy Miller* v. *Marvin Wiggins* folder, Legal Files, con. 36, post-1940, NAACP. Similarly, "Bull" Shack, who was "almost an imbecile but this circumstance was not offered in his behalf," was tried without defense counsel and sentenced to death for killing a white Coahoma County physician. His case was apparently not appealed (Jackson *Daily News*, January 20, 1912).

55. *U.S. ex rel. Goldsby* v. *Harpole*, 263 F. 2d 71 (1959).

56. Elvy E. Calloway, *The Other Side of the South* (Chicago, 1936), 16-17, 145.

57. Cortner, *A "Scottsboro" Case in Mississippi*, 46 (quotations).

58. Although the chief justice dissented, the convictions were reversed. The case history was prepared for the NAACP at the suggestion of S. D. Redmond. George L. Teat and Stewart C. Broom, "History of the Case," undated; Teat to NAACP, May 5, 1924; Stewart to NAACP, December 25, 1924, Lonnie Hunter et al. Folder, Legal Files, box D-37, NAACP; Jackson *Daily News*, December 22, 1924; *Hunter et al.* v. *Mississippi*, 137 Miss. 276.

59. See, for example, Burns to Wilkins, February 6, 1935, con. G-106, NAACP.

60. Redmond to Wilkins, December 10, 1931; August 7, 1934, Cases Sup-

ported—Tom Carraway folder, Legal Files, box D-49, NAACP; Wilson, *Make Me a Man,* 46.

61. *Carraway* v. *Mississippi,* 170 Miss. 685 at 696-697 (1934).

62. See these files generally, and for specific examples see John A. Clark to Conner, July 10, 1932, vol. 695; W. I. Munn to Conner, February 23 and October 23, 1933, vol. 702; Toxey Hall to Conner, February 25, 1933; J. A. Cunningham to Marshall T. Adams, March 2, 1933; W. D. Womack to Conner, September 1, 1935; Claude E. Conner to Conner, February 25, 1933, vol. 720, GPF.

63. Quoted in New York *Post,* April 6, 1935. On Governor Conner's Court of Mercy hearings, see Vicksburg *Evening Post,* April 19, 20, 1935; Jackson *Daily Clarion-Ledger,* April 19, 1935.

64. *Hardaway* v. *Mississippi,* 99 Miss. 223 at 224 (1911).

65. Landon, *The Honor and Dignity of the Profession,* 55, 158.

66. Stephens to Hoover, March 15, 1930, State Files—Mississippi Justice, Presidential Papers, HPL.

67. "Courting Reversal: The Supervisory Role of State Supreme Courts," *Yale Law Journal* (May, 1978), 1191-1192; Robert Haws and Michael Namarato, "Race, Property Rights, and the Economic Consequences of Reconstruction: A Case Study," *Vanderbilt Law Review,* 32 (January, 1979), 305ff.

68. Lang, *Defender of the Faith,* 94. See also Keir Nash, "The Texas Supreme Court," 622, 624; and Flanigan, "Criminal Procedure in Slave Trials," 540.

69. Under the state constitutions of 1817 and 1868 judges were appointed; under those of 1832 and (after 1914) 1890, they were elected. According to the official historian of the court, the selection method had little bearing on the quality of the judges (John Ray Skates, Jr., *A History of the Mississippi Supreme Court, 1817-1948* [Jackson, Miss., 1973], 46-57). However, Mississippi's judicial system in general has not been so well regarded by social scientists. Henry R. Glick and Kenneth N. Vines, for example, place it last among the fifty states on their "index of legal professionalism" (Glick and Vines, *State Court Systems* [Englewood Cliffs, 1973], 11-13).

70. *Clark* v. *Mississippi,* 102 Miss. 768 at 772 (1912). The Mississippi high court's long-standing insistence on this issue is suggested by Vines, "Southern State Supreme Courts and Race Relations," 11-15.

71. *Funches* v. *Mississippi,* 125 Miss. 140 at 151 (1921); *Collins* v. *Mississippi,* 100 Miss. 435 (1911).

72. *Hampton* v. *Mississippi,* 88 Miss. 257 at 259 (1906). Mollison's judgment appears in *Collins* v. *Mississippi,* 100 Miss. 435 at 438 (1911).

73. In a bootlegging case in Jones County the district attorney urged a jury to accept the uncorroborated testimony of the state's only witness because, "in the first place his skin is white while the defendant's is black" (*Hardaway* v. *Mississippi,* 99 Miss. 223 at 223 [1913]). See also *Moseley* v. *Mississippi,* 112 Miss. 854 (1916).

74. *Harris* v. *Mississippi,* 96 Miss. 397 (1909).

75. See for example, Redmond to Walter White, January 4, 1923, Administration Files—Politics, box C-389, NAACP. In the case of Sonnie Dobbs,

Redmond said, the defense could not raise the issue of self-defense "because of [the] mores of the community" (*Dobbs* v. *Mississippi,* 200 Miss. 595 at 600 [1946]).

76. *Byrd* v. *Mississippi,* 154 Miss. 742 at 754 (1929).

77. *Williams* v. *Mississippi,* 120 Miss. 604 (1919), 122 Miss. 151 at 172 (1920). Although the local sheriff refused Governor Bilbo's offer of state protection for Williams during retrial, he used the pages of the Greenville *Delta Democrat-Times* to warn the "People of Washington County" that he would not tolerate mob action ("Congratulations," *New Republic,* 20 [August 20, 1919], 93).

78. *Crisis,* 49 (March, 1942), 79, 137; *Upton* v. *Mississippi,* 192 Miss. 339 (1942).

79. *Harris* v. *Mississippi,* 96 Miss. 379 at 381 (1909); *Garner* v. *Mississippi,* 120 Miss. 744 at 752 (1919).

80. *Gore* v. *Mississippi,* 155 Miss. 306 at 308 (1929).

81. *Brown et al.* v. *Mississippi,* 173 Miss. 572; *Carraway* v. *Mississippi,* 167 Miss. 390 (1933). The chilling effect of the Carraway ruling is demonstrated in *Barton* v. *Mississippi,* 143 So. 861 (1932), in which the state appeals court in a split decision let stand the death sentence of another black convicted on the coerced testimony of his common-law wife. Available evidence suggests that Columbus Barton may have been framed for the murder of a white man, and that his wife, Selena Moore, was threatened with death, first during an unlawful search of Barton's house and then repeatedly during four months of pretrial detention, unless she agreed to "tell a false" that would lead to Barton's conviction. Barton's appeal for commutation to Governor Conner was also denied and he apparently was hanged. See letters and affidavits on the Barton Case, vol. 690, GPF.

82. *Dobbs* v. *Mississippi,* 200 Miss. 595 (1946), 331 U.S. 868, Legal File, box 48, post-1940, NAACP.

83. *Fisher* v. *Mississippi,* 145 Miss. 116 at 134 (1926).

84. *Carraway* v. *Mississippi,* 167 Miss. 390 at 408-409 (1933).

85. Wharton, *Negro in Mississippi,* 137; Mississippi *Constitution,* 1890, art. 14, sec. 264; *Laws,* 1896, chap. 84.

86. *Gibson* v. *Mississippi,* 17 So. 892 (1895), 162 U.S. 565 (1896); *Williams* v. *Mississippi,* 170 U.S. 213 (1898) (quotation); *Smith* v. *Mississippi,* 18 So. 116, 162 U.S. 592 (1896); *Dixon* v. *Mississippi,* 74 Miss. 271 (1896). The Gibson and Smith cases are often regarded as particularly flawed judgments (Louis P. Goldberg and Eleanore Levenson, *Lawless Judges* [New York, 1970], 145-149).

87. *Lewis* v. *Mississippi,* 91 Miss. 505 (1907); *Farrow* v. *Mississippi,* 91 Miss. 509 (1907). See also *Hill* v. *Mississippi,* 89 Miss. 23 (1906). Following these rulings, Rankin County supervisors at least added token black names to jury lists (Lincoln County *Times,* January 17, 1907).

88. *Patton* v. *Mississippi,* 201 Miss. 410 (1946), 332 U.S. 463 (1947), 68 S. Ct. 184 (1947). Patton was tried a second time by an all-white jury. Because three blacks appeared on his grand jury and one was included on the petit

jury *list,* the state appeals court affirmed his death sentence—and asserted that its justices "have never stayed our hand in interposing the barrier of constitutional rights between the forces of vengeance or prejudice, which are the product of over-sensitive social relationships, and the life of its humblest citizens" (*Patton* v. *Mississippi,* 207 Miss. 120 at 134 [1949]).

89. *Cameron* v. *Mississippi,* 223 Miss. 404 at 412 (1958). The state supreme court's disingenuousness on this issue is illustrated by a comparison of the ruling in the Cameron case with that of *Seay* v. *Mississippi,* 212 Miss. 712 (1951), in which a conviction was reversed and remanded after county officials openly acknowledged the deliberate exclusion of blacks from jury lists. Also see related cases: *McGee* v. *Mississippi,* 203 Miss. 592 (1948); *Flowers* v. *Mississippi,* 209 Miss. 86 (1950); *Gordon* v. *Mississippi,* 243 Miss. 750 (1961); *Kennard* v. *Mississippi,* 242 Miss. 691 (1961). Not until 1965 was the high court of Mississippi generally in line with the United States Supreme Court. In that year, for the first time, it instructed trial judges that "token summoning of Negroes for jury service does not comply with equal protection" (*Harper* v. *Mississippi,* 251 Miss. 699, at 709 [1965]).

Chapter 7. Judge Lynch's Court

1. Quoted in Baker, *Following the Color Line,* 246.

2. Quoted in William R. Ferris, "Black Folklore from the Mississippi Delta" (Ph.D. diss., University of Pennsylvania, 1969), 68.

3. Quoted in Jackson *Daily Clarion-Ledger,* September 10, 1908.

4. Samuel Alfred Beadle, *Sketches of Life in Dixie* (Chicago, 1899), quoted in Jordan, "Samuel Alfred Beadle," 110. See also Beadle's satire on Mississippi justice: "Abduction and Rape of Themis," also in *Sketches.*

5. Jordan, "Samuel Alfred Beadle," 34.

6. David Walker, *Appeal,* reprinted in Herbert Aptheker, *"One Continual Cry": David Walker's Appeal to the Colored Citizens of the World (1829-1830), Its Setting and Its Meaning* (New York, 1965), 63ff.; Henry Highland Garnet, "An Address to the Slaves of the United States of America" (1843), reprinted in Garnet, *A Memorial Discourse of Rev. Henry Highland Garnet, Delivered in the Hall of the House of Representatives* (Philadelphia, 1865), 44-51; Claude McKay, "If We Must Die," *Liberator,* 2 (July, 1919), 21.

7. Madison County *Herald,* February 18, 1916.

8. Quoted in Meridian *Star,* November 6, 1906. See also Columbus *Commercial,* November 13, 1906. Similar cases at Liberty and Gunnison are reported in Jackson *Weekly Clarion-Ledger,* April 18, 1907; and Jackson *Daily Clarion-Ledger,* February 12, 1911.

9. WPA History: Kemper County, unpaginated.

10. New York *Times,* December 25, 1906; Lincoln County *Times,* December 27, 1906; WPA History: Kemper County, unpaginated; Jackson *Weekly Clarion-Ledger,* December 27, 1906; Dwyn M. Mounger, "Lynching in Mississippi, 1830-1930" (M.A. thesis, Mississippi State University, 1961), 79-80.

11. Quoted in Williamson, *The Crucible of Race,* 187. Editor Frederick

Sullens, however, denied that Mississippi lynchers were "reckless and indiscriminate": "Our mobs go out and get the guilty and then they quit" (Jackson
Daily News, July 31, 1919).

12. For example, five blacks were killed (two of them burned alive) at
Doddsville in 1904 by a mob searching for the murderer of a white planter
(NAACP, *Thirty Years of Lynching in the United States, 1889-1918* [1919;
reprint ed., New York, 1969], 15; New York *Tribune,* February 8, 1904; Vicksburg *Evening Post,* February 13, 1904). In 1918 four black minors (two of
them female) were hanged by members of a Shubuta mob who mistook a
white suicide for murder (Chicago *Defender,* February 8, 1919; Gulfport *Daily
Herald,* December 21, 1918). In 1923, a mob at Pickins killed an eighteen-
year-old black woman while pursuing her brother who had refused to pay ten
cents interest on a fifty-cent debt to a white man ("An Analysis of 3,216
Lynchings in Thirteen States, 1889-1935," box 237, post-1940, NAACP). For
other cases in which mobs ran amuck see Batesville *Weekly Panolian,* June
9, 1904; Meridian *Star,* April 15, 1917; Jackson *Daily Clarion-Ledger,* April
15, 1917; Chicago *Defender,* October 29, 1932.

13. Greenville *Times,* October 13, 1906.

14. James Weldon Johnson, "Lynching—America's National Disgrace,"
Current History, 19 (January, 1924), 600-601; Robert R. Moton, "The South
and the Lynching Evil," *South Atlantic Quarterly,* 18 (July, 1919), 192. For
the relationship of particular acts of mob violence to out-migration from
Mississippi communities see Chicago *Defender,* February 8, 1919; July 7, 1928;
January 19, 1929.

15. Vicksburg *Evening Post,* May 16, 1919.

16. Dewey C. Bell, "One More Mississippi Lynching: May 14, 1919" (course
paper [1969]), Terry Alford Collection, Annandale, Va. (Laurel quotation);
Johnson, *Growing Up in the Black Belt,* 317 (Coahoma County quotation);
Jerry Harmon, "Death By Fire" (course paper, July 17, 1968), Alford Collection
(Rocky Ford quotation). See also Anderson, oral history, August 24, 1970,
MHC.

17. Dollard, *Caste and Class in a Southern Town,* 331, 359-360; Wright,
Black Boy, 83-84, 190. For similar expressions, see Holtzclaw, *Black Man's
Burden,* 167; Ray Sprigle, *In the Land of Jim Crow* (New York, 1949), 101.

18. Williamson, *Crucible of Race,* 117, 182-185; Mounger, "Lynching in
Mississippi," 20-27.

19. All quotations are from Mounger, "Lynching in Mississippi," 42, 49,
56-57, 75-78. On rare occasions, black Mississippians lynched people of their
own race and from time to time blacks joined in white-led "nigger hunts"
(see Port Gibson *Reveille,* January 11, 1895; Walthall *Warden,* August 1, 1885;
Wesson *Mirror,* December 13, 1890; Woodville *Republican,* July 30, 1887;
Jackson *Clarion-Ledger,* September 13, 1888; June 3, 1917; Lincoln County
Times, October 3, 1907; Chicago *Defender,* June 9, 1917).

20. Raymond *Gazette,* July 18, 1885, quoted in Wharton, *Negro in Mississippi,* 224.

21. Ibid.

22. Quoted in Memphis *Commercial-Appeal,* May 9, 10, 1919. The problem of suppressed lynchings is also suggested in Booker T. Washington to Charles Banks, January 17, 1913, con. 64, BTW; and David M. Elliott, "Negro-White Relationships in a Small Mississippi Town" (course paper, January 7, 1966), Alford Collection. From time to time, the state's white press also took note of the need to suppress lynching news. See Sunflower *Tocsin,* August 28, 1896; Vicksburg *Evening Post,* March 21, 1904.

23. James A. Burns to Roy Wilkins, February 6, 1935, box G-106, anonymous to NAACP, May 23, 1939, box C-359; and Myra Thornton to Walter White, May 31, 1939, box C-359, NAACP; Southern Commission on the Study of Lynching, *Lynchings and What They Mean* (Atlanta, 1932), 59-60; Arthur F. Raper, *The Tragedy of Lynching* (Chapel Hill, 1933), 96.

24. Unless otherwise stated, all lynching statistics used in this chapter are those compiled by the NAACP. The association's lynching materials relevant to Mississippi for the period from 1918 to 1940 are open to researchers (boxes C-359, C-360, C-361, C-371, NAACP). See also "Lynchings by States, 1882-1937," and "Known Lynchings of Women in the United States," box C-371, NAACP; NAACP, *Thirty Years of Lynching,* 74-80; NAACP, *Annual Reports,* beginning with the *Ninth Annual Report of 1918;* NAACP, *A Generation of Lynching in the United States, 1921-1946* (New York, n.d.); Walter White, *Rope and Faggot: A Biography of Judge Lynch* (1929; reprint ed., New York, 1969), 256, Table 7; *The Anti-Lynching Crusaders: "A Million Women United to Suppress Lynching,"* (n.p., n.d.). For the period 1882-1946, the Department of Records and Research of Tuskegee Institute credited Mississippi with 574 (forty-one of them white) lynching victims, followed by Georgia with 525 (Work, ed., *Negro Year Book, 1941-1946,* 306; *Lynching,* Subject File, MDAH).

25. Multiple lynchings in Mississippi for the period from 1889 through 1945 included forty-two double, eight triple, six quadruple, and three quintuple lynchings.

26. Editorials, Norfolk *Journal and Guide,* January 7, 1928; Chicago *Defender,* October 29, 1932; Greensboro (N.C.) *Daily News,* January 1, 1928; White, *Rope and Faggot,* 171.

27. After World War I (1919 excluded) there were seven lynchings in Mississippi cities of more than 10,000 population: Clarksdale (1925), Columbus (1938), Hattiesburg (1928), Laurel (1936 and 1942), Yazoo City (1923 and 1926).

28. Average black population figures for these counties (1890-1930) are: Hinds, 65 percent; Lowndes, 69 percent; Kemper, 48 percent; Desoto, 73 percent; Bolivar, 86 percent; Washington, 83 percent.

29. My computations based on NAACP data reveal that in the 1889-1939 period, lynching rates per 10,000 black population in Mississippi were: 8.36 in counties less than 24 percent black; 6.09 in counties 25 to 50 percent black; 3.89 in black majority counties; and 3.74 in Delta counties. Statewide, the figure was 4.59. See also the per capita data in Raper, *Tragedy of Lynching,* 483.

30. Some individual counties did not conform to the general pattern de-

scribed here. Lynching rates per 10,000 black population for the counties mentioned in this paragraph (in order of their appearance in the text) are: Tishomingo, 39.45; Itawamba, 8.86; Harrison, 10.45; Jackson, 10.67; Greene, 5.27; George, 7.48; Hinds, 5.11; Lowndes, 7.50; Kemper, 11.26; Desoto, 7.91; Bolivar, 3.22; Washington, 3.21; Adams, 0.54; Jefferson, 2.15; Claiborne, 2.53; Perry, 33.15; and Jones, 7.20. For an opposing view, one that concludes that in Mississippi the lynching "rate is positively related to the percent black," see John Shelton Reed, "Percent Black and Lynching: A Test of Blalock's Theory," *Social Forces,* 50 (March, 1972), 356-360.

31. Southern Commission on the Study of Lynching, *Lynchings and What They Mean,* 12; Ames, *The Changing Character of Lynching,* 14.

Seasonal data on lynching are not conclusive. White self-interest seemed to influence the timing of mob violence; regionwide, lynchings were more numerous in the summer months, in the relatively idle period of "lay-by" between chopping and harvest, when the planters' need for field hands was lower than at any time in the growing season. Statewide figures for Mississippi are consistent with the South in general: June and July, the "slack work" time, were the months with the most lynchings (see Table 7.2); the labor-intensive months of the harvest season, beginning as early as September and often running through mid- to late December, had fewer mob murders; and April and May, the planting, cultivating, and chopping months, had fewer still. Yet when we isolate the cotton-rich Delta, this statistical pattern, such as it is, all but dissolves: in Bolivar, Humphreys, Sharkey, Warren, Washington, and Yazoo counties, lynchings rarely occurred in the harvest months, but in Coahoma, Leflore, and Tunica, September and October were the mob's favored months.

TABLE 7.2. Mississippi Lynchings by Month, 1889-1945.

Month	Statewide	Delta only	Month	Statewide	Delta only
January	26	9	July	60	13
February	30	12	August	25	3
March	40	14	September	48	15
April	25	5	October	43	12
May	35	8	November	31	3
June	57	11	December	30	12

Source: Adapted from NAACP data.

32. The impact of economic forces on the number of lynchings is a complicated subject on which social scientists do not agree. Clearly the first great peak period of lynching in Mississippi coincides with the agricultural depression of the 1890s. Thereafter, however, the "frustration-aggression hypothesis" becomes more problematic, particularly during the Great Depression. See, for example, Raper, *Tragedy of Lynching,* 30-31; Carl I. Hovland and Robert S. Sears, "Minor Studies of Aggression: Correlation of Economic Indices with Lynchings," *Journal of Psychology,* 9 (1940), 301-310; and Alexander Mintz,

"A Re-Examination of Correlations between Lynchings and Economic Indices," *Journal of Abnormal and Social Psychology,* 41 (April, 1946), 154-160.

33. The most convenient sources on lynching methods are the NAACP, *Annual Reports,* but the most detailed descriptions are to be found in the lynching files, NAACP.

34. White, *Rope and Faggot,* 21-22; NAACP, *Burning at the Stake in the United States: A Record of the Public Burning by Mobs . . . during the First Six Months of 1919* (New York, 1919); NAACP, *Annual Reports,* 1918-1940.

35. The reference is to a burning in Gulfport. Richland (La.) *Beacon-News,* November 9, 1901, quoted in Hair, *Carnival of Fury,* 14.

36. Hall, *Revolt against Chivalry,* 136.

37. Vicksburg *Evening Post,* February 13, 1904. See also White, *Rope and Faggot,* 35; Greenwood *Commonwealth,* February 13, 1904.

38. Vicksburg *Daily Herald,* May 28, 1919.

39. Memphis *News-Scimitar,* September 21, 1925.

40. Jackson *Daily News,* January 1, 1929.

41. According to one editor, "The parties thus summarily dealt with in 49 cases out of 50 are negro brutes reeking with the guilt of a nameless crime" (Winona *Democrat,* quoted in Indianola *Enterprise,* June 26, 1903). See Jackson *Weekly Clarion-Ledger,* July 24, 1902; Brandon *News,* May 13, 1909; Belzoni *Banner,* August 15, 1919.

42. Holmes, *The White Chief,* 88-89 (Vardaman quote); *Anti-Lynching: Hearings before Subcommittee No. 4 of the Committee on the Judiciary, House of Representatives,* 80th Cong., 2d sess., February 4, 1948 (Washington, D.C., 1948), 126 (Rankin quotation).

43. William Hayne Levell, "On Lynching in the South," *Outlook,* 69 (November 16, 1901), 731 (minister's quotation); Powdermaker, *After Freedom,* 52, 389.

44. Wells, *Crusade for Justice,* 64-65; NAACP, *Thirty Years of Lynching,* 9, 10, 36; "An Analysis of 3,216 Lynchings in Thirteen States, 1889-1935" and "Memorandum on Lynchings for Trivial Causes in Thirteen States," box 237, post-1940, NAACP. See also William H. Glasson, "The Statistics of Lynchings," *South Atlantic Quarterly,* 5 (October, 1906), 345-358; Work, ed., *Negro Year Book, 1921-1922,* 72.

45. Stone, "The Negro in the Yazoo-Mississippi Delta," 239; Mounger, "Lynching in Mississippi," 82 (second quotation).

46. See particularly, Thurgood Marshall to Attorney General Frank Murphy, April 15, 1939, box 138, post-1940, NAACP; but also Charles Bennett files, Governors' Pardon Files, vol. 691, RG 27, MDAH; Johnson, "Lynching—America's National Disgrace," 596-597; Guy B. Johnson, "The Negro and Crime," *Annals of the American Academy of Political and Social Science,* 217 (September, 1941), 96; Dollard, *Caste and Class in a Southern Town,* 164; Chicago *Defender,* January 31, 1937; Louisville (Ky.) *News,* October 18, 1919.

47. Walter White to Byron Patton Harrison, December 8, 1938, box 138, post-1940, NAACP.

48. See the NAACP, *Annual Reports;* "An Analysis of 3,216 Lynchings in

Thirteen States, 1889-1935" and "Memorandum on Lynching for Trivial Causes in Thirteen States," box 237, post-1940, NAACP.

49. Quoted in Jessie Daniel Ames, "Editorial Treatment of Lynchings," *Public Opinion Quarterly,* 2 (January, 1938), 81. See also NAACP, *Annual Report for 1929,* 36; Chicago *Defender,* July 13, 1929.

50. *Crime of Lynching: Hearing before a Subcommittee of the Committee on the Judiciary, U.S. Senate,* 76th Cong., 3d sess., February 6-7, March 5, 12-13, 1940 (Washington, D.C., 1940), 4. On the role of lynching as an instrument of social control, see Daniel, "The Metamorphosis of Slavery," 88-99; and Allen D. Grimshaw, "Lawlessness and Violence in America," *Journal of Negro History,* 44 (January, 1959), 52-72.

51. Quoted in Jackson *Daily News,* July 1, 1919. The literature of the period abounds in similar expressions: e.g., B. F. Ward, *The Truth Regarding the South* (Greenwood, Miss., 1901); *Vardaman's Weekly,* May 5, 1919.

52. Editorial, Jackson *Clarion-Ledger,* July 1, 2, 1919.

53. Distributed by International Newsreel Photos, the photograph appeared in numerous papers outside Mississippi. See Memphis *News-Scimitar,* September 21, 1925; New York *Journal,* September 24, 1925; New York *Daily Mirror,* September 24, 1925; New York *Evening Graphic,* December 15, 1926; [J. N. Flowers], *Mississippi and the Mob* (Jackson, [1926]), 20.

54. E.g., see H. C. Brearley, "The Pattern of Violence," in W. T. Crouch, ed., *Culture of the South* (Chapel Hill, 1934), 680; and Jackson *Weekly Clarion-Ledger,* October 2, 19, 1902.

55. Street, *Look Away,* 75-76; Hodding Carter, *The Ballad of Catfoot Grimes, and Other Verses* (Garden City, N.Y., 1964), 9-10. In Carter's poem, a "respectable citizen" thought it "Too bad it happened/ But he brought it on. . . ./ Like I say, you got/ To teach 'em sense. Besides this way/ saves the town expense."

56. Williamson, *Crucible of Race,* 291-295.

57. Hall, *Revolt against Chivalry,* 173, 183, 187, 215-216, 229-230.

58. [Flowers], *Mississippi and the Mob.* For similar expressions, see Jackson *Clarion-Ledger,* February 28, 1889; editorial, Hattiesburg *American,* quoted in Chicago *Defender,* February 9, 1929.

59. Interview with one Mr. Burgess, Laurel, Miss., Summer, 1981, CPC. Black fears of the redneck are depicted by Samuel A. Beadle in his short story "Hagar," collected in *Adam Suffler* (Jackson, 1901).

60. Meridian *Star,* September 5, 1919; but see also Sunflower *Tocsin,* October 30, 1896; Batesville *Weekly Panolian,* June 9, 1904; Lincoln County *Times,* December 27, 1906; Jackson *Daily Clarion-Ledger,* February 12, 1911; April 26, 1917; January 16, 1918.

61. Editorial, Jackson *Daily News,* April 21, 1935.

62. Bell, "Child of the Delta," chap. 1, p. [7]; chap. 2, p. [11]; chap. 7, p. [2].

63. See Charles S. Sydnor, "The Southerner and the Laws," *Journal of Southern History,* 6 (February, 1940), 3-23; Richard Maxwell Brown, "Southern

Violence—Regional Problem or National Nemesis," *Vanderbilt Law Review,* 32 (January, 1979), 228; Ayers, *Vengeance and Justice,* passim.

64. Bilbo to Louise Kates, December 9, 1938, box 138, post-1940, NAACP; Bertram Wyatt-Brown, *Southern Honor: Ethics and Behavior in the Old South* (New York, 1982), 439 (Williams's quotation).

65. See for example a summary of unfavorable press coverage of the lynching of Lindsey Coleman in [Flowers], *Mississippi and the Mob,* 71-78; and Mounger, "Lynching in Mississippi," 119-120.

66. Street, *Look Away,* 62.

67. Vicksburg *Daily Herald,* May 18, 22, 1919; Vicksburg *Evening Post,* May 15, 16, 1919; Chicago *Defender,* May 24, 1919. The alleged victim, the woman who on two occasions failed to pick Clay out of a police lineup, said of the lynching: "It is terrible, but I'm not sorry. For the sake of other girls and women I'm glad" (quoted in Bell, "One More Mississippi Lynching," 7).

68. Editorial, Jackson *Clarion-Ledger,* July 19, 1935.

69. Aberdeen *Examiner,* quoted in Jackson *Clarion-Ledger,* March 22, 1889 (first quotation); Jackson *Clarion-Ledger,* July 25, 1889 (second quotation). See also Jackson *Daily Clarion-Ledger,* September 9, 1908. Following the burning of Thomas Clark (a.k.a. Will Gibson) at Corinth, one newspaper reported that while "arrangements for the [burnt] offering were being made . . . no arm of the law was interposed to stop the program which was pretty generally understood and sanctioned. Reserved seats were placed for the women. . . . Special trains were run to the scene" (Jackson *Weekly Clarion-Ledger,* October 2, 1902). Public hangings in Mississippi, outlawed in 1916, are described in Sunflower *Tocsin,* January 17, 1896, June 10, August 12, 1897; Brandon *News,* July 22, 1909; Atlanta *Constitution,* August 7, 1915; Madison County *Herald,* August 13, 1915.

70. John H. Lang, *History of Harrison County, Mississippi* (Gulfport, 1936), 132-134.

71. Dollard, *Caste and Class in a Southern Town,* 335-339. Dollard reported slightly differing versions of the same incident, one of which attributed the incident to economic rivalry between the victim and the husband.

72. Valley L. Lester, *The Mob Violence and the American Negro: My Experience* (Memphis, 1919), 34-53; Laurence Jones, *Piney Woods and Its Story* (New York, 1922), 111-113; Harrison, *Piney Woods School,* 110. The evidence also suggests that Jones thought to employ the "Mason sign" and that the white intervenor, also a Mason, was moved by this revelation. The site of the near lynching is in dispute. Early graduates of Piney Woods place the incident near Braxton. Jones himself, perhaps for public relations reasons, placed it in a neighboring state to the west of Mississippi (Lensie Braddy, September 15, 1978; and Rosie Bell Brooks, September 6, 1978, oral histories, JSU).

73. Walthall *Warden,* August 29, 1888; Jackson *Weekly Clarion-Ledger,* October 2, 1902.

74. Harmon, "Death by Fire," 5; Raper, *Tragedy of Lynching,* 85-88.

75. See, e.g., Sheriff H. C. Hinton's description of the Wilder McGowan lynching (1938) in Ames, *Changing Character of Lynching,* 44; but also the

descriptions of "orderly lynchings" in Jackson *Mississippian,* September 9, 1891; Greenwood *Commonwealth,* February 13, 1904; Biloxi *Daily Herald,* June 28, 1904; Meridian *Evening Star,* April 6, 1908; and Lincoln County *Times,* April 9, 1908.

76. The fullest account of Hartfield's lynching is Street, *Look Away,* 12-38, but see also Jackson *Daily News,* June 21, 26, 27, 1919; Memphis *Commercial-Appeal,* June 27, 1919; New Orleans *Item,* June 27, 1919; New Orleans *Times-Picayune,* June 26, 27, 1919; Birmingham *News,* June 27, 1919; New York *Times,* June 27, 1919; Hilton Butler, "Lynch Law in Action," *New Republic,* 67 (July 22, 1931), 256-57.

77. Jackson *Daily News,* June 26, 1919; New Orleans *States,* June 26, 1919; NAACP, *Annual Report for 1919,* 24.

78. Jackson *Clarion-Ledger,* February 28, 1889; [Raper], *The Mob Still Rides,* 16.

79. NAACP press release, May 7, 1937, box C-360, NAACP; Ames, "Editorial Treatment of Lynchings," 77-84; [Raper], *The Mob Still Rides,* 21-22.

80. Editorial, Webster *Progress,* July 14, 1938; [Raper], *The Mob Still Rides,* 22. At the turn of the century some editors treated lynching with "droll touches" and morbid jokes about "midnight dramas" amid the "sighing boughs" (Jackson *Weekly Clarion-Ledger,* April 18, 1907; Hair, *Carnival of Fury,* 51). During the near anarchy of the 1960s, several Mississippi journalists distinguished themselves and their state by opposing mob terror—among them notably J. Oliver Emmerich of the McComb *Enterprise-Journal* and Hodding Carter of the Greenville *Delta Democrat-Times.*

81. Minutes, Mississippi Council on Interracial Cooperation Committee Meeting, Jackson, Miss., April 28-29, 1942, box 169, CIC.

82. "Investigation of a Mississippi Lynching," file 17-B-8-d (old classification, Trevor Arnett Library, Atlanta University), CIC. Bishop Charles B. Galloway (Methodist Episcopal Church, South) was a notable early exception (Galloway, "Some Thoughts on Lynching," *Journal of Negro History,* 5 [October, 1906], 351-353).

83. Jackson *Daily News,* February 4, 1931; Hall, *Revolt against Chivalry,* 215, 232.

84. Hall, *Revolt against Chivalry,* 215; Robert M. Miller, "The Protestant Churches and Lynching, 1919-1939," *Journal of Negro History,* 42 (April, 1957), 119, 123, 126; Helene Alford to Jessie Daniel Ames, December 29, 1939, box 168, CIC. Walter White found an "almost exactly parallel curve upwards of lynchings and the Methodist-Baptist percentage of the total of church members." He reported that 87.4 percent of Mississippi's church members were Baptist or Methodist (*Rope and Faggot,* 245, 248).

85. Hall, *Revolt against Chivalry,* 215-216. However, in 1925 both the North Mississippi Conference and the Mississippi Annual Conference of the Methodist Church (South) endorsed the efforts of the Mississippi Bar Association to promote law and order ([Flowers], *Mississippi and the Mob,* 79).

86. Mounger, "Lynching in Mississippi," 123. See also David M. Reimers, *White Protestants and the Negro* (New York, 1965), 46-50, 90-97.

87. Mississippi Senate, *Journal* (1900), 88; Montgomery *Enterprise,* January 26, 1900; Chicago *World,* January 27, 1900; Vicksburg *Herald,* July 31, 1903; Jackson *Daily News,* July 2, 1919; Jackson *Daily Clarion-Ledger,* July 3, 1919; Kirwan, *Revolt of the Rednecks,* 154-155; Longino to Chadbourn, June 8, 1932, quoted in Chadbourn, *Lynching and the Law,* 115.

88. Natchez *Democrat,* July 4, 1911. Mounger notes, however, that Vardaman received "hundreds of telegrams" of support for his use of troops (Mounger, "Lynching in Mississippi," 100). See also Hamilton, "Mississippi Politics," 127-128.

89. Smith, *Congressman from Mississippi,* 110-111.

90. See lynching files, boxes C-359, C-360, C-361, NAACP. For the frustration of one grand jury foreman and several judges with grand jury negligence, see Jackson *Weekly Clarion-Ledger,* January 15, 1903; Hair, *Carnival of Fury,* 51; Jackson *Daily News,* July 13, 1919; Hazelhurst *Courier,* September 6, 1928; Jackson *Daily News,* September 4, 1928; Jackson *Clarion-Ledger,* September 5, 1928.

91. [Flowers], *Mississippi and the Mob,* 5. On the complicity of some sheriffs in lynching, see [Raper], *The Mob Still Rides,* 12.

92. Frank Shay, *Judge Lynch: His First Hundred Years* (New York, 1938), 93; Butler, "Lynch Law in Action," 256; [Raper], *The Mob Still Rides,* 12; NAACP, *Can the States Stop Lynching?* (New York, [1937]), passim.

93. "Mob Member Laughs at Probe," Memphis *Press-Scimitar,* September 21, 1925; White, *Rope and Faggot,* 26-27.

94. Although widely reported, the fullest and most accurate account of the incident is [Howard Kester], *Lynchings by Blow-Torch: A Special Report to Members of the United States Senate on the Lynchings at Duck Hill, Mississippi, April 13, 1937* (n.p., n.d.).

95. Press release, Commission on Interracial Cooperation, April 16, 1937, box C-331, NAACP; Memphis *Press-Scimitar,* April 14, 1937; Jack Hancock to Walter White, October 4, 1937; and White to Hatton W. Sumners, October 7, 1937, box C-360, NAACP; *Congressional Record,* April 13, 1937, 3434, 3437. See also cartoon, "Mississippi Sends a Message to Congress," *Crisis,* (June, 1937), 176.

96. Sunflower *Tocsin,* April 13, 1937; Jackson *Daily News,* as quoted in NAACP press release May 7, 1937, box C-360, NAACP. See also *Crisis,* 44 (June, 1937), 179; and 45 (February, 1938), 49; NAACP press release, May 7, 1937, box C-360, NAACP.

97. [Kester], *Lynchings by Blow-Torch;* Kester to Walter White, May 8, 1937, box C-360, NAACP. When word of the Duck Hill murders reached Governor White he had just finished informing a farm conference: "We are justly proud of the fact that Mississippi has not had a lynching in 15 months" (NAACP, *Annual Report for 1937,* 5).

98. See, for example, the defiant letter of one sheriff, George B. Alexander, to the "People of Washington County," Greenville *Daily Democrat-Times,* undated clipping, box D-11, NAACP; and also *New Republic,* August 20, 1919, 93; Sunflower *Tocsin,* September 9, 1897; New York *Times,* June 30, 1927;

Chicago *Bee,* July 7, 1928; Mounger, "Lynching in Mississippi," 115-116; NAACP, *Annual Report for 1920,* 42; *for 1926,* 26. For the political costs paid by Mississippi law officers who defended their prisoners, see Cohn, *God Shakes Creation,* 101-102; White, *Rope and Faggot,* 27.

99. "Shame to Mississippi," *Nation,* 128 (January 16, 1929), 62; Association of Southern Women for the Prevention of Lynching, *Death by Parties Unknown,* Bulletin no. 6 (January, 1936), 13; New York *Times,* February 21, 1926; April 15, 1927; Chicago *Sun,* November 20, 1942. Earlier governors, including Vardaman, also occasionally acted against lynching (Mounger, "Lynching in Mississippi," 89, 96-97, 111; and Greenville *Times,* March 4, 1905). Although Governor Bilbo refused to intervene to save Hartfield in 1919, he did send troops in 1917 to prevent a mob execution in Canton (Meridian *Star,* June 25, 1917).

100. ASWPL, *Death by Parties Unknown,* 13; *Southern Frontier,* February, 1940.

101. Bessie Alford, quoted in Hall, *Revolt against Chivalry,* 229.

102. Wharton, *Negro in Mississippi,* 226-227.

103. In 1929, Walter White still listed Mississippi among the "notorious states" where there was no evidence that "decent citizens are working against lynching" (*Rope and Faggot,* 184).

104. New York *World,* December 23, 1925; Chicago *Defender,* January 12, 19, February 9, 1929; January 31, 1931; Millsaps College *Purple and White,* April 22, 1937; Miller, "Protestant Churches and Lynching," 119-126; Jessie D. Ames, *Southern Women and Lynching* (n.p., n.d.); Henry Eugene Barber, "The Association of Women for the Prevention of Lynching, 1930-1942" (M.A. thesis, University of Georgia, 1967), 61-69; Lewis T. Nordyke, "Ladies and Lynchings," *Survey Graphic,* 28 (November, 1939), 686; John Shelton Reed, "An Evolution of an Anti-Lynching Organization," *Social Problems,* 16 (Fall, 1968), 174; Theodore D. Bratton to Roy Wilkins, April 13, 1934, box C-360, NAACP. The white Mississippi businessman's argument against lynching is succinctly presented in Hattiesburg *American,* reprinted in Chicago *Defender,* February 9, 1929.

105. Between 1882 and 1933, legal action was brought in only forty of the nation's 5,150 lynchings. By that date, only four southern states had convicted a lyncher (Michael R. Belknap, *Federal Law and Southern Order: Racial Violence and Constitutional Conflict in the Post-Brown South* [Athens, Ga., 1987], 9).

106. Kester to White, September 20, 1939; November 10, 1939; White to Godfrey Cabot, November 28, 29, 1939, box 138, post-1940, NAACP.

107. Although a Copiah County judge created a "profound sensation" by identifying members of a mob and asking for indictments in 1898, the first lynchers formally accused in Mississippi were probably those named in an Attala County grand jury true bill in 1903. They were not convicted and may never have been tried (Jackson *Evening News,* April 4, 1898; Jackson *Daily Clarion-Ledger,* January 1, 1903; Mounger, "Lynching in Mississippi," 100; James Elbert Cutler, *Lynch-Law: An Investigation into the History of Lynching*

in the United States [1905, reprint ed., New York, 1969], 254). After a mob stormed a Humphreys County jail and lynched Eugene Greene, the sheriff was tried for contempt of court for failing to produce his prisoner for trial (Memphis *News-Scimitar,* May 16, 1919; Chadbourn, *Lynching and the Law,* 67).

108. Southern Commission on the Study of Lynching, "Legal Punishment of Lynchers, 1899-1930," file 17-B-8-d, CIC; New York *Times,* January 14, 1926; Memphis *Commercial-Appeal,* January 2, 1926; *Fisher* v. *State,* 145 Miss. 116, (1926). Ironically, the indictments in the Coleman case are attributable to pressure on local and state authorities from the Grand Dragon of the Mississippi Ku Klux Klan, Col. T. S. Ward, Coleman's defense attorney. Charging the lynching to the neglect of duty by the sheriff and circuit judge, Ward pledged Klan support of a bill to facilitate the removal from office of sheriffs who did not protect their prisoners from mob violence. Such a law was added to the Mississippi code of 1930 (Francis Harmon to Will W. Alexander, December 13, 1925, CIC; Chadbourn, *Lynching and the Law,* 177).

109. Madison Jones to Walter White, November 7, 1942, box 236; and "Lynching is Everyone's Business," box 237, post-1940, NAACP; NAACP, *Annual Report for 1942,* 34; Chicago *Sun,* November 20, 1942.

110. Wilkins to Franklin D. Roosevelt, October 19, 1942; Randolph to NAACP, November 4, 1942, box 236, post-1940, NAACP; New York *Times,* October 21, 1942; Natchez *Democrat,* October 21, 1942.

111. One of the defendants confessed his guilt to an FBI agent (affidavit of Welborn Pryer, box 236, post-1940, NAACP). New York *Times,* October 21, 1942; January 13, April 21, 24, 1943; Jackson *Daily News,* October 20, 21, 1942; Jackson *Clarion-Ledger,* April 27, 1943; Washington *Times-Herald,* October, 18, 1942; January 13, 1943; Washington *Post,* October 21, 1942; NAACP, *Annual Report for 1936,* 6.

112. Jackson *Clarion-Ledger,* April 27, 1943; New York *Times,* April 20, 21, 24, 1943; Robert K. Carr, *Federal Protection of Civil Rights: Quest for a Sword* (Ithaca, 1947), 137, 139-140, 145, 170. Considered in context, the defense argument also suggested the legitimacy of lynch law. See New York *Times,* April 24, 1943.

113. Jackson *Advocate,* quoted in *Southern Frontier,* January, 1943; Wilkins to Godfrey L. Cabot, June 5, 1939, box 138, post-1940, NAACP. The importance of a federal antilynching statute to black Mississippians is explained in S. D. Redmond to Walter White, December 19, 1922, box C-389, NAACP. The NAACP's position is set forth in a form letter to Members of Congress, undated, box 138, NAACP; and in Robert Zangrando, *The NAACP Crusade against Lynching, 1909-1950* (Philadelphia, 1980), passim.

114. "The Passing of Judge Lynch," *Literary Digest,* 84 (January 31, 1925), 30-31; Zangrando, *NAACP Crusade against Lynching;* Carter, *Where Main Street Meets the River,* 239-244.

115. See folder, "Joe Rodgers," box 138, post-1940, NAACP; Joseph Johnson, *What Was the Lynching Record in America during 1946?* (Chicago, [1947]);

Ames, *Changing Character of Lynching,* 7; Horace B. Davis, "A Substitute for Lynching," *Nation,* January 1, 1930, 12-14.

116. Three such deaths were reported in Mississippi during 1938. "When Is a Lynching?" *Christian Century,* 55 (August 10, 1938), 957; *Indiana Catholic and Record,* August 5, 1938; NAACP press release, undated, box 138, post-1940, NAACP.

117. J. F. Lane to Walter White, August 31, 1940; White to Henry Wright, September 6, 1940, box 237, post-1940, NAACP.

118. Kester to White, September 10, October 10, 1939, box 138, post-1940, NAACP; Baltimore *Evening Sun,* March 14, 1940; [Howard Kester], "Lynching Goes Under Ground: A Report on a New Technique," January 1940, box C-359, NAACP. Kester's investigative approach is described in Kester to White, May 8, 1937, box C-360, NAACP.

119. Neil R. McMillen, "Black Enfranchisement in Mississippi: Federal Enforcement and Black Protest in the 1960s," *Journal of Southern History,* 43 (August, 1977), 354; idem, "Development of Civil Rights, 1956-1970," in McLemore, ed., *History of Mississippi,* 2: 173; Howard Smead, *Blood Justice: The Lynching of Mack Charles Parker* (New York, 1986); Jackson *Daily News,* November 5, 1959; January 14, 1960; Clayborne Carson, *In Struggle: SNCC and the Black Awakening of the 1960s* (Cambridge, Mass., 1981), 114-115. On the strength of his reputation as Medgar Evers's alleged assassin, Byron de La Beckwith launched an unsuccessful political career. During his pretrial internment, Beckwith was reportedly permitted to keep his gun collection in the Hinds County jail; during his murder trial he was visited by Governor Ross Barnett (James W. Silver, *Mississippi: The Closed Society* [New York, 1966], 30, 36, 92-93, 239).

Chapter 8. "Northboun' ": Mississippi's Black Diaspora

1. Lucy Ariel Williams, "Northboun'," *The Negro Caravan,* ed. Sterling A. Brown (New York, 1941), 377.

2. Quoted in T. Arnold Hill, "Why Southern Negroes Don't Go South," *Survey,* 43 (November 29, 1919), 185.

3. James Bryce, *The American Commonwealth,* rev. ed. (New York, 1910), 2: 513, 534, 562.

4. The second-blackest "county" was Tensas Parish (91.5 percent), immediately across the river in Louisiana. Unless otherwise noted all statistical data in this chapter are drawn from the United States Census of Population for years indicated.

5. On the failed efforts to find alternatives to black labor, see numerous letters to and from LeRoy Percy, boxes 1-3, PFP; Walter L. Fleming, "Immigration to the Southern States," *Political Science Quarterly,* 20 (June, 1905), 276-297; Rowland T. Berthoff, "Southern Attitudes toward Immigration, 1865-1914," *Journal of Southern History,* 17 (August, 1951), 328ff.; Brandfon, "The End of Immigration to the Cotton Fields," 591-611; Harris, *Day of the Carpetbagger,* 498-503; Wharton, *Negro in Mississippi,* 97-105; James Loewen,

The Mississippi Chinese: Between Black and White (Cambridge, Mass., 1971), 22-26.

6. Because the Bureau of the Census asked no questions directly relevant to population mobility prior to 1940, migration statistics are at best estimates. However, by employing "life survival ratios" and thereby eliminating from census data population changes resulting from natural increase, Simon Kuznets, Dorothy Swaine Thomas, and their associates have estimated net intercensal population changes resulting from migration. They have described their answers to questions left unanswered by the Bureau of the Census as "tentative" but "potentially useful" to other scholars. I have relied extensively on their refined data. See Kuznets et al., *Population Redistribution and Economic Growth: United States, 1870-1950,* vol. 1, *Methodological Considerations and Reference Tables* (Philadelphia, 1957), 1; but also Allan H. Spear, *Black Chicago: The Making of a Negro Ghetto, 1890-1920* (Chicago, 1967), 139n.

7. In the other half of the interchange, that with other states, there were in 1870 some 57,500 nonresident Mississippi-born blacks, most of them residing in Louisiana (17,800), Texas (13,900), Tennessee (8,600), and Arkansas (7,000). The most accessible state-of-birth population data for the period from 1870 to 1950 are to be found in Kuznets et al., *Population Redistribution,* Table P-3, pp. 271, 321.

8. Morant, *Mississippi Minister,* 9 ("fantastic" quotation); Harris, *Day of the Carpetbagger,* 509; Wharton, *Negro in Mississippi,* 108 (last quotation).

9. Harris, *Day of the Carpetbagger,* 509 ("ten thousand" quotation); Columbus *Democrat* [January, 1875], quoted in Wharton, *Mississippi Negro,* 108 (subsequent quotations). For a later expression of the same idea, see Jackson *Commonwealth,* quoted in Port Gibson *Southern Reveille,* May 16, 1890.

10. Nell Irvin Painter, *Exodusters: Black Migration to Kansas after Reconstruction* (New York, 1977), 154ff. In 1870-1880, Kansas ranked fourth among destination states for out-migrating black Mississippians; Louisiana, Arkansas, and Tennessee, the leading states, received nearly 72 percent of all black migrants from Mississippi (William Edward Vickery, "The Economics of the Negro Migration" [Ph.D. diss., University of Chicago, 1969], 183).

11. Wharton contends that black in-migration, though diminished, continued at least until 1890. Harris argues, and the statistical estimates of Kuznets and associates suggest, that 1875 was the effective termination date. Wharton, *Negro in Mississippi,* 109; Harris, *Day of the Carpetbagger,* 510; Kuznets et al., *Population Redistribution,* 1: 74, 78, 80, 87, 91, 93.

12. According to Department of Labor statistics, 80 percent of the estimated 478,700 wartime emigrants came from the four states of Mississippi, Alabama, Florida, and Georgia. Secretary of Labor to Calvin Coolidge, February 23, 1924, Chief Clerks File, DL.

13. Memphis *Commercial-Appeal,* October 5, 1916. See also Hattiesburg *News,* August 8, 1916.

14. Meridian *Star,* March 13, April 25, 1917; Jackson *Daily Clarion-Ledger,* June 7, 1917, but see also March 8, June 10, July 13, and July 22, 1917.

15. Jackson *Daily Clarion-Ledger,* February 4, March 17, May 23, 1917; Meridian *Star,* March 16, 17, June 18, 1917. See also U.S., Department of Labor, *Negro Migration in 1916-1917,* 18; Scott, *Negro Migration,* 67; Tupelo *Journal,* October 18, 1918; Biloxi *Daily Herald,* March 17, 27, April 28, 1917.

16. See Table 8.1 above and Selz Mayo and C. Horace Hamilton, "Current Population Trends in the South," *Social Forces,* 42 (October, 1963), 84.

17. See for example Everett S. Lee, "A Theory of Migration," *Demography,* 3 (1966), 47-57; William F. Stinner and Gordon F. De Jong, "Southern Negro Migration: Social and Economic Components of an Ecological Model," *Demography,* 6 (November, 1969), 455-457; Morton Rubin, "Migration Patterns of Negroes from a Rural Northeastern Mississippi Community," *Social Forces,* 39 (October, 1960), 59-60; Thomas J. Woofter, *Negro Migration: Changes in Rural Organization and Population of the Cotton Belt* (reprint ed., New York, 1971), 14; Henry J. Shryrock, Jr., *Population Mobility within the United States* (Chicago, 1964), 1.

18. Economic conditions in Mississippi are described in U.S., Department of Labor, *Negro Migration in 1916-1917,* 15-49, 93-113, 216; Scott, *Negro Migration,* 14-15; U.S., Department of Labor, *The Negro at Work during the World War and during Reconstruction: Second Study on Negro Labor* (reprinted; New York, 1969), 82-83. For wages in Chicago see Spear, *Black Chicago,* 157.

19. Emmett J. Scott, ed., "Letters of Negro Migrants of 1916-1918," *Journal of Negro History,* 4 (July, 1919), 305, 318; idem, "Additional Letters of Negro Migrants," ibid., 4 (October, 1919), 419, 435.

20. Quoted in Jackson *Daily Clarion-Ledger,* July 22, 1917. See also Biloxi *Daily Herald,* March 21, 1917, and the description of black economic conditions by a Lauderdale County white man: S. S. Coleman to Theodore Roosevelt, July 7, 1917 (microfilm, ser. 1, reel 239), TRP.

21. Quoted in George E. Haynes, "Negroes Move North," *Survey,* 40 (May 4, 1918), 120.

22. "Jim Crow Blues," quoted in Oliver, *Blues Fell This Morning,* 51.

23. See for example the letters in folder 173, Detroit Urban League, CGW, and those published in Scott, ed., "Letters of Negro Migrants," 292, 293, 308-311, 320-321, 332.

24. U.S., Department of Labor, *Negro Migration in 1916-1917,* 101; T. M. Campbell, "Report of Investigation on Negro Migration, November 11 to December 15, 1923," "Negroes" file, SAg.

25. Scott, ed., "Letters of Negro Migrants," 304, 334; idem, "Additional Letters of Negro Migrants," 452-453; Richard Johnson to F. B. Washington, May 15, 1917, folder 173, Detroit Urban League, CGW.

26. Scott, *Negro Migration,* 45-46; Charles S. Johnson, *The Negro in American Civilization* (New York, 1930), 17, 24. In some cases the Mississippi migrants literally fled slave conditions. See William M. Tuttle, Jr., *Race Riot: Chicago in the Red Summer of 1919* (New York, 1972), 77-78.

27. Quoted in Levine, *Black Culture and Black Consciousness,* 51.

28. Quoted in Litwack, *Been in the Storm So Long,* 104, 167, 230.

29. Johnson, *Growing Up in the Black Belt,* 244; Scott, *Negro Migration,* 26, 48; Chicago *Defender,* February 17, 1917.

30. Chicago *Defender,* January 15, 1916; Detweiler, *Negro Press,* 10-11, 15-16; Florette Henri, *Black Migration: Movement North, 1900-1920* (Garden City, 1976), 64-65; Spear, *Black Chicago,* 134; Scott, *Negro Migration,* 30.

31. Scott, *Negro Migration,* 34-35. See also, Biloxi *Daily Herald,* March 19, 1917.

32. Quoted in Johnson, *Negro in American Civilization,* 23.

33. Scott, *Negro Migration,* 34-35. See also the testimony of Howard Snyder, a northern-born Mississippi planter who read "a number of these letters": "Negro Migration and the Cotton Crop," *North American Review,* 219 (January, 1924), 27-28.

34. In 1890, 75.8 percent of all nonresident, Mississippi-born blacks lived in contiguous states, 29.3 percent in Arkansas alone (Kuznets et al., *Population Redistribution,* 1: 321, Table P-3). In the decade 1880-1890, Arkansas and Louisiana were the destination states of 70 percent of all out-migrating black Mississippians (Vickery, "Economics of Negro Migration," 183).

35. Kuznets et al., *Population Redistribution,* 1: 321; Louise V. Kennedy, *The Negro Peasant Turns Cityward: Effects of Recent Migration to Northern Centers* (New York, 1930), 31; U.S., Department of Labor, *Negro Migration in 1916-1917,* 16.

36. In 1910-1920, Arkansas received nearly one in every three of all out-migrating Mississippi blacks. But Illinois led all states in 1920-1930, 1940-1950, and 1950-1960 (Vickery, "Economics of Negro Migration," 183). See also C. Warren Thornthwaite, *Internal Migration in the United States: A Study of Population Redistribution* (Philadelphia, 1934), 13-16; Lyonel C. Florant, "Negro Internal Migration," *American Sociological Review,* 7 (December, 1942), 784-785.

37. From 1870 to 1950 southern blacks were more urban than southern whites in every census except 1920 and 1930. Hope T. Eldridge and Dorothy S. Thomas, *Demographic Analyses and Interrelations,* 204, vol. 3 of *Population Redistribution,* ed. Kuznets et al.

38. Ibid., but see also T. Lynn Smith, "The Redistribution of the Negro Population of the United States, 1910-1960," *Journal of Negro History,* 51 (July, 1966), 165.

39. Thornthwaite, *Internal Migration,* pl. 8, opposite p. 26; Paul B. Foreman, "Mississippi Population Trends" (Ph.D. diss., Vanderbilt University, 1939), 143-146; U.S., Department of Labor, *Negro Migration in 1916-1917,* 16-18.

40. The percentage is based on estimates of the black population in the Delta in Loewen, *The Mississippi Chinese,* 11, Table 1; but see also B. W. Harris, *Population Changes among Rural Negroes in Mississippi* (Lorman, Miss., 1956), 8.

41. The process of migration by stages was first described by Ravenstein. But see Shryrock, *Population Mobility,* 318, 421; Clyde Vernon Kiser, *Sea Island to City: A Study of St. Helena Islanders in Harlem and Other Urban*

Centers (New York, 1932), 145-189; and Florant, "Negro Internal Migration," 785.

42. Otto Klineberg, *Negro Intelligence and Selective Migration* (New York, 1935), 7, 59.

43. See Daniel O. Price, "Education Differentials between Negroes and Whites in the South," *Demography,* 5 (1968), 32; C. Horace Hamilton, "The Negro Leaves the South," *Demography,* 1 (1964), 284-285, 289; idem, "Educational Selectivity of Net Migration from the South," *Social Forces,* 38 (October, 1959), 35; Elizabeth M. Suval and C. Horace Hamilton, "Some New Evidence of Educational Selectivity in Migration from the South," *Social Forces,* 43 (May, 1965), 536-547.

44. The more refined census data available for the 1935-1940 period reveal that among black males the most mobile were those in the 25-29 age-group, followed closely by those in the 20-24 age-group (15 percent of all black male out-migrants). Eldridge and Thomas, *Demographic Analyses and Interrelations,* Table A1.37, p. 312; Foreman, "Mississippi Population Trends," 131.

45. In 1920, in Mississippi cities of 10,000 or more population, black women outnumbered black men by 32,888 to 25,941. On migration and male desertion, see Oliver, *Blues Fell This Morning,* 51-55, 64.

46. In fact, in Tupelo at least, one scholar has concluded that blacks who owned property and who enjoyed relatively high occupational status were less migratory than those who were not so advantaged (Grisham, "Tupelo," 360-361).

47. Baker, *Following the Color Line,* 81.

48. Brandon *News,* July 16, 1909 ("inconvenient" quotation); Forest *Register,* January, 1875, quoted in Wharton, *Negro in Mississippi,* 108 ("curse" quotation).

49. Vicksburg *Herald,* August 19, 1916, quoted in Scott, *Negro Migration,* 153. See also U.S., Department of Labor, *Negro Migration in 1916-1917,* 41, and Henri, *Black Migration,* 77.

50. Jackson *Daily News,* December 4, 1917; Meridian *Star,* January 4, 1917; Jackson *Clarion-Ledger,* June 15, 1917; *Madison County Herald,* October 24, 1919; *Natchez Democrat,* January 24, 1920.

51. New Orleans *Times-Picayune,* October 19, 1916; December 26, 1924; Jackson *Clarion-Ledger,* April 9, 10, 1918; Biloxi *Daily Herald,* March 3, 17, 1917; Scott, *Negro Migration,* 77-78; Henri, *Black Migration,* 64-65; Detweiler, *Negro Press,* 154-155.

52. Letter from Greenville, May 16, 1917, Scott, ed., "Additional Letters of Negro Migrants," 435.

53. U.S., Department of Labor, *Negro Migration in 1916-1917,* 31; Scott, *Negro Migration,* 40.

54. For statements by Jones, Holtzclaw, and Montgomery, see Jackson *Daily Clarion-Ledger,* July 14, 1917; and Meridian *Star,* January 28, 1917; Jackson *Daily News,* December 8, 1923. See also Harrison, *Piney Woods School,* 44; Jones, *The Bottom Rail,* 35; Isaiah T. Montgomery, *Our Great State, Mississippi: Tragic Sketch of the Past . . . and the Wonderful Possibilities of the Future*

(Mound Bayou, [1923]), passim. For examples of the white uses of conservative black opposition to the exodus see Biloxi *Herald,* June 1, July 20, 1917; Sunflower *Tocsin,* December 21, 1916; Meridian *Star,* January 4, June 25, 1917; Vicksburg *Evening Press,* August 21, 1918; Madison County *Herald,* October 31, 1919; February 20, 1920; Natchez *Democrat,* January 24, 1920; and form letter from J. M. Williamson, October 15, 1923, in "Negroes" file, SAg.

55. Mollison's anomalous role as a critic of migration can be followed in Sunflower *Tocsin,* December 21, 1916; January 4, February 1, 1917; January 29, 1919. See also the example of Dr. Joseph E. Walker of Indianola: Sunflower *Tocsin,* December 7, 1916; and chapter 5 above.

56. Although the East St. Louis riot was among the bloodiest ever, the death toll was probably no more than forty. The Jackson *Daily Clarion-Ledger* initially reported that "nearly a half hundred" blacks died but then raised the estimate to "perhaps 600" (July 5, 29, 1917). The headlines are from the *Daily Clarion-Ledger,* June 3, July 29, 1917; and Meridian *Star,* July 9, 1917. For other examples see Biloxi *Daily Herald,* July 6, 20, 1917; Madison County *Herald,* July 6, 1917; Meridian *Star,* July 8, 1917; and Belzoni *Banner,* August 15, 1919.

57. Belzoni *Banner,* August 15, 1919; Jackson *Daily Clarion-Ledger,* September 2, 1919.

58. Meridian *Star,* January 4, 14, 1917; Jackson *Daily Clarion-Ledger,* February 13, 1917; Dewey H. Palmer, "Moving North: Negro Migration during World War I," *Phylon* 28 (Spring, 1967), 59.

59. Biloxi *Daily Herald,* April 13, 28, May 23, 1917; Meridian *Star,* January 4, 1917; Belzoni *Banner,* August 15, 1919; Jackson *Daily Clarion-Ledger,* May 23, June 3, 7, 1917; May 24, September 2, 1919; Jackson *Daily News,* October 13, 1920.

60. Quoted in Jackson *Clarion-Ledger,* July 22, 1917.

61. Chicago *Defender,* March 10, 1917.

62. The formation and purposes of the league are described in the Jackson *Daily Clarion-Ledger,* July 13, 1919, and *Organization of the Mississippi Welfare League* (n.p., n.d.), unpaginated. See also Spear, *Black Chicago,* 203, and Meridian *Star,* August 8, 1919.

63. Hill, "Why Southern Negroes Don't Go South," 184; Arvarh E. Strickland, *History of the Chicago Urban League* (Urbana, 1966), 56-63.

64. The commission's report was reprinted in the Jackson *Daily Clarion-Ledger,* October 5, 1919. See also Madison County *Herald,* September 5, 1919.

65. Black Chicagoans, however, gave the report the derision it deserved (Hill, "Why Southern Negroes Don't Go South," 183-185; Chicago *Defender,* September 27, 1919). Subsequent white efforts to promote repatriation are detailed in Campbell, "Report of Investigation on Negro Migration"; Arvarh E. Strickland, "To the Manor Born: Southern White Responses to Black Migration in the 1920s" (Paper delivered at the Fifty-second Annual Meeting of the Southern Historical Association, Charlotte, N.C., November 1986), 2; and Cohn, *Where I Was Born,* 340-345.

66. U.S., Department of Labor, *Negro Migration in 1916-1917,* 32 (quotation); *American Missionary,* new ser., 9 (July, 1919), 223; Jackson *Daily News,* January 7, 1920.

67. U.S., Department of Labor, *Negro Migration in 1916-1917,* 28; Scott, *Negro Migration,* 37.

68. Sunflower *Tocsin,* December 7, 1916. For similar arguments, see also Montgomery, *Our Great State,* passim.

69. Lester, *Mob Violence and the American Negro,* 38, 52-53.

70. Banks to editor, Jackson *Daily News,* June 12, 1917.

71. J. M. Williamson to Percy, March 7, 1922 (first quotation); petition [1922], box 23, PFP (second quotation).

72. Vicksburg *Evening Post,* December 2, 1918. Similar statements appear in Meridian *Star,* April 5, 1917; and Memphis *Commercial-Appeal,* September 9, 1917. See also the example of black educator A. M. Strange (Grisham, "Tupelo," 325-326).

73. Jackson *Daily Clarion-Ledger,* February 23, 28, 1918.

74. Press release, Citizens' Mass Convention, May 2, 1923, box C-373, NAACP; "Negroes Say Why They Leave the South," *American Missionary,* new ser., 15 (September, 1923), 293.

75. Jackson *Daily News,* January 29, 1924. "Such a thing," the newspaper noted, "might not have been possible in the Mississippi Legislature fifteen or twenty years ago." Theodore Bilbo expressed amazement that the petitioners were not "bodily thrown out" of the legislature (*Free Lance,* quoted in *Crisis,* 32 [December, 1926], 102. See also S. D. Redmond's document prepared for the legislature in 1926, ibid., 90-102).

76. Montgomery, *Our Great State,* app., 6-7 (first quotation); J. E. Johnson to Mississippi Baptist State Convention, November 15, 1939 (second quotation); Johnson to Dear Members, January 15, 1928 (third quotation), JEJ.

77. O. C. Luper to Dear Representative, December 31, 1923, JEJ.

78. Snyder, "Negro Migration and the Cotton Crop," 21-24; Norfolk *Journal and Guide,* March 3, 1928; "White Southerner Tells Why Negro Goes North," press release, February 24, 1928, Administrative Files, box C-373, NAACP.

79. Jackson *Daily News,* October 27, 1923; Strickland, "To the Manor Born," 13.

80. Vicksburg *Daily Herald,* July 7, 1917; The Meridian *Star* and Jackson *Daily News* are quoted in U.S., Department of Labor, *Negro Migration in 1916-1917,* 102, 111-112.

81. Senate *Journal,* 1924, 200-201. See also Lester A. Walton, "Whitfield— Apostle of Racial Good Will," *Outlook,* 136 (April 9, 1924), 589-591; Jackson *Daily News,* January 23, 1924; Baker, *Catch the Vision,* 110.

82. P. P. Garner to Jessie O. Thomas, January 20, 1926; and R. S. Curry to Thomas, January 16, 1926, Central Office file, box A-19, National Urban League Papers, LC; *Organization of the Mississippi Welfare League,* unpaginated.

83. Scott, *Negro Migration,* 83-84, 87, 89; Daniels, *A Southerner Discovers the South,* 178-179; Crosby, "Building the Country Home," 64; Snyder, "Plan-

tation Pictures," 169-170; Holtzclaw, "The Present Status of the Negro," 341-342; *American Missionary,* new ser., 19 (January, 1927), 409; Dickens, *A Nutrition Investigation,* 11; Bunche, *The Political Status of the Negro,* 565; James E. Fickle, *The New South and the "New Competition": Trade Association Development in the Southern Pine Industry* (Urbana, 1980), 297, 329; Charles Granville Hamilton, *Progressive Mississippi* (Aberdeen, Miss., 1978), 178-179.

84. George E. Haynes, report to W. B. Wilson, June 19, 1919; Haynes to Wilson, April 5, May 1-7, 20, 1919, Chief Clerks Files, DL; U.S., Department of Labor, *The Negro at Work during the World War,* 12-13, 20, 82-87.

85. Quoted in Vicksburg *Evening Post,* September 14, 1918.

86. New York *Age,* March 15, 1919; U.S., Department of Labor, *Negro Migration in 1916-1917,* 46; Scott, *Negro Migration,* 83-84; Daniel, *Breaking the Land,* 12; Edwin Mims, comp., *A Handbook for Inter-Racial Committees* (n.p., 1926), 7.

87. Interview with Alcee L. Johnson, November, 1986.

88. Quoted in Scott, *Negro Migration,* 90.

Chapter 9. The Gathering Challenge

1. Wright, *Black Boy,* 283.

2. Levine, *Black Culture and Black Consciousness,* xiii.

3. Cohn, *Where I Was Born and Raised,* 276-277. See also similar observations in Powdermaker, *After Freedom,* 11-12; Smith, *Congressman from Mississippi,* 10; Percy, *Lanterns on the Levee,* 298-299.

4. Howard W. Odum, "Social and Mental Traits of the Negro," *Studies in History, Economics and Public Law,* 37 (1910), 565; Dollard, *Caste and Class in a Southern Town,* 173, 257.

5. Alfred Holt Stone, "Race Friction between Blacks and Whites," 693. But see also Yazoo City *Sentinel,* quoted in Greenville *Times,* March 4, 1905.

6. Davis, "Caste, Economy, and Violence," 8; Dollard, *Caste and Class in a Southern Town,* 68 (quotation); Alphonso A. Barron, oral history, March 11, 1976, JSU.

7. Wright, *Black Boy,* 88, 90-91.

8. Johnson, *Patterns of Negro Segregation,* 138-139.

9. B. Baldwin Dansby, oral history, June, 1973, JSU. See also a defense of Jones as "quite an actor" who skillfully manipulated whites, in Sylvannus P. Weathersby, oral history, October 14, 1978, JSU.

10. Wright, *Black Boy,* 204.

11. Rawick, ed., *Miss. Narr.,* 8(3), 1101. See also, Doris James, *My Education at Piney Woods* (New York, 1937), 80-81.

12. Lillie Jones, oral history, December 11, 1974, University of Southern Mississippi Oral History Project.

13. Williamson, *Crucible of Race,* 202 (quotation). On Charles and Wells see Hair, *Carnival of Fury,* passim; Wells, *Crusade for Justice,* passim; Ida B. Wells-Barnett, *Mob Rule in New Orleans: Robert Charles and His Fight to the Death* (Chicago, 1900), reprinted in Wells-Barnett, *On Lynching,* 33-42. On

Redmond, see Jackson *Daily News,* April 6, 1947; St. Louis *Post Dispatch,* May 12, 1974; Walter J. Leonard, *Black Lawyers: Training and Results, Then and Now* (Boston, 1977), 145.

14. Steven F. Lawson, *In Pursuit of Power: Southern Blacks and Electoral Politics, 1965-1982* (New York, 1985), 93.

15. Jackson *Clarion-Ledger,* May 9, 1889.

16. Machen Box, oral history, May 5, 1970, MHC; Maxine Davis, oral history, May 4, 1976, JSU; Lizzie V. Garner, oral history, April 1, 1976, JSU.

17. Quoted in Myrdal, *An American Dilemma,* 2: 741.

18. Betty Gray, oral history, April 11, 1976, JSU.

19. Harris, *Day of the Carpetbagger,* 348 ("precedent" quotation); McPherson, "White Liberals and Black Power," 1359 ("their own" quotation).

20. Editorial, New Orleans *Picayune,* reprinted in Jackson *Clarion,* June 20, 1889; Jackson *Clarion-Ledger,* July 4, 1889.

21. The complete resolution appears in Jackson *Clarion-Ledger,* July 4, 1889. The preference of some middle-class blacks for a "European system of class-cars," as opposed to the "unrighteousness of a color discrimination," is also described by the Caucasian president of Tougaloo University: Frank G. Woodworth, "Discrimination," *Southern Workman* (November, 1900), 616.

22. *Louisville, New Orleans and Texas Railway Co.* v. *State,* 66 Miss. 662 (1889), and 133 U.S. 587 (1890), 33 L. Ed. 784; *Alabama and Vicksburg Railway Co.* v. *Morris,* 103 Miss. 511 (1912); *Southern Railway Co.* v. *Norton,* 112 Miss. 302 (1916); *Payne* v. *Stevens,* 125 Miss. 582 (1921); *Joseph Waldauer* v. *Vicksburg Railway and Light Co.,* 88 Miss. 200 (1906); *Southern Light and Traction Co.* v. *Compton,* 86 Miss. 269 (1905); *City Bus* v. *Thomas,* 172 Miss. 424 (1935). That whites, too, were sometimes inconvenienced by Jim Crow is demonstrated in *O'Leary* v. *Illinois Central Railway Co.,* 110 Miss. 46 (1915).

23. The Leonard incident is described in Madison County *Herald,* October 3, 1919. On the Gloster case, cf. the slightly differing accounts of Sprigle, *Land of Jim Crow,* 105; and Walter White, *How Far the Promised Land?* (New York, 1955), 167. On similar violence aboard a streetcar, see *Mississippi Power and Light Co.* v. *Garner,* 179 Miss. 588 (1937).

24. See, for example, *Illinois Central* v. *A. M. Redmond,* 119 Miss. 765 (1919); Columbus *Commercial,* October 30, 1906; Jackson *Daily News,* January 29, 1924; Atlanta *Independent,* July 18, 1914, in Tuskegee Institute News Clipping File (reel 2, frame 1006); Banks to Washington, July 9, 1914, con. 68, BTW; Harlan, *The Wizard of Tuskegee,* 419-421.

25. Quoted in Columbus *Commercial,* October 30, 1906; Chicago *Defender,* January 29, 1916.

26. "Jim Crow on Wheels," Chicago *Defender,* November 3, 1917. See also, Work, ed., *Negro Year Book, 1918-1919,* 110; and the more positive views of Evans, *Black and White in the Southern States,* 142-143.

27. There was at least one other buyers' strike, however: "an undemonstrative but well-organized boycott" by blacks of a Natchez movie house after

a Jim Crow balcony and one section of a gallery were closed to them (Davis et al., *Deep South,* 458).

28. Jackson *Daily Clarion-Ledger,* August 28, 1902; Vicksburg *Evening Post,* January 21, 1904; Greenville *Democrat,* January 25, 1904; Sallis, "The Color Line in Mississippi Politics," 387-388.

29. Vicksburg *Evening Post,* January 28, 29, February 2, 1904; Jackson *Daily Clarion-Ledger,* July 2, 1902; Hattiesburg *Progress,* quoted in Jackson *Daily Clarion-Ledger,* August 28, 1902.

30. August Meier and Elliott Rudwick, "The Boycott Movement against Jim Crow Streetcars in the South, 1900-1906," in Meier and Rudwick, *Along the Color Line,* 267-289.

31. E. L. Richardson, quoted in Vicksburg *Evening Post,* June 22, 1904. See also Pascagoula *Democrat-Star,* June 17, 1904.

32. Vicksburg *Evening Post,* January 30, 1904; Natchez *Bulletin,* February 25, 1904, reprinted February 26, 1904; Meier and Rudwick, "The Boycott Movement," 279. See also Rabinowitz, *Race Relations in the Urban South,* 194.

33. Vicksburg *Daily Herald,* June 2, 5, 1904; Batesville *Weekly Panolian,* June 9, 1904; Pascagoula *Democrat-Star,* June 17, 1904; Aberdeen *Weekly,* June 10, 1904; Natchez *Daily Democrat,* August 23, 29, 1904.

34. Natchez *Daily Democrat,* August 23, 25, 26, 1904.

35. On Jones see Roller and Twyman, eds., *Encylopedia of Southern History,* 1345.

36. Quoted in Harris, *Day of the Carpetbagger,* 683.

37. Holtzclaw, "Present Status of the Negro Farmer in Mississippi," 344. See also Holtzclaw's position on lynching, quoted in Jackson *Weekly Clarion-Ledger,* February 21, 1907.

38. Samuel Alfred Beadle, *Lyrics of the Underworld* (Jackson, 1912), quoted in Jordan, "Samuel Alfred Beadle," 54.

39. Montgomery to Washington, September 6, 1904, in Louis R. Harlan and Raymond W. Smock, eds., *The Booker T. Washington Papers* (Urbana, 1979), 8: 62-63 (first and second quotations); Hermann, *Pursuit of a Dream,* 237 (third quotation).

40. For example, see the views of A. J. Oakes of Yazoo City, Mississippi's black "lumber king," described in Hamilton, *Beacon Lights of the Race,* 60-63; Jackson *People's Defender,* quoted in Winston County *Journal,* November 25, 1898; Charles Banks to J. A. Richardson, December 2, 1911; Banks to W. L. Park, February 6, 1911, con. 52; Montgomery to E. W. Lampton, April 25, 1904, con. 242, BTW; and Banks to editor, New York *Sun,* December 12, 1919.

41. Banks, untitled address to the Mississippi Negro Business League, 1909, con. 43, BTW. See also Perry W. Howard to LeRoy Percy, March 27, 1922, box 23, PFP.

42. Quoted in Alferdteen Harrison, *A History of the Most Worshipful Stringer Grand Lodge: Our Heritage is Our Challenge* (n.p., 1977), 52.

43. Beam, *He Called Them by the Lightning,* 178 (Montgomery quotation); Waldron, "All Black," 34 (Mayor Benjamin Green's quotation).

44. Holtzclaw, "Present Status of the Negro," 341. See also William T. Holmes, "Prophecies and Fulfillments in Mississippi," *American Missionary,* new ser., 19 (January, 1927), 408.

45. B. Baldwin Dansby, oral history, January 5, 1971, MDAH. For other examples of the importance black Mississippians assigned to their wartime participation, see: Samuel Alfred Beadle's poem, "Lines," in Beadle, *Sketches from Life in Dixie,* 63-64; "Tougaloo College in 1919-1920," *American Missionary,* new ser., 11 (February, 1920), 591; and resolution "To Governor Paul B. Johnson and the Members of the Mississippi Legislature," [1940], box C-201, NAACP. See also William Faulkner's assessment of the war's impact on black thought and action in *Flags in the Dust* (New York, 1973), a work first published in truncated form in 1929 as *Sartoris.*

46. Jackson *Daily Clarion-Ledger,* October 19, 1917 (first quotation); "What Does the Negro Want or Expect," *American Missionary,* new ser., 10 (January, 1919), 541 (second quotation; Howard is identified in this essay as a Jackson resident and president of the National Negro Bar Association).

47. Jones's remarks were paraphrased by a local correspondent in Chicago *Defender,* April 27, 1918. See also the resolution of Gulf Coast blacks juxtaposing "some laws upon our statute books" and black patriotism (Biloxi *Daily Herald,* April 17, 1917).

48. Editorial, Vicksburg *Herald,* September 22, 1917.

49. Quoted in Chicago *Defender,* April 7, 1917.

50. Jackson *Daily Clarion-Ledger,* August 26, November 15, 20, December 15, 1917; April 19, 1918; Biloxi *Daily Herald,* April 6, 1917.

51. Quoted in Sunflower *Tocsin,* August 8, 1918.

52. Miller to White, September 3, 1918; White to William G. McAdoo, October 10, 1918, box C-361, NAACP.

53. Vicksburg *Evening Post,* July 26, 28, 29, 30, 1918; Vicksburg *Herald,* July 24, 25, 27, 1918; Jackson *Daily Clarion-Ledger,* July 24, 25, 26, 1918.

54. Alice Dunbar Nelson, quoted in William J. Breen, "Black Women and the Great War: Mobilization and Reform in the South," *Journal of Southern History,* 44 (August, 1978), 425-426.

55. Miller to White, September 3, 1918, box C-361, NAACP.

56. The burning of Lloyd Clay is described in Chapter 7. On white fear following the lynching, see New Orleans *Vindicator,* July 28, 1919.

57. Vicksburg *Evening Post,* September 20, October 9, 1918; Jackson *Daily Clarion-Ledger,* June 20, September 21, October 2, 1918; July 24, 1919; Clarksdale *Register,* May 24, 27, 1918; [Walter White], "Report on Conditions Found in Investigations of 'Work or Fight' Laws in Southern States," box C-418, NAACP; idem, " 'Work or Fight' in the South," 144-146.

58. Breen, "Black Women and the Great War," 425-426.

59. Biloxi *Daily Herald,* March 20, April 5, 16, 1917; Meridian *Star,* April 5, 7, 14, 19, 1917; Jackson *Daily News,* April 6, 1917; Jackson *Daily Clarion-Ledger,* April 2, 1918; Clarksdale *Register,* January 26, April 15, 1918.

60. Quoted in Henri, *Black Migration,* 77.

61. Madison County *Herald,* September 12, 1919 ("expected" quotation); Grisham, "Tupelo," 321 (Rankin quotation); *Vardaman's Weekly,* quoted in *Literary Digest,* 62 (August 2, 1919), 25.

62. Madison County *Herald,* October 3, 1919; Chicago *Defender,* May 10, June 21, 1919; NAACP, *Annual Report for 1919* (New York, 1920), 39.

63. Of these, one reportedly gave "marked attention to a white woman"; a second had apparently attempted to enter a movie house through the white entrance; and the third may have tried to dine in a white restaurant (Ratliff, "Mississippi Replies," 126; Jackson *Daily News,* February 18, 1919; Louisville (Ky.) *News,* October 18, 1919, quoted in Robert T. Kerlin, *The Voice of the Negro, 1919* (New York, 1920), 107-108; NAACP, *An Appeal to the Conscience of the Civilized World* (New York, 1920), 8; White, *Rope and Faggot,* 112.

64. Quoted in Davis, "The Negro Church and Associations," 145-146.

65. Meier and Rudwick, *From Plantation to Ghetto,* 240.

66. Stone, "Race Friction between Blacks and Whites," 693.

67. Cohn, "How the South Feels," 48-49.

68. Quoted in Scott, *Negro Migration,* 24-25.

69. Quoted in U.S., Department of Labor, *Negro Migration in 1916-1917,* 33.

70. Grace Morris Allen Jones, *What the Mississippi Women Are Doing* (Braxton, Miss., [1922?]), 3-12; "History of Mississippi Association of Colored Women," *National Association of Colored Women, Inc., 1891-1952* (n.p., n.d.), 86-94.

71. The Old Folks Home for Colored in Vicksburg was originally owned and operated by a local organization, the Vicksburg Woman's Christian Union (Jones, *What the Mississippi Women are Doing,* 16-19, 26-27). For examples of local club activity, see Hood, *The Negro at Mound Bayou,* 33; Mrs. M. M. Hubert, "Club Women's View on National Health Week," *National Negro Health News,* 3 (April-June, 1935), 3-5.

72. State funds for the temporary school for the blind at Piney Woods were suspended during the depression, however, and a permanent facility was not completed until 1950 (Harrison, *Piney Woods School,* 82-85).

73. Atlanta *Daily World,* March 21, 1932; "History of the Mississippi Association of Colored Women," *National Association of Colored Women, Inc.,* 86-94; Melerson Guy Dunham, oral history, July 31, 1974, JSU; J. E. Johnson to Dear Friend, January 20, 1934; and Minutes, Annual Meeting of the Committee of One Hundred, December 16, 1933, JEJ; Prentiss, *Spirit of Mississippi,* January 5, 1935; *Southern Frontier,* May, 1941; January, April, May, 1942; *Report of the State Superintendent, 1939-1941,* 18; *1941-1943,* 22.

74. J. B. F., "The Story of the Committee," [1934], unpaginated, JEJ; Montgomery, *Our Great State,* app., 6-7; Jackson *Clarion-Ledger,* December 20, 1923; Prentiss, *Spirit of Mississippi,* June 1, 1934.

75. J. B. F., "The Story of the Committee"; Finch, *Mississippi Negro Ramblings,* 109; J. E. Johnson to Mary C. Booze, February 24, 1944, JEJ; Prentiss, *Spirit of Mississippi,* June 15, 1934; January 5, 26, July 15, 1935.

76. J. E. Johnson to Friend and Member, January 5, 1928, JEJ. See also Jackson *Clarion-Ledger,* February 13, 1941.

77. Jackson *Advocate,* March [?], 1943, clipping in JEJ ("ultra" quotation); Finch, *Mississippi Negro Ramblings,* 195 ("spoke" quotation). The ambiguous character of committee leadership is suggested by the reputation of Finch himself, who was often thought to be an Uncle Tom in the 1960s and who, as his biographer has written, "used praise as a strategy to get what he wanted from the White man" (Sharon Burette Bell, "Anselm Joseph Finch: Mississippian and Life Long Educator" [M.A. thesis, Jackson State University, 1976], 36).

78. Alcee L. Johnson, interviews with author, October 16, 1986 (telephone) and November 15, 1986. See also the reminiscence of Joseph H. Armstrong, oral history, n.d., JSU.

79. Quoted in Minutes, Annual Meeting of the Committee of One Hundred, February 22, 1946, JEJ. See also J. E. Johnson to Mississippi Baptist State Convention, November 15, 1939, JEJ; Anselm J. Finch, "As I Knew J. E. Johnson," *Mississippi Educational Journal* (January, 1954), 64-65, 76-77.

80. Montgomery, *Our Great State,* app., 6-7; Jackson *Clarion-Ledger,* December 20, 1923; Prentiss, *Spirit of Mississippi,* June 1, 1934; Prentiss Normal and Industrial Institute, "Founders' Day Bulletin, 1907-1980," May, 1980, JEJ.

81. Johnson, interview, October 16, 1986 (quotation). See also J. E. Johnson to R. W. Dunn, June 9, 1937, JEJ.

82. R. L. Young et al., "To the Committee of 100," [1935] (first quotation); Minutes, Committee of One Hundred, March 5, 1943; March 12, 1947 (second quotation); J. E. Johnson to T. J. Harris, February 8, 1946; "Tentative Program, 23rd Annual Session, State Committee of One Hundred," February 22, 1946, JEJ; Prentiss, *Spirit of Mississippi,* January 26, 1935.

83. Sewell and Dwight, *Mississippi Black History Makers,* 243.

84. Johnson, interview, October 16, 1986 (quotation); Minutes, Committee of One Hundred, March 5, 1943; February 22, 1944; February 25, 1948; J. E. Johnson to Dear Co-Worker, January 25, 1936; Minutes, Committee of One Hundred, February 22, 1944, JEJ; Prentiss, *Spirit of Mississippi,* January 26, 1935.

85. Dr. D. W. Sherrard, quoted in Minutes, Committee of One Hundred, January 10, 1942, JEJ.

86. UNIA chapter list, compiled by Michael Fitzgerald, from Universal Negro Improvement Association Division Lists, 1925-1926, box 2, A, 16, Schomburg Collection (New York Public Library, New York, N.Y.). See also V. L. Lewis to James Weldon Johnson, September 2, 1923; and Lewis to NAACP, September 21, 25, 1924, box G-106, NAACP; Davis et al., *Deep South,* 249.

87. Celia J. Allen to Bilbo, May 23, June 9, 1938; Mrs. M. M. L. Gordon to Bilbo, August 10, 1938, box 1091; and "Petition of American Negroes" [1938?], box 1092, Theodore G. Bilbo Papers (McCain Library, University of Southern Mississippi, Hattiesburg, Miss.).

88. T. J. Woofter and Issac Fisher, eds., *Cooperation in Southern Com-*

munities: Suggested Activities for County and City Inter-racial Committees (Atlanta, [1921]), 5; Work, ed., *Negro Year Book, 1921-1922,* 210, 212; *Southern Frontier,* February, October, 1940; September, 1943.

89. List of Members, October, 1938, List of Officers and Executive Committee [November 5, 1941], box 168; S. Truman Lewis to Ames, April 1, May 5, 1939, box 168; Minutes of Annual Business Meeting, February 29, 1940, box 68, CIC.

90. Mississippi Council on Interracial Cooperation, *Statement of Purposes* (n.p., n.d.), box 168 (quotation); Program, Regional CIC, Southern Mississippi, October 26, 1939, box 168; Annual Report of the First Vice-Chairman, January 26, 1940, box 168; Report of the Meeting of Officers, October 29, 1943, box 169; Mrs. Frank S. Sulton to Ames, February 26, 1939, box 168; Helene G. Alford to Ames, May 16, 1941, box 168, CIC.

91. S. Truman Lewis to Bessie C. Alford, July 10, 1940; Lewis to Ames, July 20, 1940; Alford to Ames, July 13, 1940; Ames to Alford, July 15, 1940, box 168, CIC.

92. Ames to R. R. Moton, January 28, 1930, box 168; Ames to Mrs. J. Morgan Stevens, July 29, 1943, box 169, CIC. See also Ames to Alexander, January 15, 1930; Ames to Moton, January 30, 1930; Ames to Mrs. Earl Chambers, January 15, 1930; Ames to Flora B. Walthall, September 3, 1943, box 169, CIC.

93. Ames to Mrs. J. Morgan Stevens, July 29, 1943, CIC.

94. Application for branch charter, Vicksburg, June 9, 1918, box G-106, NAACP. The checkered life of the Vicksburg organization can be traced in branch files: e.g., Robert W. Bagnall to V. L. Lewis, August 24, 1923; Bagnall to B. W. Currie, November 25, 1924; Cleve Johnson to Arthur Spingarn, November 8, 1933; Edwin Merrick to Pickins, September 20, 1939; W. L. Byrd to Thurgood Marshall, December 16, 1939, box G-106, NAACP; and Pickins to George Schuyler, March 29, 1940, box 205, post-1940, NAACP.

95. Application for branch charter, Mound Bayou, March 9, 1919, box G-106, NAACP. Charter members of the Mound Bayou branch included Isaiah T. Montgomery and Montgomery's daughter and son-in-law, Mary and Eugene P. Booze—but not Charles Banks, Washington's closest associate in Mound Bayou.

96. Bagnall to A. W. Wells, February 10, 1930; J. L. Calhoun to White, February 21, 1934; and Lucille Black to Calhoun, February 27, 1934, box G-105, NAACP.

97. See Branch-General Folder, box X-46, NAACP; and NAACP, *Annual Report for 1940,* 32.

98. The impact of out-migration on the Mound Bayou branch is described in R. B. Davis to Bagnall, December 30, 1924, box G-106, NAACP.

99. William Anderson to NAACP, June 21, 1932; and Anderson to White, December 20, 1933, box G-106, NAACP.

100. George Mongrun to NAACP, January 3, 1936, box G-106, NAACP. See also a similar report from Greenwood: H. M. Thompson to Lucille Black, September 3, 1934, box G-106, NAACP.

101. The occupations of founding members of NAACP branches are listed in applications for branch charters: e.g., applications for Vicksburg (June 9, 1918), Mound Bayou (March 9, 1919), Jackson (June 9, 1926), Panola County (June 4, 1932), Meridian (April 8, 1935), all box G-106, NAACP.

102. J. A. Miller to John Shillady, October 16, 1918; D. D. Foote to NAACP, July 29, 1918; and William P. Harrison to Shillady, September 25, 1918, all box C-361, NAACP.

103. Madison Price to NAACP, August 8, 1927, box G-106, NAACP. See also a report from the Gulf Coast: C. C. Hall to James Weldon Johnson, July 1, 1919, ibid.

104. NAACP, *Annual Report for 1920,* 22; Brooklyn *Daily Eagle,* April 24, 1920; Dollard, *Caste and Class in a Southern Town,* 339; Detweiler, *Negro Press,* 154-155.

105. W. L. Byrd to Marshall, August 1, 1939, box C-279, NAACP. See also Ella J. Baker to Abbie Wandlesey, February 2, 1944; and Baker to Mrs. Davis Nichols, September 20, 1944, box 278; Edward Holcomb to Arthur Spingarn, August 12, 1940, box 205, post-1940, NAACP.

106. Editorial, Jackson *Daily News,* August 21, 1946; Alexander Heard, *A Two Party South?* (Chapel Hill, 1952), 191.

107. Roy L. Young to NAACP, March 14, 1939, box G-106, NAACP.

108. Albert Lee Williams to Baker, November 29, 1943, box 272; and Williams to Baker, February 11, 1944, box 278, post-1940, NAACP.

109. William Pickins to Roy Wilkins, April 11, 1940, box 205; and Ruby Hurley, "1957 Annual Report, Southeast Region: The Fight for Freedom" (n.d.), 21, box 513, post-1940, NAACP.

110. *Crisis,* 42 (March, 1935), 79; Wilkins to Bidwell Adams, August 14, 1934, box D-49; William Pickins to Ed Holcomb, October 4, 1938, box G-106; and Pickins to J. K. Rushing, December 27, 1935, box G-105, NAACP; NAACP, *Annual Report for 1932,* 9-10.

111. See for example, William T. Anderson to A. W. Wells, January 17, 1929; White to Wells, March 26, 1931; Wells to White, July 21, 1935; and Wells to Marshall, August 3, 1937, all box G-105; R. L. Young to Du Bois, February 14, 1931, box D-20; Roy Wilkins to J. E. Gibson, August 7, 1935, box G-106, NAACP.

112. Quoted in Louis E. Lomax, *The Negro Revolt,* rev. ed. (New York, 1971), 92.

Index

Note on the Author

Neil R. McMillen, professor of history at the University of Southern Mississippi, is the author of *The Citizen's Council: Organized Resistance to the Second Reconstruction, 1954-64.*